Renewable Energy
Power for a Sustainable Future

Edited by Godfrey Boyle

The Open University   OXFORD

Oxford University Press in association with the Open University

Published by Oxford University Press, Oxford
in association with
The Open University, Milton Keynes

Oxford University Press, Walton Street, Oxford OX2 6DP

Oxford New York
Athens Auckland Bangkok Bogota Bombay Buenos Aires
Calcutta Cape Town Chennai Dar es Salaam Delhi
Florence Hong Kong Istanbul Karachi
Kuala Lumpur Mumbai Madrid Melbourne
Mexico City Nairobi Paris Sao Paolo Singapore
Taipei Tokyo Toronto Warsaw

and associated companies in
Berlin Ibadan

Oxford is a trade mark of Oxford University Press
Published in the United States by Oxford University Press, Inc., New York

The Open University, Walton Hall, Milton Keynes MK7 6AA

First published in the United Kingdom 1996
reprinted 1998

British Library Cataloguing in Publication Data

Data available

Library of Congress Cataloging in Publication Data

Data available

ISBN 0-19-856452-X
ISBN 0-19-856451-1 (Pbk)

Edited, designed and typeset by The Open University

Printed in the United Kingdom by BPC Wheatons Ltd, Hennock Road, Exeter, Devon, EX2 8RP

This book was produced as a major component of the second level Open University undergraduate course *T265 Renewable Energy*. It is also intended for use in other Universities by undergraduates studying renewables, perhaps with the aid of the learning resources contained in the Open University's *T521 Renewable Energy: A Resource Pack for Tertiary Education*.

T265 Renewable Energy

The Open University undergraduate course *T265 Renewable Energy* includes, in addition to this book, an extensive set of supplementary readings, several hours of video material, a set of computer spreadsheet based exercises and a substantial project. Study is supported by study guides, guidance from an Open University tutor and face-to-face tutorials. Students can communicate with one another and with their tutors using a computer conferencing system, and have access to the Internet for information searching purposes. Assessment consists of a set of tutor-marked assignments and a final examination. The course is available to residents of the European Union.

For further details, write to:
The Course Manager, *T265 Renewable Energy*, Faculty of Technology, The Open University, Milton Keynes MK7 6AA, United Kingdom.

T521 Renewable Energy: A Resource Pack for Tertiary Education

The Open University *T521 Renewable Energy Resource Pack* is designed to help lecturers and professors in the tertiary education sector to extend their teaching programmes to cover the renewable energy sources. The media included are text, video, slides and computer software. The Pack covers the principal renewable energy sources and is designed for use across a wide range of academic disciplines, at levels ranging from introductory to advanced. It explains the physical and engineering principles underlying each source, and discusses its environmental impact and future prospects. Also included are sections on economics, resource assessment and integration, a detailed index and an extensive set of exercises, solutions and seminar topics. The coverage throughout is detailed, authoritative and up-to-date.

For further details of *T521 Renewable Energy: A Resource Pack for Tertiary Education*, write to:
Learning Materials Sales Office, The Open University, PO Box 188, Milton Keynes MK7 6DH.

The *T265 Renewable Energy* Course Team

Gary Alexander
Alun Armstrong
Godfrey Boyle
Geoff Brown
David Crabbe
David Elliott
Bob Everett
Janet Ramage
Derek Taylor
Susan Walker

Consultants

Dr Les Duckers   (Coventry University)
Dr Jonathan Scurlock   (King's College, London)

External Assessor

Prof David Hall   (King's College, London)

Support Staff

Claire Emburey   (Course Secretary)
Sarah Hofton   (Graphic Designer)
Zoe Hoult   (Course Manager)
Susan Lapworth   (Course Manager)
Keith Cavanagh   (Editor)
Roger Moore   (Academic Computing Service)
Andrew Rix   (Audio-Visual Department)
Bill Young   (BBC Producer)

Acknowledgements

The course team gratefully acknowledges the contributions made in the development and production of T265 by the following:
Christopher Pym, Connie Tyler, Alison Cunningham, Scott Forrest, Howard Taylor, Philippa Broadbent, Linda Lynham, Alison Bannister, Mark Kesby.

PREFACE

By the end of the 21st century, according to United Nations projections, the number of people on the Earth is likely to have approximately doubled. How can a world of 10 to 12 billion people be provided with adequate supplies of energy, cleanly, safely and sustainably?

There is a growing consensus that renewable energy sources will be a very important part of the answer. The growing interest in "renewables" has been prompted, in part, by increasing concern over the pollution, resource depletion and possible climate change implications of our continuing use of conventional fossil and nuclear fuels. But recent technological developments have also improved the cost-effectiveness of many of the renewables, making their economic prospects look increasingly attractive.

A number of detailed studies (see Chapter 10), from bodies as diverse as the World Energy Council, Greenpeace International, the Shell International Petroleum Company and a team of United Nations energy specialists, suggest that the renewables could well be providing around half of the world's energy by about the middle of the next century.

If this contribution is to be realised, however, the world will need many more professional people with a thorough knowledge of the renewable energy sources, their underlying physical and technological principles, their economics, their environmental impact and how they can be integrated into the world's energy systems. Policy-makers and the general public will also need to have a broad understanding of the renewables and their potential role in satisfying the world's energy requirements.

This book has been written to address both needs. It is aimed both at undergraduates studying the Open University's second-level course *Renewable Energy* (T265) and at undergraduates in other Universities who are also studying renewables, perhaps with the aid of the learning resources in the Open University's *Renewable Energy: a Resource Pack for Tertiary Education* (T521). We have also aimed to make the book accessible, wherever possible, to non-specialists interested in learning more about the subject. We have tried to strike a balance between, on the one hand, making the principles underlying the renewables as understandable as possible, and, on the other, trying not to over-simplify important scientific, technological, economic or mathematical aspects.

We hope this book will contribute to an improved and more widespread understanding of the potential of the renewable energy sources, at all levels. We also hope we have succeeded in conveying, to specialist and non-specialist readers alike, something of the enthusiasm we feel for this complex, fascinating and increasingly-important subject.

Godfrey Boyle

Course Team Chair
T265 Renewable Energy, and
T521 Renewable Energy: A Resource Pack for Tertiary Education.

The Open University.

CONTENTS

OVERVIEW
THE CONTEXT OF RENEWABLE ENERGY TECHNOLOGIES

1.1 INTRODUCTION

STYLE AND APPROACH

Interest in the use of renewable energy sources has grown dramatically during the past few years, largely as a reaction to concerns about the environmental impact of the use of fossil and nuclear fuels. (The term 'renewable energy' is defined in Section 1.4 below.) However, the subject of renewable energy is of far wider interest than to environmental scientists alone. The use of fossil and nuclear fuels is so central to industrialised societies that any examination of the difficulties they cause or their potential solutions raises a wide range of issues: of technology and design, politics, social structure, economics, planning and even history.

The questions raised go to the heart of any examination of the nature and direction of modern society. There are no clear-cut answers to these questions at present. This is an area in which there are many views, of varying degrees of insight and expertise, but little certainty. Thus any book on renewable energy must be exploratory, questioning and creative, and that, in turn, has influenced the style and approach of the material presented in this and later chapters. It will highlight some of the more open-ended issues, which can be clarified by discussion and exploration. In the end the resolution of these issues will emerge from the collective decisions of people in the future.

One of the most exciting aspects of the study of renewable energy is that it is inherently positive. It is an area which offers the possibility of solutions to some of society's most difficult problems. Again, this appears most clearly when a broad approach to the issues is taken. Thus the study of renewable energy involves much more than the technical possibilities of the replacement of fossil and nuclear fuels. Some of the major areas of interest are:

Environmental science – the comparative impact of fossil, nuclear and renewable energy sources on the atmosphere, waterways, and the plant and animal life of the earth. This includes consideration of the greenhouse effect, acid rain and pollution of the seas. Related issues include the dynamics of climate and its relationship to the biosphere.

Earth sciences – the origins of and physical principles underlying the various forms of renewable energy.

Technology – the design and implementation of renewable energy based technologies, and their integration with existing technologies and distribution systems. Related issues include the technical possibilities for improving the efficiency of present energy use, in buildings, machinery, appliances, etc.

Social sciences – the technological/social/philosophical issue of large-scale centralised systems versus small-scale local systems. The difference between the relatively concentrated reserves of fossil fuels in some countries and the wider distribution of renewable energy sources has major political implications and may influence patterns of industrialisation and development. Changing fuel prices have a dramatic effect upon the world's economies.

Planning – the siting of power stations, transmission lines, wind farms, tidal barrages, biomass plantations or hydroelectric plant, which has a major planning impact, with legal and social implications. Transport planning, too, is intimately related to the mix of fuels and other energy sources available.

Architecture, building and design – the design of buildings and neighbourhoods for energy efficiency and to incorporate integrated energy supply systems which mix renewable and other sources.

SUMMARY OF CHAPTER 1

The purpose of this introductory chapter is to set the context for the rest of the book. It will raise some of the more general issues, and provide some of the scientific background needed to understand the material in later chapters.

The remainder of this section gives a brief historical review of fuel use, which serves to introduce the reasons for energy use and creates a context for a review of some of the principal scientific and technical concepts concerning energy.

Section 1.2, 'Present-day fuel use', concentrates on the current use of fuels and their significance in society. Fuels are now necessary to all aspects of civilised life, from agriculture to obtaining and working materials, from creating buildings, implements and machinery to communications.

Section 1.3, 'The energy problems of modern societies', looks at the problems which have come to be associated with large-scale fuel use: climate change, acid rain, oil pollution of the seas, the difficulties in disposing of nuclear waste, the dangers from nuclear and fossil fuel accidents, the dangers from declining resources of fossil fuels, the political tensions caused by concentrated reserves of fuels, and the military dangers of nuclear proliferation.

Section 1.4, 'Renewable energy sources: a way out?', looks at the possibility that renewable energy sources could provide partial or perhaps even complete solutions to the problems examined in Section 1.3. It takes a first look at renewable sources, their potential and difficulties. It starts with a brief examination of the origin of renewable sources in the natural energy flows of the earth. It then looks at the technical potential for substitution: electricity from hydro, wave, wind, solar electric, biomass, geothermal and tidal sources; heat from solar thermal, waste, geothermal and biomass sources; and transport energy from biomass, hydrogen (derived from renewable sources) and (renewably charged) batteries.

A BRIEF HISTORY OF ENERGY USE

At present, the large-scale use of fossil (and to a lesser extent, nuclear) fuels is a dominant feature of industrial societies. It is regarded as essential for the growing, distribution and preparation of foods, for construction, manufacturing, communication and organisation, and many other activities. However, the use of energy sources other than the human body has characterised human cultures for far longer than there have been industrial cultures. We shall review that use briefly, because it forms a useful way of introducing modern uses of energy, and gives a context for explaining some of the related technical concepts.

For perhaps half a million years, people have used wood fires to keep themselves warm, to provide light and to cook their food. Later, fires were used to extract and work metals (copper, bronze and iron), and to fire clay pots and bricks. Thus fuel was used to provide heat at low temperatures for people's comfort, and at high temperatures to produce light and to create chemical and physical changes in materials to make them more useful.

Animals have been used for traction since the beginnings of agriculture some ten or twelve thousand years ago. The wind has been used to power ships in the Mediterranean for between five and six thousand years. Mills powered by wind and water were used two to three thousand years ago, while tidal mills were in use in Norman times. Thus natural forces have been used for many centuries to move objects for transport or production.

These three categories of use: low-temperature heat for human comfort, high-temperature heat for light and for working materials, and force applied to create movement, are still the dominant categories of energy use.

A large number of civilisations with highly specialised systems of production and trade, spectacular cities and architecture, sophisticated art and elaborate social systems have risen and fallen using only the energy of human bodies, animals, wood, the wind, water, and tides. These sources are still predominant in many parts of the World.

The change to the present intensity of fuel use, and dependence upon fossil fuels, began with and was an intimate part of the Industrial Revolution. That era can usefully be divided into three periods.

The earliest stages were powered by watermills, built at frequent intervals along whatever streams and rivers had enough flow to power them. With the invention of the steam engine burning coke and coal, fuels began to replace running water as the power source. In the nineteenth century, the combination of coal mining which provided fuel, the casting and smelting of iron which provided materials, and steam engines which provided transport, reinforced each other to feed industrialisation. At that time coal and iron ores were plentiful, crude and inefficient industrial processes were the rule, and environmental effects were ignored.

The late nineteenth and early twentieth century saw the development of electricity and the internal combustion engine, oil and gas as additional fuels, and the development of a chemical industry that could create new materials using oil as a feedstock. At that time power was provided directly from oil or gas burned in engines, or indirectly from electricity obtained from burning coal, oil or gas, or from hydroelectric plant. Again, it was the mutual reinforcement between the availability of cheap fuels, more sophisticated materials (metal alloys and plastics), and transport that spread industrialisation.

The mid-twentieth century saw the spread of distribution networks for electricity, to the point at which it was available nearly universally in industrialised countries, and of gas pipelines to a somewhat lesser extent. With the opening of the major oil fields of the Middle East and North Africa, industrial culture had become totally dependent upon fuel use, based around centralised sources. The development of nuclear sources of electricity after the Second World War added an additional power source.

At this stage fuels were still seen as cheap and plentiful, the uses of those fuels were still predominantly crude and inefficient, and environmental effects were still ignored.

Now, in the late twentieth century, those parts of the world that have been in the mainstream of the industrial revolution are at a stage which has been called 'post-industrial'. Manufacturing has continued to increase, but is no longer the largest element of economic activity. Services, and in particular, communications and information processing, have become dominant activities, accompanied by developments in supporting technologies.

There has also been an enormous growth in scientific and technical knowledge of all sorts. Since the late 1960s, there has been a growing recognition of the environmental impact of industrial societies, and especially of the burning of fossil fuels. Galvanised by the oil crises of the 1970s, there has been a growth in understanding of a vast array of techniques for making more efficient use of energy, and also for providing energy from renewable sources. Major reductions in fuel use are now seen as technically possible, simply through care and attention to the energy aspects of the design of buildings, equipment and industrial processes, but also through sophisticated control processes, low-energy materials, biological processes, and many other methods. A broad outline of these possibilities will be given in the next section.

In the 1990s, this understanding is only beginning to be applied, but economic constraints have held it back. After the dramatic rises in 1973 and again in 1979–80, the world price of oil has since decreased. The result is that it is economically very difficult to develop and introduce renewable sources, and pressure to introduce energy conservation measures has reduced. It is very difficult for environmental pressures to compete with economic pressures.

Improved efficiency would require changes to product lines, design procedures, the training of engineers and craftspeople, and the education of consumers. New products and procedures start off at a disadvantage because at first they lack the infrastructure, supply industries, and consumer expectations to break into existing markets.

TECHNICAL INTERLUDE: WHAT ARE ENERGY, POWER, ETC?

The discussion which follows is aimed at readers who come to the study of renewable energy technologies from a non-technical background and need a simplified introduction to the main scientific and technical concepts used. For those who require a more rigorous introduction, see the Further Reading at the end of this section.

WHAT IS ENERGY?

The historical review above has described the wide variety of technologies used over the centuries by human cultures to produce warmth, light, heat for industrial processes and motion. In parallel with this technical development has come a growing awareness that these apparently quite different systems share important characteristics, and the theoretical concept of **energy** has emerged as the unifying idea. Rooted in seventeenth-century science and refined over the following 200 years, the idea of energy has served to reveal the common features in processes as diverse as burning fuels, propelling machines or charging batteries.

Diverse processes can be described in terms of diverse **forms of energy**: thermal energy (heat), chemical energy (in fuels or batteries), kinetic energy (in moving substances), electrical energy, gravitational energy, and a few more, as will be explained later. Energy is not itself a thing or a substance (fuels are substances); rather it is a theoretical concept, an idea, used to connect and explain various observations.

The word energy is derived from the Greek *en* (in) and *ergon* (work). The normal technical definition is that *energy is the capacity, or ability, to do* **work**. In the technical sense, 'to do work' means moving something against a resisting force. The work done is then defined as the product of force and distance, i.e.:

work = force × distance

In this formula, if the units in which force is expressed are Newtons (N), and the units in which distance is expressed are metres (m), then the units in which work is expressed will be **joules** (J) (see Box 1.1). The Newton is defined as that force which will cause a mass of 1 kilogram (kg) to accelerate at a rate of 1 metre per second per second (m s^{-2}).

The basic idea is that energy has many forms and that physical processes can be understood in terms of the conversion from one of its forms to another. Inherent in this idea is the assumption that the total quantity of energy remains unchanged in any transformation. If the quantity of energy in the output of a process (say electric power) is less than the quantity of energy in the input (say a fuel) then some energy must have been converted to some other form as well (usually waste heat). This principle, that the total quantity of energy is always conserved, is called the **First Law of Thermodynamics**.

If the total quantity of energy is always the same, how can we talk of *consuming* it? The answer of course is that we don't consume energy: we convert it from one form into other forms. We consume fuels, which are sources of readily-available energy. We burn fuel in an internal combustion engine, converting its stored chemical energy into heat and then into the kinetic energy of the moving vehicle. A wind turbine extracts kinetic energy from moving air and converts it into electrical energy, which can in turn be used to heat the filament of a lamp causing it to radiate light energy. A forest grows, converting the energy of sunlight into the chemical energy of the components of plant cells. A gallon of petrol, a mountain reservoir and a municipal rubbish dump are all accumulated stores of energy.

FORMS OF ENERGY

How many different forms of energy are there? The present answer is that the diversity of forms can be understood in terms of four at the most basic level.

One has already been mentioned: the **kinetic energy** possessed by any moving object. The kinetic energy of a body in motion is given by the formula:

$$\text{kinetic energy} = \tfrac{1}{2} \times \text{mass} \times (\text{speed})^2$$

Table 1.1 Common energy units and conversions

1 kilowatt-hour (kWh) = 3.6 megajoules (MJ)

1 calorie = 4.18 J

1 Therm = 105.5 MJ

1 British Thermal Unit (BTU) = 1055 J

One horsepower (HP) is equal to 746 W

Heat energy content of 1 cubic metre (m^3) of natural gas = 38 MJ

1 million tonnes of coal equivalent (Mtce) ≈ 28 PJ ≈ 7.5 TWh
     (assuming 100% conversion efficiency)

1 million tonnes of oil equivalent (Mtoe) ≈ 42 PJ ≈ 12 TWh
     (assuming 100% conversion efficiency)

1 tonne of oil ≈ 7.3 barrels of oil ≈ 260 imperial gallons of oil
     ≈ 30 sacks of coal (1.5 tonnes)
     ≈ 4.2 m^3 of dry wood (3 tonnes) ≈ 12 000 kWh of electricity
     (assuming 100% conversion efficiency)

Typical power ratings

A one bar electric fire is rated at 1 kW

A large modern wind turbine is typically rated at around 500 kW

A large modern fossil fuel power station is typically rated at around 1 GW (1000 MW)

BOX 1.1 UNITS OF ENERGY AND POWER

For historical and practical reasons, there are as many ways of measuring energy as there are forms of energy. The official, standard unit of energy is the same as the unit of work, normally the **joule** (abbreviated J), but a wide variety of other units are used too. Energy is often measured in terms of quantities of fuel: tonnes of coal, and barrels, gallons or tonnes of oil. National statistics of energy 'consumption' are often given in such units as 'Mtoe' (million tonnes of oil equivalent). Table 1.1 lists some common units and the conversion factors between them.

Power is almost universally measured in **watts** (abbreviated W), or in multiples of watts such as kilowatts, megawatts, etc. One watt is equal to one joule per second.

Watts are most familiar to us as ratings of electrical appliances. For electricity, it follows from the definition of voltage that electrical power is equal to the product of the voltage and the current at any instant, i.e.:

watts = volts × amps.

In the case of alternating current (AC), voltage and current are not always in phase with each other and the power is given by the expression
watts = volts × amps × power factor.

But other, non-electrical energy conversion processes can also be described in terms of power.

Because of the close connection between energy and power, it is common to measure energy, and particularly electricity, in terms of power and time, i.e.:

energy = power × time

Thus a kilowatt-hour (kWh) is the energy of a 1 kW (1000W) device running for 1 hour (3600 seconds), and is equal to 3.6 MJ.

where energy is expressed in joules, mass in kilograms and speed in metres per second (m s^{-1}).

Less obviously, it is also the energy which makes something hot. All matter consists of atoms, or the combination of atoms called molecules. In a gas such as the air around us these move freely. In a solid or a liquid they form a more or less loosely linked network in which every particle is constantly vibrating. **Thermal energy**, or heat, is the name given to the kinetic energy associated with this rapid random motion: hotter means faster. (See Box 1.2.)

A second fundamental form of energy is **gravitational energy**. An input of energy is required to lift anything. This is because the gravitational pull of the earth opposes the movement. (Away from the earth, the gravitational pull of other heavenly bodies is significant.) As the object is raised, whether it is an apple lifted above your head or a few thousand tonnes of water pumped to a reservoir, the input energy is stored. It is now in a form called **gravitational potential energy** (often just potential energy or gravitational energy). That this stored energy exists will be obvious if you release the apple and observe the subsequent conversion to kinetic energy. The gravitational force pulling an object towards the earth is called the *weight* of the object, and is equal to its *mass*, *m*, multiplied by the acceleration due to gravity, *g* (which is 9.81 m s^{-2}). The potential energy stored in raising the object to a height *h* is given by:

$$\text{potential energy} = \text{force} \times \text{distance} = \text{weight} \times \text{height} = m \times g \times h$$

where energy is expressed in joules, force in Newtons, mass in kilograms, and distance or height in metres.

Gravity may be the most obvious force influencing the objects around us, but it is not the only one. On a scale far too small for the eye to see, it is not gravity but electrical forces which hold together the atoms and molecules of all materials. The **electrical energy** associated with these forces is the third of the basic forms.

Every atom consists of a cloud of electrically charged particles, electrons, moving incessantly around a central nucleus. When atoms come together to form molecules or solid materials, the distribution of electrons is changed, often with dramatic effect. Thus **chemical energy**, viewed at the atomic level, can be considered to be a form of electrical energy. When a fuel is burned, the chemical energy it contains is converted into heat energy. Essentially, the electrical energy released as the atomic electrons are rearranged is converted to the kinetic energy of the molecules of the combustion products.

A more familiar form of electrical energy is **electricity**. Electric current is the organised flow of electrons in a material, most often a metal. Metals are substances in which one or two electrons from each atom can become detached and move freely through the lattice structure of the material. It is the presence of these free electrons which allows metals to carry electrical currents. To maintain a steady flow of electrons requires a constant input of energy because the electrons continually lose energy in collisions with the metal lattice. (The resulting increase in kinetic energy of the metal is why wires get hot when they carry electrical currents.)

A battery uses stored chemical energy to provide its energy input to an electric circuit. A power station involves a longer series of conversions. If the input is a fuel, the first step is to burn it, using the heat to produce high-pressure steam or hot gases. (Where the input is already in the form of a moving fluid such as wind or water, this stage is not necessary.) The steam or other moving fluid is used to drive rotating turbines, which in turn drive the electrical generator. In virtually every power station in the world, the generators operate on a principle discovered by Michael Faraday in 1832:

BOX 1.2: HEAT AND TEMPERATURE

What is heating? When the faster moving molecules in a hotter substance come in contact with the relatively slower moving molecules in a cooler substance, the collisions speed up the slower moving molecules and slow down the faster ones. This transfer of kinetic energy is described as a flow of heat. Clearly, it always takes place from hotter (faster) to cooler (slower). This direction of heat flow allows us to define scales of relative 'hotness', or **temperature**. The temperature scale which is most natural to scientific theory is one in which zero corresponds to zero molecular motion. The unit of temperature in this scale is the Kelvin (abbreviated K). The temperature scale in most common use is the Celsius scale (written as °C), in which zero corresponds to the freezing point of water and 100 to the boiling point of water. The two scales are related by a simple formula:

temperature (K) =
temperature (°C) + 273

that a voltage is induced in a coil of wire set spinning in a magnetic field. Connecting the ends of the coil to an electric circuit will then allow a current to flow. The electrical energy can in turn be transformed into heat, light, motion or whatever, depending upon what is connected to the circuit. Thus electricity is a convenient *intermediary* form of energy, used to allow energy released from one source to be converted to another quite different form some distance from the source.

Another, more subtle form of electrical energy is carried by electromagnetic radiation. More properly called **electromagnetic energy**, this is the form in which, for example, solar energy reaches the earth. Electromagnetic energy is radiated in greater or lesser amounts by every object. It travels as a wave and can carry energy through empty space. The length of the wave (its wavelength) determines its form, which includes x-rays, ultraviolet and infrared radiation, microwaves, radio waves and the small band of wavelengths that our eyes can detect which we call visible light.

The fourth and final basic form of energy is bound up in the central nuclei of atoms, and is called **atomic** or **nuclear energy**. The technology for releasing it was developed during the Second World War for military purposes, and subsequently in a more controlled version for the peaceful production of electricity. Nuclear power stations operate on much the same principles as fossil fuel plants except that the furnace in which the fuel burns is replaced by a heat-generating nuclear reactor.

ENERGY AND POWER

When discussing energy matters it is important to be clear about the difference between the *quantities* of energy involved, and the *rate* at which energy is converted from one form to another or transmitted from one place to another. The **rate** per second at which energy is converted (or transmitted) is called the **power** of the conversion (or transmission). The terms energy and power are often used informally as though they were synonymous (e.g. wind energy/wind power). This is often harmless, but can lead to meaningless statements such as a newspaper report that a new wind farm 'will produce 30 megawatts a year'.

CONVERSION AND EFFICIENCY

When we convert energy from one form to another for some purpose the useful output is never equal to the input. Some energy always ends up in some unwanted form. The ratio of the useful output to the required input is called the **efficiency** of the process. It can be as high as 90% (in a water turbine or well-run electric motor) or very much less than this (in a typical internal combustion engine, 10–20%; in a coal-fired power station without the use of the 'waste' heat, 35–40%). Some of the inefficiencies can be avoided by good design, but others are inherent in the nature of the conversion, and an understanding of these limits is central to the design of optimum ways of making use of energy sources.

The important distinction between the high- and low-efficiency conversion systems listed above is that the latter involve the conversion of heat into mechanical or electrical energy. Heat, as we have seen, is the kinetic energy of randomly-moving molecules, an essentially chaotic form of energy. No machine can convert this chaos completely into the ordered state associated with mechanical or electrical energy. This is the message of the **Second Law of Thermodynamics**: that there is necessarily a limit to the efficiency of any heat engine. Some energy must always be rejected as low-temperature heat.

More generally, energy sources can be classified along a spectrum. High-grade sources are those which provide the most organised forms of energy; low-grade sources the least organised. The highest grades are the kinetic

---

BOX 1.3: SYNCHRONISING GENERATORS

All generators in modern power stations generate **alternating current**: the current increases and decreases sinusoidally a fixed number of times per second (50 in Europe and 60 in the USA). The number of cycles per second, i.e. the **frequency**, is determined, in so-called **synchronous** generators, by the speed of rotation of the generator, and is usually controlled within close limits. This is because many motors and appliances rely for their operation on a predictable frequency.

If, as is usual, there are many power stations linked together by a high-voltage **grid** of power lines, it is necessary for all the generators to be synchronised, i.e. to operate at the same frequency, so that the peaks and troughs of current generated by each reinforce one another rather than cancelling each other out.

If generators driven by renewable sources such as wind, wave or hydro are connected to the same electricity grid, they too must be synchronised to all the others. The frequency of their output must thus be effectively constant, regardless of fluctuations in the renewable source. This is a significant design constraint on renewable sources, and can lead to lower efficiencies than could be obtained if the generators were allowed to vary in speed. (In some renewable energy systems, such as wind turbines, so-called **asynchronous** or **induction** generators are often used. The frequency of output of these generators is fixed by the frequency of the grid, but their rotation speed varies within a small percentage of the nominal speed, depending on the power output.)

energy of moving matter, gravitational potential energy and electrical energy. These can be inter-converted, or converted into lower forms, with small losses. (Large losses occur when lower forms are converted to higher forms.) Chemical energy occupies an intermediate position, then high-temperature heat and finally low-temperature heat. In the historical review above, our uses of energy were classified in this sequence. The least wasteful way to use energy resources is to match the grade of the source as closely as possible to the grade of use.

MATCHING THERMODYNAMIC GRADE BY CASCADING PROCESSES

In most modern societies, where limited attention has been paid to energy efficiency, the thermodynamic grade of energy sources is often ignored. Thus electricity is sold for low-temperature heating, in competition with directly burned fuels, even though about three times more heat is released in the power station than is delivered to the consumer. However, there is nothing to prevent the 'waste' heat from a heat engine being used for some other purpose. This is essentially the principle of combined heat and power (CHP), or 'co-generation', in which fuel is burned to generate electricity and the remaining output, which is in the form of heat, is then used to provide

---

BOX 1.4: POWER STATIONS AND EFFICIENCY

The steam turbine used in many fossil-fuelled power stations is a heat engine and its efficiency is accordingly limited by the Second Law of Thermodynamics.

The Second Law can be written as an equation which tells us how to calculate the maximum theoretical efficiency: it depends upon the temperature of the steam reaching the turbine and the lower temperature at which the departing steam is condensed. If we call these T_U and T_L respectively, then:

maximum theoretical efficiency

$$= \frac{T_U - T_L}{T_U}$$

(The Kelvin temperature scale must be used in this formula.)

Suppose that steam enters the turbines of a coal-fired power station at 550 °C and is ultimately cooled to 27 °C.

The Kelvin temperatures are $T_U = 823$ K and $T_L = 300$ K, so the maximum thermodynamic efficiency is 523 / 823 = 63.5%.

In practice the best steam turbines achieve perhaps 70% of this, or about 44% efficiency. Assuming that the efficiency of

the boiler and generator is 90%, we obtain an overall plant efficiency of 36%.

The plant will also use some of its output to run its own machinery, so the overall efficiency is unlikely to exceed 35%*. Thus a large modern power station which typically produces an **output** of 1.2 GW (1200 MW) of electrical power needs a fuel **input** of 3.4 GW, of which 2.2 GW becomes waste heat – enough to supply heating and hot water to a million or more households.

Note: the efficiency of electricity generation in the latest Combined Cycle Gas Turbine (CCGT) generating stations that are being installed in the UK is substantially higher than that of earlier steam turbine plant and is around 50% in the best installations. In a CCGT, essentially, natural gas is burned at very high temperature in a gas turbine (similar to that used in an aircraft engine), which produces shaft power to drive an electrical generator. The hot 'waste' gases leaving the turbine are then used to raise steam for use in a conventional steam turbine, which then powers a second electrical generator.

low-grade heating. The overall efficiency of a CHP plant, in terms of converting the heat released when the fuel is burned into useful forms, can be 80% or more.

Moreover, the waste heat from many high-temperature processes other than heat engines (in the chemical industry, for example) can be channelled to a lower temperature use (i.e. drying processes) so that the energy of the original source can flow or 'cascade' through two or more uses, thus providing a highly efficient use of fuel. These examples follow the principle of matching the grade of energy required as closely as possible to the available energy.

1.2 PRESENT-DAY FUEL USE

WORLD ENERGY SUPPLIES

HOW MUCH DO WE USE?

As we have seen, modern societies, and particularly industrial societies, are now totally dependent upon the use of large quantities of energy, most of it in the form of fossil fuels, for virtually all aspects of life. In 1992, the estimated total world consumption of primary energy, in all forms, was approximately 400 EJ per year, equivalent to some 9500 million tonnes of oil (mtoe) per year (see Figure 1.1). Assuming a world population of about 5300 million in that year, this gives an annual average fuel use for every man, woman and child in the world equivalent to about 1.8 tonnes of oil. In more familiar units, this is equivalent to about 470 imperial gallons of oil per person per year.

These figures are not just for direct personal use of fuel: they include all fuel used by industry, commerce, governments, etc. They also include the large quantities of wood and other biological fuels used outside the monetary economy, chiefly in the 'Third World'. It has been estimated that the use of these 'traditional' fuels contributes about 14% to the overall total (Hall, 1991). Moreover, the figures are averages over the world's population, and conceal tremendous differences between different regions. Figure 1.2 shows the consumption of commercially-traded energy (i.e. excluding traditional biofuels) per person for different parts of the world over the last 25 years. The graphs speak for themselves.

The magnitude of the energy problem that may face future generations can be illustrated by a simple calculation. The population of the world in 1990 was approximately 5 billion people. The best UN estimates of population trends show it continuing to increase to around 8 billion by 2025, but stabilising towards the end of the next century at somewhere between 10 and 12 billion people. Most of that increase will be in the less-developed countries (LDCs). Fuels are used at an average rate in the developed countries which is more than six times that in the LDCs. The present situation is summarised in Table 1.2, from which it can be seen that the developed countries use nearly twice as much fuel as the LDCs, even though they have less than a third of their population.

Now suppose that by 2025 the developed nations succeed in doubling the efficiency of their energy use, which as we will see is technically possible, so that their energy use per person is halved. Let us also suppose that the LDCs' energy use per person doubles, as living standards improve. In other words, there is a move towards convergence in the energy use per person in the two parts of the world. The results are also shown in Table 1.2. Given the expected population increase, there is still a rise of 50% in the overall level of global energy use.

A breakdown of world primary energy consumption by source in 1992 is shown in Figure 1.1. Oil is the dominant fuel, contributing some 33%, followed by coal at 23%. Coal was once the dominant world fuel, but is now losing ground rapidly to oil and to gas, which has a 19% share. Hydroelectricity and nuclear are much less used, at around 6% each. As stated earlier, the estimated share of traditional, non-commercial fuels, mainly biomass, is around 14%.

BOX 1.5: WORLD PRIMARY ENERGY CONSUMPTION

Estimates of world primary energy consumption in 1992, and the shares of the principal energy sources, are shown in Figure 1.1 below. Figures for world consumption of oil, coal, gas and nuclear fuels in terms of primary energy are from BP (1993).

In accordance with the conventions currently used until 1994 in compiling UK energy statistics, the primary energy equivalent of hydroelectricity production is expressed here in terms of the thermal energy content of the fossil fuel that would need to be burned in a conventional thermal power plant to generate the same amount of electricity. The primary energy equivalent of nuclear electricity is expressed in the same way. This convention is also used by the World Energy Council (WEC, 1993).

Other sources of energy data may quote slightly different figures because:

(a) they assume slightly different values for the thermal energy content of fuels;

(b) they adopt different conventions for estimating the primary energy equivalent of hydro and nuclear electricity;

(c) they may adopt different estimates of the contribution made by traditional biomass

fuels, or even ignore them completely.

In 1994, the UK Department of Trade and Industry (DTI) changed the basis on which the primary energy equivalent of electricity from some renewables is calculated. From 1994 onwards, the primary energy equivalents of energy from those renewables that produce 'primary electricity', such as hydroelectricity or wind power, are no longer calculated on the 'substitution' basis described above but on an 'energy supplied' basis, where production is expressed in terms of the energy content of the electricity produced. (Department of Trade and Industry, 1994). The new approach is consistent with that adopted by the International Energy Agency and the European Union. This change has the overall effect of reducing by 73% the primary energy contributions of renewables sources such as hydroelectricity, wind power and photovoltaics. (The primary energy contribution of nuclear electricity generation
is relatively unaffected by these changes).

However, the DTI continues to publish some primary energy figures calculated on the former 'substitution' basis, alongside the new 'energy supplied' figures, in order to facilitate estimates of the quantities of fossil fuel

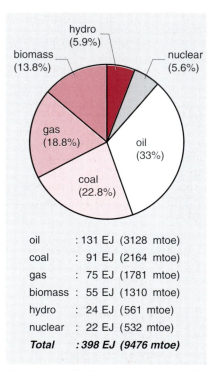

oil	: 131 EJ (3128 mtoe)
coal	: 91 EJ (2164 mtoe)
gas	: 75 EJ (1781 mtoe)
biomass	: 55 EJ (1310 mtoe)
hydro	: 24 EJ (561 mtoe)
nuclear	: 22 EJ (532 mtoe)
Total	**: 398 EJ (9476 mtoe)**

Figure 1.1 Estimated annual world primary energy consumption, 1992, by source

consumption that have been replaced by 'primary electricity' sources.

If reflected in the Figure above, the change would have the effect of reducing the estimated hydro contribution to world primary energy needs by more than two thirds, from nearly 6% to less than 2%.

Table 1.2 Increase in energy use expected as a result of population increases

Year	Population (billions)	Total energy use (EJ/y)	(TW*)	Energy use per person (GJ/y)	(kW*)
1990 (dev)	1.2	284	9.0	237	7.5
1990 (ldc)	4.1	142	4.5	35	1.1
1990 (world)	5.3	426	13.5	80	2.5
2025 (dev)	1.4	167	5.3	120	3.8
2025 (ldc)	6.8	473	15.0	69	2.2
2025 (world)	8.2	640	20.3	78	2.5

* = equivalent continuous power
dev = developed countries
ldc = less developed countries.

Note: The units used in this table and actual quantities are somewhat different from those in the sources quoted earlier in the text. One of the problems in this field is the difficulty in converting apparently similar figures, because their basis may be different.

(Source: adapted from Holdren, 1990)

ENERGY USE IN EUROPE

Even from this small amount of data, it is clear that fuel use varies enormously from country to country, and has changed rapidly over the past few decades. This variety and potential for change should be borne in mind when considering the prospects for renewable sources. To round off this sub-section, let us illustrate this variety by providing snapshots of electricity supply in France and Denmark, and a look at energy use in the United Kingdom.

Figure 1.2 Consumption per capita of commercially-traded fuels (excluding traditional biofuels) in various regions of the world, and in the world as a whole, 1967–92 (Source: BP, 1993)

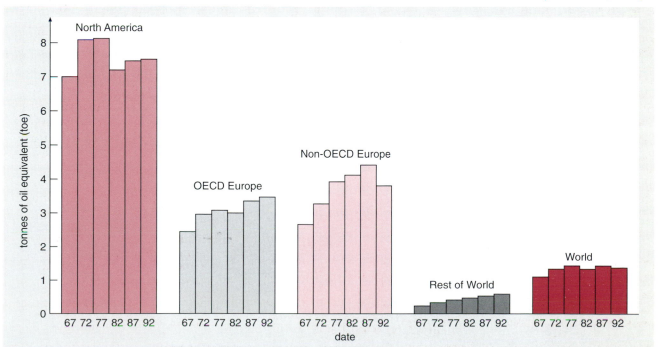

ELECTRICITY SUPPLIES IN FRANCE

France has very limited indigenous fossil fuel resources, and has for many years been pursuing a policy of substituting for fossil fuels. The strategy has been to concentrate on hydro and nuclear electricity, with nuclear forming some 75% of total electrical generating capacity and hydro 20%. France has the largest proportion of nuclear energy generation in the world, and nuclear capacity is planned to rise still further during the 1990s. France has a large excess of generating capacity over average demand, but not enough to meet peak loads. Thus it imports electricity from Spain to meet peaks, but is the largest European exporter of electricity at other times. The French Government is pursuing policies to encourage the use of electricity for domestic space heating and air conditioning.

ELECTRICITY SUPPLIES IN DENMARK

Denmark was almost totally dependent upon oil in the early 1970s but has since transformed its electricity supply industry to one which is now almost totally dependent upon coal. Coal provides 90% of the electricity produced in Denmark, making it the European Community member most biased towards one fuel. The country also imports large amounts of hydroelectricity from the Norwegian and Swedish systems. The Danish government has decided that no nuclear power will be developed in Denmark. Combined heat and power stations and district heating plants are widespread. It has also embarked on an ambitious programme of providing small-scale decentralised power plants using renewable energy sources.

ENERGY USE IN THE UNITED KINGDOM

The UK has substantial indigenous energy resources, including large reserves of coal, oil and gas, which make it reasonably self-sufficient. Figure 1.3 shows UK energy production and consumption between 1960 and 1992. Note that consumption was rising until the early 1970s but has been up and down since then, never again quite exceeding the peak value of 1973.

Gas, oil and coal are known as 'primary fuels' (see below), and all made major contributions to UK energy consumption in 1992, as shown in Figure 1.4. Electricity from hydro and nuclear plants is known as 'primary electricity', whereas electricity generated by burning primary fuels is known as 'secondary electricity'.

In 1992, about 60% of the UK's electricity was generated from coal, as shown in Figure 1.5, with nuclear as the next largest source. However, there

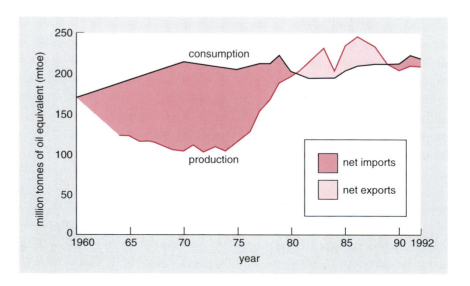

Figure 1.3 UK energy production and consumption, 1960–1992 (Source: Department of Trade and Industry, 1993)

has been a steady move away from coal. The amount of gas used for electricity generation at present is quite small, but the electricity industry is currently building substantial gas-fired capacity. In addition, one more nuclear plant (Sizewell B) was completed in 1994, although some other nuclear power stations will be decommissioned during the 1990s.

The capacities of the various types of electricity generating plant are shown in Figure 1.6. In 1992 the total capacity was around 65 000 MW, whereas the peak load the industry had to supply was some 52 000 MW, so there is around 25% excess capacity. Moreover, the average load was considerably less than the peak load, so much of that capacity was idle most of the time.

The extent to which an electricity generating plant is utilised over time is often expressed as its *capacity factor*, which is the ratio (or percentage) of the actual energy delivered by the plant, during a given period, to the energy it would have delivered had it operated at full rated capacity for the entire period. The term *load factor* is often used in this context instead of capacity factor, although strictly speaking load factor is the ratio of average to peak load, over a given period, in equipment which uses energy rather than plant which generates it.

Figure 1.4   Production and consumption of primary fuels in the UK in 1992. Differences between production and consumption are due to foreign trade, stock changes and the contents of ships' bunkers (Source: Department of Trade and Industry, 1993)

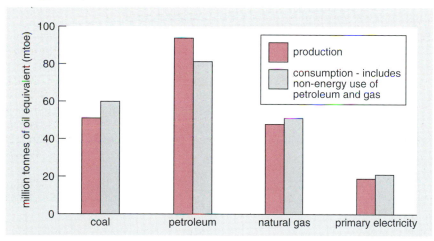

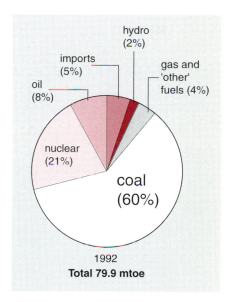

Figure 1.5   Fuels used in electricity generation in the UK in 1992 (all generating companies) (Source: Department of Trade and Industry, 1993)

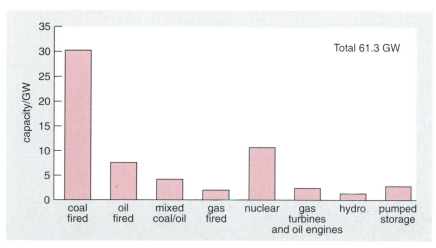

Figure 1.6   UK electricity generating plant capacity in 1992. The capacities shown are those of the major generating companies only. When the capacity of other generators (approximately 4000 MW) is added, the total capacity is approximately 65 000 MW. (Source: Department of Trade and Industry, 1993)

For an entire electricity generating system, such as that of the UK, the term *system load factor* is often used, and is the ratio of the average load on the system over a given period to the highest load. In the UK in 1992 the annual system load factor was 0.676 (67.6%). Load factors and capacity factors are often expressed as percentages rather than ratios.

Of course, there has to be some excess of total capacity over peak demand, to allow for equipment maintenance, breakdown, etc. Moreover, some generating plant is only intended for use at peak periods.

ENERGY USE AND THE POTENTIAL FOR SAVINGS

To understand how best to make use of renewable sources, and also to understand fully the problems caused by the present use of fuels, we must take a closer look at the way energy is currently used in industrial societies. At the same time, we will take a closer look at the technical possibilities for making more efficient use of energy.

To make some sense of the great variety of energy use, it is necessary to categorise it. In most official statistics human activity is divided into four main sectors:

• the *transport* sector (which includes road, rail, air and water transport, both public and private, and for both goods and passengers);

• the *domestic* sector (private households);

• the *commercial and institutional* sector (which includes government buildings, commercial offices, education, health, shops, restaurants, commercial warehouses, plus pubs, clubs, entertainment, religious buildings, and miscellaneous other energy users);

• the *industrial* sector (which includes manufacturing, iron and steel, food and drink, chemicals, building, agriculture, etc.).

The first question to consider is how much energy is used by each sector. In general, energy used by a final consumer is the end result of a series of energy conversions, so the answer to the question must consider where in

Figure 1.7 (Below) Breakdown of UK primary and delivered energy use, 1986 (Source: Blunden & Reddish)

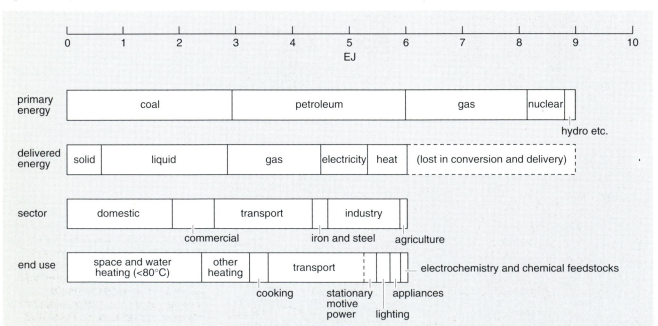

the chain the measurement is being made. For example, coal may be burned in a power station to provide electricity which is used in an immersion heater to heat water in a domestic hot water tank. The energy released when the coal is burned is called the **primary energy** required for that use. The amount of electricity reaching the consumer after conversion from the heat in the burning coal and transmission losses in the electricity grid is the **delivered energy**. After considering losses in the tank and pipes, a final quantity, called the **useful energy**, comes out of the hot tap.

Figure 1.7 gives an overall picture of energy use in the UK in 1986 in terms of primary and delivered energy, by fuel and by sector, together with the estimated proportions of delivered energy employed in various end-uses. Figure 1.8 compares the proportions of delivered energy used in various sectors in the UK, and the proportions of fuels used, between 1960 and 1992. In the UK, as in many other countries, industrial energy use was dominant but is now in decline and has been overtaken by the energy used in transport, which has been growing rapidly in recent years.

THE TRANSPORT SECTOR

Energy in the UK transport sector is dominated by road transport, which accounts for some 80% of energy used in the sector, three-quarters of which is consumed in private cars (Hughes, 1991). In terms of thermodynamic grade, virtually all the energy use in the transport sector is at the highest grade (kinetic energy), yet only 1% of the energy is supplied in the form of electricity. The remainder is almost entirely liquid fuels, turned into work in heat engines.

The main reasons for using fossil fuels, particularly oil, for transport purposes are that they are cheap, have high energy density, are easily stored in vehicles and are widely available.

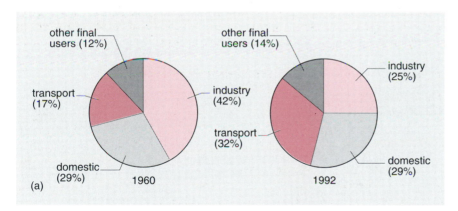

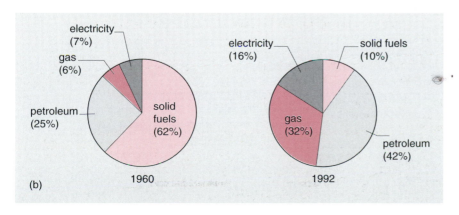

Figure 1.8 (Left) Changes in the proportions of energy delivered to different sectors in the UK (a) and changes in fuel use (b), 1960–1992. 'Other final users' denotes the commercial and institutional sector (Source: Department of Trade and Industry, 1993)

On the other hand, burning fossil fuels in the engines of vehicles is inefficient thermodynamically, as most of the energy is turned not into kinetic energy of movement but into waste heat. In principle, electricity, as a high-grade energy source, is much more suited to supplying the high-grade kinetic energy required in transport. However, if the electricity is supplied from a conventional thermal power station, there is still a great deal of waste heat generated. This is not the case, of course, if the electricity is generated from a high-grade source, such as hydro power or many of the other renewable energy sources.

A lot can be learned from a consideration of the relative fuel consumption of different forms of road transport. This is shown in Figure 1.9. The first point to notice is the large difference in fuel use per passenger kilometre between fully loaded and 'typically' loaded transport. A 2.8 litre car with one person in it can be less fuel efficient than a Boeing 737 jet aircraft. Fully loaded small cars are more efficient than mopeds and motorcycles, and not much worse than many forms of public transport. Obviously, no motorised transport is as fuel efficient as walking or cycling.

A lot of research has gone into increasing the efficiency of road vehicles. There are a large number of possible measures, each of which would produce small savings, but which cumulatively could add up to a reduction of between 40 and 70% compared to typical current vehicles. An average of 60 miles per gallon of fuel (about 4.7 litres per 100 km) for a car is not technically difficult to achieve. For example, an experimental Toyota, built in 1985, had a fuel economy of 98 miles per US gallon (about 3.5 litres per 100 km) on the combined urban/highway test administered by the US government. (See also Figure 1.10.)

Some of the measures are familiar: use of lighter weight materials, lower drag coefficients, electronic engine controls, lower resistance tyres, low friction engine coatings. There has also been research on more efficient engines. The best in current mass production are turbo-charged diesels.

Figure 1.9 Energy efficiency of different transport modes in the UK (Source: Hughes, 1993)

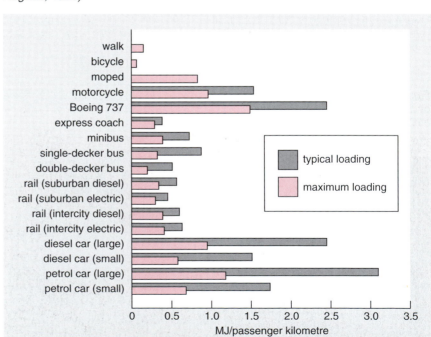

More exotic possibilities include the use of continuously varying transmissions to keep engines running at an optimum speed and hybrid fuel/electric engines with full energy recovery when braking.

The transport sector shows clearly the possibilities for considerable efficiency improvements. Not only is there substantial scope for technical improvements, but social changes, such as car sharing, increased availability and use of public transport, and more walking and cycling, could make large differences.

THE DOMESTIC SECTOR

The principal uses of energy in the domestic sector are for space heating, water heating, cooking, lighting and electrical appliances. Most of the energy used, around 85%, is for low-grade heat (at a temperature below about 80 °C) for space and water heating. This is generally provided directly by high-grade sources (burning fuels directly), or much less efficiently, from a thermodynamic point of view, by electricity from thermal power plants.

By far the greatest scope for reducing energy consumption in the domestic sector is by improving the insulation of existing buildings and designing new buildings for minimal heating requirements. In the late 1970s, the Swedish government initiated a programme to reduce space heating requirements by 30% by 1990 in the domestic sector, by the use of insulation and weatherstripping. The initial incentives were 100% grants, and the government also provided builder training programmes, technical advisers and inspectors. As people became more familiar with the techniques required the grant programme was replaced with a loan scheme. The results exceeded the 30% target. There are now many examples of houses with heating requirements so low that the heat given off by cooking, lights, appliances and the body heat of the occupants is sufficient to supply virtually all their space heating needs. Such 'superinsulated' houses have either very small or no central heating systems, which results in cost savings that largely offset any extra capital costs.

In addition to insulation, other techniques for reducing energy requirements for heating include recovery of heat from exhaust air, and design to maximise the heating effect of sunlight through windows (this is one form of 'passive solar' design – see Chapter 2).

Figure 1.10 The E-Auto, a model of a prototype fuel-efficient family car developed by a consortium of Lotus, Volvo, Alcan, APEX and Cranfield University. At 56 mph, its predicted fuel consumption is 140 mpg (1.9 litres per 100 km)

Most existing central heating boilers were not designed to maximise energy efficiency, and so the scope for improvement there is also substantial. The best boilers now available have efficiencies of over 80%, as compared to the 40–60% of older boilers. Electrical heating appears efficient, as it puts 100% of the delivered energy into a house, but its efficiency in terms of primary energy is very low if the electricity comes from conventional (thermal) power plant because of the 'waste' heat generated. Much better is the use of combined heat and power (CHP) whereby low-grade heating requirements are supplied by low-grade heat sources – in this case, 'waste' heat from thermal power plant.

Most lights and appliances, too, were not designed with low energy use as a consideration and so provide great scope for improved efficiency. Fluorescent light bulbs, including the more recent 'compact fluorescent' designs, are much more efficient than incandescent bulbs, as well as lasting several times longer. Ovens, refrigerators and freezers could be made much more efficient simply by improving their insulation.

THE COMMERCIAL AND INSTITUTIONAL SECTOR

From the point of view of energy use, the commercial and institutional sector is quite similar to the domestic sector. Energy use is currently dominated by space heating, followed by lighting and electrical appliances and equipment, air conditioning, then water heating and cooking (although there is a great deal of variation between buildings).

The prospects for improved efficiency in this sector are very great. A 50% or greater reduction in energy use is relatively easy to obtain in many cases. The first requirement is for improved insulation and draught proofing to the same high standards as described for the domestic sector. Similarly, there is great scope for improved boiler efficiency in central heating plant. Improved controls are also important to permit heating to be supplied only when and where needed. Other efficiency measures include better control of ventilation, and/or heat recovery from the exhaust air stream. Lighting efficiencies can be improved by using more efficient lamps, but also by better use of daylight and spot and task lighting to concentrate illumination when and where needed. Again, there is great scope for increased energy efficiency of appliances of all sorts.

THE INDUSTRIAL SECTOR

Finally there is the industrial sector, which is the most diverse, both within countries and between countries. Generally the largest category of end use energy is process heat, often at high temperatures, as in the iron and steel or chemicals industries. There is also a large requirement for motive power: machines for moving, shaping, forming, etc. After this come the similar requirements to those in the domestic and commercial sectors: space and water heating, lighting, appliances, cooking. One final use of fuels that is specific to this sector is the use of oil not as an energy source but as a raw material for manufacturing plastics and chemicals. This can be equivalent to a significant fraction of the energy delivered to the sector.

In industry there is a wider spread of thermodynamic grades of heat required than in other sectors, and more attention is given to thermodynamic considerations. For example, it is much more common in this sector to use combined heat and power systems to provide both heat and electricity for a factory. In many cases, hot water and steam generated from burning fuels are circulated around a plant for use by other processes.

The principal approaches to improved efficiency in industry are: shifts from more to less energy-intensive industries; more efficient motors, drives and controls; more careful use of energy-intensive materials such as aluminium; shortened process routes, which replace a large number of energy-consuming stages by a direct pathway to the end product; yield improvements on given process routes; technical changes to raise process efficiencies; and greater use of integrated energy technologies such as CHP and heat recovery schemes.

1.3 THE ENERGY PROBLEMS OF MODERN SOCIETIES

Now let us look at some of the consequences of the current scale of fuel use. Today the energy-related problems that hit the headlines most often are environmental ones. Twenty years ago it was sustainability problems: concerns that supplies of fuels would run out. These concerns, of course, are still with us, but now more in the form of anxiety about dependency upon imports from countries which may become unfriendly. A third category of problems are social, and these too often feature in the headlines.

ENVIRONMENTAL PROBLEMS

GLOBAL WARMING: CARBON DIOXIDE AND THE GREENHOUSE EFFECT

Various environmental problems loom large in the public consciousness at present. Many (though not all) of these are largely a result of large-scale fuel use. One of the most significant problems appears to be that of 'global warming', a gradual increase in the global average air temperature at the earth's surface. The majority of scientists now believe that global warming is probably taking place, at a rate of around 0.3 °C per decade, and that it is caused by increases in the concentration of so-called 'greenhouse gases' in the atmosphere. The most significant single component of these greenhouse gas emissions is carbon dioxide (CO_2) released by the burning of fossil fuels. (See Houghton *et al.*, 1990 and 1992.)

When the earth first became solid, some 5 billion years ago, it is believed that the atmosphere was composed largely of carbon dioxide, with no free oxygen. This is consistent with the nature of Mars and Venus, both of which have atmospheres which are over 90% carbon dioxide.

It was the presence of life on earth that radically changed the situation, over billions of years. This reduced the amount of carbon dioxide in the atmosphere to only a 'trace' level of some 350 parts per million (0.035%), although even at this level it is still very significant.

The earliest forms of life on earth some 3.8 billion years ago were primitive bacteria. They were followed by the ancestors of the blue-green algae, the first photosynthetic bacteria, which were the first organisms to use sunlight as their energy source. They extracted carbon dioxide from the atmosphere, and combined it with hydrogen from water to provide the carbohydrates from which they were mainly built. Oxygen was a waste product. This process, called **photosynthesis**, is the basis of all plant life.

Much of the carbon dioxide was recycled by organisms which took in oxygen and gave off carbon dioxide (as do animals), but some was absorbed by rocks in the form of carbonates, or buried as layers of the debris of life at the bottom of the oceans. The result of this process, over billions of years, was to gradually reduce the concentration of carbon dioxide from nearly all of the atmosphere to its present trace levels, and to build up the concentration of oxygen from nothing to its present level of 21% of the atmosphere (by volume).

Some of the remains of this buried ancient life eventually formed carboniferous rocks such as those in the white cliffs of Dover. Another part, the buried remains of forests and other living matter from the Carboniferous period, between 350 and 280 million years ago, turned into the coal, oil and gas which we are burning today. By burning fossil fuels today we are gradually returning to the atmosphere the carbon that was extracted by ancient life.

By returning atmospheric conditions towards what they were in the ancient past, we are certainly not threatening the viability of life on earth as a whole (which still consists predominantly of bacteria!). However, many modern ecosystems, and especially those of plants and animals important to human societies, are very closely adapted to current conditions in terms of temperature and climate, and it is these that are likely to change.

The temperature of the earth is determined by the process in which the incoming radiation from the sun is balanced by the outgoing radiation of the earth. The sun is much hotter than the earth (its effective temperature is 6000 °C), so its radiation peaks at the relatively high frequencies (short wavelengths) of visible light. The earth's temperature is about 15 °C on average, so its radiation peaks at the much lower frequencies (longer wavelengths) of the infrared.

The balance between incoming and outgoing radiation is affected by any absorption or reflection which occurs in the atmosphere. For example, cloud cover reflects back a lot of sunlight before it reaches the surface of the earth, and so keeps the planet cooler than it would otherwise be. The molecules of oxygen (O_2) and nitrogen (N_2), which form most of the atmosphere, are made up of only two atoms each and do not absorb the relatively long wavelengths of the infrared radiation. However, more complex molecules in the atmosphere do absorb the long wavelengths, and thus trap the infrared near to the surface of the earth, keeping temperatures higher.

Carbon dioxide (CO_2), water (H_2O), methane (CH_4), chlorofluorocarbons (CFCs), and other chemicals with many atoms, all absorb infrared radiation, and in general the more complex molecules absorb it more strongly than the simpler ones. All these gases are called **greenhouse gases**. Even in very small so-called 'trace' quantities they can have significant effects on average temperatures. It is estimated that the effect of the current low concentrations of greenhouse gases is to keep the earth about 32 °C warmer than it would be without them.

Measurements from air bubbles trapped in buried ice cores have been used to compare temperatures and greenhouse gas concentrations over the past 160 000 years, and these show there are strong correlations between them. Over that period, in and out of ice ages, the concentration of CO_2 has varied between 180 and 280 ppm (parts per million). The level of CO_2 in the atmosphere was about 280 ppm in the pre-industrial era before 1800 AD, but has now reached over 350 ppm. About half of that increase has taken place since 1960. If emissions of CO_2 continue at the present rate, its concentration will have doubled by 2100 AD, and currently emission rates are increasing at 1.5 ppm per year.

The second major greenhouse gas after CO_2 is methane (CH_4). It is a minor by-product of the burning of biomass and coal, and also comes from the venting of natural gas (which is nearly pure methane). It is released from the intestines of animals and from the decay of organic matter in swamps and paddy fields. Its current concentration is around 1.7 ppm, an increase from pre-industrial conditions when it was about 0.8 ppm. Methane is a much more effective greenhouse gas than carbon dioxide on a molecule-for-molecule basis, but its overall effect at present is smaller because its concentration is so much lower.

Different fossil fuels produce different amounts of carbon dioxide per unit of energy released. Coal is largely carbon, and so most of its combustion products are carbon dioxide. Natural gas, which is methane, produces water as well as carbon dioxide when it is burned, and so emits less CO_2 per unit of energy than coal. Oil falls somewhere between gas and coal in terms of CO_2 emissions, as it is made up of a mixture of hydrocarbons. This is one of the reasons why there is a move towards greater use of gas instead of coal or oil in power stations, despite the much greater abundance of coal.

From the above discussion, it is clear that human activities have had the effect of increasing the concentrations of greenhouse gases by large amounts. What is not so clear are the likely results of that increase. The problem has been widely studied in recent years by the leading scientists in all relevant fields, under the auspices of the Intergovernmental Panel on Climate Change (IPCC). Their conclusions are that:

In terms of observed change, there has been a real but irregular increase in global mean surface temperatures of 0.3 to 0.6 °C over the past 100 years, a marked but irregular recession of the majority of mountain glaciers and the margin of the Greenland ice sheet, and a rise in the average sea level of between 1.0 and 2.0 mm per year.

(Houghton *et al.*, 1990)

By using complex computer-based mathematical models of the climate, and assuming a doubling of CO_2 or equivalent greenhouse gas concentrations, which could occur by 2050 if present trends continue, the IPCC studies predict a global average warming of between 1.5 and 4.5 °C. There would probably also be increased annual precipitation, and decreased sea ice and seasonal snow cover.

The effects would principally be on agriculture: changes to what will grow where. The most severe effects on agriculture are predicted to be in regions least able to adjust, including Brazil, Peru, the Sahel, South-East Asia, and China. An increase in the risk of drought is potentially the most serious impact on agriculture. There could also be sea level rises that could inundate hundreds of thousands of square kilometres of coastal wetlands and other lowlands.

ACID RAIN

Another side-effect of the burning of fossil fuels is acid rain. Some of the gases which are given off when fuels are burned, in particular sulphur dioxide and nitrogen oxides, combine with water in the atmosphere to form sulphuric acid and nitric acid respectively. The result is that any rain which follows is slightly acidic. This acid rain can cause damage to plant life, in some cases seriously affecting the growth of forests, and can erode buildings and corrode metal objects.

About 70% of the sulphur dioxide released in the UK comes from power stations. It results mainly from the burning of coal, together with some oil, which contain sulphur in concentrations ranging from 0.5% to almost 5% per unit volume. Natural gas contains very little sulphur, and is generally not implicated in acid rain. Figure 1.11 shows the principal sources of sulphur dioxide release.

There are several techniques for reducing the sulphur dioxide emissions from coal burning. For conventional coal-fired power stations the most common process is to pass the flue gases through a calcium carbonate slurry, which absorbs the sulphur to produce calcium sulphate or gypsum. This is called flue-gas desulphurisation (FGD). It has the unfortunate side-effect of slightly reducing the overall thermodynamic efficiency of electricity production and thus slightly increasing the amount of CO_2 produced per unit of electricity and increasing its cost. An alternative form of coal-fired power station which has intrinsically lower emissions of sulphur and other harmful effluents uses pressurised fluidised bed combustion (PFBC), in

Figure 1.11 Principal sources of sulphur dioxide emissions, UK, 1991 (Source: Department of Trade and Industry, 1993)

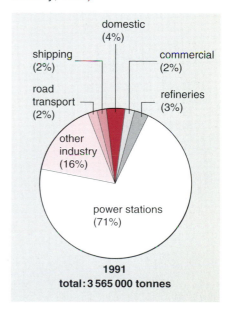

domestic (4%)
commercial (2%)
shipping (2%)
refineries (3%)
road transport (2%)
other industry (16%)
power stations (71%)

1991
total: 3 565 000 tonnes

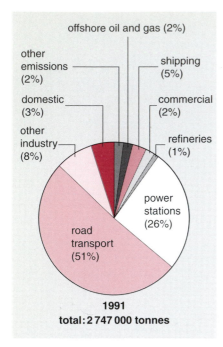

offshore oil and gas (2%)

other emissions (2%)

shipping (5%)

domestic (3%)

commercial (2%)

other industry (8%)

refineries (1%)

power stations (26%)

road transport (51%)

1991
total: 2 747 000 tonnes

Figure 1.12 *Principal ground-based sources of nitrogen oxide emissions, UK, 1991 (Source: Department of Trade and Industry, 1993)*

which air is forced through a burning bed of coal in the presence of limestone.

A second major set of effluents which cause acid rain are nitrogen oxides (NO_x). They are produced in high-temperature combustion processes, partly from the presence of nitrogenous materials in fuels such as coal or wood, and partly by oxidation of the nitrogen in the air. Nitrogen oxides are produced in greater amounts from the engines of road transport vehicles than from power stations, as shown in Figure 1.12.

OIL POLLUTION OF THE SEAS

Not all the harmful environmental effects of fossil fuels are a result of burning them. Underground coal mines can cause subsidence, and open cast mines cause great scars in the landscape – though later restoration work can minimise the long-term impact. Power stations and oil refineries, like many other major industrial installations, can cause significant visual intrusions and can produce significant smells and other effluents locally. But the category of effect that we have chosen to highlight here is the damage to the seas caused by the transport of oil.

As the scale of oil production has increased during the twentieth century, the quantity of oil transported around the world, most of it by sea, has also increased. To cope with this increase, in a highly competitive market, the size of oil tankers has increased to the point where they are by far the largest commercial ships. Even in routine operation, this results in large quantities of oil being released into the seas. The tankers fill up with water as ballast for return journeys. When this is emptied, significant quantities of oil are released as well.

Although the transport of oil is generally a safe industry, the scale of it, and the size of the tankers, means that when accidents do occur they have a large net effect. Although the number of accidents is small in proportion to the number of tanker journeys, thousands of minor incidents involving oil spills from tankers, oil rigs and oil storage facilities occur annually. Between 1970 and 1985 there were 186 major oil spills each involving more than 1300 tonnes of oil. In 1989, the tanker Exxon Valdez ran aground off Alaska, releasing 39 000 tonnes of oil to form a slick covering 1600 square miles and causing widespread environmental damage.

We tend to think of the seas as a vast reservoir which can soak up limitless quantities of whatever we put into it. In fact, the scale of pollution from oil is such that clumps of floating oil are now common almost anywhere in the world's oceans, and create a problem to at least some extent on most of the world's beaches.

RADIOACTIVE WASTES AND NUCLEAR DECOMMISSIONING

The subject of nuclear power is one of the most emotionally charged areas of environmental concern. To many environmentalists, it has become a key symbol, not only of environmental damage but of what they see as the worst aspects of industrial society: links with the military, secrecy, centralisation, etc. To its proponents, nuclear power is a liberating technology. It grew out of the Second World War nuclear weapons programmes, and so represented a 'swords into ploughshares' solution to the problems of burning fossil fuels, a peaceful justification for the dangers of nuclear weapons. It is now being promoted as a 'green' technology because no carbon dioxide is released as a direct effect of the operation of nuclear power stations.

In its early decades, nuclear power was expected by its proponents to become the world's predominant energy technology as the industry matured. That has not happened. It is the dominant electricity supply technology only in France and Belgium, and supplies significant proportions of electrical power in several other countries, but world wide is a relatively minor source, contributing less than 6% of the world's primary energy. In the United Kingdom in 1992 it supplied about 23% of the 306 TWh of electricity generated, equivalent to around 4% of the energy delivered, in all forms, to final consumers in that year.

Since the nuclear accident at Chernobyl in 1986, orders for new nuclear power stations have become relatively rare. Figure 1.13 shows the change in net nuclear generating capacity in Europe between 1980 and 1990, with projections reflecting the expected completion of nuclear power stations now under construction. It is evident that the rapid increase in the beginning of the period has not been sustained recently.

The promise that seemed so bright in the early days appears quite different now that many of the first generation of nuclear power stations are approaching the end of their designed lifetime. Many of the unsolved technical problems that at first could be left for the future have now come close and need urgent solutions.

As we saw in the historical review of energy use, the development and understanding of new materials is one of the pillars of industrial evolution. For example, new materials have enabled higher temperature, and hence more efficient, combustion processes to take place. Non-nuclear energy technologies use materials whose properties are relatively well understood. Inside a nuclear reactor, however, the combination of high radiation levels with high temperatures continuously transforms materials in ways which are extremely hard to predict accurately. The result, for example, is that cracks have been found in many ageing reactors which were unexpected, and whose potential to spread is unknown.

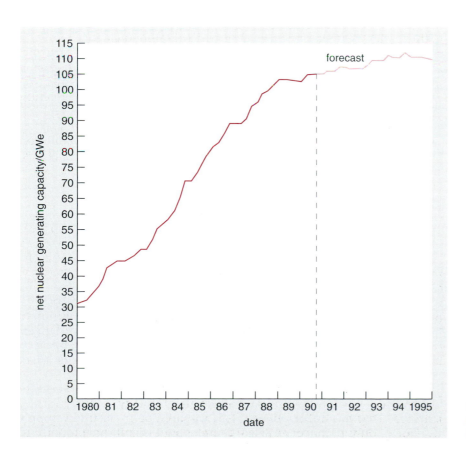

Figure 1.13 European net nuclear generating capacity since 1980 (Source: CEC, 1991)

A problem intrinsic to nuclear power is the creation of new elements, or isotopes of known elements. Some of these routine by-products of nuclear power stations are highly radioactive, and some will remain radioactive for tens of thousands of years. The safety of methods of disposal of such materials is difficult to guarantee, given the uncertainty over the properties of the materials over such long periods. The prospect of decommissioning nuclear power stations which have exceeded their useful life has exposed similar problems.

Like any other concentrated energy source, a nuclear power station, with several years' worth of fuel loaded at one time, is potentially dangerous. Major gas and oil terminals represent similar potential hazards. Nuclear power plants, like larger chemical plants, are also potentially dangerous because of the poisonous nature of the chemicals they contain.

Of course, the nuclear industry has always been very conscious of the dangers of its technology, and has probably gone to greater lengths than any other industry to counter those dangers. The cost of the containment vessel and all the other safety measures is a dominant part of the cost of a nuclear power station, and is one of the principal reasons why such stations are more expensive than fossil fuel power stations.

In all the years of nuclear power station operation, there has been only one major accident, that at Chernobyl in 1986. The earlier more limited accident at Three Mile Island in the USA in 1983 came very close to becoming a major disaster and had an effect on thousands of people. Although these major incidents are rare, there have also been hundreds of minor accidents in which significant releases of radioactivity have occurred.

It is useful to compare the Chernobyl accident with some of the other major industrial accidents of modern times. The leak from a pesticide factory at Bhopal in India caused 2000 deaths and injured 200 000 people. A liquid gas tank explosion in Mexico City killed 1000 people and left thousands homeless. The effects of these accidents were predominantly local. The Chernobyl accident spread radioactivity over large portions of Europe. One hundred and sixteen thousand people were evacuated from their homes. Only 31 people were reported to have died initially, but there are estimates that as many as 40 000 may eventually die prematurely as a result of radiation exposure. (See Medvedev, 1990.)

The reaction of the nuclear industry to the various major and minor incidents has been to increase safety standards still further. This in turn has led to still higher costs for nuclear electricity.

SUSTAINABILITY PROBLEMS

Twenty years ago the most prominent worry about fossil fuel use was the prospect of fuels running out. The influential book *Limits to Growth* (Meadows *et al.*, 1970) reported a series of computer simulations of future resource use in which world fuel consumption continued to rise exponentially. The predicted result was an ultimate collapse in fuel supplies, regardless of the amount of fuel assumed to be available. These fears came into sharp focus in the 1973 fuel crisis, when the member nations of OPEC (the Organisation of Petroleum Exporting Countries) were able for the first time to coordinate their policies and raised the price of oil dramatically. One of the factors which gave the OPEC states the power to exert their influence so strongly was that the United States, formerly a major exporter of oil, had become an importer. It had used up most of the easily obtainable oil from the Texas oil fields.

The shortages expected in the dramatic concerns of those days do not seem imminent at present. The general principle that the amount of fossil fuels remaining is ultimately limited and cannot last forever is obviously true, but estimating how long they will last is not a simple process.

In any year, published figures for 'proven reserves' of oil, gas and coal are widely available. Proven reserves are generally taken to be 'those quantities which geological and engineering information indicate with reasonable certainty can be recovered in the future from known deposits *under existing economic and operating conditions*' (BP, 1993, emphasis added). Note that these are not absolute figures. Proven reserves increase as exploration increases. Exploration for oil is a very expensive business. The amount of exploration is dependent upon economic conditions, particularly the price of oil, and upon political conditions.

The world's proven reserves of oil have increased from some 540 billion barrels in 1969 to just over 1000 billion barrels in 1992, but this is not to say that potential reserves are unlimited. The earth has been surveyed in great detail by the oil companies, and the easiest, cheapest and most promising reservoirs have all been found. Except for the huge pool of oil in the Middle East, the world's most readily exploitable sources of oil and gas have been used up. It is only because of this that such difficult sources of oil as the North Sea and Alaska have become economically viable: that is, the price of oil has risen enough to make them worth exploiting.

In physical terms, the more difficult reserves require deeper holes or extraction in more difficult environments, and the use of more materials and effort to supply the same result. This too requires energy, and there comes a point at which the energy required to extract a difficult resource becomes equal to the energy obtained from it. If this point is ever reached, further extraction will not be worth bothering with!

A useful figure of the merit for fuel reserves is the reserve/production ratio. If the proven reserves remaining at the end of any year are divided by the production in that year, the result is the length of time that those remaining reserves would last if production were to continue at the then-current level.

The reserve/production ratio for any region also gives an indication of the dependence of that area on more favoured regions. For example, for oil, the reserve/production ratio in 1992 was less than 10 years for Western Europe and for North America it was about 25 years. Obviously, both regions would be in dire straits if they could not import oil from Middle Eastern countries, where the ratio is nearly 100 years. The Middle East has some 60% of the world's reserves of oil, and Saudi Arabia alone contains about 25%.

For gas the situation is somewhat different, because of the massive reserves in the former Soviet Union. This region holds some 40% of the world's reserves of gas, and another 40% of gas is in the OPEC region. Again, the world as a whole is greatly dependent upon a limited number of regions which have most of the reserves. The reserve/production ratio for world gas supplies in 1992 was around 65 years.

The world's reserves of coal are much larger and much more evenly distributed. In 1992 the world reserve/production ratio for coal was over 200 years. Unfortunately, coal has disadvantages compared to oil and gas. As we have seen, coal burning creates more CO_2 per unit of energy released than is the case with gas and oil, and more sulphur dioxide and nitrogen oxides. Also, although it is possible to convert coal into liquid fuels for transport, the process is energy- and capital-intensive.

SOCIAL PROBLEMS

So far in this section we have looked at the principal environmental problems associated with large-scale use of fossil and nuclear fuels, and the problems of sustainability. The final category of problems to be considered consists of the associated social problems. We shall not attempt a detailed discussion, but the main issues appear to be the following:

POLITICAL AND ECONOMIC TENSIONS DUE TO CONCENTRATED RESERVES

In the earlier stages of the industrial revolution, fuel sources were local and widely distributed. Industrial activity tended to grow around suitable rivers which provided water power, and then around relatively local sources of coal and coke. As the transport associated with industrialisation spread and developed, fuels began to be transported from more and more distant places. Now, with the most accessible sources of oil and gas depleted, fuels are transported around the world from small numbers of major producing areas. The result is that the major industrial nations have become dependent upon supplies from those producing nations, in particular oil from the Middle East, and are highly vulnerable to disruption of these supplies. This vulnerability and dependence has been a major factor shaping world politics. A series of major economic and political crises has resulted – from the Suez crisis in 1956 to the 1970s oil crisis to the Gulf War in the early 1990s. Since the producing nations are generally weak militarily and the consuming nations are generally stronger, the latter are under pressure to dominate the former economically, politically – and if necessary, militarily – to maintain access to oil.

VULNERABILITY DUE TO CENTRALISATION

A related aspect of vulnerability in the present form of industrialisation is the centralised nature of fuel production and distribution. Electricity is generated in relatively few, very large power stations, and distributed throughout the country. Oil is imported in giant tankers, and converted to fuel in large refineries for further distribution. Concerns have been expressed that these large, vital installations offer potential targets for terrorists or military opponents (see, for example, Knott, 1993). As has been seen in recent years in the Middle East, the result can be massive ecological damage as well as economic devastation. The normal response to such vulnerability is to put greater resources into security and secrecy, to increase levels of protection.

MILITARY DANGERS FROM NUCLEAR PROLIFERATION

As described earlier, the nuclear electricity industries in most of the countries which use a lot of nuclear electricity (the USA, UK, France, Canada, Russia) grew out of nuclear weapons development. The earliest nuclear reactors were built to produce material for nuclear warheads. There has always been a close connection between the two in terms of the technology used, so that military spending on research and development for nuclear weapons technology has in effect been a major subsidy for civilian nuclear electricity industries. Nuclear fuel is not directly useful for nuclear weapons. Much further processing is needed. However, for a country wishing to develop nuclear weapons without publicly revealing the fact, an obvious approach would seem to be to combine weapons development with a nuclear electricity generation industry (see Large *et al.*, 1994) – although it has been argued that, in practice, most nations wishing to acquire military nuclear capability have done so directly and not under the guise of a civil nuclear programme (see Fisher, 1992).

1.4 RENEWABLE ENERGY SOURCES: A WAY OUT?

We have now considered the context in which to examine renewable energy sources. We have considered the ways in which energy is used and the scale of its use. We have looked at the various problems associated with the current use of fossil and nuclear fuels – their effects on the environment, problems of sustainability, and social problems. We are now in a position to look more closely at renewable sources, to see whether and to what extent they offer solutions to these problems.

The term 'renewable energy' can be defined in several ways: for example, Twidell and Weir (1986) define renewable energy as *'energy obtained from the continuous or repetitive currents of energy recurring in the natural environment.'*

Sørensen (1979) defines renewable energy as *'energy flows which are replenished at the same rate as they are "used"'*, adding that the term renewable energy may be taken to include, more broadly, 'the usage of any energy storage reservoir which is being "refilled" at rates comparable to that of extraction.'

More recently, the UK Renewable Energy Advisory Group (REAG) defined renewable energy as *'the term used to cover those energy flows that occur naturally and repeatedly in the environment and can be harnessed for human benefit. The ultimate sources of most of this energy are the sun, gravity and the earth's rotation.'*

Most renewable energy sources (**renewables**) are derived from solar radiation, including the direct use of solar energy for heating or electricity generation, and indirect forms such as energy from the wind, waves and running water, and from plants and animals (wood, straw, dung, and other plant wastes). Tidal sources of energy result from the gravitational pull of the moon and sun, and geothermal energy comes from the heat generated within the earth. Energy from wastes of all kinds is also often included under the heading of renewables.

In their technological development, the renewables range from technologies that are well established and mature to those that need further research and development.

The use of renewables on a more significant scale than at present would at the very least replace a further significant proportion of fossil and nuclear fuel use, thereby reducing the associated environmental impacts. Most of the renewable sources enable the forms of environmental damage discussed in the last section to be avoided, but all have some form of local environmental impact of their own, ranging from very minor to major in the case of the larger tidal and hydroelectric schemes. Almost none of them releases gaseous or liquid pollutants during operation.

Renewable sources are secure and inexhaustible, in the sense that there is no problem of reserves being depleted. With some exceptions, proposed renewable energy sources are local and so cannot be turned off by a 'foreign power'. They can also add diversity to energy supply. Some, such as large tidal and hydroelectricity schemes, can provide individual power plants much larger even than individual fossil or nuclear stations, but most are on a much smaller scale. Smaller power plants offer shorter lead times for planning and construction, and reduced transport and transmission costs.

In the remaining parts of this section, we will take an initial look at the renewable sources, their origins and technical potential. (Individual renewable energy sources will, of course, be examined in detail in the following chapters.) The section will conclude with a discussion of some of the barriers to the introduction of renewables on a more widespread basis, and some scenarios which explore their potential contribution to future energy needs.

ORIGINS AND SIZE OF RENEWABLE ENERGY RESOURCES

THE SOLAR-DERIVED TECHNOLOGIES

The overall size of the flow of solar energy to and from the earth and its atmosphere is vast. The amount of solar energy incident on the earth every year is:

- equivalent to 160 times the energy stored in the world's proven reserves of fossil fuels;
- equivalent to more than 15 000 times the world's annual use of fossil and nuclear fuels, and hydro power.

The issue is thus not one of availability of solar energy, but of the practicality of converting it to forms suitable for human use.

Figure 1.14 gives an overview of the quantity of solar energy incident on the earth and how this energy is transformed in the atmosphere and at the

Figure 1.14 How solar radiation is transformed into various forms of renewable power on earth. For comparison, the rate of world primary energy consumption is approximately equivalent to 13 TW continuous power equivalent

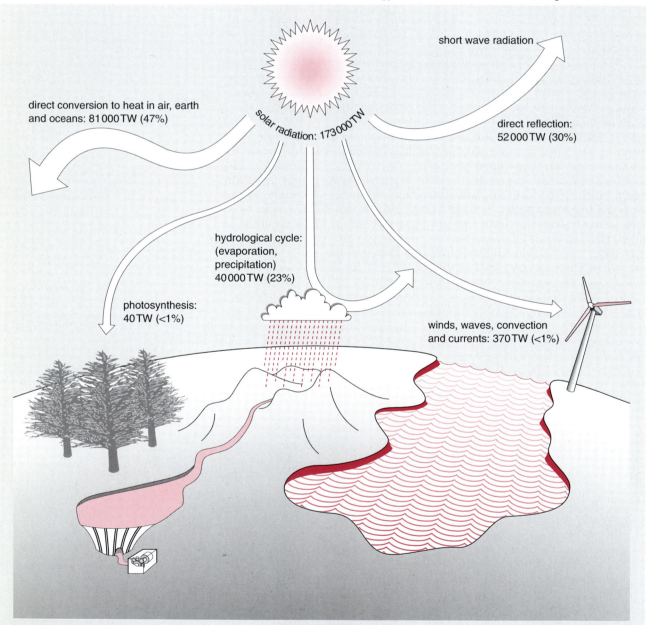

direct conversion to heat in air, earth and oceans: 81 000 TW (47%)

short wave radiation

solar radiation: 173 000 TW

direct reflection: 52 000 TW (30%)

hydrological cycle: (evaporation, precipitation) 40 000 TW (23%)

photosynthesis: 40 TW (<1%)

winds, waves, convection and currents: 370 TW (<1%)

surface of the planet. The earth's energy balance shows clearly. Of the total incoming radiation, 30% is reflected immediately back to space. Most of the remaining 70% goes to warm the earth's surface, atmosphere and oceans (47%) or is absorbed by evaporation of water (23%). Relatively small proportions are used to drive the winds and waves and are absorbed by plants in photosynthesis. Ultimately, all the energy used on earth is radiated back to space, in the form of infra-red radiation.

SOLAR ENERGY

Solar radiation can be converted into useful energy directly, using various technologies. It can be absorbed in solar 'collectors' to provide solar space or water heating at relatively low temperatures. Buildings can be designed with 'passive solar' features that allow solar energy to contribute to their space heating requirements. Small solar collectors are widely used to supply domestic hot water in several countries, including Japan, Australia and Israel. It can be concentrated by parabolic mirrors to provide heat at up to several thousand degrees Celsius, and these high temperatures may then be used either for heating purposes or to generate electricity. Solar thermal power stations are in commercial operation in the USA. Solar radiation can also be converted directly into electrical energy using photovoltaic devices (solar 'cells').

Solar thermal energy conversion and photovoltaics are described in detail in Chapters 2 and 3.

Solar radiation can be converted to useful energy *indirectly*, via other energy forms. Solar energy drives the earth's weather. A large fraction of the incident radiation is absorbed by the oceans, which are warmed and also evaporate to add water vapour to the air. Sunlight falls in a more perpendicular direction in tropical regions, and more obliquely at high latitudes, and so heats the tropics to a greater degree than polar regions. Since heat flows from hotter to colder regions, the result is a massive heat flow towards the poles. The carriers of these flows are currents in the oceans and in the atmosphere. This poleward flow of warm, moist air, when subjected to the rotation of the earth, creates the familiar patterns we see on weather maps of large-scale eddies, which appear as low-pressure 'depressions' and high-pressure regions, with associated weather fronts and storms. In particular, we experience these eddies as winds, and may choose to construct wind turbines to extract some of their energy.

The water evaporated by the sun condenses as rain to feed streams and rivers, into which we can put dams and turbines to extract some of the energy. Where the winds blow over long stretches of ocean they create the regular oscillations of its surface we know as waves. Again, we may use a variety of devices to extract that energy. Thus wind, wave and hydro power are all indirect forms of solar energy.

WIND ENERGY

More than 20 000 wind turbines are in use around the world for generating electricity, and over a million for pumping water. Although experimental wind turbines up to several megawatts in size have been built, the optimum size currently appears to be around 300–500 kilowatts. There are many areas in which wind energy is plentiful.

Wind energy conversion is described in detail in Chapter 7.

WAVE ENERGY

A variety of designs for devices for extracting energy from waves have been proposed. Experimental versions of several have been tested, but the technology has not yet reached the commercial stage. Several countries, including the UK, have significant potential for using wave energy.

Wave energy conversion is described in detail in Chapter 8.

HYDROELECTRICITY

Hydroelectricity is well established as one of the principal energy-producing technologies around the world, providing some 20% of the world's electricity. In the 'developing world', the proportion rises to around 40%. The capacity of large hydroelectric schemes can be several times that of a conventional power station. They are highly efficient, reliable, and long lasting. They are also very controllable and add an element of storage into an electricity supply system, thereby allowing compensation for the varying intensity of other renewable sources and for variations in electricity demand. However, the dams and lakes of large schemes also have major environmental and social impacts. Although there are many more potential sites for large hydroelectric dams, opposition to their effects has grown considerably in the past few decades. There are also numerous devices for extracting energy from small and medium-sized rivers and streams, with or without dams.

Hydroelectricity is described in detail in Chapter 5.

BIOMASS

Another important category of solar-derived renewable energy sources is biological. Green plants absorb sunlight in photosynthesis, which uses carbon dioxide and water to form sugars which, in turn, form the basis of all the plants' more complex molecules. So-called 'biomass' from plants is one of the major world fuel sources, especially in the 'Third World', where it provides some 40% of requirements. It is also important in some of the forest-rich parts of the industrial nations (8% in Sweden, 14% in Canada). The principal biological fuel ('biofuel') is wood, but straw and animal dung are also widely used. Wood fuel is a renewable resource if the rate at which it is consumed is no greater than the rate at which it is renewed. More often, though, it is used at a much greater rate and so leads to the destruction of forests and tree cover in marginal lands, with consequent devastation to soil structure.

Gas and liquid fuels can also be derived from biological sources. Over seven million 'biogas' units have been built, largely in China. Most of these are very small units which digest biological wastes, producing biogas – mainly methane. Some larger-scale units have been developed in the industrialised countries. There are also various methods of producing liquid fuels either from specially grown crops or from biological wastes. A major programme to produce alcohol from sugar cane for fuel use in Brazil has been underway since the mid-1970s and alcohol fuel is now used by 11 million cars. Initially, the alcohol was mixed with petrol, but is increasingly used in pure form, in cars converted to burn it. Certain vegetable oils are also being used as a substitute for diesel fuel. Other substantial programmes to produce liquid biological fuels have been implemented in the USA, France and Germany.

ENERGY FROM WASTES

Energy from wastes is often considered under the heading of biomass, as much of the waste – paper, food wastes, sewage – is directly or indirectly of organic origin. Very large quantities of waste are generated in the domestic, commercial and industrial sectors of the economy. This waste is seen as a problem rather than as an asset. Disposal by landfill is the commonest solution.

As environmental consciousness has grown in recent years, programmes to recycle paper, tin cans, glass bottles and some plastics have become commonplace, but in the UK at present they have not substantially reduced the volume of wastes needing disposal.

Landfill itself is a promising way of generating useful energy. One approach is to engineer landfill sites to encourage the natural process of decay and production of methane gas, which can be tapped with shallow wells. This is a thriving industry in the USA and increasingly in the UK. Another approach is to incinerate the wastes and recover the heat either for electricity production or for other purposes. Much waste is now incinerated, but in plants whose aim is simply to reduce the volume of the waste rather than to produce energy.

Energy from biomass, including energy from wastes, is described in detail in Chapter 4.

TIDAL POWER

The gravitational forces between the earth and the moon cause them to rotate around one another in a 28-day cycle. Another result of those forces is a tidal 'bulge' in the sea facing the moon, and another tidal 'bulge' on the opposite side of the earth, due to centrifugal force generated by the mutual rotation (see Chapter 6, *Tidal Power*, Figure 6.6). The monthly rotation should not be confused with the earth's daily rotation, which causes these two tidal bulges to move around the earth daily. Similar, but smaller, tidal bulges are caused by the gravitational attraction between the earth and the sun. The solar and lunar effects may reinforce or subtract from one another, depending upon the relative positions of the sun and moon, thereby causing the variation in height of the tides.

There are certain sites, such as the Severn Estuary, where geographical features create natural funnels and resonance effects, which concentrate and amplify the tides. Some sites, as with large hydroelectric schemes, have the potential to produce as much electricity as several large conventional power stations. The technology is similar to low-head hydroelectric technology. The output of a tidal power station is variable, though highly predictable, but does not necessarily coincide with variations in electricity demand.

The most widely used approach to harnessing tidal energy is to dam the estuary (using a tidal barrage) and use turbines to extract the ebb and/or flow of the tides; but another possibility is to use submerged rotors to tap into tidal flows in places where they are particularly fast flowing.

At present the largest tidal power station is at La Rance, in Brittany, and has a capacity of 240 MW. There are a number of smaller barrages in Canada, the former Soviet Union and China.

In principle, extracting tidal energy increases the friction of the rotation of the earth, and so would tend to slow its rotation over time. In practice, the amount of tidal energy which could be recovered is so small compared to the overall resource that this effect is negligible.

Tidal energy is described in detail in Chapter 6.

GEOTHERMAL ENERGY

The interior of the earth is very much hotter than its surface, with estimated temperatures of several thousand degrees Celsius. This high temperature was originally caused by the gravitational contraction of the earth when it was formed, but this has since been enhanced by the heat from the decay of the small quantities of radioactive materials contained within the earth's core. There are some places where the hot rock is very near or actually on the earth's surface and heats water in underground aquifers. Such places have provided hot water or steam for centuries. Over 20 countries (for example, Italy, Iceland and California, USA) use geothermal steam to produce electricity, and many others use it to heat water. The normal technique is to use naturally occurring steam, tapped from deep holes. It is also possible to drill deep holes, insert explosives or other devices to fracture the rock, and pump water through the fracture to extract the heat.

If steam or hot water are extracted at a greater rate than heat is replenished from surrounding rocks, a geothermal site will cool down after a number of years and become exhausted. New holes then have to be drilled nearby. When operated in this way, geothermal energy is not strictly renewable. However, it is possible to operate in a renewable mode by keeping the rate of extraction below the rate of renewal, just as it is possible to use biomass energy in a renewable mode, if desired.

Geothermal energy is described in detail in Chapter 9.

HOW MUCH AND FOR WHAT?

There are clearly a large number of renewable energy technologies, some of which already make a significant contribution to world energy needs and some of which are only potential sources, needing more development. They are of varying thermodynamic grade, and thus differ in their appropriateness for different purposes.

The highest-grade sources, suitable for generating hydroelectricity directly, are wind, wave, tidal and photovoltaic energy. Electricity can also be generated from lower-grade renewable sources by burning biomass or biomass-derived liquid or gaseous fuels, from geothermal heat, or from concentrating solar furnaces, using the heat to raise steam to drive a turbine and generator.

For transport, an activity that requires high-grade energy, renewable electricity can be used to power electrically powered trains and cars. Liquid and gaseous fuels from biomass can also be used for transport. A more exotic possibility is to use renewable electricity to separate water into hydrogen and oxygen, and then use the hydrogen as a transport fuel.

High-temperature heat can be obtained from burning renewable-derived fuels, from burning wastes, or from concentrating solar furnaces.

Low-temperature heat is best obtained from solar thermal collectors, but can also be obtained from geothermal sources, or by burning wastes or renewable-derived fuels.

The potential availability of renewable energy sources is as difficult to estimate as the quantity of remaining fossil fuels. Rough calculations can be made of the total resource base: the incident solar radiation, the power in the earth's winds, waves and tides, etc. These give an upper bound which may be orders of magnitude greater than any amount which may be practically recoverable. The economically recoverable amount, as with fossil fuel reserves, is a moving target which depends upon the current state of the technology, and the relative costs compared with fossil or nuclear fuels.

Above all, there are questions of infrastructure. It is much easier to add capacity to a well-established industry, with existing suppliers, maintenance procedures, professional bodies, financial support, legal procedures, and above all customers, than it is to start up a new industry.

Nonetheless, there have been numerous attempts to quantify the potential quantities of renewable energy available for human use. One such estimate is given in Table 1.3.

RENEWABLES AS THE BASIS OF A TECHNOLOGICALLY SOPHISTICATED SOCIETY

The promise of renewable energy is that it offers a solution to many of the environmental and social problems associated with fossil and nuclear fuels. Whilst it appears to be technically possible to replace all fossil and nuclear fuels with renewable sources, on the basis of present and projected costs the energy supplied would be substantially more expensive than it is now. However, there is a strong argument that conventional fuels are currently underpriced because their prices do not include provision for their

Table 1.3 Estimates of global renewable energy resources (at the surface of the earth)

Resources	Estimated as recoverable	Resource base
Solar radiation	1000 TW	90 000 TW
Wind	10 TW	1200 TW
Wave	0.5 TW	3 TW
Tides	0.1 TW	30 TW
Geothermal flow	–	30 TW
Biomass standing crop	–	450 TW years
Geothermal heat stored	>50 TW years	10^{11} TW years
Kinetic energy stored in atmospheric and oceanic circulation	–	32 TW years

Note: As these energy resources are renewable, they are described in terms of energy flow (i.e. power) in terawatts (TW), except for the standing crop of biomass, and geothermal and kinetic energy stored, which are described in terawatt years, (1 TW year = 3.16×10^{19} joules).

(Source: based on Sørensen, 1991)

environmental effects. If renewables can only replace a small fraction of current fossil and nuclear fuel use – or indeed, if the need for those fuels increases despite a renewable contribution – then the environmental and social problems will still remain.

Renewables are most valuable if they can allow a major reduction in fossil and nuclear fuel use – or, better still, if they can replace them entirely in the long term. That is the issue we would like to explore in the remainder of this section.

The amount of energy which can be supplied by renewable sources is part of the answer to this question, and was considered in the previous section. The other half of the equation is the amount of energy needed by society. To put the question starkly, is energy use on the scale now considered normal in industrialised societies *necessary* for a sophisticated, technologically-based culture? Is the only alternative a return to a low-energy, largely agricultural, peasant-style culture (as some people think desirable), or perhaps one in which technology is confined to a rich élite while the majority live in poverty (as others fear)?

Perhaps there is a third possibility, one which we think is suggested by much of the material in this section. Can we imagine a desirable future in which large-scale technical improvements in the ways in which energy is used are combined with changes in lifestyle, consumption, employment, and organisation to reduce the need for energy to levels which are well below the present norm in the richer countries and within reach of the poorer countries?

We believe the answers to these questions are still wide open. Exploring them is one of the most interesting aspects of the study of renewable energy. It raises fundamental questions about the nature of society: the balance between material and social goals, how production is organised, the kinds of economic relationships between people and political relationships between nations.

If renewable energy sources are seen as a significant part of the solution to the problems described above and begin to be used widely, they will become a major industry, with opportunities for employment and production throughout the world. They could become a very significant industry indeed.

Large-scale investment in research and development, together with market incentives and the removal of institutional and other obstacles to development, will be needed to bring some of the renewable energy technologies to maturity. As with earlier large-scale technological changes, such as the spread of telephones or electrification programmes earlier this century, their introduction will bring with it substantial new infrastructure, new distribution systems, and surely new institutions to organise and regulate their manufacture and distribution. All of these bring with them opportunities for new jobs throughout the world.

SOME ENERGY SCENARIOS

It is one thing to make broad statements about technical and social possibilities and another to try to calculate the effects and costs of those possibilities. That is the realm of the scenario maker.

A **scenario** is a hypothetical model of the future development of society. Scenarios are the main devices for constructing quantitative descriptions of the future. They are produced by governments, international bodies, industries, environmental groups, and independent research organisations. Energy scenarios tend to be long documents, full of numerical tables and graphs giving data on current energy use and projections of that use into the future. The underlying social assumptions in these scenarios are often only implicit in such documents, and are seldom the dominant aspect of them, even though they determine the nature of the projections and the shapes of the graphs.

We shall now briefly describe three documents projecting renewable energy use in the future. The first is an official report to the British Government, *Energy Paper No. 60*, by its Renewable Energy Advisory Group (REAG, 1992). The second is a briefing paper on the European Community's ALTENER (Alternative Energy) Programme (CEC, 1992 and Harrison, 1992). The third is a report commissioned by the United Nations Solar Energy Group for Environment and Development as an input to the major UN Conference on Environment and Development (UNCED) held in Rio de Janeiro in June 1992 (Johansson *et al.*, 1993). All three of these give insights into the current scientific and official views of the potential of renewable energy technology.

A major premise of the British *Energy Paper No. 60* is that 'increasing use of renewable energy sources will help to reduce environmental damage from acid rain, and to meet targets for limiting emissions of carbon dioxide and other "greenhouse gases", to which the government is committed'. Renewables are not generally competitive with other fuels now 'because current pricing systems do not take the environmental damage costs ... sufficiently into account'. By the year 2025, renewables could contribute between 5 and 45% of 1991 electricity supply, with a mid-range estimate of around 20%. To ensure that this happens 'the Government must intervene in the market ... because the market is distorted partly by written-off costs and over-supply, and also by the novelty of the relevant renewables ... the Government should underwrite a floor level of 1500 megawatts DNC (Declared Net Capacity) of new renewable electricity generation in the UK to be reached by the year 2000'. (Note that 1500 megawatts is about the same capacity as one large modern fossil fuel power station.)

The report includes many graphs and tables giving the contribution renewables could make under a variety of assumptions. The 'accessible potential', which is technically possible 'taking into account only basic constraints', is shown in Figure 1.16. Note that this is over three times larger than present conventional supply. This is seen as very unlikely, but Figure 1.17, considered more realistic, shows a graph of the contribution in 2025 for a range of different prices. At the low price end the contribution is small, but at the high price end the potential approaches the UK's current electricity requirements. (It is worth noting that the report does not give an estimate of the additional contribution renewables might make to the UK's *non*-electrical energy needs, in the form of heat or liquid fuels.)

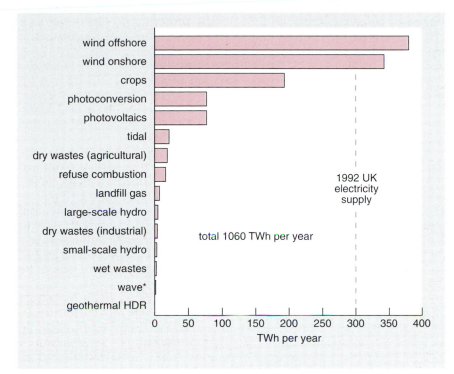

*Figure 1.16 (Right) Accessible potential of electricity-producing renewable energy technologies in the UK. (*The evaluation of wave power was incomplete) (Source: REAG, 1992)*

Figure 1.17 (Below) Estimated contribution of renewables to electricity generation in the UK in 2025 (costs based on 8% discount rate) (Source: REAG, 1992)

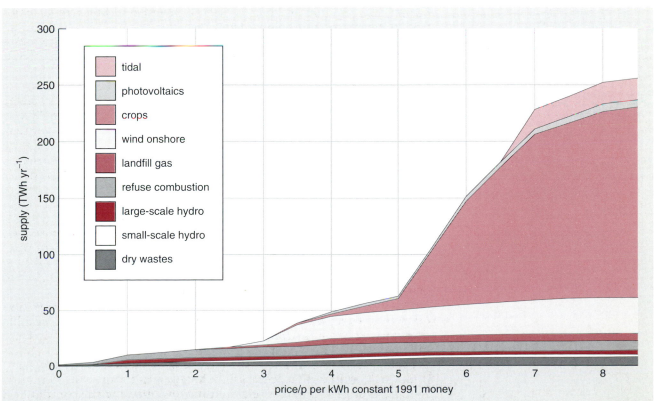

The purpose of the European Commission's ALTENER programme is 'to develop the use of renewable energy sources (REs) in the Community', in order to promote 'protection of the environment by limiting emissions of greenhouse gases' and 'to reduce the Community's dependence on imported energy'. The Commission notes that 'the growth of REs has been hampered by the falling prices of conventional energy sources' and considers that an energy tax 'levied on the final consumer of carbon-rich fuels' and 'other so-called "flanking measures"' would be appropriate.

The ALTENER programme sets targets for production from renewable energy sources for the year 2005, as set out in Table 1.4. Notice that the percentage share of renewables could more than double from an estimated 3.7% contribution to total EC energy consumption in 1991 to 7.8% by 2005, and also that the most strongly favoured technology is biomass, especially in the form of good old-fashioned firewood!

The UNCED Renewable Energy report was 'an international effort carried out by some of the world's leading specialists on renewable energy'. It describes a 'Renewables-Intensive Global Energy Scenario' (RIGES) which is optimistic regarding both the contribution of renewables and their costs. It suggests that 'by the middle of the twenty-first century, renewable sources of energy could account for three-fifths of the world's electricity market and two-fifths of the market for fuels used directly'. This could occur despite the scenario's projections of substantial economic growth and an accompanying increase in total world energy consumption.

Table 1.4 ALTENER new and renewable energy targets for 2005 in the European Union

	Production 1991			Objective 2005		
	GW	TWh	mtoe	GW	TWh	mtoe
Electricity						
Small hydro (under 10 MW)	5.0	15.0	1.3	10.0	30.0	2.6
Geothermal	0.5	3.0	1.9	1.5	9.0	5.4
Biomass and waste	2.0	6.3	2.7	7.0	20.0	8.6
Wind	0.5	0.9	0.1	8.0	20.0	1.7
Photovoltaic	0.0	0.0	0.0	0.5	1.0	0.1
Total electricity, excluding large hydro	8.0	25.2	5.6	27.0	80.0	17.6
Large hydro	74.8	154.5	13.3	88.6	198.5	17.1
Thermal						
Fuelwood			20.0			50.0
Other biomass (biogas, waste etc)			2.7			2.7
Geothermal			0.4			0.4
Solar			0.2			0.2
Total thermal			23.3			62.2
Biofuels			0.0			
Total contribution, excluding large hydro			29.3			91.6
Total contribution of renewables (including large hydro)			*42.6*			*108.7*
Total energy consumption			1160.0			1400.0
Percentage share of renewables			*3.7*			*7.8*

(Source: CEC, 1992 and Harrison, 1992)

Figures 10.25 and 10.26 in Chapter 10 show the report's projections for electricity generation and for direct fuel use. Notice that for both there is an overall increase in capacity over the period considered. Fossil fuels are reduced, but not phased out. By far the largest renewable source proposed is biomass. Large plantations would be required, especially in developing countries. The biomass would be both burned directly and converted to liquid fuels for transport.

The report lists the benefits of its scenario: social and economic development, land restoration, reduced air pollution, abatement of global warming, fuel supply diversity, reduced risks of nuclear weapons proliferation. Moreover, the scenario authors expect that renewable sources will have costs that are competitive with conventional energy sources and therefore conclude that 'such benefits could be achieved at no additional cost'.

The policy measures needed to implement this scenario include: '... subsidies that artificially reduce the price of fuels that compete with renewables should be removed, ... taxes, regulations, and other policy instruments should ensure that consumer decisions are based on the full cost of energy, including environmental and other external costs not reflected in market prices ... government support for research on and development and demonstration of renewable energy technologies should be increased '.

We thus have three projections of the contributions of renewables in the next century, one for the UK, one for the European Community, and one for the world as a whole. Although they differ in the size of the contributions they predict, and the timescales are different, all foresee a substantially increased role for renewables in the coming decades. All of the scenarios justify this increasing role primarily on environmental grounds, and all call for intervention by governments to help promote renewable technologies. One of their principal arguments for this is that current market conditions are biased against renewables because fossil fuels have hidden subsidies by virtue of not having to pay for the environmental damage they cause. In two of the three reports there is a major emphasis on biomass.

Further details of these and other energy scenarios are given in Chapter 10.

CONCLUSIONS

In this Chapter we have attempted to provide a context for the study of renewable energy technologies. We have looked at the historical development of large-scale energy use, and found that whilst it was an essential part of the creation of an advanced technological society, it also took place with little regard for environmental considerations or for the efficiency of use.

We have considered how energy is used in the world today, and found that there are great differences in levels of demand and in the ways in which they are supplied – differences not just between rich and poor, but between the richer countries. A closer look at the demand sectors highlighted the many technical possibilities for reduced energy use.

We have looked at the impact of energy use on the environment, at the problems of sustainability, and at the social problems associated with the present scale of fuel use.

We have introduced the renewable energy technologies, and examined the possibility that they could help to reduce the current problems. This would probably require significant technical and social change involving improvements in the efficiency of energy use, as well as the use of renewables to replace conventional energy sources.

This leaves the way open for the remainder of the book to help provide the detailed understanding of renewable energy technologies that is needed to enable some of these changes to take place.

REFERENCES

Blunden, J. and Reddish, A. (1989) *Energy, Resources and Environment,* Hodder & Stoughton / Open University Press.

British Petroleum (1993) *BP Statistical Review of World Energy*, BP Corporate Communications Services.

Commission of the European Communities (1991) *Energy in Europe,* May.

Commission of the European Communities (1992) Briefing Paper on ALTENER Programme.

Department of Trade and Industry (1993) *Digest of United Kingdom Energy Statistics 1992*, HMSO.

Department of Trade and Industry (1994) 'Outcome of the Review Statistical Methodologies for the Compilation of Overall Energy Data'. Insert in July issue of the monthly statistical bulletin *Energy Trends*, HMSO.

Fisher, D. (1992) 'Nuclear non-proliferation: prospects for the non-proliferation regime after the Gulf War', *Energy Policy*, July (Part 1 of two special issues on 'The first 50 years of nuclear power: legacy and lessons').

Harrison, L. (1992) 'Europe gets clean away', *Windpower Monthly*, September, pp. 18–19.

Holdren, B. (1990) 'Energy in transition', *Scientific American*, September.

Houghton, J. T., Jenkins, G. J. and Ephraums, J. J. (eds) (1990) *Climate Change: The IPCC Scientific Assessment*, Cambridge University Press, p. 365.

Houghton, J. T., Callender, D. A. and Varney, S. K. (eds) (1992) *Climate Change 1992*, The *Supplementary Report to the IPCC Assessment*, Cambridge University Press.

Hughes, P (1993) *Personal Transport and the Greenhouse Effect: a Strategy for Sustainablility*, Earthscan, London.

Hughes, P. (1990) 'Transport and pollution: what's the damage?', paper presented to *Local Transport Today*, conference on 'Environmental Policy in Local Transport', London.

Hughes, P. (1991) 'The role of passenger transport in CO_2 reduction strategies', *Energy Policy*, March.

Johansson, T. B., Kelly, H., Reddy, A. K. and Williams, R. H. (eds) (1993) *Renewable Energy: Sources for Fuels and Electricity*, Island Press, Washington, DC.

King Hubbert, M. (1971) 'The energy resources of the earth', *Scientific American*, September.

Knott, D. (1993) 'Terrorists target UK storage sites', *Oil and Gas Journal*, Vol. 91, No. 25, p. 29.

Large *et al* (1994) *Dual-Capable Nuclear Technology,* Report Ref No LA RL 2084-A for Greenpeace International, Amsterdam.

Meadows, D. *et al.* (1970) *The Limits to Growth*, Earth Island Books, London.

Medvedev, Z. (1990) *The Legacy of Chernobyl*, Basil Blackwell.

Renewable Energy Advisory Group (1992) *Report to the President of the Board of Trade*, Energy Paper No. 60, HMSO, November.

Sørensen, B. (1979) *Renewable Energy*, Academic Press.

Sørensen, B. (1991) 'Renewable energy: a technical overview', *Energy Policy*, May.

World Energy Council (1993) *Energy for Tomorrow's World*, Kogan Page/St Martin's Press.

FURTHER READING

Johansson, T. B., Kelly, H., Reddy, A. K. and Williams, R. H. (eds) (1993) *Renewable Energy: Sources for Fuels and Electricity*, Island Press, Washington, DC. Based on a major report on renewables submitted by a group of leading scientists to the 1992 UN Conference on Environment and Development, held in Rio de Janeiro.

Over 1000 pages of detailed, up-to-date, authoritative treatment of the 'state of the art' in renewable energy.

Sørensen, B. (1979) *Renewable Energy*, Academic Press.

A classic textbook on renewable energy, giving very good descriptions of the underlying physical principles.

Twidell, J. and Weir, A. (1986) *Renewable Energy Resources*, E. F. and F. N. Spon.

Another excellent textbook on renewables.

Renewable Energy Advisory Group (1992) *Report to the President of the Board of Trade*, Energy Paper Number 60, HMSO, November.

Gives the background to interest about renewable energy sources and their potential in the UK and describes policy measures needed to support that potential.

Laughton, M. A. (1990) *Renewable Energy Sources*, Watt Committee on Energy, Report No. 22, Elsevier.

Very comprehensive report; includes technical summaries of all renewables, plus economic, environmental and other aspects. Many photographs and diagrams. Sections on integration into electricity network and summaries of costs.

World Commission on Environment and Development (1987) *Energy 2000: A Global Strategy for Sustainable Development*, Zed Books Ltd.

A largely qualitative description of the problems associated with fossil fuel use on a world-wide scale, the potential of renewables and nuclear energy, plus increases in energy efficiency in the transport, industrial, and agricultural sectors.

Guilmot, J.-F., McGlue, D., Valette, P. and Waeterloos, C. (1986) *Energy 2000, A Reference Projection and Alternative Outlooks for the European Community and the World to the Year 2000*, Cambridge University Press.

A business-as-usual description of the prospects for fuel use in the EU to the year 2000. Gives detailed breakdowns by country, and includes a section which puts this in a world context. Only a passing, and largely dismissive, reference to renewable sources.

Olivier, D., Miall, H., Nectoux, F. and Opperman, M. (1983) *Energy-efficient Futures: Opening the Solar Option*, Earth Resources Research.

Very comprehensive study, although now 10 years old. Discusses risks of present energy policies, and a set of alternative scenarios: 'technical fix' and 'conserver'. Gives very detailed sector-by-sector analyses of energy demand.

British Petroleum (annual) *BP Statistical Review of World Energy*, BP Corporate Communications Services.

Multi-coloured tables and graphs of the world energy position, concentrating on fossil fuels. An authoritative reference in the field.

Department of Energy (1989) *An Evaluation of Energy Related Greenhouse Gas Emissions and Measures to Ameliorate Them*, Energy Paper No. 58, HMSO, October.

Describes present situation, and scenarios to 2020, with renewables making a small contribution. Includes assessments of the main renewable technologies, their costs and contributions, and contributions from increased energy efficiency.

Evans, R. D. (1990) *Environmental and Economic Implications of Small Scale CHP*, ETSU, Energy and Environment Paper 3, Department of Energy, March.

Includes a section with good descriptions of the emissions of CO_2, SO_2, CO, CH_4, from various types of power station.

Evans, R.D. and Herring, H. (1990) *Energy Use and Energy Efficiency in the UK Domestic Sector up to the Year 2010*, Energy Efficiency Series No. 11, HMSO.

Herring, H. and Hardcastle, R and Phillipson, R. (1988) *Energy Use and Energy Efficiency in UK Public and Commercial Buildings to the Year 2000,* Energy Efficiency Series No 6, HMSO.

Detailed descriptions of the current situation and future prospects for energy use in UK domestic, commercial and public buildings.

Digest of United Kingdom Energy Statistics (annual) and *Energy Trends* (monthly), HMSO.

Comprehensive official energy statistics for the UK.

SOLAR THERMAL ENERGY

2.1 INTRODUCTION

As we saw in Chapter 1, the sun is the ultimate source of most of our renewable energy supplies. Since there is also a long history of the sun being regarded as a deity, the direct use of solar radiation has a deep appeal to engineer and architect alike.

In this section, we look at some of the methods employed. Since they are many and varied, we can give only the briefest introduction and supply pointers to further reading for those interested in studying the subject in greater depth. Fortunately, particularly in the field of passive solar heating, some excellent reference works have been prepared by the Commission of the European Communities and others. Details will be found in the Further Reading section at the end.

What sorts of system can be used to collect solar thermal energy?

Most systems for low-temperature solar heating depend on the use of glazing, in particular its ability to transmit visible light but to block infrared radiation. High-temperature solar collection is more likely to employ mirrors. In practice, solar systems of both types can take a wide range of forms.

Active solar heating. This always involves a discrete **solar collector**, usually mounted on the roof of a building, to gather solar radiation. Mostly, collectors are quite simple and the heat produced will be at low temperature (under 100 °C) and used for domestic hot water or swimming pool heating.

Solar thermal engines. These are an extension of active solar heating, usually using more complex collectors to produce temperatures high enough to drive steam turbines to produce electric power. They can come in a wide variety of types. These range from an eight-storey-high tower and mirror assembly in the Pyrenees to 'solar ponds' covering many hectares, and even ocean thermal energy conversion (OTEC) devices that operate on the solar-induced temperature difference between the top and the bottom of the world's oceans.

Passive solar heating. This term has come to have two different meanings.

• In the 'narrow' sense, it means the absorption of solar energy directly into a building to reduce the energy required for heating the habitable spaces (i.e. for **space heating**). Passive solar heating systems mostly use air to circulate the collected energy, usually without pumps or fans – indeed the collector is often an integral part of the building.

• In the 'broad' sense, it means the whole process of integrated low-energy building design, effectively to reduce the heat demand to the point where small passive solar gains make a significant contribution in winter. A large solar contribution to a large heat load may look impressive, but what really counts is to minimise the total fossil fuel consumption and thus achieve the minimum cost.

In this section, for lack of space, we concentrate on the narrow view, although it is important to understand that implementing the broad view can produce energy savings that are five or more times greater.

Daylighting. This means making the best use of natural daylight, through both careful building design and the use of controls to switch off artificial lighting when there is sufficient natural light available.

It must be stressed at the outset that making the best use of solar energy requires a careful understanding of the climate of any particular location. Indeed, many of our present energy problems stem from attempts to produce buildings inappropriate to the local climate. This can mean that the solar technologies used in southern Europe may be disappointing when transferred, for example, to the north of Scotland.

However, most of the methods have been well tried and tested over the past century. Even the most spectacular of modern solar thermal electric power stations are just uprated versions of inventive systems built at the beginning of this century. The art of using solar thermal energy, in all its forms, perhaps lies in producing systems, glazing, solar collectors, mirrors and heat storage that are cheap enough to compete with systems based on fossil fuels at current prices.

2.2 CASE STUDY: SOLAR WATER HEATERS IN SOUTH LONDON

In 1978, the South London Consortium (SLC), a group offering energy design advice to a number of south London boroughs, suggested the installation of solar water heaters on 14 houses undergoing rehabilitation work in the borough of Southwark (Figure 2.1).

The details of a typical system are shown in Figure 2.2. It consists of the following three components:

1   A roof-mounted collector panel of 5 square metres area, covered with a single sheet of glass and tilted towards the sun. The actual panel is a steel plate bonded to copper tubing through which water circulates. It is painted with a special black paint to maximise solar absorption. The whole assembly is insulated on the back to cut heat losses.

2   A 440 litre storage tank, which also doubles as the normal domestic hot water cylinder,

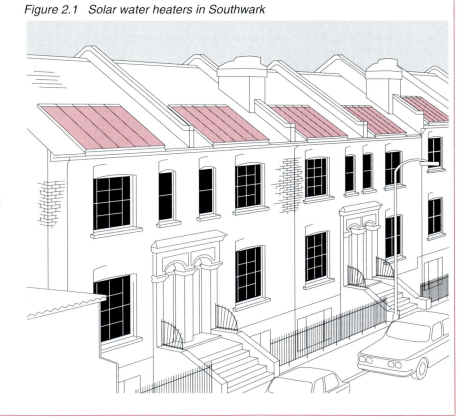

Figure 2.1   Solar water heaters in Southwark

containing an electric immersion heater for winter use. The tank is insulated all round with 50 millimetre glass fibre. The hot water from the panel circulates through a heat exchanger at the bottom of the tank.

3 A pumped circulation system to transfer the heat from the panel to the store. An electric sensor detects when the collector is becoming hot and switches on an electric circulating pump. Since the collector has to be able to survive freezing temperatures, the circulating water contains an anti-freeze. Non-toxic propylene glycol is used (instead of the poisonous ethylene glycol commonly used in car engines).

The performance of the systems was monitored during 1982. On average, each house consumed approximately 200 litres of hot water per day. Over that year, solar energy supplied over 40% of the domestic hot water needs. In the summer three months, the proportion was 66% and in the winter three months, 21%. Ten years later, in 1992, although no longer monitored, most of the systems were still in use.

Encouraged by this project, the SLC decided to incorporate solar water heaters into some of its new-build housing projects. This gave it the opportunity to integrate the systems into the houses. The SLC decided to use the simpler **thermosyphon** arrangement shown in Figure 2.3, allowing it to dispense with the electric circulating pump and its consumption of electricity.

A thermosyphon system relies on the natural convection of hot water rising from the collector panel to carry the heat up to the storage tank, which must be installed above the collector. This arrangement can make mounting the collector on the roof difficult, so instead the SLC designed the houses to have a section of roof at a lower level. This arrangement has been used on two estates in south London and one in east London.

Although the SLC has had an input to the design of a large number of houses, solar water heaters have featured in relatively few: the long payback times have been somewhat discouraging compared with those for other basic energy conservation measures.

World-wide, the thermosyphon solar water heater is the most common variety of system and is very widely used in sunnier southern European countries. A Greek government survey estimated that 15% of Greek homes had them (Eurostat, 1993).

Figure 2.2 Pumped active solar water heater

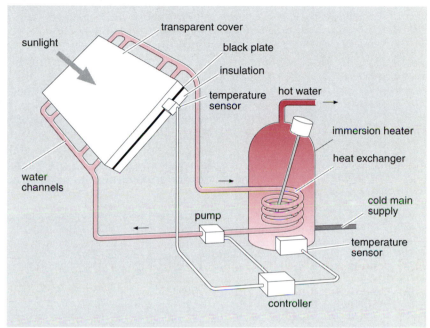

Figure 2.3 Thermosyphon solar water heater

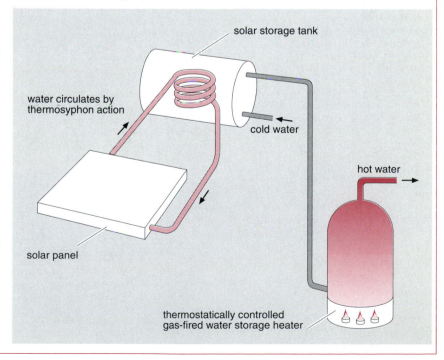

2.3 THE NATURE AND AVAILABILITY OF SOLAR RADIATION

THE WAVELENGTHS OF SOLAR RADIATION

The sun is an enormous fusion reactor, which turns hydrogen into helium at the rate of 4 million tonnes per second. It radiates energy towards the earth by virtue of its high surface temperature, approximately 6000 °C.

Of this radiation, approximately one-third of that incident on the earth is simply reflected back. The rest is absorbed and eventually retransmitted to deep space as long-wave infrared radiation. The earth re-radiates just as much energy as it receives and sits in a stable energy balance at a temperature suitable for life.

We perceive solar radiation as white light. In fact, it spreads over a wider spectrum of wavelengths, from the 'short-wave' infrared (longer than red light) to ultraviolet (shorter than violet). The pattern of wavelength distribution is critically determined by the temperature of the surface of the sun (see Figure 2.4).

The earth, which has an average atmospheric temperature of –20 °C, radiates energy as long-wave infrared to deep space, the temperature of which is only a few degrees above absolute zero, –273 °C. We tend to forget this outgoing radiation, but on a clear night a ground frost can occur as heat radiates first to the cold upper atmosphere and then out into space.

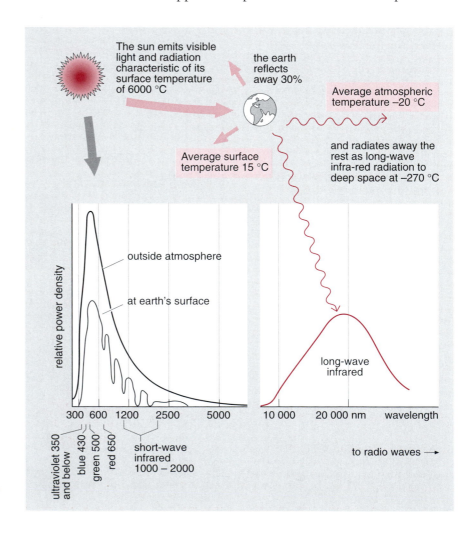

Figure 2.4   Radiation to and from the earth

As we shall see, most of the art of low-temperature solar energy collection depends on our ability to use glass and surfaces with selective properties which allow solar radiation to pass through but block the reradiation of long-wave infrared. The gathering of solar energy for high-temperature applications, such as driving steam engines, is more concerned with concentrating solar energy using complex mirrors.

DIRECT AND DIFFUSE RADIATION

When the sun's rays hit the atmosphere, more or less of the light is scattered, depending on the cloud cover. A proportion of this scattered light comes to earth as diffuse radiation. On the ground, this appears to come from all over the sky. Without it, the sky would appear black.

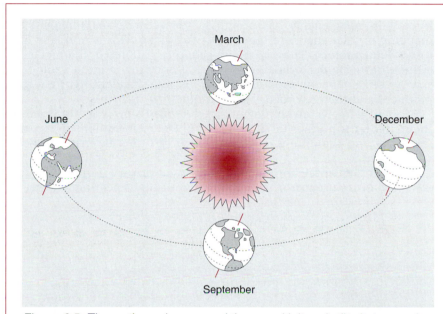

Figure 2.5 *The earth revolves around the sun with its axis tilted at an angle of 23.5°*

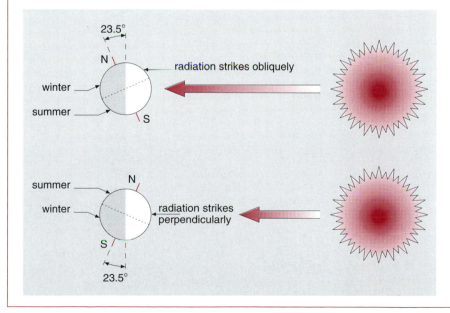

BOX 2.1 SOLAR RADIATION AND THE SEASONS

If the output of the sun is fixed, why do we receive more sun in summer than in winter?

The earth circles the sun with its polar axis tilted towards the plane of rotation (Figure 2.5). In June, the earth sits with the North Pole towards the sun. The sun's rays thus strike the northern hemisphere more perpendicularly and the sun appears higher in the sky (Figure 2.6). In December, the North Pole is tilted away from the sun and its rays strike more obliquely, giving a lower energy density. Energy density here means the number of kilowatt-hours of energy incident on a square metre of the earth's surface in a given period of time.

Another important factor is that the lower the sun in the sky, the further its rays have to pass through the atmosphere, giving them more opportunity to be scattered back into space. When the sun is at 60° to the vertical, its peak energy density on the ground will have fallen to one-quarter of that when it is vertically overhead.

Figure 2.6 *The tilt of the earth's axis creates summer and winter*

What we normally call 'sunshine', that portion of light appearing to come straight from the sun, is known as **direct radiation**. In practice, this includes a certain amount of **circumsolar diffuse radiation**, which appears to come from the region of sky immediately around the sun. On a clear day, direct radiation can approach a power density of 1 kilowatt per square metre (kW m^{-2}), known as '1 sun' for solar collector testing purposes. In the UK, practical peak power densities are just under 900 watts per square metre.

In north-western Europe, on average over the year, approximately 50% of the solar radiation is diffuse and 50% direct. Both are useful for most solar thermal applications, but only direct radiation can be focused to generate very high temperatures. On the other hand, it is the diffuse radiation that provides most of our 'daylight' particularly in north-facing rooms.

AVAILABILITY OF SOLAR RADIATION

Interest in solar energy has prompted the accurate measurement and mapping of solar energy resources over the globe. This is normally done using **solarimeters**. These contain carefully calibrated thermoelectric elements fitted under a glass cover, which is open to the whole vault of the sky. A voltage directly proportional to the total incident light energy is produced and then recorded electronically.

Most solarimeter measurements are recorded simply as **total energy incident on the horizontal surface**. More detailed measurements separate the direct and the diffuse radiation. These can then be mathematically recombined to calculate the radiation on tilted and vertical surfaces.

As we might expect, annual total solar radiation on a horizontal surface is highest near the equator, over 2000 kilowatt-hours per square metre per

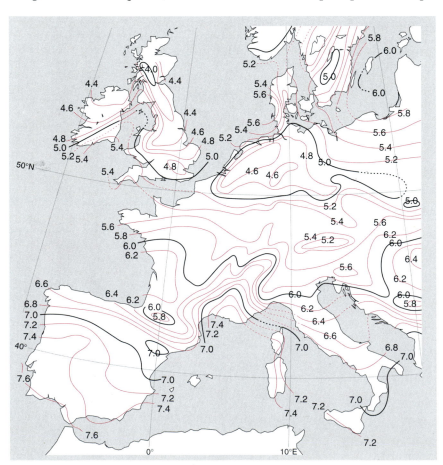

Figure 2.7   Solar radiation on horizontal surface (kWh per square metre per day), Europe, July

year (kWh m^{-2} per year), and especially high in sunny desert areas. These areas are more favoured than the UK and north-western Europe, which only receive approximately 1000 kWh m^{-2} per year. Experimental projects, such as the solar thermal power stations to be described later, tend to be built in areas such as the Pyrenees or the southern states of the USA, where radiation levels are between 1500 and 2500 kWh m^{-2} per year.

It is obvious that in the UK summers are sunnier than winters, but what does this mean in energy terms?

On average in July, the solar radiation on a horizontal surface is approximately 5 kWh m^{-2} per day (see Figure 2.7). Five kilowatt-hours is enough energy to heat the water for a hot bath. At 1995 fuel prices, we would have to pay approximately 15–20 pence for this amount of heat if we were using a normal gas boiler or off-peak electricity.

In winter, however, the amount of solar radiation is far lower. In January in central England it is only one-tenth of the July value (see Figure 2.8). In Scotland it is even less.

The implication of this is that to make best use of solar heat in the UK we need to look for applications that require energy in the summer. There is solar radiation around in the winter, but it may be difficult to gather.

TILT AND ORIENTATION

So far, we have talked about solar radiation on the horizontal surface. To collect as much radiation as possible, a surface must be tilted towards the sun. How much a surface should be tilted is dependent on the latitude and at what time of year most solar collection is required.

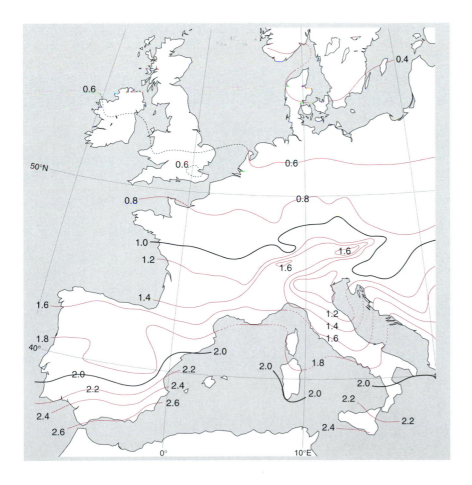

Figure 2.8 Solar radiation on horizontal surface (kWh per square metre per day), Europe, January

If a surface is tilted at an angle equal to the latitude, it will be perpendicular to the sun's rays at midday in March and September (see Figure 2.9). To maximise solar collection in the summer (when there is most radiation to be had), the surface should be tilted a little more towards the horizontal. To maximise in the winter (when more solar energy may be needed), the surface should be tilted more to the vertical (see Figure 2.10).

Fortunately, the effects of tilt and orientation are not particularly critical. Table 2.1 gives totals of energy incident on various tilted surfaces.

Similarly, the effects of orientation away from south are relatively mild. For most solar heating applications, collectors can be faced anywhere from south-east to south-west. This relative flexibility means that a large proportion of existing buildings have roof orientations suitable for solar energy systems.

2.4 THE MAGIC OF GLASS

Most low-temperature solar collection is dependent on the properties of one rather curious substance – glass. It is hard to imagine a world without glazed windows. They have been around since the time of the Romans, who invented a process for making plate glass:

Certain inventions have come about within our own memory – the use of window panes which admit light through a transparent material.

(Seneca, AD 65, cited in Butti and Perlin, 1980)

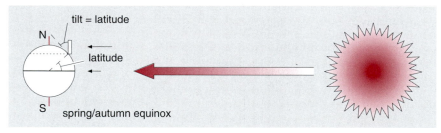

Figure 2.9 Surface tilted at latitude angle will be perpendicular to sun at spring or autumn

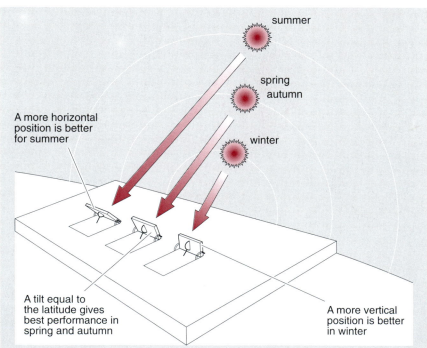

Figure 2.10 Optimising the tilt for different seasons

Table 2.1 Effect of tilting a collection surface to the south (data for Kew near London, latitude 52°N)

Tilt (°)	Annual total radiation (kWh m⁻²)	June total radiation (kWh m⁻²)	December total radiation (kWh m⁻²)
0–Horizontal	944	153	16
30	1068	153	25
45	1053	143	29
60	990	126	30
90–Vertical	745	82	29

(Source: Achard and Gicquel, 1986)

TRANSPARENCY

The most important solar property of glass is that it is transparent to visible light and short-wave infrared, but opaque to long-wave infrared re-radiated from a solar collector or building behind it (see Figure 2.11). Perhaps just as important, from Seneca's point of view, is that glass is also impervious to the wind.

Over the past few decades, an enormous amount of effort has been put into improving the performance of glazing, both to increase its transparency to visible radiation, and to prevent heat escaping through it.

Manufacturers strive to make glass as transparent as possible, usually by keeping down the iron content. Certain plastics are being developed that have optical properties similar to glass, which can be used instead, although

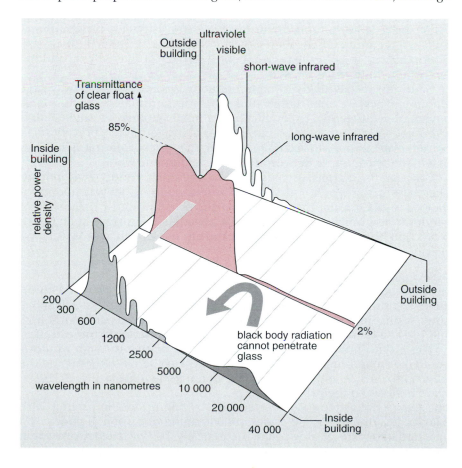

Figure 2.11 Spectral transmittance of glass

Table 2.2 Optical properties of commonly used glazing materials

Material	Thickness (mm)	Solar transmittance*	Long-wave infrared transmittance*
Float glass (normal window glass)	3.9	0.83	0.02
Low-iron glass	3.2	0.9	0.02
Perspex	3.1	0.82	0.02
Polyvinylfluoride (tedlar)	0.1	0.92	0.22
Polyester (mylar)	0.1	0.87	0.18

*Transmittance is the fraction of light incident on a transparent material that is transmitted through the material.

normally they must be protected from the damaging effects of ultraviolet light (Table 2.2).

HEAT LOSS MECHANISMS

Much development work has also gone into reducing the heat loss through windows and solar collector glazing. In order to understand this important topic, we must look at the basic mechanisms involved.

As it is heated by solar radiation, a material seeks to achieve equilibrium with its surroundings in three ways: by conduction, convection and radiation.

CONDUCTION

When solar energy is absorbed by an opaque material, the energy redistributes itself as it is **conducted** between molecules. The rate at which it can do this is proportional to both the **thermal conductivity** of the material and the temperature difference across it.

Generally, metals have very high conductivities and can carry away large amounts of heat for small temperature differences. Insulators require a large temperature differential to conduct only a small amount of heat. Still air is a very good insulator. Most practical forms of insulation rely on very small pockets of air, trapped for example between the panes of glazing, as bubbles in a plastic medium, or between the fibres of mineral wool.

Various forms of **transparent insulation** are currently under development. These use a transparent plastic medium containing large amounts of trapped insulating air. These could eventually revolutionise the notion of windows (and walls), but at present the materials are not robust and need protection from the rigours of weather and ultraviolet light (see Martin and Watson, 1992, in Further Reading).

CONVECTION

Heat can be transferred to a fluid, either a gas or a liquid, by **convection**. Energy is transferred to molecules of the fluid, which then physically move away, taking the energy with them. A warmed fluid may expand as it warms and rise as a result, creating a fluid flow known as **natural convection**.

This is one of the principal modes of transfer of heat through windows out to the environment (see Figure 2.12). It occurs between the air and the glass on the inside and outside surfaces, and, in double glazing, in the air space in between the panes.
The convection effects can be reduced by filling double glazing with heavier, less mobile gas molecules, such as argon or carbon dioxide.

Alternatively the glazing could, theoretically, be evacuated. Convection currents cannot flow in a vacuum. There are several problems still to be

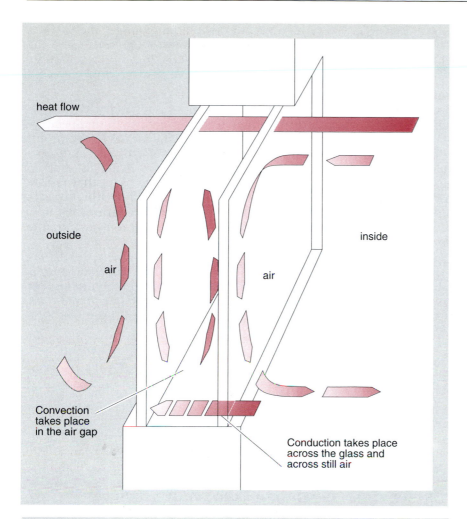

heat flow

outside

air

Convection
takes place
in the air gap

inside

air

Conduction takes place
across the glass and
across still air

Figure 2.12a *How heat escapes from a double-glazed window. If the air space is too narrow, convection will be difficult but conduction will be easy because there is only a small thickness of air to conduct across. If the space is too wide, natural convection currents can easily circulate. In addition, there is radiation across the air space. This can be reduced using low emissivity coatings.*

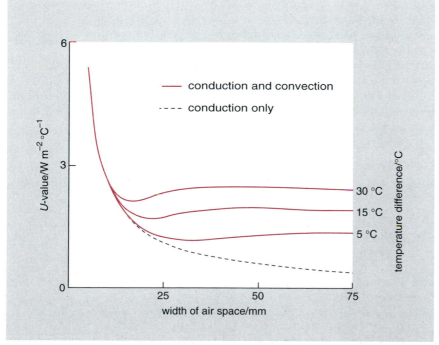

Figure 2.12b *Variation of heat loss through a double glazed window with width of air space. The minimum heat loss occurs at around 15-20 mm thickness. (Source: Hastings and Crenshaw, 1977)*

Table 2.3 Heat loss (*U*-value) of different types of window construction

Window type	*U*-value (*W m⁻² °C⁻¹*)
Single-glazed window	6
Double-glazed window	3
with 'Low-E' coatings	1.8
plus heavy gas filling	1.5
with 3 plastic films ('low-E' coated) plus heavy gas filling	0.35
For comparison: 10 cm opaque fibreglass insulation	0.4

(Sources: Granqvist, 1989 and manufacturers' literature)

solved, however. A very high vacuum would be required, the vacuum would have to last for the whole life of the window (50 years?) and the window would need internal structural spacers to stop it collapsing inwards under the air pressure on the outside.

RADIATION

Heat energy can be **radiated**, in the same manner as it is radiated from the sun to the earth. The quantity of radiation is dependent on the temperature of the radiating body and that of its destination. The roof of a building, for example, will radiate heat away to the atmosphere. It also depends on a quality of the surface known as **emissivity**. Most materials used in buildings have high emissivities of approximately 0.9, that is, they radiate 90% of the theoretical maximum for a given temperature. Other surfaces can be produced that have low emissivities. '**Low-E**' **coatings** are now commonly used inside double glazing to cut radiated heat losses from the inner pane of glass to the outer one across the air gap.

The overall heat loss through a particular building element, which may be made up of a mixture of conduction, convection and radiation, is usually specified as the **U-value**. This is expressed in terms of heat loss per unit area per degree Centigrade: for example, watts per square metre per degree centigrade (W m⁻² °C⁻¹). Table 2.3 gives typical examples (the precise values will depend on construction details).

2.5 LOW-TEMPERATURE SOLAR ENERGY APPLICATIONS

We have seen how solar radiation can produce low-temperature heat. Just how applicable is this in the UK and similar countries?

In the UK, nearly one-half of all the end-use of fuel is for low-temperature heating (see Chapter 1). Over half of energy use in the domestic sector is in this form (see Figure 2.13).

Although simple solar systems are in principle ideal for supplying this heat, other energy-saving systems are also suitable. These include:
• district heating fed from refuse incineration or waste heat from existing power stations;
• heat pumps (see Box 2.2);
• small-scale combined heat and power generation plant;
• waste heat recovery from industrial processes.

All of these merit further development, and unlike solar heating, most have the advantage of being able to run all year round. For various reasons, they are more likely to be available in commercial and industrial buildings than in the domestic sector.

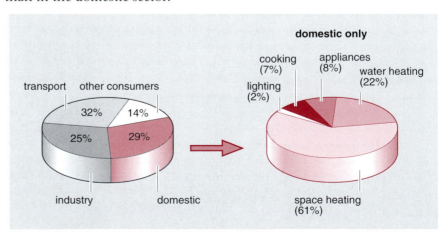

Figure 2.13 UK delivered energy consumption. Breakdown of domestic sector energy use is for 1986; other data are for 1992

BOX 2.2: HEAT PUMPS

A heat pump is essentially very similar to a refrigerator, except that it is used for heating rather than cooling.

In a domestic refrigerator, heat is 'pumped' from an 'evaporator' inside the refrigerated compartment, thus lowering its temperature, to a 'condenser' on the back of the refrigerator, where the heat is released, warming one's kitchen appreciably in the process.

In a heat pump, the evaporator is located somewhere in the external environment, usually simply in the open air. Heat is then 'pumped' from the environment to a 'condenser' in the building, the heat from which warms the building. The environment surrounding the evaporator is cooled to an appreciable degree by this process.

The heat pumping process is made possible by the use of a special refrigerant liquid that boils at low temperature. This evaporates in the 'evaporator', taking in heat from the surrounding environment as it does so. The vapour is then passed through pipes to a compressor (a form of pump, usually electrically powered), which raises its pressure. This causes it to condense (at a temperature considerably higher than that of the evaporator) in the condenser. There, it gives up the 'latent' heat which it previously acquired during the evaporation process, and this heat can be used for space or water heating.

The compressor, in effect, raises the temperature of the heat in the external environment to a level that is useful for heating purposes. Energy is, of course, required to operate the compressor, but typically the heat energy output is 2–3 times the electrical energy needed by the compressor. Ultimately, the heat energy input to a heat pump comes from the sun, which has warmed the external environment to ambient temperature (typically, 0-15 °C).

Swimming pools are a case in point. They do not use a significant proportion of the UK's total energy, since there are not very many of them, but individually they can be enormous energy users. A large, indoor leisure pool can use 1 kW for every square metre of pool area continuously throughout the year. This kind of establishment is a prime candidate for the technologies listed above.

Outdoor pools, usually unheated, are rather different. Here the aim is to make the water a little more attractive when the customers come to use them, which is usually on sunny, warm days. This is ideal solar heating territory.

DOMESTIC WATER HEATING

Domestic water heating is perhaps the best overall potential application for active solar heating in the UK and accounts for approximately 6% of the total national delivered energy use. It is a demand that continues all year round and still needs to be satisfied in the summer when there is plenty of sunshine.

Incoming water is usually at a temperature close to that of the soil, approximately 12 °C in the UK, varying only slightly over the year, and it has to be heated up to 60 °C. In many books there will be found suggestions that temperatures as low as 45 °C are adequate, but recent concerns over Legionnaires' Disease, caused by bacteria multiplying in warm water, have highlighted the desirability of choosing a higher temperature.

Most UK water heating is done in one of three ways.

- By electricity, with an immersion heater in a hot-water storage cylinder.
- Again using a storage cylinder, but with a heat exchanger coil inside connected to a gas, oil or coal-fired central heating boiler.
- By an 'instantaneous' heater, usually powered by gas or electricity.

For water heating, a UK house typically uses approximately 5 kWh per day of **useful energy** (that is, the energy content of the hot water that comes out of the taps). The precise magnitude varies enormously from house to house. However, the actual amount of **delivered energy** (that is, the energy registered on the gas or electricity meter) that is used to produce this useful energy can be considerably larger in summer.

The efficiencies of many older heating systems are notoriously low, especially in summer. Continuously burning pilot lights, uninsulated hot water cylinders and unlagged pipework are the most common causes. Even some electric immersion heaters may only manage a 50% efficiency in terms of useful energy at the tap. Without good lagging, solar water heaters can also suffer from this failing.

Because of the inconvenience of running a whole central heating system for just a little hot water in summer, there is a seasonal tendency to switch to electricity. A 1984 UK survey found that while only 30% of households used electric water heating in winter, 40% did so in summer.

Thus, in summer, a solar water heater is quite likely to be substituting for electricity. And since most UK electricity is currently generated in fossil-fuelled power stations the widespread use of solar water heating would substantially reduce the relatively high carbon dioxide emissions associated with this form of power production (Eyre, 1990). Where solar heat can be substituted for fossil-fuelled electricity used for low-temperature heating purposes, this is at least as beneficial environmentally as, say, building a photovoltaic solar power system to make an equivalent amount of extra electricity.

DOMESTIC SPACE HEATING

Space heating involves warming the interior spaces of buildings to internal temperatures of approximately 20 °C. It consumes almost 20% of the UK's delivered energy, yet with an appropriate heating system it can in principle be carried out with water at only 45 °C. It is an activity that only occurs over the **heating season**. For normal UK buildings this extends from about mid-September to April, although, as we shall see in Section 2.7 on passive solar heating, this can vary considerably with location and level of insulation.

However, there is a fundamental problem that, for this application in the UK, the availability of solar radiation is completely out of phase with the overall demand for heat (see Figure 2.14). Although the total amount of solar radiation over a whole year on a particular site may far exceed the total building heating needs, that falling during the heating season may be quite small.

Even with south-facing vertical surfaces, the amount of radiation intercepted in the UK over the winter is relatively quite small. In London, for example, over a typical six-month winter period of October to March, 1 m^2 of south-facing vertical surface will only intercept 250 kWh of solar radiation.

It is important to emphasise that the suitability of solar energy for space heating is dependent on the local climate. Textbooks may show quite grandiose solar buildings, but these may only be appropriate in particular locations, often places that are both cold and sunny in winter.

In summer, the UK has similar temperatures, and receives a similar amount of solar radiation, to other countries on the same latitude, such as Eire, the Netherlands and Denmark.

In winter, the picture is different. The UK has relatively mild winters. However, the winter solar radiation remains largely dependent on latitude alone. As can be seen in Figure 2.15, average January temperatures in London are virtually identical to those in the south of France (follow the 5 °C contour round). Why then do people go south for the winter? The answer is because it is sunnier. As we saw from Figure 2.8, the south of France receives three times as much solar radiation on the horizontal surface in mid-winter as does London.

Broadly speaking, the climate of Western Europe can be split into four regions (Figure 2.15).

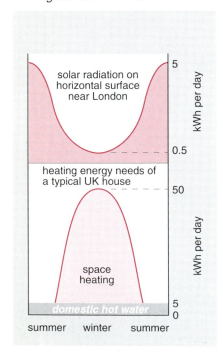

Figure 2.14 Availability of solar radiation is out of phase with space heating demand in the UK

1   Northern European coastal zone: cold winters with little solar radiation in mid-winter; mild summers.

2   Mid-European coastal zone: cool winters with modest amounts of solar radiation; mild summers.

3   Continental zone: very cold winters with modest amounts of solar radiation; hot summers.

4   Southern and Mediterranean zone: mild winters with high solar radiation; hot sunny summers.

It is no coincidence that many solar experimental projects have been built on the boundaries of regions 3 and 4, in the Pyrenees and the area around the Alps. This kind of climate is also typical of Colorado in the central USA, another area where solar-heated houses abound.

The broad view of passive solar heating is really about the subtle influence of climate on building design. Without this appreciation, it is all too easy to design buildings that are inappropriate to their surroundings.

As the Roman architect Vitruvius said in the first century BC:

We must begin by taking note of the countries and climates in which homes are to be built if our designs for them are to be correct. One type of house seems appropriate for Egypt, another for Spain ... one still different for Rome, and so on with lands of varying characteristics. This is because one part of the earth is directly under the sun's course, another is far away from it ... It is obvious that designs for homes ought to conform to the diversities of climate.

(Cited in Butti and Perlin, 1980)

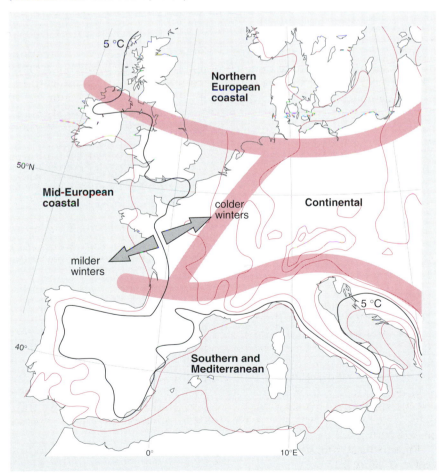

Figure 2.15 The different climatic zones of Europe. UK winters are mild compared with much of the rest of Europe. The 5 °C contour is for January

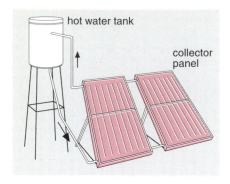

Figure 2.16 *Free-standing thermosyphon solar water heater*

VARIETIES OF SOLAR HEATING SYSTEM

In practice, the categories 'active' and 'passive' are not clear cut: they blend into each other, with a whole range of possibilities in between. The following examples illustrate the range of solar heating systems available in addition to the normal, roof-mounted solar water heater that we have considered already.

FREE-STANDING THERMOSYPHON SOLAR WATER HEATER

In the introductory case study, we saw a thermosyphon system integrated into a house. Free-standing versions, as shown in Figure 2.16, are very common in Mediterranean countries, where they can be easily installed on flat roofs. A further variant is an 'integrated package', where for ease of manufacture the storage tank has been incorporated into the top of the collector. Since the storage tank is outdoors, these systems are only really viable in frost-free regions.

SWIMMING POOL HEATING

For swimming pool heating, the solar system can be extremely simple (see Figure 2.17). Pool water is pumped through a large area of collector, usually unglazed. Typically, the collector will be about half the area of the pool itself. The best results are achieved with pools that do not have other forms of heating and are consequently at relatively low temperatures. The aim may not necessarily be to save energy as much as to make the pool temperature more acceptable to bathers.

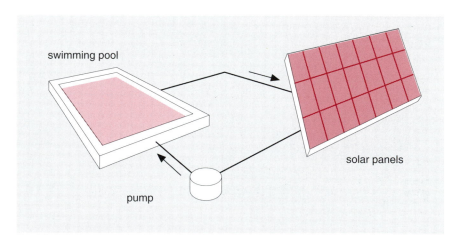

Figure 2.17 *Solar swimming pool heating system*

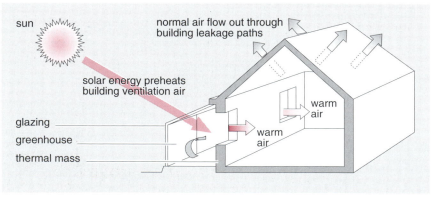

Figure 2.18 *Attached sunspace or conservatory*

CONSERVATORY (OR 'SUNSPACE')

A conservatory or greenhouse on the south side of a building can be thought of as a kind of habitable solar collector (see Figure 2.18). Air is the heat transfer fluid, carrying energy into the building behind. The energy store is the building itself, especially the wall at the back of the conservatory.

TROMBE WALL

With a Trombe wall (named after its French inventor, Felix Trombe), the conservatory is replaced by a thin air space in front of a storage wall (Figure 2.19). This is a solar collector with the storage immediately behind. Solar radiation warms the store and is radiated into the house in an even fashion from its inner side. In addition, on sunny days, air is circulated through the air space into the house behind. At night and on cold days, the air flow is cut off.

This concept can take many forms. Small collector panels can be built directly on to the existing walls of buildings. In the extreme, the air path can be omitted, and walls simply covered with 'transparent insulation'.

DIRECT GAIN

Direct gain is the simplest and most common of all passive solar heating systems. All glazed buildings make use of this to some degree. The sun's rays simply penetrate the windows and are absorbed into the interior (Figure 2.20). If the building is 'thermally massive' enough, and the heating system responsive, the gains are likely to be useful. If the building is too 'thermally lightweight', the internal temperature will rise too high and the occupants will perceive the effect as a nuisance.

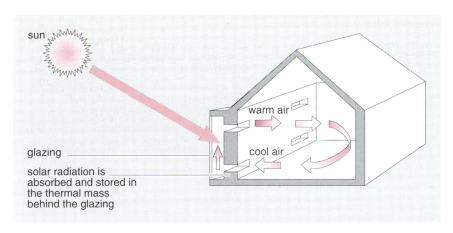

Figure 2.19 Trombe wall

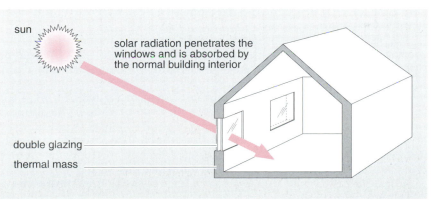

Figure 2.20 Direct gain

2.6 ACTIVE SOLAR HEATING

HISTORY

A solar water heater could be made simply by placing a tank of water behind a normal window. Indeed, many of the first systems produced in the USA in the 1890s were little more than this.

The solar water heater as we know it was patented in 1909 by William J. Bailey in California. It was very similar to the thermosyphon system described in the introductory case study. Since the system had an insulated tank, which could keep water hot overnight, Bailey called his business the 'Day and Night' Solar Water Heater Company. He sold approximately 4000 systems before the local discovery of cheap natural gas in the 1920s virtually closed his business.

In Florida, the solar water heating business flourished until the 1940s. Eighty per cent of new homes built in Miami between 1935 and 1941 had solar systems. Possibly as many as 60 000 were sold over this period in this area alone. Yet by 1950 the US solar heating industry had completely succumbed to cheap fossil fuel (Butti and Perlin, 1980).

It was not until the oil price rises of 1973 that the solar collector reappeared. The USA, Japan, Greece and Israel now all have flourishing solar water heating industries. Even in the UK, some 40 000 solar water heaters have been installed.

We have already considered the basic form of a solar water heating system, but what about the choices involved in selecting the components?

SOLAR COLLECTORS

Just as solar energy systems can have many variants, so can solar collectors. Figure 2.21 summarises most of the possibilities.

Unglazed panels. These are most suitable for swimming pool heating, where it is only necessary for the water temperature to rise by a few degrees above ambient air temperature, so heat losses are relatively unimportant.

Flat plate water collectors. Worldwide, these are the mainstay of domestic solar water heating. Usually they are only single glazed but may have an additional second glazing layer, sometimes of plastic. The more elaborate the glazing system, the higher the temperature difference that can be sustained between the absorber and the external air.

The absorber plate usually has a very black surface with a high **absorptivity**. Most normal black paints still reflect approximately 10% of the incident radiation. Some panels use a **selective surface** that has both high absorptivity in the visible region and low emissivity in the long-wave infrared, to cut heat losses.

Many designs of absorber plate have been tried with success in recent years, including pressed steel central heating radiators, specially made pressed aluminium panels and small-bore copper pipes soldered to thick copper or steel sheet. Generally, an absorber plate must have high thermal conductivity, to transfer the collected energy to the water with minimum temperature loss.

Flat plate air collectors. These are not so common as water collectors and are mainly used for space heating only. An interesting variant is to combine this type of collector with a photovoltaic panel, producing both heat and electricity.

Evacuated tube collectors. The example shown in Figure 2.21 takes the form of a set of modular tubes similar to fluorescent lamps. The absorber plate is a metal strip down the centre of each tube. Convective heat losses are suppressed by virtue of a vacuum in the tube. The absorber plate uses a special 'heat pipe' to carry the collected energy to the water, which circulates along a header pipe at the top of the array.

A heat pipe is a device that takes advantage of the thermal properties of a boiling fluid to carry large amounts of heat. A hollow tube is filled with a liquid at a pressure chosen so that it can be made to boil at the 'hot' end, but the vapour will condense at the 'cold' end. The tube in effect has a thermal conductivity many times greater than if it had been made of solid metal, and is capable of transferring large amounts of heat for a small temperature rise.

Line focus collectors. These focus the sun on to a pipe running down the centre of a trough. They are mainly used for generating steam for electricity generation (see Section 2.9). The trough can be pivoted to track the sun up and down or east to west. A line focus collector can be oriented with its axis in either a horizontal or a vertical plane.

Point focus collectors. These are also used for steam generation but need to track the sun in two dimensions.

ROBUSTNESS, MOUNTING AND ORIENTATION

Solar collectors are usually roof mounted and once installed are difficult to reach for maintenance and repairs. They must be firmly attached to the roof in a leak-proof manner and then must withstand everything that nature can throw at them – frost, wind, acid rain, sea spray and hailstones. They also have to be proof against internal corrosion and very large temperature swings. A double-glazed collector is potentially capable of producing boiling water in high summer if the heat is not carried away fast enough. It is quite an art to make something that can survive up to 20 or more years of this treatment.

Fortunately, as we have seen, panels do not have to be installed to a precise tilt or orientation for acceptable performance. This in turn means that a large portion of the current building stock, possibly 50% or more, could support a solar collector.

Figure 2.21 Types of solar collector and suitability to various temperatures

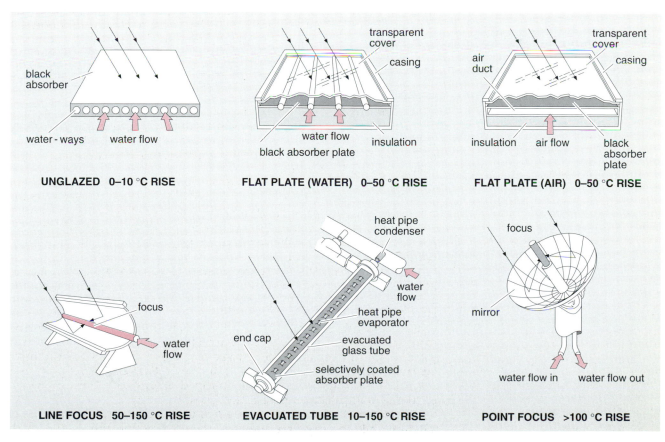

ACTIVE SOLAR SPACE HEATING

So far, we have looked in detail at domestic solar water heaters with only a few square metres of collector. If a far larger collector together with a much larger storage tank were fitted, solar energy should be able to supply far more of the annual low-temperature needs of a building. In the 1970s, many experimental systems were built with this aim around the world.

The UK house illustrated in Figure 2.22 is a good example. Built in Milton Keynes in 1975 and operational until mid 1994, it experienced a climate typical of the central UK. Thirty-six square metres of single-glazed collector were fitted to the roof of a relatively poorly insulated three-bedroomed house. The energy store took the form of two water tanks of 4.5 cubic metres total capacity in the centre of the house.

The solar energy was originally used both to heat domestic hot water and to supply some space heating. Monitoring showed that the system supplied half of the low-temperature heating needs, but that the bulk of the energy was used for domestic hot water. Only a small proportion of the space heating energy came from collected active solar energy, and that only at the sunnier ends of the heating season. In fact, almost as much came from passive solar gains through the windows.

Although the house worked largely as designed, it highlighted some basic problems.

1 In order to collect enough solar energy to supply the winter demand, the collector would have to be very large. This would mean that over much of the summer its potential output would not be used because the demand would not be there, and the capital expenditure would effectively be wasted (Figure 2.23).

2 If the house had been better insulated, it would not have required so much space heating energy, and what it did consume could have been better met by passive solar means.

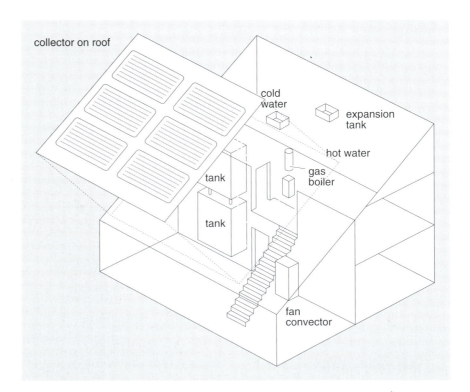

Figure 2.22 Milton Keynes active solar house – section

Here we have the key problem: whether to build poorly insulated houses and then try to find renewable energy sources to heat them, or use energy conservation to cut demands so that it is not necessary to supply so much energy.

Subsequent analysis and experiment showed that the same energy saving could be obtained from a well-insulated passive solar-heated house for a fraction of the cost of a poorly insulated one with active solar heating. Similar calculations have been made for solar-heated houses in Germany and France.

SOLAR-AIDED DISTRICT HEATING

It is tempting to think that if the storage tank of a solar-heated house was made large enough, the summer sun could be saved through to the winter. This is known as **interseasonal** storage. However, the difficulties of this should not be underestimated. The volume of hot water storage needed to supply a house is almost the same size as the house itself.

In addition, the tank would need to be well insulated. A normal domestic hot water cylinder would require insulation 4 metres thick to retain most of its heat from summer to winter. It therefore pays to make the storage volume truly enormous. This reduces the ratio of surface area to volume. For example, a project using a rock cavern with a volume of 105 000 m³ has been constructed in Sweden for connection to a communal district heating scheme feeding 550 dwellings. At this scale, solar collectors can be purchased and erected in bulk. This kind of scheme can, in principle, supply 100% solar space and water heating to buildings, but currently payback periods are very long.

The important lesson from active solar space heating experiments has been that it is essential to invest in energy conservation first and then to use solar energy to help supply the remaining reduced load. However, combining energy conservation and design for passive solar heating requires a deeper understanding of how buildings use energy, as we shall see in the next section.

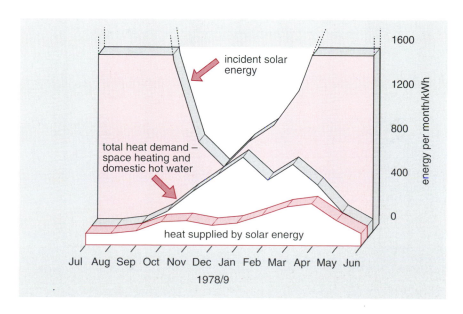

Figure 2.23 Milton Keynes active solar house – measured performance

BOX 2.3 SOLAR DISTRICT HEATING IN DENMARK

This housing project at Herlev, near Copenhagen in Denmark, incorporates solar district heating. A central solar collector field of 1025 m^2 area heats the 3000 m^3 heat store (a large insulated water tank buried in the ground) to 80 °C in summer. This solar heat provides most of the space heating requirements of the 92 housing units in the scheme. When the temperature of the heat store falls below 45 °C, heat is transferred via a heat pump, powered by a gas engine, which boosts the temperature to the required 55 °C. This process continues until the temperature of the heat store has fallen to 10 °C, at the end of the heating season. Waste heat from the engine is also delivered to the heating system, and a gas boiler is available as a back-up.

In summer, when the main heating system is shut down 90% of the domestic hot water requirements of the housing units are provided by additional 45 m^2 solar collectors situated on each of the eight housing blocks in the scheme. The total cost of the energy system was approximately 12.5 million Danish kroner, and since the estimated annual savings are 370 000 DKK, the simple payback time is 34 years. However, the system was a prototype, and it is expected that the capital costs of future systems of this type could be reduced substantially. The costs of the scheme were subsidised by the European Union, the Danish Energy Council and the building society which funded the housing project.

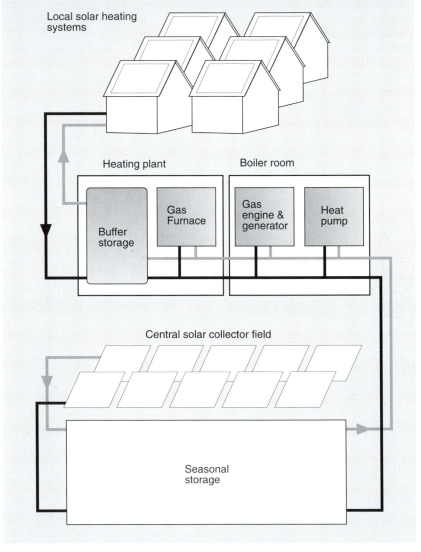

2.7 PASSIVE SOLAR HEATING

HISTORY

All glazed buildings are already to some extent passively solar heated: effectively they are live-in solar collectors. The art of making the best use of this dates back to the Romans, who put glass to good use in their favourite communal meeting place, the bath house. Window openings 2 m wide and 3 m high have been found at Pompeii.

After the fall of the Roman Empire, the ability to make really large sheets of glass vanished for over a millenium. It was not until the end of the seventeenth century that the plate glass process reappeared in France, allowing sheets 2 m square to be made.

Even so, cities of the eighteenth and nineteenth centuries were overcrowded and the houses ill-lit. It was not until the late nineteenth century that pioneering urban planners set out to design better conditions. They had an obsession with the medical benefits of sunlight after it was discovered that ultraviolet light killed bacteria. Sunshine and fresh air became the watchwords of 'new towns' like Port Sunlight near Liverpool, built to accommodate the workers of a soap factory.

The planners then did not realise that ultraviolet light does not penetrate windows, but the tradition of allowing access for plenty of sunlight continues, with recent theories that exposure to bright light in winter is essential to maintain human hormone balances. Without it, people are likely to develop mid-winter depression.

Given the UK's plentiful supply of coal, there was little interest in using solar energy to cut fuel bills until recent years. The construction of the Wallasey School building in Cheshire in 1961, inspired by earlier US and French buildings, was thus something of a novelty (see Figures 2.24 and 2.25).

Figure 2.24 Wallasey School

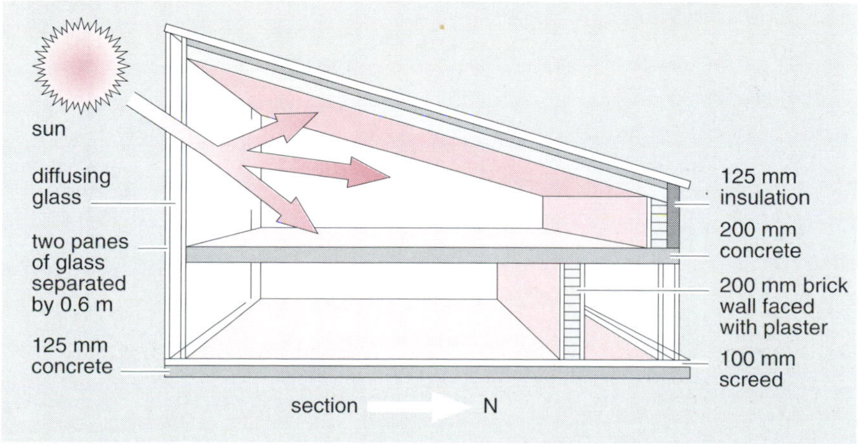

Figure 2.25 Wallasey School – section

DIRECT GAIN BUILDINGS AS SOLAR COLLECTORS

Wallasey School building is a classic direct gain design. It has the essential features required for passive solar heating:

1 a large area of south-facing glazing to capture the sunlight;
2 thermally heavyweight construction (dense concrete or brickwork). This stores the thermal energy through the day and into the night;
3 thick insulation on the outside of the structure to retain the heat.

After its construction, the oil-fired heating system originally installed was found to be unnecessary and was for a time removed, leaving the building totally heated by a mixture of solar energy, heat from incandescent lights and the body heat of the students.

PASSIVE SOLAR HEATING VERSUS SUPERINSULATION

Although the Wallasey School building is one style of low-energy building, there are others. The Wates house, built at Machynlleth in Wales in 1975 (Figure 2.26) was one of the first 'superinsulated' buildings in the UK. It features 450 mm of wall insulation and small quadruple-glazed windows. Situated low in a mountain valley, it is certainly not well placed for passive solar heating. In fact, it was intended to be heated and lit by electricity from a wind turbine.

Which of the two design approaches – passive solar or superinsulation – is better?

There are no easy answers to this. The art of design for passive solar heating is to understand the energy flows in a building and make the most of them. There need to be sufficient solar gains to meet winter heating needs and provide adequate lighting, but not so much in summer that there is overheating.

WINDOW ENERGY BALANCE

We can think of a south-facing window as a kind of passive solar heating element. Solar radiation enters during the day, and, if the building's internal temperature is higher than that outside, heat will be conducted, convected and radiated back out.

The question is whether more heat flows in than out, so that the window provides a net energy benefit. The answer depends on several things:

1 the building's internal temperature;
2 the average external temperature;
3 the available solar radiation;
4 the transmittance characteristics of the window, its orientation and shading;
5 the U-value of the window and whether it is single or double glazed.

Figure 2.26 Wates house, Machynlleth

Figure 2.27 shows the average monthly 'energy balance' of a south-facing window in the vicinity of London for a building with an average internal temperature of 18 °C. In the dull, cold months of December and January, both single- and double-glazed windows can be net energy losers. However, in the autumn and spring months, November and March, a double-glazed window becomes a positive contributor to space heating needs. Its performance can be further improved by insulating it at night.

We can compare this with a similar energy balance for Carpentras, east of Avignon, in the south of France. Although the mid-winter months there are almost as cold as in London, they are far sunnier, being at a lower latitude. The incoming solar radiation is far greater than the heat flowing out, even in mid-winter, and the energy balance is markedly positive.

To return to the UK, we need to consider how best use can be made of the solar energy available.

With a long heating season, a south-facing double-glazed window is a good thing. It can perhaps supply extra heat during October and November, March and April. On the other hand, with a very short heating season confined to the dullest months, say just December and January, it is not really much use at all.

How long is the heating season?

In order to answer this question, we must consider the rest of the building, its insulation standards and its so-called 'free' heat gains.

In a typical UK house, to keep the inside warmer than the outside air temperature, it is necessary to inject heat. The greater the temperature difference between the inside and the outside, the more heat needs to be supplied. In summer it may not be necessary to supply any heat at all, but in mid-winter large amounts will be needed. The total amount of heat that needs to be supplied over the year can be called the **gross heating demand**.

This will have to be supplied from three sources:

1 'free heat gains', which are those energy contributions to the space heating load of the building from the normal activities that take place in it: the body heat of people, and heat from cooking, washing, lighting and appliances. Taken individually, these are quite small. In total, they make a significant contribution to the total heating needs. In a typical UK house, this can amount to 15 kWh per day;

2 passive solar gains, mainly through the windows;

3 fossil fuel energy, from the normal heating system.

Figure 2.27 Window energy balance, London and Carpentras

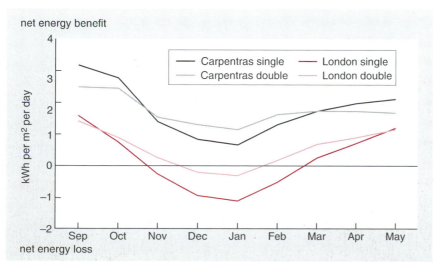

Let us now consider, for example, the monthly average heat demand of a typical, poorly insulated 1970s UK house (see Figure 2.28).

Out of a total gross heating demand of 21 000 kWh, 5000 kWh come from free heat gains and 3000 kWh from solar gains (we have arbitrarily assumed to count free heat gains before solar gains).

A perfectly ordinary house is thus already 14% passive solar heated. The **net heating demand**, to be supplied by the normal fossil fuel heating system, is simply the outstanding heat requirement, namely 13 000 kWh. This will have to be supplied from mid-September to the end of May.

It is possible to cut the house heat demand by putting in cavity wall and loft insulation and double instead of single glazing. This will reduce the gross heating demand and, as shown in Figure 2.29, allow the free heat gains and normal solar gains to maintain the internal temperature of the house for a longer period of the year. The heating season will then be reduced to between October and the end of April. Out of a total gross heat demand of 11 000 kWh, 5000 kWh still come from free heat gains, but as a result of the improved insulation, it will be possible to utilise only 2000 kWh of solar gains. Finally, 4000 kWh will remain to be supplied from the normal heating system.

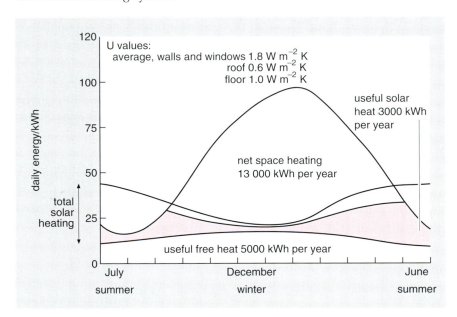

Figure 2.28 Contribution to the net space heating demand in normal houses poorly insulated

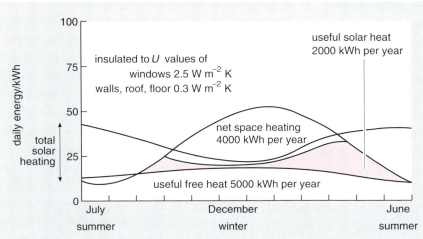

Figure 2.29 Contribution to the net space heating demand in normal houses – well insulated

By insulating the house, 9000 kWh per year will have been saved in fossil fuel heating, but the solar contribution will have fallen from 3000 to 2000 kWh.

There are two ways in which the space heating demand could be cut further.

1 By providing extra insulation. If the house was 'superinsulated', using insulation of 200 mm or more thick, the space heating load might disappear almost completely, leaving just a small need on the coldest, dullest days. Solar gains might not be needed.

2 By providing appropriate glazing to ensure that the best use is made of the mid-winter sun.

Which of these methods is chosen will depend on the precise local climate and the relative expense of insulation materials and glazing. Depending on the precise circumstances, it may be a lot easier to collect an extra 100 kWh of solar energy than to save 100 kWh with extra insulation. It also depends on the desired aesthetics of the building and the need for natural daylight inside.

GENERAL PASSIVE SOLAR HEATING TECHNIQUES

There are some basic general rules for optimising the use of passive solar heating in buildings.

1 They should be well insulated to keep down the overall heat losses.

2 They should have a responsive, efficient heating system.

3 They should face south (anywhere from south-east to south-west is fine). The glazing should be concentrated on the south side, as should the main living rooms, with little-used rooms such as bathrooms on the north.

4 They should avoid overshading by other buildings in order to benefit from the essential mid-winter sun.

5 They should be 'thermally massive' to avoid overheating in summer.

These rules were used, broadly in the order above, to design some low-energy, passive solar-heated houses at Pennyland in Milton Keynes in central England in the late 1970s. The design steps (see Figure 2.30) were carefully costed and the energy effects evaluated by computer model. The resulting houses had a form that was somewhere between the Wallasey

Figure 2.30 Design steps in low-energy housing

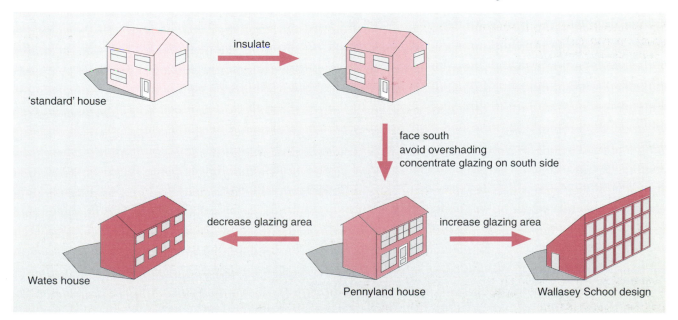

School building and the Wates house. There was not too much glazing, but not too little (Figures 2.31 and 2.32).

Figure 2.31 Passive solar housing at Pennyland, Milton Keynes – elevations. The main living rooms have large windows and face south. The north side has smaller windows.

Figure 2.32 Passive solar housing at Pennyland, Milton Keynes – plans

main living rooms are concentrated on the south side

An entire estate of these houses was built and the final product carefully monitored. At the end of the exercise it was found that the steps 1–5 listed above produced houses that used only half as much gas for low-temperature heating as 'normal' houses built in the preceding year. The extra cost was 2.5% of the total construction cost and the payback time was four years.

Here we come back to the difference between the 'broad' and 'narrow' definitions of passive solar heating. In its broad sense, it encompasses all the energy-saving ideas (1–5 above) put into these houses. In its narrow sense, it covers only the points that are rigidly solar based (3–5).

In this project, insulation and efficient heating saved the vast bulk of the energy, but approximately 500 kWh per year of useful space heating energy came from applying points 3–5 (Everett, *et al.*, 1986).

Put another way, this 500 kWh is the difference in energy consumption between a solar and a non-solar house of the same insulation standard. We call this figure the **marginal passive solar gain**. As we saw in Figures 2.28 and 2.29 above, even non-solar houses have some solar gains. What we are doing is trying to maximise them.

It is rather difficult to calculate the extra cost involved in producing marginal passive solar gains. After all, the passive solar 'heater' is an integral part of the building, not a bolt-on extra. Careful costing studies of different building designs and layouts have shown that modest marginal solar gains can be had at minimal extra cost.

Essentially, in its narrow sense, passive solar heating is largely free, being simply the result of good practice. In the 'wider' sense of passive solar heating, the energy savings have to be balanced against the cost of a whole host of energy conservation measures, some of which involve glazing and perhaps have a solar element, and some of which do not.

CONSERVATORIES, GREENHOUSES AND ATRIA

Direct gain design is really for new buildings: it cannot do much for existing ones. However, for many old buildings, conservatories or greenhouses could be added on to the south sides, just as they can be incorporated into new buildings. Figure 2.33 shows a typical example of a conservatory added to a Victorian terraced house. Monitoring of its performance suggested that it would save 800 kWh per year of space heating energy. However, not all of this is really 'solar' energy:

• 15% is due to the thermal buffering of the house, because the conservatory acts as extra insulation to the south side of the house;

• 55% is due to preheating the ventilation air to the house. Fresh air entering the house via the conservatory will be warmer than air entering another way;

• 30% is from normal solar gains entering the house via the greenhouse, principally by conduction through the intervening wall.

An extra 150 kWh per year could be obtained by using a fan to pump warm air into the house when the greenhouse became warm enough (Ford, 1982).

Add-on conservatories and greenhouses are expensive and cannot be justified on energy savings alone. Rather, they are built as extra areas of unheated habitable space. The costs can be reduced considerably for new buildings if they are integrated into the design.

A strong word of caution is necessary here. A conservatory only saves energy if it is not heated like other areas of the house. There is a danger that it will be looked on as just another room and equipped with radiators connected to the central heating system. One house built like this can easily negate the energy savings of 10 others with unheated conservatories.

Figure 2.33 Conservatory on a Victorian terraced house

Figure 2.34 Trombe wall bungalows, Bebington

Figure 2.35 Thermosyphon wall collectors, Maple Cross

Glazed atria are also becoming increasingly common. At their simplest, they are just glazed-over light wells in the centre of office buildings. At the other extreme, entire shopping streets can be given a glazed roof, creating an unheated but well-lit circulation space.

TROMBE WALLS

In a Trombe wall, the conservatory or greenhouse is replaced by a thin, glazed air space with the thermal storage immediately behind. The original Trombe wall designs were built in the 1950s in the south of France, although the idea has been tested in the UK in a set of houses at Bebington near Liverpool (Figure 2.34).

This is perhaps a technology that works best in sunnier climates, since the bulk of the building is hidden from the sun behind the storage wall, and without careful design internal lighting can be poor and direct solar gains blocked out.

Another variant of this is the small wall-mounted air collector, which treats a normal south-facing wall as a solar panel (Figure 2.35). Experiments on a typical poorly insulated house at Maple Cross, Buckinghamshire, UK, showed that a 10 m^2 solar panel could contribute 1600 kWh of heat to the space heating demand. However, the estimated payback time was long, over 40 years (Franchesi, 1985). As with water-based active solar space heating, we have to ask whether or not better overall cost-effectiveness could be achieved by investing in retrofit insulation.

AVOIDING OVERSHADING

One important aspect of design for passive solar heating is to make sure that the mid-winter sun can penetrate to the main living spaces without being obstructed by other buildings. This will require careful spacing of the buildings.

There are many design aids to doing this, but a useful tool is the sunpath diagram (see Figure 2.36). For a given latitude, this shows the apparent path of the sun through the sky as seen from the ground. In practice, the contours of surrounding trees and buildings can be plotted on it, as in Figure 2.37, to see at what times of day during which months the sun will be obscured. The Pennyland houses were laid out so that the midday sun in mid-December just appeared over the roof-tops of the houses immediately to the south.

However, we need to ask whether it is advisable to cut down all offending overshading trees in the area to let the sun through. To obtain maximum benefit from passive solar heating in its broad sense, it is necessary to follow another rule:

Houses should be sheltered from strong winter winds.

Computer modelling suggests that, in houses such as those built at Pennyland, sheltering can produce energy savings of the same order of magnitude as marginal passive solar gains, approximately 500 kWh per year per house.

Where do the winter winds come from? This is immensely dependent on the local micro-climate of the site. In large parts of the UK, the prevailing wind is from the south-west. It would thus be ideal if every house could have a big row of trees on its south-west side. But is it possible to provide shelter from the wind without blocking out the winter sun? This is where housing layout becomes an art. Every site is different and needs solutions appropriate to it.

Figure 2.36 Sunpath diagram for latitude of 56° N, approximately that of Glasgow and Edinburgh

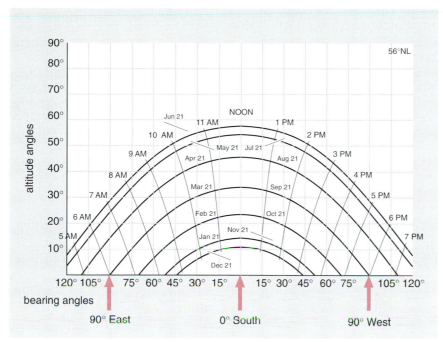

Figure 2.37 Plotting the skyline on a sunpath diagram can show how much sun a site will receive

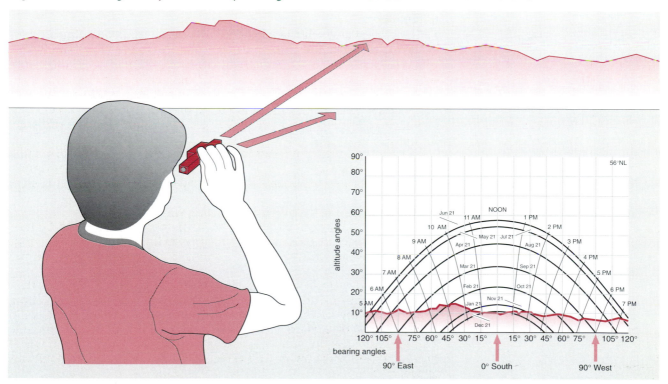

Figure 2.38 Mirrors used to catch valuable daylight in narrow London city streets before World War II

Figure 2.39 Deep-plan building

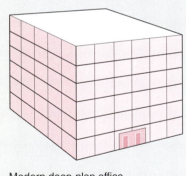

Modern deep-plan office buildings have little surface area for their volume.

They are thermally efficient but require continuous lighting in the centre of the building.

2.8 DAYLIGHTING

Daylight is a commodity that we all take for granted. Replacing it with artificial light was, before the middle of the twentieth century, very expensive. With the coming of cheap electricity, daylight has been neglected and most modern office buildings are designed to rely heavily on electric light.

Houses are traditionally well designed to make use of natural daylight. Indeed, most of those that were not have long ago been designated slums and duly demolished. In the UK, domestic lighting accounts for only approximately 2% of the delivered energy use, and even this could be cut by a factor of three or more by substituting low-energy fluorescent lamps.

In some commercial offices, however, lighting can account for up to 30% of the delivered energy use. Modern factory units and hypermarket buildings are built with barely any windows. 'Deep-plan' office buildings have central corridors and stairwells that require continuous lighting, even when the sun is shining brightly outside (Figure 2.39).

Although in winter the heat from lights can usefully contribute to space heating energy, in summer (when there is most light available) it can cause overheating, especially in well-insulated buildings. Making the best use of natural light saves both on energy and on the need for air conditioning.

Daylighting is a combination of energy conservation and passive solar design. It aims to make the most of the natural daylight that is available. Many of the design details will be found in the better-quality Victorian buildings.

Traditional techniques include:
- shallow-plan design, allowing daylight to penetrate all rooms and corridors (Figure 2.40);
- light wells in the centre of buildings;
- roof lights;
- tall windows, which allow light to penetrate deep inside rooms;
- the use of task lighting directly over the workplace, rather than lighting the whole building interior;
- deep window reveals and light room surfaces to cut the risk of glare.

More modern variants are the use of steerable mirrors to direct light into light wells, and the use of optical fibres and light ducts.

When artificial light has to be used, it is important to make sure that it is used efficiently and is turned off as soon as natural lighting is available. Control systems can be installed that reduce artificial lighting levels when photoelectric cells detect sufficient natural light.

Payback times on these energy conservation techniques can be very short and savings of 50% or more are feasible.

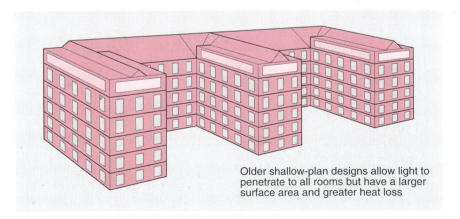

Older shallow-plan designs allow light to penetrate to all rooms but have a larger surface area and greater heat loss

Figure 2.40 Shallow-plan building

In designing new buildings, there is a conflict between lighting design and thermal design. Deep-plan office buildings have a smaller surface area per unit volume than shallow-plan ones. They will need less heating in winter. As with all architecture, there are no simple answers and compromises usually have to be made.

2.9 SOLAR THERMAL ENGINES AND ELECTRICITY GENERATION

So far, we have considered only low-temperature applications for solar energy. If the sun's rays are concentrated using mirrors, high enough temperatures can be generated to boil water to drive steam engines. These can produce mechanical work for water pumping or, more commonly nowadays, for driving an electric generator.

The systems used have a long history and many modern plants differ little from the prototypes built 100 years ago. Indeed, if cheap oil and gas had not appeared in the 1920s, solar engines might have developed to be commonplace in sunny countries, and even on space satellites (see below).

Legend has it that in 212 BC Archimedes used the reflective power of the polished bronze shields of Greek warriors to set fire to Roman ships besieging the fortress of Syracuse. Although long derided as myth, Greek navy experiments in 1973 showed that 60 men each armed with a mirror 1 m by 1.5 m could indeed ignite a wooden boat at 50 m.

If each mirror perfectly reflected all its incident direct beam radiation squarely on to the same target location as the other 59 mirrors, the system could be said to have a **concentration ratio** of 60. Given an incident direct beam intensity of, say, 800 W m^{-2}, the target would receive 48 kW m^{-2}, roughly equivalent to the energy density of a boiling ring on an electric cooker.

The most common method of concentrating solar energy is to use a parabolic mirror. All rays of light that enter parallel to the axis of a mirror formed in this particular shape will be reflected to one point, the focus (see Figure 2.41). However, if the rays enter slightly off-axis, they will not pass through the focus. It is therefore essential that the mirror tracks the sun.

Having the focus in front of the mirror can make collecting the heat a little inconvenient. A variant, the Winston mirror, concentrates the solar radiation to a more imprecise focus, but this is at the back of the mirror, which can be flat.

These mirrors can be made in either line focus or point focus forms. In the line focus form (sometimes called a trough collector), the image of the sun can be concentrated on a small region running along the length of the

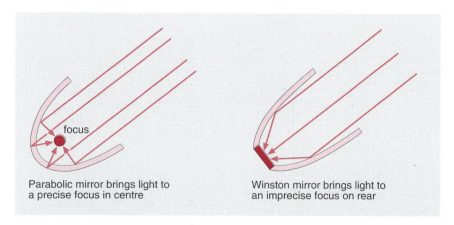

Parabolic mirror brings light to a precise focus in centre

Winston mirror brings light to an imprecise focus on rear

Figure 2.41 Concentrating mirrors – parabolic and Winston-type

mirror (Figure 2.42). In order to keep the sun focused on this, the collector normally faces south and needs only to track the sun in **elevation**, that is, up and down.

In the point focus form, the image is concentrated on a boiler in the centre of the mirror. For optimum performance, the axis must be pointed directly at the sun at all times, so it needs to track the sun both in elevation and in **azimuth** (that is, side to side).

Most mirrors are assembled from sheets of curved or flat glass, which are fixed to a framework. However, there are interesting possibilities in using light steel frames to support flexible mirrors of aluminised mylar film. These can be made extremely light and thus, in theory at least, cheaply.

There are trade-offs between the complexity of design of a concentrating system and its concentration ratio. A well-built and well-aimed parabolic collector can achieve a concentration ratio of over 1000. A line focus parabolic trough collector may achieve a concentration ratio of 50, but this is adequate for most power plant systems. The ratio required depends on the desired target temperature.

Figure 2.42 Moving mirrors – line focus and point focus

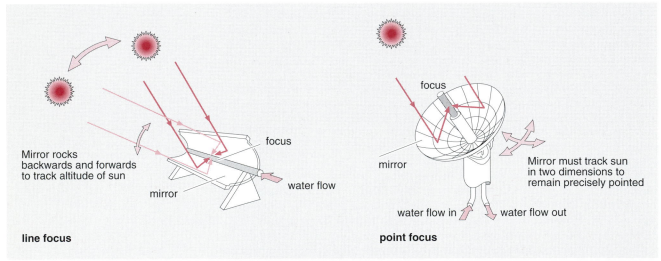

line focus

Mirror rocks backwards and forwards to track altitude of sun

focus

mirror

water flow

point focus

focus

mirror

Mirror must track sun in two dimensions to remain precisely pointed

water flow in

water flow out

Figure 2.43 Abel Pifre's solar-powered printing press

Unless the incident solar energy is carried away by some means, the target, be it a boat or a boiler, will settle at an equilibrium temperature where the incoming radiation balances heat losses to the surrounding air. The latter will be mainly by convection and re-radiation of infrared energy and will be dependent on the surface area of the target and its exposure to wind. A line focus parabolic trough collector can produce a temperature of 200–400 °C. A dish system can produce a temperature of over 1500 °C.

What is important to appreciate is that no concentrator can deliver in total any more energy than falls on it, but what it does receive is all concentrated into one small area.

THE FIRST SOLAR ENGINE AGE

The process of turning the concentrated power of the sun into useful mechanical work started in the nineteenth century. When, in the 1860s, France lacked a supply of cheap coal, Augustin Mouchot, a mathematics professor from Tours, had the answer: solar-powered steam engines. In the 1870s and 1880s, Mouchot and his assistant, Abel Pifre, produced a series of machines ranging from the solar printing press shown in Figure 2.43 to solar wine stills, solar cookers and even solar engines driving refrigerators.

Their basic collector design was a parabolic concentrator with a steam boiler mounted at the focus. Steam pipes ran down to a reciprocating engine (like a steam railway engine) on the ground.

Although these systems were widely acclaimed, they suffered from the fundamental low power density of solar radiation and low overall efficiency (see Box 2.4). It took a machine that occupied 40 m² of land just to drive a one-half horsepower engine. By the 1890s, it was clear that this was not going to compete with the new supplies of coal, which were appearing as a result of increased investment in mines and railways.

BOX 2.4: VAPOUR CYCLE ENGINES AND CARNOT EFFICIENCY

In order to understand some of the problems of engines powered by solar energy, it is necessary to consider some details.

The steam engine, especially in its railway locomotive form, is familiar enough. It is a vapour cycle engine, which works by boiling a fluid to produce a high-pressure vapour. This then goes to an 'expander', which extracts energy and from which low-pressure vapour is exhausted. The expander can be a reciprocating engine or a turbine.

Normally, to boil water, its temperature must be raised to at least 100 °C. This may be difficult to achieve with simple solar collectors. It would be more convenient to work with a fluid with a lower boiling point. In order to do this, a 'closed cycle' system must be adopted, with a **condenser** that turns the exhaust vapour back to a liquid and allows it to be returned to the boiler.

Shuman's Egyptian project (see next page) used another advantage of this arrangement. Although he used water, the whole system was depressurised so that it boiled at a temperature below 100 °C. This was before the development in the 1940s of refrigerants, stable organic chemicals with suitably low boiling points, including the now-notorious chlorofluorocarbons (CFCs). Such systems as Shuman's today might use one of the more ozone-friendly refrigerants.

As we saw in Chapter 1, all heat engines are subject to fundamental limits on their efficiency. They all produce work by taking in heat at a high temperature, T_{in}, and ejecting it at a lower one, T_{out}. In the ideal case, they could hope to achieve an efficiency of

$$1 - \left(\frac{T_{out}}{T_{in}} \right), \text{ where } T_{in} \text{ and } T_{out}$$

are expressed in degrees Kelvin (or degrees Centigrade plus 273).

For example, a turbine fed from parabolic trough collectors might take steam at 350 °C and eject heat to cooling towers at 30 °C. Its theoretical efficiency would therefore be $1 - (30 + 273)/(350 + 273)$, or 51%. Its practical efficiency is more likely to be about 25%.

By contrast, the theoretical efficiency of a heat engine that was fed with relatively low-temperature vapour at 85 °C and exhausted heat at 35 °C would be only 14%.

At the beginning of the twentieth century, in the USA, an entrepreneur named Frank Shuman applied the principle again, this time with large parabolic trough collectors. He realised that the best potential would be in really sunny climates. After building a number of prototypes, he raised enough financial backing for a large project at Meadi in Egypt. This used five parabolic trough collectors, each 80 m long and 4 m wide. At the focus, a finned cast iron pipe carried away steam to an engine.

In 1913, Shuman's system, producing 55 horsepower, was demonstrated to a number of VIPs, including Lord Kitchener. Given the expense of coal in Egypt at the time, the payback time would have been only four years.

By 1914, Shuman was talking of building 20,000 square miles of collector in the Sahara, which would 'in perpetuity produce the 270 million horsepower required to equal all the fuel mined in 1909' (see Butti and Perlin, 1980, for the full story). Then came World War I and immediately afterwards the era of cheap oil. Interest in solar steam engines collapsed and lay dormant for virtually half a century.

THE NEW SOLAR AGE

Solar engines revived with the coming of the space age. When, in 1945, a UK scientist, Arthur C. Clarke, described a possible future 'geostationary satellite', which would broadcast television to the world, it was to be powered by a solar steam engine. In fact, by the time such satellites materialised, 25 years later, photovoltaics (see Chapter 3) had been developed as a reliable source of electricity.

Elsewhere, space rockets, guided missiles and nuclear power stations needed facilities where components could be tested at high temperatures without contamination from the burning of fuel needed to achieve such temperatures. The French solved this problem in 1969 by building an eight-storey-high parabolic mirror at Odeillo in the Pyrenees (Figure 2.44). This faces north towards a large field of heliostats: flat mirrors, which, like those held by Archimedes' warriors, track the sun. This huge mirror can produce temperatures of 3800 °C at its focus, but only in an area of 50 cm^2.

POWER TOWERS

In the early 1980s, the first serious, large, experimental electricity generation schemes were built to make use of high temperatures. Several were of the

Figure 2.44 Odeillo solar furnace

central receiver system or 'power tower' type. The 10 megawatt (MW) Solar One system at Barstow, California, shown in Figures 2.45 and 2.46, is a good example. This uses a field of tracking heliostats, which reflect the sun's rays onto a boiler at the top of a central tower.

In order to carry away the heat at temperatures of over 500 °C, these systems use either special high-temperature synthetic oils or molten rock salt. The latter is a convenient heat transfer medium because of its high thermal capacity and conductivity.

The hot salt can then be used to produce high-temperature steam to drive a turbine. In theory, salt heated during the day can be stored to keep generation going at night, although in practice some recent systems find it simpler to burn gas instead.

Other large experimental schemes of this type have been built in Sicily, Spain, France and the Crimea.

Figure 2.45 Barstow central receiver system – power tower

Figure 2.46 Barstow central receiver system – heliostat field

PARABOLIC TROUGH CONCENTRATOR SYSTEMS

Most of the world's solar-generated electricity is produced at a large solar power station developed by Luz International, in the Mojave desert in California. Between 1984 and 1990, Luz brought on-line nine systems of between 13 and 80 MW rating. These are essentially massively-uprated versions of Shuman's 1913 design, using large fields of parabolic trough collectors (see Figures 2.47 and 2.48). Each successive project has concentrated on economies of scale, especially in purchasing mirror glass. The latest 80 MW scheme has 464 000 m^2 of collector.

The collectors heat synthetic oil to 390 °C, which can then produce high-temperature steam via a heat exchanger. Such temperatures give high solar-to-electricity conversion efficiencies of 22% peak and 14% on average over the day. This rivals the best commercially available photovoltaic systems.

The economies of scale also mean that the system can use well-developed, multi-megawatt steam turbines normally supplied to more conventional power stations. Estimated overall generation costs have

Figure 2.47 Luz solar collector field, southern California

Figure 2.48 Luz solar collector field – aerial view

fallen from 28 cents per kWh for the first Luz scheme to 9 cents per kWh for the eighth (1991 prices).

The Luz schemes were intended to be commercially competitive with fossil fuel generated electricity to feed the peak afternoon air-conditioning demands in California, and for several years this objective was successfully achieved. In 1992, reductions in the price of gas, to which the price paid for electricity from the plant was tied, brought financial difficulties. However the Luz solar power plants continue to operate satisfactorily, although plans for new and improved plants have been delayed.

PARABOLIC DISH CONCENTRATOR SYSTEMS

Instead of conveying the solar heat from the collector down to a separate engine, an alternative approach is to put the engine itself at the focus of a mirror (see Figure 2.49). This has been tried both with small steam engines and with Stirling engines.

Stirling engines have a long history (they were invented in 1816) and were serious competitors to the steam engine in the latter half of the nineteenth century. They are good candidates for use in space (and elsewhere) because of their few moving parts. We do not intend to describe them in detail, but briefly, they usually take the form of a piston engine in which the heat is applied to the outside of the cylinder. This heat then expands the working gas inside, which can be air, nitrogen or helium, and this moves the main power piston. A second piston, or displacer, then shifts the gas to the 'cold' side of the engine, where it contracts, and moves the power piston back again.

Although steam engines have fundamental difficulties when operating with input temperatures above 700 °C, Stirling engines, given the right materials, can be made to operate at temperatures of up to 1000 °C, with consequent higher efficiencies. Current experimental solar systems using these have managed very high overall conversion efficiencies, approaching 30% on average over the day.

(Stirling engines are also of interest because they can run on biofuels. Since combustion can take place outside the engine, it is relatively easy to optimise combustion conditions, and the engines can tolerate a wide range of fuels that normal internal combustion engines would not accept.)

Figure 2.49 Parabolic dish concentrator in Spain

The parabolic concentrating mirrors themselves are also undergoing interesting experimental developments in Germany. Instead of heavy glass mirrors, circular sheets of aluminised plastic film are being used. By creating a partial vacuum behind the film, it can be bent into a parabolic shape. This creates a very lightweight mirror, which in turn only requires a lightweight structure to support and track it.

SOLAR PONDS

A totally different approach to solar thermal electricity production is the solar pond, which uses a large, salty lake as a kind of flat plate collector (Figure 2.50). If the lake has the right gradient of salt concentration (salty water at the bottom and fresh water at the top) and the water is clear enough, solar energy is absorbed on the bottom of the pond. The hot, salty water cannot rise, because it is heavier than the fresh water on top. The upper layers of water effectively act as an insulating blanket and the temperature at the bottom of the pond can reach 90 °C. This is a high enough temperature to run a vapour cycle engine (Figure 2.51).

However, the thermodynamic limitations of the relatively low temperatures mean low solar-to-electricity conversion efficiencies, typically

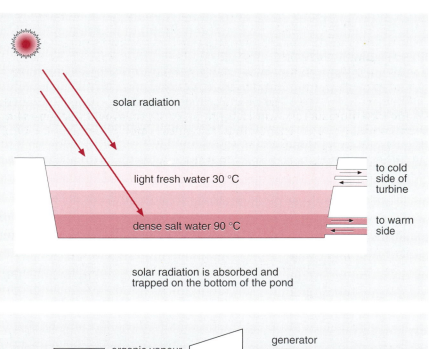

Figure 2.50 Solar pond

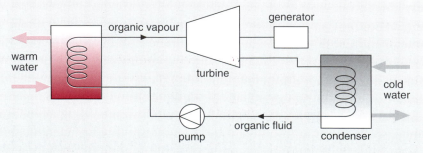

Figure 2.51 Vapour cycle turbine

less than 2%. Nevertheless, systems of 50 MW electrical output, fed from a lake of 20 hectares, have been demonstrated.

One advantage of this system is that the large thermal mass of the pond acts as a heat store, and electricity generation can go on day or night, as required.

In practice, it also has disadvantages. Large amounts of fresh water are required to maintain the salt gradient. These can be hard to find in the solar pond's natural location, the desert. Indeed, the best use for solar ponds may be to generate heat for water desalination plants, creating enough fresh water to maintain themselves and also supply drinking water. Commercial systems have been tried in the USA and Saudi Arabia.

Solar ponds are not really viable at high latitudes, since the collection surface is, by its very nature, horizontal, and cannot be tilted. Their best location is in the large areas of the world where natural flat salt deserts occur.

OCEAN THERMAL ENERGY CONVERSION (OTEC)

Ocean thermal energy conversion essentially uses the sea as a solar collector. It exploits the small temperature difference between the warm surface of the sea and the cold water at the bottom (Figure 2.52). In deep waters, 1000 m or more, this can amount to 20 °C. Although the theoretical efficiency is likely to be very small and the vapour cycle system used needs to be finely tuned to boil at just the right temperature, there is an extremely large amount of water available.

Initial experiments made on a ship in the Caribbean in the 1930s were only marginally successful. Water had to be pumped from a great depth to obtain a significant temperature difference, and the whole system barely produced more energy than it used in pumping.

More recently, large-scale experiments have been carried out in the Pacific with more success, and a large number of experimental schemes have been conceived. The engineering difficulties are enormous. An OTEC station producing 100 MW of electricity would need to pump nearly 500 cubic metres per second of both warm and cold water through its heat exchangers, whilst remaining moored in sea 1000 metres deep.

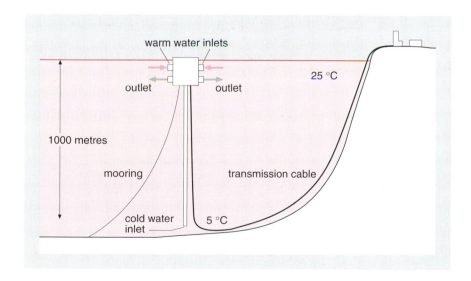

Figure 2.52 OTEC floating platform

2.10 ECONOMICS, POTENTIAL AND ENVIRONMENTAL IMPACT

ECONOMICS AND POTENTIAL

The motto of Bailey's 'Day and Night' Solar Water Heater company was: 'Solar energy, like salvation, is free'. Even so, the company still had to charge its customers money for the collection equipment.

As we have seen, there are many varieties of solar heating system. They all need to be evaluated separately. A good recent review of the economics of active solar heating in the UK can be found in Halcrow Gilbert Associates (1992).

DOMESTIC ACTIVE SOLAR WATER HEATING

Domestic water heating is the prime area for active solar systems. Analysis of collector sales in countries with flourishing solar industries, such as Greece, Israel, Japan and Australia, show that 80–90% of collectors are used for this purpose.

In the UK, approximately 40 000 systems have been installed since the 1970s. This is a minute fraction of the total potential. It is likely that around 50% of existing dwellings could be suitable to have a solar water heater fitted. If this potential were to be taken up by 2025, this would require the deployment of approximately 12 million systems (allowing for a rise in the UK housing stock). This could save an estimated 34.6 PJ (9.6 TWh) per year of oil and gas and 2.4 TWh per year of electricity, giving a saving of 5.6 million tonnes of carbon dioxide per year, or just under 1% of current UK CO_2 production.

The economics of solar water heating in the UK are rather difficult, however. Currently, sales are low, production is low and prices are high. In 1991, some 2200 domestic solar heating systems were sold in the UK. A 4 m^2 flat plate collector system typically costs approximately £2500 installed, excluding VAT. A 3 m^2 evacuated tube system of broadly equivalent performance costs approximately £4000. Of these prices, approximately £1500 is accounted for by the installer's overheads and marketing costs.

When we look further afield, things look more promising. In southern Europe, there is more sunshine, so a system may produce twice as much energy per square metre as in the UK. Indeed, approximately 50% of UK solar collector production goes for export to sunnier countries. In countries such as Greece and Israel, there is mass production and there are mass sales. The 1991 Athens *Yellow Pages* telephone directory had no less than 26 pages of advertisements for solar water heaters.

The larger the national production of systems, the lower the price. Figure 2.53 summarises collector production and price per square metre for the UK, Greece and Israel. This suggests that, with mass production, systems could be installed for under £1000 in the UK. This would be in broad agreement with earlier UK studies on possible cost reductions (ETSU, 1985). However, even at this price, payback times may be unacceptably long without some kind of financial incentive.

There is another factor that encourages the use of these systems in warmer countries. In the UK, electricity demand peaks in mid-winter. In Greece, it peaks in summer, with ever-increasing demands for refrigeration and air conditioning. In this case, every solar water heater installed saves not only on fuel, but, more important, on building new power plants.

The environmental impact of solar water heating schemes in the UK would be very small. The materials used are those of everyday building and plumbing. Solar collectors can be installed to be visually almost indistinguishable from normal roof lights. In Mediterranean countries, the use of free-standing thermosyphon systems on flat roofs can be visually intrusive. However, it is not the collector that is the problem but the storage tank above it. (Bailey's 'Day and Night' Solar Water Heater Company also had to face these problems. It offered to disguise the storage tank as a chimney!)

SWIMMING POOL WATER HEATING

Solar systems for swimming pool heating can be very simple. This is reflected in a much lower price than for solar domestic water heaters. In 1991 in the UK, a 20 m² do-it-yourself swimming pool solar heating kit cost approximately £800 and a professionally installed one £2300 (both excluding VAT).

The energy output is highly dependent on the manner of use, but it is of the same order as that for solar domestic water heaters, approximately 300 kWh per square metre of collector. If the heat is costed at current gas prices of approximately 2.5 pence per kilowatt-hour, a 20 m² system would produce £150 worth of heat per year. Again ignoring VAT, running and maintenance costs, this would allow payback times of 5.3 years for a do-it-yourself system and 15.3 years for a professionally installed one.

These payback times are short enough to encourage a steady flow of sales: 250 pool systems were sold in the UK in 1991. Overall, the total energy-saving potential for solar swimming pool heating in the UK by 2025 has been estimated at approximately 7% of that available from domestic solar water heating, producing a saving of approximately 0.4 million tonnes of carbon dioxide per year.

ACTIVE SOLAR SPACE HEATING

Although individual house solar space heating is technically feasible, it is likely that it would be far more cost effective to invest in insulation to cut space heating demands. There have been plenty of projects worldwide that have shown that even old buildings can be brought up to very high thermal standards. If this were done in the UK, given the relatively mild climate, energy demand for winter space heating would be drastically reduced.

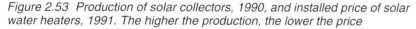

Figure 2.53 Production of solar collectors, 1990, and installed price of solar water heaters, 1991. The higher the production, the lower the price

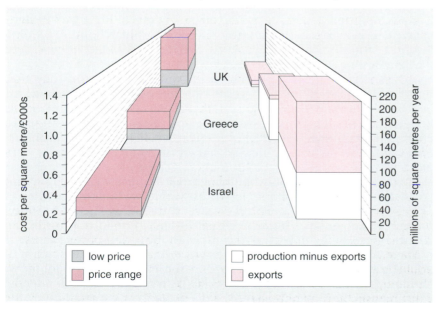

Theoretically, the remaining winter heat demand (together with a winter demand for water heating) could be met using interseasonal solar heat storage, serving large groups of buildings. A recent study (Long, 1992) has looked at the possible future costs for such a system in the UK. With favourable collector and store prices, the payback time could be brought down to 30 years, but only assuming that the solar heating system is an addition to an existing district heating system.

If district heating were as widespread in the UK as it is in Denmark and Germany now, the heating energy use of the country would be radically different. The solar heating system would face competition from other sources that deserve encouragement: waste heat from power stations (possibly biofuel fired) and refuse incineration. For these sources, heat is a by-product, which is currently simply thrown away. It would certainly pay to make sure that these sources are tapped first.

Visually, where large solar collectors for solar space heating are roof mounted, they are unlikely to be a problem. However, where there is not sufficient roof space, they may take up valuable urban ground area. More practically, they may be difficult to protect from vandalism.

PASSIVE SOLAR HEATING AND DAYLIGHTING

In its narrow sense of producing an increase in the amount of solar energy directly used in providing useful space heating, passive solar heating is highly economic, indeed possibly free. Passive solar-heated buildings have been generally well received by their occupants and are of interest to architects.

However, in the short term, the potential is relatively small, because it is limited by the low rate of replacement of the building stock. The Department of Trade and Industry has estimated the potential in the UK by 2020 as 1–2 million tonnes of coal equivalent (mtce) or approximately 0.5% of the country's fuel use.

In its broad sense of producing integrated low-energy building design, the potential for passive solar heating is enormous, but this really comes under the heading of 'energy conservation'. The magnitude of possible savings can be deduced from the fact that between 1972 and 1985 Denmark cut its national space heating energy consumption by 30%, although the actual heated floor area rose by 30% over the same period (see Norgard and Meyer, 1989).

Designing buildings to take advantage of daylighting involves both energy conservation and passive solar heating considerations. A Building Research Establishment study estimated the national potential for exploiting daylight in the UK as worth between 0.7 and 1.3 mtce by 2020. In warmer countries, daylighting may be far more important, since cutting down on summer electricity use for lighting can also save on air conditioning costs.

Designing and laying out buildings to make the best use of sunlight has been part of the architectural tradition for centuries. It is generally seen as environmentally beneficial and has already shaped many towns and cities. For example, when in 1904 the city council of Boston, Massachusetts was faced with proposals for a 100 m high skyscraper, it commissioned an analysis of the shading of other buildings that this would cause. It was not pleased with the results and imposed strict limits on building heights.

However, a word of caution is necessary. In the UK, the tradition of new town development has been based partly on Victorian notions of the health aspects of 'light and air' in contrast to the overcrowded squalor of existing cities. This has been beneficial in terms of better penetration of solar energy into buildings. On the other hand, the encouragement of low building densities has led to vast tracts of sprawling suburbs and the consumption of enormous quantities of energy in transportation.

SOLAR THERMAL ENGINES AND ELECTRICITY GENERATION

As the original pioneers realised, it pays to build solar thermal power systems in really sunny places. In order to generate the high temperatures necessary for thermodynamically efficient operation, the local climate has to have plenty of *direct* solar radiation: diffuse radiation will not do. In California, given the right financial incentives, Luz-type schemes are currently just about competitive with fossil fuel power generation.

However, recent estimates for building one such scheme in the UK (IT Power, 1992) put the generated cost of electricity at approximately 30p per kWh. For a central receiver system, it would be even higher, over £1 per kWh.

The environmental consequences of solar power stations are somewhat mixed. A major problem is the sheer quantity of land required. An 80 MW Luz-type system occupies almost 1 square mile. Although, typically, the collectors only take up one-third of the land area, it may be physically difficult to use it for anything else. This is unlike windfarms where the turbines are very widely spaced and crops can grow underneath. Similarly, solar ponds need large amounts of flat land, especially because of their low thermodynamic efficiency.

For all of these kinds of system, sunny deserts, within striking distance of large urban electricity demands, are needed. In California, the Mojave desert is ideal. In Europe, parts of central Spain and other southern Mediterranean countries are interesting possibilities.

The environmental consequences of OTEC systems may be mixed. On the one hand, it is claimed that the vast amounts of water being pumped circulate nutrients and can increase the amount of fish life. On the other, dissolved carbon dioxide can be released from the deep sea water, thereby negating some of the benefits of renewable energy generation. Only further experiments will resolve these issues.

Perhaps the best potential may be to return to Shuman's idea of thousands of square miles of solar collector in the Sahara desert, not to produce electricity, but to split water into hydrogen and oxygen. We will look at this kind of possibility in Chapter 10.

Although the UK is probably too cloudy to support economic solar thermal electricity schemes, this is not to say that they should not interest UK industry. The massive areas of mirror glass used in the US Luz schemes were not made in the USA but mainly imported from Germany. As with many other renewable energy sources, sunshine is free, but the hardware has to be manufactured by someone somewhere.

CONCLUSIONS

Solar energy is a resource that is there for the taking. All that is needed is to produce the necessary hardware. We already make plenty of use of passive solar energy and daylight, but we take it for granted. It only requires a little more care in the design and layout of our buildings to make the best use of it.

Similarly, techniques of active solar heating and solar thermal power generation are technically feasible and in many countries well proven and regarded as cost effective. Whether they can secure a foothold in the market-place in other countries, including the UK, is another matter. The economics of systems are highly dependent on the particular local climate and energy needs. The principal obstacle is that fossil fuels are too cheap and abundant at present.

REFERENCES

Achard, P. and Gicquel, R. (eds) (1986) *European Passive Solar Handbook* (preliminary edition), Commission of the European Communities, DG XII.

Butti, K. and Perlin, J. (1980) *A Golden Thread: 2500 Years of Solar Architecture and Technology*, Marion Boyars.

ETSU (eds) (1985) *Active Solar Heating in the UK*, Energy Technology Support Unit, Report R 25, HMSO.

Eurostat (1993) *Energy Consumption in Households*, HMSO.

Eyre, N. J. (1990) *Gaseous Emissions due to Electricity Fuel Cycles in the United Kingdom*, ETSU Energy and Environment Paper No. 1.

Ford, B. (1982) *Thermal Performance Modelling of a Terrace House with Conservatory*, ETSU Report 5-1056b.

Franchesi, L. (1985) *A Passive Solar Heating Facility for Existing Houses*, ETSU Report 5-1137.

Granqvist, C. G. (1989) 'Energy efficient windows: options with present and forthcoming technology', in Johansson, R. B., Bodlund, B. and Williams, R. H. (eds) *Electricity – Efficient End Use*, Lund University Press.

Halcrow Gilbert Associates (eds) (1992) *Review of Active Solar Technologies*, Energy Technology Support Unit, Report S 1337.

IT Power (eds) (1992) *A Review of Solar Thermodynamic Electricity Generation*, Energy Technology Support Unit, Report S 1369.

Johannson, T. *et al.* (eds) (1993) *Renewable Energy*, Island Press.

Long, G. (1992) *Solar Aided District Heating in the UK*, Energy Technology Support Unit, Report S 1190.

Norgard, J. S. and Meyer, N. I. (1989) 'Planning implications of electricity conservation: the case of Denmark', in Johansson, R. B., Bodlund, B. and Williams, R. H. (eds) *Electricity – Efficient End Use*, Lund University Press.

FURTHER READING

GENERAL

Flood, M. (1983) *Solar Prospects*, Wildwood House.

A very readable book on renewable energy in general.

Meinel, A. B. and Meinel, M. P. (1977) *Applied Solar Energy*, Addison Wesley.

A general textbook on solar energy.

McVeigh, C. (1983) *Sun Power*, Pergamon Press.

A general textbook on the application of solar energy.

Twidell, J. and Weir, T. (1986) *Renewable Energy Resources*, E. and F. Spon.

A general textbook on renewable energy, including solar.

Details of recent developments in solar energy research world wide can be found in two main conference proceedings: the *Proceedings of the International Solar Energy Society Conference*, and the *Proceedings of the World Renewable Energy Congress*. Both meetings take place every 1-2 years, and both Proceedings are published by Pergamon Press.

ACTIVE SOLAR HEATING

British Standards Institute (1986) *Solar Heating Systems for Swimming Pools*, BS 6785:1986.

British Standards Institute (1989) *Solar Heating Systems for Domestic Hot Water*, BS 5918:1989.

Bushell, A. (1991) *Practical Solar Handbook*.

Installation of evacuated tube systems.

Duffie, J. A. and Beckman, W. A. (1980) *Solar Engineering of Thermal Processes*, John Wiley.

A classic textbook on the physics and engineering of solar thermal energy systems.

Energy Conscious Design (eds) (1981) *Solar Water Heating*, EC Report EUR 8003. A casebook of examples.

Energy Conscious Design (eds) (1981) *Solar Space Heating*, EUR 8004. A casebook of examples.

Jager, F. (1981) *Solar Energy Applications in Houses*, Pergamon Press.

McCartney, K. and Ford, B. (1978) *Practical Solar Water Heating*, Prism Press. Simple flat-plate system installation.

Steemers, T. C. and Palz, W. (1981) *Solar Houses in Europe*, Pergamon Press.

Wozniak, S. (1980) *Solar Heating Systems for the UK*, Building Research Establishment, HMSO.

DAYLIGHTING

Baker, N. *et al.* (eds) (1993) *Daylighting in Architecture – A European Reference Book*, European Commission Handbook EUR 15006 EN, Luxembourg.

Littlefair, P. J. (1991) *Site Layout for Daylight and Sunlight*, Building Research Establishment, HMSO.

Detailed technical information.

ENERGY USE IN THE UK

Evans, R. D. and Herring, H. (1989) *Energy Efficiency in the Domestic Sector*, Energy Efficiency Office, HMSO.

Henderson, G. and Shorrock, L. D. (1989) *Domestic Energy Fact File*, Building Research Establishment, HMSO. (A 1993 update to the Fact File is also available.)

OTEC

Cavanagh, J. E., Clarke, J. and Price, R. (1992) 'Ocean energy systems', in Johannson, T. (ed.) (1992) *Renewable Energy*, Island Press.

PASSIVE SOLAR DESIGN

Achard, P. and Giquel, R. (eds) (1986) *European Passive Solar Handbook – Preliminary Edition*, Directorate General XII, Brussels, EUR 10 683.

The previous edition of Goulding *et al.* (1992b). Highly recommended.

Everett, R. *et al.* (1986) 'Pennyland and Linford Low Energy Housing Projects', *Journal of Ambient Energy*, Vol. 7, No. 2.

Goetzberger, A. (ed.) (1992) *Solar Energy* 49 (Technical Issue on Transparent Insulation).

Goulding, J. R., Lewis, J. O. and Steemers, T. C. (1992a) *Energy Conscious Design – A Primer for Architects*, Batsford/Directorate General XII, EUR 13445.

A non-technical introduction to Achard and Giquel (1986) and Goulding *et al.* (1992b).

Goulding, J. R., Lewis, J. O. and Steemers, T. C. (eds) (1992b) *Energy in Architecture – The European Passive Solar Handbook*, Batsford.

A mine of technical information, highly recommended.

Hastings, R. and Crenshaw (1977) *Window Design Strategies to Conserve Energy*, NBS Building Science Series 104, US National Bureau of Standards, Library of Congress No. 77-600018.

Practical details of window design.

International Energy Agency (1990) *Passive and Hybrid Solar Commercial Buildings*, Task XI, Energy Technology Support Unit.

A casebook of examples.

Martin, C. and Watson, M. (1992) Thermal Performance of Walls Clad with Transparent Insulation Material Under Realistic Operating Conditions, ETSU Report S 1349.

An assessment of the likely thermal performance of transparent insulation material (TIM), used as cladding for the opaque walls of UK buildings.

Mazria, E. (1979) *Passive Solar Energy Book*, Rodale Press.

A beautifully illustrated introduction to design for passive solar heating.

Yannas, S. (1993) *Solar Energy and Housing Design*, 2 vols (Book 1: *Principles, Objectives and Guidelines*; Book 2: *Examples*), Architectural Association Publications.

Detailed design information and a casebook of examples.

SOLAR THERMAL POWER

De Lacquil, P., Kearney, D., Geyer, M. and Diver, R. (1992) 'Solar-thermal electric technology', in Johansson, T. (ed.) (1992) *Renewable Energy*, Island Press.

Kreith, F. (1990) 'Solar thermal energy: current status and future potential', *Proceedings of 1st World Renewable Energy Congress*, Volume 2, Pergamon Press.

SOLAR PHOTOVOLTAICS

3.1   INTRODUCTION

In Chapter 2 we saw how solar energy can be used to generate electricity by first producing solar heat, preferably at high temperature, to drive a heat engine, which then produces mechanical work to drive an electrical generator.

This chapter is concerned with more direct methods of generating electricity from solar radiation. The most important of these is **photovoltaics**, the conversion of solar energy directly into electricity in a solid-state device.

SUMMARY

We start with an introductory case study (Section 3.2), then examine the history and basic principles of photovoltaic energy conversion, concentrating initially on monocrystalline silicon devices (Sections 3.3 and 3.4).

In Sections 3.5–3.7 we look at various ways of reducing the cost of photovoltaic electricity, including both polycrystalline and 'thin film' devices based on silicon or other semiconducting materials, the use of concentrators, and several other innovative concepts.

The electrical characteristics of photovoltaic cells and modules are described in Section 3.8, and this is followed by a review of the various current and possible future roles of photovoltaic energy systems, both in supplying power in remote locations (Section 3.9) and in feeding power into local or national electricity grids (Section 3.10).

In Sections 3.11 and 3.12 respectively, the economics and the environmental impact of photovoltaic electricity are reviewed, and in Section 3.13 we examine how photovoltaics might be integrated into the electricity supply systems of the UK in the future.

3.2 CASE STUDY: RAPPENECKER HOF

Rappenecker Hof is a small mountain inn in the Black Forest, some 15 km from Freiburg in southern Germany. Since 1987, most of its electricity has been supplied by an array of photovoltaic (PV) **solar cells** which have been integrated into the south side of the building, a converted seventeenth-century farmhouse (see Figure 3.1).

The inn is situated at an altitude of 1000 metres, some 5 km from the public electricity grid. Since the cost of grid connection was very high (some DM380 000 (£152 000)), it was decided to install an independent electricity generating system.

In such remote locations a diesel generator is often used to provide power, but this has some disadvantages. The diesel engine produces some pollution and noise, which can be a problem in a sensitive environment. Also, although the diesel generator has to be large enough to supply the peak level of demand from the building, for most of the time it is only required to supply a small fraction of the peak demand, which leads to a low overall efficiency of fuel use. Transporting diesel fuel can also be costly and inconvenient.

The photovoltaic solar **array** used at Rappenecker Hof consists of some 100 photovoltaic **modules**.

Each module, manufactured by the German company AEG, is about 0.4 m² in area and contains 40 individual photovoltaic cells, each consisting of a thin square wafer of silicon measuring approximately 100 mm by 100 mm.

Each cell produces a current proportional to the intensity of solar radiation falling on it, up to a maximum of just over 2.5 amps, at an electrical potential of around 0.5 volts. Each cell thus produces up to about 1.25 watts of power, and since there are 40 cells, this enables the module to produce a peak overall power of around 50 watts. In photovoltaic terminology, such modules are therefore rated as having an output power of 50 watts peak (50 W(p)).

The actual power produced by each module only reaches 50 watts when the sunlight intensity peaks at 1000 watts per square metre, a level reached at noon on a cloudless summer day.

There are occasions, for example on a succession of dull winter days, when the PV array does not produce enough energy to meet the demands of the residents. At such times, a standby diesel generator is used to keep the batteries charged. But, as

Figure 3.2 shows, in most months of the year the PV array provides the majority of the inn's electricity requirements. Over the 12 months from January to December 1988, for example, the inn required some 2780 kWh of electricity, of which the PV array provided 77% (2150 kWh) and the diesel generator 23% (650 kWh).

The PV array at Rappenecker Hof has a maximum output, after allowing for resistive and other losses, of some 4 kW in peak sunlight and around 1 kW when skies are overcast. The array is connected, via an electronic 'charge controller', to a lead-acid battery with a total capacity of 24 kilowatt hours (kWh), which stores the power until it is needed. The battery supplies its power to an **inverter**, a device which converts the direct current (DC) from the battery into alternating current (AC) conforming to the European standard of 220 volts, 50 hertz (see Figure 3.3). This allows conventional electrical appliances to be used in the inn. These include a dishwasher, washing machine, refrigerator, iron, TV, radio and compact fluorescent lighting.

Figure 3.1 Rappenecker Hof: a mountain inn in the Black Forest. More than three-quarters of its electricity is supplied by an array of photovoltaic cells on the side of the building

Figure 3.2 Monthly contributions from the photovoltaic array and the diesel generator to the energy demand of Rappenecker Hof during 1988

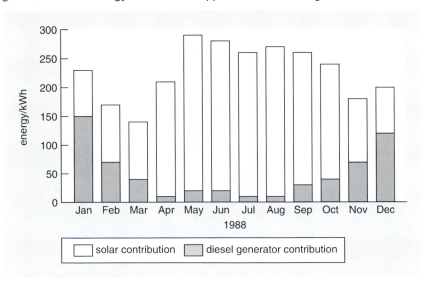

The energy system at Rappenecker Hof is, however, very expensive. The overall system cost, including PV arrays, batteries, inverter, charge controller, diesel generator and installation charges, was DM120 000 (about £48 000) – i.e. around £12 per watt of peak capacity (£12 W(p)$^{-1}$).

But the system designers, at the Fraunhofer Institute for Solar Energy Systems in Freiburg, estimate that after this initial development phase the overall system costs should reduce to between DM60 000 and DM80 000 (£24 000 and £32 000), equivalent to about £6–8 ($9–12) per peak watt. As they point out, there are an estimated one million houses isolated from the grid in the European Union, and since grid connection charges for such houses can often exceed ECU100 000 (£77 000), a photovoltaic energy system with diesel backup, like the one at Rappenecker Hof, could well be an attractive option.

A small 1 kW wind turbine was added to the Rappenecker system in 1990. The PV array still provides the majority of the inn's electricity, with the wind turbine mainly reducing the need to run the diesel generator in winter.

Note: The costs quoted above are based on 1994 exchange rates, which were approximately:
£1 = $1.50 = DM2.5 = ECU1.3.
These are not the rates that prevailed when the system was constructed.

(Sources: Schmid *et al.*, 1988 and Fraunhofer Institute, 1989 and 1991)

Figure 3.3 The main components of the energy system at Rappenecker Hof

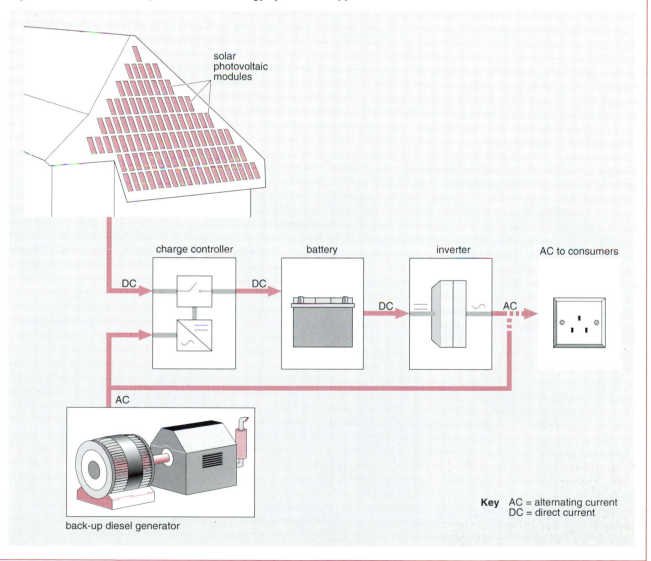

solar photovoltaic modules

charge controller

battery

inverter

AC to consumers

DC   DC   DC   AC

AC

back-up diesel generator

Key   AC = alternating current
DC = direct current

3.3 INTRODUCING PHOTOVOLTAICS

If you were asked to design the ideal energy conversion system, it would be pretty difficult to come up with something better than the solar photovoltaic (PV) cell.

In the PV cell we have a device which harnesses an energy source that is by far the most abundant of those available on the planet. As we have seen, the total annual solar energy input to the earth is more than 15 000 times as great as the earth's current yearly use of fossil and nuclear fuels.

The PV cell itself is, in its most common form, made almost entirely from silicon, the second most abundant element (after oxygen) in the earth's crust. It has no moving parts and can therefore in principle, if not yet in practice, operate for an indefinite period without wearing out. And its output is electricity, probably the most useful of all forms of energy.

HISTORICAL BACKGROUND

The term 'photovoltaic' is derived by combining the Greek word for light, *photos*, with *volt*, the name of the unit of electromotive force (the force which causes the motion of electrons). The volt was named after the Italian physicist Count Alessandro Volta, the inventor of the battery. The term photovoltaic therefore signifies the generation of electricity from light.

The discovery of the **photovoltaic effect** is generally credited to the French physicist, Edmond Becquerel (Figure 3.4), who in 1839 published a paper (Becquerel, 1839) describing his experiments with a 'wet cell' battery, in the course of which he found that the battery voltage increased when its silver plates were exposed to sunlight. (Incidentally, Becquerel's work on the effects of light on silver compounds laid the foundations for modern photography.)

The first report of the PV effect in a solid substance was made in 1877 when two Cambridge scientists, Adams and Day, described in a paper to

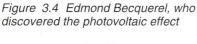

Figure 3.4 Edmond Becquerel, who discovered the photovoltaic effect

Figure 3.6 Bell Laboratories' pioneering PV researchers Pearson, Chapin and Fuller measure the response of an early solar cell to light

the Royal Society the variations they observed in the electrical properties of selenium when exposed to light (Adams and Day, 1877). Selenium is a non-metallic element similar to sulphur.

In 1883 Charles Edgar Fritts, a New York electrician, constructed a selenium solar cell that was in some respects similar to the silicon solar cells of today (Figure 3.5). It consisted of thin wafers of selenium covered with very thin, semi-transparent gold wires and a protective sheet of glass. But his cell was very inefficient. The efficiency of a solar cell is defined as the proportion of the solar radiation falling on its surface that is converted into electrical energy. Less than 1% of the solar energy falling on these early cells was converted to electricity. Nevertheless, selenium cells eventually came into widespread use in photographic exposure meters.

The underlying reasons for the inefficiency of these early devices were only to become apparent many years later, in the early decades of the twentieth century, when physicists like Max Planck provided new insights into the fundamental properties of materials.

But it was not until the 1950s that the breakthrough occurred that set in motion the development of modern, high-efficiency solar cells. It took place at the Bell Telephone Laboratories (Bell Labs) in New Jersey, USA, where a number of scientists, including Darryl Chapin, Calvin Fuller and Gerald Pearson (Figure 3.6), were researching the effects of light on **semiconductors**.

Semiconductors are non-metallic materials, such as germanium and silicon, whose electrical characteristics lie between those of conductors, which offer little resistance to the flow of electric current, and insulators, which block the flow of current almost completely. Hence the term *semi*conductor.

A few years before, in 1948, two other Bell Labs researchers, Bardeen and Brattain, had produced another revolutionary device using semiconductors – the transistor. Transistors are made from semiconductors (usually silicon)

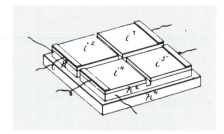

Figure 3.5 Diagram from Charles Edgar Fritts' 1884 US patent application for a solar cell

Figure 3.7(b) The first experimental application of a 'Solar Battery' by the Bell Telephone system was to power this rural telephone amplifier (mounted at the top of the pole) at Americus, Georgia, in the 1950s

Figure 3.7(a) A promotional demonstration of the Bell Solar Battery powering a telephone system at Bell Labs in the mid-1950s

in extremely pure crystalline form, into which tiny quantities of carefully selected impurities, such as boron or phosphorus, have been deliberately diffused. This process, known as **'doping'**, dramatically alters the electrical behaviour of the semiconductor in a very useful manner that will be described in detail later.

In 1953 the Chapin-Fuller-Pearson team, building on earlier Bell Labs research on the PV effect in silicon (Ohl, 1941), produced 'doped' silicon slices that were much more efficient than earlier devices in producing electricity from light.

By the following year they had produced a paper on their work (Chapin, Fuller and Pearson, 1954) and had succeeded in increasing the conversion efficiency of their silicon solar cell to 6%. Bell Labs went on to demonstrate the practical use of solar cells for powering a rural telephone amplifier in the mid-1950s, but at that time they were too expensive to be an economic source of power in most applications (Figures 3.7(a) and 3.7(b)).

In 1958, however, solar cells were used to power a small radio transmitter in the second US space satellite, Vanguard I. Following this first successful demonstration, the use of PV as a power source for spacecraft has become almost universal (Figure 3.8).

Rapid progress in increasing the efficiency of PV cells, and reducing their cost and weight, has been made over the past few decades by the aerospace and electronics industries. Their terrestrial uses are now widespread, particularly in providing power for telecommunications, lighting and other electrical appliances in locations where a more conventional electricity supply would be too expensive. PV cells are also, of course, widely used in consumer products such as watches and calculators.

A number of PV power stations connected to utility grids are now in operation in the USA, Germany, Italy, Switzerland and Japan. And a small

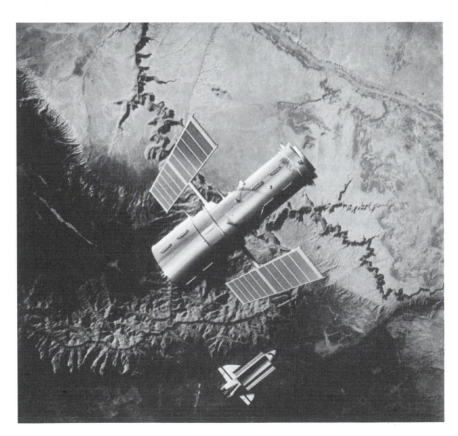

Figure 3.8 Arrays of PV cells provide electrical power for most spacecraft, including the Hubble Space Telescope

but increasing number of domestic, commercial and industrial buildings now have PV arrays providing a substantial proportion of their energy needs.

The efficiency of the best silicon solar *cells* has now reached 24% in laboratory test conditions (see Box 3.1), and the best silicon PV *modules* now available commercially have an overall efficiency of about 16%. Experience in the PV industry suggests that it takes around 10 years for the efficiencies demonstrated in the laboratory to be achieved by PV products on the market, so it is expected that by the early twenty-first century modules will be available with efficiencies of 20% or more.

As efficiencies have risen, module prices have fallen, to around $4 per peak watt (1992 prices) if purchased in large quantities. In 1959, the cost of PV cells for spacecraft was reportedly some $200 000 per peak watt (Chalmers, 1976). Although PV modules for spacecraft are more expensive than those for terrestrial use, it is clear that there has been a dramatic reduction in cost in just over 30 years. Figure 3.11 shows how PV production volumes and module efficiencies have increased, while module costs have dropped by a factor of around five, since the 1970s. Moreover, as we shall see, improvements in the cost-effectiveness of PV are likely to continue.

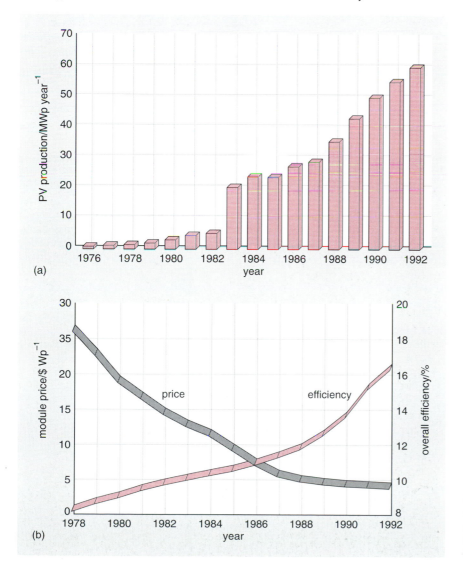

(a)

(b)

Figure 3.11(a) PV module production since 1976; (b) Increases in PV module efficiencies, and decreases in cost per peak watt, 1978–92 (Source: Derrick, 1993)

BOX 3.1: STANDARD TEST CONDITIONS FOR PV CELLS AND MODULES

There is widespread international agreement that the performance of PV cells and modules should be measured under a set of standard test conditions.

Essentially, these specify that the temperature of the cell or module should be 25 °C and that the solar radiation incident on the cell should have a total power density of 1000 watts per square metre, with a spectral power distribution known as **Air Mass 1.5**.

The spectral power distribution is a graph describing the way in which the power contained in the solar radiation varies across the spectrum of wavelengths.

The concept of 'Air Mass' relates to the way in which the spectral power distribution of radiation from the sun is affected by the distance the sun's rays have to travel though the atmosphere before reaching a PV module or array.

In space, solar radiation is obviously unaffected by the earth's atmosphere and has a power density of approximately 1365 watts per square metre. The characteristic spectral power distribution of solar radiation as measured in space is described as the **Air Mass 0** distribution.

At the earth's surface, the various gases of which the atmosphere is composed (oxygen, ozone, water vapour, carbon dioxide, etc.) attenuate the solar radiation selectively at different wavelengths. This attenuation increases as the distance which the sun's rays have to travel through the atmosphere increases.

When the sun is at its zenith (i.e. directly overhead), the distance which the sun's rays have to travel through the atmosphere to an observer (or a PV array) is clearly at a minimum. The characteristic spectral power distribution of solar radiation that is observed under these conditions is known as the **Air Mass 1** distribution.

When the sun is at a given angle θ to the zenith (as perceived by an observer at sea level), the Air Mass is defined as the ratio of the path length of the sun's rays under these conditions to the path length when the sun is at its zenith. By simple trigonometry (see Figure 3.9), this leads to the definition:

$$\text{Air Mass} \approx \frac{1}{\cos\theta}$$

An Air Mass distribution of 1.5, as specified in the standard test conditions, therefore corresponds to the spectral power distribution observed when the sun's radiation is coming from an angle to overhead of about 48 degrees, since cos 48° = 0.67 and the reciprocal of this is 1.5.

The approximate spectral power distributions for Air Masses 0 and 1.5 are shown in Figure 3.10.

(More precise definitions of the spectral power distributions for various air masses are available from the International Electrotechnical Commission (IEC), 3 rue de Varembe, Geneva, Switzerland.)

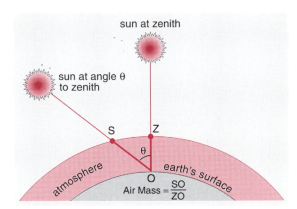

Figure 3.9 Air Mass is the ratio of the path length of the sun's rays through the atmosphere when the sun is at a given angle (θ) to the zenith, to the path length when the sun is at its zenith

Figure 3.10 The spectral power distributions of solar radiation corresponding to Air Mass 0 and Air Mass 1.5. Also shown is the theoretical spectral power distribution that would be expected, in space, if the sun were a perfect radiator (a 'black body') at 6000 °C

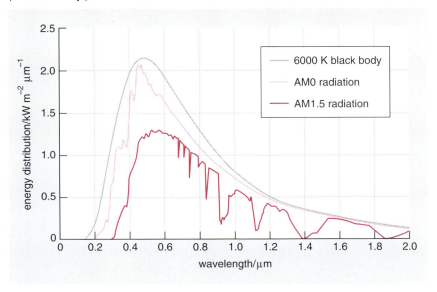

3.4 PV IN SILICON: BASIC PRINCIPLES

SEMICONDUCTORS AND 'DOPING'

PV cells consist, in essence, of a junction between two thin layers of dissimilar semiconducting materials, known respectively as 'p' (positive)-type semiconductor, and 'n' (negative)-type semiconductor. These semiconductors are usually made from silicon, so for simplicity we shall consider only silicon-based semiconductors here – although, as we shall see, PV cells can be made from other materials.

n-type semiconductors are made from crystalline silicon that has been 'doped' with tiny quantities of an impurity (usually phosphorus) in such a way that the doped material possesses a *surplus of free electrons*. **Electrons** are sub-atomic particles with a negative electrical charge, so silicon doped in this way is known as an **n (negative)-type** semiconductor.

p-type semiconductors are also made from crystalline silicon, but are doped with very small amounts of a different impurity (usually boron) which causes the material to have a *deficit of free electrons*. These 'missing' electrons are called **holes**. Since the absence of a negatively charged electron can be considered equivalent to a positively charged particle, silicon doped in this way is known as a **p (positive)-type** semiconductor (see Figures 3.12(a), (b) and (c)).

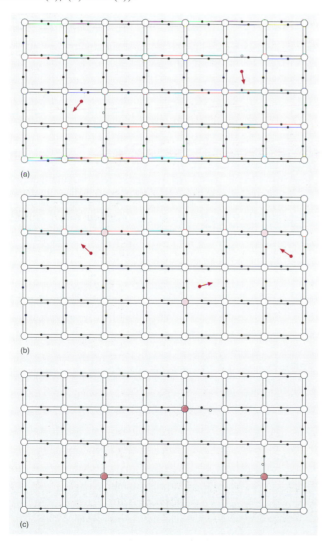

(a)

(b)

(c)

Figure 3.12(a) Crystal of pure silicon has a cubic structure, shown here in two dimensions for simplicity. The silicon atom has four valence electrons. Each atom is firmly held in the crystal lattice by sharing two electrons (black) with each of four neighbours at equal distances from it. Occasionally thermal vibrations or a photon of light will spontaneously provide enough energy to promote one of the electrons into the energy level known as the conduction band, where the electron (colour) is free to travel through the crystal and conduct electricity. When the electron moves from its bonding site, it leaves a 'hole' (white), a local region of net positive charge

(b) Crystal of n-type silicon can be created by doping the silicon with trace amounts of phosphorus. Each phosphorus atom (light colour) has five valence electrons, so that not all of them are taken up in the crystal lattice. Hence n-type crystal has an excess of free electrons (colour)

(c) Crystal of p-type silicon can be created by doping the silicon with trace amounts of boron. Each boron atom (dark colour) has only three valence electrons, so that it shares two electrons with three of its silicon neighbours and one electron with the fourth. Hence the p-type crystal contains more holes than conduction electrons (Source: Scientific American, 1976)

THE P–N JUNCTION

We can create what is known as a **p–n junction** by joining these dissimilar semiconductors. This sets up an **electric field** in the region of the junction. This electric field is like the electrostatic field you can generate by rubbing a plastic comb against a sweater. It will cause negatively charged particles to move in one direction, and positively charged particles to move in the opposite direction. (It is worth noting, however, that a p–n junction is not a simple mechanical junction: in practice, the characteristics change from 'p' to 'n' gradually across the junction, and not abruptly.)

THE PV EFFECT

What happens when light falls on the p–n junction at the heart of a solar cell?

Light can be considered to consist of a stream of tiny particles of energy, called **photons**. When photons from light of a suitable wavelength fall within the p–n junction, they can transfer their energy to some of the electrons in the material, so 'promoting' them to a higher energy level. Normally, these electrons help to hold the material together by forming so-called 'valence' bonds with adjoining atoms, and cannot move. In their 'excited' state, however, the electrons become free to conduct electric current by moving through the material. In addition, when electrons move they leave behind holes in the material, which can also move (Figures 3.12 and 3.13).

This process is similar in some ways to the two-storey 'car park' shown in Figure 3.14. In its initial state, the ground floor of the car park is full, so the cars cannot move around. If some of the cars are 'promoted' to the first floor, however, not only do they now have room to move around, but the 'holes' they leave behind, on the ground floor, can also move around.

When the p–n junction is formed, some of the electrons in the immediate vicinity of the junction are attracted from the n-side to combine with holes on the nearby p-side. Similarly, holes on the p-side near the junction are attracted to combine with electrons on the nearby n-side.

The net effect of this is to set up around the junction a layer on the n-side that is more positively charged than it would otherwise be, and, on the

Figure 3.13 A silicon solar cell is a wafer of p-type silicon with a thin layer of n-type silicon on one side. When a photon of light with the appropriate amount of energy penetrates the cell near the junction of the two types of crystal and encounters a silicon atom (a), it dislodges one of the electrons, which leaves behind a hole. The energy required to promote the electron into the conduction band is known as the band gap. The electron thus promoted tends to migrate into the layer of n-type silicon, and the hole tends to migrate into the layer of p-type silicon. The electron then travels to a current collector on the front surface of the cell, generates an electric current in the external circuit and then reappears in the layer of p-type silicon, where it can recombine with waiting holes. If a photon with an amount of energy greater than the band gap strikes a silicon atom (b), it again gives rise to an electron–hole pair, and the excess energy is converted into heat. A photon with an amount of energy smaller than the band gap will pass right through the cell (c), so that it gives up virtually no energy along the way. Moreover, some photons are reflected from the front surface of the cell even when it has an antireflection coating (d). Still other photons are lost because they are blocked from reaching the crystal by the current collectors that cover part of the front surface (Source: Scientific American, 1976)

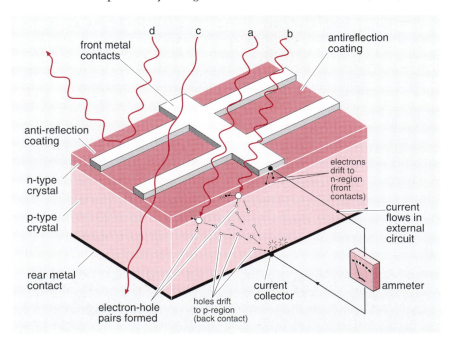

p-side, a layer that is more negatively charged than it would otherwise be. In effect, this means that a *reverse* electric field is set up around the junction: negative on the p-side and positive on the n-side. The region around the junction is also depleted of charge carriers (electrons and holes) and is therefore known as the **depletion region**.

When an electron in the junction region is stimulated by an incoming photon to 'jump' into the conduction band, it leaves behind a hole in the valence band. Two charge carriers (an **electron–hole pair**) are thus generated. Under the influence of the reverse electric field around the junction, the electrons will tend to move into the n-region and the holes into the p-region.

The process can be envisaged (Figure 3.15), in terms of the energy levels in the material. The electrons that have been stimulated by incoming photons to enter the conduction band can be thought of as 'rolling downwards', under the influence of the electric field at the junction, into the n-region; similarly, the holes can be thought of as 'floating upwards', under the influence of the junction field, into the p-region.

The flow of electrons to the n-region is, by definition, an electric current. If there is an external circuit for the current to flow through, the moving electrons will eventually flow out of the semiconductor via one of the metallic contacts on the top of the cell. The holes, meanwhile, will flow in the opposite direction through the material until they reach another metallic contact on the bottom of the cell, where they are then 'filled' by electrons entering from the other half of the external circuit.

The generation of electrical power requires both voltage and current. So in order to produce power, the PV cell must generate voltage as well as the current provided by the flow of electrons. This voltage is, in effect, provided by the internal electric field set up at the p–n junction. As we have seen, a single silicon PV cell typically produces a voltage of about 0.5 V at a current of up to around 2.5 amperes – that is, a peak power of up to about 1.25 W. (Depending on their detailed design, some PV cells produce more current or voltage than this, some less.)

MONOCRYSTALLINE SILICON CELLS

Until fairly recently, the majority of solar cells were made from extremely pure **monocrystalline** silicon (Si) – that is, silicon with a single, continuous crystal lattice structure (Figure 3.12) having virtually no defects or impurities. Mono-crystalline silicon is usually grown from a small seed crystal that is slowly pulled out of a molten mass of the less pure polycrystalline silicon

Figure 3.14 'Car parking' analogy of conduction processes in a semiconductor: (a) The ground floor of the car park is full: the cars there cannot move around. The first floor is empty. (b) A car is 'promoted' to the first floor, where it can move around freely. This also allows cars on the ground floor to move around (Source: Green, 1982)

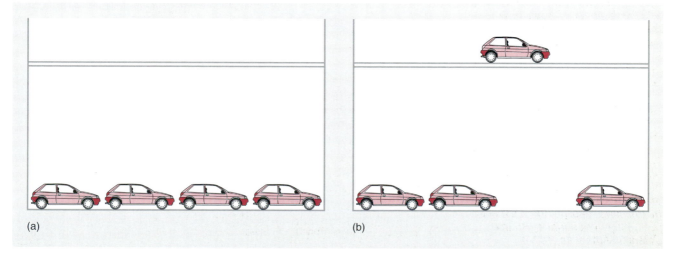

(a) (b)

BOX 3.2: BAND GAPS AND EFFICIENCY

According to the quantum theory of matter, the quantity of energy possessed by any given electron in a material will lie within one of several levels or 'bands'. Those electrons that normally hold the atoms of the material together (by being 'shared' between adjoining atoms, as we saw in Figure 3.12) are described by physicists as occupying the **valence band**.

As we shall see, some electrons may in certain circumstances acquire higher energy, sufficient to enable them to move around within the material and thus to conduct electricity. They are then described as being in the **conduction band** (Figure 3.15). There is a so-called **energy gap** or **band gap** between these bands, the magnitude of which varies from material to material, and which is measured using a unit known as the *electron volt*.

Metals, which conduct electricity well, have many electrons in the conduction band. Insulators, which hardly conduct electricity at all, have virtually no electrons in the conduction band. Pure (or 'intrinsic') semiconductors have some electrons in the conduction band, but not as many as in a metal. 'Doping' pure semiconductors with very small quantities of certain impurities can greatly improve their conductivity, however.

If a photon incident on a doped, n-type semiconductor in a PV cell is to succeed in transferring its energy to an electron and 'exciting' it from the valence band to the conduction band, it must possess an energy at least equal to the band gap. Photons with energy less than the band gap do not excite valence electrons to enter the conduction band and are 'wasted'. Photons with energies significantly greater than the band gap do succeed in 'promoting' an electron into the conduction band, but any excess energy is dissipated as heat. This wasted energy is one of the reasons why PV cells are not 100% efficient in converting solar radiation into electricity. (Another is that not all photons incident on a cell are absorbed: a small proportion are reflected.)

Because the energy of a photon is directly proportional to the frequency of the light associated with it, photons associated with shorter wavelengths (i.e. higher frequencies) of light, near the blue end of the spectrum, have a greater energy than those of longer wavelength near the red end of the visible spectrum.

The spectral distribution of sunlight varies considerably according to weather conditions and the elevation of the sun in the sky (see Box 3.1). For

Figure 3.15 (a) Energy bands in a normal ('intrinsic') semiconductor; (b) An electron can be 'promoted' to the conduction band when it absorbs energy from light (or heat), leaving behind a 'hole' in the valence band;

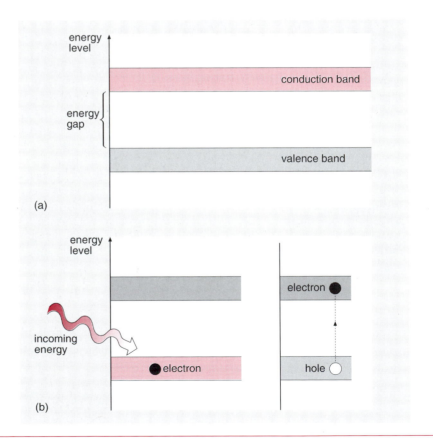

maximum efficiency of conversion of light into electric power, it is clearly important that the band gap energy of the material used for a PV cell is reasonably well matched to the spectrum of the light incident upon it. For example, if the majority of the energy in the incoming solar spectrum is in the yellow–green range (corresponding to photons with energy of around 1.5 electron volts), then a semiconductor with a band gap of around 1.5 electron volts will be most efficient. In general, semiconductor materials with band gaps between 1.0 and 1.5 electron volts are reasonably well suited to PV use. Silicon has a band gap of 1.1 electron volts.

The maximum theoretical conversion efficiency attainable in a single junction silicon PV cell has been calculated to be about 30%, if full advantage is taken of 'light trapping' techniques to ensure that as many of the photons as possible are usefully absorbed (Green, 1993). However, *multi-junction* cells have also been designed, in which each junction is tailored to absorbing a particular portion of the incident spectrum. Theoretically, such cells should have a much higher efficiency, possibly as high as 66% for an infinite number of junctions – though the efficiencies so far achieved by multi-junction cells in practice have been very much lower than this (see Section 3.7).

In practice, the highest efficiency achieved in commercially available silicon PV *modules* (as distinct from individual PV *cells*) is currently around 16%. The efficiency of PV modules is usually lower than that achieved by cells in the laboratory for various reasons, which include:

• it is difficult to achieve as high an efficiency consistently in mass-produced devices as in one-off laboratory cells under optimum conditions;

• laboratory cells are not usually glazed or encapsulated;

• in a PV module there are usually inactive areas, between cells (especially if they are circular) and due to the surrounding module frames, that decrease the effective area available to produce power;

• there are small resistive losses in the wiring between cells and in the diodes used to protect cells from short circuiting;

• there are losses due to mismatching between cells of slightly differing electrical characteristics connected in series.

Figure 3.15 (c) When the n-type and p-type semiconductors are combined into a p–n junction, their different energy bands combine to give a new distribution, as shown, and a built-in electric field is created; (d) In the p–n junction, photons of light can excite electrons from the valence band to the conduction band. The electrons 'roll downwards' to the n-region, and the holes 'float upwards' to the p-region

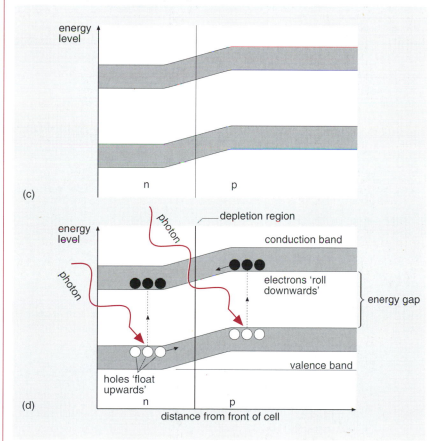

(see Section 3.5 below) in the sophisticated but expensive **Czochralski process**, developed initially for the electronics industry. The entire process of mono-crystalline silicon solar cell and module production is summarised in Figure 3.16.

The most efficient monocrystalline PV modules currently available, produced by companies such as BP Solar and AEG (Deutsche Aerospace), have an efficiency of around 16% and use the 'laser-grooved buried-grid' cell technology developed at the University of New South Wales (Green, 1993). Amongst the innovative features of these cells are their use of a pyramid-shaped texture on the top surface to increase the amount of light 'trapped', and buried electrical contacts which achieve very low electrical resistance whilst minimising losses due to overshadowing (Figure 3.17).

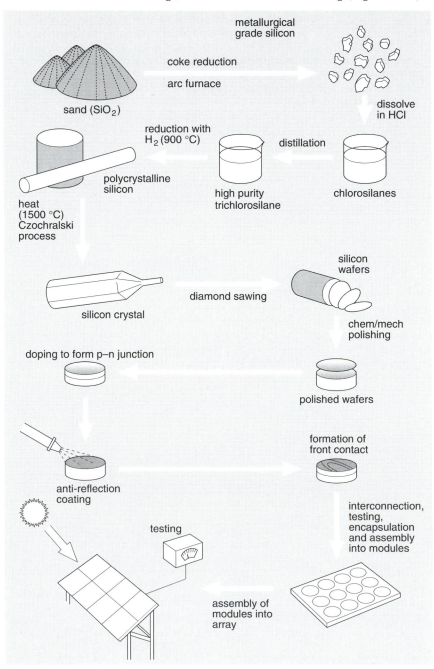

Figure 3.16 The overall process of monocrystalline silicon solar cell and module production

3.5 REDUCING THE COST OF CRYSTALLINE PV CELLS

Although the latest monocrystalline silicon PV modules are highly efficient, they are also expensive. This is because monocrystalline cells are normally manufactured by the Czochralski process which is slow, requires highly skilled operators, and is labour- and energy-intensive. Another major reason for their high cost is that until recently almost all such cells were fabricated from extremely pure 'electronic-grade' polycrystalline silicon.

However, PV cells can now be made from a less pure, so-called 'solar-grade' silicon, with only a small reduction in conversion efficiency. Solar-grade silicon can be manufactured much more cheaply than electronic-grade silicon, using a number of different low-cost processes.

But a number of more radical approaches to reducing the cost of PV cells and modules have been under development during the past 20 years or so. These include the growing of silicon in ribbon form, the development of cells using polycrystalline rather than single-crystal material, the use of other PV materials such as gallium arsenide, the development of amorphous silicon and other thin film PV devices, the use of concentrating devices, and various other innovative approaches.

SILICON RIBBON CELLS

This approach involves producing a thin 'ribbon' of monocrystalline silicon from a polycrystalline or single crystal silicon melt. The main process used is known as 'edge-defined, film-fed growth' (EFG), and was developed by the US firm Mobil Solar. It is described in Figures 3.18 and 3.19. In 1994, Mobil

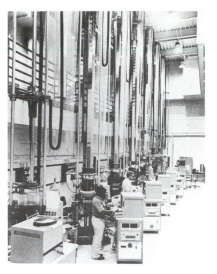

Figure 3.19 Thin polygonal tubes of crystalline silicon some 4-5 metres long being 'grown' at the Mobil Solar plant in the USA.

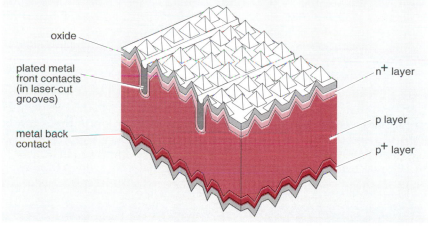

oxide

plated metal front contacts (in laser-cut grooves)

metal back contact

n^+ layer

p layer

p^+ layer

Figure 3.17 Main features of the advanced 'laser-grooved buried-grid' monocrystalline PV cell, as developed at the University of New South Wales, and used in the latest, high-efficiency PV modules produced by various companies. (The heavily-doped p^+ and n^+ layers reduce electrical resistance in the contact areas.)

Figure 3.18 Edge-defined, film-fed growth process for PV production, developed by Mobil Solar

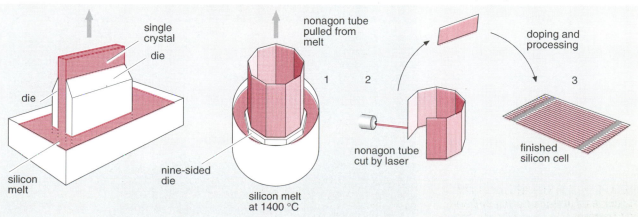

single crystal

die

die

silicon melt

nine-sided die

silicon melt at 1400 °C

nonagon tube pulled from melt

1

2

nonagon tube cut by laser

doping and processing

3

finished silicon cell

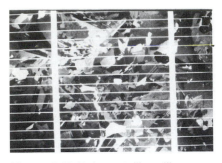

Figure 3.20 Polycrystalline silicon consists of randomly-packed 'grains' of monocrystalline silicon

sold the technology to Angewandte Solarenergie (ASE) GmbH, a joint venture of two leading German companies active in the PV field, Deutche Aerospace AG (a subsidiary of Daimler-Benz) and NUKEM GmbH, part of the RWE consortium which owns Germany's largest electricity utility.

POLYCRYSTALLINE SILICON CELLS

Polycrystalline silicon essentially consists of small grains of mono-crystalline silicon (Figure 3.20). Solar cell wafers can be made directly from polycrystalline silicon in various ways.

One of the principal technologies involves carefully controlled casting of molten polycrystalline silicon into ingots, as shown in Figure 3.21. The ingots are then cut, using fine wire saws, into thin square wafers and fabricated into complete cells in the same way as monocrystalline cells.

Although polycrystalline PV cells are easier and cheaper to manufacture than their mono-crystalline counterparts, they tend to be less efficient because light-generated charge carriers (i.e. electrons and holes) can recombine at the boundaries between the grains within polycrystalline silicon. However, it has been found that by processing the material in such a way that the grains are relatively large in size, and oriented in a top-to-bottom direction to allow light to penetrate deeply into each grain, their efficiency can be substantially improved. Commercially available polycrystalline PV modules (sometimes called 'semi-crystalline' or 'multi-crystalline') now have efficiencies of around 10% or more.

An advantage of polycrystalline silicon cells is that they can easily be formed into a square shape, which virtually eliminates any 'inactive' area between cells – in contrast to the cells produced by the Czochralski process and used in many monocrystalline PV modules, where the circular shape leads to substantial inactive areas between each adjoining cell. (In some monocrystalline PV modules, the circular silicon slices are trimmed into squares, to increase the area of active PV material that can be included in a module of given area.)

POLYCRYSTALLINE THIN FILM SILICON CELLS

Conventional silicon solar cells need to be several hundred microns thick in order to ensure that most of the photons incident upon them can be absorbed. But the US firm Astropower Inc. (see Zweibel and Barnett, 1993) has demonstrated that advanced 'light trapping' techniques can be used to maximise the interaction of photons with the material, even in thin layers or 'films' of silicon around 20 microns in thickness. These **polycrystalline**

Figure 3.21 A large polycrystalline silicon ingot and some silicon wafers

thin films, deposited on to ceramic substrates, form the basis of PV cells with reported efficiencies as high as 15%. The films used in these devices, though thin, are somewhat thicker than in other 'thin film' PV cells (see Section 3.6 below), so they are sometimes known as '*thick* film' polycrystalline cells.

The proponents of this approach believe it could soon lead to a new generation of PV modules combining the high efficiency and stability of crystalline silicon with the low material content and low processing cost of thin film devices such as amorphous silicon (see Section 3.6 below).

An array of 312 Astropower modules using this technology and delivering some 18 kW was installed in 1994 at the PVUSA test site (see Section 3.10 below) in Davis, California.

GALLIUM ARSENIDE CELLS

Silicon is not the only material suitable for PV. Another is gallium arsenide (GaAs), a so-called **compound semiconductor**. GaAs has a crystal structure similar to that of silicon (see Figure 3.12), but consisting of alternating gallium and arsenic atoms. In principle it is highly suitable for use in PV applications because it has a high light absorption coefficient, so only a thin layer of material is required. GaAs cells also have a band gap wider than that of silicon and close to the theoretical optimum for absorbing the energy in the terrestrial solar spectrum (see Box 3.2). Cells made from GaAs are therefore very efficient.

They can also operate at relatively high temperatures without the appreciable performance degradation from which silicon and many other semiconductors suffer. This means that GaAs cells are well suited to use in *concentrating* PV systems (see Section 3.7 below).

On the other hand, cells made from GaAs are substantially more expensive than silicon cells, partly because the production process is not so well developed, and partly because gallium and arsenic are not abundant materials.

GaAs cells have often been used when very high efficiency, regardless of cost, is required – as in many space applications. This was also the case with the 'Sunraycer' (Figure 3.22a), a photovoltaically-powered electric car

Figure 3.22a The 'Sunraycer', a photovoltaically-powered lightweight electric car using mainly gallium arsenide cells

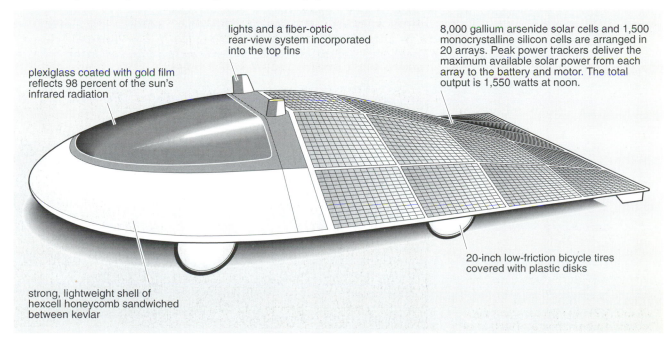

lights and a fiber-optic rear-view system incorporated into the top fins

8,000 gallium arsenide solar cells and 1,500 monocrystalline silicon cells are arranged in 20 arrays. Peak power trackers deliver the maximum available solar power from each array to the battery and motor. The total output is 1,550 watts at noon.

plexiglass coated with gold film reflects 98 percent of the sun's infrared radiation

20-inch low-friction bicycle tires covered with plastic disks

strong, lightweight shell of hexcell honeycomb sandwiched between kevlar

sponsored by General Motors, which in 1987 won the Pentax World Solar Challenge race for solar-powered vehicles when it travelled the 3000 km from Darwin to Adelaide at an average speed (in day time) of 66 km per hour. The Sunraycer was superior to the other solar cars at the time partly because of its ultra-lightweight, low drag design and high efficiency electric drive system, and partly because most of its PV cells were of the GaAs type, which gave it a speed and range advantage. However, it should be added that in the 1990 race the winning car, from the Biel School of Engineering in Switzerland, used monocrystalline silicon cells. These were of the advanced, laser-grooved buried-grid type, as described in Figure 3.17 above. The 1993 winner was the 'Honda Dream'(Figure 3.22b), powered by 20% efficient monocrystalline silicon PV cells, which achieved an average speed of 85 km per hour over the 3000 km course.

3.6 THIN FILM PV

AMORPHOUS SILICON

Silicon can not only be formed into the monocrystalline and polycrystalline structures described above. It can also be made in a less structured form called **amorphous silicon (a-Si)**, in which the silicon atoms are much less ordered than in the crystalline form. In a-Si, not every silicon atom is fully bonded to its neighbours, which leaves so-called 'dangling bonds' that can absorb the additional electrons introduced by doping, so rendering any p–n junction ineffective.

However, this problem is largely overcome in the process by which a-Si cells are normally manufactured. A gas containing silicon and hydrogen (such as silane, SiH_4), and a small quantity of dopant (such as boron), is decomposed electrically in such a way that it deposits a thin film of amorphous silicon on a suitable substrate (backing material) such as stainless steel. The hydrogen in the gas has the effect of providing additional electrons which combine with the dangling silicon bonds to form, in effect, an alloy of silicon and hydrogen. The dopant that is also present in the gas can then have its usual effect of contributing charge carriers to enhance the conductivity of the material.

Solar cells using a-Si have a somewhat different form of junction between the p- and the n-type material. A so-called 'p–i–n' junction is usually formed, consisting of an extremely thin layer of p-type a-Si on top, followed

Figure 3.22b The 1993 World Solar Challenge winner, the 'Honda Dream'

BOX 3.3: THE SUN SEEKER – A PV-POWERED AEROPLANE

One particularly interesting application of amorphous silicon PV has been in the construction of a small photovoltaically-powered aircraft, the Sun Seeker (Figure 3.24), which in the summer of 1990 flew 4060 km across the United States, setting a world record for fuel-less flight.

Piloted by her designer Eric Raymond, the Sun Seeker took off in California and, after 22 overnight stops and some breaks on rainy days, landed near Kitty Hawk, North Carolina, where the Wright Brothers made the world's first powered flight in 1903.

Power for the 2.4 metre diameter propeller on the Sun Seeker came from an array of Sanyo amorphous silicon solar cells stretched across the wings of the plane. Some 700 cells, deposited on a thin film of heat-resistant plastic, generated up to 300 watts of power to charge a nickel-cadmium battery. The battery powered a 2.2 kW electric motor to drive the propeller to enable the plane to take off.

In flight the ultra-light plane behaved as a glider, with occasional assistance from the propeller when needed. The amorphous silicon cells were only 0.12 mm thick and flexible enough to be bent, if necessary, into cylinders only 10 mm in diameter. They generated 200 milliwatts of power per gramme of weight, and cost around £5 ($8) per peak watt of power.

(Source: based on Piellisch, 1991)

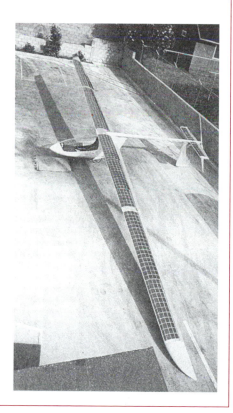

Figure 3.24 The Sun Seeker in flight; and on the ground

Figure 3.23 Structure of an amorphous silicon cell. The top electrical contact is made of an electrically-conducting, but transparent, layer of tin oxide deposited on the glass. Silicon dioxide forms a thin 'barrier layer' between the glass and the tin oxide. The bottom contact is made of aluminium. In between are layers of p-type, intrinsic and n-type amorphous silicon

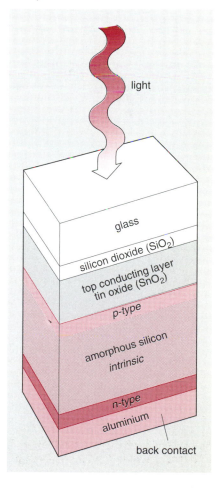

by a thicker 'intrinsic' (i) layer made of undoped a-Si, and then a very thin layer of n-type a-Si. The structure is as shown in Figure 3.23. The operation of the PV effect in a-Si is generally similar to that in crystalline silicon, except that in a-Si the band gap, although wider, is less clearly defined.

Amorphous silicon cells have various advantages and disadvantages. On the credit side, a-Si is much cheaper to produce than crystalline silicon. It is also a much better absorber of light, so much thinner (and therefore cheaper) films can be used. The a-Si manufacturing process operates at a much lower temperature than that for crystalline silicon, so less energy is required; it is suited to continuous production; and it allows quite large areas of cell to be deposited on to a wide variety of both rigid and flexible substrates, including steel, glass and plastics.

On the debit side, however, a-Si cells are currently much less efficient than their single-crystal or polycrystalline silicon counterparts: maximum efficiencies achieved with small, single junction cells in the laboratory are currently around 12%. Moreover, the efficiency of currently-available a-Si modules degrades, within a few months of exposure to sunlight, from an initial 6–7% to around 4%.

Strenuous attempts are being made by many manufacturers to improve the efficiency of a-Si cells, and to solve the degradation problem, but these difficulties have not yet been fully overcome. The most promising approach currently involves the development of multiple-junction a-Si devices (see Section 3.7 below), which should result in both reduced degradation and improved efficiency.

Nevertheless, a-Si cells have already been very successful commercially, as power sources for a wide variety of consumer products such as calculators, where the requirement is not so much for high efficiency as for low cost.

In 1990, amorphous silicon cells accounted for around 30% of total worldwide PV sales.

Amorphous silicon is by no means the only material suited to thin film PV, however. Amongst the many other possible thin film technologies some of the most promising are those based on compound semiconductors, and in particular copper indium diselenide ($CuInSe_2$, usually abbreviated to CIS) and cadmium telluride (CdTe). Modules based on both technologies have reached the pilot production stage.

COPPER INDIUM DISELENIDE

Copper indium diselenide (CIS) is a compound of copper, indium and selenium, which is a semiconductor. Thin film CIS cells have attained laboratory efficiencies of 12.5%, whilst pre-production CIS modules 30 centimetres square with efficiencies of nearly 10% have been produced by the firm Siemens Solar (Figure 3.25). In 1994, Siemens Solar announced it would be commercialising its CIS technology in partnership with the major US manufacturer Corning Glass.

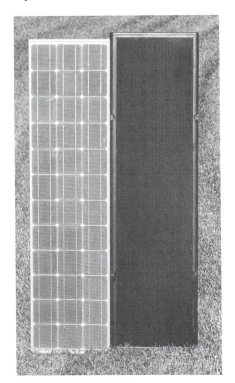

Figure 3.25 (Right) Array of copper indium diselenide (CIS) PV modules; (Below) CIS module side-by-side with crystalline silicon PV module

CIS modules with these promisingly high efficiencies do not appear to suffer from the performance degradation observed in a-Si PV modules. Somewhat thicker films are required than for a-Si, and indium is a relatively expensive material, but the quantities required are extremely small.

However, some CIS manufacturing processes involve the use of hydrogen selenide gas, which is highly toxic and could constitute a serious health hazard in the (extremely unlikely) event of an industrial accident. These and other environmental aspects are discussed in Section 3.12.

In 1994 a small US firm, Energy Photovoltaics Inc., of Princeton, NJ, announced it would be manufacturing 50 watt CIS modules of over 8% guaranteed efficiency and selling them at prices below $3 per watt for orders of 10 kW or more.

CADMIUM TELLURIDE

Another compound semiconductor suitable for thin film PV cells is cadmium telluride (CdTe), composed of cadmium and tellurium. BP Solar, a subsidiary of British Petroleum, is one of a number of companies actively involved in CdTe photovoltaics (see Figure 3.26). One advantage of CdTe modules is that they can be made using a relatively simple and inexpensive electroplating-type process. The band gap of CdTe is close to the optimum, and efficiencies of over 10% are claimed, without the performance degradation that occurs in a-Si cells.

However, since the modules contain cadmium, a highly toxic substance, stringent precautions need to be taken during the manufacture, use and eventual disposal of CdTe modules. This issue will be discussed in more detail in Section 3.12.

The US firm Golden Photon Inc., of Golden, Colorado, began production of 24 watt CdTe modules in 1994. Small-scale CdTe cells are also produced by the Japanese firm Matsushita for use in consumer products.

3.7 OTHER INNOVATIVE PV TECHNOLOGIES

MULTI-JUNCTION PV CELLS

An ingenious way of improving the overall conversion efficiency of PV cells and modules is the 'stacked' or **multi-junction** approach, in which two (or more) PV junctions, usually of the thin film type, are layered one on top of

Figure 3.26 Cadmium telluride PV modules made by BP Solar

Figure 3.27 Structure of a multi-junction (tandem) amorphous silicon cell

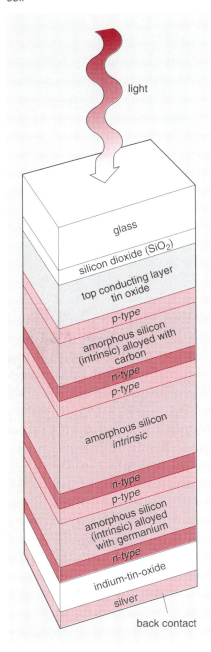

the other, each layer extracting energy from a particular portion of the spectrum of the incoming light. (Thin films of different types can also be used.) A cell with two layers is often called a 'tandem' device.

The band gap of amorphous silicon, for example, can be increased by alloying the material with carbon, so that the resulting material responds better to light at the blue end of the spectrum. Alloying with germanium, on the other hand, decreases the band gap so the material responds to light at the red end of the spectrum.

Typically, a wide band gap a-Si junction would be on top, absorbing the higher-energy light photons at the blue end of the spectrum, followed by other thin film a-Si junctions, each having a band gap designed to absorb a portion of the lower light frequencies, nearer the red end of the spectrum (Figure 3.27). In addition to increasing overall efficiency, the multi-junction arrangement also has the benefit of substantially reducing the degradation in efficiency that occurs with single-junction a-Si cells.

CONCENTRATING PV SYSTEMS

Another way of getting more energy out of a given number of PV cells is to use mirrors or lenses to concentrate the incoming solar radiation on to the cells. (The approach is similar to that described in Section 2.10, on solar thermal engines.) This has the obvious advantage that substantially fewer cells are required – to an extent depending on the concentration ratio, which can vary from as little as two to several hundred or even thousand times. The concentrating system must have an aperture equal to that of an equivalent flat plate array to collect the same amount of incoming energy.

The systems with the highest concentration ratios use complex (and expensive) sensors, motors and controls to allow them to track the sun in two axes (azimuth and elevation), ensuring that the cells always receive the maximum amount of solar radiation. Systems with lower concentration ratios often track the sun only on one axis and can have very simple mechanisms for orienting the array towards the sun.

Most concentrators can only utilise direct solar radiation. This is a problem in countries like the UK where nearly half the solar radiation is diffuse. However, some unconventional designs of concentrator, such as the Winston type (see Section 2.9) do allow some diffuse radiation, as well as direct radiation, to be concentrated (see also Boes and Luque, 1993).

There is some evidence that the latest designs of concentrating PV systems (for example, Figure 3.28) may now be more cost-effective than flat plate, non-concentrating systems in many locations (Bruton et al., 1992).

Figure 3.28 (Right) Concentrating PV array manufactured by Entech Inc. The system uses low-cost Fresnel lenses and two-axis tracking to concentrate solar radiation by a factor of around 20 on to passively-cooled, high efficiency monocrystalline cells. It provides 300 kW of power for the 3M Company's research centre at Austin, Texas, USA, and is mounted on top of a car park

FLUORESCENT CONCENTRATORS

An entirely different approach to the task of concentrating solar energy is found in the fluorescent (or luminescent) concentrator. It consists of a slab of plastic containing a fluorescent dye, or two sheets with a liquid dye sandwiched between them. The dye absorbs light over a wide range of wavelengths, but the light re-radiated when it fluoresces is in a much narrower band of wavelengths. Most of the re-radiated light is internally reflected from the front and back surfaces, and can only emerge via the edges. Reflectors are mounted on three of the edges of the slab and on the back surface, so light can only emerge along the fourth edge where it is absorbed by a strip of silicon PV cells. The frequency of the light emitted by the dye has to be reasonably well matched to the band gap of the PV cells.

Fluorescent concentrators can in principle concentrate diffuse as well as direct sunlight. But they have not yet been found to be cost-effective for power production and have so far only been used in consumer products such as clocks (Figure 3.29).

SILICON SPHERES

An ingenious way of making PV cells using tiny, millimetre-sized, spheres of silicon embedded at regular intervals between thin sheets of aluminium foil has been developed by the US firm Texas Instruments (TI) (Figure 3.30). Among the advantages claimed for this approach are that impurities in the silicon tend to diffuse out to the surface of the spheres, where they can be 'ground off' as part of the manufacturing process, and that relatively cheap, low-grade silicon can be used as a starting material. The resulting sheets of PV material are very flexible, which can be an advantage in some applications.

Prototype module efficiencies of over 10% have been achieved, and TI plans to build a pilot production plant capable of producing 15 MW of module capacity per annum in the near future.

PHOTO-ELECTROCHEMICAL CELLS

An even more radical, photo-electrochemical, approach to producing cheap electricity from solar energy has been pioneered by researchers at the Swiss Federal Institute of Technology in Lausanne. The idea of harnessing photo-electrochemical effects to produce electricity from sunlight is not

Figure 3.30 Texas Instruments 'silicon spheres' PV technology

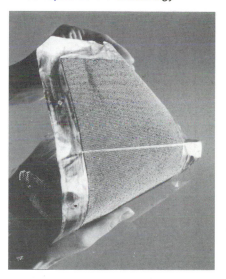

Figure 3.29 (Right) Principle of fluorescent concentrator; (Left) a photovoltaically-powered clock which uses a fluorescent concentrator

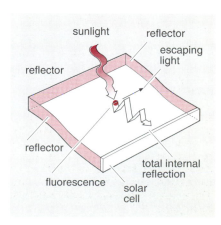

new. But the Swiss researchers claim they have achieved much higher efficiencies than before, and that their device could be extremely cheap to manufacture.

It consists essentially of two thin glass plates, both of which are covered with a thin, electrically-conducting tin oxide layer that is transparent to light (Figure 3.31). To one plate is added a thin layer of titanium dioxide (TiO_2), which is a semiconductor. The surface of the TiO_2 has been treated to give it exceptionally high roughness, in order to enhance its light-absorbing properties.

Immediately next to the roughened surface of the titanium dioxide is a layer of 'sensitiser' dye, only one molecule thick, made of a proprietary 'transition metal complex' based on ruthenium or osmium. Between this 'sensitised' TiO_2 and the other glass plate is a thicker layer of iodine-based electrolyte.

On absorption of a photon of suitable wavelength, the sensitiser layer injects an electron into the conduction band of the titanium dioxide. Electrons so generated then move to the bottom electrically-conducting layer (electrode) and pass out into an external circuit where they can do work. They then re-enter through the top electrode, where they drive a reduction-oxidation process in the iodine solution. This then supplies electrons to the sensitised TiO_2 layer in order to allow the process to continue.

The Swiss researchers claim to have achieved efficiencies of 10% in full (AM 1.5) sunlight, and that this figure can be improved substantially even in the short term. Their devices are claimed to be stable over long periods (though some researchers are not fully convinced of this), and since they use very cheap materials that are simple to manufacture, they should be very low in cost. Two major Swiss companies are reported to have invested in the technology, one with an interest in consumer products, the other in power production.

It remains to be seen what impact this new approach will have on PV technology over the coming decade. (See Gratzel, 1989, and O'Regan *et al.*, 1991, 1993.)

Figure 3.31 (Right) Principles of operation of photoelectrochemical PV cell developed at the Swiss Federal Institute of Technology, Lausanne; (Left) Two experimental photoelectrochemical cells in the laboratory at Lausanne

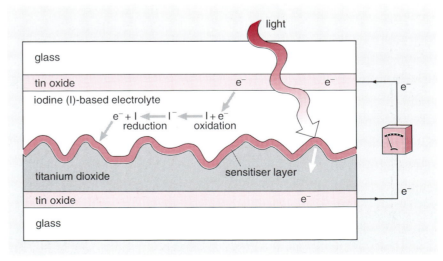

3.8 ELECTRICAL CHARACTERISTICS OF SILICON PV CELLS AND MODULES

One very simple way of envisaging a typical 100 square centimetre silicon PV cell is as a solar powered battery, one that produces a voltage of around 0.5 V and delivers a current proportional to the sunlight intensity, up to a maximum of about 2.5–3 amperes in full sunlight.

But in order to use PV cells efficiently we need to know a little more about how they behave when connected to various electrical loads. Figure 3.32 shows a single 100 cm^2 silicon PV cell connected to a variable electrical resistance R, together with an ammeter to measure the current (I) in the circuit and a voltmeter to measure the voltage (V) developed across the cell terminals. Let us assume the cell is being tested under standard test conditions (see Box 3.1).

When the resistance is infinite (i.e. when the cell is, in effect, not connected to any resistance, or 'open circuited') the current in the circuit

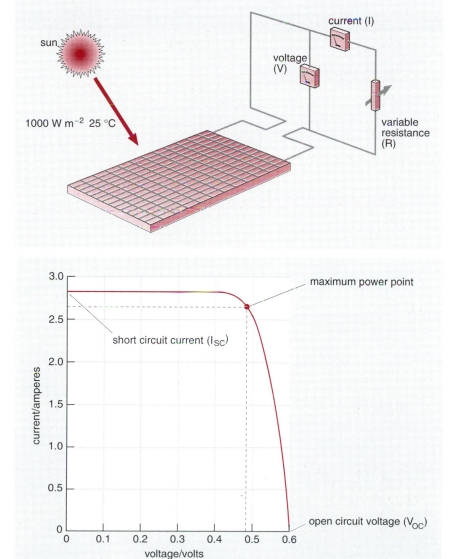

Figure 3.32 PV cell connected to variable resistance, with ammeter and voltmeter to measure variations in voltage and current as resistance varies

Figure 3.33 Current-voltage (I-V) characteristics of a typical silicon PV cell under standard test conditions

is at its minimum (zero) and the voltage across the cell is at its maximum, known as the **'open circuit voltage'** (Voc). At the other extreme, when the resistance is zero, the cell is in effect 'short circuited' and the current in the circuit then reaches its maximum, known as the **'short circuit current'** (Isc).

If we vary the resistance between zero and infinity, the current (*I*) and voltage (*V*) will be found to vary as shown in Figure 3.33, which is known

PRODUCT DATASHEET

BP275 Photovoltaic Module

PART NO. 360614

BP SOLAR

GENERAL DESCRIPTION

BP275 photovoltaic (PV) modules incorporate 36 series-connected monocrystalline silicon cells and a nominal voltage of 12 V DC.

ELECTRICAL

VOLTAGE-CURRENT CURVE (Typical)

The graph below details module performance at an insolation of 1000 W/m², air mass 1.5.

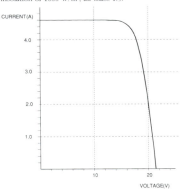

PERFORMANCE CHARACTERISTICS

The following parameters are measured under standard test conditions[1]: (Average Power measurement)

Typical Peak Power (P_{max}):	73W
Voltage @ maximum power (V_{mp}):	17.0V
Current @ maximum power (I_{mp}):	4.30A
Short-circuit Current (I_{sc}):	4.60A
Open-circuit Voltage (V_{oc}):	21.4V
Fill Factor:	0.74
Minimum Power (P_{min}):	71.3W
Maximum Power (P_{max}):	76.0W

1. Standard Test Conditions: Insolation 1000 W/m², AM 1.5, 25° C cell temp.

OPTIONAL DIODES

Two bypass diodes can be fitted within the junction box of the module, one across each string of 18 cells, one blocking diode also available.

CONNECTIONS

Electrical connections to the module are made via screw terminals within the junction box. One cable gland is fitted and 3 further knockouts (suitable for glands or conduit) are provided to facilitate series and/or parallel connection.

PRODUCT FEATURES

- High efficiency monocrystalline square silicon cells.
- Designed for maximum reliability and minimum maintenance.
- Produced using in-house technology in cell manufacturing and encapsulation.
- Highly resistant to water, abrasion, hail impact and other environmental factors.
- Lightweight anodised aluminium frame with silicone edge sealant around the laminate.
- All proven products, only materials with extensive field experienced used.
- Designed and manufactured to comply with European, American and Australian standards.

WEIGHT AND DIMENSIONS

Weight: **7.5 kg**

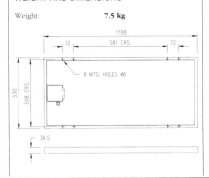

MECHANICAL

CONSTRUCTION

BP275 modules are manufactured using industry-standard materials and lamination techniques. Stainless steel fasteners are used throughout. The junction box is fastened to the module frame to avoid stressing the electrical connections between the laminate and the junction box.

Materials are as follows:

Front Cover:	Toughened glass, 3mm, high light transmission (c 92%)
Encapsulent:	Ethylene-vinyl-acetate (EVA)
Rear Cover:	Tri-laminate of PVF/Polyester/PVF
Frame:	Extruded Aluminium, Anodised
Frame Sealant:	Silicone gasket formed in-situ
Junction Box:	HPDE IP 65

Figure 3.34 Manufacturers' data sheet for the BP275 photovoltaic module

as the 'I-V characteristic' or 'I-V curve' of the cell. It can be seen from the graph that the cell will deliver maximum power (i.e. the maximum product of voltage and current) when the external resistance is adjusted so that its value corresponds to the **maximum power point** (MPP) on the I-V curve. At lower levels of solar radiation than the maximum (1000 W m^{-2}) assumed in Figure 3.33, the general shape of the I-V characteristic stays the same, but the area under the curve decreases, and the maximum power point moves to the left.

The short circuit current is directly proportional to the intensity of solar radiation on the cell, whilst the open circuit voltage is only weakly dependent on the solar radiation intensity. The open circuit voltage also decreases linearly as cell temperature increases.

When PV cells are delivering power to electrical loads in real-world conditions, the intensity of solar radiation often varies substantially over time. Many PV systems therefore incorporate a so-called 'maximum power point tracking' device, a specialised electronic circuit that automatically varies the load 'seen' by the PV cell in such a way that it is always operating around the maximum power point and so delivering maximum power to the load. Such systems can also usually compensate for the variations in electrical load that often occur in real applications outside the laboratory.

A typical 100 cm^2 silicon PV cell produces, as we have seen, a maximum current of just under 3 amps at a voltage of around 0.5 volts. Since many PV applications involve charging lead-acid batteries, which have a typical nominal voltage of 12 volts, PV modules often consist of around 36 individual cells wired in series to ensure that the voltage is usually above 13 V, sufficient to charge a 12 V battery even on fairly overcast days.

A manufacturer's data sheet for a monocrystalline PV module, the BP 275 made by the UK firm BP Solar, is reproduced in Figure 3.34.

As can be seen, the open circuit voltage is 21.4 V and the short circuit current is about 4.6 A. The peak power output of the module is 73 W under standard test conditions, achieved when the module is delivering a current of some 4.3 A at a voltage of 17.0 V.

3.9 PV SYSTEMS FOR REMOTE POWER

So how in practice are PV modules incorporated into energy systems that deliver useful power in real applications? We have already looked at one example, the 4 kW PV energy system with diesel generator backup at the Rappenecker Hof in Germany (Section 3.2).

PV cells are increasingly used to provide electrical power for a wide variety of applications, in locations where it is inconvenient or expensive to use conventional grid supplies. Examples (see Figure 3.35) range from photovoltaically-powered microwave radio repeater stations on mountain tops to PV-powered telephone kiosks, from PV battery chargers for boats and caravans to photovoltaically-powered electric fences and PV street lights.

Figure 3.36 shows a very small (50 W) PV energy system that might be used in, say, a remote holiday home in the UK to provide electricity for charging a lead-acid battery. This in turn would provide energy, when needed, for lighting and perhaps a small radio. (We shall assume that energy for cooking, space and water heating and refrigeration would be supplied by, say, bottled gas.)

But in order to be able to specify accurately how many PV modules would be required, or what the capacity of the battery should be, the PV energy

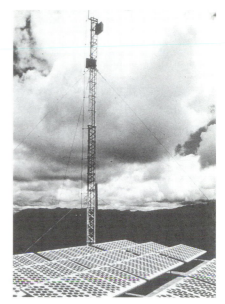

Figure 3.35 (Top) PV powered microwave repeater; (Centre) PV (and wind) power for a telephone kiosk; (Bottom) PV battery charger on a boat

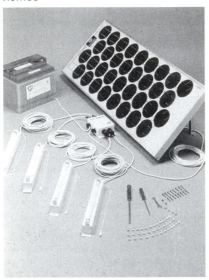

Figure 3.36 Small 50 W PV lighting kit (BP Solar) for use in remote homes

system designer needs to know the answers to such questions as:
• What are the daily, weekly and annual variations in the electrical demand of the house?
• What are the daily, weekly and annual variations in the amount of solar radiation in the area where the house is situated?
• What is the proposed orientation and tilt angle of the PV array?
• For how many sunless days do we think the battery will need to be able to provide back-up electricity?

The art of PV system sizing is quite a complex one, and most commercial PV companies have developed proprietary computer programs to help their engineers calculate reasonably accurately the size and cost of PV systems that will meet clearly specified energy requirements in given locations and climatic conditions.

System sizing and other PV system design considerations are described in detail in Imamura *et al.* (1992), Treble (1991), Roberts (1991) and Lasnier and Ang (1990). An easy to follow step-by-step procedure is also given in Treble (1993).

'AUTONOMOUS' ROOF-TOP PV SYSTEMS FOR UK HOMES

A 50 W(p) PV system like the one shown in Figure 3.36 would, of course, be far too small to supply the energy needs of a conventional UK home.

The electricity demand of a typical UK household is currently around 4000 kWh a year – say 11 kWh per day on average – but the majority of this is for resistance heating and other uses that could be supplied by non-electrical energy forms such as gas. The necessary electricity demand of a typical UK household – i.e. its demand for energy in forms, such as lighting, radio, TV and hi-fi, that *necessitate* the use of electricity – is currently around 1000 kWh a year, though this figure could be substantially reduced by the use of more energy-efficient lighting and appliances.

In order to supply this necessary electrical demand, our roof-top PV system would probably have to have PV panels of at least 10 m² in area and about 1 kW in capacity. The roofs of most UK houses could accommodate a PV array of this size, and surveys have suggested that about half of UK roofs are oriented in a direction sufficiently close to due south to enable them to be used for solar collection purposes.

But a roof-top domestic PV system like this would still be much too expensive (see Section 3.11 below) to be economically competitive with conventional sources in all but the most remote of UK locations. Another major shortcoming is that in a country like the UK its output would be at its maximum in the summer, when demand is at its lowest (except in holiday homes), and at its minimum in winter, when demand is at its peak. This might suggest the need for an extremely large battery, to store solar-generated electricity from summer, when it is available, until winter, when it is needed. But the size and cost of such a battery would currently be prohibitive in most cases.

Alternatively, at considerable extra cost, the PV array might be made much larger than is necessary for summer use, in order to provide a more adequate level of power in winter. Or a second, backup energy system (such as a diesel or wind generator) could be installed to provide power when the output of the PV array is inadequate. Or, as at Rappenecker Hof, a combination of these approaches could be adopted.

Whether or not it would be economic to install an 'autonomous' (i.e. non grid-connected) PV power system depends, clearly, on how the cost per kWh of PV electricity from it compares with that of power from other sources, whether conventional or renewable. A recent study by the Energy Technology Support Unit (Taylor, 1990) concluded that, under current economic conditions, autonomous PV power systems in remote UK locations can be cost-competitive with other energy sources if they are supplying small loads of less than 100 watt-hours (Wh) per day. For loads between about 100 Wh and 10 kWh per day, PV power was found to be similar in cost to wind turbine generation. For loads above 10 kWh per day, a conventional grid connection was found to be cheaper than PV at all but the most remote sites. (But at these very remote sites, it was found that wind generation would in many cases be cheaper than the normal substitute for mains power – a diesel generator.)

PV SYSTEMS IN DEVELOPING COUNTRIES

In most parts of the 'developed' countries, where networks for the distribution of electricity and fossil fuels are accessible almost everywhere and supplies are relatively inexpensive, it is difficult for electricity from PV to compete economically with conventional supplies.

But in the 'developing' countries, and particularly in their rural areas, electricity grids are often non-existent or rudimentary, and all forms of energy are usually very expensive. Here PV electricity can be highly competitive with other forms of energy supply – especially in the many developing countries that have high annual solar radiation levels.

In developing countries, the use of PV is growing very rapidly, in a wide variety of applications (Figure 3.37). These include PV-powered water pumping, for irrigation or drinking water supply; PV refrigerators to help

Figure 3.37 Some PV applications in developing countries: water pumping; PV powered refrigeration for vaccines; PV power for a field hospital serving the Yanomami tribe, Orinoco River basin; street lighting

keep vaccines stored safely in health centres; PV systems for homes and community centres, to provide energy for lights, radios, audio- and video-cassette players and television sets; PV-powered telecommunications systems; and PV-powered street lighting.

In Mali, for example, more than 80 photovoltaically-powered water pumping systems have been installed over the last decade, most of them under the auspices of a charity, Mali Aqua Viva (MAV), with funding from various aid agencies. As McNelis *et al.* (1992) point out, the success of these schemes is due to a combination of technological, economic, social and institutional factors:

Most of the systems installed have been for village water supplies and have been well-appreciated by the users. Arrangements for technical support have been established, so that on-going advice can be given and faults corrected. The MAV approach to all their water supply improvement projects is to involve the local people from the beginning, to ensure their full understanding and commitment. In the case of solar pumps, the villagers are expected to build as much of the local infrastructure as possible (e.g. storage tanks, access, foundations) and this means that a significant proportion of the total capital cost (up to 25 per cent) is met from local sources. The motivation generated by this initial involvement has proved to be a key factor in the successful implementation of most of the MAV projects.

The United States government is one of several that have recognised the enormous export potential of PV electricity systems for developing countries over coming decades. As part of its 'Solar 2000' initiative, aimed at installing 1400 MW of US-made PV systems by the end of the decade (900 MW in the USA and 500 MW in developing countries), the US Department of Energy is involved in several international partnerships.

One of these, called project FINESSE (Financing Energy Services for Small Scale End Users), was set up in 1989 by the World Bank. It includes the governments of the USA, the Netherlands and various other governmental and non-governmental organisations, and aims to overcome the financial and institutional constraints to implementing PV systems in developing countries. The FINESSE approach involves 'bundling' together a number of small-scale energy schemes into one larger package that can be financed as a single unit. Opportunities for funding some $800 million worth of PV and other renewable energy schemes have been identified in the Asian region alone, and an Asia Alternative Energy Unit has been set up within the World Bank to help bring these schemes to fruition.

Under the auspices of another project, the 'America's 21st Century Program', which aims to develop sustainable energy sources for the Caribbean and Latin America, US support is being given to the Mexican 'National Solidarity Program', a public anti-poverty programme which has facilitated the installation of some 18 000 PV systems in rural areas of Mexico, including systems in homes, health clinics and schools.

The America's 21st Century Program also supports an ambitious project in Brazil which aims to use PV and PV-hybrid systems to electrify some 500 000 homes, schools and health clinics, starting with 1000 homes in the State of Pernambuco and 1000 homes and a model village in the State of Ceara (see Rannels, 1992).

European Commission officials have also recognised the huge potential contribution that PV could make towards improving the living standards of the 1.1 billion people who are classified by the World Bank as 'poor'. They have proposed a 'Power for the World' programme (Palz, 1994) in which approximately 10 watts of PV capacity per person, used to meet basic health, lighting, educational and communication needs, would be installed in villages in a major collaboration between developed and developing countries over the next 20–25 years.

3.10 GRID-CONNECTED PV SYSTEMS

GRID-CONNECTED PV SYSTEMS FOR RESIDENCES

PV energy systems are not all of the 'stand-alone' or 'autonomous' type.

The Rappenecker Hof case study demonstrates that non-grid-connected PV systems can be economically justifiable in some remote locations – even in the 'developed' countries. But in most parts of the developed world, grid electricity is easily accessible as a convenient backup to PV or other renewable energy supplies. Here it makes sense for operators of PV energy systems to use the grid as a giant 'battery'. The grid can absorb PV power that is surplus to current needs (say, on sunny summer afternoons), making it available for use by other customers and reducing the amount that has to be generated by conventional means; and at night or on cloudy days, when the output of the PV system is insufficient, it can provide backup energy from conventional sources.

In these grid-connected PV systems, a so-called 'grid-commutated inverter' (or 'synchronous inverter') transforms the DC power from the PV arrays into AC power at a voltage and frequency that can be accepted by the grid, while 'debit' and 'credit' meters measure the amount of power bought from or sold to the utility.

In Germany, where there is strong support for the development of PV technologies, the Federal Ministry of Research and Technology (BMFT) and the federal States are together subsidising the installation of small (1–5 kW) grid-connected PV systems on the roofs of 2250 houses. The performance of these is being carefully monitored.

In Switzerland, the installation of domestic grid-connected PV systems is encouraged, and under 'Project Megawatt' over one hundred 3 kW grid-connected PV systems have been installed in residential and business premises since 1987.

In Japan, high land costs should make roof-mounted PV systems attractive (Figure 3.38). An extensive research programme has been

Figure 3.38 Roof-top, grid-connected PV system on the 'Eco-Energy House', near Tokyo in Japan

undertaken to determine the effects on the grid of large numbers of small, household PV systems. This includes the construction of a large experimental array of 100 individual 2 kW PV systems, each with its own inverter, by the Kansai Electric utility at its Rokko Island test site. The Japanese government is also planning to support, in its "New Sunshine" Project, a large-scale demonstration programme that could eventually lead to 70,000 roof-top PV systems.

PV CLADDING FOR THE ROOFS AND WALLS OF NON-DOMESTIC BUILDINGS

In addition to being fitted to the roofs of domestic residences, PV arrays can also be mounted on – or better still, fully integrated into – the roofs and walls of non-domestic buildings. This option is receiving an increasing amount of attention, as it offers a number of significant advantages, particularly for commercial, institutional and industrial buildings.

Firstly, PV panels can replace some of the conventional wall cladding and roofing materials that would otherwise have been needed, so reducing the net costs of the PV system. Also, commercial and industrial buildings are normally occupied mostly during daylight hours, which correlates well with the availability of solar radiation. Thus the power generated by PV cladding or roofing on a commercial building can significantly reduce a company's need to purchase electrical power from the utility. This means that PV power is replacing electricity that would otherwise have to be purchased at the 'retail' price (around 8p kWh^{-1} in the UK in 1995), rather than the 'wholesale' price (around 3p kWh^{-1} in the UK in 1995) typically paid to generators supplying to the grid.

A number of industrial and commercial buildings in Switzerland already have grid-connected PV systems integrated into their roof and wall structures (Figures 3.39 and 3.40a).

In the UK, calculations carried out by researchers at Northumbria University (Hill *et al.*, 1992) have shown that PV systems on walls and roof tops of suitable commercial and industrial buildings could in principle supply around 360 TWh (120% of 1992 electricity demand) by 2020. Their calculations took into account the unsuitability of many buildings for PV cladding, the effects of shadowing, and various other factors. On the basis of various plausible assumptions about the construction cost savings made

Figure 3.39 (Left) The Scheidegger Metallbau building at Kirchberg in Switzerland; (Right) PV modules are integrated into the south facade

possible by using PV rather than conventional cladding, and about the prospects for decreased cost and increased efficiency of PV modules, their calculations suggest that power from PV cladding of buildings might be competitive with conventional supplies in the early years of the next century.

Meanwhile, the Northumbria University researchers themselves commissioned Britain's first building with PV cladding, a 40 kW system installed on the facade of a refurbished computer centre on their own campus at Newcastle, in January 1995 (Figure 3.40b).

LARGE, GRID-CONNECTED PV POWER PLANTS

In a number of countries, relatively large PV power systems have also been built to supply power for regional electricity grids.

In Europe, one of the largest grid-connected PV power stations was commissioned in 1988 by the largest German electrical utility, RWE, at Kobern-Gondorf, on the banks of the Moselle river not far from the city of

Figure 3.40a The factory of Aerni Fenster at Arisdorf in Switzerland. Here a 65 kW PV array is integrated into skylights on the factory roof. A small array of panels is also mounted around the wall of the building. 'Waste' heat from the back of the modules is reclaimed and fed into a heat store in the basement. A diesel-powered generator and heat pump system provide backup heating and electricity. Solar energy supplies three-quarters of the building's energy needs

Figure 3.40b   Photovoltaically-clad building at The University of Northumbria, UK

Koblenz (see Figure 3.41). The location, on a hilltop just above a vineyard, was chosen because it had relatively high annual solar radiation levels for the region (around 1100 kWh m^{-2}), with minimal fog and good access to the grid. The plant has a capacity of 340 kW and its annual output is around 250 000 kWh.

The main aim of the project was to evaluate the efficiency, reliability and cost-effectiveness of various PV modules, support structures, inverters and installation techniques, and to give the utility practical experience in operating a large PV power plant connected to its network. Another aim of the project was to assess how best to integrate PV power systems into the surrounding environment.

The PV modules tested at Kobern-Gondorf are from a wide variety of European, American and Japanese manufacturers, including AEG in Germany, Chronar in France, Hoxan in Japan, and Arco Solar, Mobil,

Figure 3.41 (Top) The 340 kW RWE PV power plant at Kobern-Gondorf, Germany; (Bottom) Phase 2 of the RWE project: the 300 kW PV plant at Lake Neurath

Sovonics and Solarex in the USA. Some of the modules use monocrystalline silicon, others polycrystalline silicon and others amorphous silicon, and their efficiencies range from 4% to over 13%. The most efficient modules are those from Hoxan of Japan, which are made of monocrystalline silicon and are 13.3% efficient.

To try to optimise the integration of the overall PV plant into its environment, RWE has turned the surrounding area, which was previously fallow land, into a nature reserve for endangered species of flora and fauna. The total land area occupied by the plant is some 50 000 m^2 (0.05 km^2) – although this area was chosen to allow expansion at a later date.

To evaluate how PV modules can best be integrated into buildings, the roof of the building which houses the equipment for the plant is also used for PV power generation. The building also houses an information centre, where the company gives lectures and guided tours of the plant to 2000 visitors a month.

The performance of the Kobern-Gondorf plant has been carefully monitored, and lessons learned have been taken into account in the design of the second phase of the project, a 300 kW plant at Lake Neurath which started operation in 1991 (Figure 3.41). This plant uses large area modules, large supporting structures and a single inverter operating at high voltage. (See Beyer and Pottbrock, 1989 and Beyer, Pottbrock and Voermans, 1992.)

RWE is also part of a consortium that has constructed a large, 1 MW PV plant near Toledo in Spain. Half of the modules used are of BP Solar's high-efficiency monocrystalline type, and the plant is operated in conjunction with a hydroelectric scheme.

In Switzerland, a 500 kW grid-connected PV plant was installed in 1992 on Mont Soleil in the canton of Berne (Figure 3.42). The plant cost 8.5 million Swiss francs (£3.8 million), occupies 20 000 m^2 of land, and consists of 110 arrays of monocrystalline silicon PV modules made by Siemens Solar. Each array has a nominal capacity of 5 kW, the total area of the arrays is 4575 m^2, and the total annual output of the plant is estimated at around 700 000 kWh. It was 50% funded by a consortium of nine utilities and two industrial companies, and 50% by the Swiss National Energy Fund and the Canton of Berne (Minder, 1993).

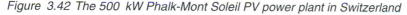

Figure 3.42 The 500 kW Phalk-Mont Soleil PV power plant in Switzerland

Another country that is actively developing large, grid-connected PV power plants is Italy. These include a 300 kW PV system which has operated successfully for a number of years on a seven hectare site at Delphos, near Foggia in southern Italy. The system was expanded to 600 kW in 1991 (Figure 3.43). An even larger, 3.3 MW plant has been built near Naples as a contribution to Italy's national energy plan, which has as one of its targets the installation of 25 MW of PV capacity by 1995.

In the USA, a number of large grid-connected PV plants have been constructed over the past decade. Two pioneering systems were constructed by the Arco Solar company in California in the early 1980s. One was a 1 MW system at Lugo, near Hesperia, the other a 6.5 MW system at Carissa Plain. Both employed an advanced, two-axis tracking array design. The Carissa plant had two reflectors on either side of each array to concentrate the solar radiation by a factor of about two. Unfortunately, the high module temperatures generated by the reflectors caused degradation of the encapsulant of some of the modules. Although the systems were successful apart from this design defect, both were dismantled in the early 1990s and their component PV modules sold off for continuing use in smaller, remote power systems.

Figure 3.43 The 600 kW PV power plant at Delphos in southern Italy

Figure 3.44 Part of the 2 MW Sacramento Municipal Utility District (SMUD) PV power plant in California

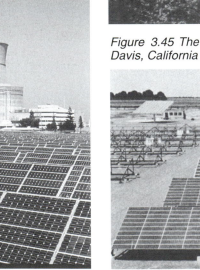

Figure 3.45 The Photovoltaics for Utility Scale Applications (PVUSA) test site at Davis, California

Other notable large US PV installations include two 1 MW plants, using single-axis tracking arrays, constructed in California for the Sacramento Municipal Utility District (SMUD) (Figure 3.44), and a 300 kW array providing power for the 3M Company's research centre at Austin, Texas (see Figure 3.28).

An increasingly important focus for PV developments in the United States is the PVUSA (Photovoltaics for Utility Scale Applications) project, which involves a number of electrical utilities, the US Department of Energy and the California Energy Commission. At the main PVUSA test site at Davis, California, there are a number of smaller arrays of around 20 kW capacity in which various 'emerging module technologies' are being demonstrated and evaluated. Several 'utility-scale' arrays of 200–400 kW capacity, each employing a different PV technology, have also been installed and are undergoing careful evaluation (Figure 3.45).

All these projects could eventually be dwarfed in scale if proposals to build a 100 MW PV power plant at a former nuclear test site in the Nevada desert come to fruition. The project has been proposed by Amoco-Enron Solar, a partnership between the major US oil company Amoco (which owns the PV manufacturer Solarex) and Enron, the largest producer of natural gas in the USA. The project would use amorphous silicon PV modules produced in a specially-built manufacturing plant nearby. The company claims that the installation would cost $150 million to build and could produce power for 5.5 cents per kWh, given the high solar radiation levels in the area.

SATELLITE SOLAR POWER

Probably the most ambitious – and some would say the most fanciful – proposal for a 'grid-connected' PV plant is the Satellite Solar Power System (SSPS) concept, first suggested more than 20 years ago (Glaser, 1972). The basic idea is to construct a huge PV array, perhaps as large as 30 km^2 and producing several GW, in geostationary orbit around the earth. The DC power generated would be converted to microwave radiation at a frequency of around 2.45 GHz and beamed, at a power density of some 250 W m^{-2}, from a 1 km diameter transmitting antenna in space to a 100 km^2 receiving antenna on earth. The received power would then be converted to 50 Hz alternating current and fed into the grid (Figure 3.46).

The advantages of the SSPS are, in theory, very substantial. In space, the PV arrays would receive a full 1365 W m^{-2} of solar power, instead of the 1000 W m^{-2} that is the maximum available at the earth's surface. Moreover, this high power would be available virtually constantly (except for occasional eclipses). And in the weightless and airless space environment, it should be possible to construct extremely large but very light structures to support the PV arrays, without having to worry about the effects of wind and weather – though meteorites might be a problem.

On the other hand, the engineering challenges in constructing an SSPS, and the associated capital costs, would be enormous. One US study estimated that a system producing 5 GW on earth would cost some $15 000 million at 1980 prices. Such an installation, clearly, could only be afforded by the richest of nations.

There are also considerable anxieties about the health effects which the microwave beam might have on anything passing through it, or around the fringes – not to mention what might happen in the event of a malfunction in the 'fail safe' control system that should ensure the beam always points at the receiving antenna. Interference with communications and radio astronomy could also be a problem.

Concerns like these have, up to now, meant that the SSPS has remained on the drawing board. (See also Glaser, 1992.)

Figure 3.46 The satellite solar power station (SSPS) concept

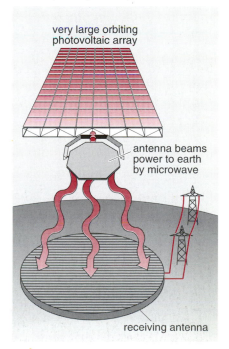

very large orbiting photovoltaic array

antenna beams power to earth by microwave

receiving antenna

3.11 ECONOMICS OF PV ENERGY SYSTEMS

As with any energy source, the price of power from PV cells consists essentially of a combination of the capital cost and the running cost.

The capital cost of a PV energy system will include not only the cost of the PV modules themselves, but also the so-called 'balance of system' (BOS) costs, i.e. the costs of the interconnection of modules to form arrays, the array support structure, land and foundations (if the array is not roof mounted), the costs of cabling, charge regulators, switching and inverters, plus the cost of storage batteries or connection to the grid.

Although the initial capital costs of PV systems are currently high, their running costs should be very modest in comparison with those of other renewable or non-renewable energy systems. Not only does a PV system not require any fuel, but also, unlike most other renewable energy systems, it has no moving parts (except in the case of tracking systems) and should require much less maintenance than, say, a wind turbine.

However, PV arrays need washing from time to time, to remove the dust and dirt that accumulates on them – particularly in urban locations. The arrays are also subject to the effects of the elements. High winds can twist and distort the support structures and cause cells or modules to become cracked or disconnected. Water can cause corrosion to metal parts and may in some cases penetrate the laminations protecting the cells, leading to increased resistive losses or even short circuits. The expansion and contraction caused by the daily solar heating and cooling of the array can also cause cracks, short circuits or disconnections.

Most of these problems can be overcome, or at least minimised, by careful attention to material specification and detailed design, and by good quality assurance during the manufacture of the system. So a well-designed PV array should need little maintenance other than washing every few months and perhaps an occasional coat of paint on its support structures every few years.

The solid-state electronic charge regulation and power conditioning equipment used in PV systems is also, in principle, very reliable. But all electronic equipment can develop occasional component failures which require specialist repair.

PV systems with battery storage have additional maintenance requirements, however. The most common PV storage battery, the lead-acid type, needs checking for terminal corrosion and 'topping-up' with distilled water every few months. ('Maintenance-free' lead acid batteries, which require attention only every few years, are available for PV systems, but cost more than conventional batteries.) These maintenance functions, though modest, still involve some cost – especially if someone has to be *paid* to carry them out.

Finally, the owner of a PV system may consider it desirable to take out insurance to cover the cost of replacing the system in case of fire, or accident or other calamity. For a small domestic system, such risks would probably be covered by an existing household insurance premium. For a large system, insurance costs could be significant – but still small in relation to the total overall costs.

In order to try to estimate what the actual costs of PV power, in pence per kWh, are likely to be under UK conditions, let's look again at the small PV system for a remote household discussed above in Section 3.9, and then at the large, grid-connected PV system described in Section 3.10.

COST OF POWER FROM A SMALL PV SYSTEM IN THE UK

Although the price of the PV modules used in large, megawatt-scale systems has now fallen to below $5 (£3) per peak watt of installed capacity (see below), smaller systems do not benefit from economies of scale in purchasing, installation and 'balance of system' components.

The capital cost of the small, single-module, 50 W(p) PV system described in Section 3.9 is around £400 ($600, or $12 per W(p): all costs are in 1994 prices), of which the cost of the 50 W module accounts for some £250. Let us assume that this capital is repaid over the lifetime of the system, which should be 20 years, and that interest on the capital is charged at a 'real' rate of 8% (i.e. 8% plus inflation). The annual cost of the capital (including both interest and repayment of principal) can be calculated using the annuity table in the Appendix, and in this case it works out at about £40.

Let us assume in this case that occasional maintenance is carried out by the householder free of labour costs, that insurance is included in the household policy, and that (for simplicity) we treat as a 'running cost' the cost of replacing the battery every five years or so. At a price of £80 per battery the latter works out at £16 per annum, and so the total cost of the system is around £56 per year.

If we assume an annual average energy conversion efficiency of 10%, the annual output of the 50 W(p) system should be around 50 kWh per year, given a typical UK annual total solar radiation level of 1000 kWh m^{-2} a year. However, we must remember that not all of the output of the PV array would actually be used, partly because of losses in the battery and wiring, and partly because the residents of the holiday home would not always be there to use it. If we assume that the net useful power is 25 kWh a year, then the cost of every kWh is £56 divided by 25, i.e. £2.24. This is 28 times the 1995 UK domestic electricity price of around 8p kWh^{-1} on-peak, and 75 times the off-peak price of 3p kWh^{-1}.

However, this calculation excludes the standing charges of around £40 per year that would be payable if the home were connected to the grid. For a grid-connected household using only 25 kWh per year of electricity (assuming half of consumption is off-peak) the total cost would be £40 + (13 × 0.08) + (12 × 0.03) = £41.40, i.e. some £1.66 per kWh. Nevertheless, the cost per kWh of power from the PV system is still about a third more than that from the grid. But this excludes the capital cost of grid connection, which as we have seen can be extremely high.

Of course, if our remote holiday home were connected to the grid, then the inhabitants would almost certainly use more electricity, the proportion of costs accounted for by standing charges would reduce, and the cost per kWh would drop rapidly as consumption increased. Nevertheless, this example underlines the point made earlier that, for low levels of energy consumption, PV systems can sometimes be competitive with grid electricity in remote locations.

COST OF POWER FROM A GRID-CONNECTED PV SYSTEM IN THE UK

The installed capital cost of a large, grid-connected PV power plant, such as the 500 kW installation at Mont Soleil in Switzerland, is typically around US$11 per peak watt of net AC output to the grid (Shugar *et al.*, 1993). This includes the cost of the PV arrays, support structures, power conditioning, grid connection, etc. The Mont Soleil plant has a total array area of some 4500 m^2, produces some 750 000 kWh a year of power for the grid, and cost some £3.8 million. It is only fair to point out that because the plant is a one-off demonstration project, this price is substantially higher than it might otherwise be.

However, solar radiation levels are higher in Switzerland than in Britain. In UK conditions, again assuming the annual total solar radiation is 1000 kWh m^{-2} and that 10% is the annual average PV array efficiency, the annual output of a 500 kW plant like the one at Mont Soleil would be around 100 kWh m^{-2}, or 450 000 kWh.

Assuming the capital cost of £3.8 million is to be repaid over 25 years and interest paid at a real rate of 8%, using the amortisation table in the Appendix we can see that the annual capital cost (interest and repayment of principal) would be about £357 000.

The running costs are difficult to calculate, since there is little or no experience of operating large PV plants in Europe, but one 'rule of thumb' estimate used in the industry is that annual running costs are likely to be around 1% of the initial capital cost, which in this case would be £38 000 a year. The total yearly cost therefore becomes £395 000 and as the total annual output is some 450 000 kWh, the cost of electricity works out at around 88p kWh^{-1}.

So the power from this large, grid-connected PV array would cost about one-third of that from the small household system we examined earlier. This is partly due to its slightly lower initial capital cost per watt of capacity, partly due to its lower running cost (because the system is grid connected and does not need batteries), and partly because all the energy produced is actually used. Nevertheless, its power is still about 10 times as expensive as conventional on-peak electricity in the UK.

How do these costs compare with the cost of power from smaller roof-top PV systems that are not autonomous but connected to the grid? A recent detailed study by Shugar *et al.* (1993) found that when all relevant factors were taken into account, the overall costs were currently about the same.

It seems that there is still some way to go before grid-connected PV systems in the UK become competitive with power from conventional sources. However, smaller grid-connected PV systems supplying power directly to users have a considerable advantage in that they are competing with power supplied at 'retail' prices, rather than the lower wholesale prices which would apply to larger PV plants supplying power for the general electricity market.

REDUCING THE COSTS OF POWER FROM PV

How, then, might the price of PV power be made more competitive?

The answers are fairly obvious. Firstly, the installed cost per peak watt needs to drop substantially. Many industry analysts are confident that PV manufacturing costs will fall to around $1.50 per watt by the early years of the next century, and that a profitable *selling* price for modules in large systems by then will be about $2 W(p)$^{-1}$.

Secondly, the overall annual conversion efficiency of the PV arrays needs to increase substantially from its present figure of around 10%, achieved by current PV modules with peak efficiencies of around 13%. It takes around 10 years for the PV efficiencies achieved in the laboratory to be reflected in the actual efficiencies of commercially available modules. So, by the early years of the twenty-first century, it may be possible to buy PV modules having a peak efficiency of around 23% and an annual average efficiency of, say, 20%.

Thirdly, the 'balance of system' costs – i.e. the costs of support structures, wiring, inverters, grid connection, etc. – need to be substantially reduced. In existing PV systems the balance of system costs are roughly equal to the module costs, so to keep this ratio these costs also need to be reduced to around $2 per watt. This seems feasible, given volume production of BOS components and the likelihood of substantially reduced installation costs when the industry has gained more experience and is installing more systems. A plausible target for overall system cost by, say, 2005 is therefore $4 (£2.66) per peak system watt.

Using this figure to recalculate the costs of the 500 kW PV power station in the example above, we get a total capital cost of £1.33 million, a total annual cost of some £138 000, an annual output of 900 000 kWh, and so a cost per kWh of delivered power of about 15p kWh^{-1}. This is still nearly twice the current on-peak price, but at least within striking distance of current prices. If a real discount rate of 5% p.a. rather than 8% p.a. were used in calculating the costs, they would reduce further to around 12p kWh^{-1}. If, as many PV advocates suggest, the full 'external' costs of conventional energy sources (acid rain, greenhouse gas emissions, oil spills, accidents, etc.) were to be taken into account, then their price might well rise to approach that of power from PV (see Hohmeyer, 1988).

The economics of PV power plants are, however, much more attractive in those areas of the world that have substantially greater annual total solar radiation than northern Europe. Areas such as north Africa or southern California not only have annual solar radiation totals more than twice those in Britain, but also have clear skies. This means that the majority of the radiation is direct, making tracking and concentrating systems effective and further increasing the annual energy output. The price of electricity from such PV installations is likely to be less than half of that from a comparable non-tracking installation in the UK, and close to being competitive with conventional sources.

In the USA and some other countries, electricity utilities have found another useful role for PV power systems: that of **grid reinforcement**. In some areas, increasing demands for electricity would normally make it necessary to install new power lines, transformers and switching equipment, or upgrade the capacity of existing electricity distribution systems. Instead, PV power systems are being installed near the point of demand. Output from the PV systems is usually highest during the day, when demand for electricity is also high. The PV system therefore effectively reduces the amount of power that has to be transmitted over the power lines from centralised generation plant. In many cases, grid reinforcement using PV would be cheaper than upgrading the electricity distribution system.

3.12 ENVIRONMENTAL IMPACT AND SAFETY

ENVIRONMENTAL IMPACT AND SAFETY OF PV SYSTEMS

Proponents of PV energy systems often claim that their environmental impact is less than that of any other renewable or non-renewable energy system.

Clearly, in normal operation PV energy systems emit no gaseous or liquid pollutants, and no radioactive substances. However, in the case of CIS or CdTe modules, which include small quantities of toxic substances, there is a slight risk that a fire in an array might cause small amounts of these chemicals to be released into the environment.

Since PV modules have no moving parts they are also safe in the mechanical sense, and they emit no noise. However, as with other electrical equipment, there are some risks of electric shock – especially if, as in some systems, the DC voltages used are substantially higher than the 12–48 volts employed in most small PV installations. But the electrical hazards of a well-engineered PV system are, at worst, no greater than those of other comparable electrical installations.

PV arrays do, of course, have some visual impact on the environment. Roof-top arrays will be clearly visible to neighbours, and may be regarded as either attractive or unattractive according to aesthetic tastes. Several companies, including Sanyo in Japan and BMC Solartechnik in Germany, have produced PV modules in the form of special roof tiles that should blend into roof structures more unobtrusively than current module designs.

Large, grid-connected PV arrays will usually be installed on land specially designated for the purpose – although this need not always be the case. As shown in Figure 3.47, the Swiss authorities are installing large PV arrays as noise barriers alongside motorways and railways. Arguably PV is here *reducing* the overall environmental impact.

Whether or not the appearance of a large PV power plant such as that at Kobern-Gondorf is aesthetically pleasing or not is again very much a matter of taste – though most people would probably regard it as more attractive than a conventional power station. RWE envisages the Kobern-Gondorf plant as one of many that could be installed on marginal land, which is not used for other purposes. The land immediately surrounding the Kobern-Gondorf PV arrays has been turned into a nature reserve – again, this is arguably an overall environmental *improvement*.

Furthermore, because of the need to space the arrays some distance from one another to avoid overshadowing, it would be possible, for example, to grow some crops on the land between the arrays – or perhaps, in a suitable location, even to include some wind turbines.

Indeed, according to some calculations (US Department of Energy, 1989) the net area of land made unavailable for other uses by PV power plants is significantly less than for coal or nuclear energy, when all associated land uses, including mining, processing, etc., are taken into account.

ENVIRONMENTAL IMPACT AND SAFETY OF PV MODULE PRODUCTION AND RECYCLING

The environmental impact of the manufacture of silicon PV cells is unlikely to be significant – except perhaps in the case of accidents at the manufacturing plant. The basic material from which 99% of the cells are made, silicon, is not intrinsically harmful. However, as with any chemical process, careful attention must be paid to plant design and operation, to ensure the containment of any toxic or potentially harmful chemicals in the event of an accident or plant malfunction. The need for a stringent approach to safety in the PV industry – as in any other manufacturing industry – is recognised by all responsible manufacturers.

Finally, even though PV arrays are potentially very long-lived devices, eventually they will come to the end of their useful life and will have to be disposed of – or, preferably, recycled. Especially in the case of PV modules containing small but not insignificant quantities of toxic metals, safe recycling and disposal methods will have to be developed to ensure that these substances are not released into the environment.

Figure 3.47 PV arrays providing sound barriers in Switzerland: (Left) alongside a motorway; (Right) alongside a railway line

ENERGY BALANCE OF PV SYSTEMS

A common misconception about PV cells is that almost as much energy is used in their manufacture as they generate during their lifetime. This was probably true in the early days of PV, when the refining of monocrystalline silicon and the Czochralski process were very energy-intensive, and the efficiency of the cells produced was relatively low, leading to low lifetime energy output.

However, with the more modern PV production processes introduced in recent years, and the improved efficiency of modules, the energy balance of PV is now much more favourable. A recent study by European Commission scientists (Palz and Zibetta, 1992) has shown that in average European conditions the energy payback time for PV modules (excluding the other elements of a PV power plant) ranges from about 2.1 years for crystalline silicon to 1.2 years for amorphous silicon. These figures were based on 1990 manufacturing conditions, and the authors believe there is considerable scope for further reductions in these payback periods in coming years.

3.13 INTEGRATION OF PV INTO FUTURE ENERGY SYSTEMS

If PV energy systems continue to improve in cost-effectiveness compared with more conventional sources, as many PV enthusiasts believe they will, how might they be integrated into national energy supply systems – and specifically that of the UK? How much energy might they supply? What areas and installed capacities of PV arrays would be required? What energy needs would they be best suited to supplying? In what way would national energy systems need to be modified to cope with the long, medium and short-term fluctuations in the output of PV arrays?

According to a UK government report (Department of Energy, 1989), a number of very large, grid-connected PV power stations, occupying some 2.5% of the UK land area, could in principle supply some 300 TWh of electricity a year – about the same as the current total annual UK electricity production. In addition, decentralised PV power systems on roof tops could, the report estimated, generate another 26 TWh a year, about 9% of current demand.

The report estimated that a land area of '200 to 300 square kilometres' would be required for a single 2 GW PV power station. However, the actual surface area of the PV arrays themselves would be very much less than this – and in any case, it is very unlikely that individual PV power stations would be built in sizes as large as 2 gigawatts. Also, as explained above, the PV arrays need to be spaced some distance apart in order to avoid overshadowing, and the land between the arrays could be used for other purposes.

To calculate the required spacing and layout of the PV arrays, various factors have to be considered, including the size and inclination of the array, the topography of the site, whether or not the arrays are fixed or track the sun, and the daily and seasonal variations in the azimuth and elevation of the sun's position. Computer programs have been developed to assist in such calculations.

The 500 kW Mont Soleil plant in Switzerland, described in Section 3.10, occupies 20 000 m^2 of land, about 4.5 times the area of the PV modules used. A hypothetical 2 GW PV power plant at Mont Soleil would occupy 4000 times as much land as a 500 kW plant – namely 80 km^2, rather than 200–300 km^2.

The discrepancy between this land area figure and that quoted in the Department of Energy report may be explained by (a) the likelihood that the UK calculation was based on the use of PV modules of somewhat lower efficiency than those at Mont Soleil; (b) the overshadowing calculations may have been based on different assumptions; and (c) there may have been a greater allowance for additional land for buildings and roads associated with the plant.

As pointed out in Section 3.11 above, the cost of power from such PV plants in the UK would be prohibitive at current prices. The DEn report suggested that the maximum achievable contribution of PV to UK generating capacity would be 2 GW by 2005 and 5 GW by 2020, respectively some 4% and 9% of current UK generating capacity. Its estimate of the range of PV power costs by 2020 was between 3 and 41 pence per kWh, with a mid-point estimate of 22p kWh^{-1} (at 1989 prices).

A more recent report (ETSU, 1994) estimated that the contribution to UK electricity demand from decentralised PV systems by 2025 could range from 0.3 Twh per year in a 'Low Oil Price' scenario to 7.2 TWh in a 'Heightened Environmental Concern' scenario (assuming an 8% discount rate in both cases).

A problem with PV power in the UK is that much of it would be produced in summer, when electricity demand is relatively low, and much less would be produced in winter, when demand is high. Also, although PV power is quite reliable (during daylight hours) in climates with mainly clear skies, it can be highly intermittent in countries like the UK, where passing clouds can reduce power output dramatically within seconds.

But as long as the capacity of variable output power sources such as PV is fairly small in relation to the overall capacity of the grid (most studies suggest a proportion of 10–20%), then there should not be a major problem in coping with the fluctuating output. The grid is, after all, designed to cope with massive fluctuations in *demand*, and similarly fluctuating sources of *supply* like PV can be treated as 'negative loads'. Fluctuations would also, of course, be substantially smoothed out if PV power plants were situated in many different locations subject to widely varying solar radiation and weather patterns.

However, if PV power stations, and other fluctuating output renewable energy sources such as wind power, were in future to contribute more than about 20% of electricity supplies, then the 'plant mix' in the grid would have to be changed to include a greater proportion of 'fast-acting' power plant, such as hydro and gas turbines, and increased amounts of short-term storage and 'spinning reserve'.

These considerations lead some analysts to suggest that without large quantities of cheap electrical energy storage, renewable energy sources like PV cannot make a major contribution. Whilst this would seem to be an exaggeration, at least for small to medium levels of 'penetration' of PV and other renewables into the system, it is certainly true that cheap storage in large amounts would make their integration easier.

There has been a recent revival of interest in the use of **hydrogen** as a medium for energy storage and distribution, particularly in connection with PV but also for use with other renewable energy sources. Hydrogen would be produced by the electrolysis of water, using PV or other renewables as the electricity source. The hydrogen would be stored and transported to wherever it was needed. It could be converted back to electricity, either in an engine-powered generator or, much more efficiently, using fuel cells. Alternatively, the hydrogen could simply be burned to release heat, or converted into heat by 'catalytic combustion' – a chemical reaction with air in the presence of a catalyst.

These issues will be examined in more detail in Chapter 10, Integration.

REFERENCES

Adams, W. G. and Day, R. E. (1877) 'The action of light on selenium', *Proceedings of the Royal Society*, London, Series A, 25, p. 113.

Becquerel, A. E. (1839) 'Recherches sur les effets de la radiation chimique de la lumière solaire au moyen des courants électriques' and 'Mémoire sur les effets électriques produit sous l'influence des rayons solaires', *Comptes Rendus de l'Académie des Sciences* 9, pp. 145–149 and pp. 561–567.

Beyer, U. and Pottbrock, R. (1989) 'Design, construction and operation of a 340 kW photovoltaic plant', *Proceedings of 9th EC Photovoltaics Conference*, Freiburg, Germany, 1989, p. 655, Kluwer Academic Publishers.

Beyer, U., Pottbrock, R. and Voermans, R. (1992) '1MW Photovoltaic Project: planning, construction and operation of photovoltaic power plants', *Proceedings of 11th European Photovoltaic Conference*, Gordon and Breach.

Boes, E. C. and Luque, A. (1993) 'Photovoltaic concentrator technology', in Johansson *et al.* (eds) (1993) *Renewable Energy Sources for Fuels and Electricity*, Island Press, Washington DC, pp. 369–370.

Bruton, T. M., Nagle, J. P., Mason, N. B. and Russell, R. (1992) 'Recent developments in concentrator cells and modules using silicon laser-grooved buried-grid cells', *Proceedings of 11th European Photovoltaic Solar Energy Conference*, Montreux, Switzerland, Gordon and Breach.

Chapin, D. M., Fuller, C. S. and Pearson, G. L. (1954) 'A new silicon p–n junction photocell for converting solar radiation into electrical power', *Journal of Applied Physics*, 25, pp. 676–677.

Chalmers, R. (1976) 'The photovoltaic generation of electricity', *Scientific American*, October, pp. 34–43.

Department of Energy (1989) *An Evaluation of Energy Related Greenhouse Gas Emissions and Measures to Ameliorate Them,* Energy Paper 58, pp 58–59, HMSO.

Derrick, A. *et al.* (1991) *Solar Photovoltaic Products*, IT Publications, London.

Derrick, A. (1993) 'A market overview of PV in Europe', *European Directory of Renewable Energy Supplies and Services 1993*, James and James Science Publishers, London, pp. 114–120.

ETSU (1994) *An Assessment of Renewable Energy for the UK* Energy Technology Support Unit, Report R82, page 119.

Fraunhofer Institute (1989) *Photovoltaics – Made in Germany,* pp. 13–14. Information brochure on PV produced for Bundesministerium für Forschung und Technologie, Fraunhofer Institut für Solar Energiesysteme, Oltmannsstr. 22, 7800 Freiburg, Germany.

Fraunhofer Institute (1991) *Der Rappenecker Hof: Tradition und Moderne Technik.* Brochure on Rappenecker Hof project.

Glaser, P. (1972) 'The case for solar energy', paper presented at the annual meeting of the Society for Social Responsibility in Science, Queen Mary College, London, September.

Glaser, P. (1992) 'An overview of the solar power satellite option', *IEEE Transactions on Microwave Theory and Techniques*, Vol. 40, No. 6, June, pp. 1230–1238.

Green, M. (1982) *Solar Cells*, Prentice-Hall.

Green, M. (1993) 'Crystalline and polycrystalline silicon solar cells', in Johansson *et al.* (eds) (1993) *Renewable Energy Sources for Fuels and Electricity*, Island Press, Washington DC, pp. 337–360.

Gratzel, M. *et al.* (1989) *The Artificial Leaf: Molecular Photovoltaics Achieve Efficient Generation of Electricity from Sunlight,* Research Report, Ecole Polytechnique Federale Lausanne, Switzerland.

Hill, *et al.* (1992) 'PV on buildings – estimation of the UK resource', *Proceedings of the 11th European Photovoltaic Solar Energy Conference*, Montreux, Switzerland, Gordon and Breach.

Hohmeyer, O. (1988) *Social Costs of Energy*, Springer Verlag, Germany.

Imamura, M. S., Helm, P. and Palz, W. (1992) *Photovoltaic System Technology: A European Handbook,* W. H. Stephens, Bedfordshire, UK, for Commission of European Communities.

Lasnier, F. and Ang, T. G. (1990) *Photovoltaic Engineering Handbook*, Adam Hilger, Bristol and New York.

Markvart, T. (ed) (1994) *Solar Electricity*, John Wiley, Chichester, 248 pp.

McNelis, B., Derrick, A. and Starr, M. (1992) *Solar Powered Electricity: A Survey of Photovoltaic Power in Developing Countries,* Intermediate Technology Publications, London, in association with UNESCO.

McVeigh, C. (1983) *Sun Power*, Pergamon, Oxford.

Minder, R. (1993) 'The Swiss 500 kW photovoltaic power plant at Phalk-Mont Soleil', *Proceedings of 11th European Photovoltaic Solar Energy Conference*, Montreux, Switzerland, Gordon and Breach.

Ohl, R. S. (1941) *Light Sensitive Device*, US Patent No. 2402622; and *Light Sensitive Device Including Silicon*, US Patent No. 2443542: both filed 27 May.

O'Regan, B. and Gratzel, M. (1991) 'A low cost, high efficiency solar cell based on dye-sensitised colloidal TiO_2 films', *Nature*, 235, pp. 737–740.

O'Regan, B., Nazeruddin M. K. and Gratzel, M. (1993) 'A very low cost, 10% efficient solar cell based on the sensitisation of colloidal titanium dioxide films', *Proceedings of 11th European Photovoltaics Conference*, Montreux, Switzerland, Gordon and Breach.

Palz, W. and Zibetta, H. (1992) 'Energy payback time of photovoltaic modules', *Yearbook of Renewable Energies 1992*, Eurosolar with Ponte Press, Bochum, Germany, pp. 181–184.

Palz, W. (1994) 'Power for the world: a global photovoltaic action plan', in McNelis and Jesch (eds) *Proceedings of UK International Solar Energy Society 20th Anniversary Conference*, January, ISES, London, pp. 7–41.

Piellisch, R. (1991) 'Solar powered flight', *Sunworld*, March–April, pp. 17–20.

Rannels, J. E. (1992) *Photovoltaics in the Developing World,* US Department of Energy, Washington DC, USA.

Roberts, S. (1991) *Solar Electricity: A Practical Guide to Designing and Installing Small Photovoltaic Systems*, Prentice Hall, London.

Schmid, J. *et al.* (1988) 'A 220 volt AC photovoltaic power supply for remote houses', *Proceedings of 8th EC Photovoltaic Solar Energy Conference*, Florence, Italy, pp. 1140–1144, Kluwer Academic Publishers.

Shugar, D. S., Real, M. G. and Aschenbrenner, P. (1993) 'Comparison of selected economic factors for large, ground-mounted photovoltaic systems with roof-mounted photovoltaic systems in Switzerland and the USA', *Proceedings of 11th European Photovoltaics Conference,* Montreux, Switzerland, Gordon and Breach.

Taylor, E. (1990) *Review of Photovoltaic Power Technology,* ETSU Report R50, HMSO.

Treble, F. C. (ed.) (1991) *Generating Electricity from the Sun,* Pergamon Press.

Treble, F. C. (1993) *Solar Electricity: a Layman's Guide to the Generation of Electricity by the Direct Conversion of Solar Energy,* The Solar Energy Society, London W3 9PP.

US Department of Energy (1989) *Energy Systems Emissions and Material Requirements,* Washington DC, USA.

Wilson, H. G., MacCready, P. B. and Kyle, C. R. (1989) 'Lessons of Sunraycer', *Scientific American,* March, pp. 90–97.

Zweibel, K. and Barnett, A. (1993) 'Polycrystalline thin-film photovoltaics', in Johansson *et al.* (eds) (1993) *Renewable Energy Sources for Fuels and Electricity,* Island Press, pp. 437–482.

FURTHER READING

Probably the most useful overview of PV is in *Renewable Energy Sources for Fuels and Electricity* (Johansson *et al.*, 1993), which contains more than 200 pages of up-to-date information on the subject, spread over six chapters entitled: 'Introduction to Photovoltaic Technology'; 'Crystalline and Polycrystalline Silicon Solar Cells'; 'Photovoltaic Concentrator Technology'; 'Amorphous Silicon Photovoltaic Systems'; 'Polycrystalline Thin-Film Photovoltaics'; and 'Utility Field Experience with Photovoltaic Systems'.

Another excellent overview, though older and rather more physics-orientated, is *Solar Cells: Operating Principles, Technology and System Applications* (Green, 1982).

A very good concise introductory text on PV is *Solar Electricity* (Treble, 1993). The territory is covered in much more detail in the same author's *Generating Electricity from the Sun* (Treble, 1991).

Engineers and others wishing to design PV energy systems will find *Photovoltaic Systems Technology: A European Handbook* (Imamura *et al.*, 1992) and the *Photovoltaic Engineering Handbook* (Lasnier and Ang, 1990) particularly useful. Equally useful, but pitched at a less advanced technical level, is *Solar Electricity: A Practical Guide to Designing and Installing Small Photovoltaic Systems* (Roberts, 1991).

Applications of PV in developing countries are covered particularly well in *Solar Powered Electricity: A Survey of Photovoltaic Power in Developing Countries* (McNelis *et al.*, 1992), and *Solar Photovoltaic Products: a Guide for Development Workers* (Derrick *et al.*, 1991).

The history of photovoltaics since the early 1950s is described in Loferski, J. (1993) 'The first forty years: a brief history of the modern photovoltaic age', *Progress in Photovoltaics,* Vol. 1, No. 1, pp. 67–78, Wiley.

CONFERENCE PROCEEDINGS

The best way of keeping up with the detailed scientific and technological advances in this rapidly changing field is to scan the proceedings of (or preferably attend) the European Community Photovoltaic Solar Energy Conferences, which are held roughly every 18 months or so. Associated with the Conference is an Exhibition at which leading manufacturers show their latest PV products and systems. (Details from the conference organisers: WIP, Sylvenstr. 2 D-8000 Muenchen 70, Germany.) A similar event, the PV Specialists Conference, is also held every 18 months in the USA.

JOURNALS

Various academic journals cover the photovoltaics field, including *Solar Energy Materials and Solar Cells* (Elsevier) and *Progress in Photovoltaics* (Wiley), and there are two highly informative industry newsletters: *PV News* (PO Box 290, Casanova, Va 22017, USA) and *PV Insiders Report* (1011 W Colorado Blvd., Dallas, TX 75208, USA).

BIOMASS

4.1 INTRODUCTION

BIOMASS

All the earth's living matter, its **biomass**, exists in the thin surface layer called the biosphere. It represents only a tiny fraction of the total mass of the earth, but in human terms it is an enormous store of energy. More significantly, it is a store which is being replenished continually. The source which supplies the energy is of course the sun. Although only a small fraction of the solar energy reaching the earth each year is fixed by organic matter on land, it is nevertheless equivalent to some eight times our total primary energy consumption. This energy stored in plants is recycled naturally through a series of conversions involving chemical and physical processes in the plant, the soil, the surrounding atmosphere and other living matter, until it is eventually radiated away from the earth as low-temperature heat – except for a small fraction which may remain in peat and a tiny proportion which may slowly become fossil fuel energy.

The importance of this cyclic process for us is that if we can intervene and 'capture' some of the biomass at the stage where it is acting as a store of

Figure 4.1   *Some routes for the solar energy absorbed by a plant*

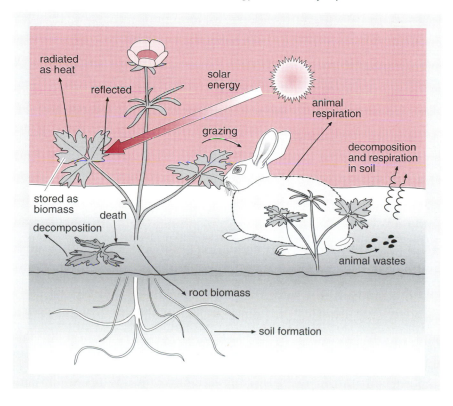

chemical energy, we have a fuel. Moreover, two facts of great environmental significance are that, provided our consumption does not exceed the natural level of recycling, in burning biofuels *we generate no more heat and create no more carbon dioxide* than would have been produced in any case by natural processes. So it seems that we have here an energy source whose use should have no deleterious environmental effect at all.

BOX 4.1: BIOMASS – SOME BASIC DATA

World totals

Total mass of living matter (including moisture)
2000 billion tonnes

Total mass in land plants
1800 billion tonnes

Total mass in forests
1600 billion tonnes

World population
c. 5.5 billion (1993)

Per capita terrestrial biomass
400 tonnes

Energy stored in terrestrial biomass
25 000 exajoules

Nett annual production of terrestrial biomass
400 000 Mt y^{-1}

World energy comparisons

The data are given in exajoules (EJ) per year and as average power in terawatts (TW)

(1 EJ = 1 million million megajoules, and 1 TW = 1 million megawatts)

Rate of energy storage by land biomass
3000 EJ y^{-1} (95 TW)

Total consumption of all forms of energy
400 EJ y^{-1} (12 TW)

Biomass energy consumption
55 EJ y^{-1} (1.7 TW)

Food energy consumption
10 EJ y^{-1} (0.3 TW)

It should be noted that most of the above data are subject to considerable uncertainty. See Section 4.3 for more detailed discussion.

BIOFUELS

The term 'biofuels' covers a very wide range of energy sources, from a simple wood fire to a thousand tonnes of urban waste feeding a multi-megawatt power station. For a more precise definition, we can quote a recent publication of the UK Energy Technology Support Unit (ETSU, 1991):

The 'biofuels' are any solid, liquid or gaseous fuels produced from organic materials, either directly from plants or indirectly from industrial, commercial, domestic or agricultural wastes. They can be derived from a wide range of raw materials and produced in a variety of ways.

The inclusion of all the energy-from-wastes processes under this heading may seem a little strange, until we notice that most present systems for deriving energy from biomass are in fact using wastes – residues associated with plant or animal products cultivated for other purposes. Urban and industrial wastes are not so evidently biomass (plastic bags and tin cans come to mind), but nevertheless much of the content of the average household dustbin is of biological origin.

SUMMARY

The extremely varied nature of the biofuels poses a problem for any account of their present use and future potential. In the following, after a brief historical excursion (Section 4.2) and an introductory case study (Section 4.3), we adopt two different approaches. Sections 4.4 and 4.5, dealing with the basic science and the technologies, are organised in terms of the **processes** involved – regardless of the particular biological material providing the energy. In Sections 4.6–4.8, concerned with present developments, the sequence is in terms of the **sources**: agricultural residues, energy from refuse, and energy crops. In Sections 4.9 and 4.10, treating the environmental effects of biofuels and the economic factors which determine their use, cases of particular relevance for discussion are selected. The chapter concludes with a survey of some new technologies and an assessment of the future potential for energy from biomass.

4.2 BIOMASS PAST AND PRESENT

FROM WOOD TO COAL

Until recent times, the history of fuels was essentially the history of biofuels. Apart from hot springs, and a little coal found on the sea shore or where seams came to the surface, biomass was until the seventeenth century the only significant source of heat energy other than the sun. The same can be said of lighting, with tallow candles and lamps using animal or vegetable oils. The main biofuel technology, of great importance because it brought within reach the high temperatures essential for extracting metals from ores, was the processing of wood to produce charcoal.

The replacement of wood by coal during the early Industrial Revolution provides an interesting case study in technological change. There is general agreement that an increasingly serious shortage of wood was a major factor, but opinions then diverge. Three contrasting views of early industrialisation and its causes might be summarised as follows.

• Growing prosperity brought conditions which favoured technical innovation. This led to the increasing use of machines, for which coal was a more suitable fuel than wood.

• Scientific inventiveness led to widespread technological change, with energy from coal replacing wood, wind and water. Increasing prosperity was one consequence of this growing industrialisation.

• Population growth, poverty and the rising price of wood forced the use of coal, which was perceived as a less desirable fuel. Surface coal was soon exhausted, deep mines became necessary, and with them the need to pump flood water from great depths. This led to the first machines of the Industrial Revolution.

At first glance this may seem to be an academic debate of interest only to historians, but when we recall that wood is still the major fuel for three-quarters of the world's population and that many regions are suffering an increasingly desperate shortage, we might feel that perhaps it has some present-day relevance.

PRESENT BIOMASS CONTRIBUTIONS

Obtaining a reliable estimate of the total world-wide energy contribution from the many biomass sources is a task fraught with difficulties. There is no large-scale organisation like OPEC keeping track of the consumption of biofuels; indeed, much of the trade in biomass is local and unrecorded, often involving no financial transaction at all. It is not perhaps surprising then that many studies of 'world energy consumption' have chosen to ignore this source altogether. Unfortunately, this gives the misleading impression that its contribution is small and relatively unimportant, which is certainly not the case.

There may be uncertainty about the detailed figures, but there is little doubt that biomass is a major energy provider over much of the world. Nepal and Ethiopia, for example, derive nearly all their energy from biomass, and the percentages in Kenya, India and Brazil are about 75%, 50% and 25%, respectively (Hall, 1991). On the basis of detailed studies of different regions, Hall estimates that *per capita* biomass consumption for energy purposes in developing countries ranges from about half a tonne to two tonnes a year, air-dry mass (see Box 4.2). With a total population of nearly four billion, the developing countries are estimated to consume in all rather more than 3 Gt (air-dry mass) of biomass a year. Assuming an average energy content of about 15 GJ per tonne, this means an annual energy of 45–50 EJ, over a third of the total energy consumption of these regions of the world.

Even in the industrialised nations the consumption of biofuels is not negligible: the *per capita* average is about a third of a tonne (air-dry) a year, representing some 3% of primary energy consumption. In countries such as Austria, Sweden, Switzerland and the USA where wood is widely used as a fuel, or where technologies for processing residues and wastes are well advanced, the figure can be considerably greater. (In the UK, by contrast, the total biomass contribution is rather less than 50 PJ a year – under 1% of primary energy consumption.) In all, the developed countries are thought to use perhaps 8 EJ a year of biomass energy, bringing the world total to a little over 55 EJ, or about 14% of primary energy consumption. It must be stressed that these figures are subject to great uncertainty, but each new detailed study, particularly in the developing world, supports the view that they are if anything underestimates of the total contribution of biomass.

Figure 4.4 Biomass contributions to primary energy.
(a) World consumption. Total energy 400 EJ/y. Per capita energy 80 GJ/y. (b) Industrialised countries. Total energy 250 EJ/y. Per capita energy 210 GJ/y. (c) Developing countries. Total energy 140 EJ/y. Per capita energy 36 GJ/y. (Source: adapted from Hall, D.O., 1991)

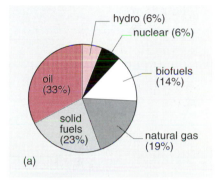

(a)

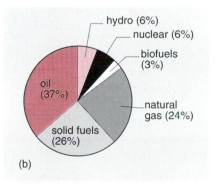

(b)

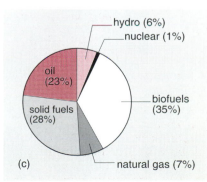

(c)

4.3 CASE STUDY: WOOD AS FUEL

It is difficult to think of a more suitable case for using wood: a country estate with some 120 hectares of semi-derelict woodland and a large house with an inadequate, inefficient and increasingly expensive oil-fired heating system.

Figure 4.2 The Drayton wood-burning system: (Below) wood chip hopper; (Bottom) the 250 kW boiler

A decade ago, faced with the need to replace the boiler, the managers of the Drayton estate in East Anglia looked at the options. Installing new oil-fired plant would be simplest, but fuel costs would be prohibitive – and uncertain. Gas was not available, but two biofuels were: straw and wood. Straw had already been selected as the best option in a similar situation at Woburn Abbey (see Box 4.8 below), but was rejected at Drayton because of the size of the storage space required and problems in siting the large heating plant.

The system finally chosen was a boiler with 250 kW heat output, designed to burn wood in the form of chips a few centimetres long. There were three possible fuel sources:

- thinnings and scrub clearance of the existing woodland;

Figure 4.3a Short rotation coppice: planting willow cuttings

- wastes from a local sawmill;
- short rotation coppice.

In the early years, the first two were the main sources, supplying 730 cubic metres of wood a year. An on-site chipper reduces the wood to chips which are stored under cover, drying naturally until the moisture content falls to about 25%, each cubic metre yielding about a quarter of a tonne of air-dry chips.

In the future, coppice wood is expected to play an increasing role. Coppicing involves planting small cuttings which are cut after one year to encourage multiple shoots. They are then harvested every few years, giving an average yield of some 10 dry tonnes a year per hectare of plantation – 10,000 square metres, or about 2.5 acres. Trials of both willow and poplar have been taking place at Drayton since 1987, and it is estimated that if about 10 hectares were planted, the estate would become entirely self-sufficient in fuel.

With all inputs – plant and labour – taken into account, the cost of the fuel at the boiler was estimated to be about £11.50 per cubic metre, £50 per dry tonne at 1991 prices. In energy terms, this

was less than half the price of heating oil (Lockhart, 1991 and 1992).

With some 1000 hectares of arable land, the estate farms are subject to EU 'set-aside' legislation which requires farmers to take land out of food production. Further legislation in recent years has recognised short rotation coppice grown for fuel as an acceptable use for set-aside land, and since 1992 coppice has also attracted UK forestry planting grants. These moves to make short rotation coppice more attractive to farmers have proved a bonus for those who had the foresight to invest in wood.

Overall, the result of this use of biomass energy has been a much more satisfactory heating system and a halving of heating costs. It has also improved derelict woodland, dealt with a disposal problem of sawmill wastes and, for the future, will provide a use for set-aside land. In addition, even after allowing for the fossil fuel used in cutting and processing the wood, this change from oil to wood-firing on the Drayton estate will have reduced atmospheric CO_2 emissions by well over 100 tonnes a year.

Figure 4.3b Short rotation coppice: second-year growth of coppiced hazel

4.4 BIOMASS AS A FUEL

WHAT ARE FUELS?

It is common experience that some materials will burn (wood, paper, straw, coal, oil, natural gas) whilst others won't (sand, table salt, water). Why? What is it that makes one material a fuel and another not? In seeking an answer, we can usefully recall a few well-known facts about combustion:

- it needs air – or to be more precise, oxygen;
- the fuel disappears – or at least undergoes a major change;
- heat is produced, i.e. energy is released.

It would appear then that a fuel is a substance which interacts with oxygen and in doing so changes chemically and releases energy. The release of energy must mean that in some way the original fuel and oxygen contain more energy than the products formed in the combustion.

We know enough about the composition of the most common fuels to be able to predict what these products will be. Consider, for instance, methane – a biofuel and also the principal component of natural gas. It consists entirely of carbon and hydrogen, each methane molecule containing one carbon and four hydrogen atoms: CH_4. Oxygen gas consists of molecules with two atoms each (O_2) and in combustion each methane molecule reacts with two of these:

$$CH_4 + 2O_2 \rightarrow CO_2 + 2H_2O + energy$$

Where does the heat energy come from? One answer is that the rearrangement of the C, H and O atoms is a sort of 'settling-down' process: the energy of the carbon dioxide and water is much lower than that of the original fuel and oxygen and the difference appears as heat. As molecules are held together mainly by electrical forces, in a sense we can say that combustion is a process in which stored electrical energy is converted into heat.

Although the reaction shown above represents the combustion of methane, it contains the essential features of the burning of any common fuel: a compound containing carbon and hydrogen interacts with oxygen from the air to produce carbon dioxide and water. (The latter of course usually appears in the form of water vapour or steam.) Indeed, if we know the relative masses of the elements, we can predict how much carbon dioxide and water vapour will be produced in burning a given amount of fuel (see Box 4.3).

Oil and coal, our other main fuels, are more complex than methane, but their combustion is a similar process. The heat produced per tonne is rather less, however, and as the ratio of carbon to hydrogen atoms is greater they produce more CO_2 per unit of heat output (Table 4.1). These fossil fuels, the result of hundreds of millions of years of slow geological change acting on plant or animal matter, are examples of **hydrocarbons** and consist almost entirely of carbon and hydrogen.

Most of the biofuels, derived from living or recently dead biomass, contain oxygen as well. The molecules of biological materials are also much larger and more complex than methane, but we can represent their combustion in a much simplified way by considering the **carbohydrates** as an example. In these the ratio of the constituents is approximately one oxygen and two hydrogens to each carbon, so $[CH_2O]$ can stand for a typical sub-unit of a carbohydrate molecule. The burning process is then:

$$[CH_2O] + O_2 \rightarrow CO_2 + H_2O + energy$$

The details will be specific to each type of biomass, but this shows the general idea, and the data in Table 4.2 are some examples of the energy which can be obtained in burning one tonne or one cubic metre of various biological materials, with the main fossil fuels for comparison.

BOX 4.2: ENERGY AND MOISTURE CONTENT

The water in plant matter contributes nothing to its stored energy. As the moisture content can be as high as 95% for some fresh plants, the useful energy *per tonne* may be a great deal less than in the same material after drying.

It is therefore essential always to indicate the moisture content when mentioning quantities of biomass. Air-dried wood, referred to frequently here, contains about 20% moisture – less than fresh-cut wood, but appreciably more than the oven-dried product. Its energy content is about 15 GJ t^{-1}.

BIOMASS AS A SOLAR ENERGY STORE

Carbon, hydrogen and oxygen are the main constituents of all our conventional fuels. (The 'fuel' in a nuclear reactor produces its heat in an entirely different way which does not involve combustion in the sense discussed here.) That C, H and O are also the main constituents of living matter is no coincidence. As we have seen, the fuel–oxygen combination is an energy store, and the energy is dissipated as heat when the fuel burns. Natural decomposition is a similar **oxidation** process, also leading to carbon dioxide and water. But the process does not finish there. Nature completes the cycle, putting energy back into these final products to create more fuel and oxygen. The mechanism is **photosynthesis** (from *photo*: to do with light and *synthesis*: putting together). This is the process by which plants take in carbon dioxide and water from their surroundings and use energy from sunlight to convert these into the sugars, starches, cellulose, etc. which make up 'vegetable matter'.

The essential features of the process can be represented:

$$CO_2 + H_2O + energy \rightarrow [CH_2O] + O_2$$

Notice that the first item on the right, the $[CH_2O]$, again indicates a sub-unit of a carbohydrate molecule. This is not necessarily the final 'vegetable matter', but as before it will serve for our simple example. The second item is of course oxygen, and it will by now be obvious that this process is exactly the reverse of the decomposition/combustion discussed above. The plant

Table 4.1 Proportions of carbon, hydrogen and oxygen in fuels

Fuel	Ratio of atoms[a]			% by weight			CO_2 per GJ of heat output
	C	H	O	C	H	O	
Coal	1	1	<0.1	85%	6%	9%	120 kg
Oil	1	2	0	85%	15%	0	75 kg
Methane	1	4	0	75%	25%	0	50 kg
Wood	1	1.5	0.7	49%	6%	45%	77 kg[b]

(a) Approximate values. Except for methane, the proportions vary.
(b) If the wood is grown sustainably (see Section 4.1), the *lifecycle* CO_2 production will be close to zero.

Table 4.2 Average energy content of fuels

Fuel	Energy content	
	GJ t^{-1}	GJ m^{-3}
Wood (air-dried, 20% moisture)	15	10
Paper (stacked newspapers)	17	9
Dung (dried)	16	4
Straw (baled)	14	1.4
Sugar cane (air-dried stalks)	14	10
Domestic refuse (as collected)	9	1.5
Commercial wastes (UK average)	16	*
Grass (fresh-cut)	4	3
Oil (petroleum)	42	34
Coal (UK average)	28	50
Natural gas (supply pressure)	55	0.04

* Wide variations depending on the type of material.

BOX 4.4: A CLOSER LOOK AT PHOTOSYNTHESIS

The essential feature of photosynthesis is the conversion of CO_2 and H_2O into carbohydrate and oxygen under the influence of light. These are indeed the inputs and the final products, but showing only the overall reaction hides some important facts. The most significant is that the breaking-up of the H_2O and the CO_2 are successive rather than simultaneous events, and that it is the first of these which needs light.

When light is absorbed by the green pigment chlorophyll, part of its energy is used to split water molecules:

$$2H_2O + energy \rightarrow O_2 + 4H^+ + 4e^-$$

The first of these products is oxygen gas, which is released. The other products are the separated parts of two hydrogen atoms (e^- stands for an electron removed from an atom and H^+ for what is left). The role of the sunlight is now essentially finished.

Energy is carried by the H^+ and e^- particles, which are passed along a chain of different molecules, ending with a compound known as NADP which thus becomes $NADPH_2$. During this stage, some of the energy is used to form a substance called ATP.

The two molecules, $NADPH_2$ and ATP, are the carriers which transport hydrogen and energy and enable the second stage to proceed: the production of carbohydrate using CO_2:

$$4H^+ + 2CO_2 \xrightarrow{ATP} 2[CH_2O]$$

This is a 'dark' process, needing no direct input of light energy. Finally, the NADP (now without its extra hydrogens) and the original constituents of the ATP are recycled to repeat the entire process.

All the plant matter on earth is formed through this process, all the CO_2 in the atmosphere is cycled through plants every 300 years and all the oxygen is recycled through photosynthesis every 2000 years.

For further details, see Hall (1987) in the Further Reading list.

---

grows by using solar energy to convert carbon dioxide and water into carbohydrate or similar material, with a release of oxygen. When it *decays* – or we burn it – oxygen is used and energy is released as heat.

It is important to appreciate the role of the living matter, the biomass, in maintaining the earth's atmosphere. If a cosmic hurricane were to sweep away all the plant life on earth, the resulting loss of mass would be no more than one part in a billion – like blowing the dust off a school globe. Yet the physical consequences of this infinitesimal change would be enormous. There would no longer be a supply of oxygen to the atmosphere, and it is the composition of the atmosphere – the particular mixture of nitrogen, oxygen and trace gases such as CO_2 – which in turn maintains the surface conditions on the earth. When we consider the possible effects of human actions on the environment it is essential to bear in mind the important fact that the biomass and the atmosphere are not two separate features of the surface layers of the earth: their interdependence is so strong that it is essential to treat them as one single system.

CONVERSION EFFICIENCIES

Data such as those in Table 4.2 are useful if we are considering using some existing plant residue or other biological material as a fuel and we know how many tonnes or cubic metres are available. If, however, the question is whether to grow a crop specifically for burning, what we need to know is the amount of energy that can be obtained from a particular area of land. And if the aim is to maximise the yield, we need to know in some detail what determines it. In practice, the quantity of biomass and its energy content depend on many factors: the location, climate and weather, the nature of the soil, supplies of water, nutrients, etc., and the choice of plant. The resulting yields vary over an extremely wide range. Even confining ourselves to situations considered for energy production, we find that the air-dry mass of plant matter produced annually on an area of one hectare can be as little as one tonne or, in extremely favourable circumstances, as much as 30. In energy terms, this could mean less than 15 GJ or nearly 500 GJ per hectare per year. (Table 4.5 in Section 4.8 below shows the yields in tonnes per hectare for various energy crops.)

These figures illustrate the extremely low energy conversion efficiency of photosynthesis. In northern Europe, where the annual average solar energy reaching one hectare is about 35 000 GJ, a good yield might be some 200 GJ per hectare: an efficiency of a little over half a percent. In order to understand why solar-to-biomass conversion efficiency is rarely greater than this, we need to look at the processes in more detail. We'll follow the successive reductions in available energy, from the incident solar radiation to the ultimate plant material (see also Box 4.5).

Firstly, there will be times during the year when the conversion efficiency is virtually zero because no growth is occurring. And secondly, even during the growing period not all the sunlight is intercepted by leaves.

Once we have an estimate of the solar energy arriving at the leaf surface, a more careful quantitative study becomes possible. Leaves don't absorb all the energy of the sunlight reaching them – if they did, they'd be black. That they are green suggests that they reflect green light, and indeed the fraction of sunlight absorbed shows a dip in this region (Figure 4.5). The light-harvesting system responsible for this selective absorption consists of an assembly of pigment molecules, of which chlorophyll is the most important and probably the most familiar. When active, they absorb about 80% of the solar energy falling on the leaf.

The next loss is again the result of selection, in this case because the photochemical reactions described above require light of only a narrow range of wavelengths. The individual photons, which are the pulses of light energy, carry more energy the shorter the wavelength, with the result that photons of the long-wavelength infrared don't have enough energy to allow photosynthesis. (A similar situation in photovoltaic cells was discussed in Chapter 3.) The overall effect of this aspect of selectivity is that only about 50% of the energy absorbed by the leaves is effective in the ultimate chemical reactions.

The end products of these reactions are the 'vegetable matter' and the oxygen which is released by the plant. The details vary from plant to plant, but the chemical energy stored in the plant matter will always be only a

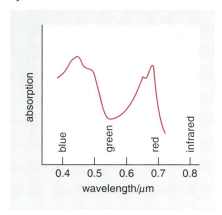

Figure 4.5 Relative absorption of different parts of the solar spectrum by a leaf

---

BOX 4.5: CONVERSION OF SOLAR ENERGY

Consider one hectare of land, in an area where the annual energy delivered by solar radiation is 1000 kWh m^{-2} y^{-1}.

1000 kWh is 3.6 GJ and 1 ha is 10 000 m^2, so the total annual energy is	36 000 GJ
One third of this is delivered during the growing period	12 000 GJ
20% of which reaches the growing leaves	2 400 GJ
After a further loss of about 20% by reflection	2 000 GJ
50% of this is photosynthetically active radiation	1 000 GJ
30% of which is converted into stored energy	300 GJ
But 40% is consumed in sustaining the plant, leaving	180 GJ

This is half a percent of the original total annual energy, and corresponds to an annual production on each hectare of a little under 10 tonnes of dry material.

fraction of that taking part in the chemical reactions – under a third on average; and then some 40% of this is consumed by the plant itself in maintaining its metabolism. This, and all the other 'lost' energy, is released by the plant into its surroundings through the process of respiration or directly as low-temperature heat. Of the solar energy which actually reaches the green leaves, less than a tenth becomes available in the final biofuel. So finally, taking all these factors into account, we reach the observed overall conversion efficiency of less than 1%.

ESTIMATING THE RESOURCE

Natural renewal of the earth's land biomass represents an energy supply of some 3000 EJ a year, of which we currently use a little under 2% as fuel. There is of course no sustainable way in which we could make use of the entire annual production even if we wished to. And fuel is in any case only one of four competing uses of biomass. **Food**, **fodder** and **fibre** must share the resource – food for humans, fodder for wild and domestic animals, and fibre for construction, paper, fabrics, etc.

Given the extremely diverse nature of biofuels, and the wide variations in local conditions, it is evident that any assessment of the world potential must rest on detailed analyses of individual contributions within specific regions or countries. As with any resource estimation, these must take into account environmental and social factors as well as technical and economic considerations.

Recent studies of renewable energy in Britain (ETSU, 1994(1) and 1994(2)) have led to estimates of the Maximum Practicable Resource for a number of electricity-generating technologies in the early years of the next century, under various financial criteria. At 8% discount rate and a unit cost not exceeding 6 p kWh^{-1} (1992), for example, the Maximum Practicable Resource for the year 2005 includes about 12 TWh a year from municipal and industrial waste combustion, 8 TWh y^{-1} from landfill gas and 5 TWh y^{-1} from agricultural and forestry wastes. But the largest contribution by far is the 90 TWh y^{-1} from energy crops, which rises to twice this by 2025. (For comparison, total UK electricity consumption is some 300 TWh y^{-1}). The above figures imply an annual total contribution of more than 1000 PJ, but it should be stressed that they are 'maximum' estimates, and that for instance the greatest projected contribution from energy crops in the year 2005, under the scenarios considered in the above studies, is no more than 22 TWh y^{-1}.

Estimates for the total biomass contribution to EU energy needs over similar periods lie between 4000 and 14 000 PJ a year. The wide ranges in these figures result from different assumptions about future prices and discount rates, and again the upper estimates would be reached only under economic regimes which were very favourable to biomass. In another study (Audubon, 1991), the 'recoverable resource' in the USA from all forms of biomass residues – not including energy crops – has been assessed as 6700 PJ a year.

On the world scale, a scenario based on a detailed analysis carried out for the 1992 United Nations Conference on Environment and Development (UNCED) suggests that the annual energy supply from biomass by the middle of the next century could reach about half the present total world primary energy consumption (Table 4.3). The assumptions lying behind these and other estimates are discussed in more detail in Section 4.12.

Table 4.3 World potential for biomass energy supplies in the year 2050

Biomass resource	Potential annual supply in EJ
Energy crops	128
Dung	25
Forestry residues	14
Cereal residues	13
Sugar cane residues	12
Existing forests	10
Urban refuse	3
TOTAL	205

After Johansson *et al.*, 1992.

4.5 EXTRACTING THE ENERGY

If biofuels are to compete with our present fuels, they must be able to meet the demand for appropriate forms of energy at competitive prices. Two important criteria are the *availability* and the *'transportability'* of the supply. The premium fuels – oil and natural gas – are valued because their energy can be stored with little loss and made available when we need it. And these fuels, together with electric power, offer the further advantage of energy that is easily transferred from place to place.

The biomass resource comes in a variety of forms: wood, sawdust, straw, rape seed, dung, waste paper, household refuse, sewage and many others. Nearly all types of raw biomass decompose rather quickly, so few are very good long-term energy stores; and because of their relatively low energy densities, they are likely to be rather expensive to transport over appreciable distances. Recent years have therefore seen considerable effort devoted to the search for the best ways to use these potentially valuable sources of energy.

In considering the methods for extracting the energy, we can order them by the complexity of the processes involved:

- Direct combustion of the raw biomass.
- Combustion after relatively simple **physical** processing. This might involve sorting, chipping, compressing and/or air-drying.
- **Thermochemical** processing to upgrade the biofuel. Processes in this category include pyrolysis, gasification and liquefaction.
- **Biological** processing. Natural processes such as anaerobic digestion and fermentation, encouraged by the provision of suitable conditions, again lead to a useful gaseous or liquid fuel.

The immediate 'product' of some of these processes is heat – normally used *in situ* or at not too great a distance, for chemical processing or district heating, or to generate steam for power production. For other processes the product is a solid, liquid or gaseous fuel: charcoal, liquid fuel as a petrol substitute or additive, gas for sale or for power generation using either steam or gas turbines. In this section we look at each of the processes in turn, whilst Sections 4.6 – 4.8 discuss their suitability and present applications for different biomass energy sources.

DIRECT COMBUSTION

Boiling a pan of water over a wood fire is a simple process. Unfortunately, it is also very inefficient, as a little elementary calculation reveals.

Table 4.2 shows that the energy content of a cubic metre of air-dry wood is 10 GJ, which is ten million kJ. To raise the temperature of a litre of water by 1 °C requires 4.2 kJ of heat energy. Bringing a litre to the boil should therefore require rather less than 400 kJ, equivalent to 40 cubic centimetres of wood – one small stick, perhaps. In practice, with a simple open fire we might need at least fifty times this amount: a conversion efficiency no better than 2%.

Designing a stove or boiler which will make rather better use of valuable fuel requires an understanding of the process – or to be more precise, the series of processes – involved in the combustion of a solid fuel. The first is one which consumes rather than produces energy: the evaporation of any water in the fuel. With reasonably dry fuel, however, this uses only a few percent of the total energy.

In the combustion process itself there are always two stages, because any solid fuel contains two combustible constituents. The **volatile matter** is released as a mixture of vapours or vaporised tars and oils by the fuel as its temperature rises. The combustion of these produces the little spurts of

BOX 4.6: ANIMAL POWER

A further 'biomass' energy resource, not usually included with the energy available from plants, is the power supplied by draught animals, mostly in the developing countries, where they are the principal source of motive power for small farmers – up to 85–90% in the case of Africa and Asia.

The data are very uncertain, but estimates suggest that draught animals world-wide number about 400 million, including 250 million cattle, with a total 'installed capacity' in excess of 100 GW – about 150 million horsepower (Kristoferson, 1991). Assuming that each animal is used on average for 8 hours per day, 100 days per year, the total energy they supply is about 90 TWh or 320 PJ per year – only a small fraction of the energy supplied directly by plants.

However, allowing for energy 'losses' in growth and maintenance, the energy consumed as fodder by these draught animals will be at least 10 times their useful output, and is probably therefore a significant proportion of world biomass consumption.

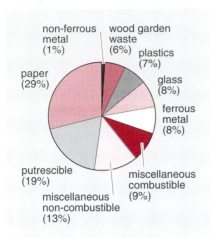

Figure 4.6 The composition of municipal solid wastes in the UK

non-ferrous metal (1%)
wood garden waste (6%)
plastics (7%)
paper (29%)
glass (8%)
ferrous metal (8%)
putrescible (19%)
miscellaneous non-combustible (13%)
miscellaneous combustible (9%)

flame seen around burning wood or coal. The solid which remains consists of the **char** together with any inert matter. The char is mainly carbon, and burns to produce CO_2, whilst the inert matter becomes clinker, slag or ashes.

A feature of the biofuels is that three-quarters or more of their energy is in the volatile matter (unlike coal, where the fraction is usually less than half). It is important therefore that the design of any stove, furnace or boiler should ensure that these vapours burn, and don't just disappear up the chimney. For complete combustion, air must also reach all the char, which is best achieved by burning the fuel in small particles. This can raise a problem, because finely-divided fuel means finely-divided ash – particulates which must be removed from the flue gases. The air flow should also be controlled: too little oxygen means incomplete combustion and leads to the production of carbon monoxide, which is a poison. Too much air is wasteful because it carries away heat in the flue gases.

Modern systems for burning biofuels are as varied as the fuels themselves, ranging in size from small stoves designed to save cooking fuel in Third World countries to large boilers with outputs of megawatts of heat (see for instance Figures 4.18 and 4.23).

Direct combustion is of course one way to extract the energy contained in household refuse, but as collected it is hardly an ideal fuel. Its contents are variable, its moisture content tends to be high (20% or more) and its energy density is low, each cubic metre containing less than a thirtieth of the energy of the same volume of coal. So it is expensive to transport, and burning it requires plant designed specifically for this type of fuel. Whilst the development of such systems has received considerable attention in a number of European countries, interest in the UK has tended to concentrate on methods for converting refuse into a fuel suitable for burning in conventional plant. The term **refuse-derived fuel** (RDF) refers to a range of products resulting from separation of unwanted components, shredding, drying and otherwise treating the raw material to improve its combustion properties. Relatively simple processing might involve separation of very large items, magnetic extraction of ferrous metals and perhaps rough shredding. The most fully processed product, known as **densified refuse-derived fuel** (or d-RDF), is the result of separating out the combustible part which is then pulverised, compressed and dried to produce solid fuel pellets with about 60% of the energy density of coal (Figure 4.7).

←5cm→

Figure 4.7 Refuse-derived fuel (d-RDF) pellets

GASIFICATION

The term **gasification** covers a range of processes in which a solid fuel is reacted with hot steam and air or oxygen to produce a gaseous fuel. Figure 4.8 shows the processes in outline. There are several types of gasifier, with operating temperatures varying from a few hundred to over a thousand degrees Celsius, and pressures from near atmospheric to as much as 30 atmospheres. The resulting gas is a mixture whose main constituents are carbon monoxide, hydrogen and methane, together with carbon dioxide and nitrogen, in proportions which depend on the processing conditions and whether air or oxygen is used.

Gasification is not a new process. 'Town' gas, the product of coal gasification, was widely used for many decades before its displacement by natural gas, and many vehicles towing wood gasifiers as their fuel supply were to be seen during the Second World War. There are several reasons for the resurgence of interest in biomass gasification in more recent years. Firstly, it can result in a fuel which is much cleaner than the original biomass, as undesirable chemical pollutants can be removed during the processing, together with the inert matter which produces particulates (smoke) when the fuel is burned. Secondly, a gas is a much more versatile fuel. Direct burning is one option, but the gas can also be used in internal combustion engines or gas turbines. And finally, gasification under suitable conditions can produce **synthesis gas**, a mixture of carbon monoxide and hydrogen which can be used to synthesise almost any hydrocarbon.

The simplest process results in gas containing up to 50% by volume of nitrogen and CO_2, and as these have no fuel value, its energy may be only a few megajoules per cubic metre – about a tenth of that of methane. But it will be a clean fuel, and although transporting such a dilute energy carrier may not be worthwhile, its improved qualities may make it worth producing for use *in situ*.

Figure 4.8 Gasification processes

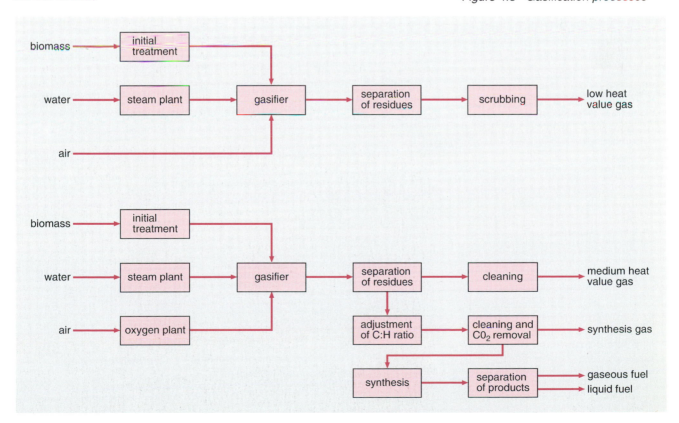

PYROLYSIS

Pyrolysis is the simplest and almost certainly the oldest method of processing one fuel in order to produce a better one. **Conventional pyrolysis** involves heating the original material in the near-absence of air, typically at 300–500 °C, until the volatile matter has been driven off. The residue is then the char – more commonly known as charcoal – a fuel which has about twice

BOX 4.7 GAS TURBINES

One potential use for the clean fuel gas from biomass gasifiers is to run **gas turbines** for local power generation. A gas-turbine power station is similar to conventional steam plant except that instead of using heat from the burning fuel to produce steam to drive the turbine, it is driven directly by the hot combustion gases (Figure 4.9). Increasing the temperature in this way improves the thermodynamic efficiency, but in order not to corrode or foul the turbine blades the gases must be very clean – which is why nearly all present gas-turbine plants burn natural gas.

Substitution of gas from biomass gasifiers would serve a double purpose, conserving a premium fuel and reducing the emission of greenhouse gases – provided the biomass cycle is CO_2-neutral, of course. This route, gasification followed by power generation using gas turbines, is receiving attention as a potentially efficient use of wood from short rotation coppice (Sections 4.8 and 4.11).

In situations where the wastes from processing of vegetable material provide the input, the requirement is often for process heat (hot steam) as well as electric power, with the heat requirement often taking precedence. For this purpose the **steam-injected gas turbine** (STIG) is very suitable. As the name suggests, the turbine is driven by a combination of combustion gases and high-pressure steam, so the plant incorporates steam generators

and can be operated much more flexibly in response to varying demands for heat. The system is

therefore a **biomass integrated gasifier/steam-injected gas turbine** – a BIG/STIG.

Figure 4.9   Types of generating system (a) conventional steam turbine: (b) simple gas turbine; (c) steam-injected gas turbine

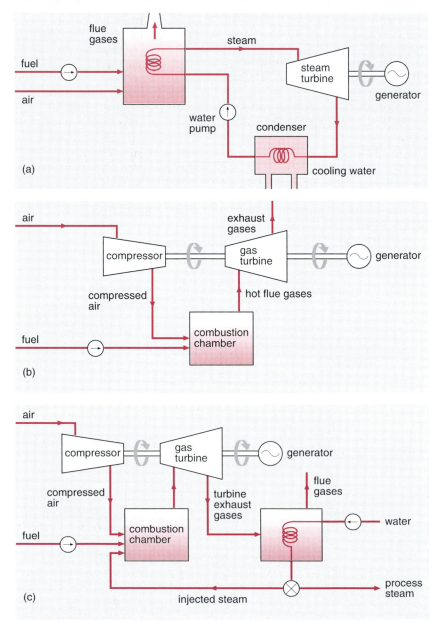

the energy density of the original and burns at a much higher temperature. For many centuries, and in much of the world still today, charcoal is produced by pyrolysis of wood. Depending on the moisture content and the efficiency of the process, 4–10 tonnes of wood are required to produce one tonne of charcoal, and if no attempt is made to collect the volatile matter, the charcoal is obtained at the cost of perhaps two-thirds of the original energy content. (The use of wood in developing countries to produce high-quality 'barbecue charcoal' for export may earn valuable foreign currency, but is not perhaps the best way to treat a decreasing resource.)

With more sophisticated pyrolysis techniques, the volatiles can be collected, and careful choice of the temperature at which the process takes place allows control of their composition. The liquid product has potential as fuel oil, but is contaminated with acids and must be treated before use. **Fast pyrolysis** of plant material, such as wood or nutshells, at temperatures of 800–900 °C leaves as little as 10% of the material as solid char and converts some 60% into a gas rich in hydrogen and carbon monoxide. This makes fast pyrolysis a competitor with conventional gasification methods (see above), but like the latter, it has yet to be developed as a treatment for biomass on a commercial scale.

At present, conventional pyrolysis is considered the more attractive technology. The relatively low temperatures mean that fewer potential pollutants are emitted than in full combustion, giving pyrolysis an environmental advantage in dealing with certain wastes. There have been some trials with small-scale pyrolysis plants treating wastes from the plastics industry and also used tyres – a disposal problem of increasingly urgent concern. (See also 'Commercial and industrial wastes', Section 4.7.)

SYNTHESISING FUELS

A gasifier which uses oxygen rather than air can produce a gas consisting mainly of H_2, CO and CO_2, and the interesting potential of this lies in the fact that removal of the CO_2 leaves the mixture called synthesis gas, from which almost any hydrocarbon compound may be synthesised. Reacting the H_2 and CO is one way to produce pure methane, for instance:

$$2CO + 2H_2 \rightarrow CH_4 + CO_2$$

Another possible product is methanol (CH_3OH), a liquid hydrocarbon with an energy density of 23 GJ per tonne. Producing methanol in this way involves a series of sophisticated chemical processes with high temperatures and pressures and expensive plant, and one might wonder why it is of interest. The answer lies in the product: methanol is that valuable commodity, a liquid fuel which is a direct substitute for gasoline. At present the production of methanol using synthesis gas from biomass is not a commercial proposition, but the technology already exists, having been developed for use with coal as feedstock – as a precaution by coal-rich countries at times when their oil supplies were threatened.

ANAEROBIC DIGESTION

As its name suggests, **anaerobic digestion**, like pyrolysis, occurs in the absence of air; but in this case the decomposition is caused by bacterial action rather than high temperatures. It is a process which takes place in almost any biological material, but is favoured by warm, wet and of course airless conditions. It occurs naturally in decaying vegetation on the bottom of ponds, producing the **marsh gas** which bubbles to the surface and can catch fire – giving rise to the myths of the 'will o' the wisp'.

Anaerobic digestion also occurs in situations created by human activities, and in two major instances these have been developed as energy sources.

One is the **biogas** which is generated in concentrations of sewage or animal manure, and the other is the **landfill gas** produced by domestic refuse buried in landfill sites. In both cases the resulting gas is a mixture consisting mainly of methane and carbon dioxide; but major differences in the nature of the input, the scale of the plant and the time-scale for gas production lead to very different technologies for dealing with the two sources. (A third system, treating municipal solid wastes in purpose-built digesters, is discussed in Section 4.7.)

The detailed chemistry of the production of biogas and landfill gas is complex, but it appears that a mixed population of bacteria breaks down the organic material into sugars and then into various acids which are decomposed to produce the final gas, leaving an inert residue whose composition depends on the type of system and the original feedstock.

BIOGAS

The dung or sewage which is the feedstock for biogas is fed into a purpose-built **digester** as a slurry with up to 95% water. Digesters range in size from perhaps one cubic metre for a small 'household' unit (roughly 200 gallons) to some ten times this for a typical farm plant (Figures 4.10 and 4.15) and as much as 2000 m³ for a large commercial installation. The input may be continuous or in batches, and digestion is allowed to continue for a period of from ten days to a few weeks. The bacterial action itself generates heat, but in cold climates additional heat is normally required to maintain the ideal process temperature of at least 35 °C, and this must be provided from the biogas. In extreme cases *all* the gas may be used for this purpose, but although the net energy output is then zero, the plant may still pay for itself through the saving in fossil fuel which would have been needed to process the wastes.

A well-run digester will produce 200–400 m³ of biogas with a methane content of 50% to 75% for each dry tonne of input – at best about 11 GJ of useful energy. Comparison with Table 4.2 shows that this is about two-thirds of the fuel energy of the original dung, and probably represents the best which can be achieved. However, even at lower conversion efficiencies, the process may be worthwhile in order to obtain a clean fuel and at the same time dispose of unpleasant wastes. The effluent which remains when digestion is complete can also be of considerable value as a fertiliser.

Figure 4.10 A farm biogas digester

LANDFILL GAS

A large proportion of ordinary domestic refuse – **municipal solid wastes**, or MSW – is biological material (Figure 4.6), and its disposal in deep landfills furnishes suitable conditions for anaerobic digestion. That landfill sites produce methane has been known for decades, and recognition of the potential hazard led to the fitting of systems for burning it off; however, it was only in the 1970s that serious attention was paid to the idea of using this 'undesirable' product.

The waste matter is more miscellaneous in a landfill than in a biogas digester, and the conditions neither as warm nor as wet, so the process is much slower, taking place over years rather than weeks (Figure 4.11). The end product, known as landfill gas (LFG), is again a mixture consisting mainly of CH_4 and CO_2. In theory, the lifetime yield of a good site should lie in the range 150–300 m^3 of gas per tonne of wastes (as collected), with between 50% and 60% by volume of methane. This suggests a total energy of 5–6 GJ per tonne of refuse, but in practice yields are much less.

In developing a site, each area is covered with a layer of impervious clay or similar material after it is filled, producing an environment which encourages anaerobic digestion. The gas is collected by an array of interconnected perforated pipes buried at depths up to 20 metres in the refuse (Figure 4.12). In new sites this pipe system is constructed before the wastes start to arrive, and in a large well-established landfill there can be several miles of pipes, with as much as 1000 m^3 an hour of gas being pumped out.

Increasingly, the gas from landfill sites is used for power generation. At present most plants are based on large internal combustion engines, such as standard marine engines. Driving 500 kW generators, these are well-matched to typical gas supply rates of the order of 10 GJ an hour. However, modern gas turbines (Figure 4.9) should give better efficiencies, and a few are coming into use at the time of writing.

Figure 4.11 The changing gas composition in a landfill site

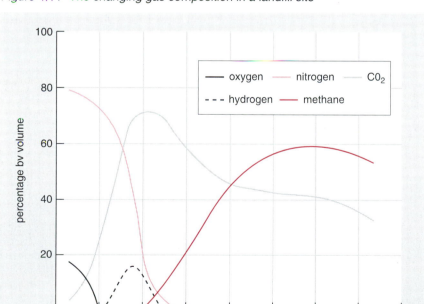

Figure 4.12 Extraction of landfill gas

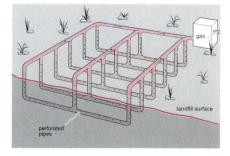

FERMENTATION

In considering the uses of synthesis gas, we have seen how an alcohol (methanol) could be produced from biomass by a series of sophisticated chemical processes. There are of course other ways to produce alcohols from biomass – as vintners and brewers have known for centuries. Fermentation is an **anaerobic biological** process in which sugars are converted to alcohol by the action of micro-organisms, usually yeast. The resulting alcohol is **ethanol** (C_2H_5OH) rather than methanol (CH_3OH), but it too can be used in internal combustion engines, either directly in suitably modified engines or as a gasoline extender in **gasohol**: gasoline (petrol) containing up to 20% ethanol.

The value of any particular type of biomass as feedstock for fermentation depends on the ease with which it can be converted to sugars. The best-known source of ethanol is sugar-cane – or the molasses remaining after the cane juice has been extracted. Other plants whose main carbohydrate is starch (potatoes, corn and other grains) require processing to convert the starch to sugar. This is commonly carried out, as in the production of some alcoholic drinks, by enzymes in malts. Even wood can act as feedstock, but its carbohydrate, cellulose, is resistant to breakdown into sugars by acid or enzymes (even in finely divided forms such as sawdust), adding further complication to the process.

The liquid resulting from fermentation contains only about 10% ethanol, which must be distilled off before it can be used as fuel. The energy content of the final product is about 30 GJ t^{-1}, or 24 GJ m^{-3}. The complete process requires a considerable amount of heat, which is usually supplied by crop residues (e.g. sugar cane bagasse or maize stalks and cobs). Table 4.4 shows the yields of ethanol obtainable per tonne of raw material and per hectare of land for several crops. The energy loss in fermentation is substantial, but this may be compensated for by the convenience and transportability of the liquid fuel, and by the comparatively low cost and familiarity of the technology.

Table 4.4 Ethanol yields

Raw material	Litres per tonne[a]	Litres per hectare per year[b]
Sugar cane (harvested stalks)	70	400 –12000
Corn (maize, grain)	360	250–2000
Cassava (roots)	180	500–4000
Sweet potatoes (roots)	120	1000–4500
Wood	160	160–4000[c]

(a) This figure depends mainly on the proportion of the raw material which can be fermented.

(b) The ranges of values reflect world-wide differences in yield.

(c) The upper figure represents the theoretical maximum.

4.6 AGRICULTURAL RESIDUES

The following three sections discuss the present uses of biomass in a sequence determined by the sources: *agricultural residues* (both plant and animal wastes), then *energy from refuse* – another form of wastes, and finally purpose-grown *energy crops*.

Crop and animal wastes provide significant amounts of energy in many countries, coming second only to wood as the dominant biomass fuel world-wide. It was estimated, for example, that 110 Mt of dung and crop residues were used as fuel in India in 1985, compared with 133 Mt of wood, and in China the mass of available agricultural residues has been estimated at 2.2 times the mass of wood fuel (Scurlock and Hall, 1990). In the UK and elsewhere in Europe, restrictions on open-field burning of straw have highlighted the magnitude of the crop wastes and the potential for using them cleanly and efficiently. Britain alone produces about 20 Mt of agricultural and forest residues every year, although only a proportion of these are economically recoverable (FOE, 1991).

WOOD RESIDUES

Operations such as thinning of plantations and trimming of felled trees generate large volumes of **forestry residues**. At present these are often left to rot on site – even in countries with fuelwood shortages. They can be collected, dried and used as fuel by nearby rural industry and domestic consumers, but their bulk and high water content makes transporting them for wider use uneconomic. In developing countries where charcoal is an important fuel, on-site kilns can reduce transport costs. Mechanical harvesters and chippers have been developed in Europe and North America over the last 15 years to produce uniform 30–40 mm wood chips which can be handled, dried and burned easily in chip-fired boilers.

The use of forest residues to produce steam for heating and/or power generation is now a growing business in many countries. American electricity utilities have more than 9 GW of biomass-fired generating plant on line, much of it constructed in the last ten years. Austria has about 1250 MW of wood-fired heating capacity in the form of domestic stoves and district heating plant, burning waste wood, bark and wood chips. Most of these district heating systems are of 1–2 MW capacity, with a few larger units (15 MW) and a number of small-scale CHP systems.

In the UK, about 2.3 Mt (air-dry mass) of forest residues are produced each year, representing about 40 PJ of energy. At present this feeds a modest fuelwood market of some 0.25 Mt per annum, but it is estimated that a further 25% of the total could be used to supply perhaps half a dozen power stations with 50 MW total capacity. The accessible resource for the year 2005, for electricity generated at less than 10p kWh^{-1}, has been estimated to be about 14 PJ, or just under 4 TWh (ETSU, 1994(2)). However, the remote location of many forests makes it improbable that more than a third of this can be regarded as a practicable resource. Finally, the investment required for new harvesting and processing machinery means that the resource is likely to become economically viable only when a market for the wood is fully established. (See also Section 4.8, 'woody crops'.)

Timber processing is a further source of wood residues. Dry sawdust and offcuts produced during the processing of cut timber make very good fuel. The British furniture industry is estimated to use 35 000 tonnes of such residues a year, one third of its production, providing 0.5 PJ of space and water heating and process heat (FOE, 1991). In Sweden, where biomass already provides nearly 15% of primary energy, forestry residues and wood industries contribute over 200 PJ y^{-1}, mainly as fuel for CHP plant.

TEMPERATE CROP WASTES

Every year, 14 million tonnes of **straw** are produced in the UK, half of it surplus to need. Until recently, this was burned in the field or ploughed back into the soil, but environmental legislation to restrict field burning from the end of 1992 has drawn attention to its potential as an energy resource – equivalent to about 100 PJ a year, or 1% of UK primary energy use, a figure which rises to 300 PJ if all other agricultural wastes are taken into account. The UK market for straw-burning systems for domestic,

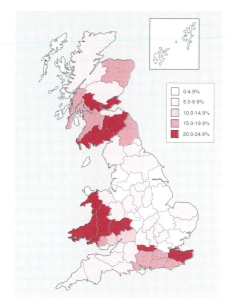

Figure 4.13 Percentage cover of woodland in Great Britain. In total, woodlands cover more than two million hectares – about 9% of the total land area

BOX 4.9: HEATING WITH STRAW

Woburn Abbey, a country estate in Bedfordshire, UK, has for nearly a decade met most of its space heating and domestic hot water requirements using surplus straw from its own and neighbouring farms. The large straw bales are delivered to a conveyor carrying them to a shredder (Figure 4.14 (Bottom)) which teases out the bales and chops the straw into 5–15 cm lengths, before it is fed automatically to the boiler. The heat produced is carried by pressurised hot water through underground pipes and transferred by heat exchangers to the heating system of each building (Figure 5.14(Top)). The system, with maximum heat output of 800 kW, replaces earlier oil-fired boilers, saving over £20 000 a year in fuel costs and with a payback time of seven years for its total capital cost of £146 000.

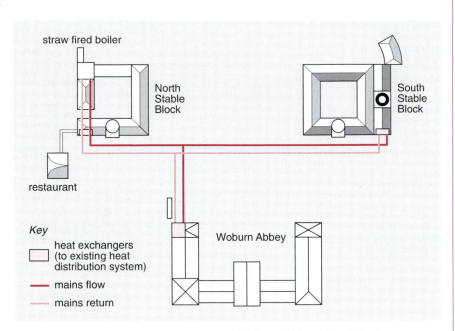

Figure 4.14 The straw-burning system at Woburn Abbey: (Top) the heat distribution system; (Bottom) straw bales entering the shredder

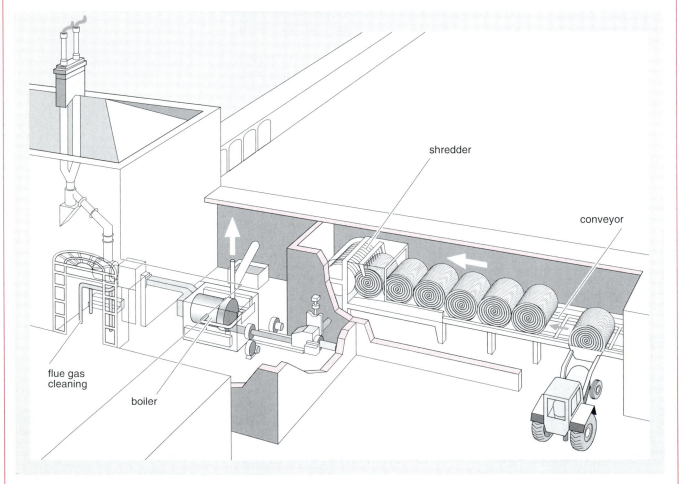

horticultural and rural industrial space heating has been slow to develop over the last 10 years because of the competition from fuel oil, which has remained a convenient and relatively cheap alternative. Nevertheless, about 200 000 tonnes of straw a year are presently used in this way in Britain, a figure projected to rise to 800 000 tonnes by 2000 (see for instance Box 4.9). Other European countries have more extensive experience with straw burning – Denmark, for instance, has set up 54 straw-fired district heating schemes in rural areas over the past decade, mostly in the range 3–5 MW.

Other crop wastes arising in Britain each year include about 1.6 Mt (fresh weight, including 60–80% moisture content) of potato and sugar beet tops, and 5 Mt of nursery and garden wastes. The EU as a whole generates 8.5 Mt (fresh weight) of reject potatoes per year, and 2.3 Mt of damaged fruit, as well as 'structural surpluses' of other food commodities amounting to tens of millions of tonnes. These 'wet' wastes may be more suitable for fermentation or anaerobic digestion than for direct combustion, but these surpluses, or the land on which they are grown, are potentially available for biomass fuel.

ANIMAL WASTES

The combination of intensive animal rearing and stricter environmental controls on odour and water pollution by manures is leading farmers to invest in **anaerobic digestion** as a means of waste management. The biogas produced by a digester (Section 4.5) can be used to produce heat or electric power as required – or in many cases both. One system uses the gas to run large internal combustion engines which drive electric generators, while their cooling water and exhaust gases are used to provide heat to the digester (Figure 4.15).

Manures from cattle, chickens and pigs are the most common wet wastes in Europe, especially in the Netherlands and Denmark, where there is insufficient land available for the spreading of pig slurry. In the UK, about 7 Mt of animal wastes are produced each year with an energy content of 110 PJ. Although only a fraction of this resource may be economically viable in terms of its energy content, biogas can be generated as a valuable by-product of waste management by anaerobic digestion.

Figure 4.15 Power from anaerobic digestion of pig slurry. This 750 m^3 plant at Piddlehinton in Dorset was one of the projects accepted in the first NFFO round, in 1990 (see Table 4.6). It can handle over 20 000 gallons of slurry a day, and the generators fuelled by the resulting biogas feed some three-quarters of a million kWh of electricity a year into the National Grid

Sewage sludge has been treated by anaerobic digestion in the UK since the first large 'sewage farms' were built at the turn of the century, but much of the biogas was simply flared in the 1950s and 1960s. More recently, with 70% of all sewage now treated, an increasing proportion of the biogas has been used for electricity and heat production on-site. By mid-1994, 26 projects with a total generating capacity of 33 MW were in operation under the NFFO scheme (see Section 4.10).

Small biogas plants for human and other animal wastes are in widespread use in China and India, where a variety of low-cost designs have been promoted by both government and non-government agencies. Rapid expansion of the Chinese biogas programme in the 1960s and 1970s resulted in more than seven million digesters, but about half of these later fell into disuse due to various difficulties such as poor construction, maintenance and lack of local involvement. Biogas plants are now becoming more common again, especially in the south and west of China. However, in many developing countries the capital cost of a digester is out of reach of the typical small farmer, and attempts to introduce community biogas plants have met with mixed fortunes, largely due to difficulties with balancing 'ownership' of animal dung against credit in the form of biogas consumption. As a result, many of the biogas plants in India are concentrated on farms with larger numbers of cattle.

Another option for extracting energy from animal wastes, if the water content is low enough, is **direct combustion**. Poultry litter, a relatively dry form of waste, is the energy source for a 12.5 MW power plant at Eye in Suffolk, UK, commissioned in 1992. It has been claimed that 'one chicken equals one watt' (Arnold, 1993), and surrounding poultry farms are providing 180 000 tonnes of litter per year as fuel – about one-tenth of UK production.

TROPICAL CROP WASTES

Bagasse (sugar cane fibre) has significant potential as a biomass fuel since it mainly arises at sugar factories where flows of materials and energy are already well organised (Figure 4.16). Most sugar factories use bagasse as a source of heat for raising steam, but deliberately burn it inefficiently in order not to accumulate surplus wastes. Many sugar factories also produce electricity for their own needs, but only a few at present export electricity because of operational and contractual difficulties with selling power only during the cane growing season. Studies conducted in Brazil, Thailand, Jamaica and Zimbabwe suggest that optimisation of bagasse combustion for energy, and utilisation of the cane trash or 'barbojo' (cane tops and leaves), could yield significant amounts of electricity and heat (Goldemberg, 1992). If the increased recovery of biomass materials were combined with improved efficiency of conversion to electricity, up to 50 GW of generating capacity could be installed in association with the sugar industry world-wide.

Rice husks are among the most common agricultural residues in the world, accounting for about one-fifth of unmilled rice dry weight. Indonesia, for example, produced 6.5 Mt of husks in 1986. Although they have a high silica (ash) content compared with other biomass fuels, the uniform texture of rice husks lends them to technologies such as gasification. Rice husk gasifiers have been successfully operated in Indonesia, China and Mali (Manurung, 1990).

In many countries, the **coconut** processing industry gives rise to large quantities of both coarse and fine wastes. Gasification of coconut fibre has been tried in Thailand, with limited success due to the very low density of the substrate material. Finely divided coco fibre ('coir dust') is more promising as a biofuel, although alternative markets for this have been found in Sri Lanka through the production of 'cocopeat'.

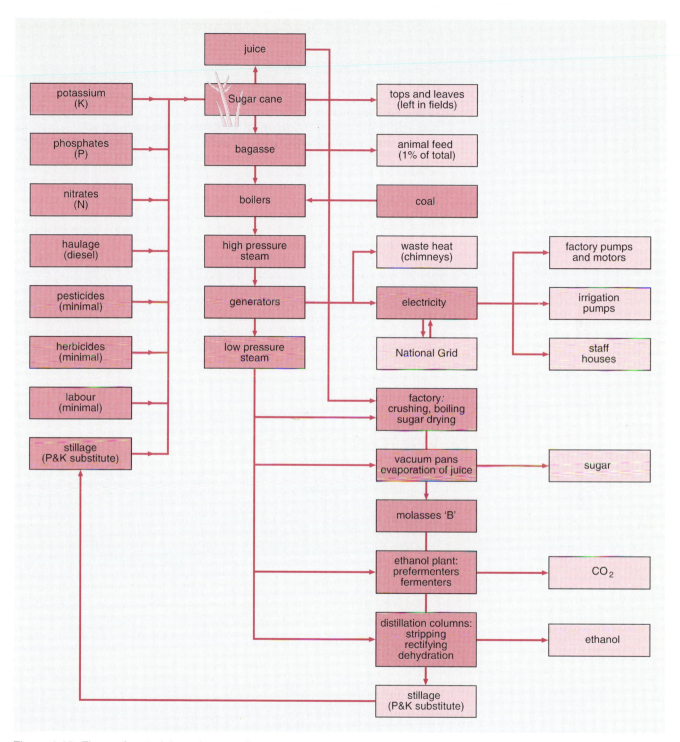

Figure 4.16 Flows of materials and energy in sugar-cane processing

4.7 ENERGY FROM REFUSE

MUNICIPAL SOLID WASTE

The UK produces 25 million tonnes of household waste each year, and a similar quantity of combustible commercial and industrial wastes. (The latter are sometimes included within the term MSW, but are treated separately here.) Over 90% of the domestic waste is currently landfilled, most of the remainder being incinerated. The presence of contaminating plastics, metals and toxins can create pollution problems, but landfill sites and incineration plant are subject to operating conditions laid down by regulatory authorities and designed to ensure that emissions are reduced to acceptable levels. Meanwhile, the increasing cost and shortage of space for well-designed non-polluting landfill disposal, both in Britain and around many cities world-wide, is leading to growing demands for waste reduction through recycling and recovery of materials from mixed waste.

Large-scale plans for waste separation, recycling and composting have yet to take effect in the UK and Europe as a whole, but in the future about half of all MSW could be subject to energy recovery through direct combustion, production of refuse-derived fuel (RDF) or utilisation of landfill gas. Energy from wastes is an attractive option in many large cities in Britain because of the shortage of suitable landfill sites and the high costs of transporting the waste to distant sites. (Transport already costs some councils more than £20 per tonne.)

MSW COMBUSTION

The technology for MSW combustion has been well tried and tested in both continental Europe and Japan (less in the USA and Britain), and collection networks already exist to ensure a continuous supply of municipal wastes. About 350 energy-from-refuse incinerators are in operation world-wide, and countries such as Switzerland and Japan already treat 80% or more of their MSW in this way.

Many industrial countries consider refuse incineration with heat recovery to be an important means of waste disposal. The heat is used both for district heating and for electricity generation, and the ash can be used for construction and road building. Emissions of dust, acids, metals and organic compounds from both new and existing incinerators are now tightly controlled by a 1990 EC Directive as well as the UK Environmental Protection Act (see also Section 4.9).

The UK has refuse-burning district heating schemes in Mansfield and Nottingham, and an incinerator in Sheffield provides district heating for a multi-storey complex containing 2450 flats and numerous public buildings including shops and a police station, all of which are owned by the local authority.

In the first three rounds of the NFFO scheme (see Section 4.10), 34 electricity-generating MSW plants with a total capacity of some 500 MW were awarded contracts. However, difficulties in obtaining planning permission delayed implementation of many of these, with less than a quarter of the contracted capacity of the 1990 and 1991 rounds in operation by late 1994.

REFUSE-DERIVED FUEL (RDF)

Six processing plants for municipal solid waste (MSW) are operating in Britain, mechanically separating non-combustibles such as metals and glass, and pelletising the remaining organic matter into RDF (Section 4.5). Coarse RDF and the more highly processed d-RDF are more convenient to handle than unprocessed MSW waste, and the reduced ash content makes them suitable for combustion in conventional power and heating plant together with coal. However, strict environmental standards on all forms of waste combustion in the UK have so far limited the size of the RDF market.

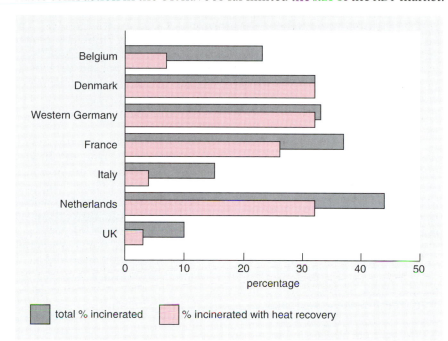

Figure 4.17 Incineration of solid wastes in some EU countries.

total % incinerated   % incinerated with heat recovery

Figure 4.18 A large MSW combustion plant

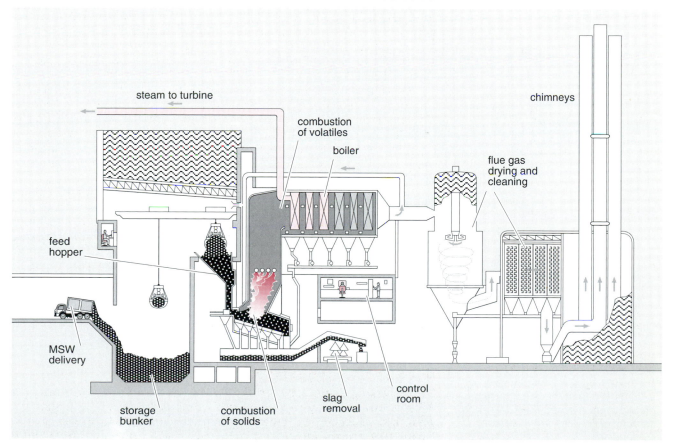

LANDFILL GAS DEVELOPMENTS

Although in the USA landfill gas is sometimes upgraded to pipeline-quality methane by 'washing' to remove carbon dioxide, in most applications world-wide it is more economic to burn the gas directly. One use is to fire kilns, furnaces or boilers nearby, but there are rarely enough large users close to a landfill site and the LFG is increasingly used to generate electricity for local use or for sale. World-wide there are more than 240 plants, incorporating a total installed generating capacity in 1992 of about 440 MW. One of the largest landfill projects in the world generates 46 MW of electricity at Puente Hills, California. In the UK, power generation from LFG attracted more contracts in the first three NFFO rounds than any other renewable source: 94 plants with a total output capacity of 166 MW (see Table 4.6 in Section 4.10).

Whilst theoretically each tonne of refuse can, over a site lifetime of 10 years or more, yield between 150 and 300 m^3 of gas, with an energy content of 5 or 6 GJ, difficulties with gas extraction and management of underground conditions can mean that only 25–50% is ultimately recoverable. At current UK extraction rates the energy per tonne of wastes (as collected) is usually less than 2 GJ, but this figure is expected to rise significantly as newer, purpose-designed sites become productive.

The economics of power generation from landfill gas are already attractive. In the UK, some 80% of the projects contracted in the 1990 and 1991 NFFO rounds were producing power within two years, and the contracted prices for the 1994 round were in the range 3.29–4p kWh^{-1}. With 25 Mt of household wastes a year, 90% of it landfilled, the resource is reasonably large. At a yield of 150 cubic metres of gas per tonne of MSW, it would produce a total electricity output of over 5 TWh a year with present gas-to-power conversion efficiencies – effectively replacing one large fossil-fuel or nuclear plant.

ANAEROBIC DIGESTERS FOR MSW

As an alternative to recovery of biogas from landfills, the organic fraction of domestic waste can be subjected to more carefully controlled processing in specially fabricated digesters. Under these conditions gas yields are much nearer the theoretical values referred to in Section 4.5, and digestion is complete within a matter of weeks rather than years. Feedstock for the

Figure 4.19 Power generation at the Appley Bridge landfill site. The top of the landfill is seen in the foreground, with the five generators below and behind them a freight train delivering containers of MSW from Greater Manchester

digester is the organic fraction of MSW diluted into a slurry – possibly mixed with sewage.

An advantage of these digesters over landfill plants is that they can be sited closer to urban areas, reducing transport costs. They also require much less land. The greater capital and processing costs are, however, a disincentive to investment. MSW digesters already exist in several European countries, and although Britain has no plants yet, interest is growing due to the rising cost of landfill. Low-solids systems have been developed particularly in the USA, and Figure 4.21 shows the full complexity of a system which first recovers useful materials from the MSW, then produces methane by digestion and finally generates electric power using the combustion heat of the residual solids.

COMMERCIAL AND INDUSTRIAL WASTES

Britain generates about 36 Mt of specialised wastes each year, about two-thirds of which are combustible. Much of this is unsuitable for combining with domestic waste, for reasons of safety or for minimising disposal costs. Where dedicated equipment must be used in order to meet environmental and safety standards, energy recovery can help to reduce total costs. For example, food processing wastes, which must be treated before discharge to reduce biological and chemical oxygen demand, may be anaerobically instead of aerobically digested, the resulting biogas being used for process heat. Hospital wastes, all of which must now be incinerated to avoid contamination, are increasingly subject to energy recovery as health authorities upgrade their waste-handling equipment. Total production of hospital wastes in Britain is equivalent to 12 PJ y^{-1}.

A large proportion of the 28 million tyres discarded in Britain every year is unsuitable for reuse, but with an energy content of 32 GJ per tonne, constitutes a potential industrial fuel (Figure 4.22). The UK Energy Technology Support Unit has estimated that scrap tyres, including recovery of tyres already dumped, have an economic potential of about 5.6 PJ a year.

Figure 4.20 Anaerobic digestion of municipal sold wastes. The flow diagram shows the processes and resulting products for an average tonne of MSW in a large (2000 m^3) high-solids system. As can be seen, the total useful output is 5 GJ per tonne

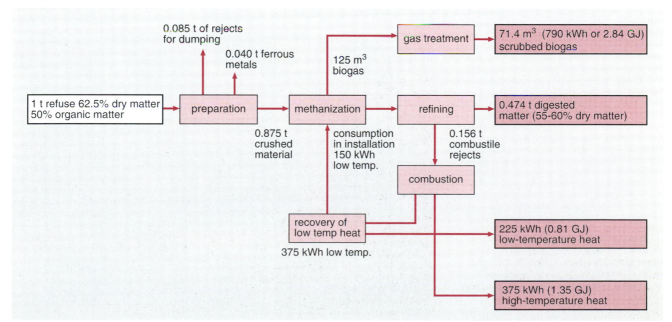

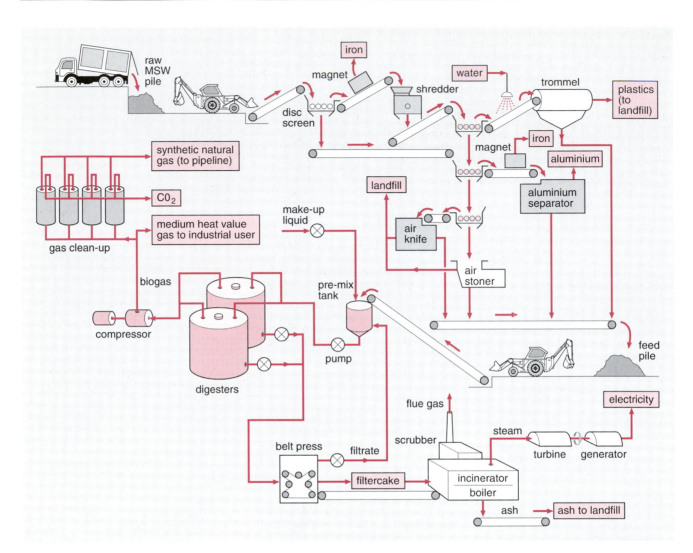

Figure 4.21 An integrated waste materials plant. This plant in Florida has facilities for recovery of metals and removal of plastics, followed by anaerobic digestion of the remainder. The solid residue from the digester serves as fuel for power production

Figure 4.22 A 25 MW tyre-burning power plant. This plant near Wolverhampton, constructed by Elm Energy, is the first in the UK using tyres as fuel for power production. Awarded a contract in the 1990 NFFO round (see Table 4.6), it consumes nearly 10 million scrap tyres a year

4.8 ENERGY CROPS

'Energy crops', plants grown specifically as energy sources, have attracted increasing attention in recent years. The reduction in net CO_2 emissions may be sufficient reason for substituting biomass for fossil fuels, but in many countries the more immediate motives for change have been the problem of surplus agricultural land and the search for indigenous alternatives to imported oil. The preferred crops, depending on the relative importance of these factors and on local conditions, include wood for burning, plants for fermenting to ethanol and crops whose seeds are particularly rich in oils (Table 4.5).

WOODY CROPS

Wood remains a major energy source in much of Asia, most of Africa and several South American countries. Wood (or charcoal) is often the main household fuel, and can also contribute appreciably to industrial energy consumption – in Brazil, for instance, where the steel industry uses over two million tonnes of charcoal a year. The wood resource is accordingly of great importance. Where a forestry industry exists, wood residues can be used, but deforestation is leading to local shortages in many areas. A possible solution, which could serve the dual purpose of helping reforestation and providing a relatively short-term return, is the planting of fast-growing trees suitable for **coppicing**. This centuries-old technique, which involves cutting the growth every few years and allowing the tree to sprout again, has been the subject of trials in a number of developing countries.

Table 4.5 Annual yields of various crops

Crop	Average yield	Best yield
Sugar cane	35	90
Maize (corn)	10	40
Wheat	5	20
Rice	4	16
Sugar beet	8	18
Cassava	8	35
Wood (temperate region)	10	20
Wood (tropics)	20	35

(All yields in tonnes of oven-dry matter per hectare per year)

Figure 4.23 A large-scale plant for generating process heat from wood-chips

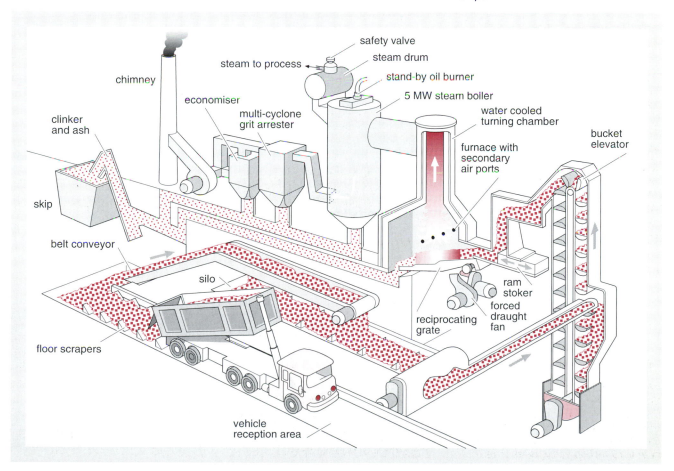

Short rotation coppice is also attracting interest in the very different context of the industrialised countries where agricultural surpluses have led to the withdrawal of land from food production. Poplar and willow are the preferred trees. Planted at a density of 5000–20 000 trees per hectare (at spacings from 0.5 × 1 metre to 1 × 2 metres) and coppiced on a two- to five-year cycle, they can remain productive for 30 years, with annual yields in excess of 10 tonnes per hectare. (See also Section 4.2.)

An alternative to short rotation coppice is **modified conventional forestry**, based on integrated harvesting techniques developed in Sweden. Coniferous trees are planted at relatively high density (5000 per ha) and vigorously thinned later, yielding an early harvest of chipped wood. Sweden aims to increase its biomass energy supply by planting 10 000 ha of coppice and short rotation forest per year during the 1990s (Hall, 1991). The Swedish government is spending US$179 million over five years to promote utilisation of biomass, predominantly within the forestry industry, and a recent assessment (IEA, 1994) suggests an annual contribution from biofuels rising from its present 250 PJ to 700 PJ by the year 2000, with forest fuels accounting for some 50% of this total.

Recent estimates (Hall, 1992) suggest a long-term potential in Europe of more than 10 000 PJ a year from energy crops on up to 5% of the total land area (50 Mha) – effectively twice the land area of the UK, producing the equivalent of the total present UK primary energy consumption.

In Britain itself the area currently considered suitable for short rotation coppice is perhaps 1–2 Mha, yielding over 200 PJ a year. In the longer term, estimates for the early decades of the next century lie in the range 2.8–5.5 Mha, with a yield between 250 and 700 PJ a year (REAG, 1992). Coppice is considered the most promising energy crop for the UK, and trials have received government support for several years. Planters, harvesters and chippers have been developed, and the potential for gasification as an alternative to conventional combustion is currently being studied (see also Section 4.11).

ETHANOL FROM SUGAR CANE

Ethanol from sugar cane or maize is perhaps the best-known of all energy crops, with many examples of its use around the world. In Brazil, over 100 billion litres have been produced since the inception of the 'Proalcool' programme in 1975, based on the existing sugar industry. Enormous savings have been made in fossil fuel imports and thus in Brazil's foreign debt. More than four million Brazilian vehicles run on pure ethanol, and the remaining 9 million use a 20% blend in gasoline. Many of the technical problems of such large-scale production (12 billion litres a year) have been overcome, but disputes over quotas and contract prices between the growers and distillers, the government and the national oil company have limited the growth of ethanol production in recent years.

On a smaller scale, Zimbabwe has a highly successful programme (40 million litres a year) based on a single integrated sugar estate which makes sugar, ethanol, carbon dioxide, cattle feed and electricity for sale, and recycles all its stillage (the effluent left over after distillation in the ethanol plant) as a fertiliser substitute on the cane fields. Similar small ethanol plants exist in Kenya and Malawi.

The decline of the sugar industry in the Caribbean region and elsewhere may be halted by the introduction of new high-biomass varieties of sugar cane, which is already one of the most productive plant species known. These would be used in conjunction with the full utilisation of the fibrous cane residues known as bagasse, generating an income from production of electricity and heat as well as sugar. Compared with typical sugar cane annual yields of 30–40 dry tonnes per hectare, 'energy cane' may produce 60–70 t ha^{-1} y^{-1}, much of this in the form of increased fibre content. Although actual sugar yield may be reduced and the wear on crushing machinery increased, these factors would be more than offset by the additional energy available in the form of bagasse residues. It is conceivable that it may even be worth burning the cane directly without extracting the sugar!

MAIZE, SORGHUM AND MISCANTHUS

Bio-ethanol production in the USA has developed around conversion of surplus **maize** into alcohol for blending into gasoline, at up to 10% by volume. In 1990, 3.4 billion litres were produced by distillation plants located in 22 states, and capacity is growing, assisted by state and federal subsidies. Although no bio-ethanol is presently produced in Britain, a recent study for the former Department of Energy, now DTI (Marrow, 1987) concluded that 5% of UK petroleum consumption (about 40 PJ) could be supplied without significantly affecting agricultural markets. An EU directive already allows up to 7% ethanol in gasoline throughout Europe, and tax incentives for liquid biofuels have been proposed.

Sweet-stemmed varieties of the grass-like grain crop, **sorghum**, are already grown in the USA and Brazil. The sugar is fermented to ethanol for

Figure 4.24 Miscanthus and sweet sorghum plantations in the EU (Top) Miscathus; (Bottom) Sweet sorghum

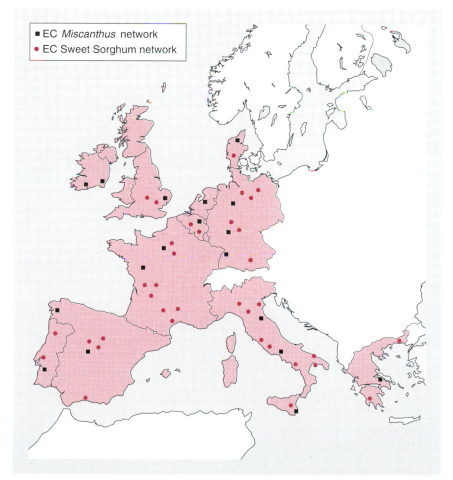

■ EC *Miscanthus* network
● EC Sweet Sorghum network

use as a fuel, using the same equipment as for sugar cane. The timing of harvest is critical, with a period of only a few weeks when the stems have maximum sugar content. However, two crops per year are possible, and sorghum has a much lower water requirement than sugar cane. There is considerable genetic potential to further increase yields, and plant breeders in Europe are presently developing hybrids which grow better at lower temperatures.

Miscanthus is a temperate climate grass adapted to moist soils, which has some of the photosynthetic characteristics of sugar cane. It may be capable of high yields (30 t ha^{-1} y^{-1}) under European conditions, especially if sewage sludge or other wastes are used as a fertiliser. The thick woody stems are suitable for direct combustion since they have a very low water content (20–30%) when harvested.

VEGETABLE OILS

Seeds of many plants can be crushed 'on the farm' to yield a range of vegetable oils, most of which are compounds of hydrocarbon-like fatty acids and glycerol. Vegetable oils have an energy content of about 37–39 GJ t^{-1}, similar to that of diesel (about 42 GJ t^{-1}) and superior in this respect to ethanol (30 GJ t^{-1}). Many vegetable oils can be burned directly in diesel engines, either pure or blended with diesel fuel. However, blends containing a high proportion of vegetable oil tend to clog the diesel injectors and form deposits in other parts of the engine. Simple chemical processing of vegetable oil, by 'esterifying', i.e. combining it with ethanol or methanol, leads to a superior diesel substitute which does not foul engines. Where rape-seed oil is used, the resulting product is called rape methyl ester, or RME.

Blends of up to 30% vegetable oil with diesel are the main applications at present. Coconut oil is used in tractors and lorries in the Philippines; palm and castor oil in Brazil; and sunflower oil in South Africa, where the annual sunflower crop from one field can produce enough oil to fuel a tractor working ten fields the same size. Current yields and processing costs limit the application of vegetable oil to places where diesel fuel is costly and in short supply – the food and cosmetics markets can usually pay a better price.

In Europe, the potential of RME from rape grown on set-aside land has generated interest, and since 1993 EU member states have been able to grant tax reductions to such vehicle biofuels developed in pilot projects. The French government in particular has implemented this, with four RME pilot plants operating and plans for a full-scale plant to process 100 000 tonnes a year (Armitage, 1994). The UK government has not adopted the tax incentive, but 1994 saw the launch of a bio-diesel consortium, producing initially 18 000 litres of RME for tests on road and agricultural vehicles.

4.9 ENVIRONMENTAL BENEFITS AND IMPACTS

The environmental impact of a sustained biomass energy programme deserves careful consideration. Although the combustion of wastes generally pays environmental dividends by solving a disposal problem, the consequences of a move towards large-scale production of energy crops may be less benign, unless care is taken in the production and use of the biomass.

CARBON DIOXIDE

Some of the proposals for reducing the impact of global warming have centred on the need to fix or sequester atmospheric CO_2 by tree planting on a very large scale. Whilst there is little doubt that the halting of deforestation and the replanting of large areas of trees would bring many environmental benefits, the adoption of a wider biomass energy strategy may be a more cost-effective way of regulating the CO_2 balance of the atmosphere.

Absorption of carbon dioxide by a new forest plantation is a once-and-for-all measure which will 'buy time' by fixing atmospheric CO_2 while the trees mature, say for 40–60 years, but the substitution of biomass fuels for fossil fuels offers a more lasting solution, since the growing and combustion of biofuels on a sustainable basis is CO_2-neutral. The cost and the potential for reducing CO_2 emissions in this way depends on the efficiency of energy conversion in the growing and the combustion of the biomass, and on the type of fossil fuel which is replaced. Coal is a potential candidate for replacement, since it produces the most carbon dioxide per unit of energy delivered (Table 4.1) and because many of the advanced 'clean coal' technologies (fluidised bed combustion, exhaust gas clean-up, etc.) can be readily adapted for biomass.

OTHER COMBUSTION PRODUCTS

Carbon dioxide and water are never the sole products of the use of fuels. It has been argued, for instance, that although bio-diesel generates 65% less CO_2 than the equivalent fossil fuel, its advantage falls to 35% when other greenhouse gases such as nitrogen oxides and methane are taken into account (Meyer, 1993; Patel, 1993). In general, by-products result from the high temperatures of combustion, and most fuels also contain some incombustible material (ash) which must be removed from the furnace or combustion chamber. For many fuels, careful attention to plant design, construction and operation is required to ensure that complete combustion is achieved and prevent the emission of poisonous products of incomplete combustion. This is particularly important for domestic and industrial wastes. Whilst a simple wood fire can be very smoky, advanced stove design drastically reduces the emission of pollutants such as particulates and poly-aromatic hydrocarbons (PAHs). Furthermore, biofuels are inherently cleaner than coal, with virtually zero sulphur content. Their more uniform energy content and greater reactivity makes it easier to optimise the design of combustion systems, and means there is no need for 'scrubbing' equipment to remove sulphur dioxide.

Biofuels are therefore 'clean' with respect to greenhouse gas emissions (carbon dioxide) and acid gas emissions (sulphur dioxide). Another constituent of acid rain, nitrogen oxides (NO_x), can be produced by the burning of any fuel, particularly where the drive for fuel efficiency has led to higher combustion temperatures. Their level can, however, be greatly reduced using modified combustion systems and/or catalysts to clean up exhaust gases. Significant advances have been made in the USA, where equipment ranging from wood-burning stoves to electricity generating plant is now available with catalytic converters fitted to the chimneys.

All types of combustion plant in Britain are now subject to both UK and EU regulations governing emissions of particulate matter and gases. 'Schedule A' combustion plant (including municipal and commercial waste incinerators) are overseen by Her Majesty's Inspectorate of Pollution (HMIP) and must meet standards on pollution of land and water, as well as the air. Less complex 'Schedule B' combustion processes are subject to local authority control of air pollution only. Where EU Directives are in force, these form the basis for minimum standards; otherwise HMIP determines the stringency of the regulations. Suggested ways of meeting pollution standards are drafted by HMIP, and set out as BATNEEC (Best Available Technology Not Entailing Excessive Costs) guidelines.

METHANE

As well as avoiding accidental explosions due to horizontal migration of methane from existing landfill sites into buildings, extracting and burning the landfill gas provides an added environmental benefit by converting a potent 'greenhouse gas' (methane) to a much less harmful one (carbon dioxide). A molecule of CH_4 is nearly 30 times as effective as a molecule of CO_2 in trapping the earth's radiated heat. It has been estimated that using the landfill gas in the UK instead of letting it leak away is equivalent to reducing the carbon dioxide reaching the atmosphere by between 38 and 55 million tonnes a year – 10% of present UK carbon dioxide emissions.

LAND USE

Proposals to use surplus agricultural land for energy crops, particularly oil-seed rape and short rotation coppice, have led to expressions of concern about the effect on the agricultural landscape of Europe. These centre on the visual impact, the possible reduction in biological diversity and the potential increase in intensive farming with high inputs of fertilisers and pesticides.

In response, the proponents of biomass energy point out that many of these problems have been anticipated. Guidelines for woodland energy cropping already consider the possibility of adjacent plots of different tree species interspersed with indigenous vegetation, to avoid outbreaks of

Figure 4.25 Coppiced woodland in Cumbria

disease. Short-rotation coppicing, involving disturbance only every few years, may actually result in the creation of useful refuges for displaced woodland and hedgerow species. Experiments have shown that diversity of both bird life and invertebrates is greater under arable coppice than with annual row-crop agriculture, and inclusion of small areas of undisturbed forest can further improve biological diversity.

Whilst some fertilisers and pesticides are necessary to achieve economic yields, it is suggested that coppice could in fact improve groundwater quality, the extensive root system acting as a biofilter. A possibility attracting interest is the use of coppice for land treatment of sewage sludge. The sludge would provide a slow-release fertiliser, and its water content would reduce the demand for irrigation. In Denmark, it is estimated that 30 000 ha of willow coppice could treat all the sewage produced by a population of over five million.

Nevertheless, research is continuing on the impact of energy cropping, especially with regard to minimising the use of resources such as chemical fertilisers, pesticides and water. In estimating the **acceptable resource** (see the Appendix), countries need to take into account both commercial and environmental criteria. In England and Wales, planning authorities are guided by Policy Planning Guidance Notes, which set out formal advice on the need to balance the benefits of renewable energy schemes and the benefits of maintaining the countryside in its present form.

ENERGY BALANCES

In the recent past, some biomass projects have been criticised because they require the input of a great deal of energy in the form of fertilisers, harvesting and processing. In the worst cases, such as the conversion of surplus US maize to ethanol fuel, it has even been shown that the **energy balance**, the ratio of outputs to inputs, is close to unity (i.e. there is no net energy gain) if the energy of the ethanol is counted as the only output.

However, the calculation of energy balances must take into account all the relevant factors. It is of course important to consider the energy content of inputs such as fuel for agricultural vehicles and the use of energy-rich nitrogen fertilisers, as well as non-biomass fuels used for processing; but outputs must also be counted carefully. For example, the fermentation of starch crops to ethanol yields useful by-products such as pure CO_2 (used for instance in the manufacture of soft drinks) and Distillers' Dried Grains (a cattle feed) which have both market and energy values.

Care must be taken to consider whether the system is actually optimised for biomass energy production. For example, many waste-to-energy schemes are designed initially to get rid of the waste, with little consideration given to the net energy yield. Energy balance analysis can be useful in this respect, highlighting areas where energy inputs need to be reduced. A recent appraisal of ethanol production from sugar cane in Zimbabwe found a favourable energy balance of 1.9:1, but recommended improvements which could more than double this, by increasing the use of bagasse and thereby reducing the need for coal to provide process heat outside the cane harvesting season (see Figure 4.16). Where only bagasse is used to provide the energy for ethanol production from sugar cane, Brazilian studies have shown that the energy balance for the entire process cycle can exceed 6:1, thus providing considerable net energy gain (Goldemberg, 1992).

An optimised biomass energy system will therefore tend to be low-input, minimising the use of energy-rich or fossil fuel-derived resources such as fertiliser or tractor fuel, and maximising recycling and energy recovery throughout the process. Recent estimates of the energy balances for energy crops have produced encouragingly high values. Analysis based on present

US yields suggests 10:1 for herbaceous crops and 15:1 for woody crops. In the UK, for chipped coppice wood delivered up to 25 miles, the figure reaches 20:1 (Foster, 1993). Further increases could result from improved crop yields and the use of less energy-intensive fertilisers such as sewage sludge.

The energy balance of a biomass energy system is also a reflection of its environmental impact. The greater the outputs, the greater the amount of fossil fuels and pollution which are displaced. The lower the inputs, the lower the extra demands put upon the environment by the biomass system. In the past, fears were expressed that any large-scale biomass energy programme would consume so many extra inputs that the undesirable environmental consequences would outweigh the benefits. Sufficient experience has now been gained world-wide to demonstrate that this is rarely the case, especially if the inputs and outputs have been properly estimated and optimised.

4.10 ECONOMICS

INSTITUTIONAL FACTORS

The institutional environment plays an important role in the development of any new technology. The tax regime, grants for research and development, agricultural subsidies, etc. can make the difference between success and failure for an innovative proposal. Before looking at individual systems, therefore, we start with a brief account of a few of these factors.

One of the most important is the extent to which the 'greenhouse-neutral' nature of biofuels is quantified in economic terms. The issue of a carbon tax has been the subject of much debate. An EU proposal would introduce a tax on combustion of fossil fuels rising to US$10 a barrel within a decade provided the USA and Japan adopt similar policies.

The Non-Fossil Fuel Obligation (NFFO) was introduced under the 1989 Electricity Act which paved the way for privatising the electricity industry in England and Wales. The aim was to promote methods of generation which do not increase atmospheric CO_2 and to encourage diversity of energy supply, by offering premium prices for power from nuclear and renewable

Table 4.6 Electricity generation from biomass under the Non-Fossil Fuel Obligation: contracts awarded and Declared Net Capacities (DNC)

Category	1990		1991		1994	
	Number of contracts	DNC (MW)	Number of contracts	DNC (MW)	Number of contracts	DNC (MW)
Landfill gas	24	35.5	28	48	42	82
Biogas	9	6.6	19	27	–	–
Municipal and industrial wastes	5	64	11	260	20	242
Agricultural and forestry wastes	2	28	3	30	6	104
Biomass gasification	–	–	–	–	3	19
Biofuels as a percentage of the NFFO totals	53%	84%	50%	79%	50%	71%

energy sources. As Table 4.6 shows, the first renewables contracts were dominated by biofuels projects.

Agricultural surpluses have led to the introduction of payments for 'non-agricultural use' of land. In the EU, energy coppice and rape grown for fuel fall into this category. Under the EU set-aside scheme, coppice in the UK qualifies for annual payments of £130–150 per hectare.

Also in the UK, the Forestry Commission has for many years provided grants to encourage the planting of woodlands. Since 1992, energy coppice has been eligible and can attract planting grants of £1000–2000 per hectare, off-setting much of the establishment cost.

Another factor, probably unique to biofuels, enters where the energy source is a waste product. Disposing of such material by other means would usually involve both capital and running costs, which are likely to increase with stricter environmental legislation. Disposal fees can thus be charged and these can be offset against the costs of the biofuel installation.

BIOGAS

Although the technical feasibility of anaerobic digestion is not in doubt, its economic viability in terms of energy production alone has often been questioned. The disincentive of relatively high capital cost has tended to limit development in Britain to dealing with sewage rather than farm wastes. Most of the business is at present with water companies which have to dispose of sewage sludge, and many are now in receipt of NFFO contracts (Table 4.6). A recent report (REAG, 1992) estimated the accessible resource for electric power from farm wastes to be three times that from sewage (2.4 TWh y^{-1} at less than 10p kWh^{-1} and 8% discount rate), and pointed out that no more than one-thousandth of this resource is currently developed.

Environmental considerations such as planning permission for new industrial or agricultural activities are important, but so are rising waste disposal costs. Constraints on the disposal of farm slurry, capital grants for improved waste disposal facilities and the likely ban on dumping of sewage sludge at sea should all contribute to reduced payback times. In the UK, the payback time on a digester in a small abattoir can be reduced from 5–6 years to as little as 18 months by taking into account fees for waste disposal.

Elsewhere in Europe there is a growing market for digesters. In Denmark, a government programme investigating the economics of anaerobic digestion has concluded after six years of trials that a large-scale biogas plant running on farm wastes, together with some industrial organic wastes, will be profitable if built with present-day technology. Three realistic conditions must be fulfilled, namely that:
- the gas is sold at a price comparable to that of natural gas;
- credit is given for the disposal of industrial organic wastes;
- the biogas plant is operated in combined heat and power mode.

A contrasting example of biogas economics is the case of Pura village in Karnataka, South India (Rajabapaiah, 1992). Here, a community biogas plant provides methane to a dual-fuel diesel engine to generate 5 kW of electricity for lighting and water pumping. Over four years, the cost of electricity worked out at about US$0.25 kWh^{-1} (about 17p kWh^{-1}), relatively expensive compared with grid-connected electricity. However, closer analysis showed that an increased supply of animal manure could raise the 'load factor' from 4 hours a day to 15 hours a day, halving the cost per unit. Furthermore, the system is more reliable than the rural electricity grid and nearly half its costs are incurred locally, bringing further benefits to the community.

WOODY ENERGY CROPS

Some of the best information on the cost of woody biomass comes from Brazil, where biomass plantations are well established commercially. Recent commercial estimates (Carpentieri, 1992) for woody energy crops planted on degraded land in north-east Brazil, where biomass production is far from optimal due to shortage of water, showed that biomass could be produced for US$1.40 GJ^{-1} (£0.90 GJ^{-1}). This low cost is a reflection of extensive experience and low labour costs, and compares very favourably with international prices of fossil fuel energy (Table 4.7). In the USA, the cost for plantation biomass has been estimated at $2.7–3.9 GJ^{-1}, although this is expected to fall to $1.9–2.7 GJ^{-1} by the year 2010.

In terms of its potential 20-year life-cycle, short rotation coppice is still a novel and rather experimental crop in the UK. Changes in the grant regime are even more recent, adding to the difficulty of assessing its economic viability. Carter (1991) suggests that with currently available grants, a 10-hectare coppice should become profitable after the second cycle of cutting, assuming a yield of 12 tonnes per hectare and a selling price of £38 per dry tonne of wood (about £2.40 GJ^{-1}).

FORESTRY WASTES

In Austria, forestry wastes such as bark and wood chips are available at very low prices (£3.50 per cubic metre air-dry, or about £0.70 GJ^{-1}), due to industry surpluses which until recently were even dumped in landfills. To stimulate the biomass market by reducing payback times, capital subsidies on wood-burning equipment for local and district heating plant are available from the federal and state governments, ranging from 10–50% of the purchase price, although only farmers' groups are eligible for the higher level of support.

ELECTRICITY FROM BIOMASS

The extent to which biomass penetrates the electricity generation market must depend on the extent to which high conversion efficiencies can be achieved with present or future conversion technology.

In the USA, a combination of low feedstock prices and enabling legislation forcing electricity utility companies to buy power from independent generators at 'avoided cost' has resulted in 9 GW of biomass-electricity

Figure 4.26 An on-site wood chipper for harvesting arable coppice

---

BOX 4.10: FUEL PRICES

Estimates of the cost of energy from biofuels are often expressed as pounds or dollars per gigajoule (£ GJ^{-1} or $ GJ^{-1}), but the prices of coal, oil and gas are normally quoted in terms of the quantities in which they are traded: tonnes, barrels, cubic metres, etc. Table 4.7 is designed to facilitate comparison. (It may be worth noting in this context that the UK householder pays about £21 GJ^{-1} for electricity and the urban householder in Africa as much as £6 GJ^{-1} for charcoal.)

Table 4.7 Fuel prices (£(1994))

Fuel	World market prices	
	In traded units[a]	Per GJ[b]
Coal	$50 per tonne	£1.20 GJ^{-1}
Oil	$15–20 per barrel (bbl)	£2.00 GJ^{-1}
Natural gas	$70 per 1000 m^3	£1.20 GJ^{-1}

	UK prices per GJ	
	Bulk buyers	Domestic users[c]
Coal	£2.30 GJ^{-1}	£8.00 GJ^{-1}
Oil	£1.50–3.50 GJ^{-1}[d]	£14.00 GJ^{-1}
Natural gas	£3.00 GJ^{-1}	£4.50 GJ^{-1}

(a) Approximate world prices at the time of writing.

(b) The terms 'coal' and 'oil' are not well defined, and even natural gas varies in composition. The figures in Columns 3–5 are based on average values of energy content: 28 GJ t^{-1} for coal, 5.6 GJ bbl^{-1} (42 GJ t^{-1}) for oil and 38 MJ m^{-3} for gas, with the currency conversion £1 = $1.5.

(c) Approximate prices at the time of writing for solid fuel and domestic gas to the householder and for unleaded petrol at the pump.

(d) The price range reflects different products, from heavy fuel oil to gasoline.

---

capacity, much of it in the form of conventional steam turbine plant of around 25 MW.

In the UK, the electricity prices contracted in the first (1991) NFFO round were 5.7p kWh^{-1} for landfill gas and 6.55p kWh^{-1} for MSW, but had fallen to 3.76p kWh^{-1} and 3.84p kWh^{-1} respectively in the 1994 round. The reduction is no doubt due in large part to the effect of extending the contract deadline from 1998 to 2014, but it also reflects a developed technology. In contrast, the average 1994 contract price for electricity produced by gas turbines running on the output from wood gasifiers was a relatively high 8.65p kWh^{-1}.

POWER FROM SURPLUS STRAW

The seven million tonnes of straw surpluses arising each year in the UK represent a potential source of some 10 TWh of electric power, equivalent to the output of a large coal-fired or nuclear power station. Until now, straw-fired generating plant has not been commercially attractive, with development of this resource limited to relatively small-scale local heating systems using some 3% of the total supply. Two factors inhibiting investment have been the low energy density of straw bales, leading to high transport, storage and plant costs, and the low conversion efficiency to electric power – only 10–20% using conventional steam plant. However, improved technology could change the situation, and one possibility is discussed in Section 4.11.

ETHANOL PRODUCTION IN BRAZIL

There is still considerable disagreement about the economics of ethanol production in Brazil. Production costs depend on the location and management of the facility, and whether it is a part of a dedicated sugarcane-ethanol plantation or simply added on to a plantation primarily engaged in sugar production. The economic value of the ethanol depends on its own market niche (anhydrous ethanol as a gasoline extender, or hydrated ethanol as a 100% gasoline substitute) as well as the world market price for crude oil.

The cost of ethanol produced in Sao Paulo State in 1990 has been estimated at US$0.185 litre^{-1} (US$7.90 GJ^{-1}), with prospects of falling further to US$0.15 litre^{-1} by the year 2000. Indeed, the production cost of ethanol has been falling by 4% per year over the past decade, due to increased cane yields and improved conversion efficiency. Full use of bagasse residues could further offset costs, making ethanol cost-competitive with gasoline, even at the low price of the early 1990s. Other price adjustments, taking into account ethanol's high octane value (which offsets oil refining costs), distortions in official currency exchange rates and the long-term benefits of price stability, further enhance the economics of ethanol production.

Nevertheless, continuing depressed oil prices and the growth in Brazilian domestic oil production, coupled with the failure of growers, distillers and government to agree on a fair price for ethanol, threaten the future expansion of large-scale liquid fuel production in Brazil, if not the entire industry.

Figure 4.27 Straw as fuel for industry. Transported from the fields in large rectangular bales to feed the fully automatic system, 2000 tonnes of straw a year are consumed by this straw-burning plant at Needham Chalks Ltd in Suffolk. It can provide up to 2.5 GJ an hour (700 kW) of process heat, carried to the chalk-drying chamber in the flue gases at a temperature of 1000°C

4.11 NEW TECHNOLOGIES

Over the next 10 years, technologies currently under development are likely to provide new ways of using biomass as a clean fuel with high conversion efficiency.

POWER FROM GAS TURBINES

Advances in gas turbine technology, driven by the aircraft industry, and the development of reliable gasification systems for clean coal combustion, have opened up a pathway for highly efficient and flexible biomass-to-electricity systems of around 20–100 MW capacity. Such systems are based on the biomass integrated gasifier/steam-injected gas turbine (BIG/STIG) technology mentioned in Box 4.7.

Steam-injected gas turbines (STIGs) were introduced in the USA in the 1980s, originally fired by natural gas, but then adapted for the gas from coal gasification. A further advanced form of this technology, **intercooled STIGs** (ISTIGs), can achieve the high efficiencies of STIGs at lower unit costs. Combining a biomass gasifier with a gas turbine to generate power is attractive for a number of reasons. The high reactivity and very low sulphur content of most biomass residues such as sugar cane bagasse, sawmill wastes or wheat straw make them an ideal gasifier fuel. Gas turbine plant of appropriate size for locally available supplies such as plant residues can use a modified aero-engine which is virtually a standard product, with well-established maintenance and replacement facilities. Since much of the technology is already available 'off the shelf', a number of pilot projects have been initiated or planned to demonstrate high-efficiency conversion of agricultural and forestry residues into electricity.

Although specially grown biomass energy crops may be used, the main applications of these technologies are likely to be for cogeneration of electricity and process heat in agricultural and forestry processing industries, where biomass residues are readily available as fuel. For example, conventional sugar mills presently generate around 15–25 kWh of electricity per tonne of cane crushed, mostly for use within the plant. Optimising the use of bagasse for electricity generation with ordinary steam turbines can yield up to 100 kWh per tonne of cane, but adoption of BIG/STIG or BIG/ISTIG technology could boost this to 240 or 280 kWh a tonne. This would enable the sugar industry in many developing countries to diversify significantly into electricity generation.

A study conducted by Shell UK in 1989 examined the feasibility of a 37 MW combined-cycle gas turbine system based on conventional combined-cycle gas turbine technology (Rolls-Royce RB211) and an air-blown Ahlstrom gasifier. The plant should achieve 42% overall conversion efficiency and produce electricity for 3–4p kWh^{-1}, assuming a delivered price for bulk straw of £20–25 a tonne and a plant capital cost of about £900 kW^{-1} installed capacity. Series production could reduce the capital cost to around £700 kW^{-1}, with corresponding reduction in the price of electricity, and the study envisages the establishment of up to 20 such plants in eastern England (Elliott, 1990). Similar power plants running on forestry wastes or specially-grown fuelwood are under construction or planned in Sweden and north-east Brazil (Williams, 1992) and, as we have seen (Table 4.6), three plants are now contracted under the UK's NFFO scheme.

BIOMASS FUEL CELLS

Combustion of biomass fuels has two drawbacks which are shared with all other combustion processes. Firstly, since air contains 78% nitrogen, burning of any fuel leads to the production of nitrogen oxides (NO_x), which contribute to both photochemical smog and the greenhouse effect. Secondly, inevitable physical limitations on the conversion of chemical energy to heat and then electricity mean that at least half the energy is lost in the process. Both of these disadvantages could be overcome if the biomass fuel were converted to electricity via a fuel cell (see Chapter 10). In the transport sector, lightweight fuel cells are under development by General Motors and other manufacturers, to meet Californian requirements for 'zero-emission' vehicles. Such cars would run on hydrogen fuel produced by electrolysis of water at remote power stations, or alternatively methanol which might be produced from biomass.

Gas from biomass might also be used in the future as a source of 'reducing power' within integrated systems for hydrogen production; powdered iron and water would be used to generate hydrogen fuel where and when required, and biomass fuels would be used to convert the spent iron oxide back into iron in a regeneration plant. Fuel cell vehicles could thus provide a clean, high-efficiency transport option, using biomass as the energy source and hydrogen as an energy carrier. It is arguable that, taking into account the higher efficiency of fuel cells (compared with internal combustion engines), hydrogen-powered cars could be economically viable against conventional gasoline-engined vehicles.

PHOTOBIOLOGICAL FUEL PRODUCTION

Fuels such as hydrogen and energy-rich compounds such as ammonia can be produced by so-called **photobiological** and **photo(electro)chemical** systems, which aim to convert solar energy into fuels and chemicals with a higher efficiency than natural photosynthesis. These highly specialised technologies involve both natural and artificial light-absorbing components, and could have great potential if they could tap even a small proportion of the huge solar energy flow.

Photobiological systems involve living organisms (higher plants, algae and cyanobacteria) or cell components such as chloroplasts, membrane particles and enzymes. In contrast, photochemical systems absorb light energy by non-living organic or inorganic molecules (pigments, semiconductors, etc.) in solution or suspension. Photoelectrochemistry is a kind of intermediate between these two – it involves similar charge separation and electron emission reactions, but uses an absorber or sensitiser material with the reactions taking place on surfaces (see Chapter 3, Section 3.7). The eventual aim is to mimic the processes of photosynthesis without the requirement for good land, water and fertilisers.

Outdoor 'photobioreactors' have been developed for both photosynthetic bacteria and cyanobacteria (blue-green algae). Apart from the commercial production of food and fine chemicals extracted from algae and cyanobacteria, most of these technologies are laboratory-scale only, with a few pilot plants in operation. Ultimately, such systems might be optimised for commercial production of hydrogen or fixation of carbon dioxide from the atmosphere, or for the clean-up of agricultural and food processing wastes. However, for commercial viability, long-lived, reliable systems will be required, together with dramatic reductions in the cost per unit area.

4.12 FUTURE PROSPECTS

THE WORLD VIEW

We have seen in Section 4.4 that, according to one scenario (Johansson, 1992), the biomass contribution to world energy by the middle of the next century could be about 200 EJ a year. This figure could be reached by:

- the use of some 400 million hectares of land (about 2.5% of the total land area) for energy crops;

- the recovery of energy from between a quarter and three-quarters of residues;

- high efficiencies of energy conversion resulting from improved combustion methods and advanced techniques for power generation from biomass.

A country-by-country analysis (Hall, 1992), carried out for the 1992 Earth Summit Conference, demonstrates that world-wide there is a total of about 2000 Mha (million hectares) of unused potential agricultural land which could be used for both food and biomass energy production. Based on UN FAO (Food and Agricultural Organisation) definitions of potential agricultural land, this study shows that Latin America could quadruple, Africa could treble, and Asia could double its existing agricultural land area. Estimates of land area with potential for biomass production from other studies include 750–800 Mha of degraded land which was once forested but has not been settled, and 1000 Mha of land affected by salt, of which 120 Mha could be used for salt-tolerant biomass crops.

World-wide, the amount of degraded land suitable for reforestation is huge – some 156 Mha in Latin America and 101 Mha in Africa. If biomass plantations with a productivity of 300 GJ ha^{-1} y^{-1} could be established on these lands, annual biomass energy production of 47 EJ and 31 EJ for Latin America and Africa respectively could make these regions into major exporters of modern biomass-based fuels within the next 30 years. In the longer term, if plantations with this productivity were established on 10% of forests, woodlands, cropland and pasture-land world-wide (890 Mha), the annual energy contribution from this source alone would amount to 270 EJ – about 80% of present world commercial energy use.

REGIONAL VIEWS

In the developing countries, demand for biomass energy seems unlikely to decrease in the near future. By the middle of the next century, some 90% of the world's population will reside in the developing countries, compared with 75% today, and if biomass remains the fuel of development, it is evidently important that it be provided in a sustainable manner. Modernisation of biomass energy supply, with improved efficiency in harvesting and energy conversion, could provide one pathway for improved energy services in the developing countries.

The issue of 'fuel versus food' – hotly debated in the past – is a complex subject somewhat outside the scope of this account. It is clear that conflicts can occur where there is demand for land for both food supply and energy supply, and there is significant scope for encouraging agricultural practice which optimises the use of land to meet both needs.

A detailed study of food and fuel ethanol production in Brazil (Rosillo-Calle, 1987) suggested that the 'food versus fuel' issue had been exaggerated, whilst the clash of interests between domestic crop production and commodity export production had been overlooked. Bio-ethanol was seen to have forced the pace of agricultural modernisation in Brazil in some areas, but the influence of sugar cane expansion on traditional staple crops had been overshadowed by the production of export crops such as soya bean.

In the industrialised countries, direct combustion of residues and wastes for electricity generation, substitution of liquid fuels by bio-ethanol and bio-diesel, and combined heat and power production from energy crops are considered the most likely major contributors to biomass energy supply in the near future. The present uptake of biomass energy in the EU is only some 330 PJ, but a trebling of this figure is thought to be attainable by the year 2000 by the conversion of surplus farm land to energy crops. The likely future total and the mix of biofuels (solid, liquid or gaseous fuel, heat or electric power) are difficult to predict, even on a regional basis, since they will depend on factors such as the nature and extent of market stimulation for individual technologies.

At present biomass contributes less than 1% of Britain's primary energy supply. The resource estimates quoted in Section 4.4 imply a gross annual input in the early years of the next century of 150–300 PJ from wastes and up to 600 PJ from energy crops. In the most favourable case, biomass would then be contributing some 8% of UK primary energy – but this assumes energy crops covering an area of some three million hectares – slightly more than all present woodlands.

REFERENCES

Armitage, R. (1994) 'Fuelling the argument', *Surveyor*, 26 May, p. 22.

Arnold, S. (1993), *The Observer*, 7 March.

Audubon (1991) *Toward Ecological Guidelines for Large-scale Biomass Energy Development*, National Audubon Society/Princeton University, New York.

Carpentieri, A. E., Larson, E. D. and Woods, J. (1993) 'Future biomass-based electricity supply in North-east Brazil', *Biomass and Bioenergy*, Vol. 14, pp. 149–173.

Elliott, P. and Booth, R. (1990) *Sustainable Biomass Energy*, Selected Paper PAC/233, Shell International Petroleum Co., London.

ETSU (1991) *Making Fuels from Wastes and Crops,* Department of Energy, Energy Technology Support Unit, Harwell, Oxfordshire.

ETSU (1994(1)) *New and Renewable Energy: Future Prospects in the UK*, Energy Paper 62, HMSO, London.

ETSU (1994(2)) *An Assessment of Renewable Energy for the UK*, Energy Paper R82, HMSO, London.

FOE (1991) *Energy without End*, Friends of the Earth, London.

Foster, C. (1993) personal communication.

Goldemberg, J., Monaco, L. C. and Macedo, I. C. (1992) 'The Brazilian fuel-alcohol program', in Johansson *et al., op. cit.*

Hall, D. O. (1991) 'Biomass energy', *Energy Policy*, Vol 19, No.8, October 1991, pp. 711–737.

Hall, D. O., Rosillo-Calle, F., Williams, R. H. and Woods, J. (1992) 'Biomass for energy: supply prospects', in Johansson *et al., op. cit.*

IEA (1994) *Bioenergy Newsletter*, Vol. 6, No. 1, pp. 2-7.

Johansson T. B., Kelly, H., Reddy, A. K. N. and Williams, R. H. (eds) (1992) *Renewable Energy: Sources for Fuels and Electricity*, Island Press, Washington DC.

Kristoferson, L.A. and Bokalders, V. (1991) *Renewable Energy Technologies – Their Applications in Developing Countries*, IT Publications, London.

Lockhart, J. (1991) 'Cost chop by chipper', *Farmers Weekly*, 27 September.

Lockhart, J. (1992) 'The estate option' in Richards, G.E. (ed), *Wood – Energy and the Environment*, Harwell Laboratories, Oxfordshire.

Manurung, R. and Beeuackers, A. A. C. M. (1990) 'Field test performance of open core downdraft rice husk gasifiers', Biomass for Energy and Industry, 5th EC Conference (Grassi, G. *et al.*, eds), pp. 2.512–2.523.

Marrow, J. E., Coombs, J. and Lees, E. W. (1987) 'An assessment of bio-ethanol as a transport fuel in the UK', ETSU R44, HMSO, London.

Meyer, C. (1993) 'Rough road ahead for biodiesel fuel', *New Scientist*, 6 February.

Network News (1991) July–August 1991, Biomass Users Network, San Jose, Costa Rica.

Patel, T. (1993) 'France placates farmers with plant fuel plan', *New Scientist*, 27 February.

Rajabapaiah, P., Jayakumar, S. and Reddy, A. K. N. (1992) 'Biogas electricity – The Pura village case study', in Johansson T.B. *et al.*, *op. cit.*

REAG (1992) *Renewable Energy Advisory Group: Report to the President of the Board of Trade*, Energy Paper Number 60, HMSO, London.

Rosillo-Calle, F. and Hall, D. O. (1987) 'Brazilian alcohol: food versus fuel?', *Biomass*, Vol. 12, pp. 97–128.

Scurlock, J. M. O. and Hall, D. O. (1990) 'The contribution of biomass to global energy use (1987)', *Biomass*, Vol. 21, pp. 75–81.

Scurlock, J. M. O., Rosenschein, A. D. and Hall, D. O. (1991) *Fuelling the Future: Power Alcohol in Zimbabwe*, ACTS Press, Nairobi/Biomass Users Network, Harare.

Williams, R. H. and Larson, E. D. (1992) 'Advanced gasification-based biomass power generation', in Johansson *et al.*, *op. cit.*

FURTHER READING

Hall, D. O. and Rao, K. K. (1987) *Photosynthesis* (4th edn), Edward Arnold, London.

This small and justly very popular textbook offers a clear account for anyone wishing to study the subject in more depth.

Johansson, T. B., Kelly, H., Reddy, A. K. N. and Williams, R. H. (eds) (1992) *Renewable Energy: Sources for Fuels and Electricity*, Island Press, Washington DC.

Prepared for the United Nations Conference on Environment and Development (UNCED) held in Rio de Janeiro in 1992, and with 300 of its 1000 pages devoted to biomass, this authoritative volume is an invaluable source. Its treatment of energy crops and agricultural residues world-wide is comprehensive, and virtually the only topic not covered in detail is energy from urban and industrial wastes.

Kristoferson, L. A. and Bokalders, V. (1991) *Renewable Energy Technologies – Their Applications in Developing Countries*, IT Publications, London.

An informed and down-to-earth account of biomass in general and biofuels for engines in particular. Contains a great deal of descriptive detail – and virtually no mathematics.

Laughton, M. A. (1990) *Renewable Energy Sources,* Watt Committee on Energy, Report No. 22, Elsevier, London.

Includes a clear and comprehensive summary of the status and potential of biofuels in the UK at the time of publication.

Patterson, W. (1995) *Power from Plants*, Earthscan.

Readable and well-informed account of recent developments in electricity generation from biomass.

Renewable Energy Advisory Group (1992) *Report to the President of the Board of Trade*, Energy Paper No. 60, HMSO, London.

Department of Trade and Industry (1994) *New and Renewable Energy: Future Prospects in the UK*, Energy Paper 62, HMSO, 114pp.

Energy Technology Support Unit (1994) *An Assessment of Renewable Energy for the UK*, HMSO, 308pp.

These three reports reflect official thinking on the state of renewables in the UK, including projections of the potential contributions to UK electricity supplies from wastes and crops in the early years of the next century.

Richards, G. E. (ed.) (1992) *Proceedings of Wood: Fuel for Thought Conference*, Harwell Laboratories, Oxfordshire.

The papers presented at this first UK wood fuel conference give a useful overview of current concerns, both technical and economic. The discussions following the papers are particularly illuminating.

HYDROELECTRICITY

5.1 SUMMARY

Like most other renewables, water power is indirect solar power. Unlike most of the others, however, it is already a major contributor to world energy supplies. Hydro-electricity is a well-established technology, which has been producing firm power at competitive prices for about a century. It is the principal source of electric power in some 30 countries, and provides about a fifth of the world's annual electrical output. Its power stations include some of the largest artificial structures in the world.

Present-day hydroelectric plant is the end-product of 2000 years of technological advance, from the creaking wooden wheel, converting a few per cent of the water power into useful mechanical output, to the modern turbo-generator spinning at 1500 revolutions per minute (rpm) and producing electric power at efficiencies which can reach 90%.

After a short introductory case study, our treatment of hydro power starts with a discussion of the nature of the resource and an account of its present contribution to world energy supplies. This is followed by a brief history of the development of water power, tracing the changing design of water-wheels and the evolution of the turbines which succeeded them. Modern turbines and the installations in which they operate are the subject of Sections 5.5–5.9, where we consider each of the main types in some detail and discuss the criteria determining their use.

The remaining sections are concerned with the problems and potentialities of hydroelectricity for the future. In discussing the potential for *small-scale* developments, we find the familiar questions relating to cost, firmness of supply and integration which arise for all the renewable sources. But for large-scale hydro systems the questions are rather different: whether there are limits to growth, what determines these limits, and whether we are already reaching them.

We start, however, with a case study: an account of a Scottish hydroelectric scheme, commissioned nearly 60 years ago and still operating with much of its original plant. The story of the initial financing and subsequent performance of this medium-scale scheme exemplifies rather well both the economic problems and the financial benefits of hydroelectricity.

5.2 CASE STUDY: THE GALLOWAY HYDROS

The Galloway Hydroelectric Scheme on the River Dee in south-west Scotland makes an interesting study for several reasons. Its six power stations are controlled as one integrated system. Initially commissioned in 1935, it was the first major UK scheme designed specifically to provide the extra power needed at times of peak demand. Several of its dams are across major salmon-fishing rivers, raising environmental issues common to many hydro schemes. And it is technically interesting because significant differences in flow conditions at the power stations mean that the system includes several types of turbo-generator.

Origins

The Galloway Hydros owe their origin to local pride and individual enthusiasm – and to an Act of Parliament. Although the first proposals to use the rivers and lochs of south-west Scotland for hydro power appeared in the 1890s, a combination of financial, political and geographical factors held up development for several decades. Then in the 1920s the government decided to co-ordinate the production of electric power on a nation-wide basis. This had two important consequences for Galloway: the establishment of a national grid meant that the great industrial conurbation of Glasgow became a potential customer, and the need for plant with fast and flexible response to meet daily and seasonal peaks in demand favoured the inclusion of some hydroelectric power in the otherwise coal-dominated national system.

The scheme

The system (Figure 5.1) has three main elements. The first is Loch Doon, which provides the main long-term seasonal storage. Its natural outflow is not into the Dee at all but to the north. However, a dam now restricts this northerly stream and the main flow is

diverted eastwards through a 2 km tunnel into the upper Dee valley. An interesting feature is the Drumjohn Valve: when demand for power is low, this directs the flow from two upper tributaries of the Dee through the tunnel in the reverse direction, *into* Loch Doon, adding to the stored volume. The level in the loch can vary by 12 metres, releasing

Figure 5.1   The Galloway Hydros

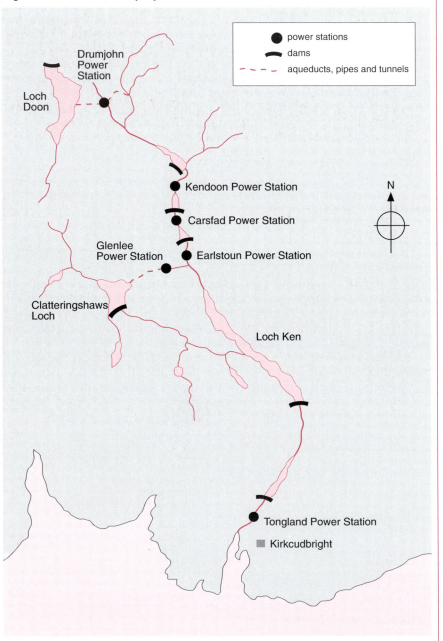

80 million cubic metres of water. Falling through the 200-metre height difference down to the final outflow at Tongland, this represents a gross release of some 150 million MJ of energy – over 40 million kWh.

Clatteringshaws Loch, the only completely artificial reservoir in the system, is the second long-

Figure 5.2 Carsfad power station and dam

term storage element. Its outflow, through a tunnel nearly 6 km long and pipes with a fall of over 100 metres, supplies the 24 MW Glenlee power station before joining the Dee.

The third element, designed for fast response to short-term demand variations in the course of a day, is the series of dams and power stations along the course of the Dee: Kendoon, Carsfad, Earlstoun and Tongland.

Power

The essential characteristics of a hydro site are the **effective head** (the height H through which the water falls) and the **flow rate** (the number of cubic metres of water per second, Q). The power carried by the water is roughly 10 times the product of these two quantities:

$$P \text{ (kW)} = 10 \times Q \times H$$

(The electric power output will of course be rather less than this input, as Table 5.1 shows. Section 5.3 discusses these factors in more detail.)

The conversion of the energy of the water into electrical energy is carried out by the **turbo-**

generator: a rotating turbine driven by the water and connected by a common shaft to the rotor of a generator.

The turbines

The head and the required power are critical in determining the most suitable type of turbine for a site. Glenlee's high head puts it at one extreme in the Galloway system, with Drumjohn's very low head and power rating at the other. Of the four river plants, Kendoon and Tongland have intermediate heads and fairly high power

Table 5.1 The Galloway power stations

Power station	Average head (m)	Maximum flow ($m^3 s^{-1}$)	Output capacity (kW)	Number of turbines
Drumjohn	11	16	2000	1
Kendoon	46	55	24 000	2
Carsfad	20	73	12 000	2
Earlstoun	20	71	14 000	2
Glenlee	116	26	24 000	2
Tongland	32	127	33 000	3

(Source: Scottish Power)

ratings, whilst Carsfad and Earlstoun have almost identical low heads and powers.

Any turbine consists of a set of curved blades designed to deflect the water in such a way that it gives up as much as possible of its energy. The blades and their support structure make up the turbine **runner**, and the water is directed on to this either by channels and guide vanes or through a jet, depending on the type of turbine.

The speed of the runner blade relative to the water striking it is critical for the efficiency of the turbine. As we see in more detail in later sections, 'propeller' types run best with their blade tips moving faster than the water, whilst the skirted Francis turbine is most efficient when the two speeds are roughly equal. So choosing the most suitable type involves comparing these speeds. The main relevant features are:

• the *available head*, which limits the water speed;

• the *rate of rotation* of the turbine runner, which depends on the desired rate of rotation of the generator – usually between about 200 and 1500 rpm;

• the *diameter of the runner*, which depends on the power output required.

Table 5.2   The turbines

Power station	Turbine rating (MW)	Turbine type	Rate of rotation (rpm)
Drumjohn	2	Propeller	300
Kendoon	12	Francis	250
Carsfad	6	Propeller	214.3
Earlstoun	7	Propeller	214.3
Glenlee	12	Francis	428.6
Tongland	11	Francis	214.3

In general, the result is that propeller types are preferred for low heads and Francis turbines for medium to high heads, a point discussed in more detail in Section 5.9. Comparison of Tables 5.1 and 5.2 shows that this is true for the Galloway scheme. Notice that at Glenlee, with its greater head, the blade speed is increased by using a higher rate of rotation.

The salmon

The principal environmental issue raised during the approval process was the possible effect on salmon fishing. Several dams blocked rivers below their salmon spawning pools, and concern was expressed about the fate of the adult salmon making their way upstream and young smolt during the reverse journey. The response was the incorporation of fish ladders at four dams. These are series of stepped pools with a constant downward flow of water to attract the fish, which leap up from pool to pool. The Doon dam had insufficient space for a long series of pools, so the fish ladder there is partly inside a round tower, but it is claimed that the fish find this spiral staircase no problem. More surprisingly, it seems that the smolt pass without harm *through* the low-speed turbines, so only at Kendoon is a by-pass needed. Glenlee presents no problem as salmon do not use the artificial Clatteringshaws Loch. (It is worth noting that a much more detailed environmental impact statement would be required today.)

Economics

The Galloway scheme was built to supply power at times of peak demand. In other words, it was designed with the expectation that it would generate for only a few hours a day: an annual plant **load factor** of no more than 25%. This would suggest a very poor return on the investment, which was in any case higher than for coal-fired plant of similar capacity. However, a number of circumstances made the scheme nevertheless financially attractive.

Figure 5.3   Turbine runners

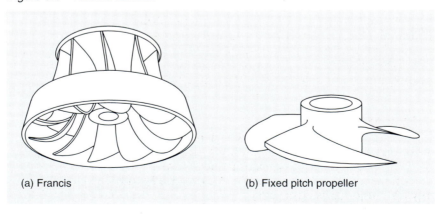

(a) Francis   (b) Fixed pitch propeller

• The company was able to assume a firm demand for the planned output.

• During its first three years the scheme received an annual treasury grant of £60 000 (close to a million pounds at present-day values), reducing the cost per unit by about 3%.

• The company also argued successfully that the local property taxes ('the rates'), which were based on capital value, should be lower for hydro than for coal-fired plant, as capital represented a smaller proportion of total costs for the latter.

From the start, demand and the consequent economic performance exceeded expectations, and only in a few years of serious drought did output fall below the planned level. This remains the case today. After nearly 60 years the original five plants are still generating power, joined in 1984 by the 2 MW plant at the Drumjohn Valve. The entire scheme is operated by the engineer at Glenlee, the only permanently staffed plant – and the original construction costs were of course repaid many years ago.

Figure 5.4   The fish ladder at Earlstoun

Figure 5.5   Clatteringshaws dam

5.3 HYDRO: THE RESOURCE

In this section we consider the sources of this particular form of renewable energy, and how much power it can offer us. Nearly a quarter of the solar power incident on the earth is consumed in the evaporation of water (see Figure 1.14). The water vapour in the atmosphere thus represents an enormous, continually renewed energy store. Unfortunately most of this energy is not available for our use: it is recycled into the atmosphere when the water vapour condenses to form rain or snow, and ultimately reradiated into space. But a small fraction, less than one tenth of a per cent of the total circulating energy, does become potentially available when the precipitation falls on high land.

STORED POTENTIAL ENERGY

Water (or anything else) held at a height represents stored energy – the gravitational potential energy discussed in Section 1.1. We find that about 10 joules are needed to lift one kilogram vertically through one metre. More formally, if M kilograms are raised through H metres vertically, the stored potential energy (PE) in joules is given by:

$$PE = MgH \qquad (1)$$

The '*g*' here is the acceleration due to gravity, whose value is 9.8 m s^{-2}. (As we rarely need better than 2% precision, we shall normally use the approximation g = 10 m s^{-2}.)

With this result we can calculate an absolute upper limit to the world's hydroelectric capacity. World-wide, the annual precipitation over land is estimated to be about 10^{17} kg, and the mean height of the land above sea level is a little over 800 metres. The annual addition to the energy store is therefore about 8×10^{20} J, or a little over 200 000 TWh a year. This is equivalent to about twice the world's total annual primary energy consumption. However, with no conceivable technology can we capture every drop of rain that falls: there will always be some inaccessible run-off and some re-evaporation before we can use the water, so this figure must obviously be regarded as quite unrealistically high.

POWER, HEAD AND FLOW RATE

In estimating the resource, the power available at any time is at least as important as the annual total. The power supplied by falling water is the rate at which it delivers energy – the *number of joules per second*, and this will obviously depend on the flow rate – the *number of kilograms per second*. It is generally more useful to consider the volume flow (*Q*) – the *number of cubic metres per second*. As each cubic metre of water has a mass of 1000 kg, the power *P* in watts is given by:

$$P = (1000Q) \times 10H$$

More conveniently, we can express *P* in kilowatts, in which case:

$$P \text{ (kW)} = 10QH$$

Resource estimates must take into account **energy losses**. In any real system the water will lose some energy as a result of frictional drag and turbulence as it flows in channels and through pipes, and the **effective head** will thus be less than the actual head. These flow losses vary greatly from system to system: in some cases the effective head is no more than 75% of the actual height difference, in others as much as 95%. Then there are energy losses in the plant itself. Under optimum conditions, a hydroelectric turbo-generator is one of the most efficient machines, converting all but a few per cent of the input power into electrical output. Nevertheless, the **efficiency** – the ratio of output to input power – is always less than 100%. With these factors incorporated, therefore, the output power becomes:

$$P \text{ (kW)} = 10\,\eta QH \tag{2}$$

where η is the efficiency expressed as a fraction and *H* is now the effective head (See Box 5.1).

THE WORLD RESOURCE

Estimates of world gross potential based on an assessment of river flows might realistically be regarded as the **total resource** in the sense discussed in the Appendix. These tend to suggest 50 000 TWh a year – only a quarter of the 'precipitation' figure calculated above, but still over four times the total annual output of *all* the world's present power stations.

There will certainly be a further reduction in the above figures when we ask how much of the 'realistic' total resource is actually exploitable. The answer will depend on local conditions such as topography and rainfall patterns. The latter are obviously very important, although the use of reservoirs can to some extent smooth out their effects. The relationship between this pattern of **supply** and the local pattern of **demand** determines how much of the annual potential can be used. In principle, a plant could deliver 8760 kWh a year for each kW of installed capacity. In practice, the

---

BOX 5.1: AVAILABLE POWER

As examples of power calculations, we may consider two systems of very different size. Both have an effective head of 100 metres and a plant efficiency of 83%.

The first site is a mountain stream with a water flow rate of 32 gallons a minute: 2.4 litres, or 0.0024 cubic metres, a second. The available power is then 83% of 10 x 0.0024 x 100, which is 2 kW.

In contrast, suppose that the flow rate is 6000 cubic metres a second – roughly the total flow over Niagara Falls. With the 100 metre head, the power becomes 5 million kW, or 5 GW.

world-wide average for hydro power is about 40% of this maximum, implying an annual **load factor** of 40%.

Current estimates of the technically exploitable hydroelectric potential of the world suggest a possible capacity in the range 2–3 TW, with an annual output of 10 000–20 000 TWh (UN, 1992). This is effectively the **technical resource** as defined in the Appendix. With the wide uncertainty in the estimates, attempting to distinguish between this and the **practical** and **accessible** resources would not appear to be justified on the broad world scale. (It is characteristic of such predictions that 50 years ago the estimated world potential was only 6000 TWh.)

Two important further questions remain: how much of the hydroelectric potential can we afford to use, and how much do we want to use? In other words, we need to consider the economically exploitable potential: the **viable** resource; and the environmentally exploitable potential: the **acceptable** resource. We return to these in Sections 5.11 and 5.13.

PRESENT WORLD CAPACITY AND OUTPUT

The world's total installed hydroelectric generating capacity is about 630 GW (Figure 5.6). The data are uncertain because the contributions from small-scale and private systems are difficult to estimate, but these are unlikely to add more than a few per cent to the total. The annual production world-wide is 2200 TWh, which means that the plant is on average running at two-fifths of its rated output – the load factor of about 40% mentioned above. Without more information, we can't of course tell whether this is due to limited demand or constraints imposed by variations in water supply.

Figure 5.6 World present and potential hydroelectric capacity Legend: 1 Asia excluding the former USSR; 2 South America; 3 Africa; 4 North America; 5 The former USSR; 6 Europe excluding the former USSR; 7 Oceania

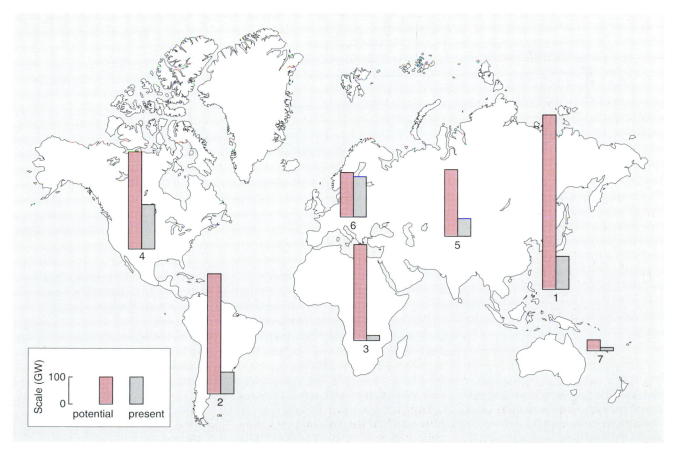

BOX 5.2: DIRECT USES OF WATER POWER

There are of course many possible uses of water power which do not involve the generation of electricity. The kinetic energy of moving water (or the potential energy of water available at a height) can be used directly – and indeed these were the sole uses of water power until the mid-nineteenth century.

In the present day, however, such direct use accounts for only a very small fraction of the total. Old watermills are still operating in a few places, grinding corn or sawing wood. And there are mountain railways whose cars are raised by filling a counter-balancing tank with water at the top and emptying it at the foot of the hill. But these are rarities in the industrialised world.

In some developing countries, direct water power plays a slightly greater role. In Nepal, for instance, a turbine has been designed which can be produced locally without sophisticated facilities, and many of these are in operation driving machinery for small-scale industries. The use of the energy of a flowing stream to raise water for irrigation (see Section 5.4) has by no means disappeared in the Middle East and Asia. Nevertheless, the world-wide energy contribution from all direct uses is negligible compared with that from hydroelectric power, and we shall therefore concentrate on the latter for the remainder of this chapter.

Compared with many other countries the hydro resource of the UK is not large. The present installed capacity of 1400 MW, 90% of which is in Scotland, produces some 5 TWh a year - about 2% of the total UK electrical output (Department of Trade and Industry, 1993).

The 2200 TWh world production represents about 10% of the upper estimate of the technically exploitable potential. Which again raises the obvious question: to what extent can we – or should we – use the remaining 90%? The final answers will certainly depend on the economics of hydro power and perhaps increasingly on social and environmental considerations, but informed discussion requires some understanding of the technology, so the following sections look at the ways we actually harness the power.

5.4 A BRIEF HISTORY OF WATER POWER

THE PRIME MOVER

Moving water was one of the earliest energy sources to be harnessed to reduce the work load of people and animals. No-one knows exactly when the water-wheel was invented, but irrigation systems existed at least 5000 years ago and it seems probable that the earliest water power device was the noria, raising water from a river into a tank or a system of channels for this purpose. This device (Figure 5.7) appears to have evolved over at least six centuries before the birth of Christ, perhaps independently in different regions of the Middle and Far East.

The earliest watermills were probably vertical-axis cornmills, known as Norse or Greek mills (Figure 5.8), which seem to have appeared during the first or second century BC in the Middle East and a few centuries later in Scandinavia. (Mills of this type are still in use in countries such as Nepal with plenty of streams but no nation-wide power system.) In the following centuries, increasingly sophisticated watermills were built throughout the

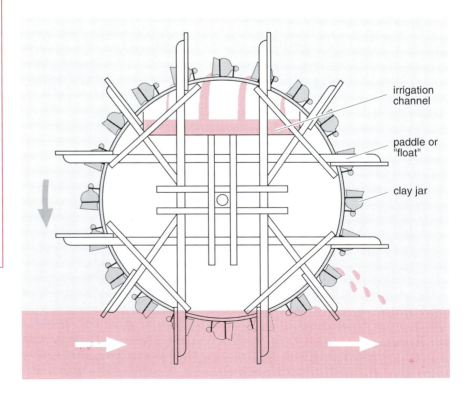

Figure 5.7   A noria. In this earliest water-wheel the paddles dip into the flowing stream and the rotating wheel lifts a continuous chain of jars, raising water for irrigation

Roman Empire and beyond its boundaries in the Middle East and Northern Europe (Figures 5.9 and 5.10). In England, the Saxons are thought to have used both horizontal- and vertical-axis wheels. The first documented mill was in the eighth century, but three centuries later the Domesday Book recorded about 5000, suggesting that every settlement of any size had its mill.

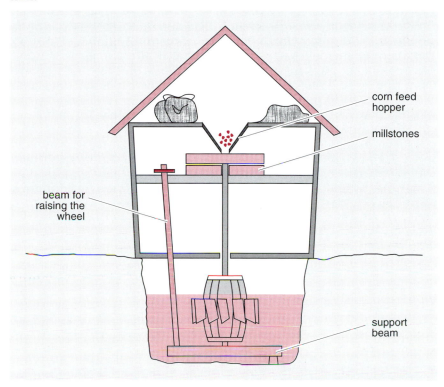

Figure 5.8 *A Norse mill. Mills of this early vertical-axis type are still in use to provide mechanical power in some remote mountainous regions*

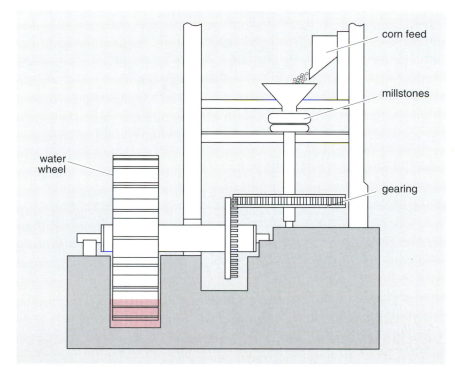

Figure 5.9 *A Roman mill. This corn mill with its horizontal-axis wheel was described by Vitruvius in the first century BC. Notice the use of gear wheels*

Raising water and grinding corn were by no means the only uses of the watermill, and during the following centuries the applications of this power source kept pace with the developing technologies of mining, ironworking, papermaking, and the range of processes associated with wool and later cotton. Water power was the main source of mechanical power almost everywhere, and by the end of the seventeenth century England alone is thought to have had some 20 000 working mills.

Over the centuries there was much debate on the relative efficiencies of undershot and overshot wheels (Box 5.3). The period from about 1650 until 1800 saw the first detailed scientific studies of the principles of water-wheels and some excellent technical investigations of different designs (see Open University, 1986). They revealed output powers ranging from about one horsepower to perhaps 60 for the largest wheels – in modern terms, roughly 1–50 kW. More importantly, they showed that for maximum efficiency the water should meet and leave the blades as smoothly as possible and should give up all its kinetic energy, falling away with minimal speed. They also proved that, in principle at least, overshot wheels should win the efficiency competition.

But then steam power entered the scene, putting the whole future of water power in doubt.

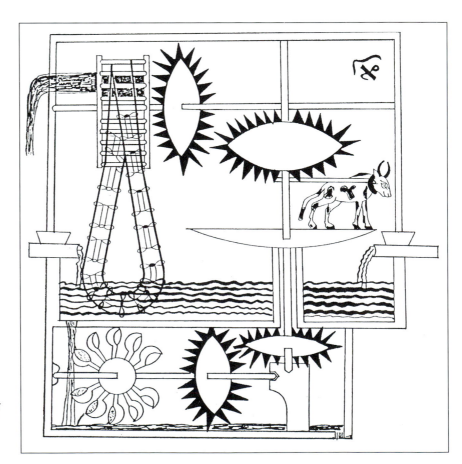

Figure 5.10 Medieval saqiya. The diagram comes from the Book of Knowledge of Ingenious Mechanical Devices of al-Jahazi, written in Mesopotamia 700 years ago. (The ox is made of wood and designed to fool the public, who can't see the hidden water-wheel)

BOX 5.3 TYPES OF WATER-WHEEL

By the end of the eighteenth century three main types of wheel were in use (Figure 5.11). It is a striking fact that two of these had remained virtually unchanged for well over 1000 years. (Vertical-axis wheels had also survived but played only a minor role in the industrially developing countries – a situation which was soon to change.)

Whilst we are not chiefly concerned here with water-wheels of the past, it may be worth looking briefly at some of their features in order to understand the problems which later developments were designed to overcome.

- The **undershot wheel** is driven by the pressure of water against its lower blades which dip into the flowing stream. This has the advantage that it can be used in almost any stream or channel, but the disadvantage that it becomes very inefficient if the water downstream backs up because of flooding, impeding the motion of the wheel.

- The **overshot wheel** is driven by water falling on the blades from above. The blades have closed sides, making them effectively buckets. Overshot wheels don't suffer the flooding problem, but do have the limitation that the height difference between the entering and departing water (the **head** of water) must be at least as great as the diameter of the wheel. This makes them unsuitable for streams and rivers with gentle gradients. They also tend to be more massive as they must withstand the weight of water falling on them from above.

- The **breastshot wheel**, a later development than the other two, is a compromise between them. The water is channelled between parallel breast walls and strikes the paddles at about the level of the wheel axle. It has the advantage of overcoming the flooding problem without requiring the high head of water and massive construction of the overshot wheel.

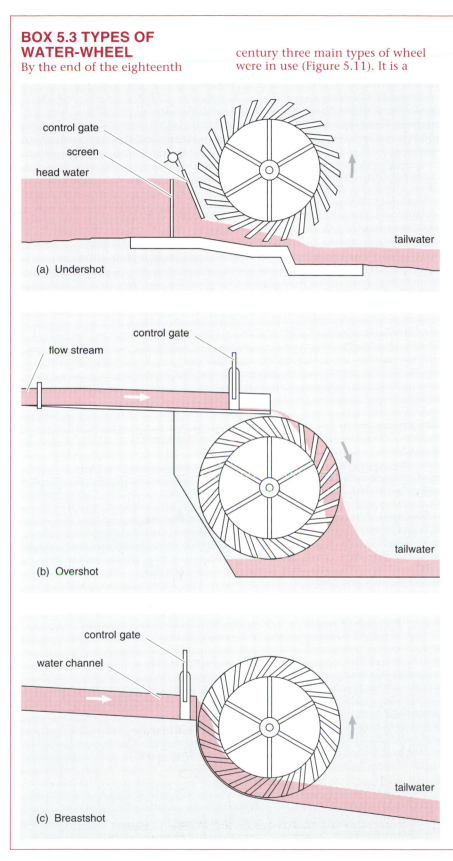

Figure 5.11 *Types of traditional water-wheel*

NINETEENTH-CENTURY HYDRO TECHNOLOGY

An energy analyst writing in the year 1800 would have painted a very pessimistic picture of the future for water power. The coal-fired steam engine was taking over, and the water-wheel was fast becoming technologically obsolete. However, like many later experts, ours suffered from an inability to see into the future, and a century later the picture was again completely different. The world now had an electrical industry with a quarter of its generating capacity water powered. The growth of the power industry was the result of a remarkable series of scientific discoveries and technical developments in electricity during the mid-nineteenth century, but significant changes in what we might now call hydro-technology also played their part. These changes are the subject of this section.

In 1832, the year of Faraday's discovery of electromagnetic induction, a young French engineer patented a new and more efficient water-wheel. His name was Benoit Fourneyron and his device was the first successful water **turbine**. (The name, which comes from the Latin *turbo*: something that spins, was coined by Claude Burdin, one of Fourneyron's teachers.) The water-wheel, essentially unaltered for nearly two thousand years, had finally been superseded.

Fourneyron's turbine (Figure 5.13) incorporates many new features. It is a vertical-axis machine, itself something of a novelty. But the most important innovations are the use of **guide vanes** to direct the water on to the blades and the fact that the turbine runs completely submerged. These are the features that ensure the smooth flow of water essential for high efficiency. The water enters centrally and is diverted across the curved faces of the stationary guide vanes so that it is travelling horizontally outwards

Figure 5.12 Calbourne Mill. The mill machinery of the corn mill at Calbourne on the Isle of Wight. The mill was mentioned in the Domesday Book of AD 1086. The present overshot iron wheel, 20 feet in diameter, was installed in 1881

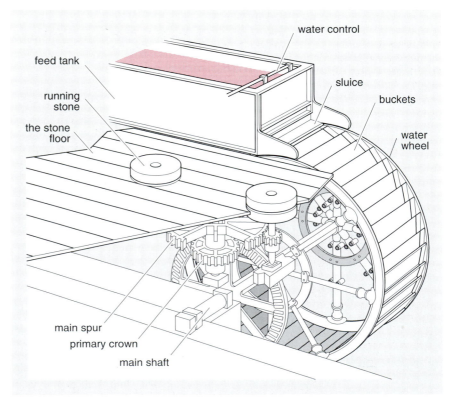

almost parallel to the curve of the runner blades as it reaches them. Deflected as it crosses the faces of the blades, it exerts a sideways pressure on them which transmits energy to the runner. Having given up its energy, it falls away into the outflow. Power control is by raising or lowering a ring between the guide vanes and the runner blades, another new feature of the design.

Tests showed that Fourneyron's turbine converted as much as 80% of the energy of the water into useful mechanical output – an efficiency previously equalled only by the best overshot wheels. The runner could also spin much faster, an advantage in driving 'modern' machines. The first pair of these turbines to come into use were installed in 1837 in the small town of St Blasien in the Grand Duchy of Baden. Development did not stop there: various other forms of turbine were investigated, and within a few years the American engineer James Francis started the series of experiments on **inward-flow** radial turbines which ultimately led to the modern machines known by his name (Section 5.6).

Half a century of development was needed before Faraday's discoveries in electricity were translated into full-scale power stations. Godalming in Surrey can claim the first public electricity supply, opened in 1881 – and the power source of this most modern technology was a traditional water-wheel. Unfortunately, this early plant experienced the problem common to many forms of renewable energy: the water flow in the River Wey was not sufficiently reliable, and the water-wheel was soon replaced by a steam engine.

From this primitive start, the electrical industry grew during the final 20 years of the nineteenth century at a rate seldom if ever exceeded by any technology. The capacity of individual power stations rose from a few kilowatts to over a megawatt in less than a decade. In 1891 power was first transmitted over a distance of 100 miles, and in homes and factories electric lights were joined by cookers, heaters, electric irons, and of course electric motors.

Figure 5.13 Fourneyron's turbine. Water flows outwards between the guide vanes and across the runner blades. The complete runner, consisting of a circular plate with the blades around its rim and a central shaft, spins under the force of the water: (a) vertical section; (b) guide vanes and runner

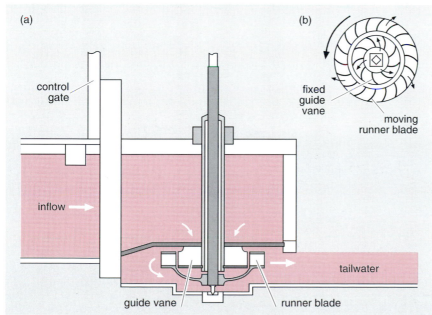

Figure 5.14 The Hoover dam. Constructed in 1936, this dam on the Colorado River was originally called the Boulder Dam. It is 200 metres high and its reservoir, Lake Mead, holds over 30 billion cubic metres of water. The power plant and switch gear are at the foot of the dam on the downstream side

Figure 5.15 The Grand Coulee Dam on the Columbia River in the state of Washington. Constructed in 1942, it is 170 metres high and creates a reservoir 240 km long, storing 12 billion cubic metres of water. Its plant has a generating capacity of 2 GW

5.5 TYPES OF HYDROELECTRIC PLANT

Present-day hydroelectric installations range in capacity from a few hundred watts to more than 10 000 megawatts – a factor of some hundred million between the smallest and the largest. We can classify installations in several different ways:

- by the effective head of water;
- by the capacity – the rated power output;
- by the type of turbine used;
- by the location and type of dam, reservoir, etc.

These categories are not of course independent of each other. The available head is an important determinant of the other factors, and the head and output largely determine the type of plant and installation. We start therefore with the customary classification in terms of head, but shall soon see that it is really the last of the above criteria which is being used.

LOW, MEDIUM AND HIGH HEADS

Two hydroelectric plants with the same power output could be very different: one using a relatively low volume of high-speed water from a high mountain reservoir and the other the huge volume flow of a slowly moving river. Sites, and the corresponding hydroelectric installations, can be classified as low-, medium- or high-head. The boundaries are a little fuzzy and tend to depend on whether the subject of discussion is the civil engineering work or the choice of turbine, but high-head usually implies an effective head of appreciably more than 100 metres, and low-head less than perhaps 10 metres. Figure 5.16 shows the main features of the three types.

The low dam or barrage of the installation shown in Figure 5.16(a) serves to maintain a head of water and also houses the plant. It may incorporate locks to allow the passage of ships (or in different circumstances a fish ladder for salmon). 'Run-of-river' power stations of the type shown, having effectively no storage capacity, are dependent on the prevailing flow rate in the river and can present problems of reliability of supply if the flow varies greatly with the time of year or weather conditions. The plant shown uses a vertical-axis turbine with the generator above, but other turbine systems are increasingly common in low-head installations. The large volume flow through a low-head plant means that all the machinery and the associated civil engineering works must be large too, which makes such installations expensive, although some saving is possible where the hydroelectric plant has a second function: flood control or irrigation, perhaps.

The plant shown in Figures 5.14 and 5.16(b) is typical of the very large hydroelectric installations with a dam at a narrow point in a river valley. The large reservoir behind the dam is designed to provide sufficient storage to meet demand in all but exceptionally dry conditions. (It will also have flooded an extensive area and may not have been entirely welcomed by the population, a topic discussed in more detail in later sections.) The USA has some of the world's largest dams of this type, including the Grand Coulee (Figure 5.15), which had the distinction when it was constructed of being the first artificial bulk structure with a volume greater than the Great Pyramid! On this scale, the civil engineering costs are obviously considerable, but the large reservoir normally ensures a reliable supply. Systems of this type don't of course have to be on a gigantic scale: quite small reservoirs can provide power for hydroelectric plant located below their dams.

To call the 220-metre head of the Hoover Dam 'medium' may seem rather surprising, but it illustrates the fact that the distinction between this

Figure 5.16 Types of hydroelectric installation

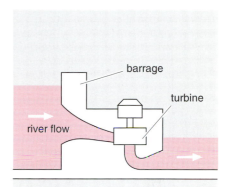

(a) low head

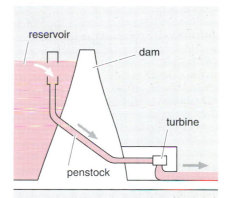

(b) medium head

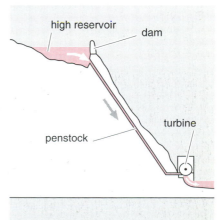

(c) high head

BOX 5.4: HEIGHT AND PRESSURE

The pressure in a liquid (or gas) is the force with which it presses on each square metre of surface of anything submerged in it.

Atmospheric pressure is due to the weight of the air above us. At sea level, the force on each square metre of any surface is equivalent to the weight of a 10-tonne mass (in more technical terms, a pressure of about 100 000 pascals or 14 pounds per square inch). The pressure decreases with altitude, by some 5% for each 300 metres.

As you move down below the surface of a reservoir or any body of water, the pressure *increases* because of the increasing weight of water above. Because water is several hundred times denser than air, the change is much more noticeable.

At a depth of just under 10 metres the pressure is twice that at the surface: a pressure of two atmospheres. This increase of about one atmosphere per 10 metres continues as the depth becomes greater (Figure 5.17).

Figure 5.17 Increase of pressure with depth

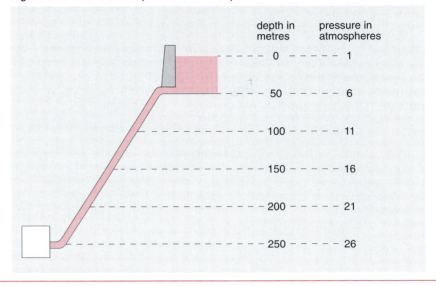

depth in metres	pressure in atmospheres
0	1
50	6
100	11
150	16
200	21
250	26

and high-head systems lies more in the type of installation. Figure 5.16 shows the difference. In the 'high-head' plant the entire reservoir is well above the outflow, and the water flows through a long **penstock** – possibly through a mountain – to reach the turbine. (The term penstock originally referred to the wooden gate or stock which controlled the flow from a millpond or pen to a millwheel. Later it came to mean the channel where the gate was located and ultimately acquired its present meaning.)

With a high head, the volume flow for a given power is much smaller than for a low-head plant, so the turbines, generators and housing are more compact. But the long penstock adds to the cost, and the structure must be able to withstand the extremely high pressures below the great depth of water – as much as 100 atmospheres for a 1000-metre head (Box 5.4).

ESTIMATING THE POWER

Reliable data on flow rates and, equally important, their variations, are essential for the assessment of the potential capacity of a site. Stopping the flow and catching the water for a measured time might be nice, but is hardly practicable for large flows or as a routine method. The preferred techniques depend on establishing empirical relationships between flow rate and either water depth or water speed at chosen points. Simple depth or speed monitoring, manually or automatically, then provides a record of flow rates. For many major rivers, particularly in developed countries, such data have been accumulated for years.

Where such records are not available, an entirely different approach is to determine the annual precipitation over the catchment area. This should give an estimate of the rate of flow into the system and is particularly suitable for large systems. Allowance must be made, however, for losses due to processes such as re-evaporation, take-up by vegetation or leakage into the ground, and as these could account for as much as three-quarters of the original precipitation they are hardly negligible corrections.

Dealing with the time variations adds further problems. In most areas there will be seasonal changes, but these may be predictable to a degree; at least they come at known times. The more serious problems are with changes over very long or very short periods. Year-to-year variations can be large: the average precipitation falling on the catchment area of the River Severn in a year, for instance, is 900 mm, but it can range from as little as 600 mm to as much as 1200 mm. Long-term weather prediction is unfortunately not yet an exact science, and for countries which depend heavily on hydroelectric power a succession of dry years can mean a serious supply shortage. In the early 1990s this has been a problem in New Zealand and some Latin American countries.

At the other extreme, any hydro installation must be designed to survive the '100-year flood', the sudden rush of water following unusually heavy rain. As in any power system, the need to guard against rare but potentially catastrophic events adds to the cost of the installation.

5.6 THE FRANCIS TURBINE

Present-day turbines come in a variety of shapes (Figure 5.18). They also vary considerably in size, with runner diameters ranging from as little as a third of a metre to some 20 times this. In the next four sections we look

Figure 5.18 Types of turbine runner

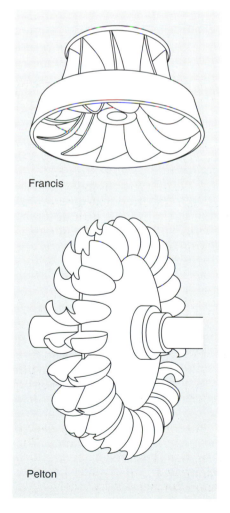

Francis

Pelton

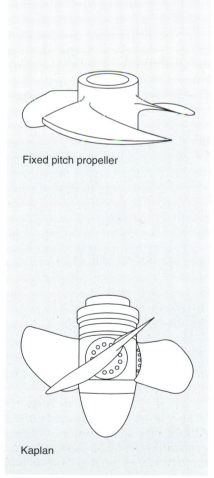

Fixed pitch propeller

Kaplan

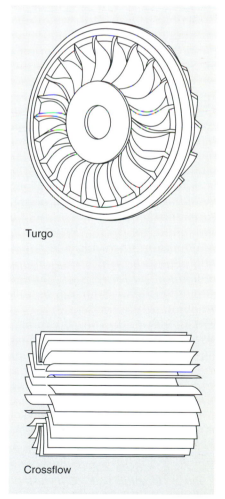

Turgo

Crossflow

at how they work, the factors that determine their efficiency and the most suitable operating conditions for each type.

The most commonly used turbines in present hydroelectric power stations are the Francis turbines (Figure 5.19). They are found in installations where the head is as low as two metres or as high as 200. These are radial-flow turbines, and although the water flow is inwards towards the centre instead of the outward flow of Fourneyron's turbine, the principle remains the same as that of their nineteenth-century predecessor.

ACTION OF THE TURBINE

The following account assumes a vertical-axis machine, but as the Francis turbine is completely submerged it can equally well run with its axis horizontal (in which case the draft tube has a right-angle bend, see, for instance, Figure 5.23). Water entering from the penstock flows around the circumference of the turbine. Directed by the guide vanes, it circles in towards the runner (Figure 5.20). As it crosses the curved runner blades it is deflected sideways, losing its whirl motion, and also downwards. It finally flows out down the central draft tube to the tail race. In medium- or high-head Francis turbines the flow is channelled in through a scroll case (also called a volute), a curved tube of diminishing size rather like a snail shell, with the guide vanes set in its inner surface. The shapes of the guide vanes and runner blades are critical in producing the smooth flow which leads to high efficiency and in ensuring that when the water leaves it has lost almost all its rotational motion.

Figure 5.21(a) shows the flow of the water as it encounters and leaves a runner blade. But we must remember that the blade itself is moving very fast, so in travelling across its face the water must also be moving sideways with it. In other words, the real path of the water is the result of adding the blade velocity to the water velocities shown in (a). The arrows in (b) show this, and demonstrate how the direction of flow is changed. (As mentioned above, the water has also been deflected towards the outflow, but this is not shown by Figure 5.21.)

Figure 5.19 Francis turbine runners. Each of these two runners is a metre in diameter and drives a generator with an output of 450 kW. They are designed to rotate at 200 rpm under a head of 10 metres and with a water flow rate of 5.8 cubic metres a second

That the water exerts a force on the blades is obvious because it has changed direction in passing through the turbine. In being deflected by the blades, it pushes on them in the opposite direction - the way they are travelling - and this reaction force transfers energy to the runner and maintains the rotation. For this reason, these are called reaction turbines. An important feature of this type is that the water arriving at the runner is usually still under pressure, and the pressure drop through the turbine accounts for a significant part of the total delivered energy.

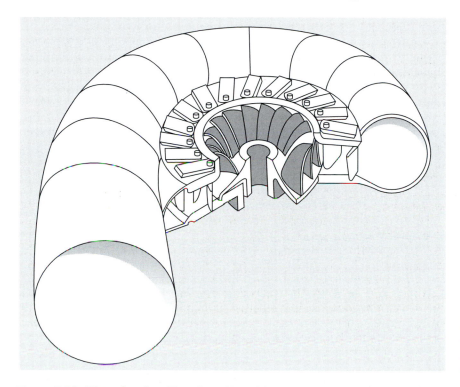

Figure 5.20 Structure of a Francis turbine. This cut-away diagram shows the volute, guide vanes and runner blades. Note that the guide vanes can be pivoted to adjust the flow rate

Figure 5.21 Water flow in a Francis turbine: (a) viewed from the spinning blade; (b) actual motion of water and blade

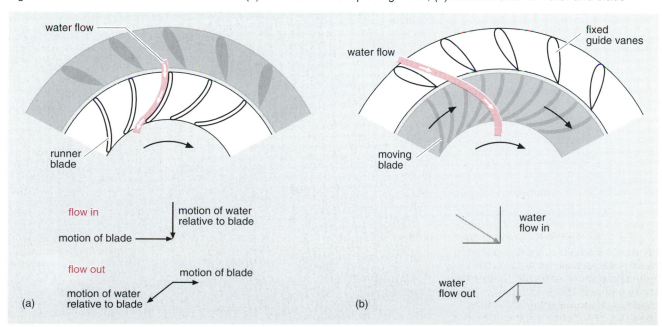

MAXIMISING THE EFFICIENCY

The power output of a turbine is less than the input for several reasons. Firstly there will be the energy losses due to friction which are inevitable in any moving machinery. Energy is also used in pushing water through pipes and channels – another type of friction which is unavoidable. These losses can't be eliminated, but good design can minimise them. A rather different reason for less than 100% efficiency is that some kinetic energy is carried away by the water as it flows out. The remedy is to flare the draft tube: as the tube becomes wider the water moves more slowly, until, by the time it reaches the tail race, its speed is almost zero (see Box 5.5).

Modern turbines operating under optimum conditions are extremely efficient machines. Efficiencies of 95% can be achieved – but only by maintaining exactly the right speed and direction of the incoming water relative to the blades, and this leads to a further problem. Suppose demand falls. The output can be reduced by reducing the water flow. (In a Francis

Figure 5.22 A small-scale hydroelectric plant in Scotland, commissioned in 1993 and supplying power to the grid. The rated electrical output is 450 kW, from a water flow rate of 2.1 cubic metres a second at a head of 25 metres.

Top: The turbine house. Water flows through underground pipes from an intake above the falls in the distance to the top of the penstock whose lower section can be seen in the centre.

Bottom: The horizontal-axis Francis turbine rotates at 750 rpm. The inflow is at the lower right and the outflow through the rear wall; the generator casing can be seen on the left. The light-coloured elements on the face of the turbine are the hydraulic mechanism for rotating the guide vanes

---

BOX 5.5: WATER SPEED, PRESSURE AND CAVITATION

The increase in pressure with depth below the surface of a reservoir has been described in Box 5.4. This was for a static body of water; but if the water is flowing, and in particular if its speed varies, the pressure can change without any change in depth at all. The reasoning is as follows.

Suppose a pipe containing flowing water narrows. The water speed must increase (because the water has to go somewhere). But as we know, an increase in speed requires more energy. Some force must act which pushes the water in the forward direction.

The required force comes from a pressure difference between the slower water behind and the faster water in front: the pressure becomes lower the faster the water moves.

Along a narrowing pipe, therefore, there is a continuous fall in pressure, and conversely, there is rising pressure along a widening pipe.

The latter occurs when the water flowing from a turbine passes through a flared draft tube (Figure 5.23), with the consequence that the pressure immediately below the turbine is lower than at the outflow. The pressure drop across the turbine is therefore greater and the energy transfer is increased, which is the aim.

There is, however, an undesired result. The pressure at the outflow is atmospheric pressure, so the pressure below the turbine blades will be less than atmospheric. It could be so low that the water boils, even at normal temperatures, and the effect of this 'cavitation' is erosion of the

blades due to impact as the air bubbles collapse.

Figure 5.23 Flared draft tube

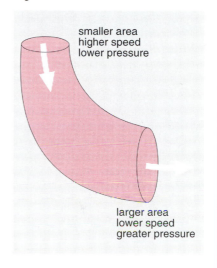

smaller area
higher speed
lower pressure

larger area
lower speed
greater pressure

---

turbine this is done by turning the guide vanes to constrict the flow.) To maintain constant supply frequency the rate of rotation of the generator needs to remain the same at any power level. But an unchanged runner speed with a lower water speed means that the angle at which the water hits the moving blades is altered, so the efficiency falls. This is a characteristic which must be accepted with this type of turbine. Ideally, the angle of the blades should be altered to match the new conditions, but this is not practicable with radial-flow turbines. (As we see below, some propeller types do allow adjustment of the pitch.)

LIMITS TO THE FRANCIS TURBINE

Selecting the best turbine for a particular purpose will depend on a number of factors, amongst which the head is particularly important. If the head is low a large volume flow is needed for a given power. But a low head also means a low water speed, and these two factors together mean that a much larger input area is required. Attempts to increase this area whilst adapting the blades to the reduced water speed and at the same time deflecting the large volume down into the draft tube led to turbines with wide entry and blades which were increasingly twisted. Ultimately the whole thing began to look remarkably like a propeller in a tube, and this is indeed the type of turbine now commonly used in low-head situations (Section 5.7).

Very high heads bring problems too. High heads mean high water speeds. Francis turbines are most efficient when the blades are moving nearly as fast as the water, so very high heads imply very high speeds of rotation, which may not be desirable, and for these conditions yet another type of turbine takes over (Section 5.8).

Figure 5.26 The runner of a 2.2 MW
Kaplan turbine

5.7 'PROPELLERS'

In the propeller or **axial-flow** turbine shown in Figure 5.24 the area through which the water enters is as large as it can be: it is the entire area swept by the blades. Axial-flow turbines are therefore suitable for very large volume flows and have become usual where the head is only a few metres. They have the advantage over radial-flow turbines that it is technically simpler to vary the angle of the blades when the power demand changes, and as we have seen this improves the efficiency under varying demand. Axial-flow turbines with this feature are called **Kaplan turbines**.

Figure 5.25 can be compared with Figure 5.21. It again shows the flow of water relative to a blade and the actual flow required to achieve this. In this case the general flow direction is not radial but *axial*, and the view is therefore at right angles to the axis, not along it. As before, the entering water is swirling round, but an important feature is that the blade speed is now appreciably greater than the water speed – as much as twice as fast. This allows a rapid rate of rotation even with relatively low water speeds. (Note that because the outer parts of the blade move faster than the more central

Figure 5.24 A 'propeller' or axial-flow turbine

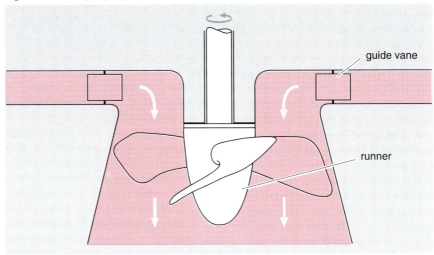

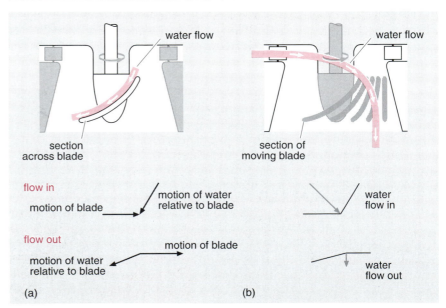

Figure 5.25 Water flow in an axial-
flow turbine: (a) viewed from a moving
blade; (b) actual motion of water and
blade

parts but swirling water moves faster near the centre, the blade angle needs to increase with distance from the axis. This is why a propeller has its familiar twisted shape.)

Once you have axial flow there is no need to feed the water in from the side. It must be better to let it flow in along the axis instead of deflecting it through a right angle. But if the water flows in along the axis of the turbine, surely the generator will get in the way and/or get wet? Several different solutions to this problem are shown in Chapter 6, Tidal Power.

5.8 IMPULSE TURBINES

PELTON WHEELS

For heads above 250 metres or so (and much lower than this for small-scale systems) the **Pelton wheel** is the preferred turbine. The Pelton wheel evolved during the gold rush days of late nineteenth century California and was patented by Lester Pelton in 1880. It is entirely different from the types described above. Essentially a wheel with a set of double spoons or cups mounted around the rim (Figure 5.27), it is driven by a jet or jets of high-speed water hitting each cup in turn. The water passes round the curved bowls, and under optimum conditions gives up almost all its kinetic energy. Because the energy is delivered in a series of short impulses, this type is called an **impulse turbine**, in contrast to the reaction turbines discussed previously. One important difference between the two types is that whereas a reaction turbine runs fully submerged and with a pressure difference across the runner, the impulse type is essentially operating in air at normal atmospheric pressure.

The power input to the Pelton wheel is determined as usual by the effective head and the flow rate of the water. If the jet area is A m^2, the volume rate of flow corresponding to an effective head H (see Box 5.6) is given by:

$Q = A \times \sqrt{(20H)}$

The input power in kilowatts is $10QH$ (Section 5.3), so we find that:

$P \text{ (kW)} = 10 \times A \times \sqrt{(20H)} \times H$

or approximately:

$P \text{ (kW)} = 45A \sqrt{(H^3)}$

If adjacent cups are not to interfere with the flow, the wheel diameter needs to be about 10 times the diameter of the jet. But Pelton wheels need not have only one jet. Two or even four can be used to give greater power

BOX 5.6: EFFECTIVE HEAD, WATER SPEED AND FLOW RATE

The kinetic energy of the water leaving a jet is equal to the potential energy which it would have lost in falling through the effective head.

We know that the potential energy (PE) lost by M kg of water in falling through H metres is given by:

$PE = MgH$

In Chapter 1 we saw that the kinetic energy (KE) of a moving object is proportional to its mass and the square of its speed:

$KE = \frac{1}{2} Mv^2$

Equating these two quantities, we have:

$\frac{1}{2} Mv^2 = MgH$

or $v^2 = 2gH$ (3)

and it follows that the water speed corresponding to an effective head H is given by $v = \sqrt{(2gH)}$, or approximately:

$v = \sqrt{(20H)}$

If this water flows through a jet with an area A square metres (Figure 5.28) the number of cubic metres flowing out in each second (Q) will be equal to A times v. So the flow for an effective head H is:

$Q = A \times \sqrt{(20H)}$

Figure 5.28 Speed, area and flow rate

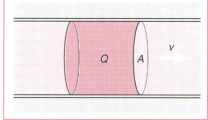

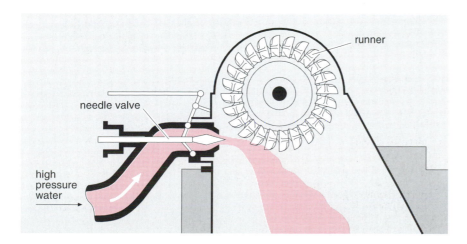

Figure 5.27 Structure of a Pelton wheel turbine

Figure 5.29 Finlarig power station on the shore of Loch Tay, draws its water from Loch na Lairige at a gross head of 415 metres. The average annual output from its 30 MW generator is 64 million kilowatt-hours. Top: the power station; Bottom: the double twin-jet Pelton wheel and horizontal-axis generator

Figure 5.30 Water flow in a Pelton wheel: (a) viewed from a moving cup; (b) actual motion of water and blade

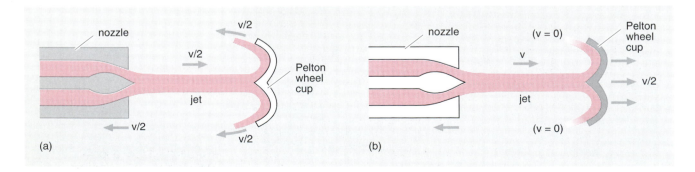

without increasing the size and therefore the cost of the turbine. If the number of jets is j, the power input becomes:

$$P \text{ (kW)} = 45jA \sqrt{(H^3)}$$

The efficiency of a Pelton wheel is greatest when the speed of the cups is half the speed of the water jet (see Box 5.7). It follows that there is an optimum rate of rotation for any head and wheel diameter. The power can be varied to meet varying demand by adjusting the jet size to change the volume flow rate.

TURGO AND CROSS-FLOW TURBINES

A variant on the Pelton wheel is the **Turgo turbine** (Figure 5.31), developed in the 1920s. The double cups are replaced by single, shallower ones, with the water entering on one side and leaving on the other. The water enters as a jet, striking the cups in turn, so this is still an impulse turbine, and like the Pelton, is most efficient when rotating at roughly half the speed of the water. However, its ability to handle a larger volume of water than a Pelton wheel of the same diameter gives it an advantage for power generation at medium heads.

The cross-flow turbine (**Mitchell-Banki**, or **Ossberger turbine**, see Figure 5.18) is yet another impulse type. The water enters in a flat sheet rather than a round jet. It is guided on to the blades, then travels across the turbine and meets the blades a second time as it leaves. As we see in the next section, cross-flow turbines are often used instead of Francis turbines in small-scale plants with output below 100 kW or so, and some ingenious technological ideas have gone into the development of simple types which can be constructed (and maintained) without sophisticated engineering facilities and are therefore suitable for remote communities, particularly in the developing world.

5.9 SPECIFIC SPEED AND RANGES OF APPLICATION

We have seen that in general Pelton wheels are most suitable for high heads, propellers for low heads and Francis turbines for the intermediate ranges. But the effective head is not the only factor determining the most appropriate turbine type for a given situation. The available power is also relevant.

The parameter normally used in selecting turbines is the **specific speed** (N_s), which is related to the output power (P in kW), the effective head

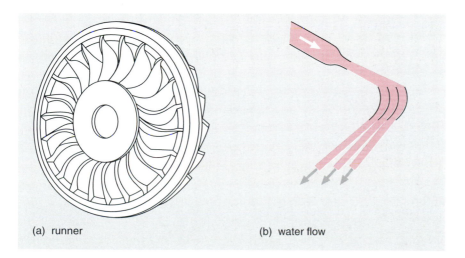

(a) runner   (b) water flow

Figure 5.31 Turgo turbine: (a) the runner; (b) water flow

Table 5.3 Specific speeds

Type of turbine	Specific speed range
Francis	70–500
Propeller	600–900
Kaplan	350–1000
Pelton, 1-jet	10–35
Pelton, 2-jet	10–45
Turgo	20–80
Cross-flow	20–90

(H in metres) and the rate of rotation (n in revolutions per minute) as follows:

$$N_s = n \sqrt{\left(\frac{P}{H^2 \sqrt{H}} \right)} \qquad (4)$$

This can be used to choose the best turbine type for a particular site. The site is assessed to find the effective head H and the available power P. The possible values for the rate of rotation n are limited by the requirement that a generator connected to the grid must rotate at a speed appropriate to the mains frequency (see Chapter 1). These data can then be used in the above formula to find a preferred value (or range of values) of N_s for the proposed plant. Finally, data such as those in Table 5.3 are used to find a turbine type matching the calculated N_s.

How does this work? The point is that specific speed, derived from the rather strange combination of P, H and n above, can be shown (see Box 5.8) to depend in a rather simple way on the features of the turbine:

$$N_s = 500 \left(\frac{r}{R} \right) \left(\frac{v_B}{v_W} \right)$$

In other words, N_s depends essentially on two things:
- the ratio of diameter of the incoming flow or jet of water to the total diameter of the turbine: d/D (or r/R which is the same);
- the ratio of the blade speed to the water speed: v_B/v_W.

As we have seen above, these two ratios reflect the most important differences between the various types of turbine. Each *type*, regardless of size, therefore has its own range of values of N_s (Figure 5.32 and Table 5.3) and matching this to the N_s calculated from the site data and preferred rpm allows the appropriate type to be chosen. The *size* of the turbine will of course be determined by the power requirements. (An intriguing feature of some of these water turbines is that essentially the same design is used in a giant 700 MW plant or a little system delivering no more than a millionth of this power.)

Figure 5.32 *Ranges of application of turbines. The diagram shows the heads, flow rates and corresponding power ranges for which each type of turbine is most suited. It should be noted however that criteria such as cost, simplicity in manufacture or ease of maintenance can lead to choices outside these ranges*

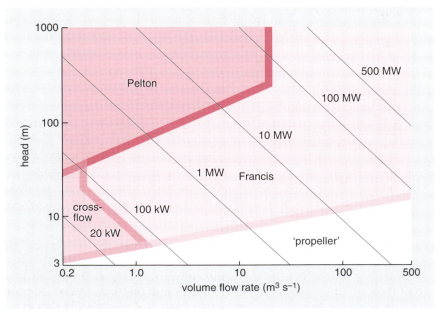

BOX 5.8: SPECIFIC SPEED

We can show that the two expressions for specific speed given in the main text are equivalent. To do this we use various results obtained earlier in the section.

We'll start with Equation 4, relating N_s to rate of rotation, power and effective head. We know that:

- the output power P (in kW) is equal to $10\eta QH$ (Section 5.3),
- the flow rate Q is equal to the water speed (v_W) times the area of the inflow,
- if r is the inflow radius, the area is πr^2,
- the head (H) is equal to $v_W^2/20$ (Section 5.8).

With a little algebra we find that

$$\frac{P}{H^2\sqrt{H}} = \frac{10 \times \eta \times (v_W \pi r^2)}{(v_W^2/20)^2\sqrt{(v_W^2/20)}} = 2800 \times \eta \times \left(\frac{r^2}{v_W^2}\right)$$

Assuming that the efficiency η is not too different from 1, the square root of the above quantity becomes

$$\sqrt{\left(\frac{P}{H^2\sqrt{H}}\right)} = 53 \times \left(\frac{r}{v_W}\right)$$

The number of complete revolutions per second is equal to the speed of the blade (v_B in metres per second) divided by the circumference of the turbine runner ($2\pi R$, if R is its radius in metres). The number of revolutions per minute is then

$$n = 60 \times \frac{v_B}{2\pi R}$$

Finally, therefore, we find that the specific speed is

$$N_S = 60 \times \frac{v_B}{2\pi R} \times 53\left(\frac{r}{v_W}\right) = 500 \times \left(\frac{r}{R}\right) \times \left(\frac{v_B}{v_W}\right)$$

which is the second expression for N_s in the main text.

This is a much simplified version of the full analysis, but it does give roughly the right specific speeds, as the following examples show.

(a) Water enters across the entire area of a Kaplan turbine, so r/R is about 1. If we assume that the maximum blade speed at the rim is twice the water speed, we obtain a maximum value for N_s of 1000.

(b) For a single-jet Pelton wheel the value of r/R cannot be greater than about one tenth. With the optimum blade speed of about half the water speed, this gives $N_s = 25$.

As you can see, these are within the ranges in Table 5.3.

5.10 SMALL-SCALE HYDROELECTRICITY

It is an interesting reflection of the scale of present-day power systems that a 50 MW plant producing enough power for a fair-sized town can be referred to as 'small-scale'. Perhaps this extreme case should be taken as an example of the varying terminology in discussions of small-scale hydro, the terms **small**, **mini-** and **micro-** being variously used for sub-sections of a range stretching down from tens of megawatts to a few hundred watts. In the following, we shall take **small-scale** to include the whole range from 5 MW downwards, unless otherwise stated.

WORLD-WIDE DEVELOPMENTS

Small-scale hydro is hardly a novel idea in the countries of Europe and North America. From the earliest days of electric power, generators in the kilowatts to megawatts range were installed on streams or rivers, often using the dams and sluices of old watermills. Many continued to deliver power for half a century or more until the growth of national transmission networks from the 1920s. The convenience and greater reliability of central supplies then led to the gradual abandoning of small plants with their variety of voltages and frequencies. For the past 70 years or so, technological development has largely centred on multi-megawatt systems, and only in recent years have turbo-generators with capacities under a megawatt again attracted serious attention. The renewed interest seems to be attributable to a coincidence of several factors:

- strategic concerns about energy supplies;
- the limited potential for further large-scale hydro development in many countries;
- advances in electronics which have greatly reduced the cost of controlling the output of small turbo-generators, enabling them to follow demand whilst meeting the voltage and frequency standards of centralised systems.

In the industrialised nations, the sites under consideration tend to fall into two main categories. There are the dams and reservoirs of water-supply systems. Many are already in use for power generation, but there is still considerable potential for small-scale systems making use of existing civil engineering works. This is obviously economically attractive and often more acceptable environmentally than completely new installations. Then there is scope for run-of-river systems on streams or small rivers. An interesting example of the latter is the growing number of small-scale hydroelectric installations in the Alps – not infrequently driving machinery which once ran on direct water power from the same mountain stream. Elsewhere in the world, the Chinese are without doubt leading in the use of small-scale hydro, having installed nearly 100 000 plants over the past 25 years. Averaging about 100 kW, these represent a total installed capacity approaching 10 000 MW.

The view is often expressed that major power stations with capacities of hundreds of megawatts are not necessarily the most appropriate for the least developed regions of the world, and that small-scale systems represent a better technological solution to the problem of bringing 'power to the people'. They have the advantage of being independent of long-distance transmission lines, and their technological requirements in terms both of facilities and of trained personnel may be more appropriate to the local situation. Programmes for the development and installation of locally manufactured hydro plants have been initiated by governments and rural development organisations in some 20 or so countries, mainly in those regions of Asia and South America which are rich in mountain streams and small rivers.

SMALL-SCALE POTENTIAL IN THE UK

With most of the potential sites in the UK for large-scale hydroelectric plant lying in areas of great natural beauty it is considered unlikely that further developments on this scale will prove acceptable (ETSU, 1994(2)). Proposals for an increased hydro contribution have tended therefore to centre on the scope for small-scale installations with outputs between a few kilowatts and a few megawatts. The introduction of the Non-Fossil Fuel Obligation (NFFO) encouraged such schemes, and by 1993 twenty plants (9 MW in total) commissioned under the 1990 order and a further 9 (10 MW) under the 1991 order were generating power (ETSU, 1994(1)). Studies in recent years have led to estimates of a total economically viable installed capacity of 100–400 MW, with an annual output ranging from 500 to 2000 GWh. (The spread of estimates is mainly the result of differences in the criteria for economic viability.)

Figure 5.33 shows the sites investigated in a detailed study carried out for the then UK Department of Energy (now part of the Department of Trade and Industry) during 1987–88 and forming the basis for subsequent DTI assessment of the potential contribution from this resource (ETSU, 1989, 1994(1) and 1994(2)). The study was limited to sites with heads of at least 3 m (2 m where civil works were already in place) and covered some 1300 sites with potential output in the range 25–5000 kW. It assumed a 40-year plant life, a load factor of 56% and annual costs equal to 2% of the capital cost. As Figure 5.34 shows, the total potential for the production of power at the 1989 average tariff price of 2.7p per kWh and 10% rate of return on capital was estimated to be about 1300 GWh a year from a capacity of 320 MW. Not surprisingly, Scotland provides 60% of the sites and nearly 90% of the capacity.

For the 90% of sites with heads greater than about 10 m (65% in the case of sites outside Scotland) the estimated capital cost was between £700 and £3000 per installed kilowatt, with a mean of about £1400 kW^{-1}. Under the assumptions of the study, the average cost of electricity would be about 4p kWh^{-1} (1989 pence), but with a range from less than 2p kWh^{-1} to nearly 20p kWh^{-1}.

Figure 5.33 Small-scale hydroelectric potential in the UK: (a) mean annual precipitation; (b) sites assessed for small-scale hydro

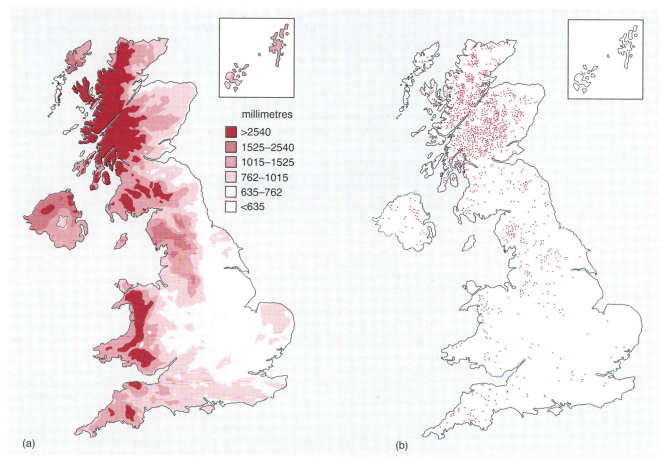

Figure 5.34 *These graphs summarise the results of the study* Small Scale Hydroelectric Generation Potential in the UK, *carried out for the then Department of Energy by Salford Civil Engineering Ltd. (ETSU, 1989). (a) cumulative installed capacity vs internal rate of return; (b) cumulative annual energy yield vs internal rate of return (IRR); (c) potential in the range 25 kW–5 MW at IRR ≥ 10%*

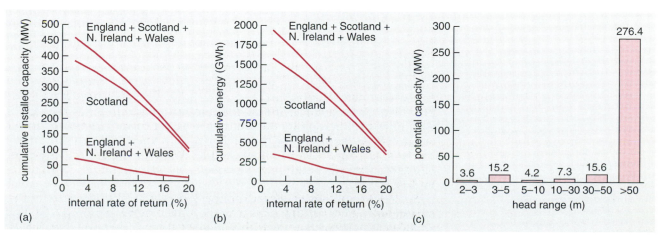

Some 23 MW of the potential capacity considered in the study comes from sites with heads less than about 10 m, and it has been estimated that if run-of-river sites with really low heads – below 3 m – were included the figure would be several times this. These sites, however, pose a technical problem. Low heads mean very slowly moving water, and present turbines become inefficient under such extreme conditions. Reduced efficiency means reduced power output which in turn means a higher capital cost for each kilowatt-hour produced. The investigation of potentially more efficient low-head systems, possibly involving new principles for extracting the energy, is an area of work which has received UK government support. For the present, however, this is one factor which limits the total viable potential.

The 10% discount rate used as the criterion for viability is another, and it is worth noting that at 5% discount rate the potential rises to 1700 GWh a year from an installed capacity of 400 MW – a 30% increase. (See also Section 5.14.)

5.11 ENVIRONMENTAL CONSIDERATIONS

The environmental impacts of a hydroelectric project must be thoroughly analyzed since, after it is completed, they are essentially irreversible.

(Dorf, 1978)

The ecological damage per unit of energy produced is probably greater for hydroelectricity than for any other energy source.

(CONAES, 1979)

Most people would probably agree with the first of the above statements, although some might point out that by implication it refers to major projects rather than small-scale hydroelectricity. How many would accept the conclusions of the second report is less certain.

In discussing the factors which could enter into an assessment of the **acceptable resource**, we might usefully start by summarising the environmental benefits of hydroelectricity. It produces no CO_2 and has little other effect on the atmosphere – apart perhaps from a local increase in water vapour and some temperature effects. (Vegetation rotting under water produces methane, but it has yet to be shown that hydro installations have appreciably increased the rate of release of this greenhouse gas.) The noise pollution is negligible too, and there is little to explode, catch fire or emit noxious materials.

We can consider the environmental and related social effects which hydroelectricity does produce under three headings:

• the hydrological effects – water flows, groundwater, water supply, irrigation, etc.;
• the ecological effects – on the land and its plants and animals;
• the social effects.

HYDROLOGICAL EFFECTS

The three categories of effect listed above are not of course independent of each other. Hydrological changes, in any of the senses mentioned, will certainly be significant for the ecology and for the local community – particularly in the case of a major installation. A hydroelectric scheme is not basically a consumer of water, a fact now taken into account by legislation in Britain, where water abstraction charges are no longer levied on small hydro schemes. The installation does however 'rearrange' the water resource. Diverting a mountain stream into a pipe may not greatly change the flow at the valley bottom, but it will have a marked effect at intermediate levels.

BOX 5.9: TWO DANUBE PROJECTS

The flow of the Danube is already used for hydroelectric power generation at a number of sites. One development in particular which has been criticised on environmental grounds is the major dam completed in the early 1970s near Turnu-Severin, where the river forms the border between Romania and Serbia. The resulting lake, stretching some fifty miles upstream, has completely obliterated the unique and spectacular Iron Gates gorge, famous for centuries as one of Europe's most dramatic landscapes.

Another Danube project which has been the subject of controversy for more than a decade is the development on the Slovak-Hungarian border downstream from Bratislava

(Figure 5.35). The 880 MW scheme, agreed in 1977, included barrages with power plants at Gabcikovo and Nagymaros, the Dunakiliti reservoir (large enough to hold two days' average flow of the river) and an 18 km canal to carry diverted water to Gabcikovo. Work proceeded for about a decade, but with the political changes of the late 1980s, opposition on environmental grounds became increasingly vocal, particularly in Hungary. Construction on the Hungarian side effectively stopped in 1989, and finally, in May 1992, the government officially announced cancellation of the 1977 agreement (Fleischer, 1993).

The newly established Slovak state, however, remained committed to the scheme, declaring that the agreement could not legally be

cancelled. In October 1992, Slovak engineers used the window of opportunity when the river was at its lowest to complete the diversion into the new canal. Lined with asphalt and with concrete walls rising to a height of 15 metres above the surrounding land, this carries the water to the main plant at Gabcikovo. (Dodd, 1993)

The resulting fall in the water table, with village wells drying up, vegetation dying and unique forms of wild life in danger, has reinforced calls for legal limits to the amount of water which may be diverted. However, despite a number of meetings, and intervention by the EU, the situation remains unresolved at the time of writing.

Figure 5.35 The proposed Danube scheme

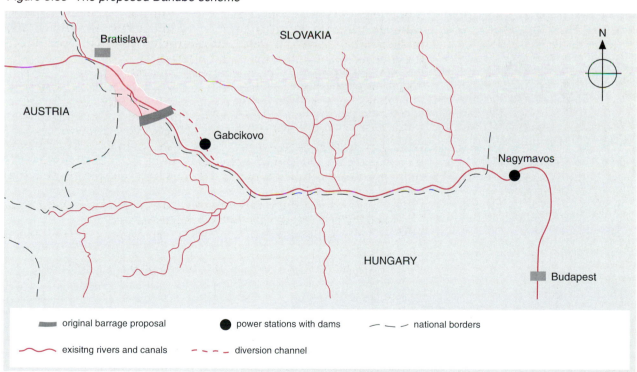

Storing water in a reservoir may reduce the final flow as a result of evaporation from the large exposed surface. One of the concerns about the Danube scheme (see Box 5.9) is that groundwater levels will be altered in the surrounding countryside. The depletion of the Colorado River along its length until virtually no flow remains at its mouth in the Gulf of California has been the subject of inter-state and international conflict for many decades. Whilst this has centred mainly on the diversion of water for other uses, the major hydroelectric plant served by the river has also played a role.

DAMS AND THEIR EFFECTS

Any structure on the scale of a major hydroelectric installation must affect its environment in many ways not directly linked to the hydrology. The construction process itself can cause widespread disturbance, and although the building period may be only a few years, the effect on a fragile environment can be much longer-lasting. Even if we confine ourselves to the time when the initial disturbance has disappeared, the change from an environment suitable for flowers, worms and furry creatures to one which suits only fish and boating enthusiasts can hardly be negligible. Whether it is seen as detrimental, beneficial or neutral will depend on the situation – in the geographical and biological sense – and undoubtedly on the point of view and interests of those concerned.

Unfortunately, it is not only the desirability of the predicted change which is the subject of debate. There is often considerable disagreement in advance about the predictions themselves, and unpredicted consequences resulting from large-scale schemes are not uncommon. Following the construction of the Aswan High Dam in Egypt, the land downstream no

---

BOX 5.10: ITAIPU

The hydroelectric plant at Itaipu, on the Parana River between Brazil and Paraguay, is the world's largest single power station. The effective head is about 120 metres and the average water flow is 9000 tonnes a second, peaking at times to more than 30 000. The first generators came on-line in 1984, each unit having a capacity of 700 MW. The final total is 18 such sets, representing a capacity of 12.6 GW.

Noting that 1 tonne of water is the same as 1 cubic metre, we find that the average power delivered (see Section 5.3) is 10 x 9000 x 120 = 11 million kW, or 11 GW. This surprising result, suggesting that the installed output capacity is greater than the input, may be the consequence of using approximate values, but a more likely explanation is that the plant is designed to make use of the flow during above-average periods.

It is claimed that the sceptics who called Itaipu a white elephant, producing unwanted power in the wrong place, have been proved wrong and that there is sufficient demand to require its full capacity.

(Source: Helps, 1990)

Figure 5.36 The Itaipu dam

Table 5.4 Dams and seismicity

Dam	Country	Height of dam (m)	Reservoir capacity (billion m³)	Earthquakes since construction
Glen Canyon	USA	220	33	Nil
Hoover	USA	220	38	Medium
Kariba	Zambia, Zimbabwe	130	160	Strong
Oroville	USA	240	4	Slight
Warragamba	Australia	140	2	Medium

longer receives the soil and nutrients previously carried by the annual Nile floods. A long-established agricultural system based on this natural phenomenon has largely been destroyed, to be replaced by reliance on constant irrigation and the use of fertilisers, causing deterioration of the soil and pollution of the river water. Meanwhile the silt is accumulating behind the dam and reducing its useful volume and hence the hydroelectric potential of the site. The problem of silt is not confined to Aswan, and its magnitude is only gradually being appreciated. The Hoover Dam, for instance (Figure 5.14), has lost over half its original storage capacity in its 55-year life.

Dams themselves are often the subject of concern, both for their visual impact and the possibility of catastrophic failure. Many people feel that the risks associated with different energy systems should be quantified in order to include them in the economic assessment, but there is less agreement on the methods to be adopted.

We might look at the data on dam failures. There are some 15 000 dams in the world. Over recent decades the frequency of major disasters involving significant loss of life seems to be about one per 6–10 years. We might therefore say that the current rate is one disaster per 120 000 dam-years. By a strange coincidence the CONAES Report (CONAES, 1979) in its much-criticised attempt at risk analysis, assessed the chance of a nuclear accident involving similarly significant loss of life as one per 120 000 reactor-years. What, if anything, can we conclude from these two pieces of quantitative information?

That dams in regions subject to earthquakes are particularly at risk is obvious, but recent debate has also centred on the question whether the weight of a major dam and its associated large volume of water can actually *cause* earthquakes. Measurements made as the water level of the Zambesi rose behind the newly-completed Kariba Dam in the early 1960s revealed changes in ground level as much as 36 km away, and the year or so after the reservoir reached its final level saw a striking rise in the number of earthquakes, including some at magnitude 5 or more on the Richter scale. This is by no means always the case, however, as Table 5.4 shows.

SOCIAL EFFECTS

From a child's book on energy:

They built a dam and made a lake in the place where Ahmed lived. Ahmed and his family had to leave the farm. His grandfather had lived there. Ahmed was born in that place. He was sad to go.

Just so. Cost-benefit analysis, it has been said, usually means that I pay the cost and you get the benefit.

Even for the people immediately affected, the building of dams can have very different consequences. For those living in a valley which will become a reservoir it means the loss of your family home and entire village. The Aswan Dam, for instance involved the relocation of 80 000 people and the Kariba Dam of nearly 60 000, whilst the proposed Three Gorges hydroelectric system on the Yangzi river, half as large again as the Itaipu plant described in Box 5.4, will submerge about 100 towns and displace over a million people. In contrast, however, we should remember that for people living on a river which periodically overflows its banks, the barrier and embankments of a hydroelectric sheme can bring freedom at last from devastating floods. And on the smaller scale, changes which mean the loss of a beloved riverside walk to some may be welcomed by others as the opportunity for exciting new leisure activities.

It should not be forgotten either that the choice may not be hydroelectricity or nothing but hydroelectricity or some other form of power station. As with the issue of risk discussed above, there is little agreement on how to translate environmental gains and losses into the economic data which are used in comparing options. A current issue of particular relevance is the costing of long-term compensation for the large numbers of people displaced by major new hydroelectric installations.

5.12 INTEGRATION

Even if the resource is available and environmentally acceptable there remain factors other than the basic generating cost which affect the viability of a particular source of electric power. In the industrialised world at least, few power stations operate in isolation, and the extent to which the proposed source can form a useful part of a supply **system** is important.

POWER STATIONS AS ELEMENTS IN A SYSTEM

From the point of view of the operator of the system, the characteristics of the ideal power station would be:

1 constant availability;
2 a reserve energy store to ballast input variations;
3 no correlation in input variations between power stations;
4 rapid response to changing demand;
5 an input which matches annual variation in demand;
6 no sudden and/or unpredictable changes in input;
7 a location which does not require long transmission lines.

The purpose of this list is not of course to rule out any source which doesn't satisfy all the criteria. It is rather that each compromise with these requirements adds to the effective cost: the need for back-up supply, or storage, or long transmission lines, etc. One can safely say that any type of power plant will require some compromises to be made and these must be taken into account in assessing the total cost.

Almost all hydroelectric plants score very well on the fourth criterion, and in those parts of the world with cold, dark, wet winters, on the fifth as well. (But not if the water is locked up as ice.) And sudden unplanned fluctuations in input are rare, at least in large conventional systems.

How well hydroelectricity performs on the first three criteria depends in part on the type of plant. A high-head installation with a large reservoir will normally have little difficulty in maintaining its output over a dry period, whereas the water held behind the low dam of a run-of-river plant cannot compensate for periods of reduced flow. A serious drought will of course affect all hydroelectric plant in the region concerned, and although this may be rare, hydro cannot be said fully to satisfy the third requirement. The final criterion is however the real hurdle. Locations for hydro plants are determined in the first instance by geography, and whilst run-of-river plant can sometimes be located near major centres of population this is rarely possible for high-head systems.

Much of the above assumes a conventional large-scale installation. Is the situation different for small-scale plant? It is, of course, but not solely in favour of one or the other. Smaller plant is predominantly run-of-river, or perhaps served by a relatively small reservoir. Either of these means a less reliable supply. On the other hand, many small sites could result in increased reliability if different regions of a country experienced different rainfall variations. Local small-scale plants can bring further benefits by reducing the need for high-voltage transmission lines: cutting costs and also reducing the energy dissipated as heat in these lines. As we shall see in the next section, the capital costs of both large- and small-scale systems vary so widely that generalisations are of little use and meaningful comparisons can only be made on the basis of specific proposals.

Overall, hydroelectricity ranks well in comparison with both conventional and other renewable sources of power in terms of the criteria discussed in this section. And under suitable circumstances, it can offer a bonus. A hydro installation with a large reservoir can not only maintain its own reserve of energy – it can provide a store for the spare output of other power stations as well.

PUMPED STORAGE

Pumped storage systems (Figures 5.37 and 5.38) are being developed increasingly in a number of countries, often in association with 'normal' hydroelectric power generation but also where the local water flow alone would not justify the installation. The growing concern with the means of storing large quantities of electrical energy is a consequence of two very different factors. The first is the rise in nuclear power. The output of a nuclear reactor cannot easily be made to follow large hour-by-hour variations in demand, so if the nuclear input to a national supply rises above base-load level, it becomes important to find a means of storing the excess power which is generated at times of low demand. The requirement is not in fact confined to nuclear power stations: any generating plant runs most efficiently at its full rated power, and the energy (and financial) cost of frequently reducing and increasing the output can be appreciable.

The second reason for the present concern with storage is rather different. It arises with the increase in the use of renewable sources for electricity generation, and here the problem is that the output often *does* vary – sometimes suddenly and usually for reasons which we cannot control. Back-up power is therefore needed which can be brought on-stream very quickly.

Figure 5.37 Pumped storage: (a) at time of low demand (b) at time of high demand

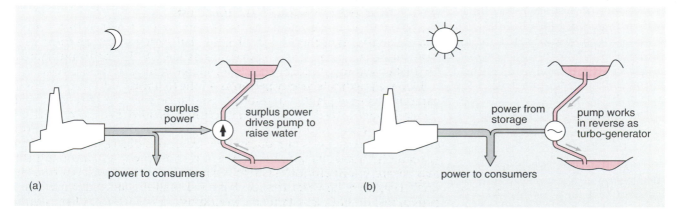

(a) surplus power — surplus power drives pump to raise water — power to consumers

(b) power from storage — pump works in reverse as turbo-generator — power to consumers

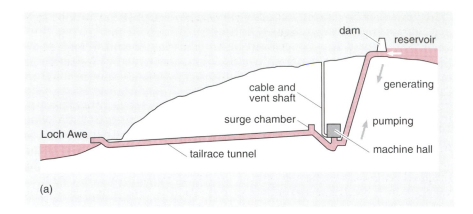

(a)

(b)

Figure 5.38 Cruachan pumped storage plant. The reservoir of the Cruachan plant in Scotland, which was commissioned in 1965, can hold 10 million cubic metres of water at an operating head of 365 m. The mass of each cubic metre is l000 kg, so the total stored energy (see Section 5.3) is 10 000 x 10 x 365 million joules, or about 10 million kilowatt-hours. Running the four 100 MW reversible machines for an hour at full capacity, as electric pumps or turbo-generators, raises or lowers the reservoir level by about a metre. (a) the installation; (b) aerial photograph; (c) the dam

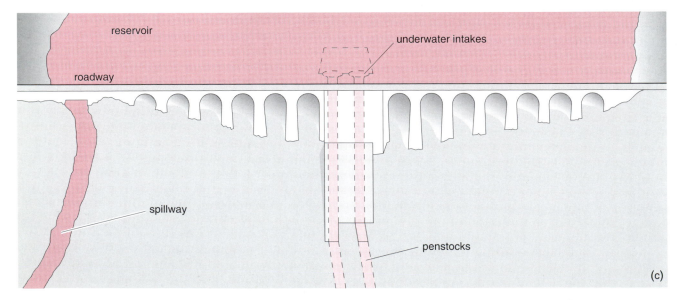

(c)

At present the only practicable and economically viable way to store electrical energy in very large quantities is to use it to pump water up a mountain. One alternative would be to use electric power to produce hydrogen, retrieving the power by burning the hydrogen in fuel cells (see Section 11.9); but whilst this is a possibility for the future, pumped storage remains the only available method at present.

The principle is obvious enough. Electrical energy is converted into gravitational potential energy when the water is pumped from a lower reservoir to an upper one, and the process is reversed when it runs back down driving a turbo-generator on the way (Figure 5.37). The economics of the method depend on two nice technological facts. The first is that a suitably designed generator can be run 'backwards' as an electric motor: the machine which converts mechanical energy into electrical energy can equally well carry out the reverse process. And a suitably designed turbine can also be run in both directions: extracting energy from the water as a turbine and delivering energy to the water as a pump. The complete reversal is thus **turbo-generator** to **electric pump**. The machines must of course be designed for this dual role, but the cost saving is obviously significant.

There will, as always, be losses associated with the conversion processes, but turbines and generators are very efficient machines, and it is possible to retrieve nearly 80% of the input electrical energy. The value of the system is enhanced by the speed of response of hydroelectric generators: any of the six 300 MW Francis turbines of the Dinorwig storage plant in Wales can be brought to full power in just 10 seconds if it is initially spinning in air, and even from complete standstill takes only one minute. This makes pumped storage particularly useful as back-up in case of sudden changes, whether for the reasons discussed above or due to failure elsewhere in the system.

There are of course requirements on the location of systems. To make full use of the pumping facility, a low-level reservoir of at least the capacity of the upper one must be available – or must be constructed. Sites such as Cruachan (Figure 5.38), where the mountains rise from a loch, obviously meet this criterion. Using the sea as the lower reservoir is a further possibility, but questions then arise of the effect of sea water on the ecology of the upper reservoir and on equipment corrosion. Pumped storage systems can of course be combined with 'normal' hydroelectric generation in locations where there is already a potential for this. The upper reservoir will in any case have a local catchment area, so there may be a positive net output of electrical energy from the plant. Although a high head has the advantage of requiring smaller reservoirs for a given energy storage capacity, the Pelton wheels and Turgo turbines most suited to high heads cannot be used as pumps. At the other extreme, if the head is sufficiently low for propeller-type turbines, there is the advantage that the switch from pumping to generating can be achieved by reversing the pitch of the blades instead of changing the direction of rotation.

5.13 ECONOMICS

We now return to the questions raised at the end of Section 5.3 and ask about the **viable** hydroelectric resource. No matter how elegant the technology, few will buy it if it is going to lose money. The potential investor needs to know how much each kilowatt-hour of output will cost, taking all relevant factors into consideration.

COSTS

Unlike many of the other renewables, hydroelectricity is a very well-established technology. The water-control systems and the turbo-generators to extract the power are standard items. The many existing installations cover a power range from hundreds of watts to thousands of megawatts. Nevertheless, despite all the available data, it is very difficult if not impossible to generalise meaningfully about 'the cost of hydroelectric power'.

The reason lies in the combination of heavy front-end loading and extremely site-specific construction costs. In other words, the dominant factor in determining the total cost per unit of output is the initial capital cost, and a major part of this can be the civil engineering costs which vary greatly from site to site. On average, the civil works account for perhaps two-thirds of the total capital cost. But it could be over 80% – or at the other extreme, if the plant can make use of existing dams and reservoirs, as little as 25%. If we regard the machinery cost as a fixed amount for a given plant capacity, we see that the total capital cost can vary between less than half and more than twice the average. This could certainly make the difference between viability and non-viability.

Where a specific new proposal is concerned, past experience means that the capital cost can be estimated rather accurately, using the methods discussed in the Appendix. But Figure 5.39, based on the relatively detailed study of the scope for small-scale hydro in the UK described in Section 5.10 above, shows the wide range of estimates which can result from different plant sizes and sites. At the other extreme of size, a few examples might give an idea of the capital cost of large schemes. Canada and the USA are continuing to develop the resources of the Niagara River, with major civil engineering work to redirect water flows and extract the maximum power from this oldest of large-scale installations. The $500 million upgrade on the US side, to increase the capacity by 330 MW, had an estimated capital cost of $1500 (1990) per kilowatt (Prins, 1991). In Europe, the original 1989 estimate for the new Danube scheme was about $1200 per installed kilowatt (*New Civil Engineer*, 1989). It is claimed that the capital cost of the huge Itaipu plant was as low as $800 kW^{-1} (Helps, 1990), but on the other hand, World Bank figures indicate an average $1900 kW^{-1} (1988) for 'Third World' hydro developments (Munasinghe, 1989).

When we come to calculating the effect of capital cost on the cost per unit of output (p kWh^{-1}) the critical non-economic factor is the load factor of the plant. Clearly it makes a great deal of difference to the return on the investment whether the plant runs constantly at full power, or intermittently, using on average only a fraction of its installed capacity. In Section 5.3 we saw that hydroelectric plant world-wide runs with an average load factor of 40%, compared with perhaps 60%–80% for conventional (fossil fuel or nuclear) base-load plant in general. There are three main reasons why the load factor of any power plant will be less than 100%: shortage of input, lack of demand, and outages during maintenance or due to equipment failure. Bare data on load factors may not distinguish between these, and can be misleading. The speed of response of hydroelectric plant favours its use for rapid load-following rather than base load in systems where it coexists with the other types, and its load factor will obviously be low in these circumstances. Other factors can enter, however, such as reduced capacity due to drought,

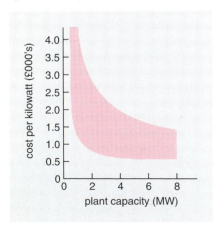

Figure 5.39 Capital cost and plant capacity for small-scale hydroelectricity in the UK. The graph, based on ETSU,1989 (Figures 5.33 and 5.34), shows the range of estimated capital costs for potential small-scale hydroelectric plants in the UK

or to the silting-up of reservoirs. To calculate the anticipated cost per unit of output it is necessary to estimate:

- the capital cost and anticipated time-scale for construction;
- the annual operating and maintenance costs;
- the load factors over the life of the plant;
- the appropriate discount rate.

An approximate cost can be obtained in the case of hydro power by assuming that the running costs are small compared to the cost of the capital investment, and that the load factor remains the same throughout the life of the plant. The cost in pence per kilowatt-hour on these assumptions, and using the method of calculation described in Box 5.11, is approximately equal to the capital cost in £ kW^{-1} divided by 350.
We return to these results and their significance for investment in hydro power in the next section.

It is possible, of course, to look at the cost data for existing installations, and these are on the whole much more encouraging for hydro power. Well-established plants are undoubtedly producing some of the cheapest power in many different countries. In Scotland, for instance, with its large proportion of hydro power, the average unit cost (1994) is only 1.5p kWh^{-1} - roughly two-thirds of the UK average for all types of power station. The same is true for many installations in the USA, and is the motivation for the widespread policy of upgrading existing structures by putting in new turbo-generator sets. This of course involves a much lower investment of capital than for a completely new plant.

BOX 5.11: CAPITAL COST AND COST PER KILOWATT-HOUR

Once we know the estimated capital cost of a proposed hydro plant, we need to estimate the cost per kilowatt-hour of the electricity it will produce.

As there are no fuel costs and maintenance costs are small, it is essentially the capital cost that matters. Call this £C per installed kilowatt.

The other relevant data are the load factor and the life of the plant. For simplicity we assume a load factor of 0.4 throughout the plant life. There are 8760 hours in a year, so each installed kilowatt will deliver 3500 kWh a year. We assume a plant life of 50 years and therefore a total lifetime output of 175 000 kWh per installed kW.

As a first attempt, suppose we were to adopt the simple view that the cost per kilowatt-hour is the total cost divided by the total number of kilowatt-hours: C divided by 175 000. If C is

£1000 kW^{-1}, for instance, the cost will be 0.57p kWh^{-1}.

However, as the Appendix shows, cost calculation in practice is not quite so simple, and can lead to a very different result.

The future income – in our case, the value of the kilowatt-hour produced – must be properly discounted. Suppose that the price obtained per unit is u pence per kWh. In the absence of other information, we assume that this remains constant in real terms throughout the life of the plant. The present value of the 50 years of output, for each installed kilowatt, is

$$PV = \frac{1-(1+r)^{-50}}{r} \times 3500 \times u$$

If we assume a 10% discount rate ($r = 0.1$), the value of $(1 + r)^{-50}$ is less than 0.01 and can be ignored. The PV is then

$$\left(\frac{1}{0.1}\right) \times 3500 \times u = 35\,000\ u$$

pence, or £350 × u.

For simplicity we assume that the capital is spent over a short period and need not be discounted. If the capital cost £C per installed kilowatt is to be covered by the present value of the output per installed kilowatt, we have

$C = 350 \times u.$

and the cost per unit becomes

$$u\,(\text{p kWh}^{-1}) = \frac{C(\text{£ kW}^{-1})}{350}$$

If C is £1000 per installed kilowatt, the cost per unit is now 2.9p kWh^{-1}, or about five times the previous figure! (It is worth noting that it rises still further, to about 3.4p kWh^{-1}, if we assume only a 20-year lifetime.)

INVESTING IN HYDROELECTRICITY

If hydroelectricity has so many of the desirable features listed in Section 5.12 and existing plant is producing cheaper power than from any other source, why are the utility companies and private producers in so many countries rushing to build gas turbine plants instead?

The answer seems to lie in the fact discussed above, that hydroelectric plant is capital-intensive. In contrast, a gas-turbine plant has relatively low initial capital cost but greater annual costs because they must include the fuel. So whilst most of the costs of the hydro plant are concentrated in a few years at the start, those of the gas turbine are spread more uniformly over its life. Unfortunately for hydroelectricity, the accepted methods for assessing the viability of a scheme, together with the high interest rates of recent years, have favoured the more uniform distribution of costs. Consider the four graphs in Figure 5.40.

Each of the upper two graphs shows the actual cost per year over the life of the plant together with the output per year. They are of course much simplified, but the pattern on the left is characteristic of hydro plant and that on the right of a gas turbine system. In this example both have the same total lifetime costs (construction, maintenance, operation, fuel) but the hydro plant has a longer life and therefore a greater total lifetime output. It seems obvious therefore that the hydro plant produces the cheaper power.

But observe the effect of adopting the discounting procedure and changing to present values. The value of the power which the hydro plant produces during its later years is discounted almost to nothing. It now appears that the two plants have about the *same* lifetime output, but the hydro has *higher*

Figure 5.40 Some effects of discounting. (See the text for discussion of these graphs). (a) actual costs and output – hydro; (b) present value – hydro; (c) actual costs and output – other power plant; (d) present values – other power plant

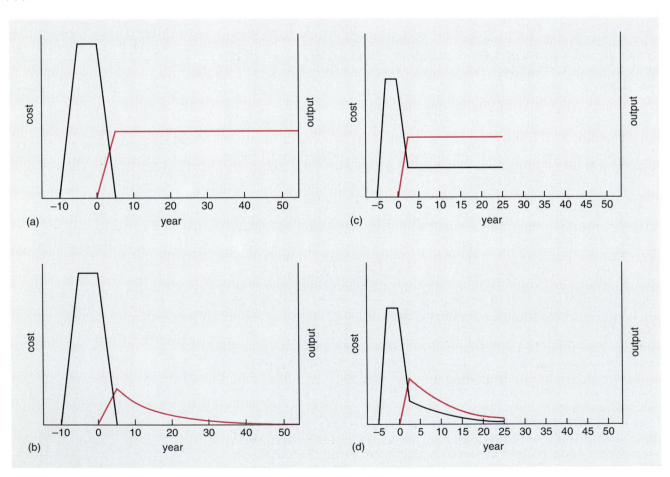

lifetime cost. On this basis, there is no doubt that the gas turbine is the better investment.

In the words of a recent report:

It is paradoxical that investment in hydro schemes looks extremely favourable in retrospect ... but extremely uncertain in prospect.

(Munasinghe, 1989)

Or in one specific case:

The Puueo plant (in Hawaii), first operated in 1918, is still generating electricity. ... Long ago, the plant paid off its initial capital costs and completed its economic life. Therefore, according to a cost–benefit economic study, the electricity which the plant is producing has no value. But the fact is that the plant continues to produce ... the same power that it did 60 years ago and there should be some way to place a value on it ...

(Miyabara, 1981)

There is much truth in the observation that all power producers wish they had invested in hydroelectricity 20 years ago, but unfortunately can't afford to do so now – and that they held this same view 20 years ago!

5.14 FUTURE PROSPECTS

World total electricity production is currently about 12 000 TWh per annum, from an installed generating capacity of 2700 GW, implying a world-wide annual load factor of 50%. As we saw in Section 5.3, the corresponding figures for hydroelectricity are 2200 TWh from a capacity of 630 GW – just over 18% of the total output from 23% of the total capacity. World-wide, electricity consumption rose by 40% during the 1980s, an average annual increase of 3.4%. Significantly, however, consumption in the developing countries has risen at about twice this rate.

CONVENTIONAL LARGE INSTALLATIONS

It is not surprising that most of the world's undeveloped hydroelectric potential is found in its less developed regions, or that many of the very large-scale developments recently completed or currently under consideration are in the parts of South America, Asia and Africa which have this potential. These major plants are undoubtedly supplying power to large areas of the world, as can be seen from the 7% growth in per capita electricity consumption in the developing countries, with a comparable rate of increase in the number of connections to the supply. However, the low overall economic growth indicated by GDP annual increases of only a per cent or two makes it doubtful whether investment in power plant is succeeding in one of its main aims, encouraging industrial growth. Concern has been expressed that power station construction alone has been accounting for a quarter or more of government investment in many countries, with rates of return which show a steady fall over the past two decades. Plant load factors are frequently poor, in part because distribution systems have failed to keep pace with plant capacity. A recent paper expressed the view that:

It seems apparent ... that there is a strong argument in favour of putting greater emphasis on efficiency and restructuring issues, rather than concentrating solely on continued power-sector expansion.

(Munasinghe, 1989)

These comments do not of course imply a total stop to power development. Nor do they invalidate the argument that where major expansion is still seen as necessary, hydroelectricity at least does not add to the world's atmospheric pollution or deplete its fuel resources. Large-scale hydro installations are bound to alter the landscape, and in populated regions their socially disruptive effects may be considered unacceptable, but their supporters argue that other deleterious environmental effects discussed in Section 5.11 are avoidable with care and good planning. Unlike many of the by-products of power from fossil or nuclear fuels, these are not, it is claimed, *necessary* consequences of hydroelectric power production.

In the industrialised nations, future large-scale development is of course already constrained. Some countries have little or no potential for large-scale hydroelectricity, whilst in others such as Norway, Switzerland or the USA, the installed capacity may already be approaching the full potential of the resource, or at least the point where environmental criteria over-ride other considerations. In the USA, the existing hydroelectric capacity of 72 GW is predicted to rise by about 20% before the end of the century, but much of the increase will come from the up-grading of existing schemes, installing more modern equipment to improve their efficiency. Where available this option has the obvious attraction of providing additional capacity without the full costs of major civil engineering work.

The present total hydroelectric capacity of the EU countries is about 60 GW – equivalent to the total generating capacity of the UK. The predicted increase in the EU for the next decade is a little less than 10% – again much of it through up-grading of existing installations. The largest current development in Europe is the Danube scheme, whose completion is in some doubt, as we have seen.

SMALL-SCALE PLANT

Not surprisingly, the world potential for small-scale hydroelectricity has not been estimated in detail, although studies have been carried out in a number of individual countries. These have found small-scale potentials ranging from a tenth to perhaps a quarter of the total hydro potential, suggesting an additional capacity of perhaps 500 GW - comparable with the 600 GW of all existing hydro plant. The present small-scale capacity world-wide in plants of 5 MW or less is thought to be about 25 GW, of which 10 GW is in China. If these estimates are reliable, it would appear that whereas some 10–20% of the large-scale technically exploitable potential has been developed, for small-scale plant the figure is only 5%.

Some 70 countries now have small-scale programmes, with plans for some 5 GW of plant, 10% of which is under construction. Nevertheless the extent to which the world will develop the remaining potential remains uncertain. China, with about half its annual hydro output of 80 TWh already coming from small-scale plant, is unique. For the rest of the world the fraction is less than 1%.

Recent studies of the UK potential have suggested that, on both cost and environmental grounds, there is little likelihood of major large-scale hydroelectric development. Small-scale installations, however, may be more acceptable environmentally, and could contribute as much as 2000 GWh a year at a unit cost of 3p kWh^{-1} or less. This figure assumes a 56% load factor, annual costs equal to 2% of the capital cost and 8% discount rate. At 15% discount rate, it falls to less than 1000 GWh a year, but at 8% and a unit cost of 6p kWh^{-1}, rises to nearly 4000 GWh (ETSU 1994(2)).

Worldwide, there appear to have been two main factors acting against development on the Chinese scale. One has been the predilection of most governments and major utilities companies everywhere for large centralised systems. The other is financial.

The problem is that hydro plant is capital-intensive. As we have seen, by conventional investment criteria, it compares unfavourably with fuel-consuming alternatives whose costs are more evenly split over the life of the plant. From the investors' point of view the fact that the hydro plant will still be producing power in the year 2050, long after its capital is paid off, is of little immediate interest. (It may however interest their great-grandchildren, particularly when they realise that the alternatives have exhausted the world's gas reserves.)

To see large-scale growth in small-scale hydro, therefore, some change is necessary. The options appear to be:

• a reduction in the initial cost – perhaps as a result of technological improvements or by greater standardisation of systems;

• a change in the purely financial factors – perhaps a tax structure reflecting environmental and long-term benefits, or government policies favouring lower interest rates;

• government investment in small-scale systems, accepting a lower rate of return.

Each of these options probably requires expenditure. In the UK, the support which renewable energy has received in the early 1990s through the NFFO scheme (Section 5.10) has been financed by a levy on electricity consumers. An encouraging move, but the actual figures give cause for reflection; the NFFO contributions to small-scale hydro for 1994 added rather less than thirty pence to the average household electricity bill for the entire year.

REFERENCES

CONAES (1979) National Research Council Committee on Nuclear and Alternative Energy Systems, *Energy in Transition 1985–2010*, W. H. Freeman, San Francisco.

Department of Trade and Industry (1993) *Digest of United Kingdom Energy Statistics*, HMSO, London.

Dodd, Christopher (1993), *Damming of the Danube*, The Guardian, February 12.

Dorf, R. C. (1978) *Energy, Resources and Policy*, Addison-Wesley, New York.

ETSU (1989) *Small Scale Hydroelectric Generation Potential in the UK*, Department of Energy, Energy Technology Support Unit, Report No. ETSU-SSH-4063, London.

ETSU (1994(1)) *New and Renewable Energy: Future Prospects in the UK*, Energy Paper 62, HMSO, London.

ETSU (1994(2)) *An Assessment of Renewable Energy for the UK*, Energy Paper R82, HMSO, London.

Fleischer, Tamas (1993), *Jaws on the Danube: Water Management, Regime Change and the Movement Against the Middle Danube Hydroelectric Dam*.

Helps, F. C. (1990) 'Itaipu – the rock that sings', *IEE Review*, July/August.

Miyabara, T. and Goodman, L. J. (1981) 'Hawaii, USA: hydroelectric development', in Goodman, L. J. *et al.*, *Small Hydroelectric Projects for Rural Development*, Pergamon, London.

Munasinghe, M. (1989) 'Power for development, electricity in the Third World', *IEE Review*, March.

New Civil Engineer (1989), 24 August.

Open University (1986) *T362 Design and Innovation*, Units 3–5, 'Water Turbines', The Open University, Milton Keynes.

Prins, A. (1991) 'Niagara, falling for power', *IEE Review*, October.

UN (1992) *1990 Energy Statistics Yearbook*, United Nations, New York.

FURTHER READING

Webber, N. B. (1971) *Fluid Mechanics for Civil Engineers*, Chapman and Hall.
Streeter, V. L. and Wylie, E. B. (1979) *Fluid Mechanics*, 7th edition, McGraw-Hill, New York.
Either of these well-established textbooks could provide useful further reading for a student of the physical sciences or related technologies wanting a more detailed mathematical account of the operation of different types of turbine.

Open University (1993) T236 *Introduction to Thermofluid Mechanics*, Block 5, 'Fluid momentum', The Open University.
The treatment in this section of the Open University course T236, rather shorter than in the above textbooks, leads to a useful detailed discussion of the Francis and Pelton turbines.

Fraenkel, P. *et al.* (1991) *Micro-Hydro Power*, Intermediate Technology.
In contrast to the above recommendations, this down-to-earth and very interesting book has almost no mathematics but a great deal of practical detail. Its emphasis on the potential for hydro-power in the developing world also provides a useful contrast in technology.

Strandh, S. (1979) *The History of the Machine*, Bracken Books.
Open University (1986) T362 *Design and Innovation*, Units 3–5, 'Water turbines', Open University Press

Hill, G. (1984) *Tunnel and Dam: the story of the Galloway Hydros*, South of Scotland Electricity Board (now Scottish Power).
These three books, very different in style and approach, offer interesting accounts of some of the developments leading to today's hydro-technology. They might prove attractive both to those whose main concerns lie outside the sciences and to scientists and technologists who are interested in the wider aspects of their subject.

TIDAL POWER

6.1 INTRODUCTION

The rise and fall of the seas represents a vast, and as King Canute reputedly discovered, relentless natural phenomenon.

The use of tides to provide energy has a long history, with small tidal mills on rivers being used for grinding corn in Britain and France in the Middle Ages. More recently, the idea of using tidal energy on a much larger scale to generate electricity has emerged, with turbines mounted in large **barrages**, essentially low dams, built across suitable estuaries. This colourful 1938 account of tidal power by Ritchie Calder focuses on the scheme proposed at that time for the Bay of Fundy in Canada (see Figure 6.1).

MIGHTY ENGINES DRIVEN BY THE MOON

BY RITCHIE CALDER

The Moon rides high but there are ways of harnessing it and taming it to the docility of a trace-horse. Or, rather, 12 000 000 000 horses.

You might guess that a large-scale rodeo like that – a circus such as even 'The Mighty Barnum' never dreamed of – would appeal to the Americans. So they set about harnessing the Moon.

And the way they intended to do it was through the tides.

Up the Bay of Fundy races a tidal bore like the one in the Bristol Channel. In Passamaquoddy inlet at Eastport, Maine, it rises sharply, between 18 and 26 feet at each tide.

Dexter Cooper, a visionary promoter, had a summer residence at Eastport, and his near neighbour was Franklin Roosevelt. When the depression hit Maine,

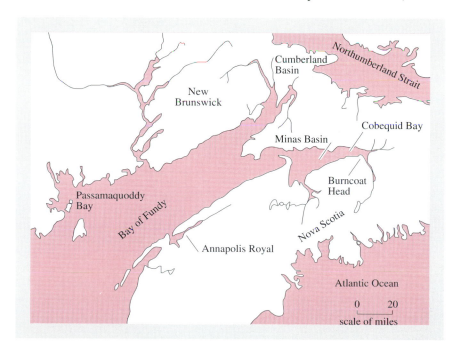

Figure 6.1　Tidal power sites in the Bay of Fundy

Cooper conceived the idea of turning the giant horses of the Fundy Bore into power and the backward areas of Maine into an industrial region.

He submitted his plan to the Public Works ('New Deal') Administration but it was turned down as impracticable. Then Mrs. Cooper thought of Neighbour Roosevelt, now translated to the White House, Washington, DC, so she put on her best hat and went off to see him.

Roosevelt OK'd the scheme, turned the US Army engineers on to the job with £1 million in their knapsacks. They examined the draft schemes and discarded them, spending nearly half their money allocation in evolving new ones.

But, at last, they planned a way of 'coralling' the Moon and putting it into harness. A barrage was to be built, the tide was to rush in, fill the giant reservoir and rush out again, through the turbines. A secondary station was to 'level-out' the tides, which unfortunately do not run, like industries, throughout the whole day, by maintaining a relief supply.

The work began. Millions of tons of rock and rubble were piled into Passamaquoddy Bay.

And then it stopped abruptly. Congress did not like the idea of harnessing the Moon to a New England buggy. The Senate liked it even less, for it saw little prospect of that enormous power being used. And £8 million is a lot of money to spend on Moon-chasing, even in America.

So the scheme was dished. Passamaquoddy is just a dismal monument to an ambitious scheme which the politicians did not like.
But that does not prove that it was 'phoney'. On the contrary, Passamaquoddy may yet prove more than a dream. But it will mean a treaty with Canada. Look at an atlas, and you will see how the tidal race of Fundy, translated into power may yet bring industry and prosperity to New Brunswick and Nova Scotia, two parts of the British Empire still backward from the point of view of industrial prosperity.

Take cheap power over the frontier from Quoddy and the two provinces could be galvanised into life.

Meanwhile the scheme is just one stage farther on than the British plan for 'harnessing the Moon' in the Bristol Channel – which lies in some Whitehall pigeon-hole. Here, too, there is a mighty tidal bore, plunging like a million bucking broncos, careering into the funnel-shaped mouth of the Severn.

A government committee, appointed 12 years ago, examined a scheme for building a barrage across 'The Shoots' where the estuary narrows to 1500 feet, with a depth of 60 feet. It is estimated that it would supply one-thirteenth of the total requirements of Great Britain in 1941. It could supply 2 207 000 000 units of electricity a year.

The actual tides would generate about half, but the reservoir and a secondary station, balancing, as at Quoddy, the action of the tides would supply the rest and keep up a steady supply during the whole 24 hours.

The secondary reservoir would be in the hills, 500 feet up. The water would be raised by electric driven centrifugal pumps. These same pumps would be used as turbines to generate the power when the water 'went into reverse'.

In this way we could generate in the Severn about a third of the power which can be produced at Boulder Dam. The cost of generation per kilowatt hour, would be 0.2372d but the cost of construction would be nearly £40 million.

(Source: Calder, 1938)

Subsequently, as we shall see, interest in tidal power has continued. One medium-scale scheme has been built at the Rance Estuary in France (see Figure 6.2) and a number of small schemes have been built around the world. There have also been proposals for barrages with several gigawatts of generating capacity. An artist's impression of the proposed 8.6 gigawatt (GW) Severn Barrage, stretching 16 kilometres across the Severn Estuary, is shown in Figure 6.3. If built, this would generate 17 terawatt-hours per year (TWh y^{-1}), the equivalent of some 6% of the electricity generated in the UK in 1992.

Tidal barrages thus potentially represent the utilisation of renewable energy on a very large scale, and, as Figure 6.4 illustrates, there are several possible sites for large-scale projects around the world.

Figure 6.2   Aerial view of La Rance tidal scheme

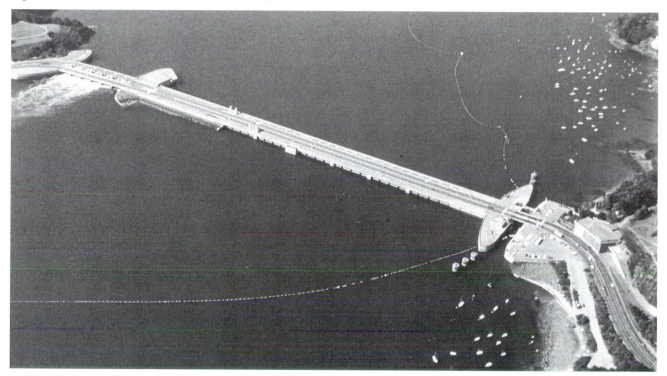

Figure 6.3   Artist's impression of the proposed Severn Barrage

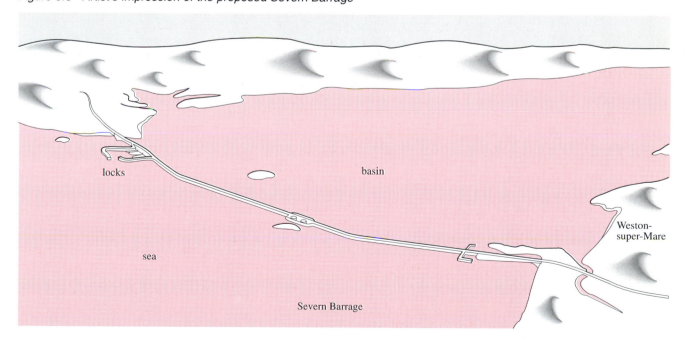

THE NATURE OF THE RESOURCE

It is important at the outset to distinguish tidal energy from hydro power. Tidal energy, as we shall see, is the result of the interaction of the gravitational pull of the moon and, to a lesser extent, the sun, on the seas. As we saw in Chapter 5, hydro power is derived from the hydrological climate cycle, powered by solar energy, which is usually harnessed via hydroelectric dams. Schemes that use tidal energy rely on the twice-daily upstream flow and/or downstream ebb of the tides.

Equally, we must distinguish between tidal energy and the energy in waves. This distinction is not helped by the use of the term 'tidal wave' to describe the occasionally dramatic surges of water (which are neither waves nor tides!) that are sometimes produced by storms or undersea earthquakes.

Conventional waves are caused by the action of wind over water, this in turn being the result of the differential solar heating of air over land and sea. If we consider wave energy, like hydroelectric energy, to be a form of solar power, tidal energy could be called 'lunar power'.

The rise and fall of the tides can be exploited without the use of dams across estuaries, as in some traditional **tidal mills** on the tidal sections of rivers. A small pond or pool is simply topped up and closed off at high tide and then, at low tide, the head of water is used to drive a water wheel, as with traditional watermills.

There is also the possibility of using the rapidly flowing **tidal streams** at sea. These are strong surface currents created due to the effects of concentration in narrow channels, for example between islands or other constrictions. Some recent developments in this area are discussed later in Box 6.11.

Figure 6.4   Locations of possible sites for tidal barrages

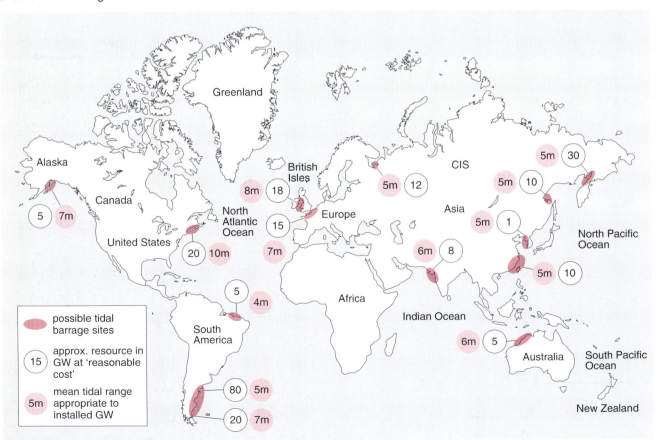

More usually, however, the upstream **tidal flow** in an estuary (usually called the 'flood' tide) is trapped behind a barrage. The incoming tide is allowed to pass through sluices, which are then closed at high tide, trapping the water. As the tide ebbs, the water level on the downstream side of the barrage reduces and a 'head' of water develops across the barrage. The basic technology for power extraction is then similar to that for low-head hydro, that is, the head drives the water through turbine generators. The main difference, apart from the salt-water environment, is that the power-generating turbines in tidal barrages have to deal with regularly varying heads of water.

BASIC PHYSICS

The variation in tidal height is due primarily to gravitational interaction between the earth and the moon. As the earth rotates on its axis, gravitational forces produce, at any particular point on the globe, a twice-daily rise and fall in sea level, this being modified in height by the gravitational pull of the sun, and by the topography of land masses and oceans.

The detailed analysis of the interaction between earth, moon and sun is quite complex. However, in simple terms, starting first with just the earth and the moon, the gravitational pull of the moon draws the seas on the side

---

BOX 6.1: THE EARTH AND THE MOON

A useful mathematical analysis of the generation of tides is given in *Renewable Energy Resources* (Twidell and Weir, 1986). This identifies *two* processes at work in relation to the earth and the moon: a centrifugal effect as well as a gravitational effect.

The first process, the centrifugal effect (that is, the tendency of any mass in motion to try to continue in a straight line rather than be constrained to move in a circle), is the result of the fact that the earth and the moon rotate around each other, somewhat like a 'dumb-bell' being twirled. In reality, this giant dumb-bell does not rotate around the half-way point between the earth and the moon. Since the earth is much larger than the moon, their common centre of rotation is close to the earth; in fact it is just below its surface (see Figure 6.5). The mutual rotation around this point produces a relatively large *outward* centrifugal force acting on the seas on the side of the earth *furthest* from the moon, bunching them up into a bulge. There is also a smaller centrifugal force, directed *towards*

the moon, that acts on the seas *facing* the moon. (This force is smaller since here the distance from the earth's surface to the common rotation point, just below the surface, is smaller.)

The second process, the gravitational effect, relates to the gravitational pull of the moon, which draws the seas on the side of the earth *nearest* to the moon into a bulge *towards* the moon, whilst the seas *furthest* from the moon experience a less than average lunar pull and bulge *away* from the moon.

There is thus, to summarise, a small centrifugal force and an increased lunar pull acting on the seas facing the moon, and a larger centrifugal force and a decreased lunar pull acting on the seas on the other side of the earth. The end result, on the basis of this analysis, is essentially a symmetry of forces, small and large, on each side of the earth, producing tidal bulges of (in theory) the same size on each side of the earth. In practice, the bulges may differ, due, for example, to the tilt of the earth's axis in relation to the orbit of the moon and to local topographic effects.

For further discussion, see *Waves, Tides and Shallow Water Processes* (Open University, 1989).

Figure 6.5   Relative rotation of the earth and the moon (not to scale)

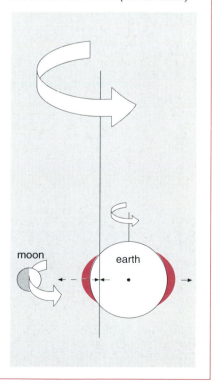

of the earth *nearest* to the moon into a bulge *towards* the moon, while the seas *furthest* from the moon experience a less than average lunar pull and bulge *away* from the moon.

As the earth rotates on its axis, the lunar pull will maintain these high tide patterns, as it were 'under' the moon. That is, the two high tide configurations will in effect be drawn around the globe as the earth rotates, giving, at any particular point, *two* tides per day (or, more accurately, two tides in every 24.8-hour period), occurring approximately 12.5 hours apart. Since the moon is also moving in orbit around the earth, the timing of these high tides at any particular point will vary, occurring approximately 50 minutes later each day. For a somewhat more detailed analysis, see Box 6.1.

This basic pattern is modified by the pull of the sun. Although the sun is much larger than the moon, it is much further away from the earth, and the moon's influence on the seas is approximately twice that of the sun, the final impact depending on their relative orientation.

When the sun and the moon pull together (in line), the result is the very high 'spring tides'; when they are at 90° to each other, the result is the lower 'neap tides'. The period between neap and spring tides is approximately 14 days – that is, half the 29.5-day lunar cycle (Figure 6.6). The ratio between the height of the maximum spring and minimum neap tides can be more than two to one.

The gravitational pull of the sun is larger, by a factor of approximately 177, than the pull of the moon, and yet its influence on the tides is much less.

The explanation, as outlined by Baker (1991b), is that the ratio of the earth's diameter to the distance between the earth and the moon is much greater than the equivalent ratio for the sun, making the gravitational gradient across the earth higher for the moon than for the sun. It is the net *difference* in the gravitational fields of the moon and the sun on either side of the earth that is the defining factor.

The analysis of interactions presented above is simplified. In reality, there are other factors that complicate the tidal patterns and can alter them dramatically.

Some of the other factors do not have much direct relevance to tidal power generation. For example, although the tides are not seasonal in climate terms, the weather can play a significant (and sometimes destructive) role, with high winds and major storms occasionally combining with high tides to produce very high 'surge' tides. Barrages have to be designed to withstand these surges, but any energy gains from them would be marginal.

However, there are other factors that *are* more relevant to power generation, even if their significance is usually relatively small. For example, the basic twice-monthly moon/sun, spring/neap tide pattern outlined above is modified by the fact that the moon's orbit is not circular but *elliptical*. There are also longer-term orbital variations, for example a semi-annual cycle caused by the inclination of the moon's orbit in relation to that of the earth (around the sun), which gives a variation of approximately 10% in the height of the tides.

Finally, to complete the complex picture of the nature and cause of tides, the tides are modified in some locations by **Coriolis forces**. These are due to the spin of the earth, and deflect tidal currents from the paths that they would otherwise have taken.

Apart from relatively minor perturbations such as these, the overall effect of the basic sun–moon–earth interaction is that, *in mid-ocean*, the typical tidal variation or **tidal range** should be approximately 0.5 metres. However, the tidal ranges experienced in practice at coastal sites are sometimes significantly modified and amplified by *local* topographic variations, for example in shallow coastal waters and in estuaries. As the tide approaches the shore, and the water depth decreases, the tidal flow is concentrated and can be increased to reach up to, typically, 3 m. If the tide then enters a suitably shaped estuary, it can be funnelled and therefore heightened even further, up to 10–15 m at some sites, with complex resonance effects playing a major role.

Resonances are like the vibrations that can be set up in the sound boxes of some musical instruments, amplifying certain frequencies of the original sound. Whether any particular resonance can be set up depends on the shape of the 'cavity' in which it is established. The size of the cavity has to be matched to the wavelength of the sound, or some multiple of it. Given the variations in depth and width of estuaries, it is hardly surprising that in practice the resonance patterns that emerge, when and if tidal resonances occur, are often very complicated. This point is discussed further in Box 6.2, which also opens up the intriguing idea of resonance across entire oceans.

Even without a full understanding of resonances, it is fairly easy to see that, given the right 'funnel' configuration, the tidal range will increase as the tide moves upstream, and as the depth and width of the estuary reduces. However, there are also frictional effects: for example, energy is lost as the tidal flow moves over differing estuary bed materials.

In practice, the extent to which the tidal range is magnified at any point depends on the balance between the energy losses and the concentration of the tidal flow by the topography. The frictional losses will usually begin to outweigh the concentration gains at some point upstream when the funnel-like layout of an estuary gives way to a more parallel-sided, flat-bottomed river configuration. On the Severn, this 'natural' optimal point normally occurs around the site of the existing Severn Bridge, where the tidal range reaches 11 m.

Figure 6.6   Influence of the sun and the moon on tidal range (not to scale)

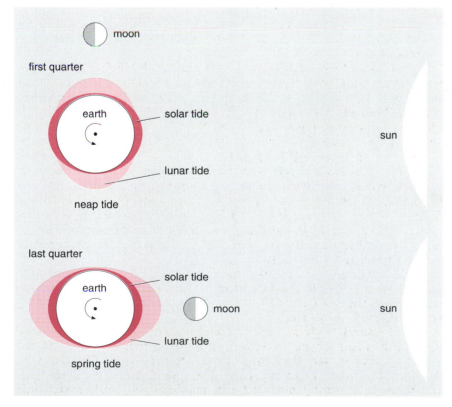

BOX 6.2: RESONANCES

Resonance effects, occurring both locally (for example, in estuaries) and also across the width of oceans, can play a major role in increasing tidal range.

An estuary or a complete ocean basin can behave like a *resonant cavity*: an enclosure or box in which resonances occur when the dimensions of the box match the wavelength of an impinging vibration or oscillating 'signal'. If the dimensions are right, the waves trapped in the cavity reflect off the walls and reinforce or *amplify* the original signal. These 'standing waves' can also have wavelengths that are *multiples* of the original wavelength, as long as they are exact multiples. Similarly, resonances can occur with waves at half or one quarter of the original wavelength.

The cyclic rise and fall of the tides represents an oscillating signal or vibration that can enable amplified resonances to be created in an ocean basin or estuary of appropriate dimensions. In very crude terms, this is something like the 'sloshing' effect you can create by moving with the right rhythm when lying in a bath. The height you can obtain depends on the amount and the phasing of the energy you put in, but also on the shape of the bath.

As it happens, the distance between North America and Europe, approximately 4000 km, turns out to be just about right for creating a resonance, given the 12-hour tidal cycle, with a wavelength of twice the width of the ocean.

In practice, the tidal range that results at each coast will depend on local effects. In the simple picture given above, the oscillating cavity, that is, the ocean basin, was assumed to have vertical sides, which could reflect the standing waves perfectly. In reality, the sea bed rises near the coast and this will modify the resonance effect, with local resonances, driven by the changes at deep sea level, sometimes resulting. In the case of the North Atlantic, the end result is that the initial open sea tidal range (of 0.5 m) is enhanced to approximately 3 m at each side of the Atlantic.

Modified resonances of this sort, albeit at different frequencies, should also occur in the Pacific, which is about four times the width of the Atlantic, the tidal cycle's wavelength in this case being *half* the width of the ocean. However, the width is irregular, and the result in practice is that resonant effects around the Pacific are often more complex and less dramatic. In some locations around the Pacific, the result is that only very small tides occur, that is, there is little resonatory enhancement. Interestingly, in some sites there is only one significant tide per day, since the resonances occur only on the basis of 24-hour periods.

Local resonances

In addition to the resonances created *across* complete ocean basins, *local* resonances in shallower coastal areas are possible, for example in the smaller basins defined by some land masses and in estuaries. These can increase the tidal range from its typical coastal height of 3 m to over 10 m.

For example, the Irish Sea, Bristol Channel and Severn Estuary complex has a total length of approximately 600 km and a natural resonant period of approximately six hours, and resonances at a quarter wave length (twice the tidal wave frequency) are therefore possible. There is also a half-cycle resonance in the area from Land's End to Dover along the English Channel (approximately 500 km at an average depth of approximately 70 m).

Resonance can be very much greater in estuaries, since they are more like closed cavities, but the resonances are often very complex, since the width and depth varies, and changes in the nature of the estuary bottom introduce varying frictional losses (see Figure 6.7).

For more detailed discussion of resonance effects, see *Tidal Power* (Baker, 1991a).

Figure 6.7   Tidal resonance in the Severn Estuary

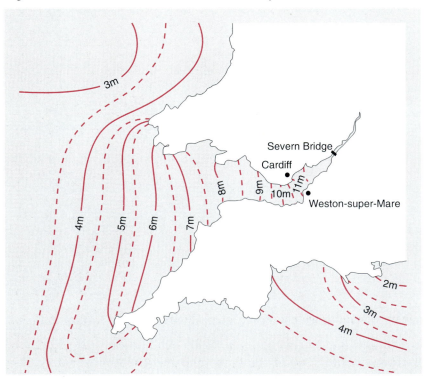

Occasionally, in some long estuaries, dramatic tidal effects can occur further upstream. For example, rather than producing a relatively slow rise, as normally happens in the main part of the Severn Estuary, the upstream tidal flow further up the Severn can be concentrated so abruptly that it rises into an almost vertical step or wave, the so-called Severn Bore. A similar effect occurs on other long estuaries, including the Humber and the Hoogly near Calcutta in India.

As can be seen, even leaving aside freak effects like the Severn Bore, there is a complex range of tidal phenomena. Fortunately for the designers of tidal barrages, the end results – that is, the tidal patterns in estuaries – although very much site-specific, are predictable and reliable. The tides will continue to ebb and flow, on schedule, indefinitely.

Is the energy in the tides really renewable?

As we have seen, the primary mechanism in tide generation is the gravitational interaction between the earth and the moon, but the energy in the tidal flow comes from the rotation of the earth, which, in effect, draws the tidal bulges across the seas. The rotation of the earth is being very gradually slowed (by approximately one-fiftieth of a second every 1000 years) by this process, because of friction, but the extra frictional effect that would be produced even by the widespread use of tidal barrages would be extremely small. The influence on the moon's orbital velocity (which is also being very slowly reduced by the tidal interaction) would be even smaller.

POWER GENERATION

The basic physics and engineering of tidal power generation are relatively straightforward.

Tidal barrages, built across suitable estuaries, are designed to extract energy from the rise and fall of the tides, using turbines located in water passages in the barrages. The *potential energy*, due to the difference in water levels across the barrages, is converted into *kinetic energy* in the form of fast-moving water passing through the turbines. This, in turn, is converted into *rotational kinetic energy* by the blades of the turbine, the spinning turbine then driving a generator to produce electricity.

The average power output from a tidal barrage is roughly proportional to the square of the tidal range. The mathematical derivation of this is fairly simple, as is demonstrated by the analysis in Box 6.3.

Clearly, even small differences in tidal range, however caused, can make a significant difference to the viability and economics of a barrage. A mean tidal range of at least 5 m is usually considered to be the minimum for viable power generation, depending, of course, on the economic criteria used. As the analysis in Box 6.3 indicates, the energy output is also roughly proportional to the area of the water trapped behind the barrage, so the geography of the site is very important. All of this means that the siting of barrages is a crucial element in their viability.

To date, the only tidal power plant of any size to have been installed is the 240 megawatt (MW)-rated prototype barrage on the Rance Estuary in Brittany, on the west coast of France, which has been operating successfully for more than 25 years. A single 18 MW-rated turbine was installed in the mid-1980s at Annapolis Royal in Nova Scotia, Canada, and there are a number of other much smaller projects around the world, including a prototype in a small estuary off the White Sea near Murmansk in Russia and several in China.

Many studies have been carried out on tidal power in the UK, dating from the early 1900s onwards (see Box 6.4). This is hardly surprising, since the UK has about half the total European potential for tidal energy, including one of the world's best potential sites, the Severn Estuary. There is also a range of possible medium- and small-scale sites, including locations

BOX 6.3: DERIVATION OF POWER OUTPUT FROM A TIDAL BARRAGE

Assume that the high-to-low tidal range is R and that the basin behind the barrage has a constant surface area A, which remains covered in water at low tide (see Figure 6.8). The trapped water, having a mass ρAR at a centre of gravity $R/2$ above the low tide (where ρ is the density of water), is all assumed to run out at low tide. The maximum potential energy E available per tide if all the water falls through a height of $R/2$ is therefore given by the mass of water (ρAR) times the height ($R/2$) times the acceleration due to gravity (g), that is, $E = \rho ARg(R/2)$. If this energy is averaged over the tidal period T, the average potential energy for one tide becomes $\rho AR^2g/2T$.

Figure 6.8 Power generation from tides

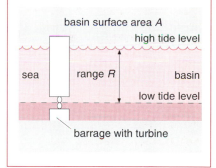

basin surface area A

high tide level

sea   range R basin

low tide level

barrage with turbine

BOX 6.4: A BRIEF HISTORY OF TIDAL POWER

Small tidal mills, not unlike traditional watermills, were used quite widely on tidal rivers in the Middle Ages for grinding corn, but the idea of exploiting the full power of the tides in estuaries is relatively recent.

There have been a number of proposals for various types of crossing for the Severn Estuary, the UK's largest tidal site. For example, a barrage concept (albeit with no provision for power generation) attributed to Thomas Telford was put forward in 1849. The first serious proposal involving electricity production came in 1920 from the Ministry of Transport. This was followed by a major study by the Brabazon Commission, which was set up in 1925 and reported in 1933, which focused on a barrage on the English Stones line, not far from the modern Severn Bridge. It was to have 72 turbines with a total installed capacity of 804 MW and to incorporate road and rail crossings. The scheme was not followed up. It was reassessed in 1944, but again not followed up.

In the 1960s and 1970s, a range of schemes was proposed, each on different lines, culminating in a new government-supported study by the Severn Barrage Committee, which was set up in 1978 under Professor Sir Hermann Bondi. The Committee reported in 1981 (Department of Energy, 1981), concluding that it was 'technically feasible to enclose the estuary by a barrage located in any position east of a line drawn from Porlock due North to the Welsh Coast'. From all the possible lines, three were favoured, the most ambitious being from Minehead to Aberthaw, which, it was estimated, could generate 20 TWh y^{-1} from 12 GW of installed capacity.

In the event, the less ambitious, but still very large, so-called 'inner barrage', on a line (first proposed by E. M. Wilson in 1966) from Weston-super-Mare to Lavernock Point, became the favourite, and was pursued by the Severn Tidal Power Group industrial consortium. It was initially conceived of as generating approximately 13 TWh y^{-1} from 7 GW installed, although this has since been upgraded to 17 TWh y^{-1} from 8.64 GW installed.

Enthusiasm for tidal schemes was fuelled in part by the success of the French scheme on the Rance Estuary in Brittany, near St Malo (Figure 6.2). It was constructed between 1961 and 1967 and the first output from its 240 MW turbine capacity was achieved in 1966. It includes a road crossing. Apart from a problem with the generator mountings in 1975, it has operated very successfully. Subsequently, a much larger 15 GW scheme was proposed, to enclose a vast area of sea from St Malo in the south to Cap de Carterel in the north, the so-called Isle de Chausey project. This has not been followed up.

Although large-scale schemes have been proposed for the Bay of Fundy in Canada and in the former USSR, the only significant tidal plants to be built to date, other than La Rance, are an 18 MW single unit, using a 'rim generator' (see Figure 6.14), at Annapolis Royal in Nova Scotia, completed in 1984; a 400 kilowatt (kW) unit in the Bay of Kislaya, 100 km from Murmansk, completed in 1968; and a 500 kW unit at Jangxia Creek in the East China Sea.

Whilst a number of other schemes have been considered around the world, the main focus in recent years in the field of tidal power has been on the Severn Barrage 'inner barrage' concept and on the Mersey Barrage. However, as we shall see, barrages on the Humber and several smaller UK estuaries have also been considered.

For further information on the history of tidal power, see the 'Further Reading' section.

on the Mersey, Wyre and Conwy. The total UK theoretical tidal energy potential is estimated at approximately 53 TWh y^{-1}, about 17% of current UK electricity generation. The contribution to electricity consumption that could be achieved in the UK and elsewhere in practice would depend on a range of *technical*, *environmental*, *institutional* and *economic* factors. Although these factors interact, we can explore each in turn before attempting a synthesis.

6.2 TECHNICAL FACTORS

The input energy source for a barrage, the rise and fall of the tides, follows a roughly sinusoidal pattern (see the sea level curves in Figure 6.9). As we have seen, the tides have a 12.4-hour cycle, with the peak-to-trough height variation (that is, the tidal range) varying from site to site, due to complex resonances.

Given the complexity of estuary configurations, the actual resonances and funnelling effects are very hard to model accurately, with variations in depth, width and friction over differing estuary bed materials introducing many local variations.

However, it is well worth the effort required to analyse these effects when deciding on the precise siting and orientation of a barrage, since they will have a major effect on its output. Indeed, it may be possible to locate and/or operate a barrage so as to 'tune' the estuary to be more nearly resonant, and thus to increase power output. Certainly, disturbance to existing resonance should be avoided.

In addition to the basic issues of location and orientation, a second set of factors that influence the likely power output of a barrage relates to its *operational pattern.*

Power can be generated from a barrage either by passing the incoming tide through the turbines mounted in the barrage (this is called '**flood**' generation; Figure 6.9); or by allowing the flow to pass through sluices (with the turbines idling, that is, without generating power) and then trapping the high tide behind the barrage by closing the sluices. The head of water is then passed back through the turbines on the outgoing ebb tide (this is called '**ebb**' generation; Figure 6.10). In either case, two bursts of power are produced in every 24.8-hour period (Figure 6.9). Ebb generation is, as we shall see, the most popular, but two-way operation, on the ebb and the flood, is also possible (Figure 6.11).

The basic technology for power production is well developed, having much in common with conventional low-head hydro systems (see Chapter 6). Figure 6.12 is an artist's impression of the typical layout of a power generation scheme.

A number of different configurations are possible. At La Rance, a so-called '**bulb**' system is used, with the turbine generator sealed in a bulb-shaped enclosure mounted in the flow (Figure 6.13). However, the water has to flow around the large bulb and access (for maintenance) to the generator involves cutting off the flow of water.

These problems are reduced in the '**Straflo**' turbine (as used at Annapolis Royal), with the generator mounted radially around the rim and only the runner (that is, the turbine blades) in the flow (Figure 6.14). However, it is difficult to regulate the performance of the Straflo turbine and to use it for pumping.

Alternatively, there is the '**tubular**' turbine configuration, with the runner set at an angle so that a long (tubular) shaft can take rotational power out to an external generator (Figure 6.15).

Turbine rotational speeds are usually relatively low (50–100 revolutions per minute, rpm), so wear is reduced compared with high-head hydro plants. Since large volumes of water have to be passed through in a relatively short time, large numbers of turbines are required in a large-scale barrage. For example, the proposed ebb generation Severn Barrage would have 216 turbines, each rated at 40 MW, giving a total installed (or 'nameplate') capacity of 8640 MW and delivering 17 TWh y^{-1}.

In simple ebb or flood generation, this large installed capacity is used only for a relatively short period (three to six hours at most) in each tidal cycle, producing a short burst of power which may not match demand. However, it is possible to operate on both the ebb and the flood, in a two-

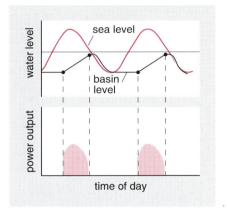

Figure 6.9   Schematic diagram of water levels and power outputs for a flood generation scheme

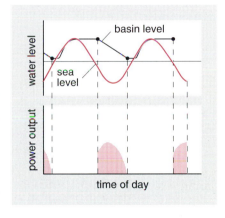

Figure 6.10   Schematic diagram of water levels and power outputs for an ebb generation scheme

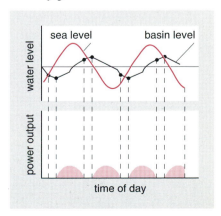

Figure 6.11   Schematic diagram of water levels and power outputs for a two-way generation scheme

way operation, giving a more nearly continuous output, by using reversible-pitch turbines. These are more complex and costly, and, although the output will be more evenly distributed in time, there will be a net decrease in power output for each phase compared with a simple ebb generation scheme. This is because, in order to be ready for the next cycle, neither the ebb nor the flow generation phases can be taken to completion: it is necessary to open the sluices and reduce water levels ready for the next flood cycle and vice versa for ebb generation (see Figure 6.11). Furthermore, the blade design cannot be optimised for flow in both directions, and would have to be compromised for two-way operation.

Flood pumping is another option. The turbine generators are run in reverse as motor-pump sets, powered with electricity from the grid. Water is thus pumped behind the barrage into the basin, to provide extra water for the subsequent ebb generation phase.

Figure 6.12 Artist's impression of the typical layout of a power generation scheme

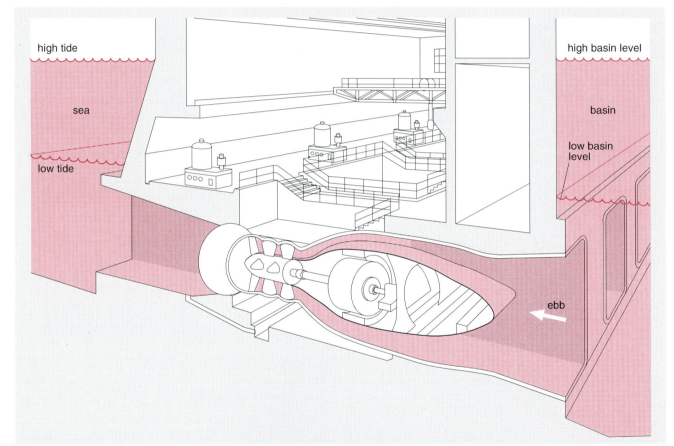

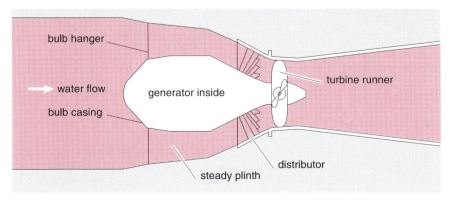

Figure 6.13 Bulb turbine

In addition, as will be discussed in more detail later, many different types of **double-basin** system have been proposed (see, for example, Figure 6.16), often using pumping between the basins. Excess power generated during periods of low demand by the turbines of the first basin can be used to pump water into the second basin, ready for the latter to use for generation when power is required.

Whatever the precise configuration chosen for a barrage, the basic components are the same: *turbines*, *sluice gates* and, usually, *ship locks*, all linked to the shore with *embankments*.

The turbines are usually located in large concrete units. For the Severn Barrage, the use of large concrete (or steel) **caisson** structures to house the

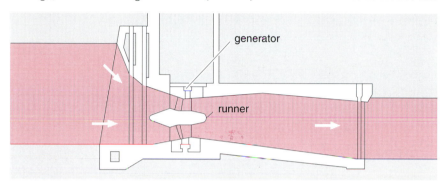

Figure 6.14 Rim generator turbine

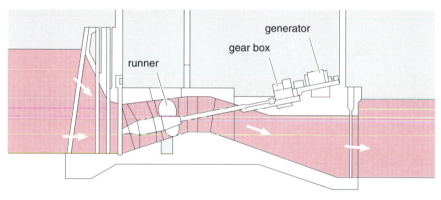

Figure 6.15 Tubular turbine

Figure 6.16 Severn Estuary with possible double-basin schemes

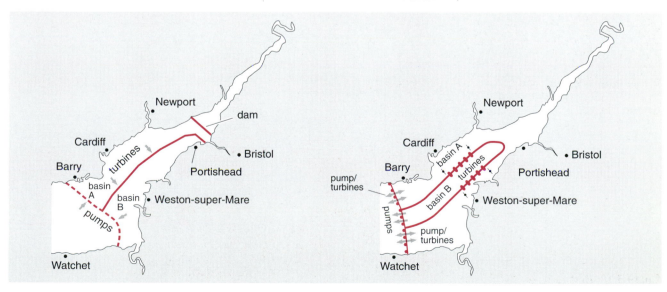

turbines has been proposed. These can be constructed on shore within impounded fabrication yards, floated onto site and sunk into place (Figure 6.17).

Sluices gates are another essential operational feature of a barrage, to allow the tide to flow through ready for ebb generation, or back out after flow generation. These can also be mounted in caissons (Figure 6.18).

The rest of a barrage is relatively straightforward to construct. La Rance, for example, has a rock-filled embankment, whilst the proposed Severn Barrage would have a different form of construction, using sand-filled embankments faced with suitable concrete or rock protection (Figure 6.19).

Details of the existing Rance Barrage and of the proposed Severn and Mersey barrages are given in Boxes 6.5, 6.6 and 6.7.

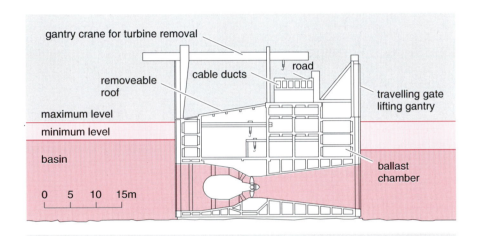

Figure 6.17 Turbine caisson

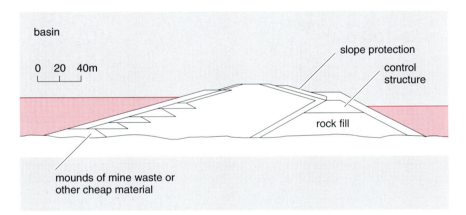

Figure 6.19 Cross-section of the embankment design proposed for the Severn Barrage

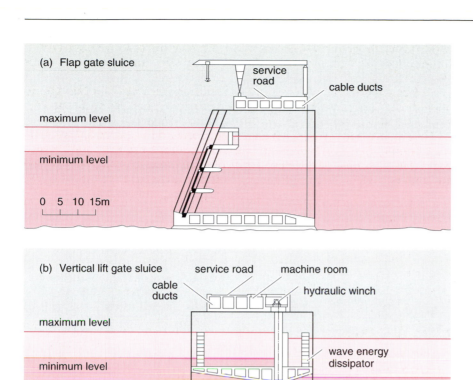

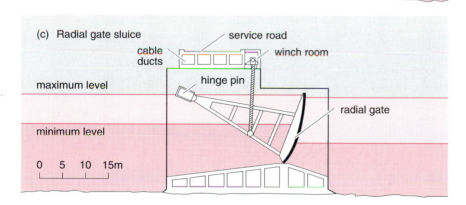

Figure 6.18 Types of sluice caisson

BOX 6.5: LA RANCE

The 740 m long Rance Barrage was constructed between 1961 and 1967. It has a road crossing and a ship lock (see Figures 6.20 and 6.21) and was designed for maximum operational flexibility. It contains 24 reversible (that is, two-way) pump turbines (10 MW), operating in a tidal range of up to 12 m, with a typical head of approximately 5 m.

The operational pattern initially adopted at La Rance was to optimise the uniformity of the power output by using a combination of two-way generation (which meant running the turbines at less than the maximum possible head of water) and incorporating an element of pumped storage. For spring tides, two-way generation was favoured; for neap tides and some intermediate tides, direct pumping from sea to basin was sometimes carried out to supplement generation on the ebb.

Although some mechanical problems were encountered in 1975, which subsequently led to two-way operation mostly being avoided, overall the barrage has been very successful. Typical plant availability has often been more than 90% and net output has been approximately 480 GWh per year, with, in some years, significant gains from pumping.

The construction of the barrage involved complete closure of the estuary (apart from sluices), via temporary coffer-dams on each side, with the water being pumped out to allow work to be carried out in dry conditions. This resulted in effective stagnation of the estuary and the subsequent collapse of the ecosystem within it. Since construction, exchange of water between the open sea and the estuary has restored the estuarine ecosystem, but because there was no monitoring it is difficult to establish what changes the barrage caused to the original environment in the estuary.

Figure 6.20 La Rance coffer-dam

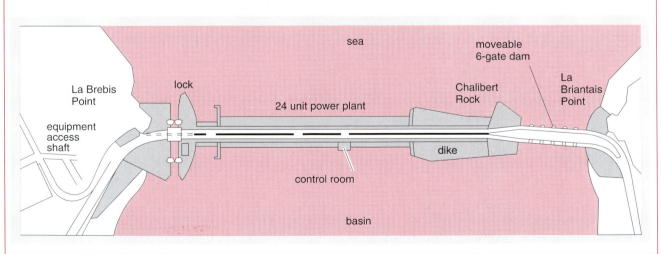

Figure 6.21 Layout of the Rance Barrage

BOX 6.6: THE SEVERN BARRAGE 'REFERENCE PROJECT'

Basic data for the Severn Barrage 'reference project' are as follows.

Number of turbine generators	216
Diameter of turbines	9.0 m
Operating speed of turbines	50 rpm
Turbine generator rating	40 MW
Installed capacity	8640 MW
Number of sluices, various sizes	166
Total clear area of sluice passages	35 000 m^2
Average annual energy output	17 TWh
Operational mode	Ebb generation with flood pumping
Length of barrage, total including:	15.9 km
powerhouse caissons	4.3 km
sluice caissons	4.1 km
other caissons	3.9 km
embankments	3.6 km
Area of enclosed basin at mean sea level	480 km^2
Construction cost, excluding public roads and grid strengthening (at April 1988 prices)	**£8280 million**

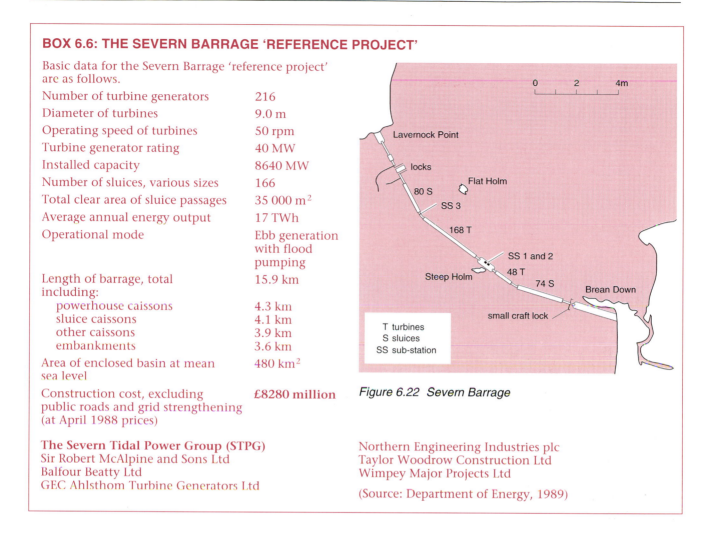

Figure 6.22 Severn Barrage

The Severn Tidal Power Group (STPG)
Sir Robert McAlpine and Sons Ltd
Balfour Beatty Ltd
GEC Ahlsthom Turbine Generators Ltd

Northern Engineering Industries plc
Taylor Woodrow Construction Ltd
Wimpey Major Projects Ltd

(Source: Department of Energy, 1989)

6.3 ENVIRONMENTAL FACTORS

The construction of a large barrier across an estuary would clearly have a significant effect on the local ecosystem. Some of the effects would be negative, and some would be positive. Much research has gone into trying to ascertain the likely final balance, focusing mainly on the proposed Severn Tidal Barrage. This, following one of the lines reviewed by the 1981 Severn Barrage Committee (Department of Energy, 1981), would stretch 16 km from Weston-super-Mare to Lavernock Point near Penarth (Box 6.6) and would operate on the ebb.

The Department of Energy (1987) summarised the environmental effects of the Severn scheme as follows:

The construction of a barrage would result in higher minimum water levels and slightly lower high water levels in the basin. Currents will be reduced and extreme wave conditions will, in many places, be less severe. The changes that will occur to the tides and currents during construction and then later during the operation of a barrage will cause changes in sediment characteristics and in the salinity and quality of the water. These factors have a major bearing on the estuary's environment and ecology. Thus predictions relating to the environment must be preceded by work aimed at defining the likely changes in the pattern of water movement. …

BOX 6.7: THE PROPOSED MERSEY BARRAGE

As initially conceived by the Mersey Barrage Company, a station would have 700 MW installed capacity comprising 28×25 MW turbines and 20 deep venturi sluices. The preferred method of construction would be *in situ* construction of the New Ferry Lock, and caisson construction for turbine and sluice housings, either *in situ* or off-site (dry dock at Cammell Laird or similar facility) for the Dingle Lock.

Construction cost (at July 1989 prices) was estimated to be £880 million.

The construction period would be about five years following parliamentary approval and detailed design.

The barrage would generate 1.4 TWh of electricity per annum throughout its operational life of at least 120 years.

A revised configuration subsequently reduced the estimated cost to £847 million (at October 1992 prices) and increased the output to 1.45 TWh y^{-1}.

The founding subscribers to the Mersey Barrage Company were:
Allied Steel & Wire Ltd
Barclays Bank plc
Blue Circle Industries plc

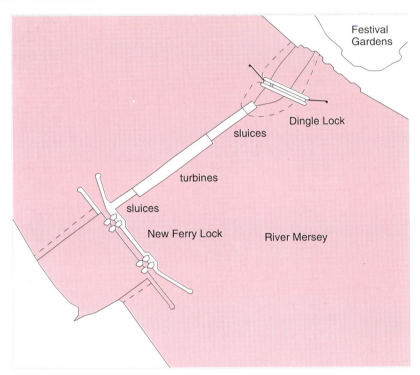

Figure 6.23 *Mersey Barrage*

Cammell Laird Shipbuilders Ltd
Costain Civil Engineering Ltd
Littlewoods Organisation plc
Mersey Docks & Harbour Company
Merseyside & North Wales Electricity Board
Northern Engineering Industries plc

Ocean Marine Ltd
Royal Insurance (UK) Ltd
Straflo Ltd
Tarmac Construction Ltd
Trinity International Holdings plc
Tunnel Cement, now Castle Cement (Padeswood) Ltd

Figure 6.24 *Tide level curves with and without the barrage (Source: Department of Energy, 1989)*

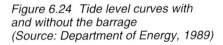
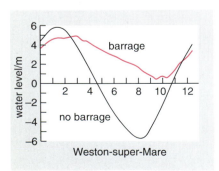

Mathematical models will be used extensively to describe the water levels and currents before and after construction of a barrage. Local data will be collected to calibrate the models and to improve the accuracy of the predictions. The behaviour of the estuaries of the rivers feeding into the main estuary will also influence the environment.

The most obvious potential impact would be on local wildlife, that is, fish and birds, many of the latter being migratory. The UK's estuaries play host to approximately 28% of European swans and ducks and to 47% of European geese. There are also large populations of fish: the Severn, for example, is well known for its salmon and eels (elvers). Many of these species rely on the estuaries for food, and access to that supply might be affected by a tidal barrage.

The proposed Severn Barrage would decrease the currently large area (200 km² or more) of mud flats exposed each day, since the water level variations behind the barrage would be reduced (see Figure 6.24). Some species (for example, mud-wading birds) feed on worms and other invertebrates from the exposed mud flats, and could be adversely affected.

However, the barrage could have a compensating impact on the level of silt and sediment suspended in the water. The waters in the Severn Estuary currently carry in suspension much silt churned up by the tides, making the water impenetrable to sunlight. With the barrage in place and the tidal ebbs and flows reduced, some of this silt would drop out, making the water clearer. Given this change in '**turbidity**', sunlight would penetrate further down, increasing the biological productivity of the water, and therefore increasing the potential food supplies for fish and birds. The net impact for some species might thus be positive: some might not find a niche in the new ecological balance, whilst others previously excluded from the estuary might become established. Similar issues apply in the case of salt marshes.

This rather simplified example illustrates the general point that there are complex interactions at work, often making it hard to predict the net outcome. For a more detailed analysis, see Box 6.8.

Similar interactions occur in relation to other impacts. Clearly, the construction of a barrage across an estuary would impede any shipping, even though ship locks are likely to be included. However, the fact that the sea level behind the barrage would on average be higher could improve navigational access to ports, the net effect depending on tidal cycles and the precise location of the barrage and of any ports.

Visually, barrages present fewer problems than comparable hydro schemes. Even at low tide, the flank exposed would not be much higher than the maximum tidal range. From a distance, all that would be seen would be a line on the water.

Barrages could play a useful role in providing protection against floods and storm damage, since they could be operated to exclude very high tidal surges and would limit local wave generation. However, for some sites, due to the changed tidal patterns (with the tide upstream staying above mid-level for longer periods), there might be a need for improved land drainage upstream.

A barrage would, of course, have some effects on the local economy, both during the construction phase and subsequently, in terms of employment generation and local spending, tourism and, in particular, enhanced opportunities for water sports. Depending on the scale and the site, there could also be the option of providing a new road (or rail) crossing, as has happened with the Rance Barrage. Public roads (but not motorways) have been proposed for both the Severn and the Mersey barrages.

Whether these local infrastructural improvement options represent environmental benefits or costs depends, of course, on your views on industrial and commercial development (some conservation and wildlife groups, for example, baulk at the prospect of increased tourism), but many people would be likely to welcome local economic growth. Indeed, that has been the message from local populations faced with barrage proposals. Whilst a minority of special interest groups, including conservationists and preservationists, have opposed barrages, local commercial and civic interests are usually in support, as is the public at large (see Box 6.9).

The environmental case against barrages is, however, a far from trivial one. For example, the prospect of barrages on UK estuaries has been opposed by the Royal Society for the Protection of Birds, which sees them as inherently damaging, reducing habitats for key species, particularly migrant birds. This problem could clearly be compounded if several barrages were to be built.

The debate has become quite heated at times, with some national and local environmental pressure groups coming out strongly against barrages. Friends of the Earth, for example, argues that whilst each project should be assessed on its merits (see Box 6.9), in general large barrages are likely to have a net negative impact, and the organisation currently opposes the proposed Severn and Mersey barrages.

BOX 6.8: ENVIRONMENTAL IMPACT

In a review of tidal power issues, Baker (1991b) identifies the most important environmental issues as probably water quality and sediment movements, 'because these govern to a large extent the ecology of the estuary'. He continues:

'One unavoidable change in water quality behind a barrage is that, in the upper estuary away from the immediate effects of the barrage, salinity will reduce as a result of the reduction in the volume of sea-water entering the estuary each tide. Thus freshwater species will extend their domain seawards, while the brackish water zone, which tends to be relatively impoverished, will move downstream.

'In the basin behind and clear of a barrage, tidal current velocities will be reduced, particularly during the ebb. This will have a major effect on the power of the currents to erode and transport sediments. The effect will be a general 'freezing' of sediments which are normally mobile, especially during spring tides. This will in turn reduce the turbidity of the water and provide a more stable regime for organisms which live in muddy deposits. One result could be an increase in invertebrate populations which would benefit wading birds.

'Because a tidal barrage would lie across the path of mobile sediments, there is a risk that the sediments moving upstream with the flood tide would be deposited inside the basin at high water and would not be re-suspended during the ebb because the strength of the currents would be reduced markedly. The importance of this will depend on the availability of fresh supplies of fine sediment seaward of the barrage. This aspect has been studied in great detail with the aid of computer models of water movement.'

Severn Barrage
The Severn project has so far been the main focus of study in the UK, although there have also been studies on the Mersey.

The Severn Barrage Project: General Report (Department of Energy, 1989) includes summaries of some of the key ecological and conservation problems. It indicates that, whilst the levels of micro-organisms (phytoplankton, etc.) and even inter-tidal plants are relatively low, due to the harsh hydro-dynamic and sedimentary regime in the area around the proposed barrage (with high turbidity being a major feature), there are significant populations of invertebrates, and of fish and birds, which feed off them. The area is a major site for waders and shelduck, there being four overwintering bird species of international importance and two of national importance.

Parts of the estuary are protected as a Site of Special Scientific Interest, and there are also a number of other areas with potential protected status.

The Severn Barrage Project: General Report identifies a number of opportunities for 'ameliorative and creative conservation measures', ranging from the relatively straightforward provision of wildlife sanctuaries, coastal lagoons and protected intertidal areas, to the more complex provision of a quasi-tidal regime for those plant and animal species dependent on tidal rhythms.

It concludes 'The continuation of a formal dialogue between the development and conservation interests is recommended in order to achieve a nature conservation strategy' and suggests that the primary objective should be the conservation of natural resources 'with ameliorative and creative measures as secondary options where necessary'.

Comparisons with other schemes
Whilst it is, of course, important to remember that the impacts will be site-specific, in relation to environmental impact the French experience with La Rance is of interest.

Evidently no detailed preliminary environmental studies were done, but as noted earlier (Box 6.5), the construction phase caused some dislocation, and the operator (Electricité de France) reported that initially the barrage had a significant effect on the estuary's biological productivity. However, gradually most flora and fauna returned, and some new species appeared. The fishing is now said to be better and there are more migratory birds. The effects on sedimentation are said to be low.

If the turbines are brought up to speed rapidly, this can cause waves along the shore and there are some strong undercurrents, which can present hazards, for example to leisure craft, but otherwise the operation of the barrage seems unproblematic. Leisure sailing has increased, and to aid navigation the barrage operator publishes details of operational plans three days in advance.

The potential damage to fish passing through the turbines or sluices has proved to be a problem for some hydroelectric plants (see Chapter 5). In the case of tidal barrages, there has been no evidence of damage at La Rance, but there has been significant mortality to shad (a local fish) at Annapolis Royal in Canada. Consequently, a sonic generator, producing one-second 'hammer blow' pulses, has been installed and appears to be effective at warning fish. A special fish pass has been installed, as with some run-of-river hydro schemes, and as has been proposed for the Severn Barrage.

Mersey Barrage
Initial studies of the proposed Mersey Barrage (stage 1) indicated that water quality should not deteriorate to affect flora or fauna, but that the barrage could affect the ornithological habitats of the estuary, although such effects could be 'considerably offset as the design and operations regime of the barrage is developed'. Although siltation might increase, it was felt that the barrage should not significantly affect fish life in the river.

See *Tidal Power from the River Mersey: A Feasibility Study Stage 1* (ETSU, 1988) and subsequent MBC/ETSU reports.

BOX 6.9: SOME REACTIONS TO UK BARRAGE PROPOSALS

Reactions to hypothetical schemes, rather than actual projects, are, of course, somewhat unreliable, but the rather drawn-out and intermittent public debate over the Severn Barrage, dating from the 1981 Bondi Report (Department of Energy, 1981) onwards, has thrown up some interesting responses.

Although it carried out a consultation exercise (Department of Energy, 1991), which reviewed responses from some 300 individuals and organisations in 1990/91, in general the STPG industrial consortium has adopted a relatively low public profile, leaving the field relatively free for objectors to express their views. Some have been quite harsh, even fearing the creation of a 'stinking lake'.

For example, during a parliamentary debate on the Severn Tidal Barrage in October 1987, Michael Stern, MP for Bristol North West, said:

'The Severn barrage has been compared to a large, inefficient, activated sewage treatment plant. It operates by aeration and agitation by wind and tidal coverage, and variation of that agitation from violent on stormy days and spring tides to relatively mild on neap tides and during calm weather. When the waters of the Severn estuary are quiescent, large pools of liquid mud with a high affinity for pollutants settle in the estuary.

'One effect of the interposition of a barrage in the estuary will be greatly to increase the frequency and depth of those pools of liquid mud. That in itself may not be too much of a worry, but the pools have an affinity for pollutants, and if they remain anaerobic for 14 days or more because of the process of stratification – they will undoubtedly do so once the tidal range of the Severn is cut off – large amounts of toxic, evil-smelling gases such as hydrogen sulphide, methane and other reduced sulphur compounds will begin to be emitted. Imagine the extension of that process over a period of years, and having to live anywhere along the shores of the Severn estuary with the build-up of these vast smells which are an inevitable risk when the tide is cut off in an area that has been subject to one of the greatest tidal ranges in the world.'

(*Hansard*, 1987)

Although these anxieties may be exaggerated, others feared that the quiet retirement town of Weston-super-Mare might be disrupted, not least as a consequence of the presence, albeit only temporary, of the tens of thousands of construction workers needed. This was estimated at 35 000 at peak by the STPG, although not all these would be in or near Weston.

On balance, however, most local opinion, on the English side, seemed to favour the project, often on the grounds of local economic and indirect employment benefits (tourism, etc.), but also as an alternative to the construction of more nuclear power plants. This view is reinforced, for some, by Weston's proximity to the nuclear site at Hinkley.

On the Welsh side, there was also strong support on the basis of employment and economic gains, although some nationalists tended to portray the project as a scheme for the benefit of English power consumers. The main objections, however, came from environmental and wildlife groups, nationally and locally. The Royal Society for the Protection of Birds strongly opposed barrages on any estuaries.

Friends of the Earth has been striving over recent years to define a policy on tidal power, which reflects on one hand its commitment to renewable energy and on the other its concern for environmental protection. Currently, it has quite a sophisticated policy, which essentially puts the onus of proof of net benefit on intending developers. Friends of the Earth is unconvinced that there is a case, on balance, for large schemes like the Severn or Mersey barrages, but leaves the door open for smaller schemes.

Part of this opposition is motivated by strategic issues. Many environmentalists, for example, feel that in general smaller projects are preferable, not just for environmental reasons, but since they might provide an opportunity for more decentralisation. Although barrages are portrayed as inevitably centralised, in reality some of the smaller barrages might be owned and managed by regional or even local bodies, including municipalities.

For its part, the MBC attempted to involve local environmental pressure groups in a negotiation process from the start, but even so some strong objections emerged, with wildlife groups concerned that the barrage would endanger large areas of salt marsh, which are of international importance to wintering waders and other birds. Shipping interests also expressed concern, as did some local industrialists, concerned about maintaining access.

For further information on responses to the Severn Barrage, see the Further Reading section.

Some of this opposition relates not so much to specific points about the potential environmental impact, as to more general strategic questions relating to 'opportunity cost' aspects. For example, Friends of the Earth argues that any money spent on large barrages would be better spent on energy conservation.

In the end, should barrage proposals proceed in the UK, what are likely to emerge (assuming outright opposition is avoided) are compromises over siting, design and operation. For example, as we shall see, there are operational patterns that could allow larger areas of mud flats to be exposed for longer periods, albeit perhaps with some cost penalties. There are also other, non-barrage, costs. For example, as the quotation from the speech by Michael Stern MP in Box 6.9 highlights, it would be vital to invest in cleaning up sewage plant outflow clean up and the reduction of emissions from industrial plants, since the tides could no longer be relied on to flush the estuaries so vigorously. Although there would still be significant flushing effects (for instance, the Severn Barrage would involve a water exchange of 0.5 cubic miles twice a day), most proposals so far have included plans for cleaning up emissions, and the fact that current waste disposal policies are inadequate should not be seen as an argument against barrages. Rather, the advent of barrages could ensure that emissions into estuaries are cleaned up. Indeed, investment in cleaning up is likely to occur in any case, to meet rising European Union standards.

A final point on scale should be made. Barrages are inevitably fairly large structures, but some environmentalists argue that smaller barrages are preferable to large ones, in that they might have less environmental impact. That could clearly be true on a *pro-rata* basis, but the net effect of a lot of small units compared with, say, one large unit, is far from clear, with the site-specific nature of impacts complicating any general analysis. To take the Severn as an example, there has been some support for a smaller barrage on the English Stones line, near the existing Severn Bridge. This would be cheaper to build and could also provide a base for another river crossing (motorway or rail). However, initial studies indicated that at that site, further up the river, siltation could be a major problem, and the scale of the local environmental impact has yet to be ascertained.

Clearly, whether we are talking about small or large barrages, the environmental questions must be treated seriously and certainly much work is currently under way to try to reduce uncertainties. In the end, however, it would seem to come down to a matter of strategic choice. Assuming that there are significant negative local impacts, they would have to be compared with the role that barrages can play in resolving some of the global environmental problems, such as global warming. For example, the Severn Barrage would, according to the STPG, avoid the production of 17.6 million tonnes of carbon dioxide per annum.

The Severn Barrage Project: General Report summed up this aspect as follows:

If renewable energy sources are to be utilised to increase diversification of electricity generation and to reduce pollution, the Severn Barrage remains the largest single project which could make a significant contribution on a reasonable time scale. Once completed, the project would represent an insurance against escalation of fuel prices.

(Department of Energy, 1989)

Although much more needs to be done, the environmental impact issues have been studied in considerable detail; the results of this work have been published in a number of Department of Energy/Energy Technology Support Unit (ETSU) reports. Of particular interest are *The Severn Barrage Project: General Report* (Department of Energy, 1989) and *Severn Barrage Project: Detailed Report*, Vols I and II (ETSU, 1989a and b) (see 'Further Reading' for details).

6.4 INTEGRATION

The electricity produced by barrages must normally be integrated with the electricity produced by the other power plants that feed into the national grid power transmission network.

The key problem in feeding power from a tidal barrage into national grid networks is that, with conventional ebb or flow generation schemes, the tidal energy inputs come in relatively short bursts at approximately 12-hour intervals. Typically, power can be produced for five to six hours during spring tides and three hours during neap tides, within a tidal cycle lasting 12.4 hours (Figure 6.25).

Clearly, the availability of power from a barrage would not always match the pattern of demand for power on the grid. With a large, well-developed grid, as in the UK, with a large load and many other types of power plant connected into it, this problem might not be too severe, depending, of course, on the size of the barrage output. The two daily bursts of tidal power could be used to off-load older, less efficient and/or more expensive 'low merit order' plants, for example older coal-fired plants. The barrage would thus be operating in a 'fuel-saving' mode, the predictability of the tides allowing for the process of substitution to be planned well in advance. Even so, with a barrage the size of that proposed for the Severn, absorbing all the power would clearly represent a significant task. At peak, it would be generating 8 GW of power, which represents a sizeable proportion of the UK's total installed (1993) capacity of approximately 65 GW.

In some other countries, with smaller grids and relatively low demands, weaker interconnections, longer transmission distances and relatively few other types of generating plant, a large burst of tidal power input could represent a major integration problem. In this situation, the option of two-way generation, on the incoming flood as well as the ebb, could be attractive, since that would give *four* bursts of power for each 24-hour cycle. However, as was noted earlier, although the phasing of the power is improved in two-way generation, there is no net energy output advantage

Figure 6.25 Operation over a spring–neap tide cycle (Source: Watt Committee on Energy, 1990)

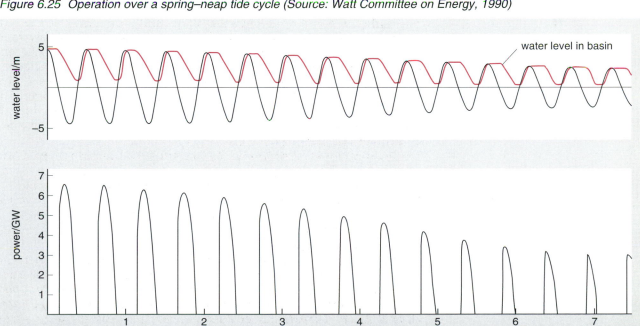

over simple one-way generation, since, in order to be ready for the reversed flow, neither the ebb nor the flood generation phase can be taken to completion. There is a trade-off between continuity and net output. The installation of the much more complex two-way turbines also involves extra cost and it is difficult to optimise the design of the turbines for two-way operation. The end result is that two-way generation could cost 10–15% more, and in the case of the Severn Barrage the overall benefit is currently seen as negligible.

As already noted, there is also the option of pumping, using modified turbines run on grid power (e.g. during off-peak periods) to pump extra water behind a barrage during the flood phase. This could, to a limited extent, help to re-phase the power output, the extra head and extra volume of water helping to increase the subsequent ebb generation period. The barrage would thus be used as a short-term pumped storage reservoir. More importantly, a bonus would be obtained by pumping at low head, since the incoming tide in effect lifts the extra water to high-tide level, ready for subsequently generating power on the ebb. Typically, between 5 and 15% extra output can be gained, with little additional capital cost and with no loss of generating efficiency. This is now the favoured option for all proposed UK tidal energy schemes (Severn, Mersey, Conwy, Wyre) and, as we have seen, is carried out on the Rance Barrage. That said, the economic advantages of pumping seem fairly small, and depend crucially on tidal timing, which will not necessarily coincide with off-peak grid power availability.

Another option for providing more nearly continuous power is to construct two basins. In one version of this concept, one basin is filled at high tide, whilst the other is kept low (by emptying it regularly at low tide level), so that the power output from turbines running between them can be more nearly continuous. Another possibility is to have two separate basins, each with their own set of turbines. The first operates on ebb generation, whilst the second acts as essentially a reservoir, filled at high tide and used for generation only when no ebb power from the first basin is available.

Figure 6.26 Double-basin pumped storage scheme

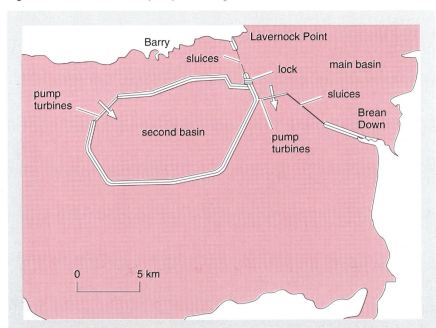

There are many other double-basin concepts, with most of them using (modified) turbines to pump water 'uphill'. For example, the first basin could operate in the normal manner, but any excess power, during low demand periods, could be used to pump water out of the second basin to keep it below tide level, so that power could be generated from the second basin when needed by filling it through its turbines (Figure 6.26).

However, with or without pumping, these configurations all involve building what amounts to two barrages, which increases the overall cost significantly. To date, no double-barrage systems have been seriously considered, simple ebb generation being seen as the most economic option overall.

In addition to these basic design options, there is, of course, a variety of adjustments that can be made to detailed design (for example, optimising the number, location and size of the turbines and sluices) to give maximum efficiency, as well as ways of optimising operational performance.

Ebb generation schemes usually start up when the difference in level between the basin and the sea is approximately half the tidal range, with generation continuing until the levels are equalised, when the next tide is allowed in. However, other patterns are possible, taking the local tidal patterns into account.

Clearly, the system design and operation pattern will have an environmental as well as integration and economic implications: for example, it will define the duration of the low sea level behind the barrage. Flood generation is seen as less attractive than ebb generation in part because the estuary behind the barrage would be kept at low level for longer periods (as power was absorbed from the incoming flow), leaving the mud flats uncovered for longer periods.

By contrast, double-basin schemes would probably be left at near, or even above, high tide level overnight, since that is a low demand period. Either way, wildlife feeding patterns and food supplies would be affected.

With two-way generation, the water in the basins would remain closer to mean sea level. Even so, where navigation must be maintained to ports upstream of a barrage (for example, on the Severn and the Mersey), two-way generation would not be likely to be acceptable because there would still be a reduced high water level within the basin. This applies even more to flood generation.

Whichever system is used, the overall economic viability of tidal power might be enhanced, in theory at least, if several barrages were in operation, given the fact that the tidal maxima occur at slightly different times around the coast. For example, the Solway Firth and Morecambe Bay are approximately five to six hours out of phase with the Severn, so that the output from these and other possible barrage sites could be fed into the grid to provide a more nearly continuous net contribution.

Finally, the linking of power from barrages to the national grid could present some practical problems. As with many other types of large, new, power plant, extra grid connections would have to be made, and in some circumstances existing local grid lines strengthened to carry the extra power. Fortunately, most potential barrage sites in the UK are reasonably near to existing power lines, so the sorts of problem facing deep-sea wave power (much of which would have to be transmitted from the north of Scotland) would be avoided. However, in the case of the proposed Severn Barrage new power lines, perhaps stretching as far as the Midlands, would probably be required. These extra grid connections would add to the total system cost. For the Severn Barrage, these costs have been estimated at some £850 million, out of a total barrage cost of £8280 million at 1988 prices (see Table 6.1), although the STPG has argued that some grid strengthening in the area is needed anyway.

Table 6.1 Severn Barrage 'reference project' capital and annual recurring costs (£ million)* (1988 prices)

Pre-construction phase	
Feasibility and environmental studies, planning and parliamentary costs	60
Design and engineering	130
Barrage construction	
Civil engineering works†	4900
Power generation works	2400
On-barrage transmission and control	380
Management, engineering and supervision	300
Land and urban drainage sea defences	30
Effluent discharge, port works	80
Barrage capital cost total	**8280**
Off-barrage transmission and grid reinforcement	
With all transmission lines overhead	850
Extra cost for 10% of transmission lines underground	380
Annual costs	
Barrage operation and maintenance	40
Off-barrage costs	30
Annual costs total	70

* In April 1988 money terms. Estimated figures are rounded and include contingencies but exclude interest during construction.

† Excluding public road across the barrage (estimated to cost from £135 million to £207 million depending on links provided into road network).

(Source: Department of Energy, 1989)

As can be seen, the key issue in terms of integration is *cost*, whether this is in terms of basic grid linkages or in terms of systems for allowing power to be produced on a more nearly continuous basis.

The discussion above has been based on the assumption that the UK's existing national power system remains basically unchanged, with single or multiple barrage inputs simply fed into the grid. However, if renewable energy systems of various types were to proliferate, with the problem of intermittent inputs therefore growing, it could be that the pumped storage capacity that barrages potentially represent would become more attractive economically. The pumped storage option has not been followed up fully because there are disagreements about the value of this option, a key issue being that 'carrying' an extra head of (stored) water beyond the next ebb phase would interfere with the normal cycle of operations. Pumping to extend the ebb can make sense, particularly if cheap off-peak electricity can be used and the stored power employed to meet demand peaks. However, the tidal cycle will shift in and out of phase with the electricity supply and demand cycle. Overall, it is argued, that if longer-term storage is wanted, it is better to build a separate conventional, high-head pumped storage reservoir, on land, like the 1800 MW Dinorwig scheme in Wales.

The same type of argument applies to double-basin pumped storage schemes. Building a low-head pumped storage facility in an estuary (with an efficiency, in terms of the ratio of energy input to output, of, say, 35–40%) is likely to be less cost effective than building a conventional high-head pumped storage system (with an efficiency of, say, 75%) on land. There might also be other forms of synergy between tidal and other renewable systems, for example the installation of wind turbines along barrages, in the same way as some wind farms have been constructed on causeways in harbours. The wind plant might even be used at times for pumping water behind the barrage, although the energy contribution that could be made, even if wind turbines were located regularly along the entire length of a barrage, would be relatively small. A 1994 study by a team from Cranfield University suggested that up to 67.5 MW of wind capacity could be accommodated, generating 177.5 GWh p.a. They also proposed tethering 150 floating wave energy devices off the seaward side of the barrage. The circular Clam (p. 334) was considered suitable and it was thought they could generate 34 GWh p.a. and help reduce wave damage to the barrage.

Broader, multi-system integration issues of this type are discussed further in Chapter 10.

For a useful discussion of the integration issue in relation to tidal energy, see *Renewable Energy Sources* (Watt Committee on Energy, 1990) and *Tidal Power from the Severn Estuary*, Vol. I (Department of Energy, 1981).

6.5 ECONOMIC FACTORS

The overall economics of tidal barrages depends not only on their operational performance, but also on their initial capital cost. Table 6.1 gives a breakdown of the STPG's 1989 basic capital and running cost estimates for the Severn Barrage (Department of Energy, 1989). Note that civil engineering works are the single largest element in the total cost, closely followed by turbine manufacture and installation.

Subsequently, the total estimated capital cost of the Severn Barrage has been increased, in line with inflation, from the 1988 figure of £8280 million shown in Table 6.1, to approximately £10 200 million in 1991, as reported in the STPG's evidence to the House of Commons Select Committee on Energy in November 1991 (House of Commons Select Committee on Energy, 1992). These figures exclude interest during construction, although interest *is* taken into account in the calculation of generation costs given in Table 6.2. We shall be coming back to this key issue shortly.

Although, as Tables 6.1 and 6.2 indicate, there are running costs (approximately 1% of the total capital cost), like all renewable energy systems that are based on natural flows, barrages have no fuel cost. They can generate power for many years without major civil engineering effort, the low-speed turbines needing replacement perhaps every 30 years.

However, as we have seen, the initial capital cost is very significant. Even so, the capital costs of barrages, at approximately £1300 per kilowatt of installed capacity, are broadly comparable to those of many other generating systems – for example, wind power at around £1000 per installed kilowatt.

The period during which power can be produced, at least for simple single-basin ebb or flow systems, is clearly less than for a conventional power plant. For example, since it would only operate during tidal cycles, the 8.6 GW turbine capacity of the Severn Barrage could, very roughly, only offer the same 'equivalent firm capacity' as a 1–2 GW conventional plant. In other words, the barrage requires a large investment in expensive capacity which is only used intermittently and can therefore only replace a limited amount of conventional plant output. The precise 'capacity credit' that can be allocated to barrages (in effect, their value as replacements for conventional plants) will depend in practice on the scale and timing of the outputs of the plants they can off-load: after all, not all of *these* will be able to generate continuously. Perhaps the most convenient way to compare systems is therefore by using their load factors. The average annual load factor for the Severn Barrage is estimated at around 23%; in comparison, the average annual plant load factor for coal-fired power stations in the UK in 1992 was 63%, and for nuclear stations, 74% (Department of Trade and Industry, 1993).

Table 6.2 Severn Barrage generation costs (pence per kilowatt-hour)* (1988 prices)

Discount rate	2%	5%	8%	10%	12%	15%
Basic capital†	1.05	2.25	3.42	4.15	4.83	5.77
Time component‡	0.11	0.63	1.64	2.60	3.82	6.18
Total capital cost	1.16	2.88	5.06	6.75	8.65	11.95
Annual cost	0.53	0.50	0.47	0.47	0.46	0.46
Total cost of energy at barrage boundary	1.70	3.37	5.53	7.22	9.12	12.42
Off-barrage transmission (all overhead lines)	0.12	0.28	0.49	0.64	0.80	1.08
Total cost of energy including overhead transmission lines	1.81	3.65	6.01	7.85	9.92	13.50
Extra cost for 10% of transmission lines being underground	0.05	0.11	0.18	0.23	0.28	0.36

* In 1988 money terms. Figures rounded.

† On the basis that all the capital cost is incurred instantaneously at the time when capital spending ceases.

‡ Extra cost arising from the actual timing of the incidence of capital expenditure (equivalent to interest during construction).

(Source: Department of Energy, 1989)

Tidal projects have a relatively high capital cost in relation to the usable output, compared with most other types of power plant, with, consequently, long capital payback times and low rates of return on the capital invested, the precise figures depending on the price that can be charged for the electricity.

For the Severn Barrage, the STPG has estimated that, depending on the price at which the electricity could be sold, the internal rates of return on the large capital outlay would be around 6–8% (1989 figures). But this is unlikely to be attractive to the private sector, where much higher rates are expected. To put it the other way around, if commercial rates of return were expected, the price charged for electricity would have to be substantially higher than is currently considered acceptable (see Table 6.2 and Figure 6.27).

The most recent estimate by the government's Renewable Energy Advisory Group put the cost of electricity from the Severn Barrage at 5–7 pence per kilowatt-hour (p kWh^{-1}) at an 8% discount rate, or 10–14p kWh^{-1} at a 15% discount rate, both at 1991 prices (Renewable Energy Advisory Group, 1992).

Another perspective is given by Table 6.3, based on evidence given to the House of Commons Select Committee on Energy. This is a comparison of costs of electricity and capital repayment times for three UK schemes currently proposed. As can be seen, payback times run up to 20 years or more, with the smaller barrages, which generally have higher generation costs, having to charge higher electricity prices.

The capital payback times in Table 6.3 are the times that it would take to pay back, from sales of electricity at the stated prices, the full capital cost, plus interest charges on the borrowed capital, including interest during construction.

Of course, once the capital and interest costs had been paid off, a tidal barrage would be generating profit for the rest of its life (at least 100 years), apart from the relatively small operation and maintenance costs.

It is therefore sometimes argued that it is misleading to try to assess barrages just on a conventional 'discount rate' basis over a financial project period, which may be relatively short compared with the life of the barrage. For example, the House of Commons Select Committee on Energy, when reviewing tidal power as part of the review of renewable energy that it carried out in 1991/92 (House of Commons Select Committee on Energy, 1992), was keen for a 'total life cost' approach to be adopted, at least for use in comparisons. In this approach, the capital cost would be averaged out over a plant's lifetime, to give the 'levelised cost' (to use US jargon).

On this sort of basis, capital projects with very long lives, like barrages or hydroelectric plants, appear to be very good long-term investments. The average cost of the Mersey Barrage if spread over its lifetime, for example, works out at only about 2p kWh^{-1}. The STPG has argued that, given reasonable maintenance and regular turbine replacements, the Severn Barrage could, in fact, last almost indefinitely.

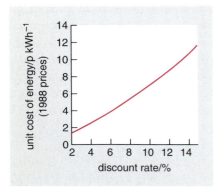

Figure 6.27 Severn Barrage electricity cost versus discount rate (Source: Department of Energy, 1989)

Table 6.3 Tidal power electricity cost comparisons and capital repayment periods (November 1991 estimates)

	Capital cost (£ million)	Running costs per annum (£ million)	Electricity price (p kWh^{-1})
Severn (17 TWh y^{-1})	10 200	86	6p (16.5-year payback) 5p (20-year payback)
Mersey (1.4 TWh y^{-1})	966	17.6	6.75p (25-year payback)
Conwy	72.5	0.6	8.6p (15–20-year payback)

(Source: House of Commons Select Committee on Energy, 1992)

However, given the 'short-termism' of many UK financial institutions, such arguments are unlikely to appeal to the private sector, which normally takes the view that the maximum loan period for large-scale industrial investments should not exceed 20 years. It is usually argued that the state should invest in long-term projects of this sort, for the long-term benefit of the nation as a whole.

The benefits that could flow from the construction of tidal barrages are more than just the provision of relatively cheap power: they include environmental benefits, for example reduction in carbon dioxide emissions, diversity, security and sustainability of supply, local and regional employment gains and, in some cases, possible new road or rail transport crossings.

However, to date, the UK government has been unwilling to provide financial support for tidal barrage construction, preferring, as a matter of policy, to leave such developments to the private sector, although some funds have been allocated for tidal research and feasibility studies (approximately £14 million since 1979, at 1992 prices; see Box 6.10).

It would seem that, in this context, small schemes such as the Mersey Barrage (rated at 700 MW) or even the Wyre Barrage (64 MW) might be more likely to go ahead, because of their lower capital cost (less than £1 billion at 1991 prices for the Mersey, £90 million for the Wyre), at least part of which could conceivably be raised from private finance.

The MBC has argued that the prospects for the Mersey Barrage would be greatly improved if it could receive support under the government's non-fossil fuel obligation (NFFO) cross-subsidy scheme, under which a levy on fossil-fuelled power generation is used to subsidise non-fossil based generation. For example, in 1991, the MBC proposed that it should be paid a 6.75p kWh^{-1} unit cost for 25 years, of which 2p kWh^{-1} for 25 years at zero discount rate would be paid 'up front' as an advance during construction, through the NFFO cross-subsidy. This advance would be equivalent to over £700 million of the £1 billion construction cost. To meet part of the remaining £300 million cost, the MBC proposed a price of 4.75p kWh^{-1} over 25 years. However, this would require a continuing NFFO payment, since the pool price for electricity is currently around 3p kWh^{-1}. Subsequently MBC proposed some alternative approaches avoiding an advance payment, but inevitably this involved an even higher NFFO payment, e.g. 11p kWh^{-1} over 7.5 years (Haws and McCormick, 1993). However, the government felt that overall the project was too costly and it has decided not to support further development work.

Approaching the problem from a somewhat different angle, in 1993 the STPG submitted a funding proposal based on the idea of joint private/public support, possibly using a 'Hybrid Bill' (Wardle *et al.*, 1993). This proposal was also turned down, and, according to the STPG, the option of 'going it alone' with just private finance, was 'a trifle unlikely'. (*Electrical Review* 15-28 April 1994.)

As can be seen, the economics of tidal power are complex. Quite apart from the problems of funding and the vagaries of finance capital, interest rates, etc., as it were on the 'supply' side, there are technical and environmental uncertainties, with trade-offs between operational efficiency and likely impact. To these uncertainties must be added the 'demand' side uncertainties, with estimates having to be made of the price that can be charged for tidal electricity in relation to the price of conventional fuel saved decades ahead.

Although it is possible that fossil fuel and nuclear electricity prices will increase over time, so that tidal energy projects become more attractive, under present conditions tidal energy appears to be a relatively unattractive commercial investment option.

BOX 6.10: GOVERNMENT SUPPORT FOR TIDAL BARRAGE FEASIBILITY STUDIES

Severn Barrage

The government has provided the following assistance to the project.

1 It funded completely the study leading to the Bondi Report in 1981 (Department of Energy, 1981) (approximate cost £2.25 million).

2 It funded 50% of the interim study carried out by the STPG, reported in 1986 (STPG, 1986): government contribution £375 000.

3 It funded 33% of the study carried out by the STPG that was reported in 1989 (Department of Energy, 1989): government contribution £1.3 million.

4 It funded 88% of the work on responses and consultation following publication of *The Severn Barrage Project: General Report* in 1989 (Department of Energy, 1991): government contribution £79 000.

5 It is committed to funding 85% of the further environmental regional and financing studies currently in hand: government contribution £88 000.

6 It has directly commissioned generic work of relevance costing about £1.6 million.

Mersey Barrage

Just under £1 million was provided jointly (on a 50/50 basis) by the MBC and the (then) Department of Energy for initial Phase 1 and 2 feasibility studies, followed by £1.5 million (out of £3 million) for Phase 3, which was extended in 1991 with the allocation of a further £1.2 million (out of £1.5 million).

Small barrages

Departmental funding for work on small barrage options has included £65 000 for a study of the Loughor Estuary, together with two-thirds of the £155 000 cost of a study on the Duddon Estuary (1992) and of the £220 000 cost of a study of the Wyre Barrage proposal (1991). The same proportion has also been met for a £180 000 project on the Conwy Estuary.

6.6 POTENTIAL

UNITED KINGDOM

In general, the best potential tidal energy sites in the UK are on the west coasts of England and Wales, where the highest tidal ranges are to be found. Despite its indented coastline, the tidal energy potential of Scotland is very small (1–2 TWh y^{-1}), due to its generally low tidal range.

As we have seen, the practical potential of tidal power in the UK depends crucially on economics, and on environmental factors. The technically exploitable potential, assuming that every practical UK scheme was developed, could rise to approximately 53 TWh y^{-1}, or around 17% of current (1992) electricity generation. Approximately nine-tenths of this potential (48 TWh y^{-1}) is at eight large sites, each yielding 1–17 TWh y^{-1}, while one-tenth is at 34 small sites, each yielding 20–150 gigawatt hours per year (GWh y^{-1}) (ETSU, 1990).

The Severn Barrage, if built, would make the largest contribution, approximately 17 TWh y^{-1}, but initial estimates suggested that the Wash, the Mersey, the Solway Firth, Morecambe Bay and possibly the Humber could also make significant contributions (Table 6.4 and Figure 6.28). Subsequently, the emphasis was on the Severn and the Mersey, but a privately funded pre-feasibility study has also been carried out on the Humber.

In addition, as indicated, there are many smaller estuaries and rivers that could be used. Preliminary estimates of costs have been obtained for more than 100 small schemes, with the former Department of Energy subsequently focusing on eight estuaries: the Severn, Mersey, Morecambe Bay, Solway Firth, Humber, Wash, Thames and Dee. Table 6.5 gives some preliminary data on five of these, and Figure 6.29 indicates their locations. Detailed feasibility studies have now been carried out on the Loughor (8 MW) and

Table 6.4 An early assessment of the potential medium- and large-scale tidal sites in the UK

	Range (m)	Length (m)	Capacity (MW)	Output (GWh)	Cost (p kWh^{-1})*
Severn – Outer line	6.0	20 000	12 000	19 700	4.3
Severn – Inner line	7.0	17 000	7200	12 900	3.7
Solway Firth	5.5	30 000	5580	10 050	4.9
Morecambe Bay	6.3	16 600	3040	5400	4.6
Wash	4.45	19 600	2760	4690	7.2
Humber	4.1	8300	1200	2010	7.0
Thames	4.2	9000	1120	1370	8.3
Dee	5.95	9500	800	1250	6.4
Mersey	6.45	1750	620	1320	3.6
Milton Haven	4.5	1150	96	180	10.0
Cromarty Firth	2.75	1350	47	100	11.8
Loch Broom	3.15	500	29	42	13.9
Loch Etive	1.95	350	28	55	11.7
Padstow	4.75	550	28	55	4.2
Langstone Harbour	3.13	550	24	53	5.3
Dovey	2.90	1300	20	45	7.2
Hamford Water	3.0	3200	20	38	8.5

* In 1983 money terms, at 5% discount rate. Note: these figures are now out of date.

(Source: Baker, 1986, p. 260)

Conwy (33 MW) in Wales, the Wyre (64 MW) in Lancashire, and a new study has been initiated on the Duddon (100 MW) in Cumbria.

The costings in Table 6.5 are at 1983 prices and are based on simple parametric modelling (see the Appendix). Subsequently, more detailed, 'bottom-up' costings were carried out in the feasibility studies of the Wyre, Conwy and Loughor. One of these, the preliminary feasibility study of the Wyre Barrage, estimated that electricity could be generated at a cost of 6.5p kWh^{-1}(1991 prices), assuming an 8% discount rate over a 120-year period (ETSU, 1991).

Overall, the UK potential for small tidal schemes (that is, schemes of up to 300 MW capacity), is estimated at 2% of electricity requirements, with the most economic of them providing 1.5% of requirements.

Table 6.5 Early data on small-scale sites in the UK

Location	Mean tidal range (m)	Basin area (km)	Barrage length (m)	Maximum water depth (m)	Cost function*	Indicated cost of energy (p kWh^{-1})†
Taw/Torridge Estuary (Appledore)	5.45	13	950	11	158	3.5-4.0
Wyre Estuary (Fleetwood)	6.4	7.6	480	15	182	3.5-4.0
Conwy Estuary (North Wales)	5.2	6.0	225	13.6	175	3.5-4.0
Loughor Estuary (South Wales)	6.55	46.3	3375	18	277	4.5
Lawrenny Quay (Upper Milford Haven)	4.57	2.82	200	10.5	301	4.5-5.0

* The cost function is an indication of relative capital costs.

† In 1983 money terms, at 5% discount rate.

(Source: Baker, 1986)

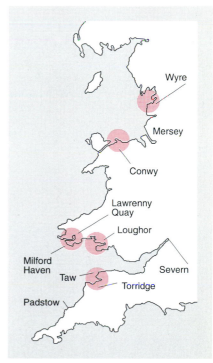

Figure 6.28 UK barrage options

Figure 6.29 Some small barrage options in the UK

WORLD

Tidal power availability is clearly very site-specific. However, as Table 6.6 indicates, there are numerous major sites around the world, in Russia, Canada, the USA, Argentina, Korea, Australia, France, China and India, with an estimated total potential of perhaps as much as 300 TWh y^{-1}. Figure 6.30 indicates the locations of some of these sites.

Although the main potential for tidal energy is from a small number of large barrages, there are also many potentially suitable sites for small- to medium-scale units.

Currently, in terms of large schemes, the main sites of interest outside the UK are the Bay of Fundy in Canada, and Mezen and Tugur in Russia. Smaller schemes of interest include Garolim Bay in Korea, the Gulf of Kachchh in India, Secure Bay in Australia and a project at São Luís in Brazil.

The pace of development of tidal energy may be relatively slow compared with that of some of the other renewables, but the potential is nevertheless substantial. The total energy dissipated from tides globally is approximately 3000 GW, of which approximately 1000 GW is dissipated in accessible shallow sea areas.

In practice, the overall world tidal potential is estimated at at least 120 GW installed capacity (producing approximately 190 TWh y^{-1}). Even though this is only about 10% of the world's total hydro power potential, it still represents a significant resource.

Indeed, this might well be an underestimate. For example, an ETSU report for the European Union (Commission of the European Communities, 1992) has suggested that the total tide energy resource in Europe is of the order of 300 TWh y^{-1}.

Figure 6.30 Map of world tidal power sites

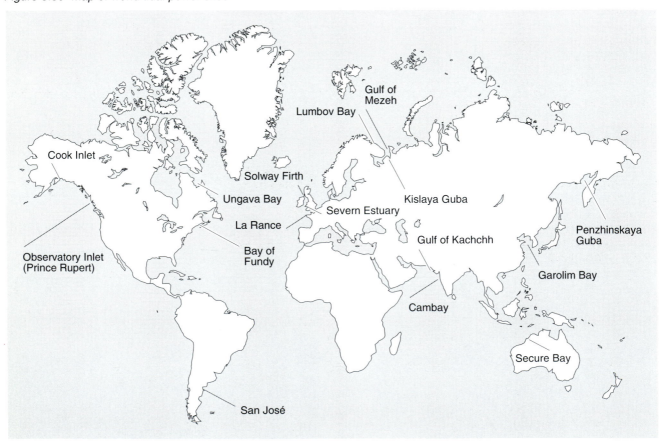

Table 6.6 Potential tidal power sites (1991)

Site	Area (km²)	Maximum depth (m)	Length (m)	Mean range (m)	Turbines (number × diameter)	Annual energy (TWh)	Estimated unit cost (p kWh⁻¹)*
Argentina and Chile							
Golfo San José	788	25	7000	5.78	270 × 7.5	10.9	2.1
San Julián	77	13	810	5.66	40 × 6	1.04	1.8
Río Santa Cruz	215	32	2070	7.48	60 × 9	5.05	2.3
Río Coig	46	12	1800	7.86	30 × 6	0.61	1.9
Río Gallegos	140	12	3400	7.46	85 × 6	3.27	1.6
Bahía San Sebastian	580	30	19 300	6.5	145 × 9	10	3.8
Australia							
Secure Bay	140	50	1300	7	37 × 9	2.9	3.6
Walcott Inlet	260	75	2500	7	70 × 9	5.4	5.1
Canada							
Bay of Fundy	282	42	8000	11.7	106 × 7.5	11.7	2.2
South-east China							
Damao shan	200	24	3550	4.8	100 × 6	2.05	3.7
Dong' an Dao	210	21	3900	5.1	100 × 6	2.26	3.2
Santu Ao	680	35	3000	4.8	150 × 9	3.7	2.8
India							
Gulf of Cambay	1055	22	25 000	6.1	570 × 6	16.4	2.5
Gulf of Kachchh	50?	18	2000	4.8	24 × 6	0.48	5
South Korea							
Garolim Bay	100	28	1850	4.8	24 × 8	0.893	4.5
Gulf of Asam	130	24	2350	6.06	72 × 6	2.05	3.1
(Former) USSR (Sea of Okoskh)							
Zaliv Tugurskiy	1400	30	26 000	4.74	200 × 9	12	4

* In 1983 money terms, at 5% discount rate.

(Source: Baker, 1991b)

Such calculations also do not take into account the possibility of harnessing the energy in tidal streams (see Box 6.11) and exclude some of the larger and more ambitious (if very speculative) 'open coast' tidal schemes that have been proposed. These include proposals for a barrage across the Wash (see Figure 6.31) and even huge barrages across the Bering Straits and the Irish Sea, though the latter proposals would be considered by many engineers to be technologically unrealistic.

BOX 6.11: TIDAL STREAMS

Instead of using costly barrages and low-head turbines located in estuaries, it may be possible to harness the kinetic energy of the tides in fast, free-flowing tidal currents or streams at suitable sites, using relatively simple, submerged, wind turbine-like rotors.

The idea is as yet relatively undeveloped, but it has been estimated that, for example, the power flowing through the North Channel of the Irish Sea is equivalent to 3.6 GW. Flows of this sort could be harnessed using arrays of large-diameter rotors, supported on pontoons tethered to the sea bed, or fixed to the bottom. One advantage of this concept would be that, unlike barrages, units could be constructed on a modular basis and installed incrementally.

There would be problems of fouling (for example, by seaweed, fishing nets, etc.), tethering and power take-off to overcome, as with wave energy systems, but on the other hand, expensive barrages are not required. The energy potential, for the UK and elsewhere, could be significant. For example, it has been estimated that the flow through Pentland Firth is the equivalent of 6.1 GW, although by no means all of this flow could be absorbed and converted into useful energy.

Several sites around the world have been discussed, including around Alderney off the French coast, the straits of Messina in Italy and in Western Australia.

By way of comparison with other technologies, submerged free stream-driven tidal rotors would operate at lower rotational speeds than wind turbines (since typical sea current velocities are approximately 3 m s^{-1} compared with, say, 7 m s^{-1} for wind machines). However, given that the density of the working fluid is much higher, the power output for a tidal stream machine would be much larger than for a wind machine of equivalent blade size.

However, the output from a tidal stream turbine would be likely to be lower than from an equivalent-sized conventional turbine in a barrage, which would have the advantage of the funnelling effect of estuaries and the creation of an enhanced head of water, but, to compensate, it might be possible to use larger rotors in free streams than is possible in barrage-mounted turbines.

Figure 6.31 UK 'open coast' barrage sites

6.7 CONCLUSIONS

The technology of tidal power generation is well developed, and useful operating experience has been obtained from the Rance Barrage and other smaller projects. Although La Rance involved a relatively expensive coffer-dam construction technique, the scheme produces electricity at costs comparable with those from French nuclear plants (see Table 6.8). Construction techniques have developed since La Rance was built. There is now much experience with large-scale civil engineering at sea in relation to oil rig and flood protection projects, for example in the use of large concrete caissons floated into place. Such new techniques could cut civil engineering costs by up to 30%, although there could be difficulties in placing caissons in high currents.

The main uncertainties are *environmental impact* and *investment provision*. Some of the environmental impacts will, of course, be positive and of global significance, for example the avoidance of carbon dioxide emissions that would occur if fossil fuel plants were used instead. The negative impacts are more localised and it is hoped that further research will show how these can be reduced. One of the key factors will probably be how people perceive barrages, in which case prior public consultation is vital. This has been done to a limited extent for both the Severn and the Mersey projects, but more will need to be done to avoid unnecessary conflicts if and when these projects go ahead, with design compromises perhaps emerging in response.

By contrast, it is much harder to respond to the financial constraints. Despite all attempts to cut capital costs, they remain stubbornly high. No doubt design and technology improvements could improve plant economics, and, more importantly, new construction technology could reduce capital costs, but the potential for cost reduction is considered to be limited. Certainly that is currently the view of the government which, in its response to the House of Commons Select Committee on Energy report on renewable energy in 1992, commented that it saw 'little scope for cost reductions via an R&D programme' (DTI 1992). In many ways, the issue is now out of the hands of the engineers, and depends much more on the attitudes of both the public and the private sectors towards investment in large-scale projects in the UK.

The STPG indicated (House of Commons Select Committee on Energy, 1992) that, on the most optimistic projections, to launch the Severn Barrage it would still need either a government subsidy of between £2 billion and £3 billion or some other form of support (such as loan guarantees) to reduce the risk as perceived by private sector financiers.

Proportionate subsidies or support arrangements would also probably be required to enable the smaller barrages to go ahead. For while the cost of electricity from some of the smaller barrages might be slightly less sensitive to high discount rates, since they can be constructed more rapidly (Commission of the European Communities, 1992), this advantage seems in many cases to be offset by the generally higher generating cost of small barrages. This is primarily because, in the main, they have lower tidal ranges. Overall, currently, it is thus believed that no clear economies of scale exist.

In general, tidal power, on a small or a large scale, would seem to require at least some state support if it is to be developed significantly in the UK.

However, State support for UK tidal barrages looks unlikely at present. In March 1994 the DTI announced that its tidal programme would be closed, with tidal power being relegated to 'watching brief' status (Department of Trade and Industry, 1994).

As indicated above, there had been hopes that some of the smaller barrages might offer somewhat better economic prospects. However a report from the Energy Technology Support Unit noted that, although the

Table 6.8   La Rance cost comparisons (1989)*

Type of power plant	Cost (centimes kWh^{-1})
Nuclear	21.46
Tidal	22.71
Hydro	23.57
Coal	32.32

* Excluding miscellaneous charges. Note: these comparisons need careful interpretation, in the absence of detailed information on the financial regime and in view of the substantial state subsidies provided in France for nuclear power and for La Rance.

(Source: Figures provided by Electricité de France to an Australian Select Committee on Energy and Processing of Resources. (Report of the Legislative Assembly (of Western Australia) Select Committee on Energy and Processing of Resources, 1991, p. 49.))

BOX 6.12 TIDAL STREAM TECHNOLOGY IN THE UK

Table 6.7 Estimates for cost of energy from tidal stream devices

Machine size at site	Discount rate (%)	*Unit costs of energy* Cheapest site (p kWh^{-1})	Most expensive site (p kWh^{-1})
Over 100 kW	5	7.7	48.0
	8	9.9	61.2
	15	16.2	100.9
Under 100 kW	5	26.0	160.1
	8	33.2	204.1
	15	54.7	336.2

(Source: ETSU, 1993)

A prototype two-bladed 10 kW tidal current turbine was tested in 1994 in the Corran Narrows in Loch Linne, near Fort William, by a consortium involving IT Power, the National Engineering Laboratory and Scottish Nuclear.

The £200 000 project was based on a 3.9 m diameter rotor submerged in 10 m depth of sea, operating at around 35–40 rpm in tidal currents at up to 2–5 m s^{-1}. The rotor unit was supported by a cable attached to a floating buoy and was tethered to the sea bed. It swivelled around on the change of the tide to absorb power from tidal currents in either direction (see Figure 6.32). Full-scale systems could be up to 1 MW each, with 20 m diameter rotors.

Indications are that, if fully developed, up to 19% of the UK's electricity could in principle come from this source. This estimate comes from an ETSU report (ETSU, 1993), which identifies the total UK tidal stream resource as some 58 TWh y^{-1}, of which 46.5 TWh is attributed to sites where machines of over 100 kW size would be installed.

However, the cost of electricity could be high. The report's preliminary estimates were that bottom-mounted, fixed-orientation 'tide mill' devices of 100 kW or more rated power, located at the best sites (Pentland Firth and the Channel Islands) would produce electricity at some 10p kWh^{-1} (at 8% discount rate) or 16p kWh^{-1} (at 15% discount rate) (see Table 6.7). However, it is believed that economies of scale in series production of turbines could reduce these figures, albeit only after a substantial development programme. Bottom-mounted, fixed-orientation devices of the sort assessed in the ETSU report would seem to be more robust, but the free-floating, mid-depth swivelling system being tested by IT Power may have cost advantages in some locations (where there is sufficient room for it to swing around), despite the need for flexible marine cable power take-off arrangements.

For further information on tidal streams, see the Further Reading section.

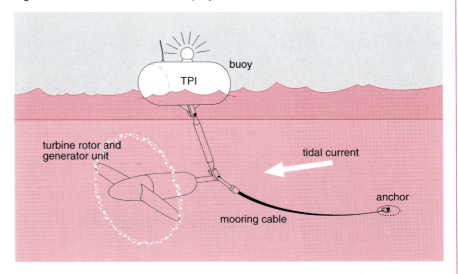

Figure 6.32 Tidal current turbine project

Wyre Barrage was the most economic of the smaller schemes, with generation costs at 8% discount rate put at 6.8p/kWh compared to 7.1p for the Mersey, 7.2p for the Severn, and 8.2p for the Conwy, "Ministers have declined to support further development of the project" (ETSU, 1994).

A subsequent ETSU report on the 100 MW Duddon scheme put its generation cost significantly higher than that of the Wyre (8.7p/kWh even given an allowance for regional and environmental benefits).

Over all, ETSU's conclusion was that, on the assumption of a 'zero commercial potential by current UK criteria', there was no justification for further R & D work, although the door was left open by the suggestion that it might still be worth investigating 'whether reverse economics of scale apply to tidal barrages' so as to 'see if small schemes are more financially attractive'. As already indicated, the evidence is mixed. Interestingly, a major study produced for the European Commission commented

'The net effects of lower capital and annual costs for large schemes give these a distinct economic edge over small projects, a bias which is only partly offset by lower interest charges attributable to the more readily constructed small schemes'. (CEC, 1994)

This debate will no doubt continue, given that there are still some signs of interest in barrages. For example, following the demise of the Mersey scheme, Tarmac Construction, initially part of the Mersey Barrage consortium, proposed a new Forth Road Bridge at Kincardine in Scotland which would include tidal turbines rated at 34 MW and which it was claimed would generate at 10p/kWh. However, to be commercially viable earnings from a road toll would be required, as would support from the Non-Fossil Fuel Obligation levy scheme.

Finally, a new focus of interest in the tidal energy field is the **tidal stream** concept. In addition to the 10 kW prototype tidemill, which has been tested in Scotland (see Box 6.12), there is an EC supported project based on a proposal for a tidemill system with 100 turbines to be installed at 100 metres depth on the sea bed in the Straits of Messina between Sicily and mainland Italy (Figure 6.33). The EC is providing 300,000 ecu to support the project.

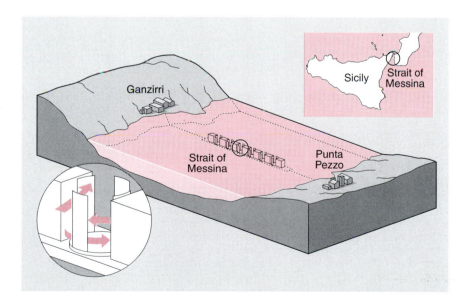

Figure 6.33 The Straits of Messina Project

REFERENCES

Baker, A. C. (1986) 'The development of functions relating cost and performance of tidal power schemes and their application to small scale sites', *ICE Symposium on Tidal Power*, Thomas Telford, pp. 331–44.

Baker, A. C. (1991a) *Tidal Power*, Peter Peregrinus.

Baker, A. C. (1991b) 'Tidal power', *Energy Policy*, Vol. 19, No. 8, pp. 792–7.

Calder, R. (1938) 'Mighty engines driven by the moon', *Modern Wonders*, 29 January.

Carson, J. L. and Samuelson, R. S. (1978) *Power*, March, pp. 54–7.

Commission of the European Communities (1992) *The Potential for Tidal Energy within the European Community*, Thermie Programme Action Report, Directorate General XVII.

CEC, (1994) *The European Renewable Energy Study* Report to the EC DG XVII, Commission of the European Communities.

Department of Energy (1978) *Severn Barrage Seminar* (Energy Paper 27), HMSO.

Department of Energy (1981) *Tidal Power from the Severn Estuary*, Vol. I (Energy Paper 46) (the Bondi Report), HMSO.

Department of Energy (1987) *Information Bulletin on the Severn Barrage*, Issue 2, HMSO.

Department of Energy (1989) *The Severn Barrage Project: General Report* (Energy Paper 57), HMSO.

Department of Energy (1991) *The Severn Barrage Project Report on Responses and Consultations*, TID 4090 p1, Severn Tidal Power Group/Energy Technology Support Unit.

Department of Trade and Industry (1992) *Government Response to the Energy Select Committee Report on Renewable Energy*, 16 July, HMSO.

Department of Trade and Industry (1993) *Digest of United Kingdom Energy Statistics*, HMSO.

Department of Trade and Industry (1994) *New and Renewable Energy: Future Prospects for the UK* Energy Paper 62, HMSO.

ETSU (1988) *Tidal Power from the River Mersey: A Feasibility Study Stage 1*, Mersey Barrage Company Limited/Energy Technology Support Unit.

ETSU (1990) *Renewable Energy Research and Development Programme* (Report R56), Energy Technology Support Unit.

ETSU (1991) *River Wyre – Preliminary Feasibility Study*, TID 4100, Energy Technology Support Unit.

ETSU (1993) *Tidal Stream Energy Review* (Report 05/00155), Energy Technology Support Unit.

ETSU (1994) *An Assessment of Renewable Energy for the UK* Energy Technology Support Unit Report R82.

Hansard (1987) Vol. 121, No. 34, columns 564–623, 30 October.

Haws, T. and McCormick, J. (1993) 'Economic and financial development of the Mersey Barrage', *IEE Conference Proceedings 'Clean Power 2001'*, Conference Paper 385, November 17–19, pp. 72–77.

House of Commons Select Committee on Energy (1992) *Renewable Energy*, Fourth Report Session 1991–2, HMSO.

IT Power News (1993) No. 10, February.

Lewis, G. L. (1963) 'The tidal power resources of the Kimberleys', *The Journal*, December, reproduced in Report of the Legislative Assembly (of Western Australia) Select Committee on Energy and Processing of Resources (1991), 12 November.

MBC (1991) Memorandum submitted by MBC to the House of Commons Select Committee on Energy, 20 November, reprinted in Energy Committee Fourth Report *Renewable Energy*, Vol. III, Minutes of Evidence and Appendices, 43-III, 11 March 1992, HMSO.

New Scientist (1988) 'Barrages to harness the power of the open sea', 3 December, p. 38.

Open University (1989) S330 *Oceanography*, Book 4 *Waves, Tides and Shallow Water Processes*, The Open University in conjunction with Pergamon Press.

Open University (1993a) U206 *Environment*, Book 3 *Energy Resources and Environment*, The Open University.

Open University (1993b) T362 *Design and Innovation*, Block 4 *Local and National Government*, The Open University.

Renewable Energy Advisory Group (1992) *Report to the President of the Board of Trade* (Energy Paper 60), HMSO.

Report of the Legislative Assembly (of Western Australia) Select Committee on Energy and Processing of Resources (1991), 12 November.

Sathiamoorthy, M. and Probert, D. (1994) 'The Integrated Severn Barrage Complex: Harnessing Tidal, Wave and Wind Power' *Applied Energy*, 49 pp. 17-46.

Saunders (1975) *Kimberley Tidal Power Revisited*, IE (Aust), quoted in Report of the Legislative Assembly (of Western Australia) Select Committee on Energy and Processing of Resources (1991), 12 November.

STPG (1986) *Tidal Power from the Severn*, Severn Tidal Power Group.

Taylor, R. H. (1983) *Alternative Energy Sources for the Centralised Generation of Electricity*, Adam Hilger.

Twidell, J. W. and Weir, A. J. (1986) *Renewable Energy Resources*, E and F Spon.

Wardle, D. G., Gibson, J. P., McGlynn, R. F. (1993) 'The present status of the Severn Barrage project studies', *IEEE Conference Proceedings 'Clean Power 2001'*, Conference Paper 385, November 17–19, pp. 78–83.

Watt Committee on Energy (1990) *Renewable Energy Sources*, Report 22, Elsevier Applied Science.

Wickert, G. (1956) 'Tidal power, Part I', *Water Power*, Vol. 8, No. 6, June, pp. 221–5, and 'Tidal power, Part II' No. 7, July, pp. 259–63, quoted in Report of the Legislative Assembly (of Western Australia) Select Committee on Energy and Processing of Resources (1991), 12 November.

FURTHER READING

GENERAL

Probably the most comprehensive introduction to tidal energy is Charlier, R. H. (1982) *Tidal Energy*, Van Nostrand.

For a good, short general introduction to tidal power, see Taylor, R. H. (1983) *Alternative Energy Sources for the Centralised Generation of Electricity*, Adam Hilger.

For an interesting critique of tidal power policy, see Wilson, E. (1988) 'A tide in the affairs of men', *International Journal of Ambient Energy*, Vol. 9, No. 3, pp. 115–17.

See also the more recent review of tidal power: Baker, C. (1991b) 'Tidal power', *Energy Policy*, Vol. 19, No. 8, pp. 792–7.

A useful review of tidal energy technology is given by Price, R. (1991) 'Tidal energy', *Proceedings of the World Clean Energy Conference*, Geneva, 4–7 November, pp. 277–95.

Perhaps the most comprehensive recent study of tidal power is Baker, C. (1991a) *Tidal Power*, Peter Peregrinus.

HISTORY

For a brief history of tidal power, see Charlier, R. H. (1979) 'Tidal power plants: sites, history and geographical distribution', *Proceedings of the First International Symposium on Wave and Tidal Energy*, Canterbury, September, paper A1-9, BHRA.

For details of traditional tidal mills, see Wailes, R. (1957) *Tide Mills*, Society for the Protection of Ancient Buildings.

For an interesting if controversial review of past schemes and institutional reactions, see Watson, W. (1992) 'Tidal power politics', *International Journal of Ambient Energy*, Vol. 13, No. 3, pp. 1–10.

LA RANCE

Allary, R. (1965) *L'Usine marémotrice de la Rance*, Electricité de France, pp. 22–46.

Banal, M. and Bichon, A. (1981) 'Tidal energy in France. The Rance tidal power station – some results after 15 years of operation', *Proceedings of the Second International Symposium on Wave and Tidal Energy*, Cambridge, September, paper K3, BHRA.

Cotillon, J. (1978) 'La Rance tidal power station – review and comments', *Proceedings of the Colston Symposium on Tidal Energy*, Bristol, Scientechnica, pp. 49–66.

Holland, M. B. (1978) 'Power from the tides', *Chartered Mechanical Engineer*, July, pp. 33–9.

RESPONSES TO THE SEVERN BARRAGE

A preliminary review of local responses to the Severn Barrage can be found in Barac, C., Spencer, L. and Elliott, D. (1983) 'Public awareness of renewable energy: a pilot study', *International Journal of Ambient Energy*, Vol. 4, No. 4, pp. 199–211.

Also see Department of Energy (1991) *The Severn Barrage Project Report on Responses and Consultations*, TID 4090 p1, Severn Tidal Power Group/Energy Technology Support Unit.

TIDAL POWER OPTIONS – DETAILED REPORTS

The UK's tidal power options and the Severn Barrage proposal in particular have been studied in considerable detail over many decades, so there is much detailed analysis, notably the series of Energy Papers from the Department of Energy.

Department of Energy (1977) *Tidal Power Barrages in the Severn Estuary* (Energy Paper 23), HMSO.

Department of Energy (1978) *Severn Barrage Seminar* (Energy Paper 27), HMSO.

Department of Energy (1981) *Tidal Power from the Severn Estuary*, Vols I and II) (Energy Paper 46) (the Bondi Report), HMSO.

Department of Energy (1989) *The Severn Barrage Project: General Report* (Energy Paper 57), HMSO.

There are also many useful summary pamphlets and brochures available free of charge from ETSU, including the 'Severn Barrage Project Summary' and a series of 'Severn Barrage Bulletins' on different aspects of the project.

In addition, the contractors and developers have produced detailed reports, for example the following.

STPG (1986) *Tidal Power from the Severn*, Severn Tidal Power Group.

ETSU (1988) *Tidal Power from the River Mersey: A Feasibility Study Stage 1*, Mersey Barrage Company Limited/Energy Technology Support Unit.

ETSU (1989a) *Severn Barrage Project: Detailed Report*, Vol. I. *Tidal Hydrodynamics, Sediments, Water Quality, Land Drainage and Sea Defence*, TID 4060 p1, Severn Tidal Power Group/Energy Technology Support Unit.

ETSU (1989b) *Severn Barrage Project: Detailed Report*, Vol. II. *Ecological Studies, Landscape and Nature Conservation*, TID 4060 p4, Severn Tidal Power Group/Energy Technology Support Unit.

For an analysis of the UK's small-scale tidal options, see Binnie & Partners (1989) *The UK Potential for Tidal Energy from Small Estuaries*, Energy Technology Support Unit.

For a review of possible schemes around the world, see:

Baker, C. (1991a) *Tidal Power*, Peter Peregrinus.

Taylor, R. H. (1983) *Alternative Energy Sources for the Centralised Generation of Electricity*, Adam Hilger.

Wilson, E. M. (1987) 'Tidal power generation', in *Developments in Hydraulic Engineering* IV, ed. Novak, P., Elsevier Applied Science.

TIDAL STREAMS

Charlier, R. H. (1982) *Tidal Power*, Van Nostrand, p. 38.

Fraenkel, P. and Musgrove, P. (1979) 'Tidal and river current energy systems', *Proceedings of the IEE Conference on Future Energy Concepts*, London, 30 January–1 February, pp. 114–17, IEE.

Peachy, C. and Wyman, P. (1979) 'Tidal current energy conversion', *Proceedings of the IEE Conference on Future Energy Concepts*, London, 30 January–1 February, IEE.

WIND ENERGY

7.1 INTRODUCTION

Wind energy offers the potential to generate substantial amounts of electricity without the pollution problems of most conventional forms of electricity generation. Its environmental costs, mainly in the form of visual intrusion, are different from those of conventional electricity generation. The scale of its development will depend critically on the care with which wind turbines are selected and sited.

Wind energy has been used for thousands of years for milling grain, pumping water, and other mechanical power applications. Today, there are over one million windmills in operation around the world; these are used principally for water pumping. Whilst the wind will continue to be used for this purpose, it is the use of wind energy as a pollution-free means of generating electricity on a potentially significant scale that is attracting most current interest in the subject. Strictly speaking, a wind*mill* is used for milling grain, so modern 'windmills' tend to be called **wind turbines**, partly because of their functional similarity to the steam and gas turbines that are used to generate electricity, and partly to distinguish them from their traditional forebears. They are also sometimes referred to as **wind energy conversion systems (WECS)** and those used to generate electricity are sometimes described as **wind generators** or **aerogenerators**.

Currently, there are few traditional windmills in the landscape, so new wind turbines are unfamiliar yet potentially highly visible new structures in the countryside. Amenity groups have an interest in assessing the impact that large numbers of these new wind turbines will have on the landscape.

Attempts to generate electricity from wind energy have been made (with various degrees of success) since the end of the nineteenth century. Small wind machines for charging batteries have been manufactured since the 1940s (see Figure 7.1). It is, however, only since the 1980s that the technology has become sufficiently mature to enable viable industries to evolve, based both on the manufacture of wind energy equipment and on the generation of electricity from wind energy. An extensive range of commercial wind turbines is currently available from over 30 manufacturers around the world.

The cost of wind energy equipment fell steadily between the early 1980s and the early 1990s. The technology is continually being improved to make it both cheaper and more reliable, so it can be expected that wind energy will tend to become more economically competitive over the coming decades.

An understanding of machines that extract energy from the wind involves many fields of knowledge, including meteorology, aerodynamics, electricity and planning control, as well as structural, civil and mechanical engineering.

This section begins with case studies of a medium-scale wind turbine at a rural animal welfare centre, and of a wind farm in Cornwall. These highlight some of the key factors involved in wind energy conversion.

Figure 7.1 The 70 watt rated Marlec 'Rutland Windcharger'. Many thousands of small wind turbines like this are in use world-wide

7.2 CASE STUDIES: Wood Green Animal Shelter Wind Turbine; Delabole, The UK's First Wind Farm

Wood Green Animal Shelter Wind Turbine

Figure 7.2 shows a 27-metre diameter wind turbine which contributes to the electrical needs of a rural centre concerned with animal welfare, near Huntingdon in the UK.

This machine is a horizontal axis wind turbine (HAWT), a type that evolved out of the traditional form of windmill from northern Europe. HAWTs are the most successful and numerous of wind energy conversion devices in use today.

In terms of physical size and power rating the wind turbine employed at Wood Green Animal Shelter can be classified as 'medium scale'. This term is currently used to describe wind turbines with power ratings between approximately 100 and 700 kilowatts (kW). Wind turbines with lower power ratings are usually referred to as 'small scale' and those above approximately 700 kW as 'large scale', although there are no generally agreed definitions of these terms. Currently, medium-scale wind turbines are the most viable commercially, although both small- and large-scale machines may become more viable with

improvements in technology and in the means of manufacture.

The 20 hectare (50 acre) site includes a large cattery, kennels, stables, veterinary clinic, incineration plant, indoor horse arena, restaurant, shop, college building, administration block and residential accommodation, as well as paddocks and a lake. The centre is extremely popular: in 1991 some 500 000 visitors were attracted to the site.

The buildings at the centre have been designed with energy conservation very much in mind and the incineration plant on the site heats water as a by-product

Figure 7.2 Vestas V27/225 kW wind turbine at Wood Green Animal Shelter, Huntingdon

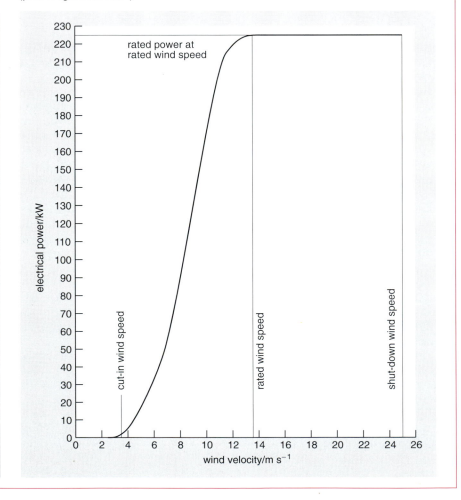

Figure 7.3 Wind speed–power curve for Vestas V27/225 kW wind turbine (pitch regulated rotor)

when operating. The centre is also considering making use of another renewable resource – dung – to feed a special digester in order to produce methane on the site.

The energy systems on the site demonstrate what a group with sufficient funds and a commitment to energy conservation and renewable energy can achieve with current technology.

Power output

The maximum power produced by the Wood Green wind turbine is 225 kW. This is known as its **rated power**, and the wind speed at which it reaches this power output, 13.5 metres per second, is known as its **rated wind speed**. Above this, there is a maximum wind speed (known as the **shut-down** or **cut-out wind speed**) at which the turbine is designed to shut down. The lowest wind speed at which a wind turbine will operate is known as the **cut-in wind speed**.

At or above the rated wind speed, the power output remains constant whatever the wind speed (below the shut-down speed), but below the rated wind speed the power varies with the wind speed. Each wind turbine of a particular design has a specific relationship between the power it produces and the wind speed. This relationship describes the amount of power generated at each wind speed, and can be represented by a graph known as the **wind speed–power curve**, often referred to simply as the 'power curve'. The power curve for the Wood Green wind turbine is shown in Figure 7.3. The power values in kilowatts refer to the electrical power output of the wind turbine's generator.

Coping with changes in wind direction

As the blades of the wind turbine rotate through their circular path, they sweep through a disc-like area which is referred to as the **swept area**. The power that a wind turbine can extract from the wind at a given wind speed is directly proportional to its rotor's swept area, which in the case of the Wood Green wind turbine is 573 square metres.

It is extremely important that the maximum swept area is presented to the wind and this is achieved by making sure that the rotor's axis is aligned with the direction from which the wind is blowing. As the wind does not always blow from the same direction, a mechanism of some kind is needed to realign the rotor axis in response to changes in wind direction. This aligning or slewing action, about a vertical axis that passes through the centre of the tower, is known as **yawing**, from the term used to describe the rotation of an aeroplane or ship about a vertical axis.

Spinning the blades

When the wind turbine is correctly aligned, the turbine's control computer checks that the wind speed is within the operating range

Figure 7.4 Three-dimensional view of machinery and housing (nacelle) of Vestas V27/225 kW wind turbine

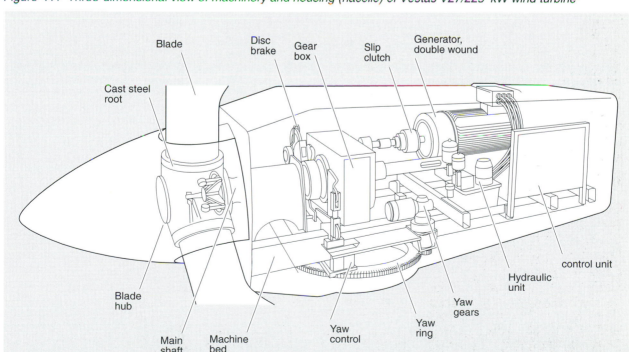

for which it is designed. If this is so, each blade is then rotated about its longitudinal or 'span-wise' axis (called the **pitch axis**), until it reaches the optimum **pitch angle**, at which it will produce the maximum power at that wind speed.

A wind turbine blade has a distinctive curved cross-sectional shape, which is rounded at one end and sharp at the other. The shape of the blade's cross-section is the key to how modern wind turbines extract energy from the wind (see Sections 7.4 and 7.5). This special profile is known as an **aerofoil section** and is already familiar as the cross-sectional shape of aeroplane wings.

The moving blades, having converted energy from the wind stream, rotate a shaft, which is mechanically coupled via a gear box to an electrical generator.

Many electricity-generating wind turbines utilise a single generator running at just one speed, but the Wood Green wind turbine uses a special kind of generator which is in effect two generators in one: it is both a 50 kW generator and a 225 kW generator. A generator of this type improves the wind turbine's energy capture at lower wind speeds.

The small generator operates at a lower rotation speed, permitting the wind turbine rotor to operate at a lower rotation speed when wind speeds are low. The turbine would otherwise have a higher **cut-in wind speed**, and energy from the more frequent light winds at this site would not be extracted.

Figure 7.4 shows a three-dimensional view of the wind turbine machinery and the technical specifications for the turbine are shown in Table 7.1. Important factors that appear to have contributed to the project's viability include the following:

• that the site is on a slight hill compared with the surrounding area (wind accelerates when passing over a hill);

• that the turbine is the latest refinement in a well-established model; and

• that the turbine has been designed to cut in at the relatively low wind speed of 3.5 m s^{-1} (7.8 miles per hour) – a gentle breeze.

The use of a low-speed generator for low wind speeds and a high-speed generator for high wind speeds improves the turbine's energy capture, as does its pitch-regulated rotor, which optimises the blade pitch setting for best performance at each wind speed. The relatively tall (30 m) tower also means that the turbine is operating in slightly higher wind speeds than it would be with a shorter tower.

All of the electricity that the wind turbine generates is sold to the local electricity company (Eastern Electricity), but electricity consumed by the centre is purchased back from Eastern Electricity. Fortunately for the centre, the price at which its electricity is sold is currently about 30% more than the purchase price of the electricity consumed. This is because the turbine is registered under a special support scheme established by the UK government known as the **Non-Fossil Fuel Obligation (NFFO)**. This requires the various regional electricity companies to purchase specified amounts of electricity from non-fossil sources, such as wind energy. Those contracted under the scheme receive a premium price for each unit of electricity sold to the local regional electricity company.

Between 29 September 1990 and 1 March 1993 the animal shelter wind turbine produced approximately 1 187 919 kilowatt-hours (kWh) of electricity, equivalent to approximately 490 000 kilowatt-hours per year.

Table 7.1 Wind turbine (Vestas V27/225 kW) at Wood Green Animal Shelter, Huntingdon

Turbine type	Horizontal axis wind turbine
Rotor type	Upwind of tower
Number of rotor blades	3
Blade type	Variable pitch
Blade material	Glass-reinforced polyester
Rotor diameter	27 m
Rotor swept area	573 m^2
Hub height	33 m
Rotation speeds	32/43 rpm*
Cut-in wind speed	3.5 m s^{-1}
Rated wind speed	13.5 m s^{-1}
Cut-out wind speed	25 m s^{-1}
Rated power	225 kW
Generator 1	50 kW @ 760 rpm (8 poles)
Generator 2	225 kW @ 1008 rpm (6 poles)
Gearbox	Speed ratio 1:23
Tower	Tapered tubular steel 30 m tall
Cost installed (September 1991)	£175 000

* rpm: revolutions per minute.

(Source: Vestas DWT, 1991)

Delabole, the UK's First Wind Farm

The power density of wind is relatively low and so the maximum power output of an individual commercial wind turbine is usually rated in hundreds of kilowatts, rather than the hundreds of megawatts that characterise conventional thermal power stations.

Whilst individual wind turbines can make a small but useful contribution to the energy production of the UK, and to the economy of local communities, the generation of significant amounts of electricity from wind energy on a national scale will probably only be feasible with wind turbines arranged in clusters or arrays known as wind farms or wind parks.

Grouping wind turbines together in this way permits much larger amounts of energy to be produced from a given site. There are other advantages in having wind turbines installed in wind farms. These include the following:

• The capital invested in the project is spread over a number of machines, so that if a turbine has to be shut down for any reason, the other machines can still continue operating, continuing to produce energy and generate revenue.

• Infrastructure and maintenance costs can be spread over all the machines. It is more cost effective to connect several wind turbines to the grid than one.

• Running an operation and maintenance crew is also cheaper, per machine, if the crew is managing or maintaining a group of machines.

Whilst wind farms have been installed in relatively large numbers overseas, the first wind farm did not appear in the UK until the end of 1991. This was the Delabole wind farm, established by the Edwards family on their mixed farm in north Cornwall. They first became interested in exploiting wind energy in 1980, when they became opposed to a plan to build a nuclear power station in Cornwall. Rather than simply saying 'No' to nuclear power, they felt that they should take positive steps to encourage renewable energy and thought that wind energy might be practicable on their farm.

In the late 1980s, the Edwards family felt that wind energy technology was sufficiently mature to consider the development of a wind farm on their land. They were successful in obtaining a grant from the Commission of the European Communities towards the establishment of a wind farm and managed to raise the rest of the capital from a bank, together with investments obtained from National Wind Power and South Western Electricity.

After discussions with a number of wind turbine manufacturers, they decided on a wind farm consisting of ten 400 kW Vestas wind turbines.

In order to keep the infrastructure costs to a minimum they decided not to build roads on the site, and to avoid the loss of productive agricultural land they decided to locate each wind turbine within a hedgerow.

The installation was quite rapid. Digging of the first foundation hole commenced on 30 August 1991; the first wind turbine was installed on 15 November 1991 and the last on 17 December 1991. Figure 7.5 shows the completed 4 megawatt (MW) wind farm at Delabole.

The mean annual wind speed at hub height on the Delabole site is 7.6 m s^{-1}. The predicted electricity production from the wind farm was between 11 and 12 million kWh per year, but only 85% of this, i.e. about 10 million kWh, was assumed for budget purposes, to allow for various energy losses. The first year's production was approximately 10 million kWh; this was within the financial tolerance allowed by the bank. The wind farm operated for 77% of the time and the turbines had an availability (that is, were available to generate if the wind speed was within their operating range) of 97%. 'The wind farm was on time, on cost and also within budget' (Edwards, 1993).

This amount of wind-generated electricity would avoid the release of approximately 50 tonnes of sulphur dioxide, 30 tonnes of nitrous oxides and 8900 tonnes of carbon dioxide, if it replaced electricity produced in a coal-fired power station.

Under the NFFO scheme (see Section 7.8), the Edwards are selling electricity at approximately 10 pence per kilowatt-hour to South Western Electricity and the expected payback time on their investment is about six years.

In addition to the revenue generated from the sale of the electricity, the wind farm has provided income for local contractors during its construction phase and has generated five part-time jobs on an ongoing basis.

A visitor's centre was established near the wind farm and the project has attracted a great many visitors; as a result the local town of Delabole has benefited from the increased trade that these visitors have brought. In the first nine months over 35 000 people had visited the site (Edwards, 1993).

Figure 7.5 The UK's first wind farm at Delabole, Cornwall, which began generating electricity in December 1991. The wind farm consists of ten 400 kW wind turbines, each 34 m in diameter

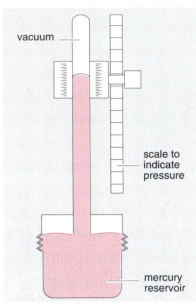

vacuum

scale to
indicate
pressure

mercury
reservoir

7.3   THE WIND

Atmospheric pressure is the result of the weight of the column of air that rests on a specified surface area on the ground, and it is measured by means of a barometer (Figure 7.6). The unit of atmospheric pressure is known as the bar. One bar is approximately normal atmospheric pressure at sea level. Barometers are usually calibrated in millibars (mbar), that is, thousandths of a bar. The average atmospheric pressure at sea level is about 1013.2 mbar. Pressure is also measured in pascals (Pa), or in newtons per square millimetre (N mm^{-2}).

The following conversion factors may be useful:

1 bar = 100 000 Pa = 100 kilopascals (kPa)

1 mbar = 100 Pa

1 Pa = 1 newton per square metre (N m^{-2})

1 N mm^{-2} = 1 million Pa = 1 megapascal (MPa)

Figure 7.6 (Left) Fortin barometer, an example of a barometer used to measure atmospheric pressure. Variations in atmospheric pressure acting on the mercury in the reservoir cause the mercury in the column to rise or fall

Figure 7.7 Typical weather map showing regions of high (H) and low (L) pressure

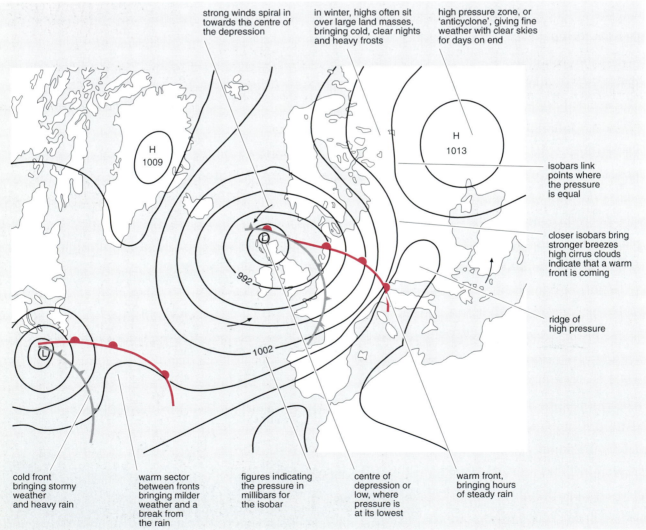

strong winds spiral in towards the centre of the depression

in winter, highs often sit over large land masses, bringing cold, clear nights and heavy frosts

high pressure zone, or 'anticyclone', giving fine weather with clear skies for days on end

isobars link points where the pressure is equal

closer isobars bring stronger breezes high cirrus clouds indicate that a warm front is coming

ridge of high pressure

cold front bringing stormy weather and heavy rain

warm sector between fronts bringing milder weather and a break from the rain

figures indicating the pressure in millibars for the isobar

centre of depression or low, where pressure is at its lowest

warm front, bringing hours of steady rain

On the weather maps featured in television weather forecast programmes, you will notice that there are regions marked 'high' and 'low', surrounded by contours (Figure 7.7). The regions marked 'high' and 'low' relate to the barometric pressure and the contours represent lines of equal pressure called **isobars**. The high pressure regions on the weather forecaster's map tend to indicate fine weather with little wind, whereas the low pressure regions tend to indicate changeable windy weather and precipitation.

The earth's wind systems are air masses that are moving around as a result of variations in air pressure. The variations in air pressure are due to differences in solar heating over the earth.

As explained in Section 2.3, a solar panel absorbs much more of the sun's energy when it is positioned so that its collection surface is perpendicular to the sun's rays than if it is positioned at an oblique angle to the rays. Similarly, one square metre of the earth's surface on or near the equator receives more solar radiation per year than one square metre at higher latitudes. The curvature of the earth means that its surface becomes more oblique to the sun's rays with increasing latitude. In addition, the sun's rays have further to travel through the atmosphere, so more of the sun's energy is absorbed *en route* before it reaches the surface. As a result of these effects, the tropics are considerably warmer than the high latitude regions. A simplified explanation of the way in which this differential warming creates the earth's wind systems is given in Box 7.1.

In addition to the main global wind systems there are also local wind patterns, sea breezes and mountain–valley winds.

Sea breezes (Figure 7.9) are generated in coastal areas as a result of the different heat capacities of sea and land, which give rise to different rates of heating and cooling. The land has a lower heat capacity than the sea and heats up quickly during the day, but at night it cools more quickly than the

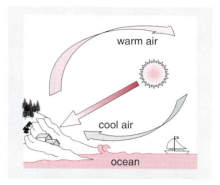

Figure 7.9 (above) Sea breezes. During the day, the wind blows towards the shore. At night, this reverses and the wind blows towards the sea

Figure 7.8 (below) Simplified representation of world wind circulation

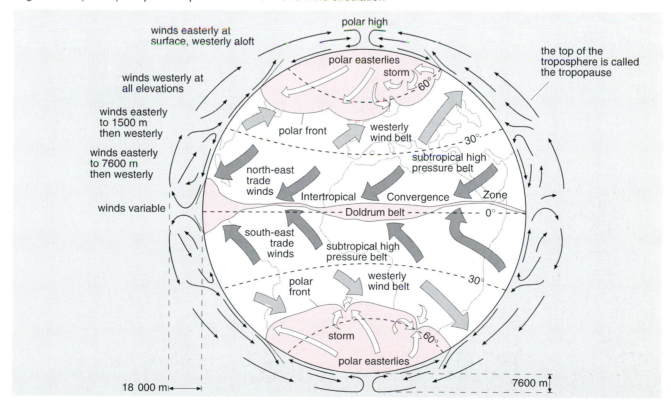

BOX 7.1: THE EARTH'S WIND SYSTEMS

Like all gases, air expands, or increases in volume, when heated; and contracts, or decreases in volume, when cooled. In the atmosphere, warm air is lighter and less dense than cold air and will rise to high altitudes when strongly heated by solar heating of the earth. Warmed air near the equator will flow upward and then outward towards the poles where the air near the surface is cooler. The regions of the earth near the poles then have more air 'pressing down' on them, and the cooler surface air tends to slide away from these areas and move towards the equator.

The circulation of the atmosphere

The movement or circulation of the atmosphere, which results from uneven heating, is profoundly influenced by the effects of the rotation of the earth (at a speed of approximately 1600 kilometres (1000 miles) per hour at the equator, decreasing to zero at the poles) and by the proportion of land to sea, the location of the continents, and such features as mountain ranges. In addition, as is to be expected, the periodic variations in the distribution of solar heat with the seasons of the year give rise to variations in the circulation.

The actual wind pattern that results is shown in Figure 7.8. Both north and south of the equator the circulation breaks into three distinct zones, called 'cells'. The first is the tropical cell, which extends from the equator to about 30° north and south latitude. The air over the equatorial region is heated by the sun, rises to the top of the **troposphere** (the **tropopause**), and starts moving towards the poles. The troposphere is the lower part of the atmosphere. The tropopause is the top of the troposphere and lies in between the troposphere and the stratosphere. Eighty per cent of the atmosphere's gas and all weather occurs in the troposphere. At the surface the equatorial region is called the 'doldrums'. The air is hot and sultry, and any winds quickly sink to stagnation, but light breezes may develop from any direction. The sky is overcast and showers and thunderstorms are frequent.

The position and width of the doldrum belt varies with the season. During February and March, the doldrum belt hugs the equator and is very narrow. By July and August, the doldrum belt may have moved farther north, and may become quite wide, covering several degrees of latitude even at its narrowest point.

At the northern and southern fringe of the tropical cells, at about 30° north and south latitude, there is a subtropical high pressure belt of subsiding or sinking air that descends to the surface creating a zone of dry, warm air called the 'horse latitudes'. Winds are light and variable, and may be stagnant for several days. Almost all of the earth's deserts are located in these regions. The name 'horse latitude' dates back to when the western hemisphere was being colonised. The crews of sailing ships, becalmed for long periods in the light and variable winds, were forced to throw horses overboard to preserve their drinking water supply.

Sinking air over the horse latitudes spreads out in both southerly and northerly directions. In the northern hemisphere, the southerly moving winds become deflected to the west and become the persistent north-east trade winds. Their counterparts in the southern hemisphere are the northerly moving south-east trade winds. (Winds are identified by the direction *from* which the wind is coming.) The trade winds are the most constant of winds: they often blow for days or even weeks with only slight variation in direction and strength.

Between 30° and 60° north latitude, the northerly winds from the horse latitudes become the westerly wind belt, and between 30° and 60° south latitude, the southerly winds become another westerly wind belt. Only in the southern hemisphere do these westerly winds exhibit a persistence approaching that of the trade winds. Their course in the northern hemisphere is interrupted by the greater land areas and mountain ranges of this area compared with the large expanse of ocean in the southern hemisphere.

The polar cells extend from about 60° latitude to each pole. Each polar cell is the result of the extreme coldness in these regions, particularly during the long winter night when there is no solar heating. These regions of cold, dense air produce surface winds called the polar easterlies, which spread toward the equator from the fringe of the polar cell, the polar front. These easterly winds are literally pushed out of the polar region by the high pressure near the poles as high altitude westerly winds cool and subside over the poles. It is the warmth brought by these high altitude winds that keeps the polar region from becoming colder each year.

The most violent and varied weather takes place in the temperate, or mid-latitude, mixing cell between 30° and 60° latitude, particularly in the northern hemisphere. Over this region tongues of warm tropical air and cold polar air meet, producing a climate over land areas most favourable to agriculture. Since human progress as we know it depended on the successful development of agriculture where only a small percentage of the population could provide food for all, it is no accident that the most advanced civilisations have flourished beneath the mid-latitude mixing cells.

(Source: Kovarik *et al.*, 1979)

sea. During the day, the sea is therefore cooler than the land and this causes the cooler air to flow *shorewards* to replace the rising warm air on the land. During the night the direction of air flow is reversed.

Mountain–valley winds are created when cool mountain air warms up in the morning and, as it becomes lighter, begins to rise: cool air from the valley below then moves up the slope to replace it. During the night the flow reverses, with cool mountain air sinking into the valley (Figure 7.10).

ENERGY AND POWER IN THE WIND

As we saw in Chapter 1, **power** is defined as the rate at which energy is used or converted and it can therefore be expressed as energy per unit of time, for example as joules per second (J s^{-1}). The unit of power is the watt (W) and one watt equals one joule per second, i.e.

1 W = 1 J s^{-1}

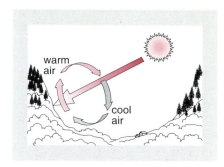

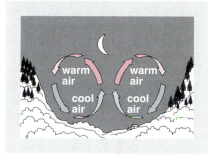

Figure 7.10 Mountain–valley winds

The energy contained in the wind is its kinetic energy and the kinetic energy of any particular mass of moving air is equal to half the mass, m, of the air times the square of its velocity, V:

kinetic energy = half mass × velocity squared   (1)

$$= {}^{1}/_{2}\, mV^2$$

where m is in kilograms and V is in metres per second.

We can calculate the kinetic energy in the wind if, first, we imagine air passing through a circular ring (enclosing a circular area A, say 100 m^2) at a velocity V (say 10 m s^{-1}) (see Figure 7.11). As the air is moving at a velocity of 10 m s^{-1}, a cylinder of air with a length of 10 m will pass through the ring each second. Therefore, a volume of air equal to $100 \times 10 = 1000$ cubic metres (m^3) will pass through the ring each second. By multiplying this volume by the density of air (r) (1.2256 kg m^{-3} at sea level), we obtain the mass of the air moving through the ring each second. In other words:

mass (m) of air per second = air density × volume of air passing each second

= air density × area × length of cylinder of air passing each second

= air density × area × velocity

i.e. $m = \rho A V$

Figure 7.11 Cylindrical volume of air passing at velocity **V** (10 m s^1) through a ring enclosing an area, A, each second

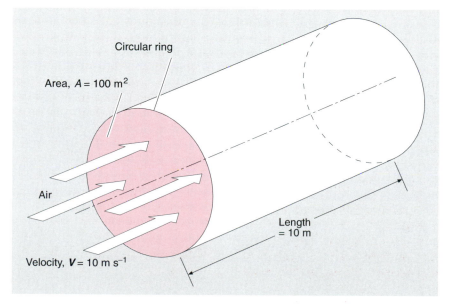

Example 7.1
Air is passing through a circular ring enclosing a circular area of 150 m^2, at a speed of 12 m s^{-1}. What is the volume of the air passing through the ring per second? If the density of air is approximately 1.20 kg m^{-3}, what is the mass of this volume of air?

Solution
Volume of air moving through the ring each second = 150 × 12

$= 1800 \text{ m}^3 \text{ s}^{-1}$

Mass of air moving through the ring each second = volume × density

$= 1800 \times 1.20$

$= 2160 \text{ kg s}^{-1}$

Example 7.2
How much power is contained in a wind stream travelling at 13 m s^{-1} and through an area of 150 m^2?

Solution
Power contained in the wind

$= \frac{1}{2} \rho A V^3$

$= \frac{1}{2} \times 1.20 \times 150 \times 13^3$

$= 197\,730 \text{ W}$

$\approx 198 \text{ kW}$

Substituting for m in (1) above:

kinetic energy per second =

$\frac{1}{2} \rho A V^3$ (joules per second)

where ρ is in kilograms per cubic metre, A is in square metres and V is in metres per second.

However, energy per unit of time is equal to power, so this is also the expression for the power in the wind:

power in the wind, P (watts) = kinetic energy in the wind per second (joules per second)

i.e. $P = \frac{1}{2} \rho A V^3$

The main relationships that are apparent from the above calculations are that *the power in the wind is proportional to:*

(a) the area through which the wind is passing;

(b) the cube of the wind velocity.

Note that the power contained in the wind is *not* the amount of power that can be extracted by a wind turbine. This is because losses are incurred in the energy conversion process (see Section 7.5 on aerodynamics).

7.4 WIND TURBINES

HISTORY OF WIND ENERGY

Wind energy was one of the first non-animal sources of energy to be exploited by early civilisations. It is thought that wind was first used to propel sailing boats, but the static exploitation of wind energy by means of windmills is thought to have been going on for about 4000 years.

Windmills were traditionally used for milling grain, grinding spices, grinding dyes and paintstuffs, papermaking and sawing wood. Wind pumps were used for pumping water, although they were also often referred to as windmills, particularly in East Anglia.

If you imagine an undershot water wheel (see Chapter 5), or a paddle wheel from a Mississippi paddle steamer, turned on its side so that its axis is vertical, you will have an idea of what the first windmills are believed to have looked like. Figure 7.12 shows an example. Looking at one of these windmills from above, it is apparent that, at any time, half the sails of the windmill will be travelling away from the wind and the other half will be travelling towards the wind.

In the case of the water-wheel, only part of the wheel is submerged. This means that for the part of its cycle in which it is moving 'forwards' with the water flow, it is in the water. For the part of its cycle in which it is moving 'backwards', it is out of the water, and since air is almost 800 times less dense than water, the resistance to the backward-moving water-wheel is insignificant. However, if the wheel were completely submerged, there would be no difference in resistance on the 'forward' and 'backward' sides, so the forces would be in balance and the wheel would not rotate.

The same thing would happen to a 'paddle wheel'-type vertical axis windmill, if various means were not employed to reduce the resistance to the 'paddle wheel' on the 'backward' part of its cycle. Some examples of the methods used are shown in Figure 7.13 and include the following.

• **Screened windmills**. These employ screens or walls around the windmill as shown in Figures 7.12 and 7.13, which are positioned to screen the windmill sails from the wind during the backward part of their cycle.

• **'Clapper' windmills**. These are so called because the moveable sails 'clap' against stops as the rotor turns with the wind (forwards), maximising their air resistance, but align with the wind (like a weather-vane), on the part of their cycle for which they are moving into the wind (backwards), so reducing their air resistance (Figure 7.13).

• **Differential resistance windmills**. In these windmills, the blades are shaped to offer greater resistance to the wind on one surface compared with the other (Figures 7.13a and b). This results in a difference in wind resistance on either side of the windmill axis, so allowing the windmill to turn. An example of this type of wind-driven device is the cup anemometer, an instrument used for measuring wind speed.

The more familiar traditional windmills are thought to have appeared in Europe in the twelfth century. The first recorded reference to such a windmill in England dates from 1185 AD and mentions a windmill in the village of Weedley in Yorkshire (Reynolds, 1970). These machines consisted of radial arms supporting sails that rotated about a horizontal axis, in a plane that faced into the direction from which the wind was blowing. Unlike the blades or sails of the traditional *vertical* axis windmills, which moved essentially in the same direction as the wind when they were on the 'working' part of their cycle, the sails or blades of these *horizontal* axis windmills were set at an oblique angle to the wind and moved in a direction perpendicular to the wind direction.

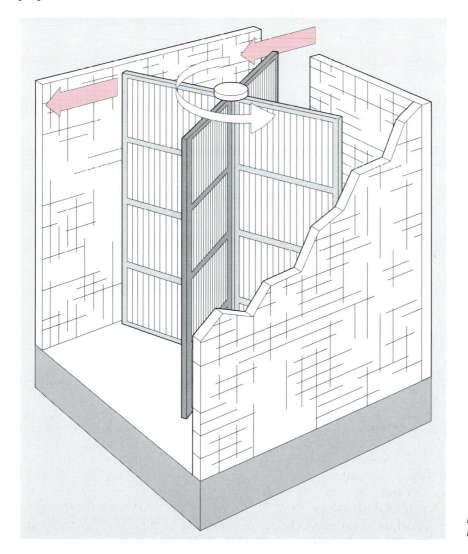

Figure 7.12 Artist's impression of a Persian windmill

Figure 7.14 Traditional north European tower windmill

In the Mediterranean regions of Europe, the traditional windmills took the form of triangular canvas sails attached to radial arms. In northern Europe, these windmills were characterised by long rectangular sails (usually four in number), consisting of either canvas sheets on lattice frameworks, so-called 'common sails', or 'shutter-type sails', which resembled venetian blinds. The latter were closed when the windmill started to operate, progressively opened to regulate the speed of the mill in different wind strengths and opened fully when the windmill was 'parked'.

In northern Europe there were two main forms of windmill in use. One was the less common 'post mill', in which the whole body of the windmill was moved about a large upright post when the wind direction changed; the other was the much more common 'tower mill' (Figure 7.14), in which the rotor and cap were supported by a relatively tall tower, usually of masonry. In the tower mill, only the cap (and rotor) were rotated in response to changes in wind direction. The sails turned fairly slowly to provide mechanical power.

At their zenith, before the Industrial Revolution, it is estimated that there were some 10 000 of these windmills in Great Britain (Golding, 1955) and they formed a familiar feature of the countryside.

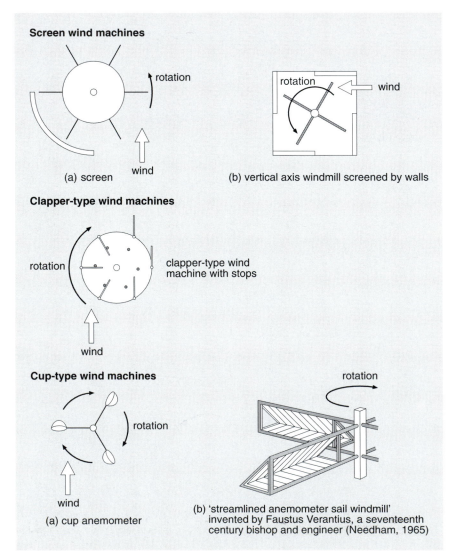

Figure 7.13 Some examples of traditional vertical axis windmills

Figure 7.15 Some of the machines that have been proposed for wind energy conversion
(Source: based on Eldridge, 1975. For further information on these machines see Eldridge, 1975 and Golding, 1955)

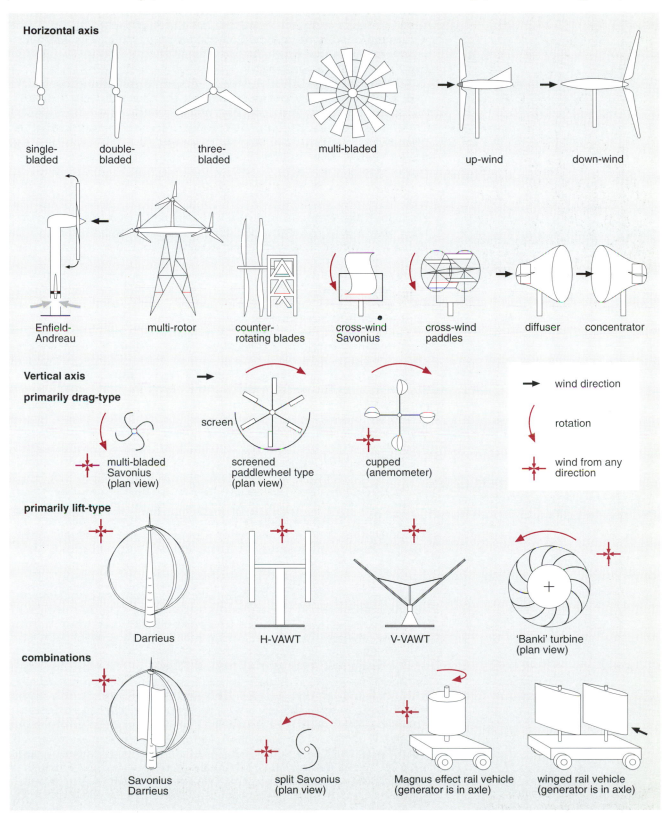

Horizontal axis

single-bladed   double-bladed   three-bladed   multi-bladed   up-wind   down-wind

Enfield-Andreau   multi-rotor   counter-rotating blades   cross-wind Savonius   cross-wind paddles   diffuser   concentrator

Vertical axis

primarily drag-type

screen

multi-bladed Savonius (plan view)   screened paddlewheel type (plan view)   cupped (anemometer)

→ wind direction

↷ rotation

✛ wind from any direction

primarily lift-type

Darrieus   H-VAWT   V-VAWT   'Banki' turbine (plan view)

combinations

Savonius Darrieus   split Savonius (plan view)   Magnus effect rail vehicle (generator is in axle)   winged rail vehicle (generator is in axle)

WIND TURBINES

The variety of machines that has been devised or proposed to harness wind energy is considerable and includes many unusual devices. Figure 7.15 shows various types of machine that have been proposed over the years.

As mentioned in the Introduction, modern windmills are usually referred to as wind turbines or wind energy conversion systems to distinguish them from their traditional forebears.

Apart from a few innovative designs, modern wind turbines come in two basic configurations: horizontal axis turbines and vertical axis turbines.

The majority of modern wind turbines are electricity generating devices. They range from small turbines that produce a few tens or hundreds of watts of power to relatively large turbines that produce 1 MW or more. Larger, multi-megawatt wind turbines have also been built, but these have almost all been research prototypes.

HORIZONTAL AXIS WIND TURBINES

Horizontal axis wind turbines (HAWTs) generally have either two or three blades or else a large number of blades. Wind turbines with large numbers of blades have what appears to be virtually a solid disc covered by solid blades and are described as **high-solidity** devices. These include the multi-blade wind turbines (Figure 7.16) used for water pumping on farms.

In contrast, the swept area of wind turbines with few blades is largely void and only a very small fraction appears to be 'solid'. These are referred to as **low-solidity** devices (see Box 7.2).

Modern low-solidity HAWTs evolved from traditional windmills and are by far the most common wind turbines manufactured today. They have a clean, streamlined appearance, due to wind turbine designers' improved understanding of aerodynamics, derived largely from developments in aircraft wing and propeller design. Their rotors generally have two or three wing-like blades (Figures 7.17 and 7.18). They are almost universally employed to generate electricity.

These turbines are commercially manufactured in power ratings of up to around 1 MW, and are produced principally in Denmark, the USA, the UK, the Netherlands, Germany, Italy, Spain, Belgium, Japan, Austria and in China. There are estimated to be in excess of 20 000 medium-scale HAWTs and considerably more small-scale HAWTs installed around the world.

Single-bladed HAWTs are also produced, mainly in Germany and Italy. Whilst these turbines may have an unusual appearance, they have characteristics that their proponents believe could eventually lead to cheaper wind turbines and more lightly stressed rotors (Figure 7.19).

VERTICAL AXIS WIND TURBINES

Vertical axis wind turbines (VAWTs) have an axis of rotation that is vertical, and so, unlike their horizontal counterparts, they can harness winds from any direction without the need to reposition the rotor when the wind direction changes. A description of how VAWTs operate is given in Section 7.5.

The modern VAWT evolved from the ideas of the French engineer, Georges Darrieus, and his name is used to describe one of the vertical-axis turbines that he invented in 1925. This device, which resembles a large egg beater, has curved blades (each with a symmetrical aerofoil cross-section) attached at one end to the top of a vertical shaft and attached at the other end to the bottom of the same shaft. Figure 7.20 shows an example of this type of wind turbine. The Darrieus VAWT is the most advanced of modern VAWTs. Several hundred have been manufactured in the USA and installed in wind farms in California. A small number have also been produced in Canada. Research on the design has been carried out elsewhere, particularly in Germany, France and Spain. More recently, Flowind Corporation have developed the EHD (extended height-to-diameter) series Darrieus rotor, to upgrade their installed base of 500 Darrieus turbines in Californian wind farms. Each turbine's existing base unit is retained but the rotor height has been increased to achieve an increased swept area.

The blades of a Darrieus VAWT take the form of a 'troposkien' (the curved shape taken by a spinning skipping rope). This shape is a structurally efficient one, well suited to coping with the relatively high centrifugal

Figure 7.16 Multi-bladed wind pump

Figure 7.18 Three-bladed HAWT (Howden 330 kW turbine)

Figure 7.17 Two-bladed HAWT (WEG MS400 turbine)

Figure 7.19 Single-bladed HAWT (MBB 600 kW turbine)

forces acting on VAWT blades. However, the shape causes difficulties in the manufacture, transportation and installation of the curved blades. In order to overcome these, a number of straight-bladed VAWTs have been proposed: these include the 'H'-type vertical axis wind turbine (H-VAWT) and the 'V'-type vertical axis wind turbine (V-VAWT).

The H-VAWT (Figure 7.21) consists of a tower housing a vertical shaft, capped by a hub to which is attached two horizontal cross arms that support, at their ends, straight, upright, aerofoil blades. In the UK, this type of wind turbine was developed by VAWT Ltd, which built 125 kW and 500 kW prototypes at Carmarthen Bay and a 100 kW turbine on the Isles of Scilly.

The V-VAWT consists of straight aerofoil blades attached at one end to a hub on a vertical shaft and inclined in the form of a letter 'V'. Its main features include short tower, ground-mounted generator and ground-level blade installation. The V-VAWT is at an early stage of development and is being researched at the Open University and at Queen Mary and Westfield College, London. An experimental prototype has been tested at the Open University (see Figure 7.22).

At the present time, VAWTs are not economically competitive with HAWTs.

Figure 7.20 (Below) Seventeen metre diameter, Darrieus-type VAWT at Sandia National Laboratories, New Mexico

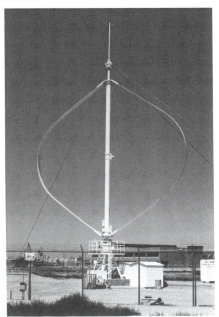

Figure 7.21 'H'-type VAWT on the Isles of Scilly

Figure 7.22 'V'-type VAWT prototype at the Open University test site, Milton Keynes

BOX 7.2: EFFECT OF THE NUMBER OF BLADES

The speed of rotation of a wind turbine is usually given in either revolutions per minute (rpm) or radians per second (rad s^{-1}). The **rotation speed** in revolutions per minute is usually symbolised by N and the **angular velocity** in radians per second is usually symbolised by Ω.

$$1 \text{ rpm} = \frac{2\pi}{60} \text{ rad s}^{-1}$$
$$\approx 0.10472 \text{ rad s}^{-1}$$

Another measure of a wind turbine's speed is its **tip speed**, U, which is the tangential velocity of the rotor at the tip of the blades, measured in metres per second. It is the product of the angular velocity, Ω, of the rotor and the **tip radius**, R (in metres). Alternatively, it can be defined as:

$$U = \frac{2\pi RN}{60}$$

By dividing the tip speed, U, by the undisturbed wind velocity, V_0, upstream of the rotor, we obtain a very useful non-dimensional ratio known as the **tip speed ratio**, which is usually symbolised by λ. This ratio provides us with a useful measure with which to compare wind turbines of different characteristics.

A wind turbine of a particular design can operate over a range of tip speed ratios, but will operate with its best efficiency at a particular tip speed ratio, i.e. when the velocity of its blade tips is a particular multiple of the wind velocity.

The optimum tip speed ratio for a given wind turbine rotor will depend upon both the width of the blades and their number. As we have seen, the term 'solidity' describes the fraction of the swept area that is solid. Wind turbines with large numbers of blades have highly-solid swept areas and are referred to as high-solidity wind turbines; wind turbines with small numbers of narrow blades are referred to as low-solidity wind turbines. Multi-blade wind pumps have high-solidity rotors and modern electricity-generating wind turbines (with one, two or three blades) have low-solidity rotors.

In order to extract energy as efficiently as possible, the blades have to interact with as much as possible of the wind passing through the rotor's swept area. The blades of a high-solidity, multi-blade wind turbine interact with all the wind at very low tip speed ratios, whereas the blades of a low-solidity turbine have to travel much faster to 'virtually fill up' the swept area, in order to interact with all the wind passing through. If the tip speed ratio is too low, some of the wind travels through the rotor swept area without interacting with the blades; whereas if the tip speed ratio is too high, the turbine offers too much resistance to the wind, so that some of the wind goes around it. A two-bladed wind turbine rotor with blades of the same width as those of a three-bladed rotor will have an optimum tip speed ratio one-third higher than that of the three-bladed rotor. A one-bladed rotor with a blade width the same as that of a two-bladed rotor will have twice the optimum tip speed ratio of the two-bladed rotor. Optimum tip speed ratios for modern low-solidity wind turbines range between about 6 and 20.

In theory, the more blades a wind turbine rotor has, the more efficient it is. However, large numbers of blades can interfere with each other, so high-solidity wind turbines tend to be less efficient overall than low-solidity turbines. Of low-solidity machines, three-bladed rotors tend to be the most energy efficient; two-bladed rotors are slightly less efficient and one-bladed rotors slightly less efficient still.

The mechanical power that a wind turbine extracts from the wind is the product of its angular velocity and the torque imparted by the wind. **Torque** is the moment about the centre of rotation due to the driving force imparted by the wind to the rotor blades. Torque is usually measured in newton-metres (Nm). For a given amount of power, the lower the angular velocity the higher the torque; and conversely, the higher the angular velocity the lower the torque.

The pumps that are used with water pumping wind turbines require a high starting torque to function. Multi-bladed turbines are therefore generally used for water pumping because of their low tip speed ratios and resulting high torque characteristics.

Since conventional electrical generators run at speeds many times greater than most wind turbine rotors, they generally require some form of gearing when used with wind turbines. Low-solidity wind turbines are better suited to electricity generation than high-solidity turbines, because they operate at high tip speed ratios and therefore do not require as high a gear ratio to match the speed of the rotor to that of the generator.

Figure 7.23 (a) and (b) An object in an air stream is subjected to a force, F, from the air stream made of two component forces: the drag force, D, acting in line with the direction of air flow; and the lift force, L, acting at 90° to the direction of air flow

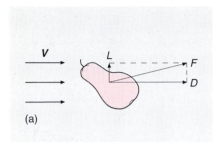

(a)

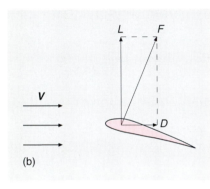

(b)

Figure 7.24 Some examples of streamlined shapes

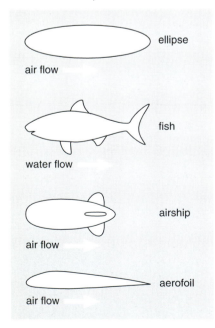

ellipse

air flow

fish

water flow

airship

air flow

aerofoil

air flow

7.5 AERODYNAMICS OF WIND TURBINES

AERODYNAMIC FORCES

To understand how modern wind turbines work, two terms from the field of aerodynamics will be introduced. These are 'drag' and 'lift'.

An object in an air stream experiences a force that is imparted from the air stream to that object (see Figure 7.23). We can consider this force to be equivalent to two component forces, acting in perpendicular directions, known as the *drag* force and the *lift* force. The magnitude of the drag and lift forces depends on the shape of the object, its orientation to the direction of the air stream, and the velocity of the air stream.

Drag forces are those forces experienced by an object in an air stream that are in line with the direction of the air stream. A flat plate in an air stream, for example, experiences maximum drag forces when the direction of the air flow is perpendicular (that is, at right angles) to the flat side of the plate; when the direction of the air stream is in line with the flat side of the plate, the drag forces are at a minimum.

A number of devices have been designed that make use of drag forces in their function. One example is the parachute, which relies on drag forces to slow down the rate of descent of a parachutist.

Objects designed to minimise the drag forces experienced in an air stream are described as *streamlined*, because the lines of flow around them follow smooth, stream-like lines. Examples of streamlined shapes are teardrops, the shapes of fish such as sharks and trout, and aeroplane wing sections (see Figure 7.24).

Lift forces are those forces experienced by an object in an air stream that are perpendicular to the direction of the air stream. They are termed 'lift' forces because they are the forces that enable aeroplanes to 'lift' off the ground and fly. Lift forces acting on a flat plate are smallest when the direction of the air stream is at a zero angle to the flat surface of the plate. At small angles relative to the direction of the air stream (that is, when the so-called *angle of attack* is small), a low pressure region is created on the 'downstream' or 'leeward' side of the plate as a result of an increase in the air velocity on that side. In this situation, there is a direct relationship between air speed and pressure: the faster the air flow, the lower the pressure. This phenomenon is known as the **Bernoulli effect** after Daniel Bernoulli, the Swiss mathematician who first explained it. The lift force thus acts as a 'suction' or 'pulling' force on the object, in a direction at right angles to the air flow.

Lift forces are used to propel modern sailing yachts, and to support and propel helicopters. They are also the principal forces that cause a modern wind turbine to operate.

AEROFOILS

The angle which an object makes with the direction of an airflow, measured against a reference line in the object, is called the **angle of attack**, α. The reference line on an aerofoil section is usually referred to as the **chord line**. Arching or cambering a flat plate will cause it to induce higher lift forces for a given angle of attack, but the use of so-called **aerofoil sections** is even more effective. When employed as the profile of a wing, these sections accelerate the air flow over the upper surface. The high air speed thus induced results in a large reduction in pressure over the upper surface relative to the lower surface. This results in a 'suction' effect which 'lifts' the aerofoil-shaped wing. The strength of the lift forces induced by aerofoil sections is perhaps demonstrated most dramatically by their ability to support jumbo jets in the air.

There are two main types of aerofoil section: asymmetrical and symmetrical, as shown in Figure 7.25. Both of them have a markedly convex upper surface, a rounded end called the 'leading edge' (which faces the direction *from* which the air stream is coming), and a pointed or sharp end called the 'trailing edge'. It is the undersurface of the sections that distinguishes the two types. The asymmetrical aerofoils are optimised to produce most lift when the underside of the aerofoil is closest to the direction from which the air is flowing, whereas the symmetrical aerofoils are able to induce lift equally well (although in opposite directions) when the air flow is coming from either side of them. Aerobatic display aeroplanes have wings with symmetrical aerofoil sections, which allow them to fly equally well when upside down. When air flow is directed towards the underside of the aerofoil, the angle of attack is usually referred to as positive.

The lift and drag characteristics of many different aerofoil shapes, for a range of angles of attack, have been determined by measurements taken in wind tunnel tests, and catalogued (e.g. Abbott and Von Doenhoff, 1958). The lift and drag characteristics measured at each angle of attack can be described using non-dimensional **lift** and **drag coefficients** (C_L and C_D), or as **lift to drag ratios** (C_L/C_D). These are defined in Box 7.3. Figure 7.28 shows typical lift and drag coefficients, and lift to drag ratios, for one aerofoil section. The knowledge of these coefficients is essential when selecting appropriate aerofoil sections for wind turbine blade design. Lift and drag forces are both proportional to the energy in the wind.

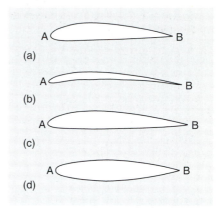

Figure 7.25 Types of aerofoil section. (a), (b) and (c) are various forms of asymmetrical aerofoil section and (d) is a symmetrical aerofoil section

Figure 7.26 Streamlined flow around an aerofoil section

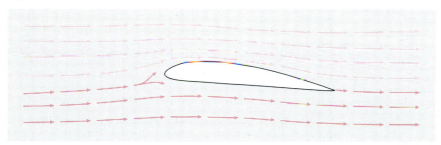

Figure 7.27 Zones of low and high pressure around an aerofoil section in an air stream

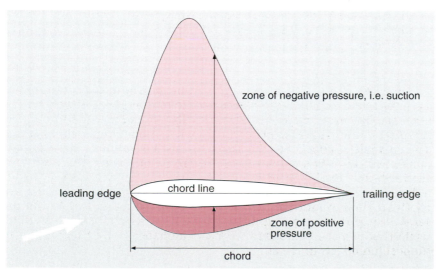

285

BOX 7.3: AEROFOIL SECTIONS AND LIFT AND DRAG COEFFICIENTS

The 'length' (from the tip of its leading edge to the tip of its trailing edge) of an aerofoil section is known as the **chord** (see Figure 7.27). The chord is also the width of the blade at a given position along the blade.

DRAG COEFFICIENT (C_D)

The drag coefficient of an aerofoil is given by the following expression:

$$C_D = \frac{D}{0.5 \rho V^2 A_b}$$

where:

D is the drag force in newtons

ρ is the air density in kilograms per cubic metre

V is the velocity of the air approaching the aerofoil in metres per second

A_b is the blade area (chord × length) in square metres.

LIFT COEFFICIENT (C_L)

The lift coefficient of an aerofoil is given by the following expression:

$$C_L = \frac{L}{0.5 \rho V^2 A_b}$$

where L is the lift force in newtons.

The lift and drag coefficients of an aerofoil can be measured in a wind tunnel at different angles of attack and wind velocities. The results of such measurements can be presented either in tabular or graphical form as in Figure 7.28.

Each aerofoil has an angle of attack at which the lift to drag ratio (C_L/C_D) is at a maximum and this angle of attack results in the highest efficiency of the blades of a HAWT.

Another important characteristic relationship of an aerofoil is its **angle of stall**. This is the angle of attack at which the aerofoil exhibits **stall** behaviour. Stall occurs when the flow suddenly leaves the suction side of the aerofoil (when the angle of attack becomes too large), resulting in dramatic loss in lift and an increase in drag (Figures 7.28 and 7.29). When this happens during an aeroplane flight, it can be extremely dangerous unless the pilot can make the plane recover. Some wind turbine blades are designed to take advantage of this phenomenon as a means of limiting the power extracted by the rotor in high winds.

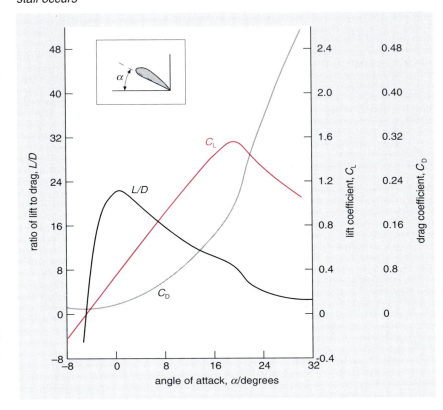

Figure 7.28 Lift coefficient, C_L, drag coefficient, C_D and lift to drag ratio (L/D) versus angle of attack, a, for a Clark Y aerofoil section. The region just to the right of the peak in the C_L curve corresponds to the angle of attack at which stall occurs

Figure 7.29 (Right) Aerofoil section in stall

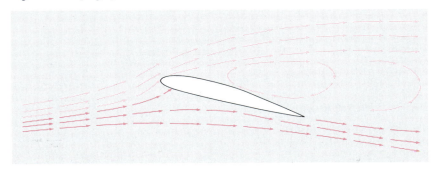

RELATIVE WIND VELOCITY

When a wind turbine is stationary, the direction of the wind as 'seen' from a wind turbine blade is the same as the undisturbed wind direction. However, once the blade is moving it has velocity, and this can be graphically represented as a two-dimensional vector. A two-dimensional vector is a quantity that has both magnitude and direction. A velocity vector can be represented graphically in the form of an arrow, the length of which is proportional to speed, and the position of which indicates the direction.

The velocity of the wind as seen from a point on a moving blade is known as the **relative wind velocity** (usually symbolised by W). This is a vector which is the resultant of the undisturbed wind velocity vector, V_0, and the tangential velocity vector of that point on the blade, U. (Note, the tangential velocity, measured in metres per second (m s^{-1}), is distinct from the angular velocity which is measured in radians per second.)

Figure 7.30(a) shows a simple example of a motor boat, first of all moored when there is no wind blowing. The boat has a flag flying. Now, let us

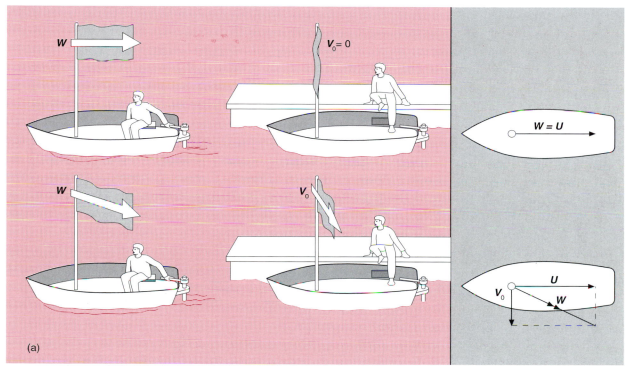

(a)

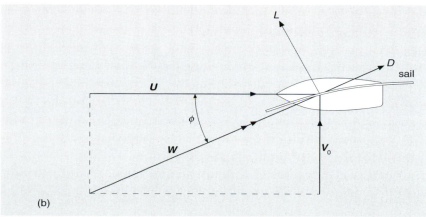

(b)

Figure 7.30 (a) Velocity vector diagram for a motor boat: (top) when there is no wind; (bottom) when wind of velocity V_0 is blowing in direction shown. (b) Velocity and force vector diagram for a sailing boat

287

assume that there is a wind blowing, with velocity V_0, from one side of the boat. When the boat is moored and motionless, the flag flies in line with the direction of undisturbed wind, V_0. However, when the boat is moving at a velocity U, the direction of the flag alters to align with the perceived wind direction. The latter is known as the **apparent wind** W, (sailing parlance for the **relative wind velocity**) and the angle which it makes with the direction of the boat is a function of the ratio of the undisturbed wind velocity, V_0, to the velocity of the boat, U. The same effect can be noticed if a flag is attached to a moving bicycle when the wind is blowing.

Now, let us consider the example of a sailing boat travelling at a velocity, U, of 10 m s^{-1} across (that is, perpendicular to) a wind stream with an undisturbed wind velocity, V_0, of 5 m s^{-1} (Figure 7.30(b)). The relative or apparent wind velocity, W, is the resultant of the velocity vectors of the boat and the undisturbed wind, U and V_0, respectively. The relative wind velocity is the actual wind, both in speed and direction, that is felt on board the boat and used by the sails to propel a sailing boat. When a boat is moving, the relative wind is always different from the undisturbed wind. The angle that the relative wind velocity vector makes with the boat's velocity vector is known as the **relative wind angle** (usually represented by ϕ), and given by the formula:

$$\tan \phi = \frac{V_0}{U}$$

In the above example:

$$\tan \phi = \frac{5}{10} = 0.5$$

Using the tangent function on a scientific calculator, we can calculate that $\phi = 26.5$.

From the relative wind angle, ϕ, we can determine the magnitude of the relative wind velocity, W, using the simple trigonometric relationship:

$$W = \frac{V_0}{\sin \phi} = \frac{5}{\sin 26.5} = \frac{5}{0.4462} \approx 11.2 \text{ m s}^{-1}$$

HOW DO WIND TURBINES WORK?

Horizontal and vertical axis wind turbines both make use of the aerodynamic forces generated by aerofoils in order to extract power from the wind, but each harnesses these forces in a different way.

In a fixed-pitch HAWT, assuming the rotor axis is in constant alignment with the (undisturbed) wind direction, for a given wind speed and constant rotation speed, the angle of attack at a given position on the rotor blade *stays constant throughout its rotation cycle*.

In a VAWT, under the same conditions, the angle of attack at a given position on the rotor blade is *constantly varying throughout its rotation cycle*.

During the normal operation of a *horizontal* axis rotor, the direction from which the aerofoil 'sees' the wind is such that the angle of attack remains positive throughout.

In the case of a *vertical* axis rotor, however, the angle of attack changes from positive to negative and back again over each rotation cycle. This means that the 'suction' side reverses during each cycle, so a symmetrical aerofoil has to be employed to ensure that power can be produced irrespective of whether the angle of attack is positive or negative.

HORIZONTAL AXIS WIND TURBINES

Horizontal axis wind turbines operate with their rotation axes in line with the wind direction and are so-called *axial flow* devices. The rotation axis is maintained in line with wind direction by a *yawing* mechanism that constantly realigns the wind turbine rotor in response to wind direction.

BOX 7.4 HAWT ROTOR BLADES

WIND FORCES AND VELOCITIES

Figure 7.31 shows a section through a moving rotor blade of an HAWT. Also shown is a vector diagram of the forces and velocities at a position along the blade at an instant in time.

Because the blade is moving, the direction from which the blade 'sees' the relative wind velocity, W, is the resultant of the tangential velocity, u, of the blade at that position and the wind velocity, V_1, at the rotor.

The tangential velocity, u (in metres per second) at a point along the blade is the product of the angular velocity, Ω (in radians per second) of the rotor and the local radius, r (in metres), at that point, that is:

$$u = \Omega r$$

The wind velocity at the rotor, V_1, is the undisturbed wind velocity upstream of the rotor, V_0, reduced by a factor that takes account of the wind being slowed down as a result of power extraction. This factor is often referred to as the **axial interference factor**, and is represented by a.

Albert Betz showed in 1928 that the *maximum* fraction of the power in the wind that can theoretically be extracted is 16/27 (59.3%). This occurs when the undisturbed wind velocity is reduced by one-third, in other words, when the axial interference factor, a, is equal to $^1/_3$. The value of 59.3% is often referred to as the **Betz limit**.

The relative wind angle, ϕ, is the angle that the relative wind makes with the blade (at a particular point with local radius r along the blade)

and is measured from the plane of rotation. The angle of attack, α, at this point on the blade can be measured against the relative wind angle, ϕ. The **blade pitch angle** (usually represented by β) is then equal to the relative wind angle minus the angle of attack.

Because the rotor is constrained to rotate in a plane at right angles to the undisturbed wind, the driving force at a given point on the blade is that component of the aerofoil lift force that acts in the plane of rotation. This is given by the product of the lift force, L, and the sine of the relative wind angle, ϕ (that is, $L \sin \phi$). The component of the drag force in the rotor plane at this point is the product of the drag force, D, and the cosine of the relative wind angle, ϕ (that is, $D \cos \phi$).

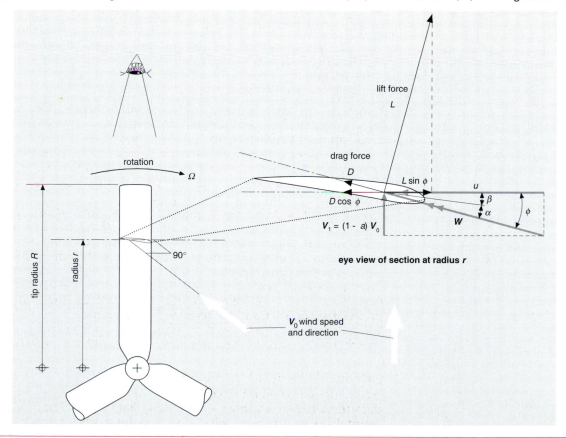

Figure 7.31 Vector diagram showing a section through a moving HAWT rotor blade. Notice that the drag force, D, at the point shown is acting in line with the direction of the relative wind, W, and the lift force, L, is acting at 90° to it

The torque, *q* (that is, the moment about the centre of rotation), in newton-metres (Nm) at this point on the blade is equal to the product of the net driving force in the plane of rotation (that is, the component of lift force in the plane of rotation minus the component of drag force in the rotor plane) and the local radius, *r*. The **total torque**, **Q**, acting on the rotor can be calculated by summing the torque at all points along the length of each blade and multiplying by the number of blades. The power from the rotor is the product of the total torque, **Q**, and the rotor's angular velocity, Ω.

The magnitude and direction of the relative wind angle, ϕ, varies along the length of the blade according to the local radius, *r*. This is because the local tangential speed, *u*, of a given blade element is equal to the rotor's angular velocity (Ω) times the local radius, *r*, of the blade element. As the tangential speed decreases towards the hub, the relative wind angle, ϕ, progressively increases. If a blade is designed to have a constant angle of attack along its length, it will have to have a built-in twist, the amount of which will vary progressively from tip to root. Figure 7.32 demonstrates the progressive twist of a HAWT rotor blade. Most manufacturers of HAWT blades produce twisted blades, although it is possible to build adequate HAWT rotor blades that are not twisted. These are cheaper, but less efficient.

Stall control

Let us assume that a wind turbine is rotating at a constant rotation speed, regardless of wind speed, and that the blade pitch angle is fixed. As the wind speed increases the tip speed ratio decreases. At the same time, the relative wind angle increases, causing an increase in the angle of attack.

It is possible to take advantage of this characteristic to control a turbine in high winds, if the rotor blades are designed so that above the rated wind speed they become less efficient because the angle of attack is approaching the stall angle. This results in a loss of lift, and thus torque, on the regions of the blade that are in stall.

This method of so-called 'stall-control' has been employed successfully on numerous fixed-pitch HAWT rotors. It is also employed on most VAWT rotors.

Figure 7.32 Three-dimensional view of an HAWT rotor blade design showing the changing angle of the relative wind angle, ϕ, along the blade span

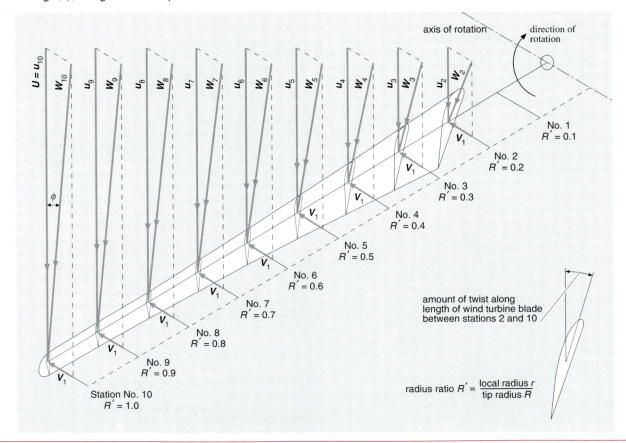

The performance of a horizontal axis wind turbine rotor is dependent on the number and shape of its blades and the choice of aerofoil section, together with the length of the blade chord, the relative wind angle and blade pitch angle at positions along the blade, and the amount of twist between the hub and tip.

Box 7.4 explains how the relative wind velocity, W, and relative wind angle, ϕ, vary along the blade, together with their influence on the optimum blade pitch angle.

VERTICAL AXIS WIND TURBINES

Modern VAWTs, unlike HAWTs, are 'cross-flow devices'. This means that the direction from which the undisturbed air flow comes is at right angles to the axis of rotation, that is, air flows across the axis. As the rotor blades turn, they sweep a three-dimensional surface, as distinct from the single circular plane swept by a HAWT's rotor blades.

In contrast to traditional vertical-axis windmills, the blades of modern vertical axis wind turbines extract most of the power from the wind as they pass across the front and rear (relative to the undisturbed wind direction) of the swept volume.

When the blade is moving at a velocity several times greater than the undisturbed wind velocity, the angle of attack from which it 'sees' the relative wind velocity, though varying, remains small enough to enable it to absorb aerodynamic forces, which impart a tangential driving force and torque to the rotor.

The vertical axis wind turbine will function with the wind blowing from any direction, but let us assume initially that it is blowing from one particular direction and also that the setting angle of the blade is such that its chord is in line with a tangent to the circular path of rotation (that is, it has 'zero set pitch'). Clearly, the angle of the blade to the direction of the undisturbed wind changes from zero to 360° over each cycle of rotation. It might appear that the angle of attack of the wind to the blade would vary by the same amount, and so it might seem impossible for a VAWT to operate at all. However, we have to take into account the fact that when the blade is *moving*, the relative wind angle 'seen' by the blade is the *resultant* of the wind velocity V_1 at the rotor and the blade velocity u. Provided that the blade is moving sufficiently fast, relative to the wind velocity (in practice, this means at a tip speed ratio of three or more), the angle of attack that the blade makes with the relative wind velocity W will only vary within a small range (see Figure 7.33).

Figure 7.33 The lift and drag forces acting on rotor blades can be resolved into two components: 'normal' (N) (that is, in line with the radius) and 'tangential' (T) (that is, perpendicular to the radius). The magnitude of both components varies as the angle of attack varies during the rotation cycle and, as a result, the torque output fluctuates as the turbine rotates.
(a) Blade forces and relative velocities for a VAWT, showing angles of attack at different positions;
(b) Detail: aerodynamic forces on a blade element of a VAWT rotor blade;
(c) Normal (radial) and tangential (chord-wise) components of force on a VAWT blade

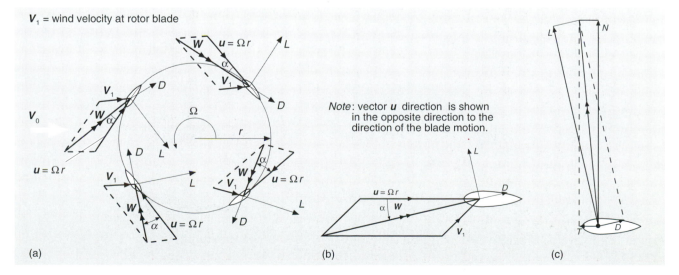

7.6 POWER AND ENERGY FROM WIND TURBINES

HOW MUCH POWER DOES A WIND TURBINE PRODUCE?

The power output of a wind turbine varies with wind speed and every turbine has a characteristic **wind speed–power curve**. An example of such a curve is shown in Figure 7.34. A power curve for the wind turbine at the Wood Green Animal Shelter was shown in Figure 7.3. The power curve will primarily determine how much energy can be produced by a particular turbine on a given site under given wind conditions.

HOW MUCH ENERGY WILL WIND TURBINES PRODUCE?

If the mean annual wind speed at a site is known or can be estimated, the following formula (EWEA, 1991; Anderson, 1992) can be used to make a *rough initial estimate* of the electricity production (in kilowatt-hours per year) from a number of wind turbines:

Annual electricity production = $KV_m^3 A_t T$

where:

$K = 2.5$ and is a factor based on typical turbine performance characteristics, an average turbine availability of 90%, losses of 5% from the wind shadow effect of machines sited in arrays, and an approximate relationship between mean wind speed and wind speed frequency distribution (see below)

V_m is the site annual mean wind speed in metres per second

A_t is the swept area of the turbine in square metres

T is the number of turbines.

This formula should be used with caution, however, because it is based on an average of the characteristics of wind turbines currently available and assumes an approximate relationship between annual mean wind speed and the frequency distribution of wind speeds that may not be accurate for an individual site. It does not allow for the different power curves of wind turbines that have been optimised either for low or high wind speed sites.

The energy that a wind turbine will produce depends on both its wind speed–power curve and the **wind speed frequency distribution** at the site. The latter is essentially a graph showing the number of hours for which the wind blows at different wind speeds, during a given period of time. Figure 7.35 shows a typical wind speed frequency distribution curve.

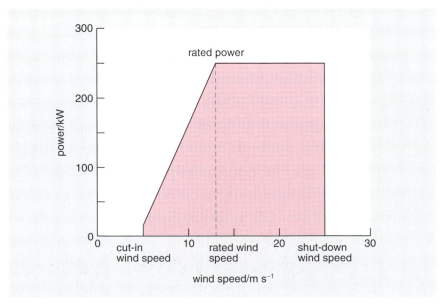

Figure 7.34 Typical wind turbine wind speed–power curve

For each wind speed within the operating range of the turbine (that is, between the cut-in wind speed and the shut-down wind speed), the energy produced at that wind speed can be obtained by multiplying the number of hours of its duration by the corresponding turbine power at this wind speed (given by the turbine's wind speed–power curve). These data can then be used to plot a **wind energy distribution curve** such as that shown in Figure 7.36. The total energy produced is then calculated by summing the energy produced at all the wind speeds within the operating range of the turbine.

The best way to determine the wind speed distribution at a site is to carry out wind speed measurements with equipment that records the number of hours for which the wind speed lies within each given speed band (e.g. 0–1 m sec^{-1}, 1–2 m sec^{-1}, 2–3 m sec^{-1}, etc.). The longer the period over which measurements are taken, the more accurate is the estimate of the wind speed distribution. Because of the V^3 **law** (the power in the wind is proportional to the cube of the wind velocity), a small error in estimating the wind speeds can produce a large error in the estimate of the energy yield.

Additional factors that affect the total energy generated include transmission losses and the **availability** of the turbine. Availability is an

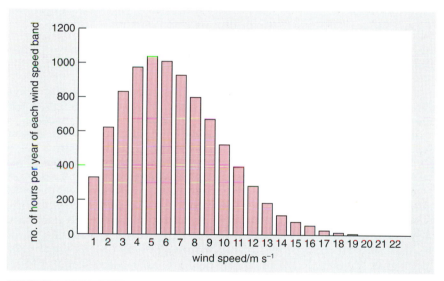

Figure 7.35 A typical wind speed frequency distribution curve

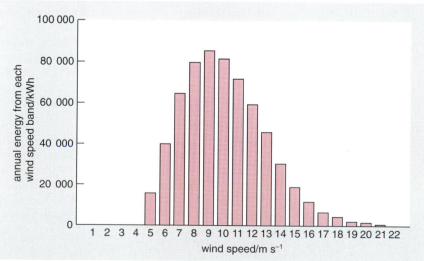

Figure 7.36 Wind energy distribution curve for the same site as in Figure 7.35, showing energy produced at this site by a wind turbine with the wind speed–power curve shown in Figure 7.34

indication of the reliability of the turbine installation and is the fraction or percentage of a given period of time for which a wind turbine is available to generate, when the wind is blowing within the turbine's operating range. Current commercial wind turbines typically have annual availabilities in excess of 90% and many have operated at over 95%.

ESTIMATING WIND SPEED CHARACTERISTICS OF A SITE

It is expensive to carry out detailed measurements at a site, but there are a number of techniques that can be employed to give an approximate estimate of the wind speed characteristics of a site. These techniques cannot at present give the more precise information that long-term site measurements are able to provide. However, they can give an indication of the potential of a wind energy site and indicate whether it might be worth taking detailed measurements. Estimation techniques currently used include the following:

USING WIND SPEED MEASUREMENTS FROM A NEARBY LOCATION

This involves making use of existing wind speed measurements from one or more locations nearby and deriving the data for the proposed site by interpolation or extrapolation, taking into account differences between the proposed site and the sites for which measurements are available.

MAKING USE OF WIND SPEED MAPS AND ATLASES

Maps are available that give estimates of the mean wind speeds over the UK. However, most of these maps were made using data from meteorological stations, which tend to be located in places that are not appropriate for wind energy.

More recently, a *European Wind Atlas* (Troen and Petersen, 1989) was produced by the Riso Laboratory in Denmark for the Commission of the European Communities. This extensive document (over 650 pages) includes maps of various areas within the European Union (EU) (for example Figure 7.37), which show the annual mean wind speed at 50 m above ground level for five different topographic conditions: sheltered terrain, open plain, sea coast, open sea, hills and ridges. The atlas includes a whole series of procedures for taking account of site characteristics to estimate the wind energy likely to be available. It works quite well on sites with gentle topography but is not so good for very hilly terrain. None the less, it is a very useful document.

Also useful are the onshore and offshore maps of the UK prepared by the former Central Electricity Generating Board (CEGB) (Bennett *et al.*, 1983). These give annual mean wind speeds at 60 m height for each 10 km Ordnance Survey grid square, based on wind speed measurements in the upper atmosphere.

A wind atlas of the UK has also been prepared by the Energy Technology Support Unit (ETSU). Using wind speed data from meteorological stations, a digital terrain model of the UK and a wind speed prediction computer model, ETSU has estimated an annual mean wind speed value for each 1km Ordnance Survey grid square in the UK (Burch and Ravenscroft, 1993).

WIND FLOW SIMULATION COMPUTER MODELS

A number of computer models have been developed that attempt to predict the effects of topography on wind speed. Data from the nearest wind measurement station, together with a description of its site, are required and local effects are taken into account to arrive at estimated wind data for the proposed wind turbine site. Used with care, such models can be useful for carrying out initial assessments to identify potential wind energy sites.

Figure 7.37 Wind energy resources over Europe (EU countries) (Source: Troen and Petersen, 1989)

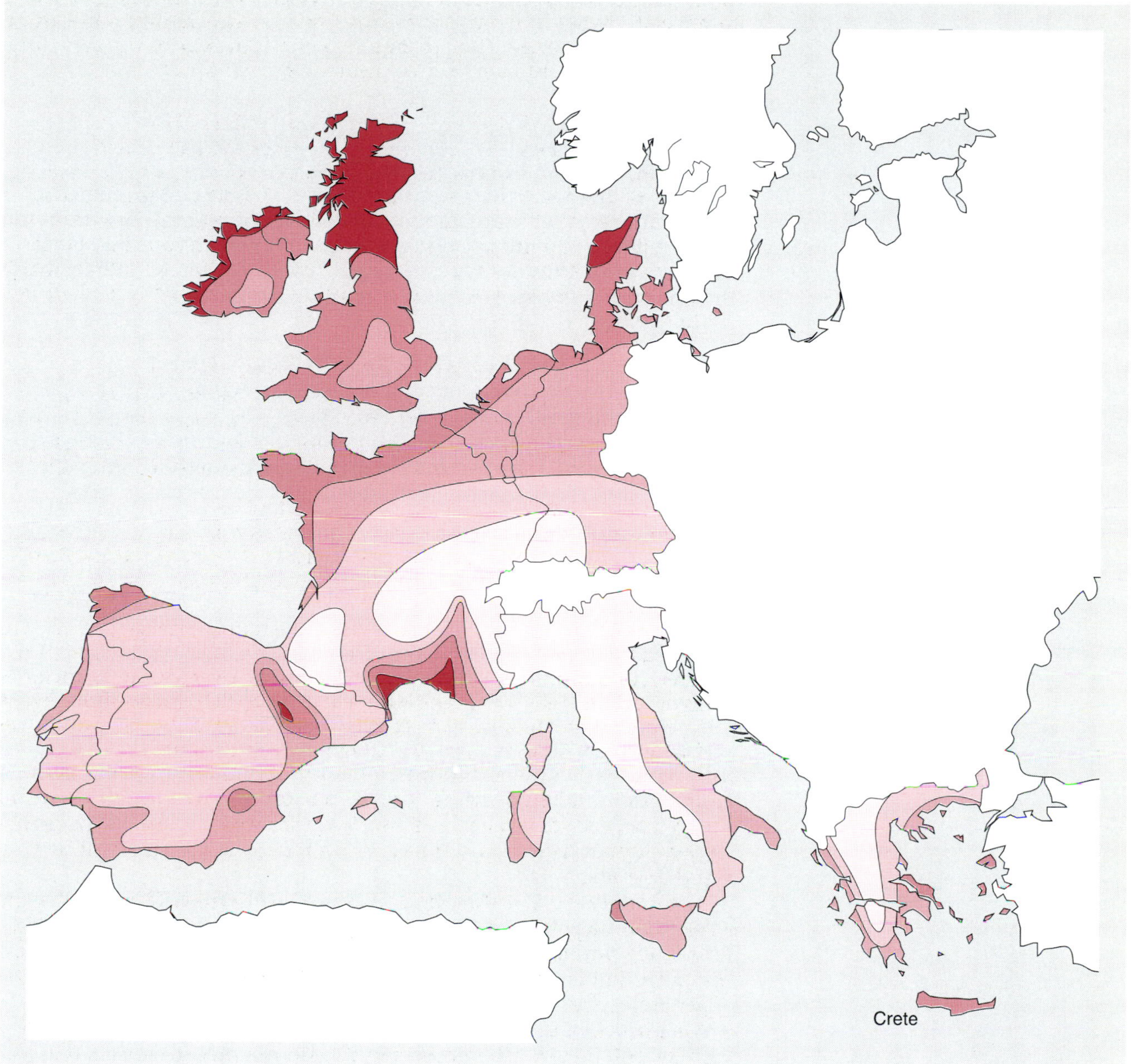

	Wind resources at 50 m above ground level for five different topographic conditions									
	Sheltered terrain		Open plain		At a sea coast		Open sea		Hills and ridges	
	m s^{-1}	W m^{-2}	m s^{-1}	W m^{-2}	m s^{-1}	W m^{-2}	m s^{-1}	W m^{-2}	m s^{-1}	W m^{-2}
	>6.0	>250	>7.5	>500	>8.5	>700	>9.0	>800	>11.5	>1800
	5.0–6.0	150–250	6.5–7.5	300–500	7.0–8.5	400–700	8.0–9.0	600–800	10.0–11.5	1200–1800
	4.5–5.0	100–150	5.5–6.5	200–300	6.0–7.0	250–400	7.0–8.0	400–600	8.5–10.0	700–1200
	3.5–4.5	50–100	4.5–5.5	100–200	5.0–6.0	150–250	5.5–7.0	200–400	7.0–8.5	400–700
	<3.5	<50	<4.5	<100	<5.0	<150	<5.5	<200	<7.0	<400

7.7 ENVIRONMENTAL IMPACT

Wind energy development has both positive and negative environmental impacts. The scale of its future implementation will rely on successfully maximising the positive impacts whilst keeping the negative impacts to the minimum.

ENVIRONMENTAL BENEFITS OF ELECTRICITY GENERATION BY WIND ENERGY

The generation of electricity by wind turbines does not involve the release of carbon dioxide, acid rain, smog or radioactive pollutants. The use of wind energy reduces dependency on conventional fossil and nuclear fuels. In addition, wind turbines do not require water supplies, unlike many conventional (and some renewable) energy sources.

ENVIRONMENTAL IMPACTS OF WIND TURBINES

Any development in the countryside will have an environmental impact of some kind, and wind energy is no exception.

Possible environmental impacts of wind turbines are noise, electromagnetic interference and visual impact, possibly including 'flicker' caused by sunlight interacting with rotating blades on sunny days.

WIND TURBINE NOISE

In general, wind turbines are not especially noisy compared with other machines of similar power rating (see Table 7.2). However, there have been incidents where wind turbine noise has been cited as a nuisance.

There are two main sources of wind turbine noise. One is that produced by mechanical or electrical equipment, such as the gearbox and generator, known as **mechanical noise**; the other is due to the interaction of the air flow with the blades, referred to as **aerodynamic noise**.

The mechanical noise is usually the main problem, but it can be fairly easily remedied by the use of special quieter gears, mounting equipment on resilient mounts, and by using acoustic enclosures.

AERODYNAMIC NOISE

The aerodynamic noise produced by wind turbines can perhaps best be described as a 'swishing' sound. It is affected by: the shape of the blades; the interaction of the air flow with the blades and the tower; the shape of the blade trailing edge; the tip shape; whether or not the blade is operating in stall conditions; and turbulent wind conditions, which can cause unsteady forces on the blades, causing them to radiate noise.

Aerodynamic noise will tend to increase with the speed of rotation. For this reason, some turbines are designed to be operated at lower rotation speeds when wind speeds are low. Noise nuisance is usually more of a problem in light winds than at higher wind speeds, when the background wind noise tends to mask wind turbine noise. Operating at a lower rotation speed will help to minimise any aerodynamic noise problem in low wind conditions.

Most commercial wind turbines undergo noise measurement tests according to either the recommended procedure developed by the International Energy Agency (Ljunggren and Gustafsson, 1988) or a procedure conforming to the Danish noise regulations. The measured noise level values from such tests provide information which enables the turbines to be sited at an adequate distance from habitations to avoid noise nuisance. This standard procedure also allows manufacturers to identify

Table 7.2 Noise of different activities compared with wind turbines

Source/activity	Noise level in dB(A)*
Threshold of pain	140
Jet aircraft at 250 m	105
Pneumatic drill at 7 m	95
Truck at 48 km h⁻¹ (30 mph) at 100 m	65
Busy general office	60
Car at 64 km h⁻¹ (40 mph)	55
Wind farm at 350 m	35–45
Quiet bedroom	20
Rural night-time background	20–40
Threshold of hearing	0

* dB(A): decibels (acoustically weighted).

(Source: Department of the Environment, 1993)

any noise problem and take remedial action before the commercial launch of the machine. Figure 7.41 shows a typical wind turbine noise pattern.

In Denmark, in order to control the effects of noise from wind turbines, there is a standard that specifies that the maximum wind turbine noise level permitted at the nearest dwelling in open countryside should be 45 dB(A). At habitations in residential areas a noise level of only 40 dB(A) is permitted. The Danes have experience with over 4000 wind turbines and this noise limit has been demonstrated to be achievable with commercial turbines. In the UK, the noise limit at buildings near to roads is 68 dB(A), a value that must not be exceeded for more than 10% of the time over an 18 hour period.

At present there are no standard maximum permitted noise levels specifically for wind turbines in the UK.

BOX 7.5: NOISE

Sound waves are sequences of variations in air pressure that can be detected by the human ear. The frequency range that is audible to human hearing is from approximately 20 to 20 000 hertz (Hz) (1 Hz = 1 cycle of vibration per second). **Noise** is unwanted sound.

Sound level is measured on a logarithmic scale in units known as decibels (dB). The threshold of hearing is defined as 0 dB. On this scale, a car passing 100 m away at 64 km h^{-1} (40 mph) has a sound level of approximately 55 dB. Doubling the sound power of the noise source increases the sound level by 3 dB.

A-weighted sound pressure level

The so-called *A-weighted* (accoustically weighted) sound pressure curve (Figure 7.40) describes the relative responsiveness of the ear to sound of different frequencies. Noise measurements are usually expressed not simply in decibels (dB) but on a scale in which the sound levels are adjusted for different frequencies, in accordance with the A-weighted sound pressure curve. The units used in this case are dB(A) (decibels, acoustic).

Sound levels decrease the further you are away from the source of the noise: a simple rule of thumb is that noise levels reduce by 6 dB for every doubling of distance. There are complications to this, though, as the noise level at a given distance from the source tends to be greater downwind than at a similar distance upwind.

Sound is absorbed as it passes through the air, but in a manner that varies according to frequency, humidity and temperature. It is also absorbed over long grass, vegetation and trees, but it is reflected, focused or 'shaded' by hard surfaces such as roads, walls of buildings, etc.

Figure 7.40 The 'A'-weighted sound pressure level curve

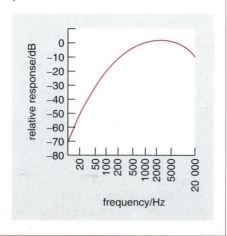

The *Annex on Wind Energy* to the UK Government's Planning Policy Guidance Note (PPG 22) on *Renewable Energy* (Department of the Environment, 1993) suggests that planning applications for wind turbines in the UK could usefully be accompanied by the following information:

(a) technical details of the turbine;

(b) hub height and rotor diameter;

(c) location of rotor: upwind or downwind of the tower;

(d) speed(s) of rotation;

(e) cut-in wind speeds;

(f) predicted noise levels at specific properties closest to the wind turbine over the most critical range of wind speeds;

(g) measured background noise levels at the properties and wind speeds outlined in (f) above;

(h) a scale map showing: the proposed wind turbine(s); the prevailing wind conditions; nearby existing development;

Figure 7.41 Wind turbine noise pattern from a typical wind turbine (Source: EWEA, 1991)

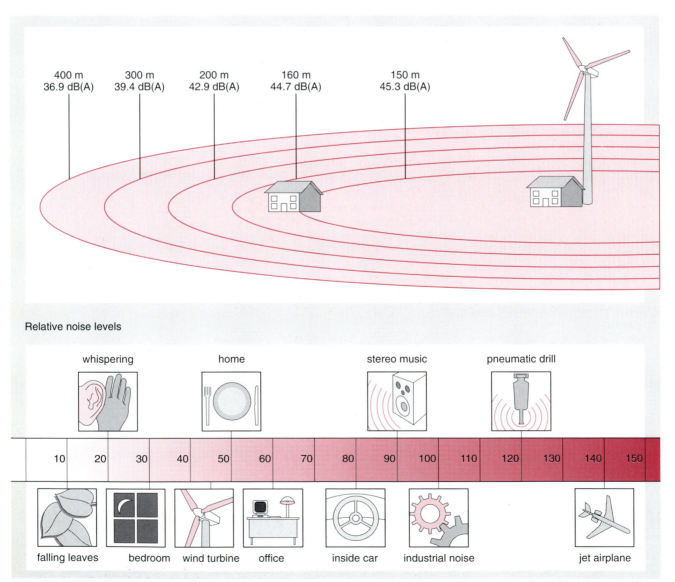

(i) results of independent measurements of noise emission from the proposed wind turbine, including the sound power level. In the case of a prototype turbine where no measurements are available, predictions should be made by comparison with similar machines.

Noise is a sensitive issue and opposition to wind energy development is likely unless it is given careful consideration both at the wind turbine design and the project planning stages, taking into account the concerns of people who may be affected.

There is much ongoing research to reduce wind turbine noise. For a useful overview of this work, see Legerton (1992).

ELECTROMAGNETIC INTERFERENCE

When a wind turbine is positioned between a radio, television or microwave transmitter and receiver (Figure 7.42), it can sometimes reflect some of the electromagnetic radiation in such a way that the reflected wave interferes with the original signal as it arrives at the receiver. This can cause the received signal to be distorted significantly.

The extent of electromagnetic interference caused by a wind turbine depends mainly on the blade materials and on the surface shape of the tower. If the turbine has metal blades (or glass-reinforced plastic (GRP) blades containing metal components), electro-magnetic interference may occur if it is located close to a radio communications service. Wooden blades absorb rather than reflect radio waves and faceted towers reflect more than smooth rounded towers, due to their flat surfaces.

The most likely form of electromagnetic interference is television interference. However, this is relatively easily dealt with by the installation of relay transmitters or by connecting cable television services to those viewers who may be affected.

Apart from television interference, microwave links, VHF Omni-directional Ranging (VOR) and Instrument Landing Systems (ILS) are the most sensitive. The Radio Communications Agency at the Department of Trade and Industry holds information about such radio services and can advise if there are such services within a sensitive radius of proposed wind turbines.

VISUAL IMPACT

The visual perception of a wind turbine or a wind farm is determined by a variety of factors. These will include physical parameters such as turbine size, turbine design, number of blades, colour, the number of turbines in

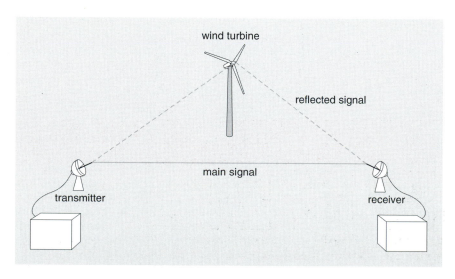

Figure 7.42 Scattering of radio signals by a wind turbine

a wind farm, the layout of the wind farm and the extent to which moving rotor blades may attract attention.

Figure 7.43 compares wind turbines and other structures in the landscape.

An individual's perception of a wind energy project will also depend on a variety of less easily defined sociological parameters. These may include the individual's level of understanding of the technology, opinions on what sources of energy are desirable and his or her level of involvement with the project. Newspaper and television reports are usually the only source of information most people have access to about wind energy and may well influence their opinions on the subject.

A public attitude study conducted in the UK (Lee *et al.*, 1989) indicated that only 35% of the respondents felt that a wind farm would spoil the view, 75% of respondents felt that, like electricity pylons, wind turbines are 'just there' and 90% of respondents preferred turbines to be painted in neutral colours.

More recently, a public attitude survey was carried out around the Delabole wind farm (Section 7.2) by Exeter University and funded by ETSU (Edwards, 1993). The survey was carried out in two phases. Phase one was carried out before construction of the wind farm and phase two after the wind farm had commenced operation.

The phase one survey indicated that 17% approved of the concept of a wind farm, 32% disapproved and 51% were not sure. The phase two survey indicated that a marked change of opinion had occurred since the wind farm had commenced operation. This time, 85% approved of the concept of a wind farm, 4% disapproved and 11% were not sure.

In Wales, three independent detailed surveys have been carried out around five geographical areas, each containing a commercial wind farm, to measure local public attitudes to wind farms. These were sponsored by ETSU (Esslemont, 1994), the Countryside Council for Wales (Chris Blandford Associates, 1994) and BBC Wales (Cymru) (Bishop & Potter, 1994).

All three studies indicate significant support from the Welsh public towards wind farms. The ETSU sponsored study indicated that 86% of the people around the Cemmaes wind farm (in Montgomeryshire) were in favour and only 4% of respondents were disturbed by the visual effects. The Countryside Council for Wales study found that 70% of those interviewed would "be prepared to see further wind farm development. Comparison

Figure 7.43 Comparison of wind turbines and other structures in the landscape

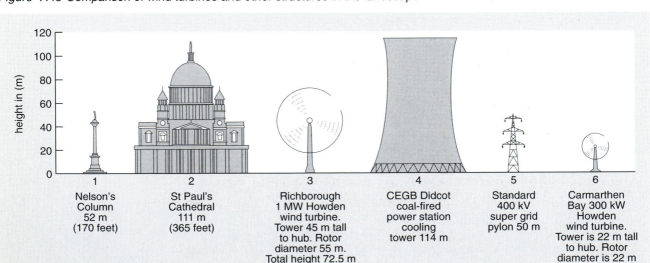

with the control sample seemed to reveal that attitudes towards wind farms became more positive where and when they have actually taken place."

The BBC Wales sponsored study found that, overall, 67% of those interviewed were generally in favour of wind power in Wales, with 76% of those interviewed in the area of the large Llandinam wind farm in favour. The majority of respondents (over 83% in the Llandinam study area) were in favour of further expansion in Wales. "The research indicated an overwhelming degree of support for wind power in Wales. Respondents had become more positive towards wind power following construction of their local wind farm and even where the turbines could be heard inside or outside the respondents' homes, this did not necessarily turn them against the wind farm." (Bishop & Potter, 1994).

ADDITIONAL ENVIRONMENTAL FACTORS

Additional environmental factors that should be considered in assessing the impact of a wind turbine installation include safety, shadow flicker and the possible impact on flora and fauna. See the government's Planning Policy Guidance Note (PPG 22) (Department of the Environment, 1993).

PLANNING AND WIND ENERGY

Planning controls have a major influence on the deployment of wind turbines. Until recently, only certain local authorities had attempted to develop policy guidelines about the planning aspects of wind energy (Taylor and Rand, 1991; Devon County Council et al., 1993). As a result, the planning aspects of wind energy have been treated differently in different locations.

As already mentioned, the UK government's recently released planning guidelines for renewable energy projects (Department of the Environment, 1993) encourage planners to look upon wind energy projects favourably, in part because of the importance of the environmental benefits of wind energy in terms of national commitments to reducing CO_2 emissions. The document includes comments about noise, electromagnetic interference, visual aspects, shadow flicker, ecology, etc.
A planning checklist has also been compiled (Taylor and Rand, 1991) to enable planners and developers to check a wind turbine planning application and take appropriate action to avoid potential environmental and nuisance problems.

Friends of the Earth have also produced guidelines on wind energy for developers and planners (F.O.E., 1994).

The British Wind Energy Association has also published Best Practice Guidelines for Wind Energy Development (BWEA, 1994) in order to promote more sensitive wind energy development. These were drawn up in consultation with a wide variety of interested parties, including a number of local authorities, the Council for the Protection of Rural England, the Countryside Commission and Friends of the Earth. It contains useful flow charts which indicate recommended actions at various stages of a wind energy development.

A good deal of what resistance there is to wind farms may be due to misunderstandings and misinformation about the technology. More explanation of and information about the environmental benefits of wind energy would probably enable those who may be affected by a wind farm to make a more objective analysis of the impact of the development.

BOX 7.6: A COST CALCULATION PROCEDURE FOR WIND ENERGY

The cost per unit of electricity generated, g, by a wind farm can be estimated using the following formula:

$$g = CR/E + M$$

where:

C is the capital cost of the wind farm

R is the capital recovery factor or the annual capital charge rate (expressed as a fraction)

E is the wind farm annual energy output

M is the cost of operating and maintaining the wind farm per unit of energy output

The capital recovery factor, R, is defined as:

$$R = \frac{x}{1 - (1 + x)^{-n}}$$

where:

x is the required annual rate of return net of inflation (expressed as a fraction)

n is the number of years over which the investment in the wind farm is to be recovered.

An estimate of the energy, E (in kilowatt-hours), can be made using the following formula:

$$E = (hP_rF)T$$

where:

h is the number of hours in a year (8760)

P_r is the rated power of each wind turbine in kilowatts

F is the net annual capacity factor of the turbines at the site

T is the number of wind turbines

The operating and maintenance cost, M, per unit of output is defined by:

$$M = KC/E$$

where K is a factor representing the annual operating costs of a wind farm as a fraction of the total capital cost. The European Wind Energy Association (EWEA) has estimated this to be 0.025, that is, 2.5% of capital cost. (Source: EWEA, 1991)

7.8 ECONOMICS

COST CALCULATION

A general approach to calculating the cost of energy from renewable energy sources based on discounted cash flow analysis is described in the Appendix. The economic appraisal of wind energy involves a number of specific factors, which are defined below. These include:

- the annual energy production from the wind turbine installation;

- the capital cost of the installation;

- the annual capital charge rate (which is calculated by converting the capital cost plus any interest payable into an equivalent annual cost, using the concept of 'annuitisation' discussed in the Appendix);

- the length of the contract with the purchaser of the electricity produced;

- the number of years over which the investment in the project is to be recovered (or any loan repaid), which may be the same as the length of the contract;

- the operation and maintenance costs, including maintenance of the wind turbines, insurance, land leasing, etc.

A detailed procedure for calculating the cost of wind energy is shown in Box 7.6.

As we have seen, the annual energy produced by a wind turbine installation depends on the wind speed–power curve of the turbine, the wind speed frequency distribution at the site, and the availability of the turbine.

The **capacity factor** is a another term widely used to describe the productivity of a power plant over a given period of time, and was defined in Chapter 1.

If a wind turbine were able to operate at full rated power throughout the year, it would have a capacity factor of one (i.e. 100%). However, in reality, the wind does not blow constantly at the full rated wind speed throughout the year, so in practice a wind turbine will have a much lower capacity factor. On moderate wind speed sites in the UK, with annual mean wind speeds of around half a turbine's rated wind speed, a capacity factor of 0.25 (i.e. 25%) is typical. However, on better wind sites, such as Carmarthen Bay in Wales, St Austell in Cornwall or the Orkney Islands, capacity factors of 0.35–0.40 or more are achievable.

As the cost of wind energy does not include the cost of fuel, it is relatively straightforward to determine, compared with the cost of energy from fuel-consuming power plants, which are dependent on future fuel costs. High or escalating fuel prices tend to favour zero (or low) fuel cost systems such as wind energy, but steady or falling fuel prices are less favourable to them.

Wind turbines are very quick to install, so they can be generating before they incur significant levels of interest during construction.

CAPITAL COSTS

The capital cost of wind turbines currently ranges from approximately £600 to £1000 per kilowatt of output, or £280 to £420 per square metre of rotor swept area. A breakdown of the components of the cost of energy from a typical wind turbine is shown in Figure 7.44. With 15 to 20-year contracts and on sufficiently windy sites, wind energy may be competitive with conventional forms of electricity generation, if the costs of the latter are calculated on a comparable basis.

ANNUAL CHARGE RATE

The cost of wind-generated electricity is very dependent on the way that the plant is financed and this can strongly affect the price of the electricity produced. The importance of the rate of return is shown in Table 7.3, which is based on a 20-year loan period, different annual mean wind speeds and installed costs of 400, 500 and 600 ECU m^{-2} for fairly good, good and very good sites respectively.

Table 7.3 Costs per unit of wind-generated electricity (ECU* kWh^{-1}) for various internal rates of return (1990 prices) and various wind speeds

Annual mean wind speed (m s^{-1})	Required internal rates of return (%)			
	5	8	10	15
6.5 (fairly good site)	0.061	0.074	0.083	0.108
7.5 (good site)	0.050	0.060	0.067	0.088
8.5 (very good site)	0.034	0.041	0.046	0.060

* At the time of preparation, 1 ECU was approximately equal to £0.70.

(Source: EWEA, 1991)

THE NON-FOSSIL FUEL OBLIGATION (NFFO) AND WIND ENERGY

As part of the privatisation of the UK electricity industry, in 1991 the government introduced the Non-Fossil Fuel Obligation (NFFO), which is described in more detail in Chapter 10. The NFFO scheme has stimulated

Figure 7.44 Breakdown of energy costs from wind plant (Source: EWEA, 1991)

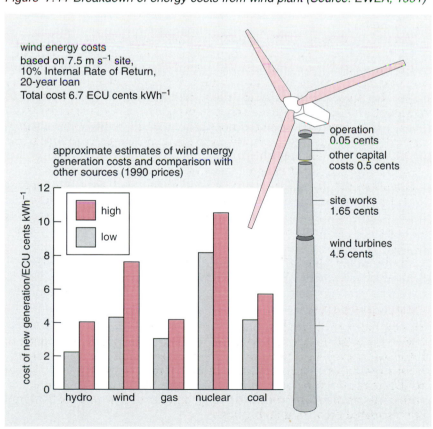

wind energy costs
based on 7.5 m s^{-1} site,
10% Internal Rate of Return,
20-year loan
Total cost 6.7 ECU cents kWh^{-1}

approximate estimates of wind energy generation costs and comparison with other sources (1990 prices)

operation
0.05 cents

other capital
costs 0.5 cents

site works
1.65 cents

wind turbines
4.5 cents

considerable development of wind energy in the UK and provided an economic framework that has encouraged investment in wind farms. By the end of 1994 some 170 MW of wind generating capacity was either operational or under construction, and substantial further capacity was planned (BWEA, 1995).

At the end of 1994, 55 further contracts for 166 MW of Declared Net Capacity (equivalent to 386 MW installed capacity) of wind energy projects were announced for England and Wales under the third order of the Non Fossil Fuel Obligation (NFFO 3). (The term "Declared Net Capacity" (DNC) is explained in Chapter 10.) At the same time 12 wind energy contracts for 45.6 MW of Declared Net Capacity (76 MW installed capacity) were announced under the Scottish Renewables Order.

The unit prices for electricity from these projects ranged from 3.98 to 4.8 p/kWh for the larger schemes, and 4.9 to 5.99 p/kWh for smaller schemes. In Scotland the prices ranged from 3.79 to 4.17 p/kWh, with an average of 3.99 p/kWh (Massy,1995). Whether all of the projects prove to be viable at these prices remains to be seen, but if so they suggest that wind energy represents an increasingly competitive of form of electricity provision in the UK.

7.9 COMMERCIAL DEVELOPMENT AND WIND ENERGY POTENTIAL

WIND ENERGY DEVELOPMENTS

The present relatively-healthy state of the wind energy industry is due largely to developments in Denmark and California.

Unlike most other European countries that historically employed traditional windmills, in Denmark the use of wind energy never ceased completely, largely because of the country's lack of fossil fuel reserves. In Denmark, windmills for electricity generation were researched and manufactured from the nineteenth century until the late 1960s. Interest in wind energy took on a new impetus in Denmark (as in many other countries, including the UK) in the 1970s, as a result of the oil crisis of 1973. The development of a new generation of wind turbines for farm-scale operation in Denmark was then undertaken by small agricultural engineering companies.

California, however, was responsible for giving wind energy the push needed to take it from a small, relatively-insignificant industry to one with the potential for generating significant amounts of electricity. A rapid flowering of wind energy development took place in the mid-1980s, when wind farms began to be installed in large numbers. This occurred as a result of generous tax credits introduced to stimulate electricity generation from the wind. An environment was created in which it was possible for companies to earn revenue from the sale of wind-generated electricity to Californian utilities, and from the manufacture of wind turbines.

Whilst many companies did not survive and quite a few turbine failures occurred, the Californian wind farms became a proving ground which led to the fairly rapid evolution of more reliable and economically competitive wind turbines. Tax credits were withdrawn in the late 1980s, but development continued, although at a much slower rate. As well as stimulating American manufacturers, the Californian developments have provided opportunities for companies from several other countries, principally Denmark, but also including the UK, Belgium, the Netherlands, Germany and Japan.

By the end of 1991, there were approximately 15 500 wind turbines operating in the state, representing 16 200 MW of generating capacity. During 1991, they produced 2700 million kWh of electricity (Gipe, 1992).

Danish manufacturers were able to take advantage of experience acquired within their home market to develop a successful export industry, which shipped over 7000 machines to California. At the peak of the Californian wind energy boom, the value to Denmark of the exports of Danish wind energy equipment to the USA, worth £130 million per year, was second only to the export value of Danish ham to the USA.

However, the period just after the Californian tax credits ceased in 1988 was an extremely difficult time for wind turbine manufacturers and many companies were forced to close down. Since then, wind energy development has been gathering momentum in Europe, particularly in Denmark itself, where over 2880 wind turbines with a 343 MW capacity had been installed by the end of 1990. These produced 604 million kWh, equivalent to 2% of Danish electricity consumption.

More recently, commercial wind energy developments have begun to take place in the UK. These were initially one-off individual installations, such as the 225 kW wind turbine at the Wood Green Animal Shelter in Huntingdon described in Section 7.2. In December 1991, as described in Section 7.2, the UK's first commercial wind farm began supplying electricity to the grid from a farm in Cornwall. The first UK wind farm to use wind turbines manufactured in the UK (by the Wind Energy Group) was developed by National Wind Power at Cemmaes in Powys. It consists of twenty-four 300 kW WEG MS3 turbines and commenced operation in 1992 (Figure 7.45). From 1992 onwards, further wind farms were installed in Cornwall, Wales, Northumberland, Cumbria, Yorkshire and Norfolk (see Figure 7.46).

In 1993, 202,000 MWh were generated from UK wind energy projects. In 1994, this figure rose to 317,000 MWh. It was estimated that the average output from the 170 MW of wind capacity installed by the end of 1994 would avoid the release of 400,000 tonnes of carbon dioxide each year (BWEA, 1995/b).

Figure 7.45 The first UK wind farm (at Cemmaes in Powys) to utilise UK-manufactured wind turbines (24 WEG MS3 300 kW turbines) was developed by National Wind Power Ltd

Figure 7.46 Location of wind energy projects with NFFO contracts

SMALL-SCALE WIND TURBINES

From the early days of wind-generated electricity, small-scale wind turbines have been manufactured to provide electricity for remote houses and farms, remote communities, for trickle charging batteries on boats, caravans and holiday cabins, and also more recently for providing the power for remote telephone boxes. British Telecom estimates that there is potential for some 10 000 of the latter applications in the UK.

Small-scale wind turbines are more expensive per kilowatt than medium-scale wind turbines. In most cases, they are currently unable to compete with mains electricity and, because so much of the UK is now connected to the National Grid, their potential has been limited. The need for batteries also tends to greatly increase the cost of such systems.

However, the steady demand from people interested in obtaining electricity from pollution-free sources, or in locations where conventional supplies are not available, provides enough support to sustain a significant number of manufacturers of small-scale wind turbines around the world.

At the 'micro' wind turbine scale (under 500 W power rating), one British company, Marlec Engineering Ltd, has developed a successful international business in manufacturing small battery-charging wind turbines and has sold in excess of 20 000 such turbines around the world, most of them rated at around 50 watts (see Figure 7.1).

There is also considerable ongoing activity in the development of small to medium-scale 'autonomous' wind turbine-based systems which utilise diesel engines as a back-up source of energy, combined with short-term storage, usually in the form of battery banks. These systems tend to be expensive but can be economically viable in locations such as island communities which are a long distance from the nearest mains supply. A number of such systems have been installed for island communities around the UK, notably on Fair Isle, Lundy and Foula.

LOCAL COMMUNITY WIND TURBINES

Another application of wind energy that is gaining support is that of local community wind turbines. This usually involves a group of people from a local community buying a wind turbine or group of wind turbines. The local community benefits from the sale of the electricity produced, or makes use of it for its own purposes locally (Taylor, 1993).

Over 50% of the wind turbines in Denmark are owned and operated in this way and there is an active Danish Windmill Owners' Association which provides support for the many people involved. Such wind energy co-operatives are also active in the Netherlands and Germany.

This approach can encourage a positive attitude towards wind energy in communities that might be opposed to commercial wind energy developers from outside the area. A number of organisations are attempting to develop such projects in the UK.

WIND ENERGY POTENTIAL

By determining the total land area that has annual mean wind speeds appropriate for wind energy, Van Wijk *et al.* (1991) have estimated the theoretical global potential for electricity production from land-based wind turbines to be approximately 20 000 terawatt-hours per year (TWh year^{-1}). This corresponds to about twice the 1987 global electricity consumption of 9000 TWh. Taking into account infrastructure limitations and other constraints, Van Wijk *et al.* concluded that it would be possible to install 450 000 MW of wind turbine capacity on a global scale up to the year 2020. It is predicted that this capacity could generate approximately 900 TWh year^{-1}, which is about 10% of current world electricity consumption and 3.5% of the projected consumption in 2020, as estimated by the World Energy Council. This would avoid the release of 800 million tonnes of carbon dioxide, assuming that it replaced coal-fired electricity.

The European Wind Energy Association (1991) has calculated that it would be feasible to achieve a target of 10% of the EU's electricity needs (based on 1990 levels) by the year 2030 using land-based wind turbines with a combined capacity of 100 gigawatts (GW). These turbines would be distributed throughout the EU and would occupy a gross land area equivalent to the island of Crete (approximately 5400 square kilometres, km^2). Ninety-nine per cent of that area would still be available for agriculture around the turbines, as only 1% would be needed for turbine foundations, access roads, etc. (see Figure 7.47). It is estimated that the construction of this capacity would generate about 50 000 jobs (see Figure 7.48) in the manufacture of wind turbines by 2030 and a further 100 000 jobs in rural areas for the operation and maintenance of the wind power plant. The same study compared the unit cost of electricity from wind energy with other energy sources (Figure 7.44).

The UK has very substantial wind energy potential: it has about 40% of the total realisable wind energy resource in the EU. An assessment of the UK's land-based wind energy resource has been carried out by ETSU (Department of Energy, 1988). When the physical, institutional and environmental constraints on the resource are taken into account, the study estimated that there is space for approximately 143 000 wind turbines of 33 m diameter, that is, approximately 43 GW capacity. These would be capable of generating 122 TWh year^{-1}, which is equivalent to almost 45% of the UK's current electricity demand.

When other factors such as proximity to the grid and economic constraints are taken into account, the exploitable UK land-based wind energy resource was estimated to be between 45 and 55 TWh year^{-1}, which corresponds to approximately 20% of current UK electricity demand. Using the same criteria as those used in the European study, this level of activity would generate approximately 8000 jobs in manufacturing and approximately 15 000 jobs in operation and maintenance of wind power plant.

The theoretical UK offshore wind energy resource is much larger than the land-based resource. The Department of Trade and Industry estimates the technical potential for offshore wind energy around the coasts of the UK to be of the order of 140 TWh year^{-1} (Department of Energy, 1988).

Energy from offshore wind farms would be likely to be more expensive than from onshore installations, because of the extra costs of civil engineering

Figure 7.47 Projected growth of wind turbine installed capacity to 100 000 MW, to achieve 10% of the current EU electricity demand by 2030. Turbines would be spread throughout Europe but would take up land area equivalent to the island of Crete, 99% of which would still be available for agriculture (Source: EWEA, 1991)

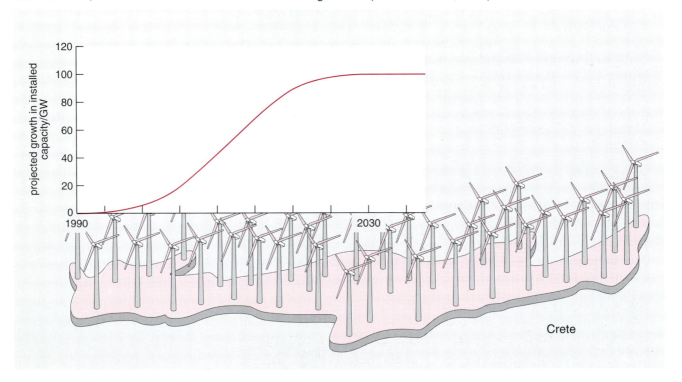

for substructure, higher electrical connection costs, and the higher specification materials needed to resist the corrosive marine environment. However, offshore wind speeds are generally higher than onshore ones, and this, together with possible reduction in offshore costs as experience is gained in this environment, might make offshore wind energy costs competitive in the longer term. Meanwhile, a demonstration offshore wind farm of eleven, 450 kW wind turbines has been installed off Vindeby in Denmark (Figure 7.49) and has been generating electricity since 1991. A single 220 kW wind turbine was also installed in 1991 off the coast of Nogersund in the south of Sweden. An offshore wind farm consisting of four 500 kW wind turbines was constructed in 1994 in the Ijssel Lake in Dutch coastal waters. Further offshore wind farms are planned in Denmark and in the Netherlands. In the UK, a novel floating, pontoon-mounted, offshore wind turbine design is being developed by Technomare, with some initial support from the DTI

In 1992, the Renewable Energy Advisory Group (REAG) produced its report on renewable energy for the Department of Trade and Industry (REAG, 1992). It identified the accessible UK wind-generated electricity resources to be 340 TWh per annum from turbines on land and 380 TWh per annum from offshore turbines. Each of these figures exceeds current UK electricity demand. They are based on a cost of electricity of less than 10p kWh^{-1} with an 8% discount rate and exclude areas of environmental sensitivity. See Figure 1.16 in Chapter 1.

Figure 7.50, from the REAG report, shows the potential contribution of various renewables to UK electricity needs in 2005. It amply demonstrates the potential significance of land-based wind energy for electricity generation for the UK.

REAG estimated that the total land-based wind energy resource that could feasibly be harnessed in the UK was 55 TWh year^{-1} (12 TWh year^{-1} in England and Wales; 5 TWh year^{-1} in Northern Ireland; 38 TWh year^{-1} in Scotland assuming 10%, 15% and 20% respectively of potential sites are successfully developed). Taking into account the assumption that there is a 20% limit to the amount of non-firm power that the National Grid can accept, the maximum contribution that was felt to be acceptable was 32 TWh year^{-1} for the UK. This also assumes sufficient strengthening of the National Grid system to fully integrate the Scottish and Northern Ireland resource, which may or may not be feasible. A contribution of 32 TWh year^{-1} would require over 38 000 330 kW machines and 4000 km^2

Figure 7.49 Offshore wind farm located off the coast of Vindeby in Denmark (eleven 450 kW Bonus wind turbines)

Figure 7.48 For wind energy to provide 10% of current EU electricity demand, 100 000 MW of wind turbine capacity would need to be installed, which by 2030 would have created 50 000 long-term jobs (Source: EWEA, 1991)

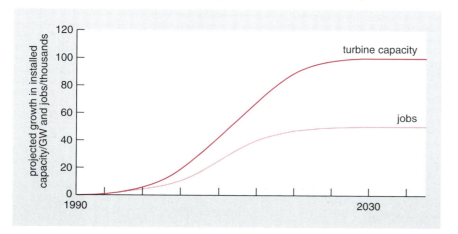

of land, or about 1.3% of the UK land area, 98% of which could still be used for agricultural purposes. Figure 7.51 shows the estimated contribution from land-based wind energy in the UK under different views of the future in 2025 (excluding any costs for National Grid reinforcement).

We can see that wind energy is potentially of great importance from the point of view of electricity production, reduction of pollution (especially of carbon dioxide and acid rain) and resource conservation. For manufacturing industry, it has considerable home and export market potential. It could also have a significant influence on the economic viability of rural communities.

Figure 7.50 Estimated contribution from renewable energy to electricity generation in the UK: supply curves in 2005, 8% discount rate. (Source: REAG, 1992)

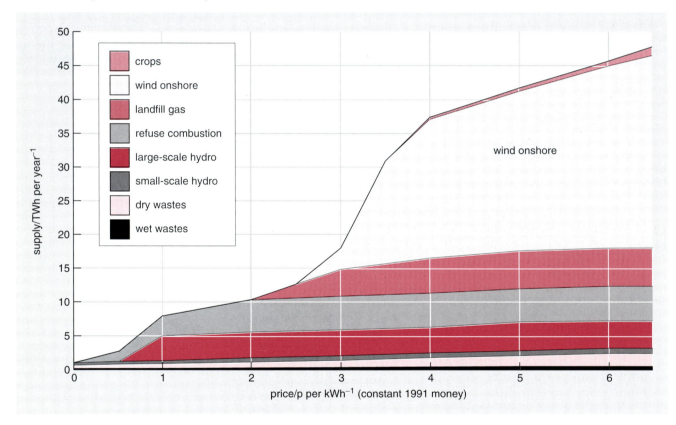

Figure 7.51 Estimated wind energy contribution in the UK in 2025 for a range of views of the future (Source: REAG, 1992)

7.10 RECENT DEVELOPMENTS

Wind turbines have been deployed on an ever increasing scale around the World: by 1994 there was more than 3.5 GW of installed wind generation capacity world wide, with the major US and Danish programmes being followed by significant programmes in countries like the UK, Germany, Spain and India.

The UK programme, supported by the NFFO scheme, led to something of a Californian-style 'wind rush', with more than 20 wind farms having been installed, chiefly in Wales and Cornwall, by 1994. Danish and Japanese machines in the range 300-400 kW dominated, only 16% being of UK origin. The pace of the programme led to some initial planning problems. Although public opinion was generally in favour of wind power, at some locations noise problems emerged, and some planning applications were turned down on the basis of visual intrusion. Some of the problems were perhaps due to lack of proper consultation, rather than technical errors, and in some cases local objections were very strong, with anti-wind lobby groups, sometimes aided by the media, creating an impression of a significant 'wind backlash'. Subsequent detailed studies of local and national opinion however indicated that wind farms were overwhelmingly popular, even amongst people who lived nearby, the objectors being a small minority. That said, it is clear that wind farm developers will need to take more care to minimise any potential impacts, with low noise turbines being an obvious priority. The House of Commons Welsh Affairs Committee (1994), in its 1994 review of wind farm developments in Wales, was supportive of wind energy development but pointed out that the Welsh topography differed from (relatively flat) Denmark and (relatively isolated) California passes, so that wind farm deployment in Wales thus required more careful attention.

The structure of the NFFO had also presented some problems. The first two NFFO rounds offered contracts only until 1998, and this arguably led some developers to opt for sensitive, high wind speed upland sites, in order to recoup their investment quickly. The third NFFO round, which offered 10-15 year contracts should help to avoid this problem. The opening up of wind farm developments in Scotland via the introduction of a Scottish Renewables Order modelled on the NFFO should also help, since the generally higher wind speeds in Scotland should enable developers to choose less invasive sites while still making a profit. The higher wind speeds occurring in Scotland have resulted in some projects appearing to be economically viable at electricity prices below 4p/kWh.

On-land wind power is currently seen in the UK as one of the near-market renewable energy options, likely to be commercially viable soon, as reflected above. However it is not clear if the UK will be able to maintain a significant manufacturing capacity in this field. To date only one UK company, the Wind Energy Group, have been manufacturing wind turbines used in wind farms. Conventional horizontal-axis machines also seem to be winning out against current commercial vertical-axis designs in the UK.

Offshore wind energy developments are seen by the UK DTI as a 'long shot'. The Department of Trade and Industry (1994) in its Energy Paper 62 put them in the 'watching brief' category. However, as mentioned above, a novel floating, offshore wind turbine design is being researched in the UK with some initial support from the DTI. Otherwise, offshore wind energy is being left to Denmark, Sweden and the Dutch to develop. Initial results from the Danish Vindeby offshore wind farm suggested that electricity costs were around 60% more than for an equivalent on-land wind farm, although that figure ought to reduce as the technology improves and more construction experience is gained.

REFERENCES

Abbott, I. H. and Von Doenhoff, A. E. (1958) *Theory of Wing Sections*, Dover.

Anderson, M. (1992) *Current Status of Wind Farms in the UK*, Renewable Energy Systems.

Bennett, M., Hamilton, P. M. and Moore, D. J. (1983) 'Estimation of low-level winds from upper air data', *IEE Proceedings*, Vol. 130, Pt A, No. 9, pp. 517–20.

Bishop, K. & Potter, A (1994): *Love Them or Loathe Them? Public Attitudes Towards Wind Farms in Wales*, Report of research commissioned by BBC Wales, Environmental & Countryside Planning Unit, Department of Regional Planning, University of Wales

Burch, S. F. and Ravenscroft, F. (1992) *Computer Modelling of the UK Wind Energy Resource: Final Overview Report,* ETSU WN7055, ETSU.

BWEA (1994): *Best Practice Guidelines for Wind Energy Development*, British Wind Energy Association

BWEA (1995a) 'Annual Wind Energy Output up by 56%', News Release, January.

BWEA (1995b) 'UK Wind Energy Output up by 56%', Wind Directions, April, p.3.

Chignell, R.J. (1987) *Electromagnetic Interference from Wind Turbines – A Simplified Guide to Avoiding Problems*, National Wind Turbine Centre, National Engineering Laboratory, East Kilbride.

Chris Blandford Associates (1994): *Wind Power Station Construction Monitoring Study*, Countryside Council for Wales

Clarke, A. (1988) *Wind Farm Location and Environmental Impact*, Network for Alternative Technology and Technology Assessment, c/o EERU, The Open University.

Creagh-Osborne, R. (1984) *This is Sailing – A Complete Course* (second edition revised by S. Sleight), United Nautical Publishers, Basel.

Department of Energy (1988) *Renewable Energy in the UK: The Way Forward*, Energy Paper 55, HMSO, June.

Department of the Environment (1993) Planning Policy Guidance Note (PPG 22) *Renewable Energy, Annex on Wind Energy*, HMSO.

Department of Trade and Industry (1993) *Renewable Energy Bulletin No. 5: Information on the Non-Fossil Fuel Obligation for Generators of Electricity from Renewable Energy Sources*, Department of Trade and Industry, REB-5, October.

Department of Trade and Industry (1994) *New and Renewable Energy: Future Prospects for the UK*, Energy Paper 62, HMSO.

Devon County Council/West Devon Borough Council/ETSU (1993) Planning for renewable energy in Devon, April.

Edwards, P.D. (1993) 'The performance and problems of and the public attitude to the Delabole wind farm', in Pitcher, K. F. (ed.) (1993) *Wind Energy Conversion 1993*, Mechanical Engineering Publications, pp. 23–5.

Eldridge, F.R. (1975) *Wind Machines*, Mitre Corporation.

Esselmont, E. (1994): *Cemmaes Wind Farm Sociological Impact Study*, Energy Technology Support Unit

EWEA (1991) *Time for Action: Wind Energy in Europe*, European Wind Energy Association.

Farndon, J. (1992) *How the Earth Works*, Dorling Kindersley, London.

F.O.E. (1994): *Planning for Wind Power: Guidelines for Project Developers and Local Planners*, Friends of the Earth.

Gardner, P., Morgan, C. A., Noakes, J. and French, R. G. (1992) 'Feasibility study for an offshore wind turbine', in *Wind Energy Conversion 1992*, Mechanical Engineering Publications.

Gipe, P. (1992) *1992 Wind Technology Status Report – US Sets New Wind Energy Record as Domestic Market Stagnates*, American Wind Energy Association, Washington, September.

Golding, E. W. (1955) *Generation of Electricity by Wind Power*, E. and F. Spon.

Kovarik, T., Pipher, C. and Hurst, C. (1979) *Wind Energy*, Quality Books and Prism Press.

Lee, T., Wren, B. and Hickman, M. (1989) *Public Responses to the Siting and Operation of Wind Turbines*, Robens Institute and Department of Psychology, University of Surrey.

Legerton, M. (ed.) (1992) *Wind Turbine Noise Workshop Proceedings*, ETSU-N-123, Department of Trade and Industry/British Wind Energy Association.

Ljunggren, S. and Gustafsson, A. (eds) (1988) *Recommended Practices for Wind Turbine Testing: 4. Acoustics: Measurement of Noise Emission from Wind Turbines*, 2nd edition, International Energy Agency Programme for Research and Development on Wind Energy Conversion Systems.

Massy, J. (1995) 'Contracts for Nearly 500 MW Win Through', Wind Power Monthly, January, pp. 28–29.

Mays, I. (1993) BWEA press release, British Wind Energy Association, 23 December.

Needham, J. (1965) *Science and Civilisation in China*, Vol. 4: 'Physics and Physical Technology', Part II: 'Mechanical Engineering', Cambridge University Press.

Park, J. (1981) *The Wind Power Book*, Cheshire Books.

REAG (1992) *Report to the President of the Board of Trade*, Energy Paper No. 60, Renewable Energy Advisory Group, HMSO.

Reynolds, J. (1970) *Windmills and Watermills*, Hugh Evelyn Ltd Publishers, London.

Taylor, D. A. (ed.) (1993) 'One-day Workshop on Local Community Wind Energy Projects held at the Open University and sponsored by the DTI, BWEA and EERU', Altechnica, Milton Keynes, April.

Taylor, D. A. and Rand, M. (1991) *Planning for Wind Energy in Dyfed*, Altechnica.

Troen, I. and Petersen, E. L. (1989) *European Wind Atlas*, Riso, Denmark for Commission of the European Communities.

Van Wijk, A. A., Coelingh, J. P. and Turkenburg, W. C. (1991) 'Global potential for wind energy', *Proceedings of EWEC'91 Conference*, Amsterdam, pp. 367–71.

Vestas, D.W.T. (1991) V27-225 kW Product Description Brochure.

Welsh Affairs Committee (1994) *Wind Energy*, House Of Commons 1993-94 Paper 336-1, HMSO.

FURTHER READING

BWEA (1982) *Wind Energy for the Eighties*, British Wind Energy Association and Peter Perigrinus.

This is an excellent overview of many aspects of wind energy and includes a high technical content. It is somewhat dated in some respects but is still nonetheless worth reading to understand the main factors affecting wind energy technology.

Department of the Environment (1993) Planning Policy Guidance Note (PPG 22) *Renewable Energy, Annex on Wind Energy*, HMSO.

This is an important document for those interested in finding out about the government's policy on the planning aspects of wind energy. It includes a number of recommendations on planning procedures.

EWEA (1991) *Time for Action: Wind Energy in Europe*, European Wind Energy Association.

This publication provides a good overview of current wind turbine technology and the potential wind energy resource within the EU. It further describes how a sustained programme of wind energy development could provide 10% of the EU's electricity requirements (1990 levels) by 2030 from 100 GW of wind-generating capacity.

Freris, L. L (ed.) (1990) *Wind Energy Conversion Systems*, Prentice-Hall.

A very comprehensive overview of topics related to wind energy with high technical level, authored by a number of contributors.

Golding, E. W. (1955) *Generation of Electricity from Wind Energy*, E. and F. Spon.

Whilst this book is somewhat out of date, it provides a good historical overview of early attempts to utilise wind energy for electricity generation.

Lancashire, S., Kenna, J. and Fraenkel, P. (1987) *Windpumping Handbook*, IT Publications.

An excellent book on the practicalities of pumping water by means of wind power.

Legerton, M. (ed.) (1992) *Wind Turbine Noise Workshop Proceedings*, ETSU-N-123. Department of Trade and Industry/British Wind Energy Association.

The proceedings of this workshop provide a good overview of work on wind turbine noise in the UK.

Sharpe, D. J. (1986) 'Layman's guide to aerodynamics of wind turbines', in *Wind Energy Conversion 1986*, Mechanical Engineering Publications, pp. 229–42.

An informative publication on the aerodynamic aspects of wind turbines by one of the UK's leading experts on wind turbine aerodynamics. Technically fairly advanced despite the title.

Taylor, D. A and Rand, M. (1991) *Planning for Wind Energy in Dyfed*, Altechnica.

Whilst produced for the county of Dyfed, the guidelines proposed are applicable elsewhere in the UK. Extensive overview of the planning and environmental aspects of wind energy developments. Includes a useful planning checklist.

WAVE ENERGY

8.1 INTRODUCTION

The possibility of extracting energy from ocean waves has intrigued people for centuries. Although there are concepts over 100 years old, it was only in the 1970s that viable schemes began to emerge. In general, these modern wave energy conversion schemes have few environmental drawbacks. The prospects that some of them may make a significant energy contribution are promising in the longer term. In areas of the world where the wave climate is energetic and where conventional energy sources are expensive, such as remote islands, some of them may already be competitive.

As concern over carbon dioxide emissions from the burning of fossil fuels increases, the search will intensify for clean, economic and plentiful energy sources. In some countries solar energy may provide an ideal energy source; for other countries – and the UK may be one example – wave energy offers a very large potential resource.

Further technological developments are needed to enable wave energy to fulfil this promise, but some shore-mounted prototypes are already in operation. Refinements of these prototype designs, and the development of floating offshore structures, could open up the possibility of harvesting vast quantities of energy from the oceans.

RECENT HISTORY

The 'energy crisis' of 1973 prompted an increased interest in renewable energy, and especially in wave energy, as a potential source of electricity for the UK National Grid. Because of the enormous wave energy resource potentially available to the UK (see below and Section 8.6), a large number of device concepts were 'invented', mathematically modelled and experimentally tested, with support from commercial sponsors and the then Department of Energy (DEn), which is now part of the Department of Trade and Industry. Unfortunately, insufficient time and money were allocated to bring the various concepts and the associated technologies to maturity. In 1982, acting on advice from ACORD (the Advisory Committee on Research and Development for Fuel and Power), the DEn curtailed the UK wave energy programme.

However, a minimal effort has been sustained by some of the research teams, and a prototype oscillating water column (OWC) wave energy converter has been commissioned on Islay in Scotland. This was fully funded by the DEn following ACORD's recommendation (ETSU, 1985) that small-scale devices should be investigated as a source of energy for islands and remote communities where diesel normally provides the main energy source.

During the period of reduced funding in the UK, a number of other countries, notably Norway and Japan, increased their research and development programmes. Norway has little immediate domestic need for wave energy since it enjoys an electricity supply almost totally derived from hydro resources. It would, however, like to export wave energy technology. Japan, on the other hand, urgently needs more clean energy sources, but is surrounded by only a modest wave climate.

Table 8.1 Electricity generation costs *(p/kWh)** for the main wave energy devices

Device	Discount rate	
	8%	15%
Offshore devices		
Bristol Cylinder	12	20
Edinburgh Duck	16	26
NEL OWC	16	29
SEA Clam 8	12	
Shoreline device		
OWC	6	9

* These are median costs expressed in 1990 prices and assume successful completion of all outstanding R&D.

(Source: Thorpe, 1992)

In the 1990s there has been increasing awareness amongst politicians and others of the potential of wave energy. A European Union initiative has been launched (Garratti *et al.*, 1993), which will provide funding for a small number of projects, probably a prototype OWC in the Portugese Azores and an 'OSPREY' OWC at Dounreay in Scotland. A new Review of UK Wave Energy, conducted by the ETSU Chief Scientists' Group (Thorpe, 1992) has been published. Five representative 'main devices' were assessed in this review, which estimated the generating costs for each device, as shown in Table 8.1 and discussed later (Section 8.10).

The review concluded that the technically achievable UK offshore wave energy resource is large (7–10 GW annual average, equivalent to 61–87 TWh year^{-1}), but that the practical resource will be much smaller because of operational and economic constraints. It further concluded that the main devices are unlikely to generate electricity competitively in the short to medium term, but that there might be some scope for reduction in generating costs (with changes to the design of devices in most cases). In the longer term, the development of wave energy could help to reduce the threat of global warming.

In this section we will explore the nature of ocean waves and look at methods of extracting energy from them. A number of prototype schemes have been tested at various locations around the world, but so far there has been little exploitation of wave energy's vast potential. During the next decade we may expect to see further prototype testing and the development of some commercial schemes.

The section begins with a case study of TAPCHAN (a name which describes the appearance of a tapered channel), which illustrates that wave energy schemes are already feasible. TAPCHAN is a shoreline scheme: it is constructed on land and captures the waves that approach the mouth of its tapered channel.

8.2 CASE STUDY 1: TAPCHAN

In 1985 a 350 kW demonstration prototype wave energy converter was completed and commenced operation on a small Norwegian island some 40 km north-west of Bergen. TAPCHAN, as it is called, was built by the company Norwave, and could reasonably be regarded as the most successful wave energy scheme in the world (Figure 8.1).

'TAPCHAN' stands for TAPered CHANnel, and it is the design of this tapered channel that enables the scheme to harvest energy from the ocean waves which arrive at the mouth of the channel. The mouth is a 40 m wide horn-shaped collector which is able to accept energy from waves with a range of frequencies and directions. Waves entering the collector are fed into the wide end of the tapered channel where they propagate towards the narrow end with increasing wave height. The channel walls on the prototype are 10 m high (from 7 m below sea level to 3 m above) and 170 m long. Because the waves are forced into an ever-narrowing channel, their height is amplified until the crests spill over the walls into the reservoir at a level of 3 m above the mean sea level. The kinetic energy in the waves has been converted into potential energy, and is subsequently converted into electricity by allowing the water in the reservoir to return to the sea via a low-head Kaplan turbine system (see Chapter 5 on Hydroelectricity for details of the Kaplan turbine). This powers a 350 kW induction generator which delivers electricity into the Norwegian grid.

The TAPCHAN concept is simple. With very few moving parts, it has a low maintenance cost and a high reliability. The storage reservoir also helps to smooth the electrical output. We shall see later that ocean waves have a random nature and so most wave energy converters produce a fluctuating power output. TAPCHAN 'collects' waves in the reservoir, and so the output from the Kaplan turbine is dependent on the relatively steady difference in water levels between the reservoir and the sea. TAPCHAN therefore has an integral storage capacity which is generally not found in other wave energy converters. Several TAPCHANs are being planned, in Indonesia, Tasmania and Shetland (see Table 8.4, Section 8.10).

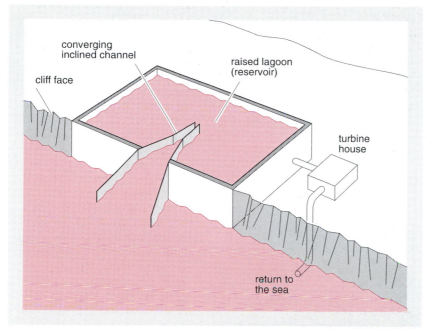

Figure 8.1 (Above) The tapered channel wave energy conversion device: TAPCHAN; (Below) Aerial photograph of the Norwegian TAPCHAN

Norwave has recently been considering methods for reducing the cost of construction of future Tapchans. Among those methods is wave prediction, to allow the Kaplan turbine to run at a greater output for some short time before the arrival of a number of large waves. This reduces the level of water in the reservoir and so makes room for those large waves. This technique may permit the designers to build schemes with smaller reservoirs and hence reduce the construction costs. A second cost-reduction method is to fabricate a shorter channel, and this has been tried out at Bergen by reducing the length of the existing channel. There have been some commercial difficulties with this exercise as the contractor went bankrupt during the operation.

TAPCHAN cannot be exploited everywhere in the world, simply because the features which make it so successful have to all coincide at an intended location. These requirements are:

• a good wave climate, i.e. high average wave energy, with persistent waves;

• deep water close to shore;

• a small tidal range (less than 1.0 m), otherwise the low-head hydro system cannot function properly for 24 hours a day (this excludes most of the UK south of the Shetland Isles)

• a convenient and cheap means of constructing the reservoir, usually requiring a natural feature of the coastline.

8.3 CASE STUDY 2: The Islay shoreline gully oscillating water column

Queen's University, Belfast (QUB) has been working on the development of a shoreline gully oscillating water column (OWC) device for the Scottish Isles since 1985. After surveying several sites, the island of Islay was chosen and a 150 kW OWC scheme incorporating a novel unidirectional turbine, called a Wells turbine (see Box 8.2) after its inventor, Professor Alan Wells, was installed in 1989. The system is an experimental prototype, not an optimised design. It was built to obtain experience with a working wave energy device and to test the turbine and grid connection of wave energy devices.

The approach was to develop a device which could be built cheaply on islands using established technology and techniques. It consists of a wedge-shaped chamber made of reinforced concrete, open at the bottom, into which sea water is free to flow (Figures 8.2 and 8.3). The sea water is contained as a water column which rises and falls with the waves. This acts as a piston, drawing air into and out of the top chamber with the rise and fall of the water column, through a 1 m diameter cylindrical tube. The moving air drives a Wells turbine (see Box 8.2 in Section 8.5), which is directly coupled to a 75 kW electrical generator.

As is often the case with novel projects, the Islay wave energy converter has not been without its problems. These have included difficulties in protecting workers in the gully during the construction, and a loss of energy (estimated at over 50%) caused by the roughness of the floor of the gully, which might have been improved by smoothing its surface. Problems were also experienced with the mechanical and electrical plant during the installation and commissioning phase, which led to loss of some turbine blades on the original rotor (a second rotor of a different design was fitted without further problems). The wave climate also proved to be less energetic than originally estimated, because of strong tidal influence. The chamber was originally installed without the Wells turbine/generator in order to assess the air power, and as a result the estimate of the power was revised. A 75 kW electrical generator was chosen. Nonetheless the Islay OWC has supplied the local grid with electricity on an intermittent

Figure 8.2 Outline of the Islay shoreline natural gully OWC

Figure 8.3 The Islay OWC

basis since 1991. It has provided considerable in-service experience and several significant achievements: electricity from a wave power device has been fed into a UK grid for the first time, and the device has remained operational through severe storms.

With experience gained from this natural gully project the development team are developing what is referred to as a 'designer gully' OWC to overcome some of the limitations of the Islay project (Figure 8.4).

Figure 8.4 Construction sequence proposed by Queen's University, Belfast for the 'designer gully' OWC

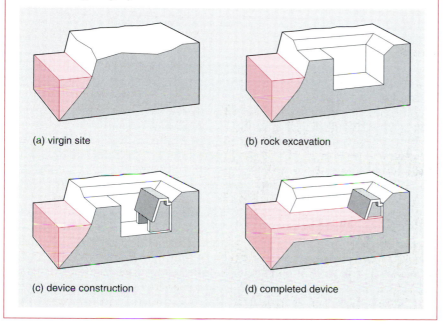

(a) virgin site

(b) rock excavation

(c) device construction

(d) completed device

Other shoreline prototypes are generally of the oscillating water column (OWC) type. An example of this type will be described in some detail in a second case study.

Shoreline devices are easier to construct and maintain than offshore devices. The latter will be deployed away from the shore, where they can harvest greater amounts of energy, since the waves in deep water have a greater energy content than those in the shallower water near to land. Also, by using an area of ocean a few kilometres offshore as a 'wave farm', it would be possible to deploy an array of wave energy converters and hence capture large quantities of energy, which could then be transmitted back to shore by subsea electrical cables. These and many other aspects of wave energy conversion will be discussed later in this section.

In order to examine wave energy technology in more detail, and to consider the possible alternatives to TAPCHAN and OWCs for those locations which do not meet the TAPCHAN or OWC criteria, we need to understand the nature of ocean waves.

8.4 PHYSICAL PRINCIPLES OF WAVE ENERGY

Ocean waves are generated by wind passing over stretches of water. The precise mechanisms involved in the interaction between the wind and the surface of the sea are complex and not yet completely understood. Three main processes appear to be involved.

1 Initially, air flowing over the sea exerts a tangential stress on the water surface, resulting in the formation and growth of waves.

2 Turbulent air flow close to the water surface creates rapidly varying shear stresses and pressure fluctuations. Where these oscillations are in phase with existing waves, further wave development occurs.

3 Finally, when waves have reached a certain size, the wind can exert a stronger force on the upwind face of the wave, causing additional wave growth.

Because the wind is originally derived from solar energy we may consider the energy in ocean waves to be a stored, moderately high-density, form of solar energy. Solar power levels, which are typically of the order of $100 \, Wm^{-2}$ (mean), can be eventually transformed into waves with power levels of over 100 kW per metre of crest length.

Waves are characterised by their wave length, L, wave height, H, and wave period, T. The size of the waves generated by any wind field depends upon three factors: the wind speed; its duration; and the 'fetch' or distance over which wind energy is transferred into the ocean to form waves (Figure 8.5).

Waves located within or close to the areas where they are generated are called 'storm waves'. They form a complex, irregular sea. However, waves can travel out of these areas with minimal loss of energy to produce 'swell' waves, at great distances from their point of origin.

Although the continental shelf results in a large loss of power, the UK is attractively situated with respect to wave energy. In addition to being surrounded by very stormy waters, it lies at the end of a long fetch (the Atlantic Ocean) with the predominant wind direction being towards the UK. The country therefore benefits from both storm and swell waves.

Larger waves contain more energy per metre of crest length than small waves. It is usual to quantify the power of waves rather than their energy

Figure 8.5 Characteristics of a monochromatic wave

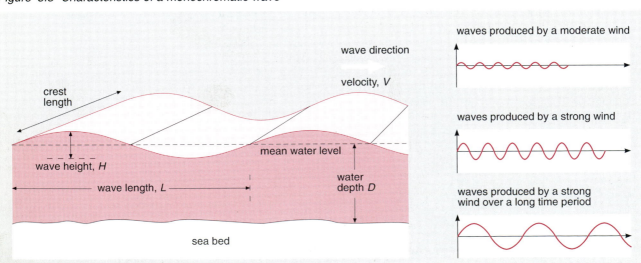

content. The power P (in kilowatts per metre) in an idealised ocean wave is approximately equal to the square of the wave height H (m) multiplied by the wave period T (s). (See Box 8.1.) The exact expression is the following:

$$P\ (\mathrm{Wm^{-1}}) = \frac{\rho g^2 H^2 T}{32\pi}$$

where ρ is the density of water and g is the acceleration due to gravity.

TYPICAL SEA STATE

A typical sea state is actually composed of many individual components, each of which is like the idealised, 'monochromatic' wave described above. Each has its own properties, i.e. its own period, wave height, and direction. It is the combination of these waves that we observe when we view the surface of the sea, and the total power in each metre of wave front of this irregular sea is of course the sum of the powers of all the components. It is obviously impossible to measure all the heights and periods independently, so an averaging process is used to estimate the total power.

By deploying a wave-rider buoy it is possible to record the variation in surface level during some chosen period of time. We can calculate the **significant wave height** H_s (Figure 8.6a), which is approximately equal to the average of the highest one-third of the waves (this generally corresponds to the estimation of wave height made by eye, since the smaller waves tend not to be noticed), and the **zero-up-crossing period** T_e, defined as the average time between upward movements of the surface through the mean level. For a typical irregular sea, the average total power is then given by:

$$P_s\ (\mathrm{kW\ m^{-1}}) = \alpha_s H_s^2 T_e$$

where α_s is a constant which conveys information about ρ, g and π and is equal to 0.49 kW s^{-1} m^{-3}.

Figure 8.6 (a) A typical wave record: H_s is the significant wave height and is defined as: $H_s = 4 \times$ root mean square of the water elevation. The mean level of the water corresponds to a surface level of 0 m. In this example $H_s = 3$ m. T_e is the 'energy period' or 'zero crossing' period and is the average time interval between successive zero values of the surface level when the surface level is moving upwards. Note that including the downward movements would give the half period. The successive upward movements are indicated with small circles. In order to obtain a reasonable average for T_e, it is best to count over 10 or more crossings. In this case there are 15 crossings in 150 seconds, so $T_e = 150/15 = 10$ seconds Then $P_s = 0.49 \times 3^2 \times 10$ kWm^{-1} = 44 kWm^{-1}

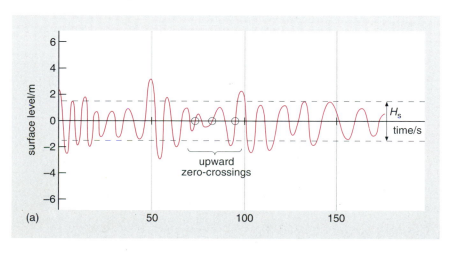

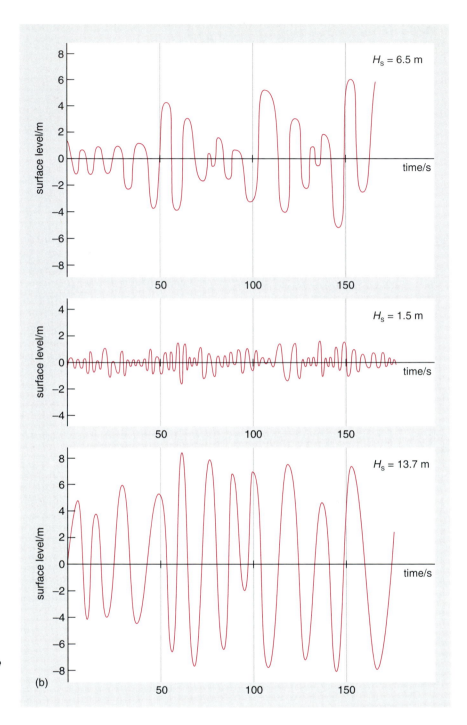

Figure 8.6(b) Three wave records are shown here for the same location but represent recordings taken on different days.

BOX 8.1: WAVE CHARACTERISTICS AND WAVE POWER

How much power is contained in ocean waves? The shape of a typical wave is described as *sinusoidal* (that is, it has the form of a mathematical *sine* function). The difference in height between peaks and troughs is known as the *wave height, H* and the distance between successive peaks (or troughs) of the wave is known as the *wave length, L*. Suppose that the peaks and troughs of the wave move across the surface of the sea with a *velocity V*. The time in seconds taken for successive peaks (or troughs) to pass a given fixed point is known as the *period, T*. (The frequency ϕ of the wave describes the number of peak-to-peak (or trough-to-trough) oscillations of the wave surface per second, as seen by a fixed observer, and is the reciprocal of the period. That is, $\phi = 1/T$.)

If a wave is travelling at velocity V past a given fixed point, it will travel a distance equal to its wave length L in a time equal to the wave period T. So the velocity V is equal to the wave length L divided by the period T, i.e. $V = L/T$.

Deep water waves

If the depth of water is greater than about half of the wave length, the velocity of a long ocean wave can be shown to be proportional to the period,

i.e. $V = \dfrac{gT}{2\pi}$

Here g is the acceleration due to gravity (9.81 m s^{-2}), leading to the useful approximation that the velocity in metres per second is about 1.5 times the wave period in seconds.

If both the above relationships hold, we can find the deep water wave length for any given wave period:

$L = \dfrac{gT^2}{2\pi}$

An interesting consequence of these results is that in the deep ocean the long waves travel faster than the shorter waves.

Intermediate depth waves

As the water becomes shallower, the properties of the waves become increasingly dominated by water depth. When they do reach shallow water, the properties of the waves are completely governed by the water depth, but in intermediate depths (i.e. between

$D = \dfrac{1}{2}L$ and $= \dfrac{1}{4}L$) the properties

of the waves will be influenced by both water depth D and wave period T.

Shallow water waves

As waves approach the shore, the sea bed starts to have an effect on their speed, and it can be shown that if the water depth D is less than a quarter of the wave length, the velocity is given by:

$V = \sqrt{gD}$

In other words, the velocity under these conditions is equal to roughly three times the square root of the water depth D: it no longer depends on the wave period.

Wave power

For waves in deep water, the power in watts delivered by each metre width of a wave is given by the following expression:

$P = \dfrac{\rho g^2 H^2 T}{32\pi}$

Using the value of $\rho = 1025$ kg m^{-2} for the density of sea water, and converting to kilowatts per metre, we obtain another useful approximation:

$P \approx H^2 T$

In other words, the power in kilowatts per metre width of wave front is approximately (within a few percent) equal to the square of the wave height $\times$ the period of the wave.

Real waves

The results in this box apply to an idealised wave, with a constant height and well-defined period and wave length (that is, a **monochromatic** wave). However, the wave patterns found in a real sea can be considered to consist of many such waves, each having a different period and height, superimposed upon one another.

VARIATIONS IN THE WAVE POWER AT ANY LOCATION

Sea level recordings made at different times or dates will of course differ, leading to different values of H_s and T_e. Suppose that each recording represents a time period of one-thousandth of a year. If we record the sea states at our chosen location over a whole year, characterising each of them by their values of H_s and T_e, we can build up a statistical picture of the distribution of wave conditions at our chosen location. This picture, or scatter diagram, gives the relative occurrences in parts per 1000 of the contributions of H_s and T_e. The example of a scatter diagram shown here (Figure 8.7) is from the north Atlantic and clearly shows that the waves at this location have a high average power density. In water 100 m deep at South Uist, for example, the average is around 70 kW m^{-1} (or 613 000 kWh m^{-1} per year), whereas closer to shore where the depth is 40 m, the average power density is about 50 kW m^{-1} (or 438 000 kWh m^{-1} per year). These figures are regarded as reasonably high, and indicate that the north Atlantic is indeed a valuable wave energy resource.

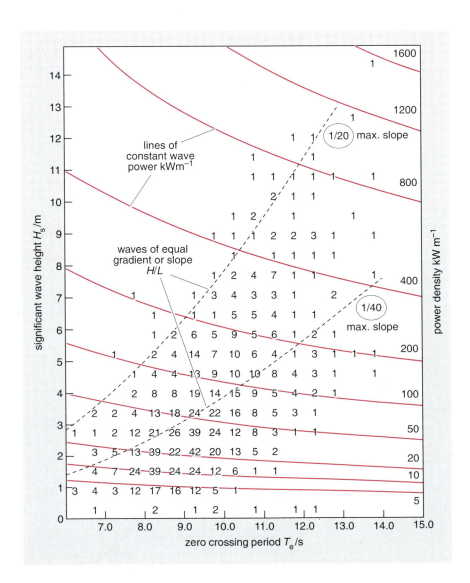

Figure 8.7 Scatter diagram of significant wave height (H_s) against zero crossing period (T_e) for 58°N 19°W in the mid-Atlantic. The numbers on the graph denote the average number of occurrences of each H_s, T_e in each 1000 measurements made over one year. The most frequent occurrences are at $H_s \sim 3$ m, $T_e \sim 9$ s

Figure 8.8 shows estimates of the wave power density at various locations around the world. The areas of the world which are subjected to regular wind fluxes are those with the largest wave energy resource. Wind from the Gulf of Mexico blowing in a predominantly north-easterly direction across the Atlantic has several thousand kilometres in which to transfer some of its energy into the Atlantic Ocean and hence form the large waves which arrive off the European coastline.

WAVE DIRECTION

It must be emphasised that so far we have only been concerned with waves in deep water – that is, where the depth exceeds about 50 m. More on this later. The direction of waves travelling in deep water is dictated by the direction of the wind which generated them. Waves can travel vast distances across open water without much loss of energy. At a given location we can therefore expect to observe waves arriving from different sources, and hence different directions. For example, we might see waves approaching us from the south-west which were produced by the wind crossing the Atlantic, but at the same time find that some waves have been generated by a storm to the north of our position. It is easy to imagine that the resulting wave pattern will be complex, and indeed such patterns are commonly observed. A representation of the average power as a function of direction at a given location can be given by a 'directional rose' (Figure 8.9): the length of each arrow indicates the relative contribution to the annual average power density at this location.

Figure 8.9 A directional rose for waves. The length of the arrow in each sector represents the average annual power in that sector. The orientation of the arrow indicates the direction from which the wave is coming. In this case most of the waves are coming from the South-West

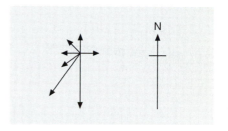

Figure 8.8 Annual average wave power in kilowatts per metre (kW m⁻¹) of crest length, for various locations around the world

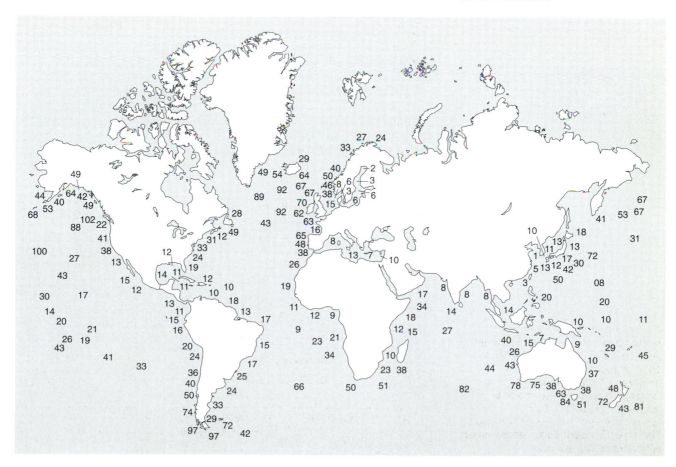

WHAT HAPPENS BENEATH THE SURFACE?

The surface profile of the ocean is the obvious evidence of waves, but we also need to understand the sub-surface nature of waves if we are to design schemes to capture energy from them (Figure 8.10).

Waves are composed of orbiting particles of water. Near to the surface, these orbits are the same size as the wave height, but the orbits decrease in size as we go deeper below the surface. The size of orbits decreases exponentially with depth.

To capture the maximum energy from a wave we could construct a device to intercept all of the orbiting parts of the wave. But this would probably be impractical and uneconomic, since the lowest orbits actually contain very little energy. Note, though, that this is a simplified view since some wave energy devices, such as the 'Bristol cylinder' (see Section 8.5 below), are able to follow the orbits. In deciding how deep a structure to extract wave energy should be, it is useful to know that 95% of the wave energy is contained in the layer between the surface and a depth h equal to a quarter of the wave length L (i.e. $h = L/4$). Note: this layer depth h should not be confused with the depth D of the sea bed.

MOVING INTO SHALLOW WATER

There are a few areas in the world where the shoreline is formed by a steep cliff which drops into reasonably deep water. These are the areas most suitable for shore-mounted wave energy converters because the incident waves have a large energy content. However, for most of the coastlines around the world the near-shore water is quite shallow.

As deep water waves approach land they often move into shallow water, and of course eventually run up the shore of the beach.

The waves gradually give up their energy as they move into shallow water. At first this is due to the frictional coupling between the deeper water particle and the sea floor, and this becomes significant when the water depth is less than a quarter of a wave length. The power loss can be several watts per metre of crest length, for every metre travelled in-shore.

This loss of energy is very important since it reduces the wave energy resource. Typically, waves with a power density of 50 kW m^{-1} in deep water might contain 20 kW m^{-1} or less when they are closer to shore in shallow water, depending on the distance travelled in shallow water and the

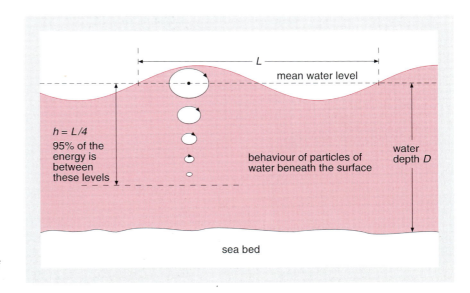

Figure 8.10 Behaviour of particles of water beneath the surface

roughness of the sea bed. However, storm waves are also attenuated and are therefore less likely to destroy shoreline devices.

There is a further mechanism for energy loss as the waves run up the beach: they form breaking waves, which are turbulent and energy-dissipating. We are usually happy to use breaking waves ('breakers') for leisure activities such as swimming and surfing, but they can be very damaging to structures and so should be avoided as far as wave energy converters are concerned. Structures must be carefully designed not only to perform their energy conversion tasks at an economic cost, but also to be able to withstand the worst wave loadings, which can add substantially to the capital cost.

REFRACTION

Ocean waves are refracted as they move through water of reducing depth. This is because, as is explained in Box 8.1, the velocity, V, of waves in shallower water which has a depth, D, less than a quarter of a wave length is given by $V = \sqrt{gD}$.

The effect of refraction, caused by the reducing depth and hence velocity, is gradually to change the direction of the propagation of the wave so that it will approach the shore almost at 90° (Figure 8.11).

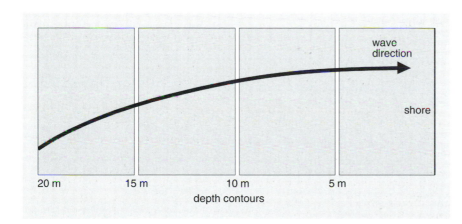

Figure 8.11 Refraction of waves. As the velocity of waves is dependent on water depth when the water is shallow compared to wave length, waves undergo refraction as they approach a shoreline. This diagram illustrates how this generally causes waves to approach a beach at right-angles to the shore

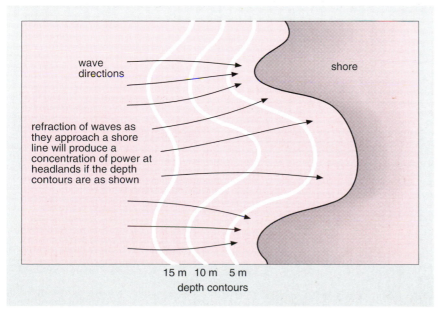

Figure 8.12 Concentration effects of refraction around a shoreline with headlands

Consider a shoreline with headlands (Figure 8.12). Notice how the varying water depth, as shown by the contours (white lines), causes refraction to occur. This concentrates the waves onto the headlands, and leaves the other areas with reduced wave density. Knowledge of the depth contours allows us to carry out a 'ray tracing' procedure, and with it we can identify those areas where the waves will be concentrated. This can also be useful for identifying the location of 'hot spots' of high energy concentration on the shoreline, and also for identifying some offshore positions which are likely to benefit from the concentrating effects of refraction. Clearly developing such sites, which have more energetic waves, would be more cost-effective.

8.5   WAVE ENERGY TECHNOLOGY

In order to capture energy from sea waves it is necessary to intercept the waves with a structure which can respond in an appropriate manner to the forces applied to it by the waves. If the structure is fixed to the sea bed or sea shore then it is easy to see that some part of the structure may be allowed to move with respect to the fixed structure and hence convert the wave energy into mechanical energy, which is usually then converted into electricity.

Floating structures can also be employed, but then a stable frame of reference must be established so that the 'active' part of the device moves relative to the main structure. This can be achieved by taking advantage of inertia, or by making the structure so large that it spans several wave crests and hence remains reasonably stable in most sea states.

The physical size of the structure of a wave energy converter is a critical factor in determining its performance. It is easy to estimate the appropriate size by considering the volume of water involved in the particle orbits. In most circumstances a wave energy converter will have to have a swept volume which is similar to this volume of water in order to capture all of the energy contained in the wave. A variety of wave energy concepts is discussed below, and the precise physical size and shape of each will be governed by its mode of operation, but as a rough guide the swept volume must be of the order of several tens of cubic metres per metre of device width.

Figure 8.13 Schematic representations of various types of wave energy converter (Source: based on Falnes, 1991)

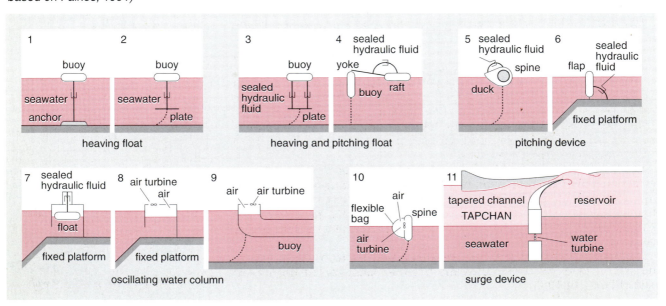

There are many different configurations of wave energy converter, and a number of ways of classifying them have been proposed. One schematic representation of the various types is shown in Figure 8.13.

Wave energy converters can also be classified in terms of their geometry and orientation, as either *terminators, attenuators* or *point absorbers.*

Terminator devices have their principal axis parallel to the incident wave front, whereas in *attenuators* the principal axis is perpendicular to the wave front. *Point absorbers* are devices which have small dimensions relative to the incident wave length, and are usually designed to absorb power from waves in the area surrounding them by the application of suitable control strategies such as latching, which holds the device until it interacts with the wave at the optimum moment.

FIXED DEVICES

Fixed sea-bed and shore-mounted devices are (with the exception of the Swedish FWPV and the Japanese Kaimei see Table 8.3, Section 8.9) the only wave energy converters to have been tested as prototypes at sea. Having a fixed frame of reference and with good access for maintenance, they have obvious advantages over the floating devices, but do operate in reduced wave power levels and may ultimately have a limited number of sites for future deployment.

The majority of devices tested and planned are of the **oscillating water column (OWC)** type. In these devices, an air chamber pierces the surface of the water and the contained air is forced out of and then into the chamber by the approaching wave crests and troughs. On its passage from and to the chamber, the air passes through an air turbine generator and so produces electricity. A novel axial flow air turbine, the Wells (Figure 8.14), which continues to rotate in one direction irrespective of whether the air flow is into or out of the chamber and has aerodynamic characteristics particularly suitable for wave applications, is used in and proposed for many OWCs. Box 8.2 explains the action of the Wells turbine.

Figures 8.16(a), (b) and (c) give a schematic representation of the operation of a fixed OWC. Floating OWCs work in a similar manner.

Air fills the upper part of the column. The water in the lower part of the column is coupled to the sea by an opening beneath the mean water level. As a wave approaches the structure, the internal water level is raised and this forces the air upwards and through the Wells turbine. The turbine extracts energy from the air flow and because it is rotating on the generator shaft, electricity is generated.

When the wave trough arrives, the internal water level falls, drawing air back into the column. The air passes through the Wells turbine in the opposite direction, but since the Wells is a 'self-rectifying' turbine, it continues to rotate in the same direction, energy is extracted from the air and is again used to generate electricity. Not all OWC designs employ Wells turbines. Figures 8.17 and 8.18 show the UK National Engineering Laboratory's proposed OWC which uses a system of rectifying valves and a more conventional air turbine.

The Kaimei, a converted barge fitted with a number of floating OWC devices, was first tested in Japan in 1977. Fixed oscillating water columns have been built in Norway, Japan, India and Scotland (see Duckers, 1989; Miyazaki *et al.*, 1991; Carmichael *et al.* (in press); Miyazaki, 1991 and Whittaker *et al.*, 1991) and are proposed for the Azores by the Portuguese (Falcao *et al.*, 1989).

Four fixed OWC type devices have been tested as prototypes in Japan. The first of these was constructed and tested at Sanze on the north-west coast of Japan in 1983.

Figure 8.14 (Below) The Wells turbine

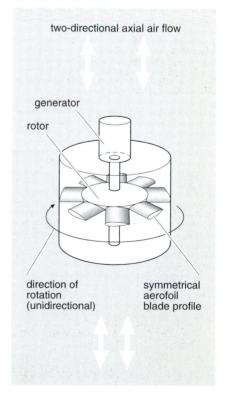

two-directional axial air flow

generator

rotor

direction of rotation (unidirectional)

symmetrical aerofoil blade profile

BOX 8.2: WELLS TURBINES

The Wells air turbine, invented by Prof Alan Wells, is self-rectifying, that is to say it can accept air flow in either axial direction. To achieve this, the aerofoil-shaped blade profile must be symmetric about the plane of rotation, untwisted and with zero pitch, i.e. the chord line must be in line with the plane of rotation. The vector diagram shows how this occurs. As the blade moves forward, the angle of attack, which is the resultant of the air flow velocity and the rotor velocity, is small and this produces a large lift force (FL). The forward component of FL provides the thrust which drives the blade forwards.

The Wells turbine operates in much the same way as would a horizontal axis wind turbine with symmetrical, untwisted blades and with zero pitch angle. Consider the nearest blade with air flowing in an upward direction (Figure 8.15(a)). If we now work in the frame of reference of the blade – we do this by making the blade appear to be stationary to us (even though it is moving) by considering the blade velocity vector to be in the opposite direction to the blade's direction of movement – we get Figure 8.15(b). Note that because the blade chord is in line with the plane of rotation the angle of attack α is the same as the relative wind angle ϕ referred to in Section 7.5. If we now combine these vectors we get Figure 8.15(c). From this diagram we can see that there will be a net forward force on the blade acting in the plane of rotation if

$$FL \sin \alpha - FD \cos \alpha$$

is greater than zero. The reaction components are of little interest but the rotor bearings must be capable of carrying these forces. If the net forward thrust is greater than zero, then the blade will be driven forwards and can usefully extract energy from the airflow.

The shape of the blade is extremely important here since it will dictate the values of the lift and drag coefficients C_L and C_D and hence the magnitude of the forward thrust.

There is a linear relationship between air flow and pressure drop for the Wells rotor rotating at a constant speed. This makes the Wells ideally suited to wave energy applications. A further beneficial characteristic of the Wells is that, at the sizes typically employed, it can rotate at high speed (1500 rpm–3000 rpm) and so the electrical generator can be attached directly to the shaft of the turbine, obviating the need for a gear box to raise the speed.

Figure 8.15 (a) Wells turbine: airflow and blade velocity; (b) Wells turbine: relative air velocity and lift and drag forces; (c) Wells turbine: forces in the plane of rotation

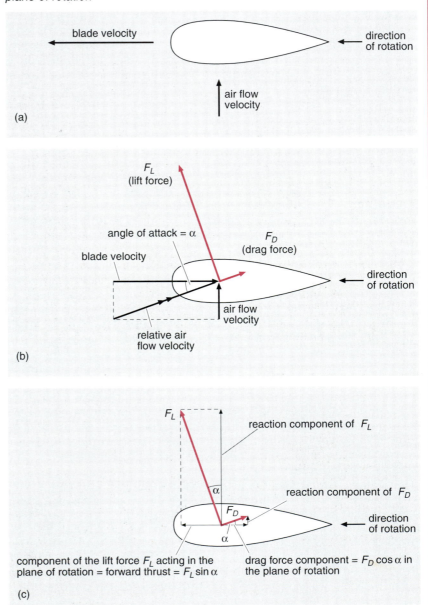

A more recently installed Japanese OWC is at Sakata, also on the north-west coast. Here an extension to the harbour wall has had one 20 m section constructed as a wave energy converter, again incorporating a Wells turbine rated at 60 kW. The Japanese believe that, by functioning as both a breakwater and an energy generator, the system is cost effective. They envisage further exploitation of such schemes when the results of this prototype are firmly established.

Other, non-OWC prototypes have been tested in Japan. A number have used a mechanical linkage between a moving component, such as a hinged flap, and the fixed part of the device. An example of this approach is the **pendulor**. (See Figure 8.19.)

The pendulor is a gate, hinged at the top, which is fitted one-quarter of a wave length from the back wall of a caisson. This is at the antinode (i.e. the point of maximum displacement of a series of standing waves) and so

Figure 8.16 (a), (b) and (c) Principle of operation of a shore-mounted OWC

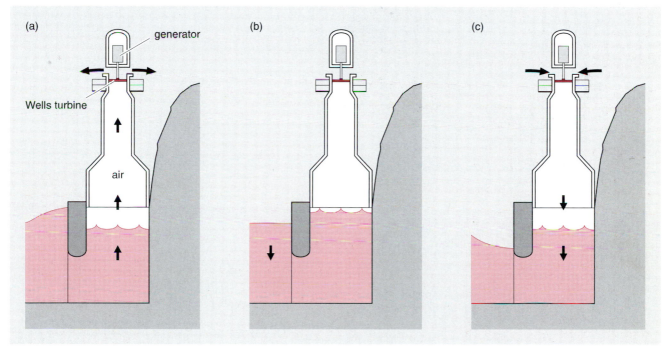

Figure 8.18 A breakwater consisting of a row of NEL OWC wave energy converters

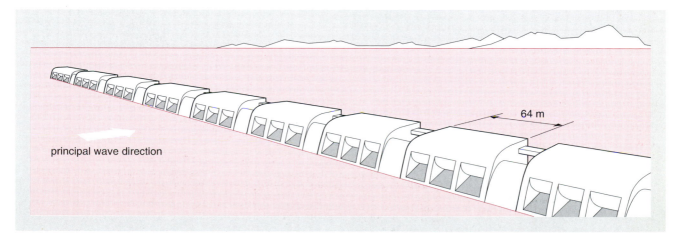

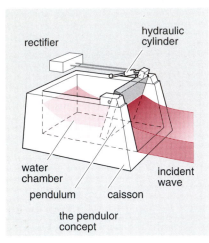

Figure 8.19 Japanese pendulor device

rectifier

hydraulic cylinder

water chamber
pendulum
caisson
incident wave

the pendulor concept

the gate is subjected to maximum movements resulting from the standing wave. Note that the gate can be located at the antinode for only one particular wave length. In the regions of Japan where pendulor devices have been tested, the seas generally have wave lengths close to the design wave length for much of the year.

Energy is extracted from the movement of the gate by a push–pull hydraulic system. Two examples with nominal power outputs of 5 kW have been operational on Hokkaido, Japan since the early 1980s.

The Norwegian OWC (see Figure 8.16) was a multi-resonant oscillating water column (MOWC) designed and manufactured in 1985 by Kvaerner Brug, one of Norway's leading engineering companies. It was located on the same island as the TAPCHAN prototype. The oscillating water column chamber was set back into a cliff face which falls vertically to a water depth

Figure 8.17 The proposed UK National Engineering Laboratory (NEL) Oscillating Water Column wave energy converter. This uses a system of rectifying valves to make the air flow in a single direction, so a conventional air turbine can be used

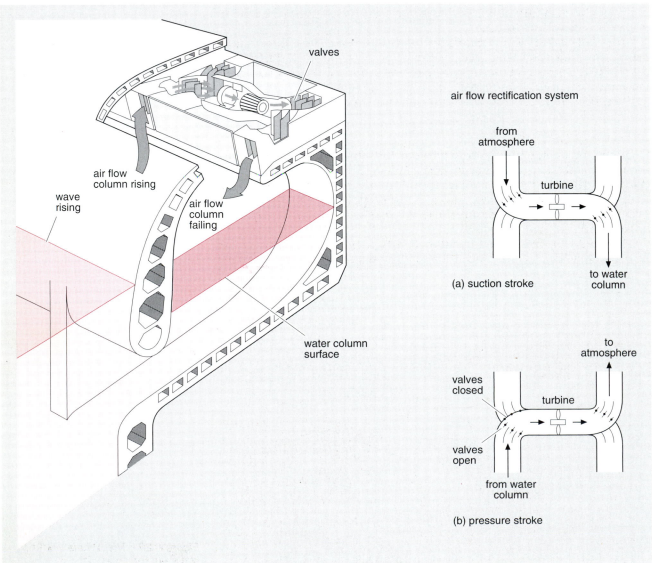

valves

air flow rectification system

from atmosphere

turbine

to water column

(a) suction stroke

air flow column rising
air flow column failing
wave rising

water column surface

to atmosphere

valves closed
turbine
valves open

from water column

(b) pressure stroke

of 60 m. Setting back the column produced two harbour walls at the entrance to the device, which had the effect of broadening the frequency response curve for the water column, allowing the system to absorb energy over a wider frequency band. The oscillating air flow was fed through a 2 m diameter Wells turbine rotating within the speed range 1000–1500 rev/min. The turbine was directly coupled to a 600 kW generator, and the output passed through a frequency converter before being fed to the grid. The performance exceeded predictions and provided electricity at relatively low cost.

However, two severe storms in December 1988 tore the column from the cliff, and to date the system has not been replaced. Future designs would be much more robust, and would probably involve setting the column into the body of the cliff, as has been done with the small UK OWC on the island of Islay in Scotland, as already described in Section 8.1. The Islay OWC has been set into a natural narrowing gully in the rocks and so is able to benefit from the tapered channel effect.

As we have seen, shore-mounted devices often have to be located in shallow water and so have a lower wave power density incident upon them. They have the advantage of being closer to a grid and more easily maintainable. In addition, the sea bed attenuates storm waves which could otherwise destroy the turbine.

Their only other major drawback is that of geographical location: to optimise output, they need to be positioned in an area of small tidal range, otherwise their performance may be adversely affected. Mass production techniques are unlikely to be totally applicable to shore-mounted schemes, as site-specific requirements will demand a tailored design for each device.

FLOATING DEVICES

Floating wave energy conversion devices include the **Clam** and **Duck** from the UK, and floating OWCs such as the **Whale** and the **Backward bent duct buoy (BBDB)** from Japan. These should be able to harvest more energy than fixed, on-shore devices, since the wave power density is greater offshore than in shallow water and there is little restriction to the deployment of large arrays of such devices.

The Whale and BBDB are illustrated in Figures 8.20 and 8.21. These floating OWC designs have been tested at model scale and the Japanese

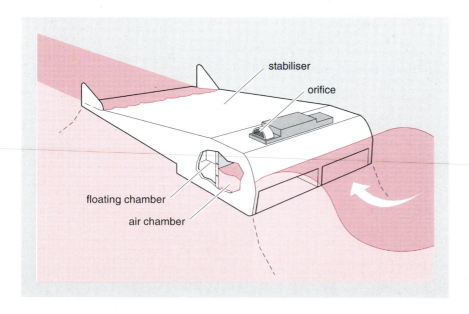

stabiliser

orifice

floating chamber

air chamber

Figure 8.20   The 'Whale' floating wave energy converter

would like to take the Whale version to a full-scale prototype. A rather massive structure is required to provide a reasonably stable frame of reference, but since the concept incorporates uses such as a breakwater and leisure provision in addition to the generation of electricity, the research team believes that the Whale will prove cost-effective.

The circular Clam consists of 12 interconnected air chambers, or cells, arranged around the circumference of a toroid (see Figure 8.22). At full scale this would be 60 m or so in diameter, and would be deployed in deep water (40–100 m). Each cell is sealed against the sea by a flexible reinforced rubber membrane; the device floats in deep water. Waves cause the movement of air between cells. Air, pushed from one cell by the incident wave, passes through at least one of the 12 Wells turbines on its way to fill other cells. As the air system is sealed, this flow of air will be reversed as the positions of wave crest and trough on the circle change.

The Edinburgh Duck concept (Figure 8.23), conceived by Professor Stephen Salter, was originally envisaged as many cam-shaped bodies linked together on a long flexible floating spine which was to span several kilometres of the sea. More recently, interest has centred on the case of a

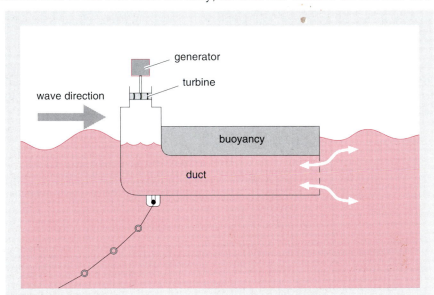

Figure 8.21   The Backward Bent Duct Buoy (BBDB)

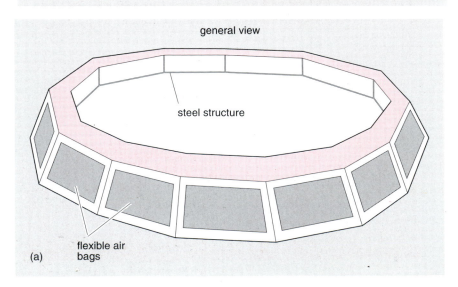

Figure 8.22a   General layout of the circular Clam

single Duck, which would demonstrate the technology at full scale and which, because it would operate as a point absorber, should be more

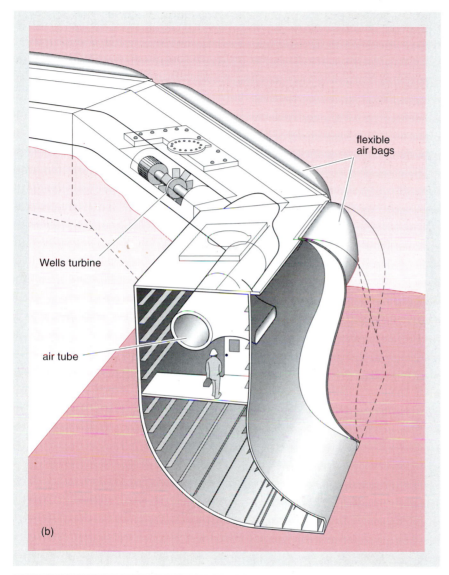

(b)

Figure 8.22b Cross-section of the circular Clam

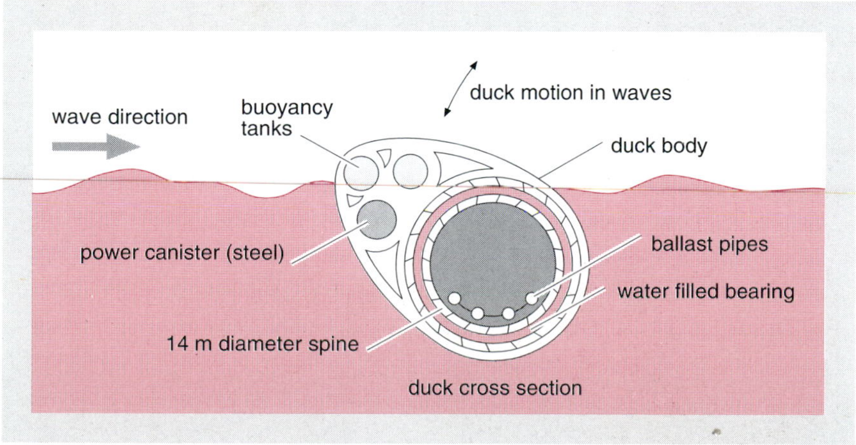

Labels in figure 8.22b:
- flexible air bags
- Wells turbine
- air tube

Figure 8.23a The Edinburgh Duck wave energy converter

Labels in figure 8.23a:
- wave direction
- buoyancy tanks
- duck motion in waves
- duck body
- power canister (steel)
- ballast pipes
- water filled bearing
- 14 m diameter spine
- duck cross section

efficient. The Duck was designed to match the orbital motion of the water particles that was discussed earlier. This matching can be nearly 'perfect' at one wave frequency and the efficiency in long waves can be improved by control of the flexure of the spine through its joints. The concept is theoretically one of the most efficient of all wave energy schemes, but it will take some years to develop fully the engineering necessary to utilise this concept at full scale. In Figure 8.24, the approximate energy capture efficiency of the NEL OWC, Duck and Clam wave energy converters is plotted against wave period T_e. These results are based on experimental data (Thorpe, 1992).

Figure 8.23b A scale model of the Duck being tested in Loch Ness

Figure 8.24 Comparisons of energy capture efficiency of NEL OWC, Duck and Clam wave energy converters

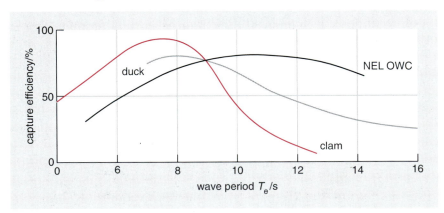

WAVE ENERGY RESEARCH ACTIVITY AROUND THE WORLD

JAPAN

Currently, Japan has the most substantial wave energy research programme, with many teams working on a variety of projects, some of which have been mentioned. Further details can be found in Miyazaki, Hotta *et al.*, 1991, Miyazaki, 1991 and Kondo, 1993. One of the most interesting new developments involves the use of focusing devices, consisting of shaped plates two metres beneath the water surface, which concentrate the waves towards the centre of a circle. A sea trial is proposed.

NORWAY

Important work is continuing on various ways of improving wave energy capture, including Budal's proposal to use rotating cylinders as a means of optimising the capture of a 'Bristol cylinder' type wave energy converter (see below). Rotating the cylinder in one direction increases its effective size and improved energy capture can be obtained. Rotating the cylinder in the opposite direction decreases its effective size, reduces energy capture, and can be used to protect the device in storm conditions.

Twin, or duplex, linked OWCs are also being studied in Norway as they may have a wider frequency response than single OWCs.

UNITED KINGDOM

In addition to the UK wave energy projects that have already been mentioned, other UK wave energy research projects include the Bristol cylinder, and the pitching and surging FROG.

The Bristol cylinder (Figure 8.25) is a submerged cylinder which follows the orbital water paths of the waves but is constrained by mooring cables attached to the sea floor. A number of sea bed mounted hydraulic pumps locate the cylinder and extract energy from its orbital motion which is excited by the waves. The hydraulic power take-off can be used to control the motion of the cylinder and to damp this motion for maximum energy extraction.

The pitching and surging FROG (Figure 8.26), developed by Professor French and his colleagues at Lancaster University, is a reaction wave energy converter which achieves energy-absorbing behaviour by the movement of internal inertial mass. Hence it is a compact structure which does not require a large spine to provide a stable frame of reference.

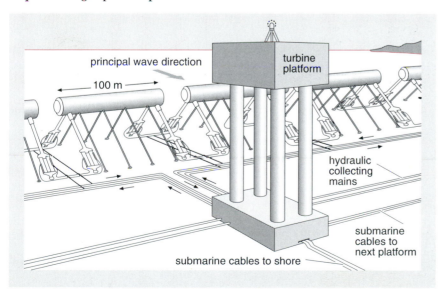

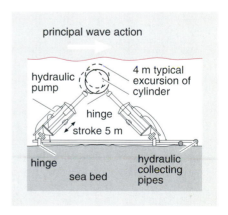

Figure 8.25 The Bristol cylinder wave energy converter

Some other devices in the early stages of research in the UK include Retzler's cylinder turbine, being researched at City University (Webb, 1992); Edinburgh University's 'Mace' design (Figure 8.27); the Applied Research and Technology (ART) steel OSPREY, a bottom-standing OWC being planned as a 2 MW pilot plant (Figures 8.28 and 8.29); and the Ecovision Lilypad (Figure 8.30).

Figure 8.26 The pitching and surging Frog wave energy converter

Figure 8.27 Edinburgh University's 'mace' wave energy converter ('belofram' is a rolling seal)

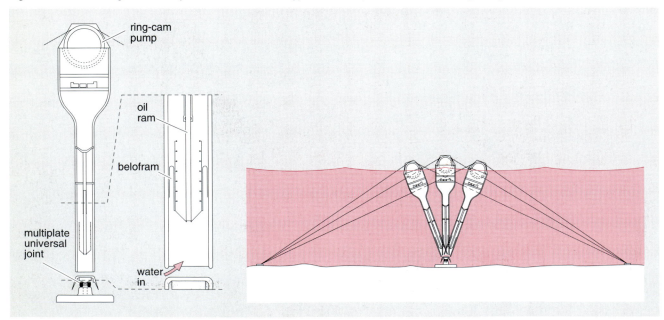

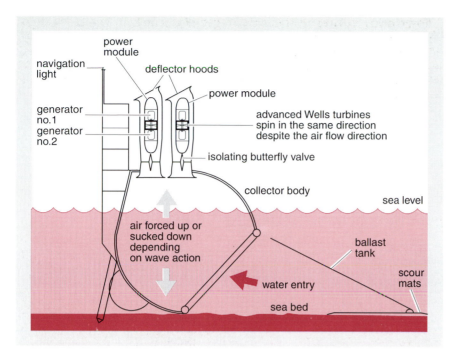

Figure 8.28 (Above) ART's OSPREY bottom standing OWC (OSPREY stands for Ocean Swell Powered Renewable Energy)

Figure 8.29 Artist's impression of the ART OSPREY

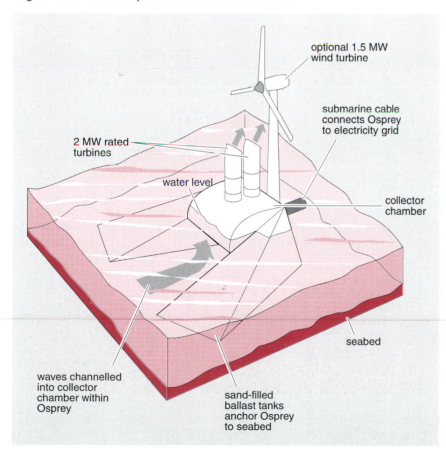

Figure 8.30 Ecovision Lilypad wave energy converter

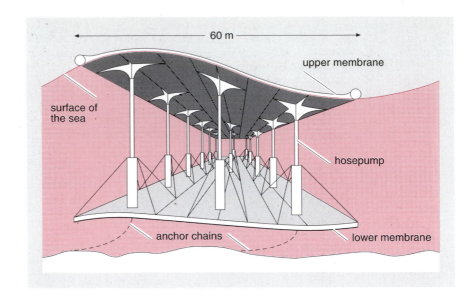

Figure 8.31 (Right) Cross-section through Indian breakwater OWC

Figure 8.32 (Below) Tethered buoy wave energy converter

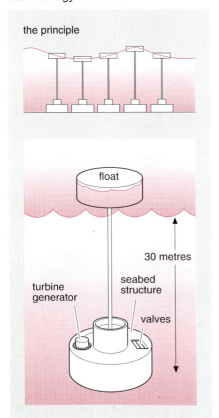

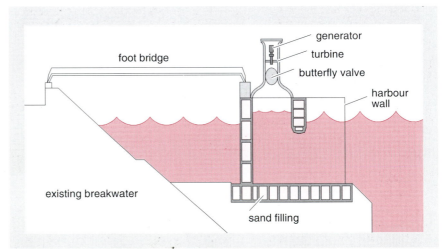

Figure 8.33 (Below) Swedish hosepump wave energy converter

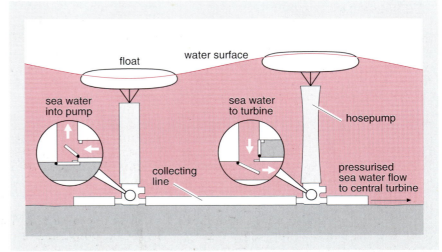

CHINA

Wave energy activity is developing in China; several papers were presented at the 1991 Japanese Symposium (Miyazaki *et al.*, 1991 and Kondo, 1993). Much of the Chinese work is linked to Japan, either in concept or by the exchange of ideas and staff. Some of the work concentrates on navigation buoys, some on theoretical modelling, but one group has deployed a small shoreline OWC of about 8 kW installed capacity in the Pearl River estuary. A 5.3 W navigation buoy based on the Backward Bent Duct Buoy (see Figure 8.21) has also been tested on the Pearl River.

INDIA

Trials of a multi-resonant OWC device, installed in a breakwater and employing a 2.0 m diameter Wells turbine driving a 150 kW induction generator (Figure 8.31), have commenced off the Trivandrum coast. As the cost of the breakwater is shared between the harbour wall and the power plant, the cost of electrical production may be economically attractive. The device is expected to deliver an average of 75 kW from April to November and 25 kW from December to March.

Since the annual average wave power density along the Indian coast is only 5 to 10 kW per metre, it is perhaps surprising to see such research and development activity. However, many more harbours are planned on the Indian coastline and this has led to consideration of the potential application of OWC wave energy converters.

DENMARK

Research effort in Denmark includes work on a tethered buoy system, as illustrated in Figure 8.32. The floating buoy responds to wave activity by pulling a piston in a sea bed unit. This piston pumps water through a submerged turbine. An array of these buoys could be deployed and arranged to have an integrated output. There have been some difficulties with seals on the prototype, but these should be overcome with further development.

SWEDEN

A concept similar to the Danish buoys has been investigated in Sweden, but using reinforced rubber hose as both the tether and pumping mechanism (Figure 8.33). The reinforcing cords in the hose are arranged at a carefully chosen angle to the main axis of the hose. As the buoy rises with a wave, the hose is stretched and the cord angle changes in such a way that it causes the internal volume of the hose to be reduced. This raises the pressure of the working fluid (sea water) contained within the hose. The working fluid is thus pumped into a high pressure reservoir where it will subsequently be used to generate electricity.

More recently, a floating wave power vessel (FWPV) has been tested off the west coast of Sweden. This steel vessel resembles a floating TAPCHAN in that waves run up a sloping ramp and are collected in a raised internal basin. The water flows from the basin back into the sea via low-head turbines. This device is not sensitive to tidal range, and by varying its ballast the device can be tuned to different wave heights.

PORTUGAL

An OWC with a capacity of 500 kW to 1 MW is planned for the island of Pico, part of the Azores, in the north Atlantic. This will be located on the sea bottom, close to the rocky shoreline. A Wells turbine will be incorporated into the column.

SPAIN

A Spanish project utilising the hose pump and buoy approach is being undertaken as part of a programme called OLAS-1000, in which an array of seven hose pumps is being designed to produce 1000 kW.

REPUBLIC OF IRELAND

The west coast of the Republic of Ireland is particularly suitable for the deployment of both shore-mounted and offshore wave energy converters. Research in Ireland has concentrated on OWCs, and on other forms of self-rectifying air turbines as alternatives to the Wells turbine.

UNITED STATES

A small amount of work has been carried out in the USA. Government support has been modest, but commercial organisations have promoted several concepts to preliminary design and model testing stage. These have included a scheme based on the OWC and also the Seamill concept, which resembles an OWC but has a float on top of the internal water surface. The motion of this float is used to provide hydraulic power which drives a turbine and hence generates electricity. Tank tests are being conducted, and a 200 kW prototype is planned (Bueker, 1991).

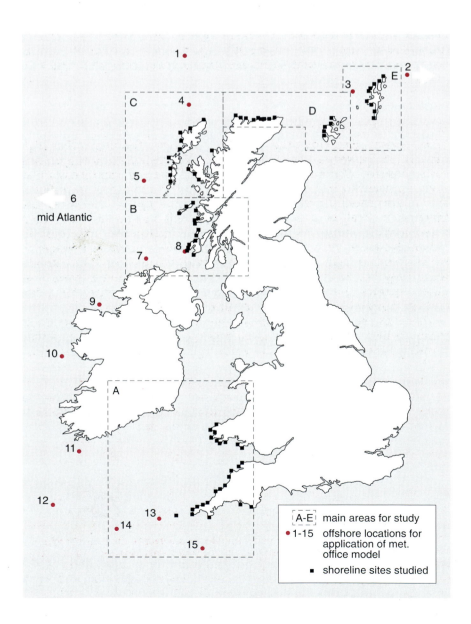

Figure 8.34 Wave power sites studied in the DTI review of wave energy

8.6 RESOURCES

Wave power resources (in annual average kW per metre of crest length) around the world were shown in Figure 8.8. The total wave energy resource around Britain and Ireland has been estimated at an annual average power of 120 GW, equivalent to 1050 TWh year^{-1} (ETSU, 1985).

It has been estimated (ETSU, 1992) that the total annual average wave power along the north and west side of the United Kingdom (i.e. from the south-west approaches to Shetland) ranges from less than 30 GW (equivalent to 260 TWh year^{-1}) at the shoreline to about 80 GW (equivalent to 700 TWh year^{-1}) in deep water.

Figure 8.34 shows the areas of British waters and coastline included in the ETSU 1992 assessment of the UK wave energy resource, and Table 8.2 gives a breakdown of the resource at different water depths.

The proportion of this resource that could actually be harnessed to produce electrical power depends on various practical and technical constraints. ETSU (1992) estimates that the 'technical resource' (i.e. the resource technically available regardless of cost) is between 7 GW and 10 GW annual average power (equivalent to 61 to 87 TWh year^{-1}), depending on the water depth. The proportion of the technical resource that could be harnessed economically depends, of course, on the cost of wave energy relative to other energy sources (see Sections 8.7 and 8.10 below).

8.7 ECONOMICS

Wave energy, like many other renewable energy technologies, has high capital costs. However, shoreline devices are expected to have low operating costs: those for offshore devices will be higher. The high capital costs arise from the need to build and deploy large structures to capture significant amounts of energy. On the other hand, the operating costs are low because there are no fuel costs, and operational, repair and maintenance costs together might amount to only a few (3 to 8) per cent of the capital cost per annum. However, there will be costs resulting from insurance requirements, which could be high at least in the early years when experience with the technology is limited. Wave energy technology, in common with most other renewable energy technologies, can only be economic if the capital cost per installed kW is less than about £1000 (1993 prices).

One consequence of high capital cost is a long payback period, and this seems to be a major drawback as far as government and commercial investors are concerned. But as wave energy, in common with most other

Table 8.2 The natural and technical wave energy resource for the UK

Water depth (m)	Average natural resource		Average technical resource	
	GW	TWh	GW	TWh
100	80	700	10	87
40	45	394	10	87
20	36	315	7	61
Shoreline	<30	<262	0.2*	1.75

*The technical shoreline resource is very dependent on details of the local shoreline structure, for example the nature and shape of the rock formations and of gullies and beaches.

(Source: Thorpe, 1992)

renewables, is an environmentally clean technology, it may be that the value of the output of wave energy converters should be enhanced with respect to electricity derived from some of the conventional sources.

As with other capital-based renewable energy sources, the cost of energy from wave energy converters is very dependent upon discount rates (see Table 8.1 and Figure 8.35). The power density of the resource, the local cost of conventional energy and the possibilities for secondary uses for the wave energy converters (such as breakwaters or leisure activities) are also important considerations. Clearly, these parameters vary from country to country, and even within a country. Assessments of the economic viability of wave energy schemes will therefore differ widely from site to site. It is clear, though, that predicted electricity costs from wave power devices, and in particular the clam and the shoreline OWC, are already approaching the costs of electricity from new coal powered stations, which would have to incorporate gas emission control systems to avoid excessive atmospheric pollution.

8.8 ENVIRONMENTAL IMPACT

Wave energy converters may be among the most environmentally benign of energy technologies because:

• they have little potential for chemical pollution. At most, they may contain some lubricating or hydraulic oil, which will be carefully sealed from the environment;

• they will have little visual impact except where shore-mounted;

• noise generation is likely to be low – generally lower than the noise of crashing waves. (However, there might be low-frequency noise effects on cetaceans, but this has to be confirmed.);

• they should present a small (though not insignificant) hazard to shipping;

• they should present no difficulties to migrating fish;

• floating schemes, as they are incapable of extracting more than a small fraction of the energy of storms, will not significantly influence the coastal environment. Of course, a scheme such as a new breakwater incorporating a wave energy device will provide coastal protection, and may result in changes to the coastline. Concrete structures will need to be removed at the end of their operating life.

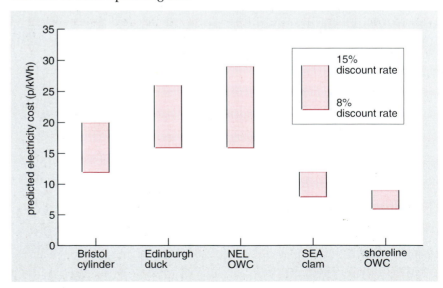

Figure 8.35 Summary of cost of electricity from wave power devices (Source: Thorpe, 1992)

8.9 INTEGRATION

Almost all wave energy schemes are designed to generate electricity. This electricity can be used directly but it is much more likely that the electricity will be fed into a grid.

WAVE ENERGY FOR ISOLATED COMMUNITIES

If the grid is small and serves a small remote community, great care must be taken in integrating the electrical output from the wave energy scheme into the grid. This care is needed because the output from the scheme will fluctuate wildly (except in the case of schemes such as the TAPCHAN) and may cause swings in voltage or frequency on the grid unless precautions are taken (Figure 8.36).

Many small communities depend on diesel generators for their electricity. The diesel generator is best run at a constant output close to its design capacity – say 50 kW. If this diesel unit is the sole source of electricity, the load from the grid should always be matched to 50 kW. Clearly, the consumers will cause the load to vary as they switch appliances on and off. To cope with this, a 'dump' load can be incorporated into the system. The diesel output voltage of 240 V a.c. rises if the load falls much below 50 kW – for instance at night when the demand is low. The grid line voltage also rises, and in order to protect other appliances and make use of the diesel output, a voltage sensor set at 250 V allows electricity to be sent to a 'dump' load consisting of electrical space and water heaters. When other appliances are switched on again, the line voltage falls and the dump load is disconnected.

In a similar way, the incorporation of a varying electrical output from a wave energy scheme into the grid can partially be accommodated by the use of such dump loads to stabilise the grid voltage (Figure 8.37). Note that a series of voltage sensors could be used to refine the control.

By careful overall design of an integrated scheme, a remote community could enjoy substantial gains in electricity supply from a wave energy scheme. The reduction in diesel oil consumption would be substantial, and since it is costly to transport diesel oil to remote locations, the cost savings could be large.

WAVE ENERGY FOR LARGE ELECTRICITY GRIDS

When the electrical outputs of several wave energy units are added together, the total output will be generally smoother than for a single unit. If we extend this to an array of several hundred floating devices, then the summed output will be smoother still. This happens to be less important if the electricity is to be delivered to national systems like those of the UK,

Figure 8.36 Integration of a wave energy/diesel system

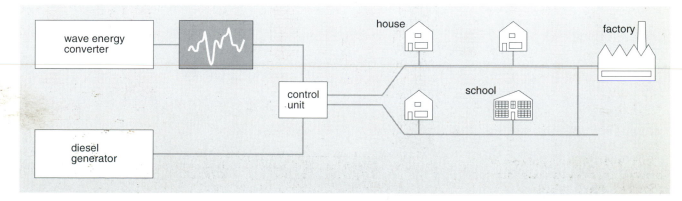

Figure 8.37 Use of voltage sensors and dump loads

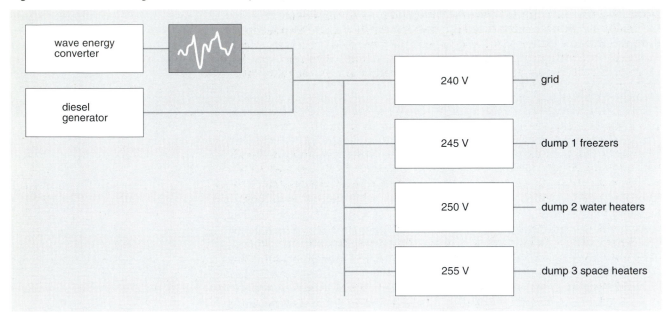

Figure 8.38 Electrical connections for an array of wave energy devices

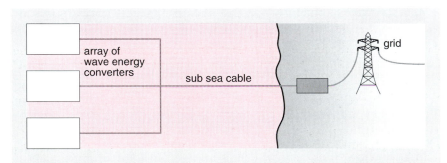

Figure 8.39 Seasonal availability of wave energy and electrical demand for the UK

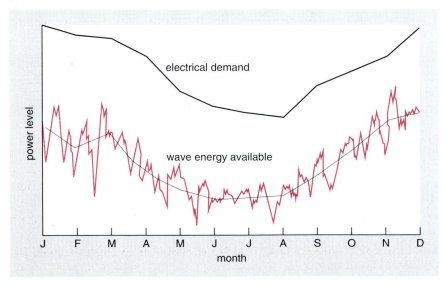

where in most locations the grid is 'strong' enough to absorb contributions from a fluctuating source. Figure 8.38 illustrates a typical scheme.

Finally, although we have dwelt upon short-term fluctuations of seconds or minutes, the wave resource also varies on a day-to-day and season-by-season basis. For the UK the seasonal variation is actually favourable, as the more energetic waves appear in the bad weather of winter when the electrical demand is greatest (Figure 8.39).

8.10 FUTURE PROSPECTS

The development of wave energy technology is a long-term process. It will take years of research and development to produce prototypes of some devices and refine the design of others. Further optimisation of the designs to improve their cost-effectiveness would need to be a part of these R&D programmes.

As Table 8.3 shows, a considerable number of prototypes have been already tested. The output rating of these has varied from the 50 W of the navigation buoys to a 600 kW OWC. Some of the prototypes have suffered setbacks whilst others have been very successful.

Some proposed future prototypes are listed in Table 8.4.

Wave energy is already being utilised experimentally in some parts of the world. Where a remote island has expensive conventional energy and a reasonable wave climate, it is likely that wave energy devices can be economically competitive.

THE DTI WAVE ENERGY REVIEW

As mentioned in Section 8.1, a review of wave energy commissioned by the Department of Trade and Industry was completed in 1992 by ETSU (Thorpe, 1992). It had the following aims:

- to review the technical feasibility, commercial viability and prospects for wave energy;

- to review the economic classification of wave energy technologies in order to determine whether they are 'economically attractive', 'promising but uncertain' or 'long shot'.

To carry out the review, five representative 'main devices' were selected: the SEA Clam, Bristol cylinder, Edinburgh Duck, NEL OWC and Shoreline OWC. This covered shoreline, small-scale offshore and large-scale offshore schemes. The review also included three newer devices which were examined in less detail: the Ecovision Lilypad; the Lancaster PS Frog; and the ART OSPREY.

All the devices reviewed are still at the research stage and require further R&D to establish their practicality and to improve confidence in cost and performance predictions.

In order to estimate the device generating costs, the Review assumed that, given sufficient R&D, the devices would prove technically viable and perform as predicted. In addition the following assumptions were included in the calculation of costs:

- Operation and maintenance costs were minimal, with no allowance for specialised equipment, maintenance facilities, repairs to civil structures, etc.

- The capital cost model allowed for savings associated with large-scale replication.

- Transmission costs excluded additional costs arising from the need for grid strengthening.

Table 8.3 Prototypes

Year	Type	Location	Owner	Installed capacity (kW)	Comments
1965	Navigation buoy OWC	Japan	Maritime agency	0.05	Several hundred now deployed around the coastline of Japan
1978–1986	Kaimei	Japan	IEA	375–1000	Vessel motion compromised the system performance. No further interest in energy testing but fundamental data on moorings and materials
1983	OWC	Sanze, Japan	Mitui and Fuji	40	Low output, decommissioned after one year
1983	Pendulor	Muroran, Japan	Muroran Institute of Technology	5	Still operational
1984	Kaiyo floating terminator	Okinowa, Japan	Institute of Ocean Environmental Technology	Not known	Research programme completed
1985	OWC	Toftestallen, Norway	Kvaerner Brug	600	Good performance. Destroyed by storms in December 1988
1985	TAPCHAN	Toftestallen, Norway	Norwave	350	Good performance, still operational
1985	Pendulor	Mashike, Japan	Mashike Port	5	Supplies hot water, still operational
1985	OWC	Neya, Japan	Taisei Corp.	40	Wells turbine driving a heat generating eddy current-type device. Tests finished in 1988
1988	OWC array	Kujukuri, Japan	Takenaka Komuten Co.	30	Array of 10 OWCs, with rectifying valves feeding a common high-pressure reservoir. Planned to continue until 1995
1989	Hinged flap	Wakasa Bay, Japan	Kansai Electric Power Co.	1	Under test
1989	Tethered float	Hanstholm, Denmark	Danish Wave Power aps	45	Problems with rubber seals. Further trials are planned
1989	OWC	Sakata, Japan	Port and Harbour Research Institute	60	The OWC is an integral part of a new harbour wall. Now operational
1991	OWC	Islay, UK	Queen's University, Belfast	75	Still operational. Over 1000 hours of testing
1991	OWC	Trivandrum, India	IIT Madras	150	Latest available information in 1992 was that device was nearing completion
1992	FWPV	West coast of Sweden	Sea Power AB	110	Successful operation, not sensitive to tidal range like TAPCHAN
1992	OLAS-1000	West coast of Spain	Union Fenosa, Madrid		Array of seven hose pumps/buoys
1995	OSPREY	UK	ART	2000	Pilot plant designed to operate near shore

• R&D costs to deployment stage were not included in capital costs.

• Several devices were optimised to reduce their costs and the modified designs were used in the economic assessment.

The results of the analysis based on these assumptions were summarised in Table 8.1 and in Figure 8.35. These show the DTI's predicted costs (based on 8% and 15% discount rates) for the cost of electricity from wave energy devices at the location of South Uist. In 1990 prices, the generating costs for the shoreline devices assessed in the Review were estimated to be 6 to 9 p kWh^{-1}, at 8% to 15% discount rates respectively. For the four offshore main devices, predicted electricity generating costs ranged from 8 to 16 p kWh^{-1} (at 8% discount rate) and 12 to 29 p kWh^{-1} (at 15% discount rate).

In the light of this Review the DTI considers that wave energy exploitation in the UK, utilising the devices considered, is unlikely to be economically competitive in the short term.

The various device teams generally assess their predicted costs to be less than the DTI's figures but are in broad agreement with the outcome of the review. They are seeking support for further R&D to reduce costs and hence make wave energy competitive in cost for the UK grid in the medium term.

8.11 CONCLUSION

Wave energy converters are being developed and tested in many countries. The TAPCHAN system and shore-mounted OWCs are simple and easily maintained. They could be economically attractive in some locations where diesel fuel supplies are expensive.

Table 8.4 Future prototypes

Type	Location	Owner	Installed capacity (kW)	Comments
OWC	Pico Island, Azores	Portugal	350–500	Currently at planning stages
Whale floating OWC	Japan	Japan Marine Science and Technology Centre	100–400	Funding requested from Japanese authorities
BBDB	Japan and/or Hawaii	Ryokuseisha Corp.	330	1:10 model tested at sea
Pendulor	Yagishiri, Japan	Muroran Institute of Technology	125	Three cells with a total frontage of 25 m used to provide heat
Clam	West coast of Scotland	Coventry University	2000	1:15 model tested in Loch Ness. Component development and theoretical modelling proceeding
TAPCHAN	Indonesia, Tasmania	Norwave	1000–1500	Under consideration
Seamill	California, USA	Hydropower Corp.	200	Early stages of planning
OWC	Scotland	UK Government	500–1000	Early stages of planning
TAPCHAN	Shetland, Scotland	Norwave/ACER/Shetland	3000	Funding requested
FWPV	Sweden	Sea Power AB	1000	Under discussion
Hose pump	Greek island	Technocean	600, 1000, 6000	Phased programme to install array of hose pumps/buoys

In the longer term, a major contribution from wave energy could probably come from arrays of floating offshore or near-shore devices if the development of new, low-cost concepts is successful. Additional research and development work will be needed, however, to bring these to the prototype stage. The size of the UK wave energy resource is such that it is likely to be of importance in the longer term.

THE CURRENT STATE OF PLAY

Although projects in Japan and Norway have continued, the UK has now demoted wave energy research to the 'long shot' category, and is just maintaining a watching brief on developments.

In March 1994 the Department of Trade and Industry announced that 'no further commitments' were to be undertaken, as this technology has limited potential to contribute commercially to energy supplies in the next few decades'.

Offshore/deep-sea wave power, which had already been assessed as economically unattractive by previous UK reviews was clearly out of the race, but further work on in-shore and on-shore systems was also now to be abandoned.

This came as something of a blow to the project team working on the follow up to the £1m 75kW Islay prototype: a 600kW version had been proposed and EC support had been obtained. But is was conditional on matching UK funding being found and it had been proposed that at least some would come from the DTI.

The EU-backed 2M OSPREY unit, developed by Applied Research and Technology (ART), for a site off Dounreay may survive the DTI's policy change, since it had obtained significant independent industrial support. A first prototype was constructed and towed to site in 1995, but was unfortunately damaged by strong seas before its ballast tanks could be flooded. ART are planning a second prototype for probable deployment in 1996.

ART have also indicated that they might be able to provide the necessary matching support for the Islay project, so that it too could receive EU funding. So some UK projects still seem likely to go ahead.

REFERENCES

Bueker, R. A. (1991) 'Project Seamill' in *Oceans 91 Symposium*, Honolulu, Hawaii.

Carmichael, A. D. and Falnes, J. 'State of the art in wave power recovery' in Seymour, R. J. (ed.) *Ocean Energy Recovery: The State of the Art* (in preparation).

Duckers, L. J. (ed.) (1989) *Wave Energy Devices*, Meeting C57, Coventry, The Solar Energy Society.

Duckers, L. J., Lockett, F. P., Loughridge, B. W., Peatfield, A. M., West, M. J. and White, P. R. S. (1992) 'Towards a prototype floating circular Clam energy converter', *Proceedings of World Renewable Energy Congress II*, September 1992, Pergamon Press.

ETSU (1985) *Wave Energy: The Department of Energy's R&D Programme 1974–1983*, ETSU Report R26, March.

Falcao, A. F., Gato, L. M. C., Teresa Pontes, M. and Sarmento, A. J. N. A. (1989) 'Wave energy project in Portugal: OWC demonstration plant', *Proceedings of ISES Solar World Congress*, Kobe, Japan, Pergamon Press.

Falnes, J. (1991) 'Ocean wave energy', *Energy Policy*, October.

Garratti, G., Lewis, A. and Howett, D. (ed.) (1993) 'Wave energy R&D', Proceedings of a workshop held at Cork, October 1992, published by CEC, EUR15079EN (1993).

IMI (1991) *Wave Energy*, One day meeting S027, Institution of Mechanical Engineers, London.

Kondo, M. (1993) *Proceedings of International Symposium on Ocean Energy Development*, 26–27 August, Muroran Institute of Technology, Japan.

Lewis, A. (1985) *Wave Energy*, Evaluation for CEC, Graham & Trotman Ltd.

Miyazaki, T. (1991) 'Wave energy research and development in Japan' in *Oceans 91 Symposium*, Honolulu, Hawaii.

Miyazaki, T. and Hotta, H. (eds) (1991) *Third Symposium on Ocean Wave Energy Utilization*, Tokyo, Japan. (Largely in Japanese.)

Open University (1992) S330 *Waves, Tides and Shallow Water Processes*, Pergamon/Open University.

Salter, S. H. (1989) 'World progress in wave energy – 1988', *International Journal of Ambient Energy*, Vol. 10, No. 1.

Thorpe, T. W. (1992) *A Review of Wave Energy*, ETSU Report R72, December.

Twidell, J. and Weir, A. (1986) *Renewable Energy Resources*, E. and F. Spon.

Webb, J. (1992) 'Swirling cylinders spin power beneath the waves', *New Scientist*, 12 December.

Whittaker, T. J. T., Long, A. E., Thompson, A. E. and McIlwaine, S. J. (1991) *Islay Gully Shoreline Wave Energy Device Phase 2: Device Construction and Pneumatic Power Monitoring*, Contractor Report to ETSU (ETSU WV1680).

FURTHER READING

For those who wish to find out more about wave energy, some suggested publications include:

Duckers, L. J. (ed.) (1989) *Wave Energy Devices*, Meeting C57, The Solar Energy Society, Coventry.

A series of papers from the main UK proponents of wave energy covering many of the main wave energy devices, and aspects such as the available wave energy resource.

Genus, A. (1992) 'Political construction and control of technology: wave power renewable energy technologies', *Technology Analysis and Strategic Management*, Vol. 5, No. 2.

An interesting paper which analyses wave energy from a sociological point of view and dwells on the policy aspects of the subject.

Institution of Mechanical Engineers (1991) *Wave Energy*, Mechanical Engineering Publications Ltd.

A series of papers presented at a seminar on wave energy held at the Institution of Mechanical Engineers in November 1991. Includes overview papers on such topics as the UK wave energy resource, wave energy research and development around the world, the PS Frog, CLAM and NEL OWC wave energy converters and the Wells turbine.

Kondo, H. (1993) *Proceedings of International Symposium on Ocean Energy Development*, Muroran Institute of Technology, Muroran, Hokkaido, Japan.

The proceedings of this symposium include some 21 papers on extracting energy from ocean waves.

Wave energy topics include bottom-standing, floating, and OWC wave energy converters. Also included are papers on newer types of wave energy converter.

This was the most recent document on wave energy available at the time of writing.

Open University (1992) S330 *Waves, Tides and Shallow Water Processes*, Pergamon/Open University.

This text is from an Open University third level course unit on oceanography. The section on wave energy provides a detailed description of ocean waves and the physics underlying them.

Ross, D. (1995) *Power from the Waves*, Oxford University Press.

A very readable and informative account of the subject by a professional journalist who has bought his earlier book '*Energy from the waves*' up to date. It is highly recommended to those interested in wave power.

Salter, S. (1989) 'World progress on wave energy – 1988', *International Journal of Ambient Energy*, Vol. 10, No. 1.

Though slightly dated, this paper provides a useful overview of current developments in wave energy around the world.

Salter, S. (1992) 'Wave energy – some questions and answers', *International Journal of Ambient Energy*, Vol. 14, No. 1.

Adopts an interesting approach to explaining many aspects of wave energy in an easy-to-understand manner.

Thorpe, T.W. (1992) *A Review of Wave Energy: Volume 1: Main Report*, ETSU Report R72.

An ETSU report covering the current status of wave energy and its potential for electricity generation in the UK.

The review of wave energy described in the report was carried out under the guidance of an independent Steering Committee and with considerable involvement from the wave energy community. As explained in the text, it includes an assessment of the UK offshore and shoreline wave energy resource, together with a detailed analysis of five representative devices. The economic potential of the various wave energy devices was analysed to identify the most promising wave energy converters and to identify areas of future research required to develop commercially viable devices.

Twidell, J. W. and Weir, A. D. (1986) *Renewable Energy Resources*, E. F. Spon.

Chapter 12 on Wave Energy covers the physical principles of wave energy and wave energy conversion and provides a good introduction to this aspect of the topic.

GEOTHERMAL ENERGY

9.1 INTRODUCTION AND SUMMARY

Geothermal energy results from heat stored in rock by the earth's natural heat flow which (a) is highly concentrated in 'high-enthalpy' regions at volcanically active plate margins (see Section 9.3); (b) is sufficiently concentrated in the 'low-enthalpy' resources of sedimentary basins with shallow rock strata that conduct a low amount of heat energy; or (c) is potentially concentrated enough for exploitation in certain granite areas where heat may be extracted by opening up pre-existing joints of hot dry rocks.

The word **enthalpy** occurs frequently in this chapter. It means the total thermodynamic heat content of a system.

The technology to exploit high-enthalpy resources is well established and continues to improve. In the early 1990s, 6 GW of installed geothermal electric capacity existed worldwide, a figure that is thought likely to double by the end of the decade.

Superheated dry steam resources are mostly easily converted into useful energy, generally producing electricity which is cheaper than that from conventional sources. Many wet steam fields are also attractive economically, even though the water must be turned into steam, sometimes at the surface. The process of turning the water into steam is called **flashing**. In each case, the steam is used to drive electricity-generating turbines – though geothermal energy can also be used for other purposes.

New technologies have been developed to produce power at competitive rates from lower grade, but still high-enthalpy, resources and are likely to become more important in the future. The design of plant is critically dependent on the exact nature of the water resources and, in turn, this affects the cost of producing electricity because imposing limits on environmental pollution, or reinjecting the water after use, adds to operational costs.

Geothermal energy for direct use in industrial processes, space heating, and domestic and leisure applications has been developed on the flanks of high-enthalpy zones, and also to exploit low-enthalpy resources in sedimentary basins. 'Doublet' systems (involving both production and injection wells) are designed to have a lifetime of 30–50 years and the efficiency of energy extraction can be improved with the use of geothermal heat pumps. Overall, the economics of using low-enthalpy resources are marginal when seen in direct competition with conventional energy sources, but their attractiveness lies in the unspent fossil fuels they save. A conservative estimate is that 4 GW thermal is currently being exploited; however, low-enthalpy resources are not suitable for electricity production.

Hot dry rock (HDR) technology has been the subject of much recent research. Although vast potential resources exist, the technology has yet to be fully developed. Experiments in opening up the pre-existing joints of hot dry rocks have only been partially successful; lower resistances to the flow of liquid, better underground heat transfer surface areas and lower water loss rates need to be developed, along with a better understanding of sub-surface stress regimes.

Geothermal research in the UK has identified large warm water 'reserves' in several sedimentary basins which currently (1994) are deemed unprofitable to develop, given their poor location with respect to existing heat loads. Similarly, large areas could be developed by hot dry rock methods if and when technological and economic circumstances improve. Geothermal energy in all forms is relatively benign and by saving on the consumption of other fuels is generally regarded as having a positive environmental impact. Factors such as environmental taxes on relatively unclean energy and/or further escalation of fossil fuel prices would probably stimulate additions to the existing small-scale demonstration projects in the UK, at Southampton and Penryn, the first of which is described in Section 9.2 below.

Following this introductory case study (Section 9.2) we examine the earth's geothermal resources, early attempts at exploiting them (Section 9.3) and their physics and chemistry (Section 9.4). The technologies of extracting energy from wet and dry steam fields and hot dry rocks are covered in Section 9.5. Sections 9.6 and 9.7 concentrate on the environmental and economic implications, and we conclude with a look at the potential resources in sedimentary basins and granite zones in the UK (Section 9.8).

9.2 CASE STUDY: THE SOUTHAMPTON GEOTHERMAL DISTRICT HEATING SCHEME

The city of Southampton is located in one of several areas in the United Kingdom known to be underlain by rock strata containing hot water. The Southampton scheme demonstrates how it is possible to make direct use of the hot water beneath the city. This scheme was not designed to produce electricity for the National Grid – it simply serves the city by providing a supply of hot water. It provides a useful case study within the UK of a small-scale geothermal scheme which actually works.

A single geothermal well, a kind of borehole, was drilled in 1981 to a depth of just over 1800 m beneath a city centre site in Southampton (Figure 9.1). Near the bottom of the hole, a 200 million year old geological formation, known as the Sherwood Sandstone, containing water at 70 °C was encountered. This particular formation is both porous and permeable, meaning

that it holds water and can transmit considerable volumes. It therefore behaves like a giant rigid sponge, and is a good geothermal **aquifer** (see Section 9.4). The fluid itself contains dissolved salts and, as in most geothermal areas, is more accurately described as **brine**. Within the aquifer the brine is pressurised and so it rises unaided to within 100 m of the surface. However, a turbine pump, located at 650 m depth in the well, brings the hot brine to the surface where its heat energy is exploited.

The brine passes through coils in a heat exchanger where much of its heat energy is transferred to clean water in a separate district heating circuit. Heat exchangers operate on a similar principle to many domestic hot water tanks in which a working fluid (also usually water passing through a coil of pipes in the tank) is used to heat water for washing.

In this case, the cooled geothermal working fluid (brine) is discharged

via drains into the Southampton marine estuary. The heated 'clean' water is then pumped around a network of underground pipes to provide central heating to radiators, together with hot water services, in several city centre buildings.

The Southampton geothermal well was originally drilled by the former Department of Energy as an exploration borehole with an agreement that the City Council would develop an extensive district heating scheme, beyond the limits shown in Figure 9.1, if the well was successful. It was hoped that a sustainable brine flow of 30 litres per second would be obtained whereas, in fact (as explained in Section 9.8 below), only 12 litres per second can be exploited if the scheme is to secure a planned 20 year lifetime. So a scaled-down district heating network was installed and since January 1989 the Civic Centre, Central Baths and several other buildings within a 2 km radius of the well have been connected to the geothermal resource. There are plans to add several other buildings to the scheme and this will be complemented by improved heat extraction from the geothermal brine, using heat pump technology.

The geothermal heat supply, originally 1 megawatt thermal (1 MW$_t$), has now been increased to 2 MW$_t$ using heat pumps, and this is capable of satisfying the base load demand. However, during periods of higher demand, fossil fuel boilers augment the plant's heat output to a maximum of 12 MW$_t$. A further technical aspect is the inclusion of a diesel generator which supplies electrical power to the various circulation pumps and the monitoring equipment. Heat from the generator is fed directly into the district heating scheme and any surplus power is sold to Southern Electric plc – an interesting contribution to combined heat and power (CHP) concepts.

The Southampton Geothermal Heating Company, which now runs the operation, charges the modest sum of about 1 penny per kWh of heat energy consumed, but it must be emphasised that neither the drilling nor the testing costs were met by the company, and the scheme is still partly financed as an EC demonstration project. Moreover, most similar geothermal district heating schemes require the drilling and operation of a waste brine reinjection well. Nevertheless, the scheme is seen as environmentally acceptable, and it is saving the equivalent of over a million cubic metres of gas (or 1000 tonnes of oil) a year.

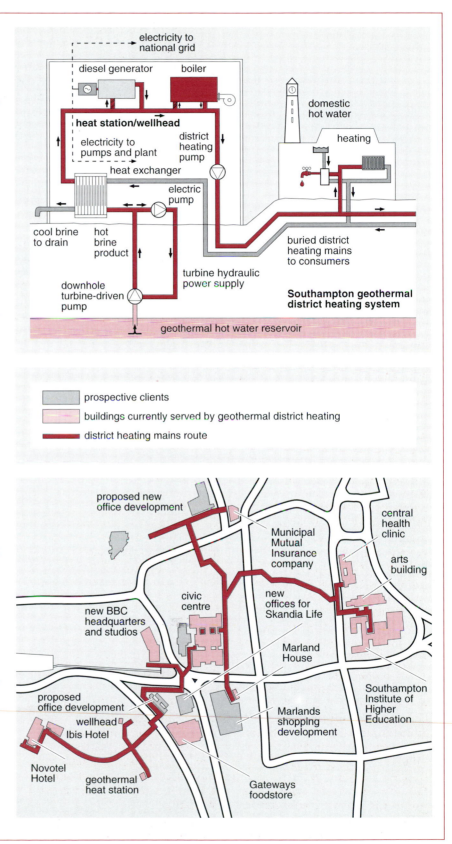

Figure 9.1 The Southampton geothermal district heating system showing technology schematic and layout of plant on the ground

9.3   GEOTHERMAL ENERGY – AN OVERVIEW

THE MINING OF GEOTHERMAL HEAT

In the continuing search to find cost-effective forms of energy that neither contribute to global warming nor threaten national security, geothermal energy has become a significant player. Geothermal is the only form of 'renewable' energy that has its ultimate source within the earth. Yet the amount of heat flowing through the earth's surface, 10^{21} joules per annum $(J\ a^{-1})$, is tiny in comparison with the massive $5.4 \times 10^{24}\ J\ a^{-1}$ solar heating of the earth which also drives the atmospheric and hydrological cycles. Fortunately, there are many places where the earth's heat flow is sufficiently concentrated for us to exploit natural geothermal resources suitable for electricity generation, in the form of steam and hot water (150–200 °C) which is available in shallow rocks. These are the so-called 'high-enthalpy' resources. By 1990 world electrical power generating capacity from these geothermal resources had reached almost 6 gigawatts electrical (6 GW_e), a small but significant contribution to energy needs in some areas (Table 9.1). About a further 4 gigawatts thermal (4 GW_t) had also been harnessed in non-electrical, direct use applications, principally space heating, agriculture, aquaculture and a variety of industrial processes. Some of these applications occur outside high-enthalpy regions where geological conditions are nevertheless suitable for pumping warm water (less than 100 °C) to the surface: these are 'low-enthalpy' resources.

Table 9.1   World geothermal resources exploited in the early 1990s

	Electrical (MW_e)	Direct use (MW_t)
Americas		
USA	2800	160
Mexico	680	8
El Salvador	95	–
Nicaragua	35	–
Western Pacific		
Japan	228	970
China	11	610
Taiwan	3	10
Philippines	894	–
Indonesia	140	–
New Zealand	280	200
Europe, Asia, Africa		
Former Soviet republics	11	340
Iceland	39	480
France	4	270
Italy	545	210
Hungary	–	375
Turkey	21	70
Azores	3	–
Kenya	45	–
Others	–	420
TOTALS	5834	4123

Adapted from Garnish *et al.*, 1992, where original source references are quoted.

In all these circumstances, but particularly in low-enthalpy applications, heat is being removed faster than it is replaced and the concept of 'heat mining' is appropriate. Although geothermal resources are non-renewable on the scale of human lifetimes and, strictly, fall outside the remit of this book, they are included because they share many features with the true 'renewable' resources. For example, geothermal is a natural energy flow rather than a store of energy, as are fossil fuels and nuclear fuels. At one time, it was thought that many high-enthalpy resources were indeed renewable, in the sense that they could be exploited indefinitely, but experience of declining temperatures in producing steam fields and simple calculations of heat supply and demand show that heat is being mined on a non-sustainable basis. (See Box 9.1)

THE EARTH AS A HEAT ENGINE

Heat flows out of the earth because of the massive temperature difference between the surface and the interior: the temperature at the centre is around 7000 °C. So why is the earth hot? There are two reasons: first, when the earth formed from accreting particles around 4600 million years ago the interior was heated rapidly, largely because the kinetic energy of accreting material was converted into heat; second, the earth contains tiny quantities of long-lived radioactive isotopes, principally thorium 232, uranium 238 and potassium 40, all of which liberate heat as they decay. Cumulative heat production from these radioactive isotopes (approximately 5×10^{20} J a^{-1} today) amounts to about half the surface heat flow, but the exponential decay laws for radioactivity imply that heat production was about five times greater soon after the earth formed. Heat is transferred through the earth principally by convection, involving motion of material mainly by creep processes in hot deformable solids. This is a very efficient heat transport process resulting in rather small variations of temperature across the depth of the convecting layer. But close to the surface, in fact across the

---

BOX 9.1: EXTRACTION AND RECHARGE RATES

The following simple calculations show the order of magnitude discrepancy between commercial geothermal extraction rates and thermal recharge by the earth's natural heat flow. They demonstrate that it is *not the heat flow but the heat store that is being exploited*, even in high-enthalpy areas.

(a)   The currently exploited area of Tuscany, northern Italy, totals about 2500 km^2. This is a generous estimate which ignores the fact that the active fields are only a small sub-set of this. The average heat flow is about 200 mW m^{-2}, so the total heat flow through this surface is 500 MW$_t$. The region currently supports generating capacity of >400 MW$_e$; at a mean generating efficiency of 13%, this requires 3000 MW$_t$. Moreover, steam supplies have been proved to support an electricity generating capacity of 1500 MW$_e$ which would require an input of approximately 12 000 MW$_t$. So the ratio of forecast commercial production rate to thermal recharge is at least $\dfrac{12\ 000\ \text{MW}_t}{500\ \text{MW}_t}$, or 24:1.

(b)   In the Imperial Valley of California, USA, a commercial lease of 4 km^2 is expected to support generating capacity of some 40 MW$_e$ (which will require at least 250 MW$_t$). Assuming an average heat flow of 200 mW m^{-2}, the thermal recharge is less than 1 MW$_t$, giving a ratio of 250 MW$_t$/1 MW$_t$ or 250:1.

(c)   The well field in Krafla, Iceland, covers an area of 4.5 km^2. It currently generates some 30 MW$_e$ implying heat extraction of some 200 MW$_t$. To recharge the field on a sustainable basis, the heat flow would have to be 45 W m^{-2}. Again, this is much higher than could be expected even in this very active area.

Of course, there *is* recharge by the earth's natural heat flow but a thermally depleted reservoir may take many tens or even hundreds of years to regenerate. However, in regions of large geothermal resources this is generally a minor problem.

outer 100 km or so of the earth, the material is too stiff to convect because it is colder, so heat is transported by conduction and there are much larger increases of temperature with depth (i.e. larger 'thermal gradients': see Section 9.4). This rigid outer boundary layer, or shell, is broken into a number of fragments, the lithospheric plates, which move around the surface at speeds of a few centimetres a year, in concert with the convective motions beneath (Figure 9.2(a)). The kinetic energy of the plates is thus derived from internal heat production and so the earth is operating as a heat engine.

From our point of view, it is at the boundaries between plates, mainly where they are in relative extension or compression, that heat flow reaches a maximum (Figure 9.2(b)). Here, the heat energy flowing through the surface is typically around 300 milliwatts per square metre (300 mW m^{-2}) as compared with a global mean of 60 mW m^{-2}.

Figure 9.2 (a) Map of the earth's lithospheric plates indicating the relative speed of motions by the size of the arrows (generally 1–10 cm per annum). Large dots indicate major high-enthalpy geothermal energy producing areas

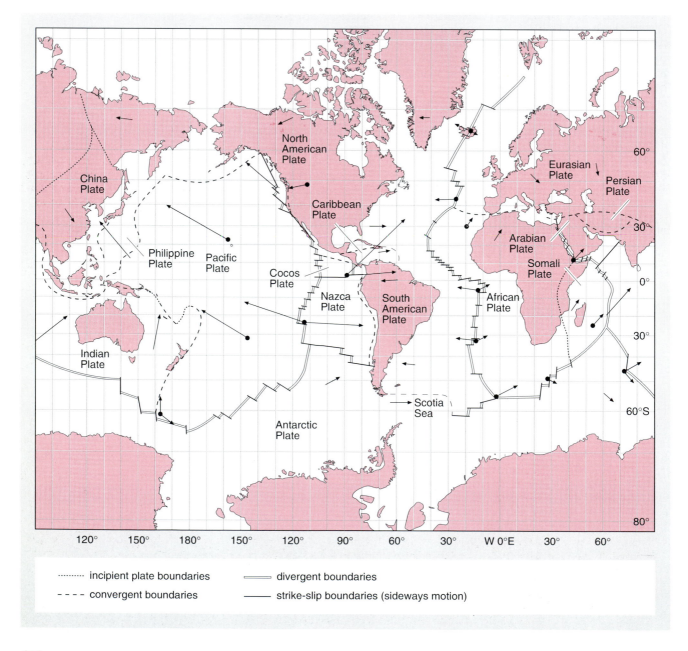

.... incipient plate boundaries   ════ divergent boundaries

‒ ‒ ‒ ‒ convergent boundaries   ——— strike-slip boundaries (sideways motion)

However, along plate margins heat flow is even more concentrated locally because rock material reaches the surface in a molten form, resulting in volcanic activity that is often spectacular. Storage of molten, or partially molten, rock at about 1000 °C just a few kilometres beneath the surface strongly augments the heat flow around even dormant volcanoes. These high heat flows result in high thermal gradients, really the hallmark of high-enthalpy areas, which are further enhanced in the upper regions by induced convection of hot water. Over geological periods of time, this high heat flow has resulted in large quantities of heat being stored in the rocks at shallow depth, and it is these resources that are mined by geothermal exploitation and commonly used for electricity generation. In areas of lower heat flow, where convection of molten rock or water is reduced or absent, temperatures in the shallow rocks remain much lower, and the resources are suitable only for direct use applications. So we see that high-enthalpy resources, including all those currently exploited for geothermal electric power (see Figure 9.2(a)), are confined to volcanically active plate margins. Boiling mud pools, geysers and volcanic vents with hot steam are characteristic features of such geothermal areas.

A HISTORICAL PERSPECTIVE

The exploitation of geothermal resources dates back to Roman times, with early efforts made to harness hot water for medicinal, domestic and leisure applications. Roman spa towns in Britain generally sought to exploit natural warm water springs with crude but reliable plumbing technology. The early Polynesian settlers in New Zealand, who lived for 1000 years undisturbed by European influence until the eighteenth century, depended on geothermal steam for cooking and warmth, and hot water for bathing, washing and healing. Indeed, the healing properties of geothermal waters are renowned throughout the modern world and have important medical benefits.

Figure 9.2 (b) Heat flow map of the world (smoothed) showing that zones of highest heat flow occur over active ocean-ridges and some volcanically active continental margins (convergent plate boundaries)

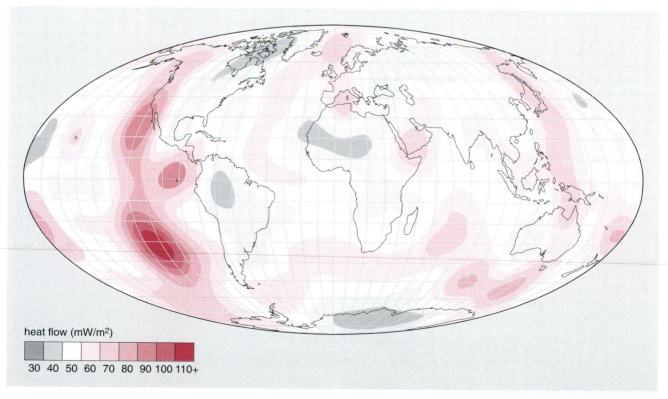

heat flow (mW/m²)

30 40 50 60 70 80 90 100 110+

By the nineteenth century, progress in engineering techniques made it possible to observe the thermal properties of underground rocks and fluids, and to exploit these with rudimentary drills. In Tuscany, natural thermal energy was used in place of wood for processing boron and ammonium compounds; indeed, the original use of geothermal fluids in Tuscany was as a source of boron and the heat was incidental. An ingenious steam collection device, the *lagone coperto* ('covered pool'), sparked a rapid growth in the Italian chemical industry, resulting in flourishing international trade. The generation of electrical power started in 1904, fostered by Prince Piero Ginori Conti, and 1913 saw the arrival of the first 250 kW power plant at Larderello, marking the start of new industrial activity (Figure 9.3). Today the Larderello power station complex (Figure 9.4) has a capacity exceeding 400 MW and a rebuilding programme is in progress that will take the capacity to 885 MW.

The Wairakei field in New Zealand was the second to be developed, but not until the early 1950s, and it was followed closely by the Geysers field in

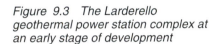

Figure 9.3 The Larderello geothermal power station complex at an early stage of development

Figure 9.4 The Larderello 3 station which produces 120 MW from six turbine units. The geothermal pipeline network consists of an inner steel pipe lagged with asbestos fibre and covered with aluminium plate

northern California where the first electricity was generated in 1960. With an installed capacity of 2800 MW, the Geysers field is now the most extensively developed in the world: indeed, there is evidence that it has been over-developed.

With the notable exceptions of Italy, the most volcanically-active European country, and Iceland, which lies on the volcanic ridge of the central Atlantic, the chief geothermal nations are clustered around the Pacific rim. Japan, the Philippines and Mexico have shared in recent technological developments; the installations in El Salvador and Nicaragua are strategically vital to the economies of those nations, and several other countries, notably Costa Rica, Ecuador and Chile, will shortly join the list of geothermal electricity producers.

Meanwhile, schemes making direct use of geothermal heat, for district heating and agricultural purposes, have advanced, with Japan, China, the former Soviet republics (mainly Kamchatka in the Far East, and the Georgia and Dagestan regions between the Caspian and Black Seas), Hungary and Iceland being the major producers. Some of the most fascinating new technology has been developed in France and other western European nations, including the UK.

9.4 THE PHYSICS OF GEOTHERMAL RESOURCES

PRIMARY INGREDIENTS

Geothermal resources of most types must have three important characteristics, as shown in Figure 9.5: an **aquifer** containing water that can be accessed by drilling; a **cap rock** to retain the geothermal fluid; and a **heat source**.

Figure 9.5 Simplified schematic cross-section to show the three essential characteristics of a geothermal site: an aquifer (e.g. fractured limestone with solution cavities); an impermeable cap rock to seal the aquifer (e.g. clays or shales); and a heat source (e.g. crystallising granite). Steam and hot water escape naturally through faults (F) in the cap rock, forming fumaroles (steam only), geysers (hot water and steam), or hot springs (hot water only). The aquifer is unconfined where it is open to the surface in the recharge area, where rainfall infiltrates to keep the aquifer full, as indicated by the water table just below the surface. The aquifer is confined where it is beneath the cap rock. Impermeable crystalline rocks prevent downward loss of water from the aquifer

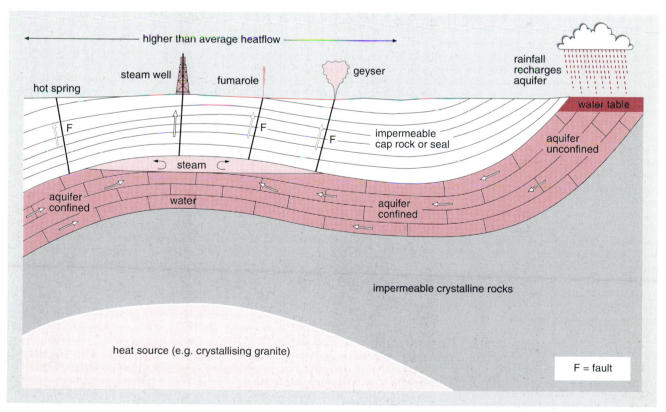

First, what is an aquifer? Natural aquifers are porous rocks that can store water and through which water will flow. **Porosity** refers to the cavities present in the rock, whereas the ability to transmit water is known as **permeability**. A geothermal aquifer must be able to sustain a *flow* of geothermal fluid, so even highly porous rocks will only be suitable as geothermal aquifers if the pores are interconnected. In Figure 9.6, rocks (a) and (c) are porous and likely to be highly permeable, whilst (b) and (d) have low porosity and permeability. Example (e), however, has low permeability despite its high porosity whereas solution cavities developed in (f) give high porosity and permeability. Permeability due to fracturing, as in (g), is particularly important in many geothermal fields.

The hydraulic conductivity (K_w) of a rock is a good measure of its permeability. Darcy's Law states that the speed (v) of a fluid moving through a porous medium is proportional to the pressure gradient causing the flow:

$$v = K_w \frac{H}{L} \qquad (1)$$

Here, H is the effective head of water driving the flow, and is measured in metres of water. The pressure gradient, or hydraulic gradient (H/L) is the change in this head per metre of distance L along the flow direction.

The volume of water (Q) flowing in unit time through a cross-sectional area A m^2 is v times A. So Darcy's Law may also be written:

$$Q = K_w A \frac{H}{L} \qquad (2)$$

and K_w may be interpreted as the volume flowing through one square metre in unit time under unit hydraulic gradient. Some values of hydraulic conductivity for different rocks are given in Table 9.2. Notice that the

Table 9.2   Typical porosities and hydraulic conductivities

Material	Porosity (%)	Hydraulic conductivity (m day^{-1})
Unconsolidated sediments		
Clay	45–60	$<10^{-2}$
Silt	40–50	10^{-2}–1
Sand, volcanic ash	30–40	1–500
Gravel	25–35	500–10 000
Consolidated sedimentary rocks		
Mudrock	5–15	10^{-8}–10^{-6}
Sandstone[a]	5–30	10^{-4}–10
Limestone[a]	0.1–30	10^{-5}–10
Crystalline rocks		
Solidified lava[a]	0.001–1	0.0003–3
Granite[b]	0.0001–1	0.003–0.03
Slate	0.001–1	10^{-8}–10^{-5}

(a) The larger values of porosity and hydraulic conductivity apply to heavily fractured rocks and, for limestones, may also reflect the presence of solution cavities (see Figure 9.6(f)).

(b) Granite is a coarsely crystalline rock that has cooled down slowly from a melt at depth in the earth. Such rocks are generally non-porous and impermeable, but occasionally they may be fractured and acquire limited permeability.

highest values occur in coarse-grained unconsolidated rocks, such as volcanic ashes which are particularly common in volcanic areas, but that values are also quite high in some limestones and sandstones. These are good aquifer rocks, with high permeability, and it is important to remember that fracture permeability is often important in geothermal aquifers (see Figure 9.6(g)).

Of course, in a confined aquifer such as in Figure 9.5, the fluid pressure beneath the extraction point is high because there is a relatively impermeable cap rock, or seal, to prevent fluid escape upwards. Mudrocks, clays and unfractured lavas are ideal. The importance of cap rocks was discovered by the Italians in the early 1980s when exploring for geothermal resources in a very obvious place, the flanks of Vesuvius volcano. Unfortunately, only small amounts of low pressure fluid were discovered because the volcanic ashes that form its flanks are apparently quite permeable throughout. This illustrates the point that, over time, alteration of the uppermost deposits or overlying sediments by hot water and steam can create clays or deposit salts in pore spaces, which produces a seal over the aquifer. Thus, many geothermal fields eventually develop their own cap rocks. This helps to explain why the youngest volcanic areas, like Vesuvius, are not necessarily the most productive from a geothermal viewpoint.

The third prerequisite for exploitable geothermal resources is the presence of a heat source. In high-enthalpy regions, abundant volcanic heat is available, but in low-enthalpy areas the heat source is less obvious. In such regions there are two main types of resource: (a) those located in deep **sedimentary basins** where aquifers carry water to depths where it becomes warm enough to exploit, and (b) those located in **hot dry rocks** where natural heat production is high but an artificial aquifer must effectively be created by fracturing the rocks in order that the geothermal resource may be exploited. Let us now look at each type of resource in more detail.

BOX 9.2: CHEMICAL FEATURES OF GEOTHERMAL WATERS

Figure 9.7 illustrates how the chemistry of geothermal solutions can vary according to distance from a magmatic heat source.

Gases escaping from solution in the magma include hydrogen chloride (HCl), sulphur dioxide (SO_2) and carbon dioxide (CO_2), while the rainwater contains dissolved CO_2 from the atmosphere (mainly as bicarbonate, HCO_3^-). HCl from the magma reacts with surrounding rocks and forms neutral chloride groundwaters (containing mainly sodium chloride, NaCl, and also some potassium chloride, KCl); some of these waters escape at the surface as chloride hot springs.

SO_2 reaches the surface to form the acid sulphate hot springs and the acid waters attack the rocks ('acid alteration' on Figure 9.7). The steam-heated geothermal waters nearest the surface are richer in sulphate than those beneath, which have mixed with the deeper chloride-rich solutions. There is progressive increase in bicarbonate content with distance from the magmatic centre, because of mixing with CO_2-saturated rainwater.

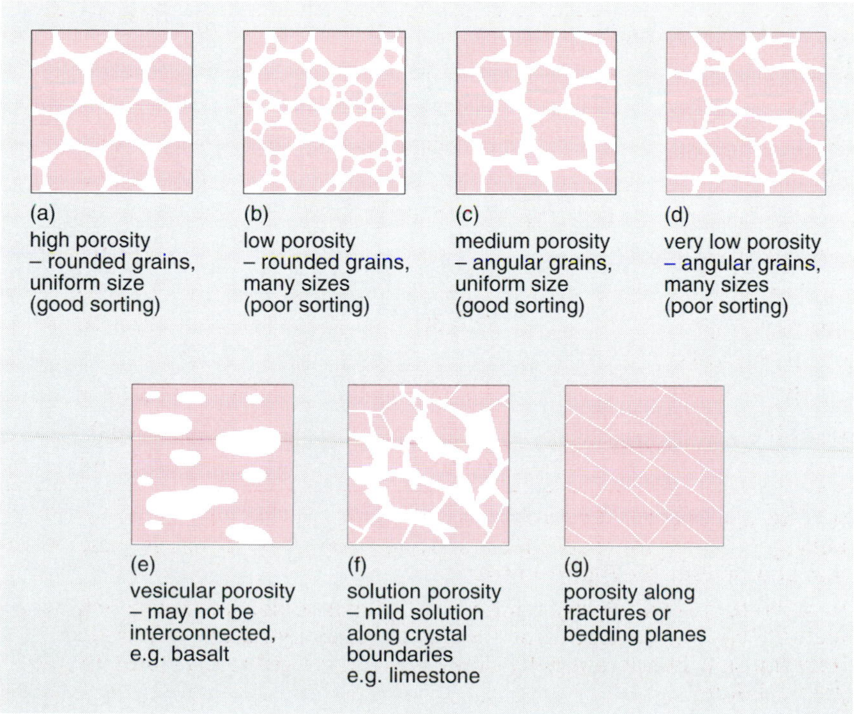

(a) high porosity – rounded grains, uniform size (good sorting)

(b) low porosity – rounded grains, many sizes (poor sorting)

(c) medium porosity – angular grains, uniform size (good sorting)

(d) very low porosity – angular grains, many sizes (poor sorting)

(e) vesicular porosity – may not be interconnected, e.g. basalt

(f) solution porosity – mild solution along crystal boundaries e.g. limestone

(g) porosity along fractures or bedding planes

Figure 9.6 The relationship between grain size, shape and porosity in sedimentary rocks, especially sandstones (a–d); vesicular porosity in crystallised lava flows due to original presence of gas bubbles (e); and solution porosity resulting from rock dissolution, especially where acid groundwaters attack limestone (f). Porosity also develops in rocks along original planes of weakness, especially bedding planes and fractures (joints and faults) (g)

VOLCANO-RELATED HEAT SOURCES AND FLUIDS

Heat is usually derived from a crystallising body of magma (partially molten rock) which need not necessarily be centred directly beneath the geothermal field (Figure 9.7). It may seem surprising that much of the magma rising beneath a volcano is not erupted but instead reaches only a level of neutral buoyancy at which its density is the same as that of the surrounding rocks. Two factors conspire to halt the rising magma: first the pressure of overlying rocks reduces as the magma ascends; this promotes the separation of liquid magma from its dissolved gases which are lost, increasing the density of the remaining magma; second, shallower rocks are inherently less dense than rocks at greater depth, usually because they are less compressed. So, whereas volcanic eruptions are driven by exceptionally high gas pressures, many magmas form 'intrusions' which crystallise beneath the surface at 1–5 km depth.

Experiments have been undertaken in the USA to drill directly into or very close to magma bodies where temperatures may be up to 1800 °C, and to harness geothermal power by cycling water through their outer margins. For example, the US Magma Energy Program succeeded in drilling into molten lava in the Kilauea (Hawaii) lava lake and ran successful energy extraction experiments; circulating water solidified the lava ahead of the drill bit, and the resulting tube of solid but fractured rock acted as a heat exchanger, with heat being transferred to the drill hole by convecting magma. A close encounter with magma occurred during the evaluation of the Krafla field in northern Iceland (Figure 9.8) when, in 1977, rising magma reached the depth of a borehole at 1138 m and three tonnes of magma was erupted through the hole in 20 minutes! Quite by chance, the

Figure 9.7 Conceptual model of a typical volcanic geothermal system in which meteoric (rain) waters percolate deep into the volcanic superstructure where they are heated by a body of magma which loses dissolved gases as it rises, and forms an intrusion (see text). The hot aqueous fluid rises and may reach the point at which water boils to form steam, producing a two-phase (steam + water) zone. The hydraulic gradient causes the geothermal fluid to migrate through any permeable rocks in the volcano flank. Here the fluids may be accessed by drilling (see drill rig symbols); the chemistry of the fluid changes during migration due to mixing with CO_2-saturated rain water (see Box 9.2)

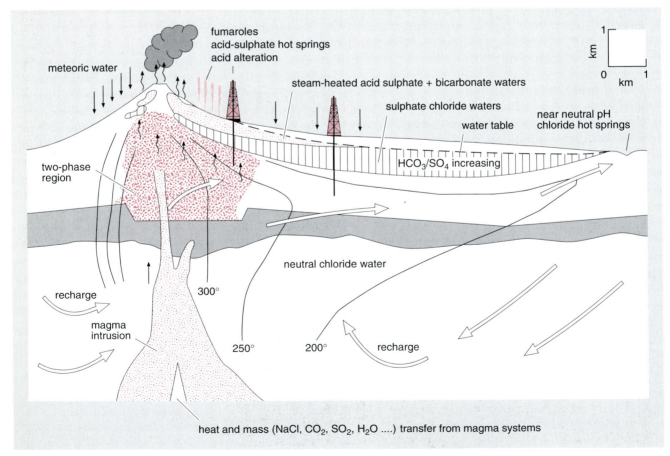

development history of this field has been dogged by a series of eruptions between 1975 and 1984, the first at Krafla for over 250 years, but progress has improved since the eruptions ceased.

Several of the world's most advanced geothermal sites (for example in northern Italy and the western USA) are located in extinct volcanic areas. Fortunately for geothermal exploitation, because rocks are such good insulators, magmatic intrusions may take tens of millions of years to cool back to ambient conditions. Such intrusions, therefore, continue to act as the focus for 'hot fluid', or hydrothermal convective cycles in permeable strata as in Figure 9.7. The nature of the resource then depends on the local conditions of pressure and temperature (P–T) in the aquifer, and this determines the extraction technology and profitability of the site.

The range of P–T conditions in which we are interested geothermally lies between 100 and 300 °C, below the critical point at which liquid water and water vapour become indistinguishable, and in the pressure range up to about 20 megapascals (MPa).

Typical P–T depth curves in a vertical profile (such as in a borehole) through a geothermal field are illustrated in Figure 9.9. At shallow depths, in this case down to about 250 m, the temperature is too low for any water present to boil, and pressure increases hydrostatically. But in the depth interval 250–575 m the temperature is high enough for water to vaporise, so that the temperature curve lies slightly to the right of the boiling point curve in Figure 9.9. Across this region pressure increases are small because the pores are occupied by convecting water vapour rather than liquid water. So it is the weight of gas that causes the small pressure increase. Because the water vapour is convecting vigorously this is also an isothermal zone (i.e. with unvarying temperature). Between 575 m and 700 m the rate of temperature increase with depth only just keeps pace with that required to boil the water as pressure continues to increase, so we have a liquid-dominated zone; pressure then increases more rapidly below 700 m as the P–T path of the geothermal fluid departs from the boiling point curve for

Figure 9.8 The Krafla geothermal power plant in north Iceland, planned as a 60 MW station which currently generates 30 MW except in the summer months. Further development of this volcanic field since the 1975–84 eruption sequence will soon bring the plant up to planned capacity

BOX 9.3: PRESSURE AND DEPTH

Hydrostatic pressure increases by about 1 atmosphere for an increase of 10 metres in depth (Box 5.3, Chapter 5). It follows that a geothermal aquifer 1 km thick will produce a pressure increase of 100 atmospheres (100 bar). (A pressure of 1 **bar** is approximately equal to 1 atmosphere.)

An alternative unit for pressure is the **pascal**, or more appropriately for the high pressures in geothermal systems, the megapascal (MPa). One megapascal is approximately 10 atmospheres, and the 20 MPa mentioned in the text is thus 200 atmospheres.

Many geothermal aquifers also contain a steam zone, and since steam has a much lower density than water, the **vapourstatic** increase in pressure with depth is much smaller than the hydrostatic increase. This helps to explain the pressure-depth profile of Figure 9.9.

Note that it is not strictly correct to refer to water vapour as steam. Steam is condensed droplets of water (as in clouds), which is why it can be seen. Water vapour is an invisible gas. However, steam is often used as a synonym for water vapour, though the meaning should generally be clear from the context.

water. The separation between liquid and steam zones is rarely so clear cut as illustrated in Figure 9.9. That is because between 250 m and 700 m in Figure 9.9 the fluid is very close to its phase transition temperature (between liquid and vapour) where large amounts of energy input or extracted cause no change in temperature. (It takes much longer to boil a kettle dry at 100 °C than to bring the water to the boiling point.)So this is really a two-phase zone in which liquid and vapour coexist, but in which the low density phase, water vapour, tends to be concentrated above the water.

In simple terms, high-enthalpy systems are subdivided into vapour-dominated and liquid-dominated, depending on the main pressure-controlling phase (i.e. steam or liquid water) in the reservoir. At first sight, the reservoir in Figure 9.9 might be classed as vapour-dominated, though it is more normal for such systems to carry even higher enthalpy vapour in the form of superheated steam because the temperature has risen *above* the boiling point curve. These are the best and most productive geothermal resources, largely because the steam is dry (free of liquid water) and is of very high enthalpy. Where reservoir rocks are at pressures below hydrostatic, which promotes steam formation (perhaps 3–3.5 MPa at depths down to 2 km), they must be sealed from direct vertical groundwater infiltration. The Larderello field in Figures 9.3 and 9.4 is of this type.

Figure 9.9   Simplified pressure–temperature (P–T) depth profile through the Wairakei geothermal field, New Zealand, along with the boiling point curve for water (i.e. the P–T curve for the transition between liquid water and water vapour). Note that the steam zone is almost isobaric (i.e. pressure is invariant), because of the low steam density compared with liquid water, and is also almost isothermal (i.e. temperature invariant) because of convection

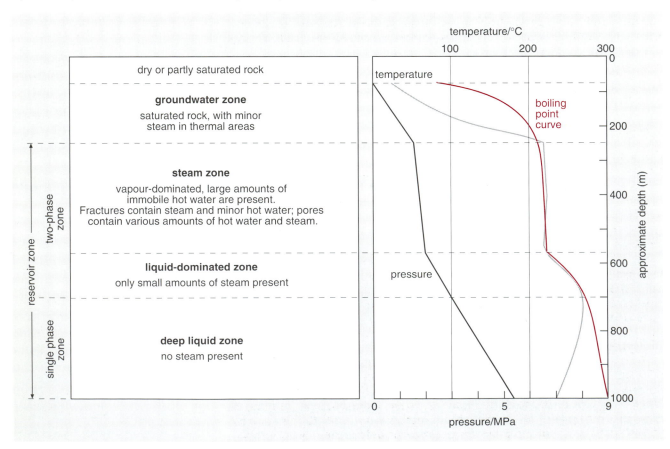

In contrast, liquid-dominated systems are at higher hydrostatic pressures, perhaps exceeding 10 MPa at depths below 1 km (because at 1 km depth the hydrostatic pressure is about 100 bars, i.e. 10 MPa, see Box 9.3). Production of electricity from liquid-dominated systems benefits from the higher fluid pressures at depth, and water is 'flashed' into steam as it crosses the boiling point curve (towards lower pressures) *en route* to the surface. That is to say, the P–T curve in liquid-dominated systems is *below* the boiling curve for water at all depths (unlike the situation in Figure 9.9), but when the geothermal aquifer is punctured by boreholes, the reduced pressure in the well means that the rising water crosses the boiling point curve on its way to the surface. However, the steam is often wet and of lower enthalpy which adds to the technical problems for electricity production. The famous Wairakei field in New Zealand is liquid-dominated but, typically for such systems, has developed a two-phase zone (Figure 9.9) as pressures have fallen during exploitation. Fortunately, the groundwater zone has a relatively low permeability which suppresses the tendency for natural venting of steam over most of the Wairakei area.

A final question we have not yet addressed is how heat is transferred from crystallising (or crystallised) magma to promote hydrothermal circulation as in Figure 9.7. The answer is complex and is the subject of much contemporary research. Yet it is clear that direct interaction between magma and groundwater rarely occurs. Instead, heat is conducted away from the magma body across a boundary layer, albeit sometimes a very thin layer with high thermal gradients, whereupon it is available for water heating. In some cases, water also escapes directly from the magma, bringing with it various other volatile chemical species which mix with the more abundant groundwater and, ultimately, generate a potential pollution problem for those exploiting the resource. Geochemical data indicate, however, that most geothermal waters are of meteoric (rainwater) origin and that juvenile magmatic water is a minor component. (See also Box 9.2.)

THE HEAT SOURCE IN SEDIMENTARY BASINS

An important key to understanding many geothermal resources is the heat conduction equation:

$$q = K_T \frac{\Delta T}{z} \qquad\qquad (3)$$

This is analogous to Darcy's Law, but here q is the one-dimensional vertical **heat flow** in watts per square metre (W m^{-2}). ΔT is the temperature difference across a vertical height z, and $\Delta T/z$ is thus the **thermal gradient**. The constant K_T relating these quantities is the **thermal conductivity** of the rock (in W m^{-1} °C^{-1}) and is equal to the heat flow per second through an area of 1 square metre when the thermal gradient is 1 °C per metre along the flow direction.

So, even under conditions of average heat flow (60 mW m^{-2}), it is possible to obtain temperatures of 60 °C within the top 2 km of the earth's crust. Box 9.4 demonstrates how the differing insulating properties of rocks influence the way the temperature varies with depth. To maintain the same vertical heat flow, low-conductivity rocks require a steeper temperature gradient than a relatively good conductor, and are accordingly important in augmenting temperatures.

Now values of K_T for most rock types are quite similar, in the range 2.5–3.5 W m^{-1} °C^{-1} for sandstones, limestones and most crystalline rocks. However, mudrocks (clays and shales) are the exceptions, with values of 1–2 W m^{-1} °C^{-1}. Referring back to Table 9.2, these are also among the most impermeable rocks, so mudrocks contribute two of the essential characteristics for geothermal resources: they act as impermeable cap rocks and enhance the geothermal gradient above aquifers in regions with otherwise normal heat flow.

This has led to exploration programmes aimed at locating natural warm waters in areas of thick sedimentary rock sequences containing both mudrocks and permeable limestones or sandstones. For example, the Paris area is at the centre of a 200 km depression in the crystalline basement rocks

---

BOX 9.4: THERMAL GRADIENT AND HEAT FLOW

Consider the situation where there is a steady upward flow of heat through the top few kilometres of the earth's crust. We can use Equation 3 to relate this flow to the temperature at any depth if we know the thermal conductivity of the rock.

If, for instance, the temperature is found to be 58°C at a depth of 2 km (2000 metres) and the surface temperature is 10°C, the temperature gradient is

$$(58 - 10)/2000 = 0.024 \ ^\circ C \ m^{-1}$$

and if the thermal conductivity of the rock is 2.5W m^{-1} $^\circ C^{-1}$, the heat flow rate is

$$2.5 \times 0.024 = 0.060 \ W \ m^{-2}$$

or 60 milliwatts per square metre.

Suppose, however, that this same 60 mW flows up through several layers with different thermal conductivities. Equation 3 tells us that the thermal gradient must be different in each layer, with the temperature changing most rapidly through the layer with the lowest conductivity, as in Figure 9.10 below.

We can check that the diagram shows the correct temperatures by using Equation 3 to calculate the temperature gradient for each layer and comparing this with the gradient read from the graph:

Layer 1

The calculated gradient is

$$0.060 / 2.5 = 0.024 \ ^\circ C \ m^{-1}$$

The measured gradient is

$$(34.5 - 10.0) / 1000 = 0.0245 \ ^\circ C \ m^{-1}$$

Layer 2

The calculated gradient is

$$0.060 / 1.5 = 0.040 \ ^\circ C \ m^{-1}$$

The measured gradient is

$$(54.5 - 34.5) / 500 = 0.040 \ ^\circ C \ m^{-1}$$

Layer 3

The calculated gradient is

$$0.060 / 3.0 = 0.020 \ ^\circ C \ m^{-1}$$

The measured gradient is

$$(64.5 - 54.5) / 1000 = 0.020 \ ^\circ C m^{-1}$$

Within the precision of the data, therefore, the temperatures shown are consistent with a heat flow rate of 60 mW per square metre through each layer. Comparing this case (Figure 9.10) with the uniform rock considered above, it is obvious that the presence of the thin layer with low thermal conductivity has appreciably enhanced the temperature at a depth of 2 km.

Figure 9.10 Variation of temperature with depth across three zones of differing thermal conductivity, K_T

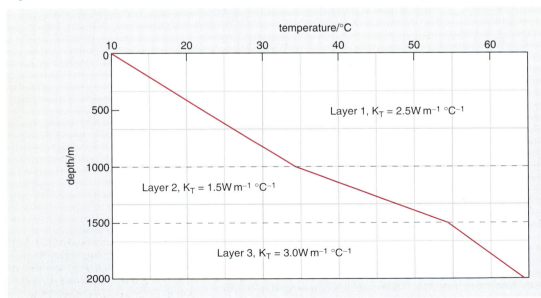

(Figure 9.11). Exploration for hydrocarbon resources in the 1960s and '70s was extremely successful in locating hot water, between 55 and 70 °C, at depths of 1–2 km, but found very little oil or gas! Of course, while such water resources are unsuitable for power generation (no high pressure steam can be produced) and must be located close to a heat load, the Paris area is ideal for exploiting them. Similar resources occur in some of the sedimentary basin areas of the UK, such as beneath the Yorkshire–Lincolnshire coast and in Hampshire, where the only commercial UK-based geothermal scheme operates in Southampton. However, most are remote from suitable heat loads.

Finally, there are two extensions of the criteria discussed above which make some sedimentary basin resources more attractive:

1 Large-scale non-electrical applications of geothermal energy world-wide (Table 9.1) arise in basins where the background heat flow is above average. The geological reasons for the association of high heat flow with sedimentary basins are not altogether surprising: extensional processes within the earth's outer plate layer induce thinning which can radically raise the heat flow as well as creating a topographic surface on which sedimentation occurs. Beneath the south Hungarian Plain, for example, geothermal gradients as high as 0.15 °C m^{-1} have been recorded and 120 °C water occurs at 1 km depth.

2 In other areas, larger sedimentary thicknesses may occur. For example, high-pressure fluids at temperatures of 160–200 °C occur at 3–5 km depth in the Gulf of Mexico, southern Texas and Louisiana. Because of their burial, the efficient sealing of the aquifers by impermeable rocks, and geothermal heating, pressures greatly exceed hydrostatic, and 100 MPa has been recorded in local pockets of fluid. The fluids are highly saline brines with trapped gas, especially methane. So-called 'geopressured brines' are a potentially important geothermal resource for power generation, a resource that has remained untapped to date but on which there is intermittent government funding for research in the USA. The great advantage of geopressured resources is that they offer three kinds of energy: geothermal heat, hydraulic energy because of the high pressure, and the large quantities of methane that are found dissolved in the fluid.

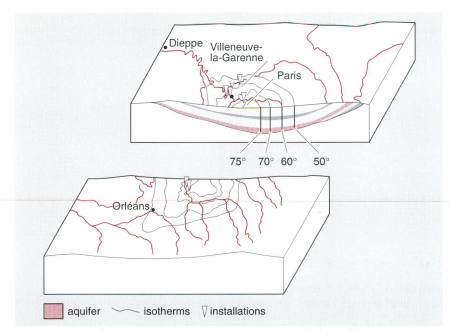

Figure 9.11 Block model of the Paris Basin showing cross-sectional structure, isotherms at the bottom of the sedimentary sequence projected onto the surface, and major river drainage

WHY ARE THERE HOT DRY ROCKS?

Our attention now turns from sedimentary strata to the underlying crystalline 'basement'. 'Hot dry rock' (HDR) resources refers to the heat stored in impermeable (or poorly permeable) rock strata and to the process of trying to extract that heat. What is required is the creation of an artificial fracture zone within suitably hot rocks; water is circulated through such a zone so that heat may be extracted, ideally to generate steam and, hence, electrical power. Although the technology does not yet exist to create suitable arrangements for reproducible heat recovery, in theory at least HDR technology could be applied over a significant proportion of the earth's surface. Drilling is expensive, so only the top 6 km of the earth's crust is generally used in calculating geothermal energy potential (though some drilling has gone as deep as 15 km). Given current technical and economic constraints on drilling depths, a minimum geothermal gradient of around 0.025 °C m^{-1} is required. With a typical thermal conductivity of 3 W m^{-1} °C^{-1}, this requires (from Equation 3) a heat flow of 75 mW m^{-2}, only a little above the earth's average. In practice, however, it is customary to look for rocks with much higher heat flows (as at experimental sites in the UK, USA, Japan and France) and ideal targets are granite bodies. This is because such rocks occupy large volumes of the upper crust and they crystallised from magmas that had naturally high concentrations of the chemical elements with long-lived radioactive isotopes – uranium, thorium and potassium.

Now we reach a situation in which heat flow through the earth's surface itself is augmented because of the heat production within certain shallow crystalline rocks. Take the situation in Figure 9.12 (Box 9.5), which refers to a granite body that crops out at the surface in south-west England. Heat production is 4.5 µW per cubic metre - even higher than that calculated in Box 9.5 and more than twice the 2.0 µW m^{-3} of the surrounding sedimentary country rocks into which the granite body was intruded. In consequence the surface heat flow is increased to about 110 mW m^{-2}, compared with the 75 mW m^{-2} of the surroundings. The size of the gravity anomaly across the granite has been used in conjunction with the density contrast between the two rock types to calculate the shape of the intrusion, which extends to a depth of 15 km.

The important feature of this area in an HDR context is that a heat flow of 110 mW m–2 through the granite implies a temperature rise of some 30 °C per kilometre, so the temperature at 5 km depth should be over 170 °C, well within the area of interest for HDR development and power production. It is for this reason that during the 1980s there was substantial investment in HDR technological research (described later) in Cornwall, at a site operated by the Camborne School of Mines (CSM).

Analogous HDR research is under way at two European sites, at Soultz in the Alsace region of France and at Urach in the German Rhineland. The most advanced research and development is at Fenton Hill in New Mexico where the Los Alamos National Laboratory (LANL) has been conducting long-term feasibility tests. These three sites all have higher geothermal gradients (0.05–0.07 °C m^{-1}) than the granites of south-west England. Both

BOX 9.5: SURFACE HEAT FLOW

We can calculate the total surface heat flow by adding the effect of the heat-producing layer to the background heat flow q_m (i.e. the heat flow from the earth's interior, the mantle, below the heat-producing layer) for the area:

$$q = bA_o + q_m \qquad (4)$$

where A_o is the rate of surface heat production per cubic metre in a layer of thickness b metres.

We'll take as an example a layer 15 km thick of 'radiothermal granite' containing the following radioactive materials:

* 4.5% potassium, of which 0.012% is radioactive potassium-40 which generates 0.028 mW of heat per kilogram

* 20 ppm (parts per million) of thorium-232 which generates 0.026 mW of heat per kilogram

* 8 ppm of uranium-238 which generates 0.096 mW of heat per kilogram.

Converting the potassium-40 content to ppm, we obtain

(4.5 / 100) x (0.012 / 100) x 1,000,000 = 5.4 ppm

The total rate of heat generation per million kilograms of granite is therefore

5.4 x 0.028 + 20 x 0.026 + 8 x 0.096 = 1.44 mW

One cubic metre of granite has a mass of 2600 kg, so the rate of heat generation per cubic metre of granite is

A_0 = 1.44 x 2600 / 1,000,000 = 0.00374 mW m^{-3}

Assuming that the background heat flow (q_m) is 40 mW per square metre, we have for the total heat flow at the surface

q = 15,000 x 0.00374 + 40 = 96 mW m^{-2}

In other words, the presence of the radioactive material has more than doubled the heat flow.

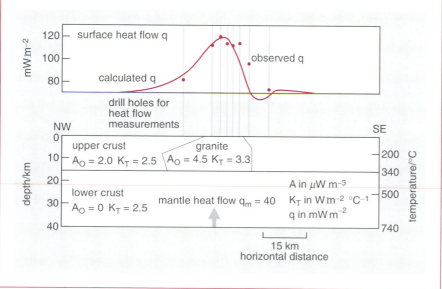

Figure 9.12 Comparison between observed and calculated heat flow (top) across a granite body in SW England where the sub-surface shape (bottom) was deduced from gravity observations and surface heat production (A_o), and thermal conductivity values (K_T) were obtained from laboratory measurements on field samples. A (heat production) and K_T for the lower crust and q_m are assumed values. The horizontal axis represents distance. (See text for discussion)

the LANL and Soultz sites benefit from the blanketing effect of 1000 m of sedimentary rock above the crystalline basement. The geothermal gradients through the sediments average 0.08–0.1 °C m^{-1}, falling to 0.028–0.05 °C m^{-1} in the crystalline basement beneath. The Fenton Hill site has the additional advantage of being located just outside the Valles volcanic caldera where one of the best developed and most extensively researched active geothermal systems in the world is located. (A caldera is a very large (up to, say, 20 km across) volcanic depression – a sort of shallow crater – which is formed by a massive volcanic explosion followed by subsidence of the volcanic superstructure. Krakatoa (1886) is the best recent example.) Studies of this area demonstrate that 95% of the thermal resource associated with such an active volcanic area is actually located in hot dry rock rather than hot water, thus illustrating the importance of continuing research to extract this energy.

9.5 TECHNOLOGIES FOR GEOTHERMAL RESOURCE EXPLOITATION

RESOURCES IN HIGH-PRESSURE STEAM FIELDS

The first stage in the exploitation of geothermal resources in volcanic areas involves a range of geological studies aimed at locating rocks that have been chemically altered by hot geothermal brines, and surface thermal manifestations such as hot springs or mud pools. Fluid chemical investigations and, increasingly, the release of gases through fractured rocks provide means of assessing the composition and resource potential of trapped fluids. However, geophysical prospecting techniques, particularly resistivity surveying and other electrical methods designed to detect zones with electrically conducting fluids (i.e. brines), are probably the most effective for locating buried geothermal resources. Once a suitable geothermal aquifer has been located, exploration and production wells are drilled using special techniques to cope with the much higher temperatures and, in some cases, harder rock conditions than in oil and water wells. Since fluid pressures in the aquifer range up to about 10 MPa, dense drilling muds are required to counteract these pressures and avoid 'blow out', where an uncontrollable column of gas is discharged. The well diameter decreases with depth from perhaps 50 cm near the surface to 15 cm at production depths. The well is cased with steel tubing and concrete, often leaving a perforated open steel casing at production depths. A well-head with valve gear is either welded to the steel casing or bolted to the concrete collar at ground level. This allows the well to be connected to a power plant via the network of insulated pipes that are a familiar sight in geothermal areas (as in Figure 9.4).

Technologies for electrical power generation depend critically on the nature of the resource – not just the fluid temperature and pressure but also its salinity and content of other gases, all of which affect plant efficiency and design. Today there are about 250 installations operating worldwide and these include four main types, described below.

DRY STEAM POWER PLANT

As the name implies, this type of system (Figure 9.13(a)) is ideal for vapour-dominated resources where steam production is not contaminated with liquid. Superheated steam is produced, typically at 180–185 °C and 0.8–0.9 MPa, reaching the surface at several hundred km h⁻¹ and, if vented to the atmosphere, sounding like a jet engine at close proximity. Temperatures up to 300–350 °C and correspondingly greater pressures are increasingly being exploited, leading to greater efficiency in electricity production. Passing through the turbine, the steam expands, causing the blades and shaft to rotate and hence generating power.

The simplest form of power plant, a 'back-pressure' unit, then vents the low-pressure steam to the atmosphere. But in the more normal 'condenser' plant shown in Figure 9.13(a), greater efficiency is achieved by condensing the exhaust steam to liquid, thus dramatically increasing the pressure drop across the turbine because liquid water occupies a volume roughly 1000

Figure 9.13 Simplified flow diagrams (a–d) showing the four main types of geothermal electrical energy production

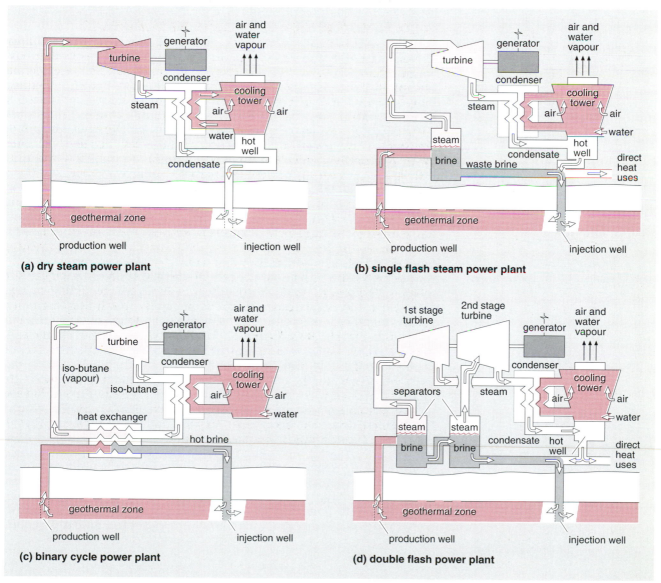

(a) dry steam power plant

(b) single flash steam power plant

(c) binary cycle power plant

(d) double flash power plant

times less than the same mass of steam. Of course, the cooling towers generate 'waste heat' in just the same way as conventional coal- and oil-fired power stations. In common with most vapour power cycles, efficiencies are also low, and despite the use of high temperature superheated steam, rarely exceed 30%. Nevertheless, whereas a 1960s plant required almost 15 kg of steam per saleable kWh in optimum conditions, modern dry steam plants, with higher temperature steam and better turbine designs, can achieve 6.5 kg kWh^{-1}, so a 55 MW plant requires 100 kg s^{-1} of steam.

Plant efficiency, and therefore profitability, is strongly affected by the pressure of so-called 'non-condensable' gases such as carbon dioxide and hydrogen sulphide. When the water component of the geothermal fluid is cooled, achieving a suction effect on the turbine as it condenses into liquid at around 100 °C, gases that do not similarly condense cause higher residual pressures in the turbine exhaust. A small percentage of such gases reduces suction efficiency and so impacts on the economics of the system. Non-condensable gases have another economic impact for environmental reasons, since they must either be removed from the waste water or reinjected into the ground to avoid pollution. These gases can be removed by gas ejectors on the condenser. However, the ejectors themselves require electric power from the turbine-generator and, consequently, reduce its output.

In general, dry steam plant is the simplest, most common and most commercially attractive. For that reason, dry steam fields were exploited early and have become disproportionately well known. Only the USA and Italy have extensive dry steam resources, though Indonesia, Japan and Mexico also have a few such fields. (In these countries and elsewhere, liquid-dominated fields are far more common.) While in some areas it is common practice to reinject the spent fluid, until recently this was not undertaken in the largest field, the Geysers in the USA. However, falling fluid pressures have led to concern among the various private operators that the field is being over-exploited, and they are rapidly being forced towards a uniform reinjection policy to make the resource more sustainable. Economic justification for reinjection requires that the short-term costs of new injection wells will be more than offset by longer-term resource availability.

SINGLE FLASH STEAM POWER PLANT

Here (Figure 9.13(b)) the geothermal fluid reaching the surface may be wet steam, water that has flashed within the well during ascent, or hot water at high (close to reservoir) pressure. In the first case, a separator is installed simply to protect the turbine from a massive influx of water should conditions change. However, it is often better to avoid flashing in the well because this can lead to a rapid build-up of scale deposits as minerals dissolved in the fluid come out of solution, leading to the plugging of the well. For this reason, the well is often kept under pressure to maintain the fluid as liquid water. To deal with hot, high-pressure water requires more complex equipment designed to reduce the pressure and induce flashing so that steam may be separated. Again, a conventional steam turbine is at the heart of the plant, but lower steam pressures and temperatures (0.5–0.6 MPa, 155–165 °C) are common, so the plant typically requires more steam, around 8 kg kWh^{-1}. However, the bulk of the fluid produced, often up to 80%, may remain as unflashed brine which is then reinjected, unless there are local direct use heating systems available. In general, therefore, reinjection wells must be available for fluid disposal both at single flash plants and at plants incorporating the newer types of technology described below.

BINARY CYCLE POWER PLANT

This type of power plant (Figure 9.13(c)) uses a secondary working fluid with a lower boiling point than water, such as pentane or butane, which is vaporised and used to drive the turbine. The obvious advantage is that low-temperature resources can be developed where single flash systems have proved unsatisfactory. Moreover, chemically impure geothermal fluids can be exploited, especially if they are kept under pressure so that no flashing ever takes place. The geothermal brine is pumped at reservoir pressure through a heat exchange unit and is then reinjected. Ideally, the thermal energy supplied is adequate to superheat the secondary fluid. Although higher efficiencies have been produced than in low-temperature steam flash plants, and 60 units of this type are in operation today, the capital costs are high. Moreover, keeping the geothermal fluid under pressure and repressurising the secondary fluid consumes some 30% of the overall power output of the system because large pumps are required. Large volumes of geothermal fluid are also involved; for example, the Mammoth geothermal plant in California uses around 700 kg s^{-1} to produce 30 MW.

DOUBLE FLASH POWER PLANT

Recently, several attempts have been made to develop improved flashing techniques, particularly to avoid the high capital costs of binary plant. Double flash (Figure 9.13(d)) is ideal where geothermal fluids contain low levels of impurities and so the scaling and non-condensable gas problems that affect profitability are at a minimum. Quite simply, unflashed liquid remaining after the initial high-pressure flashing flows to a low-pressure tank where another pressure drop provides additional steam. This steam is mixed with the exhaust from the high-pressure turbine to drive a second turbine (or a second stage of the same turbine), ideally raising power output by 20–25% for only a 5% increase in plant cost. Even so, extremely large fluid volumes are required and, for example, the East Mesa plant in southern California, opened in 1988, uses brine at 1000 kg s^{-1} from 16 wells to generate 37 MW; that is over 10 times more fluid than for similar dry steam plant.

As the geothermal industry continues to expand, there will be a need to develop technologies that can produce geothermal power from a variety of resources that are less ideal than dry steam. Increasing exploitation is being made of geothermal fluids which are either at lower temperature than (but similar pressure to) those in dry steam fields, or at the same or higher temperature and much higher pressure. These are essentially liquid-dominated resources, albeit of high enthalpy, and they exist in large volumes. Inevitably, variants on the binary and double flash systems will continue to be developed; they are at the leading edge of current research.

RESOURCES FOR DIRECT USE GEOTHERMAL ENERGY

Many of the countries listed in Table 9.1 as exploiting geothermal resources for non-electrical purposes have chosen to develop these direct use applications in areas flanking the main steam fields. Japan, New Zealand, Iceland (Figure 9.14) and Italy are obvious examples where wet steam or warm water at a range of temperatures is readily available for industrial, domestic and leisure applications (Table 9.3 gives examples). Here, however, we are concerned principally with the low-temperature resources found in sedimentary basin areas, several of which have been developed across central Europe. Drilling techniques resemble those discussed earlier, but the process is generally less hazardous since the geothermal fluid is found at much lower pressure–temperature conditions than in hot steam fields and pumps are usually required to bring the fluid to the surface. However, the hot water is certainly too saline and corrosive to be allowed directly into

Figure 9.14 Drilling for warm water for domestic heating on the outskirts of Reykjavik, Iceland

heating systems, so once again corrosion-resistant heat exchangers are widely used. The secondary circuit might be a vast greenhouse complex, using both aerial and underground pipes, or it might be a domestic heat load with a combination of underfloor and radiator pipes. The dense multi-storey apartment blocks of the Paris suburbs are ideal heat loads for these local resources.

The French have led the development of these 'low-enthalpy' resources and over the last 30 years have installed no less than 55 group heating schemes in the Paris Basin, with several more in south-western France. At

Table 9.3 Temperature ranges for direct uses of geothermal energy

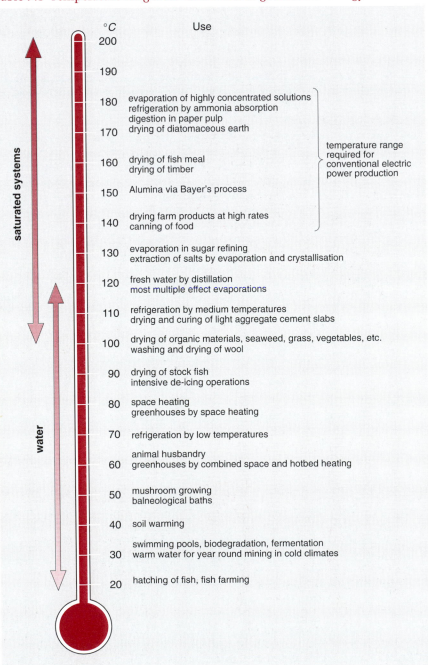

Figure 9.15 *The Creil district heating scheme, the first to be developed in France, installed in 1976 north of Paris:*
(a) Map showing location of two production and reinjection wells, and the various apartment blocks served by the system.
(b) This shows how the geothermal heat is exchanged to a secondary freshwater circuit. The circuit is used first to heat
2000 apartments by underfloor heating; the residual energy is then transferred to a second circuit using heat pumps and is
used for radiator heating in a further 2000 apartments

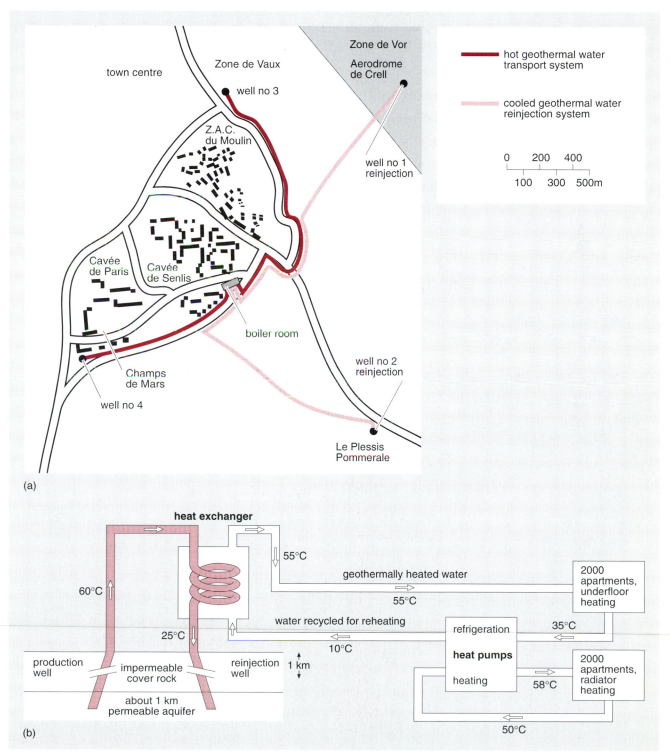

the design stage, a twin production and reinjection borehole system would be planned on the basis of supplying between 3 and 5 MW of heat energy (25–50 l s⁻¹ of water at 60 °C) over a lifetime of 30–50 years. This means that groundwater flow conditions need detailed study, and the spacing of the wells must be designed to maintain high fluid pressures by reinjection while avoiding the advance of a 'cold front' (i.e. fluid at reinjection temperatures) towards the production well until capital costs are amortised. A typical layout for a twin production well scheme, with a schematic of the heat transfer technology, is shown in Figures 9.15(a) and (b). Note the interesting application of heat pumps to enhance the system efficiency by reducing the reinjection temperature in Figure 9.15(b). Heat pumps work on the same principle as refrigerators, but here produce a concentrated high temperature output. Of course, they consume electrical energy but, in the example shown in Figure 9.15(b), they enable the number of heated apartments to be doubled.

In the longer term, heat pumps may allow the widespread economic development of even shallower, cooler geothermal aquifers. For example, some 4000 individual dwellings in Switzerland have been using geothermal heat pumps (GHPs), as shown in Figure 9.16, to draw on 100 m deep geothermal fluids for their heating needs quite satisfactorily now for over 10 years. In 1992 the number of Swiss GHPs rose to 9000, including some that obtain heat simply by conduction from the sub-soil. Strictly speaking, the conduction of heat from the sub-soil should not be classified as geothermal since it is actually stored solar energy which is being exploited. It is reported that energy from these schemes currently costs 30% more than oil heating, but they were installed because the Swiss are environmentally conscious.

Although the French group heating schemes have been a great practical success, their economic benefits are only marginal at times of low oil prices and high interest rates. For this reason, development work stopped during the period 1989–92. Nevertheless, they are producing a national saving of over 200 000 tonnes of oil (or equivalent in other fossil fuels) per year in an area which, 30 years ago, had no obvious geothermal potential. The same concept applies to the analogous UK scheme in Southampton.

HOT DRY ROCK TECHNOLOGY

The familiar concept of twin production and injection boreholes, but here drilled into relatively hard granite and terminating several hundred metres apart, provides the basis of HDR system designs, as shown in Figure 9.17. A suitable heat exchange surface is then created by opening pre-existing joints (fractures) by some means of stimulation. Water is circulated down the injection well, through the HDR reservoir and up the production well where the aim is to provide thermal energy for electricity generation, using a heat exchanger and binary turbine – though lower-temperature district heating schemes are also under consideration. The concept is much simpler to state than to bring into practice for, despite the investment of $250 million since 1970, principally in the USA, UK, Germany and Japan, HDR has not yet been demonstrated commercially on a large scale.

The principal costs in the construction of an HDR system lie in drilling wells in hard crystalline rocks and creating the artificial heat exchanger. We are dealing with rocks at higher temperatures and under higher stresses, at 3–6 km depth, than in more conventional geothermal areas. Modern approaches to this problem are derivations of the Los Alamos National Laboratory (Fenton Hill, New Mexico) method of pumping water down a borehole, drilled to production depths, at increasing pressure until fractures in the rock are opened. This technique is used in the oil industry and is

Figure 9.16 The geothermal heat pump (GHP) concept used to extract heat from warm shallow groundwater to supply a single domestic dwelling. In the winter heat is removed from the earth and delivered in a concentrated form via the heat pump. Because electricity is used, in effect, to increase the temperature of the heat, not to produce it, the GHP can deliver three to four times more energy than it consumes

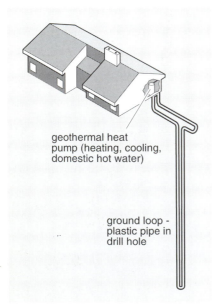

geothermal heat pump (heating, cooling, domestic hot water)

ground loop - plastic pipe in drill hole

known as hydro-fracturing. A second borehole is drilled to intersect this stimulated zone several hundred metres above its base and a closed circuit for water circulation through the fracture system is thereby generated. The first HDR energy loop was completed at 3000 m depth beneath Fenton Hill in 1977, enlarged in 1979 and tested successfully by running a small (60 kW$_e$) binary cycle plant on 140 °C water.

During the 1980s much HDR research focused on developing rock fracture technologies, principally at Fenton Hill and at the Camborne School of Mines (CSM) site, a disused quarry at Rosemanowes, Cornwall (Figure 9.18). The aim has been to deviate the twin boreholes at depth by up to 35° from the vertical so that they intersect natural joints and fissures, leaving a vertical spacing of several hundred metres between them. The key stage, stimulation, involves pumping large volumes of water or low-viscosity gel, via the lower section of the injection well, at a pressure high enough to induce the required permeability between the two wells to gain access to the main fissures, which occur about 20 m apart at Rosemanowes.

Using this approach, hydraulic connections were established at about 3 km depth beneath Fenton Hill and 2 km depth beneath Rosemanowes, both in 1985. Initial surface water temperatures were 192 °C and 70 °C respectively; the wells at Rosemanowes were drilled to less than half the depth required for any commercial electricity production, simply to undertake rock mechanics tests and avoid the problems of high pressures and temperatures. A new circulation loop at 5 km depth in rocks at 320 °C was also tested at Fenton Hill. Both systems were subjected to long-term circulation tests, during which time detailed seismic monitoring was used to pinpoint the position and development of fracturing in three dimensions. The tests revealed that the natural fractures could be stimulated by hydraulic pressure, and that artificial fractures are difficult to induce except in close proximity to the wells. But, while good circulation results were achieved, there were also several very significant problems.

First, despite the effort invested in opening the fracture networks, both systems maintained a higher resistance to flow than was desirable. This is measured by **impedance**, defined here as the pressure difference across the two boreholes, maintained by pumping, divided by the production flow rate. Since the pumps represent a parasitic electrical load in a commercial system, and for other reasons that will become clear below, target figures need to be set. For example, the target impedance at Rosemanowes was 0.1 MPa per litre per second (MPa l^{-1} s^{-1}), so if the target flow rate of 100 l s^{-1} were achieved, the pumping pressure required would be 10 MPa. The best results from Cornwall were a maximum flow rate of 24 l s^{-1} and a minimum impedance of 0.5 MPa l^{-1} s^{-1}, and even then the production temperature fell from 70 °C to 55 °C during a three year test from 1985 to 1988. This indicates that 'short-circuits', where cooling advances much more rapidly than is desirable, must exist between the wells. So, a second problem is that effective heat transfer surfaces must be increased to give commercial lifetimes of 20–30 years. This has led to suggestions that a multiplicity of independent flow paths of comparable impedance will need to be created through the lower third of the system; a heat transfer area of 10^7 m^2 would be ideal. It is also recognised that there is a critical pumping pressure (which is about 10 MPa for most systems so far examined) above which shear

Figure 9.17 Conceptual model of a hot dry rock circulation system in which wells are developed from boreholes deviated to intersect the natural fracture systems of crystalline rocks. The heat exchange surface, or artificial reservoir created at depth, ideally consists of several fluid pathways between the production and injection wells. The vertical separation between these wells is about 300 m

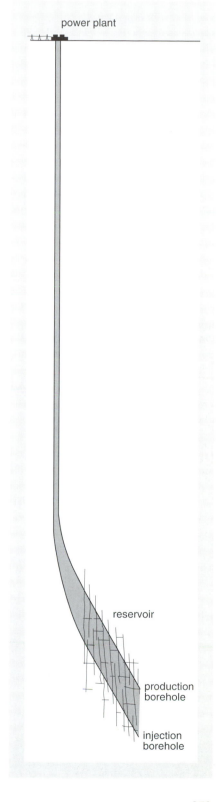

power plant

reservoir

production borehole

injection borehole

Figure 9.18 (Top) Deep drilling, to about 2 km depth for hot dry rock geothermal research at the Rosemanowes granite quarry, near Penryn (outside Truro), Cornwall, in 1981; (Bottom) Natural permeable fissure in otherwise solid impermeable granite from the quarry face at Rosemanowes
(Length of scale at centre of photograph = 1 m)

failure results, with runaway growth of the fracture network. So, for a flow rate of $100 \, l \, s^{-1}$, this limits the acceptable impedance to $<0.1 \, MPa \, l^{-1} \, s^{-1}$.

A third, related, problem is that of water loss which, for economic purposes, should be kept below 10%. Diffusion losses into the rock matrix and direct flow into the natural fracture system, perhaps itself leading to its expansion in undesirable directions, seem to be occurring: both systems have experienced losses of 20–30% during circulation, although this has reduced to <10% at both sites after well treatments. This is a particularly worrying problem at Fenton Hill, for water is increasingly scarce and expensive in the southern USA.

Despite these technical difficulties, much of the geothermal industry is optimistic about the progress of HDR research during the last decade. Although work at the two other European sites, Soultz and Urach, is less advanced than in Cornwall, single deep boreholes have been used for initial studies of 'reservoir' characteristics. At the time of writing a decision is awaited on which of the three European sites will attract EU funding to develop a single commercial prototype using joint British, French and German expertise. On the broader scale, there is also a suggestion that the next logical step might be to undertake a new generation of HDR experiments on the otherwise unproductive margins of existing fractured high-enthalpy fields, such as at Larderello, Italy.

9.6 ENVIRONMENTAL IMPLICATIONS

Significant environmental concerns associated with geothermal energy include those to do with site preparation, such as noise pollution during the drilling of wells, and the disposal of drilling fluids, which requires large sediment-settling lagoons. Noise is also an important factor in high-enthalpy geothermal areas during well-testing operations when steam is allowed to escape, but once a field comes into production noise levels rarely exceed those of other forms of power plant. Accidents during site development are rare, but a notable exception in 1991 was the failure of a well originally drilled in 1981 at the Zumil geothermal station on the flanks of Santiaguito volcano in Guatemala. Hundreds of tonnes of rock, mud and steam were blown into the atmosphere when the well 'blew its top', apparently because of gravitational slippage of the ground beneath the site.

Longer-term effects of geothermal production include ground subsidence, induced seismicity and, most important, gaseous pollution. In dry steam fields, where the reservoir pressures are relatively low and the rocks are self-supporting, subsidence is rare (as at the Geysers and Larderello). But significant reduction of the higher pressures in liquid-dominated systems, for example due to inadequate fluid reinjection, can induce subsidence, usually on the millimetre to centimetre scale (although a maximum of 3 metres has occurred at Wairakei).

The question of whether there is induced seismicity around geothermal sites has been much debated, and it must be recognised that most steam fields are located in regions already prone to natural earthquakes. Yet there is evidence that fluid injection lubricates fractures and increases pore pressures, creating small earthquakes (microseismicity), especially where reinjection is not at the same depth as the producing aquifer (mainly for reasons of fluid disposal). However, in cases where reinjection is designed to maintain reservoir pressures, seismicity is not greatly increased by geothermal production.

Geothermal 'pollutants' are chiefly confined to the non-condensable gases: carbon dioxide (CO_2), with lesser amounts of hydrogen sulphide (H_2S) or sulphur dioxide (SO_2), hydrogen (H_2), methane (CH_4) and nitrogen (N_2). In the condensed water there is also dissolved silica, heavy metals, sodium and potassium chlorides and sometimes carbonates, depending on the nature of the water–rock interaction at reservoir depths. Today these are almost always reinjected and this also removes the problem of dealing with waste water, though, as noted earlier, the presence of solutes and gases does add to the cost of producing geothermal energy. Traditionally, geothermal sites have received a bad press on account of their association with the 'rotten eggs' smell of H_2S. However, this and other gaseous products of old leaking plant have now been reduced so that the environmental impact of geothermal production is at a minimum. Interestingly, the level of atmospheric H_2S in the air over the Geysers field is now lower than that produced from hot springs and geysers before geothermal developments

BOX 9.6: ENVIRONMENTAL CONCERNS

Two new geothermal stations brought on line in the late 1980s in the western USA illustrate contemporary reactions to environmental concerns at the planning stage. At Dixie Valley (Nevada) the liquid-dominated geothermal resource is relatively clean with only small amounts of carbonate, chloride and sulphide. So the water is allowed to flash and a polyacrylate inhibitor is used to prevent carbonate scaling in the production wells. This is a dual flash plant producing 62 MW from about 800 kg s^{-1} of fluid, only about 25% of which flashes to produce steam for the turbines. Condensed steam joins the unflashed liquid and is reinjected to maintain reservoir pressures; there is evidence that fluid passes

through the underground system and back to the surface in just a few years, so a large heat store is being mined with a small fluid volume. About 5 kg s^{-1} of steam is used to force the accumulating non-condensable gases out of the condensers. This mixture is vented with the cooling tower steam plume adding, for example, about 150 tonnes a year of hydrogen sulphide to the atmosphere. This is environmentally acceptable because this is a remote location and the non-condensable gas component is a small fraction of the geothermal fluid.

In contrast, the Mammoth plant in California (see photo) lies just outside a popular ski resort and

exploits a shallow reservoir with abundant but relatively impure geothermal fluid. A similar fluid volume to that at Dixie (about 900 kg s^{-1}) is used to produce 40 MW in a binary cycle operation. The geothermal fluid is kept under pressure, requiring expensive pumping, so that it does not flash and the pollutants stay in solution. Because the producing reservoir has high sustainable flow rates, reinjection is directed considerably beneath the reservoir and is done solely to avoid pollution. The Mammoth plant also incorporates an air cooling system for the post-turbine isobutane gas, so avoiding all forms of visible gas emission from the plant. Again, this is a more costly form of condensation system and environmental restrictions on the height of the cooling towers mean that on warm days condensation is inefficient, thus reducing the electrical power output. The plant is coloured green to blend with the landscape and a screening embankment with trees reduces the visible impact from the Mammoth Lakes ski resort. Despite all these environmental restrictions, this low-level, totally self-contained and emission-free geothermal plant makes a profit through fixed-price contracts with the Southern California electric utility company.

began: this has been achieved mainly by gas extraction or chemical conversion, involving the production of huge quantities of unwanted sulphur compounds rather than reinjection, which is only now being introduced in California. Nevertheless, the image of polluting geothermal systems has slowed developments at several new sites. For example, environmental legislation covering the Miravalles plant, located on the periphery of a rainforest conservation area in northern Costa Rica (Figure 9.19), has delayed completion of the plant until 1995/96 instead of 1992 as originally planned. A project on Mount Apo on Mindanao Island in the Philippines was turned down by the World Bank and the Asian Development Bank on social and environmental grounds. Objectors claimed that 111 hectares of forest would be threatened, 28 rivers polluted and a national park destroyed.

Overall, the facts are now quite plain – geothermal developments have a net *positive* impact on the environment compared with conventional

Figure 9.19 (Top) Geothermal well head and valve gear with steam–water separator (cylinder behind the valves) at a new field being developed on the flanks of Miravalles volcano, Costa Rica (in the distance); (Bottom) Steam venting from a well head at Travale, Tuscany; note condensation of the fluid which is 'raining out' over the trees behind

energy systems because of their much smaller pollution effects. In producing the same amount of electrical power, modern geothermal plants emit less than 0.2% of the greenhouse gas CO_2 of the cleanest fossil fuel plant (Figure 9.20). Comparable figures for the acid rain gas SO_2 and for particulates are less than 1% and 0.1% respectively. In terms of social developments, geothermal plant requires very little land, taking up just a few acres for plant sizes of 100 MW or more. Geothermal drilling, with no risk of fire, is safer than oil or gas drilling, and although there have been a few steam 'blow out' events, there is far less potential for environmental damage from drilling accidents. In direct use applications, geothermal units are operated in a closed cycle, mainly to minimise corrosion and scaling problems, and there are no emissions. So while the acidic briny fluids are corrosive to machinery such as pumps and turbines, these represent technological challenges rather than environmental hazards.

There is an interesting social footnote which emphasises that geothermal energy developments are not always entirely benign when viewed at short range. Not surprisingly, drilling of direct use geothermal wells in the heart of Paris suburbs led to interesting conflicts over noise pollution. During the preparation of the new site in 1980, for example, an enormous poster was hoisted on an apartment block which nicely summarised the Parisian attitude: 'Oui à la géothermie, non aux nuisances'. The ideal geothermal development site is either in a remote location or is well screened like the quarry at Rosemanowes in Cornwall; unfortunately, not all commercially viable sites have this advantage.

9.7   ECONOMICS AND WORLD POTENTIAL

On an international scale, geothermal is one of the most significant 'renewable' energy resources. This results from quite spectacular growth at approximately 14% p.a. following the oil embargoes of the early 1970s, at a time when conventional generating capacity grew at between 0 and 3% p.a. Stabilisation of oil prices brought the growth rate down to about 8% p.a., so the 6 GW of geothermal electricity capacity of the early 1990s should have approximately doubled by the year 2000. Environmental factors and the relatively sound cost-effectiveness of high-enthalpy resources have combined to sustain this high growth rate. For example, discounting interest costs on capital loans, it is estimated that the new project in Costa Rica mentioned above will produce electricity at 25% of the cost of oil-fired plant and will satisfy 8% of the electricity needs of that country. The project should 'break even' when capital cost amortisation is included. Although geothermal resources make a similarly significant contribution in other high-enthalpy areas (e.g. 1.5% in Italy, 10% in New Zealand), even 10 GW is a minute fraction (about 0.2%) of global electrical generating capacity. Yet the long-term potential, especially in volcanically active countries, is much higher and may be realised as the technology improves.

The Geysers field (Table 9.4) provides a useful illustration of *historical* economic improvements engendered by falling plant costs as planned lifetimes and operational returns have increased (note that current electricity *prices* are 10–15 cents per kWh in most of the developed world).

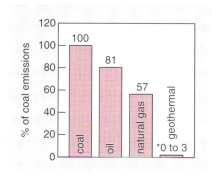

Figure 9.20 Comparative CO_2 emissions for fossil fuel and geothermal power plants. 100% is equivalent to 7700 tonnes of CO_2 per megawatt year (0.24 tonnes per GJ). *The newest geothermal plants use reinjection of gases and produce no emissions

Table 9.4 The Geysers field: improvements in cost-effectiveness

	Capital cost per kW of capacity	Operational/maintenance costs per kWh	Overall energy production cost per kWh
1981	$3000	4.0 cents	8.5 cents
1991	$2600	2.2 cents	5.7 cents

By the year 2000 it is planned that production costs will have fallen further, to 4.8 cents per kWh, as advanced drilling, exploration and conversion technologies are introduced. However, it is not yet known how much the need for further reinjection will add to costs during the present decade. Sharing of experience and R&D costs among the different operators will be a vital factor in achieving targets. The obvious economic advantages of high-enthalpy resources in providing a good return on capital have stimulated loan investments by international agencies such as the World Bank in geothermal developments, especially in Central and South American countries. But perhaps the greatest economic gain to society in general lies in the 150 million barrels of oil a year which is already being saved. Moreover, in some areas, geothermally generated steam is cheap (e.g. $2.50 a tonne in Iceland compared with $15.00 a tonne from oil-fired boilers).

The economics of lower-grade geothermal resources are much more marginal and depend on local political and economic conditions, such as the availability and price of fossil fuels, the willingness of governments to invest in new energy concepts, the degree of environmental awareness and the related tax incentives to promote 'clean' energy commercially. Future European HDR research might provide a suitable focus, and since this is clearly the most expensive form of geothermal energy, and technically the most 'distant', it is worth dwelling briefly on HDR cost modelling. (See Box 9.7.)

Taking the worst case scenario with the lowest thermal gradient of all proposed sites, several estimates have been made of energy production costs in south-west England based on experience at the Rosemanowes site. The models start from the point at which successful R&D justifies building a 4 MW net output prototype plant, which absorbs 0.82 MW for pumping. Various assumptions have been made about the geometry of the heat exchange surface (five separate stimulated zones in the depth interval 4–6 km are included in the 'Sunderland model', prepared by the University of Sunderland), the thermal lifetime of the system, its hydromechanical behaviour and the performance of the (assumed) binary cycle power plant. At 1990 prices (Figure 9.21) capital costs are £32.7 million ($15 000 per kW), with operating and other costs of £13.1 million (4 cents per kWh) over an assumed 18 year lifetime. If the rate of return on capital invested is taken

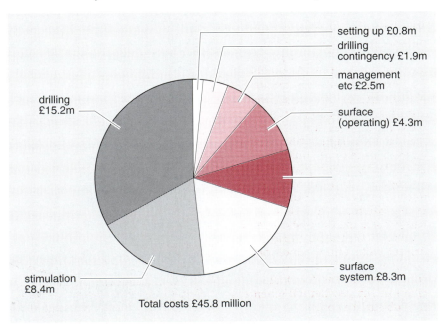

Figure 9.21 Cost breakdown of preparing and operating over an 18 year lifetime a mature hot dry rock 4 MW geothermal electric system based on current understanding of conditions in Cornwall. This is based on the Sunderland cost model; 1990 costs are assumed

setting up £0.8m
drilling contingency £1.9m
management etc £2.5m
surface (operating) £4.3m
drilling £15.2m
surface system £8.3m
stimulation £8.4m
Total costs £45.8 million

BOX 9.7: COST MODELLING OF GEOTHERMAL ENERGY SCHEMES

Cost modelling (see the Appendix) is a simplified way of calculating the likely cost of a complex project. Essentially, it involves the use of a set of (usually simple) mathematical equations in which the costs of the various elements of the project are expressed in terms of a number of parameters, the values of which can be specified or readily determined.

Detailed cost modelling of geothermal schemes is subject to a large number of variables, many of which have already been mentioned. They include:

• the costs of drilling to intersect the reservoir – increasingly expensive at greater depth (Figure 9.22);

• the cost of generating electricity, which depends on reservoir characteristics such as pressure, temperature, salinity, non-condensable gas content, etc.;

• the costs of dealing with environmental factors, especially those of reinjecting spent fluids;

• the capital outlay on plant;

• operating and maintenance costs over a lifetime of perhaps 30 years.

The costs of geothermal schemes differ in nature from those of conventional power generation and heat production. Generally, the costs of the surface component of a geothermal scheme are well known and are amenable to some control, although, as we have seen, actual design options depend on the nature of the fluid. For any given design, power plant capital and operation/maintenance costs depend primarily on output rating, whereas in a district heating scheme the costs depend principally on the heat load density and climatic conditions. However, apart from fluid conditions, the most variable factor in any geothermal scheme is the sub-surface cost.

The costs of drilling and maintaining wells and, where necessary, stimulating aquifers or fracture zones, and of pumping fluid, can be extremely important and variable. Low- and high-enthalpy sources will be economically sensitive in different ways. For example, unit costs in aquifer developments will be sensitive to aquifer temperature at different depths. As higher temperatures occur, so unit costs will fall, but eventually returns will diminish when heat rises above a certain point.

In simple terms, costs are much higher outside dry steam fields than within them. Nowhere is this better illustrated than in the western USA where there is 800 MW of installed capacity outside the Geysers dry steam field. Revenues from sales of geothermal electricity at these plants could become inadequate to cover costs once fixed-price contracts expire during the period 1994–2001, at which time the industry may be forced to compete directly with electricity generated from cheap natural gas.

Figure 9.22 US onshore oil and gas well costs

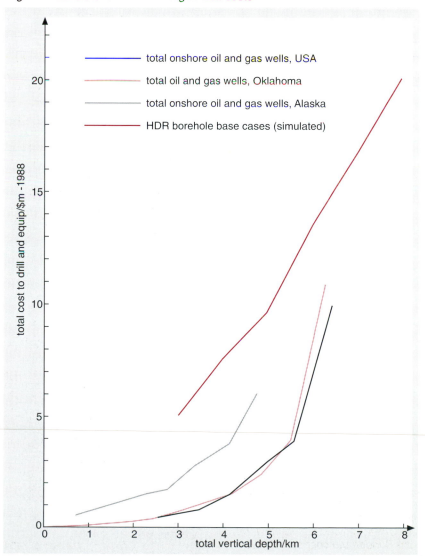

as 8%, then the overall cost of electricity production is 17p per kWh, falling to 12p per kWh if the discount rate were only 2%. The costs implied by the Sunderland model fall neatly between other more optimistic and pessimistic scenarios. Clearly, the economics are at best *extremely* marginal, and at worst have led to the conclusion that HDR research should be abandoned. However, the cost estimates are very sensitive to the geothermal gradient in the upper crust. High thermal gradients dramatically reduce unit costs simply because drilling is such an important component of the overall cost profile. This will be a factor in deciding whether European R&D investment should be focused at Soultz (just north of Strasbourg) where adequate temperatures occur at 3.5 km depth, or at Urach where they occur at 4.5–5 km depth, rather than in Cornwall. As a final caveat, note that although we can make reasonable estimates of the capital costs of HDR schemes, we still do not know how to construct a good reservoir, so we can only base our estimates on what its performance and properties *ought* to be. So predictions of HDR costs are arguably premature until further technological developments have provided better reservoir performance data.

9.8 GEOTHERMAL POTENTIAL IN THE UNITED KINGDOM

SEDIMENTARY BASIN AQUIFERS

Along with many other countries, geothermal resource evaluation in the UK followed the mid-1970s oil crisis. By 1984, new maps of heat flow (Figure 9.23(a)) and of promising geothermal sites (Figure 9.23(b)) had been produced. Three radiothermal granite zones stand out with the highest heat flow values, but significant heat flow anomalies also occur over the five sedimentary basins identified, partly because these are regions of natural hot water upflow. Many shallow heat flow boreholes were drilled during this period, together with the four deep exploration well sites of Figure 9.23(b) and Table 9.5.

In each case the main aquifer is the permeable Triassic Sherwood Sandstone (named after its most notable outcrops in the East Midlands). The shallower intersections with this aquifer at Larne and Cleethorpes are at a rather low temperature for geothermal exploitation but have reasonably high flow rates on account of the large aquifer thickness. But, unfortunately, the other two wells, which intersect the aquifer at a better temperature, produce rather low flow rates because of the restricted vertical height of good aquifer rock. The yield is reduced not just because the sedimentary sequence is thinner in the Southampton area, but also because much of the Sherwood sandstone proved to be more highly cemented and therefore less

Table 9.5 Characteristics of deep exploration well sites

Location	Completion	Well depth (m)	Bottom temp.	Main aquifer depth(m)	Temperature
Marchwood	Feb 1980	2609	88 °C	1672–1686	74 °C
Larne	July 1981	2873	91 °C	960–1247	40 °C
Southampton	Nov 1981	1823	77 °C	1725–1749	76 °C
Cleethorpes	June 1984	2092	69 °C	1093–1490	44–55 °C

permeable. During well tests the two high temperature wells in Southampton successfully yielded 30 litres per second ($l\,s^{-1}$), a value consistent with Paris Basin exploitation, but hydrogeological modelling showed that this would be too high if an operational life of 20 years was required without reinjection to maintain reservoir pressure.

The Marchwood borehole was drilled in a power station yard on the opposite side of the Test estuary from Southampton, with the aim of using the geothermal fluid as pre-heat feedwater in the Marchwood power station. The subsequent closure of this oil-fired plant by CEGB prevented this and the well has since been used for a succession of scientific experiments rather than commercially. The Southampton borehole has quite a different history and, as described in Section 9.2 above, has now been exploited at low flow rates ($12\,l\,s^{-1}$), without reinjection, for local space heating. Experience in Southampton, and cost modelling based on Paris Basin data, suggest that if the real costs of developing district heating schemes in the UK were absorbed by the operators (i.e. if there were no subsidies) then, depending on site conditions, the price would range up towards 5p per kWh of delivered heat. This is very marginally economic for a commercial concern, especially given the risk of drilling unsuccessful wells.

Figure 9.23 (a) Heat flow map of the UK based on all available measurements to 1984 compiled and published by the British Geological Survey; (b) Distributions of radiothermal crystalline rocks (granites) and major sedimentary basins likely to contain significant geothermal aquifers in the UK. (Sites of four major wells already drilled are indicated in the key)

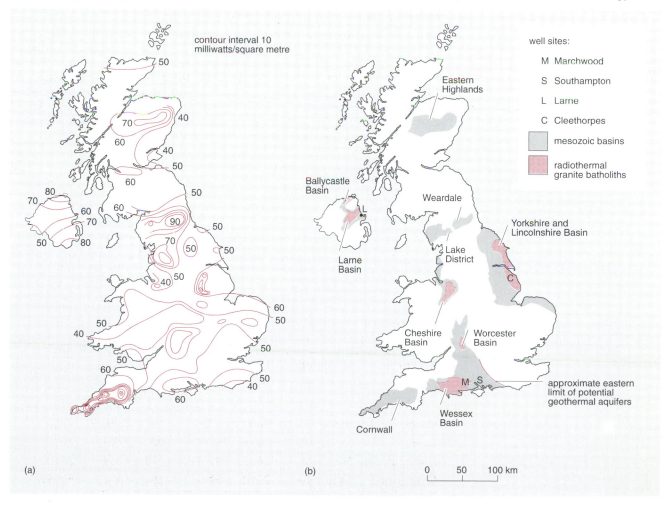

Table 9.6 Potential UK geothermal energy resources at different temperatures

Basin	Potential resource at 40–60 °C (10^{18} J)	Potential resource at >60 °C (10^{18} J)
East Yorks and Lincs	26.2	0.2
Wessex	2.8	1.8
Worcester	3.0	–
Cheshire	8.9	1.5
Northern Ireland	6.7	1.3
TOTALS	47.6	4.8

. Other assumptions are that the 40–60 °C resource (Table 9.6) would be exploited with the use of heat pumps, producing a reject temperature of 10 °C, whereas the >60 °C resource would not, giving a 30 °C reject temperature. The latter resources could be doubled with heat pumps. For comparison, UK electrical energy demand is around 10^{18} J a year (about 30 GW as equivalent continuous power), so we are considering here enormous reserves of renewable energy, but as heat rather than electricity.

So why are geothermal aquifers not being exploited much more widely?

The problem is not just one of marginal economics and geological uncertainty, but is to do with the mismatch between resource availability and heat load, itself a function of population density. Over half the resources are located in east Yorkshire and Lincolnshire, essentially rural areas lacking the concentrated populations of the Paris basin. The other UK areas are little better, though several large conurbations in the Midlands and North West could benefit from geothermal schemes such as that at Southampton. For example, there has been much discussion about reopening and exploiting the Cleethorpes well if high flow rates could be maintained at around 50 °C. Should fossil fuel prices ever escalate again, no doubt geothermal aquifers in the UK will receive much more attention than at present.

HOT DRY ROCKS

Of the three principal granite zones in the eastern Highlands, northern England and south-west England, the latter is characterised by the highest heat flow, as shown in Figure 9.23(a). However, large areas of the more northerly granite masses are covered by low thermal conductivity sedimentary rocks and so, from Equation 3 (Box 9.4), temperatures will be higher at depth than if the granite bodies came to the surface. Nevertheless, by the mid-1980s detailed evaluation of the radiothermal and heat conduction properties of all the granite areas still demonstrated, as shown in Figure 9.24, that the south-west England granite mass is the best HDR prospect. Substantial areas of Cornwall and Devon are projected in Figure 9.25 as having temperatures above 200 °C at 6 km depth and it has been estimated that the HDR resource base in south-west England alone might match the energy content of current UK coal reserves. One recent estimate suggested that 300–500 MW (about 10^{16} J a^{-1}) could be developed in Cornwall over the next 20–30 years with much more to follow later. However, for technological and economic reasons, explained earlier, the pace of progress is unlikely to be that fast.

A few historical notes on the Rosemanowes rock mechanics experiments serve to demonstrate some of the outstanding uncertainties in HDR projects, and hence the risk factor that may be inadequately covered by the drilling contingency in the cost breakdown shown in Figure 9.22. Phase 1 of this project (1977–80) saw the drilling of four 300 m deep boreholes to demonstrate that controlled explosions within the boreholes could improve permeability and initiate new fractures which might then be stimulated hydraulically. This was highly successful and target impedances of 0.1 MPa l^{-1} were achieved. (Incidentally, 22 °C water from a measurement borehole now supplies a small-scale, commercial horticultural scheme at nearby Penryn – a second, albeit minor, UK use of geothermal resources.)

The fractures opened during Phase 1 were essentially in the horizontal plane since compressive stresses at 300 m are at a minimum in the vertical direction and fractures develop most readily at right angles to the direction of minimum compressive stress. However, at depths exceeding 500 m the

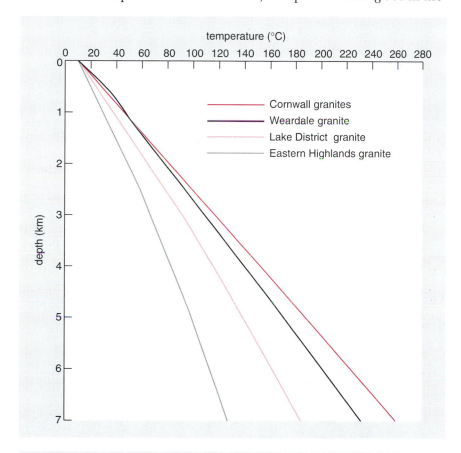

Figure 9.24 Comparison of predicted temperature–depth profiles in four major UK granite bodies in Figure 9.23(b)

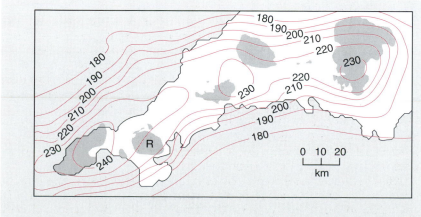

Figure 9.25 Projected temperature (°C) at 6 km depth beneath south-west England. Granite bodies that crop out at the surface are shaded (R = Rosemanowes)

minimum compressive stresses become closer to horizontal, and so near-vertical cracks will dominate. The mode of water flow, and of water loss, will therefore be very different below 500 m from what it is at a shallower depth. It is this aspect that Phase 2A (1981–89) was designed to investigate. Two 2 km deep, 30° deviated boreholes were drilled in the same plane, but after suitable fracturing the system did not behave as predicted. Water losses were excessive and the pumping required, even for poor circulation, was too high. Microseismic sensors positioned around the site were used during stimulation and circulation to pinpoint the cracking events in three dimensions. The results, plotted in Figure 9.26, show a cloud of events indicating crack propagation *beneath* the boreholes and to some extent at right angles to the plane in which they were deviated. Little wonder, then, that there were large water losses! From this it was concluded that rather few natural fractures had been intersected and that the choice of deviation direction had been unfortunate. In Phase 2B a further, deeper borehole was drilled to cross the earlier cloud of microseismic positions at right angles; stimulation was much more successful with good connections being made

Figure 9.26 Vertical section through the deep wells beneath the Rosemanowes quarry showing the seismic sources generated during Phase 2A reservoir stimulation and Phase 2B reservoir stimulation

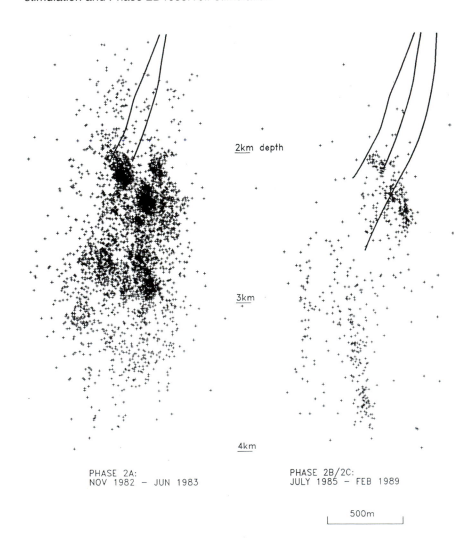

2km depth

3km

4km

PHASE 2A:
NOV 1982 – JUN 1983

PHASE 2B/2C:
JULY 1985 – FEB 1989

500m

to one of the previous wells. Although this is not the ideal HDR geometry, the subsequent circulation of water over a five year period, with associated testing, means that the Rosemanowes work has made an outstanding contribution to HDR technology. Clearly, for commercial applications, *in situ* rock stresses need to be better understood to minimise drilling and engineering uncertainties.

If and when drilling and hydrofracturing technology is improved, large areas of the UK are potentially available for HDR development. One estimate by the British Geological Survey is that 360×10^{18} J could ultimately be available from this source, enough to provide UK electrical energy needs for 200 years! However, major technological breakthroughs, coupled to a significant increase in the market price of conventional energy resources, would be needed to make HDR a viable source of power for the UK. The Renewable Energy Advisory Group concluded in 1992 that, within the UK, market penetration by geothermal aquifer-based energy systems will be difficult and that hot dry rock systems would not be economically viable in the foreseeable future. Indeed, at the time of writing, the Rosemanowes project was due to be closed down, the UK government having abandoned support for the scheme in favour of committing funds to joint research with the Germans and French (see the end of Section 9.4).

FURTHER READING

THE INTERNATIONAL SCENE

Di Pippo, R. (1988) 'International developments in geothermal power production', *Geothermal Resources Council Bulletin* 17, pp. 8–19.

Falcone, D. J. and Short, W. P. (1992) 'Living on the cliff', *Geothermal Resources Council Bulletin*, 21, pp. 325–328.

Freeston, D. H. (1990) 'Direct uses of geothermal energy in 1990', *Geothermal Resources Council Bulletin*, 19, pp. 188–198.

Huttrer, G. W. (1990) 'Geothermal electric power – a 1990 world status update', *Geothermal Resources Council Bulletin* 19, pp. 175–187.

The *GRC Bulletin* is a valuable continuing source of new ideas and data on international developments. The Council address is: 2121 Second Street, Suite 101A, Davis, California 95617, USA.

Harrison, R., Mortimer, N. D. and Smarason, O. B. (1990) *Geothermal Heating: A Handbook of Engineering Economics*, Pergamon Press.

An extremely comprehensive account with particular focus on technology and economics; good general introduction chapter.

EUROPE AND THE UK

Cross, B. (1992) *European Directory of Renewable Energy*, London, James and James.

Sections by Garnish and Batchelor cover geothermal developments in Europe and power generation from low-grade geothermal resources. There is also a useful US Supplement to the European directory with an article about geothermal energy in the USA by Anderson, Kraft and Liddell. Available from James and James Science Publishers, 5 Castle Rd, London NW1 8PR.

Downing, R. A. and Gray, D. A. (eds) (1986) *Geothermal Energy: The Potential in the United Kingdom*, London, HMSO.

A comprehensive account of a full decade of UK research into aquifers and HDR including much more technical data than it is possible to provide in this section.

Garnish, J. D., Vaux, R. and Fuller, R. W. E. (1986) *Geothermal Aquifers: Department of Energy R & D Programme, 1976–1986*, ETSU Report R-39. Summary of research on UK aquifers; see below for information on ETSU publications.

Laughton, M. A. (ed.) (1990) *Renewable Energy Resources*. Watt Committee Report No. 22. Section 7 is devoted to geothermal and includes objective comment on the UK scene; Watt Committee reports are available from Elsevier Scientific Publishers Ltd., Crown House, Linton Road, Barking, Essex IG11 8JU.

Major, K. (1991) 'The Southampton story', *Review* 15, pp. 8–9.

Review covers the whole renewables scene and contains occasional articles of geothermal interest. It is available through the Energy Technology Support Unit, Renewable Energy Enquiries Bureau, Building 149, Harwell Laboratory, Oxfordshire OX1 0RA.

HOT DRY ROCKS

Armstead, H. C. H. and Tester, J. W. (1987) *Heat Mining*, Chapman and Hall.

An authoritative text based mainly on experiences in the USA.

Baria, R. (ed.) (1990) *Hot Dry Rock Geothermal Energy*, London, Robertson Scientific Publications.

This book contains the proceedings of an international conference held in Cornwall in June 1989. It contains comprehensive technical summaries of progress in HDR, resources, technology, economics, reservoir creation and development. Robertson Scientific Publications are at 122 King's Cross Road, London WC1X 9DS.

Clark, J. H., Litt, J., Stedman, A. M. and Symons, G. D. (1991) *Geothermal Hot Dry Rock: Department of Energy R & D Programme, 1976–1991*. ETSU Report R-59.

Comprehensive account of research in SW England at the Rosemanowes site.

ETSU (1994) *The Economics of HDR Geothermal Energy* Report ETSU1/035/00052/REP Energy Technology Support Unit.

Garnish, J., Batchelor, T. and Ledingham, P. (1992) 'Hot dry rock in Europe', *Geothermal Resources Council Bulletin*, 21, pp. 167–173.

Useful source of information on Soultz together with an evaluation of the future of HDR.

Symons, G. D. (1991) *The 1990 Geothermal HDR Programme Review*. ETSU Report R-53.

Essentially an account of the engineering problems and economics of HDR at Rosemanowes.

INTEGRATION

10.1 INTRODUCTION

As we saw in Chapter 1, various studies have suggested that renewable energy sources could be making very significant contributions to the energy needs of the United Kingdom, the European Union and the world as a whole during the early part of the next century. Indeed, as we also saw in Chapter 1, renewables are already making substantial contributions to the world's primary energy needs, approximately 14% of which are supplied by traditional biomass and 6% by large-scale hydro power (1992 estimates: see Figure 1.2).

A useful summary of the status of the main renewable energy technologies was given in a report by the Watt Committee on Energy (Laughton *et al.*, 1990) which divided the different technologies into four classes:

1 *Economic*. These are well developed and economically viable technologies, at least in some markets and locations. Further market penetration will require technological refinements, mass production and/or economies of scale.

2 *Commercial with incentives*. These technologies are available in some markets but can compete with conventional technologies only if given preferential treatments such as subsidies. They need further refinements, mass production and economies of scale.

3 *Under development*. These technologies need more research and development to improve efficiency, reliability or cost in order to become commercial. This includes materials and systems development, pilot plants or field experiments to resolve operational problems and reduce environmental impacts, and demonstration plants to illustrate performance and establish costs.

4 *Future technology*. These are technologies which have not yet been technically proven, even though scientifically feasible. At this stage of development, applied R&D on components would typically be carried out, as would bench-scale model development in the laboratory to establish the technical viability.

The Watt Committee's summary of the status of the main renewables under these four headings is given in Table 10.1.

In Chapters 2-9, we reviewed each major renewable energy source in turn, and quoted various estimates of the contributions that each could make to national, regional or world energy needs during the coming decades. We also looked briefly at how each renewable source might be integrated into existing and future energy supply systems.

But what are the conditions under which these contributions might be realised in practice, and what are the most promising strategies for incorporating the many different forms of renewable energy into our systems of energy supply?

Modern societies, as we have seen, demand energy not only in extremely large quantities but in many different forms. In order to meet these quantitative and qualitative requirements, a vast, world-wide network of energy supply and distribution systems has been built up. If renewables are to make an increasing contribution to twenty-first century energy needs, to what extent will these existing energy networks need to be modified and supplemented?

Can renewables deliver our energy, not only in significant *amounts* and at an acceptable *price*, but also in the right *form*, at the right *time*, and in the right *place*?

What are the factors that currently make it difficult for renewable energy sources to compete with conventional sources? Is it just that they are often relatively expensive? Or are there various institutional, regulatory or other barriers that 'unfairly' inhibit them from becoming competitive? If so, how might governments create a 'level playing field' that could enable them to achieve a 'fairer' share of the energy market in future? And what is a 'fair share' in this context?

These are some of the questions we shall be attempting to answer in this final chapter. In it, we return to many of the topics discussed in earlier chapters, but try to draw some of the threads together and to describe the main factors that are likely to determine the overall contribution that renewable energy sources can make to the world's energy needs in coming decades.

Table 10.1   Watt Committee classification of current status of development of renewable energy technologies

ECONOMIC
(in some locations – not necessarily the UK)
Solar water heaters, for swimming pools or replacing domestic electric water heating, or with seasonal storage
Solar industrial process heat with parabolic trough collectors or large flat-plate collectors
Residential passive solar heating designs and daylighting
Solar agricultural drying
Small remote photovoltaic systems
Small to medium wind systems
Direct biomass combustion
Conventional geothermal technologies (dry and flashed steam power generation, higher-temperature hot water and low-temperature heat)
Tidal power
Hydro power

COMMERCIAL WITH INCENTIVES
Solar water and space heating replacing natural gas or oil
Solar electricity generation with parabolic trough collectors
Non-residential passive solar heating and daylighting
Biomass liquid fuels (ethanol) from sugar and starch feedstocks
Binary cycle hydro-geothermal systems

UNDER DEVELOPMENT
Solar space cooling (active and passive)
Solar thermal power systems (other than parabolic trough collectors)
Photovoltaic power systems
Biomass gasification
Hot dry rock geothermal
Wave energy systems

FUTURE TECHNOLOGY
Photochemical and thermochemical conversion
Fast pyrolysis or direct liquefaction of biomass
Biochemical biomass conversion processes
Ocean thermal energy conversion (OTEC)
Geopressured geothermal and geothermal magma

(Source: based on Laughton *et al.*, 1990)

As we shall see, although the integration of renewables into our energy supply systems may pose some technical problems, the main challenges are economic, social, institutional and political.

Firstly, we will look briefly at existing energy systems and how they currently supply our various demands (Section 10.2). Then we will review some estimates of the quantitative contribution that renewables might make to the future energy needs of the UK (Section 10.3) and investigate the extent to which renewables can deliver energy in suitable forms, in the right place and at the right time, to meet our needs (Sections 10.4 and 10.5).

In Section 10.6 we will look at how the patterns of energy use in three countries have changed over recent decades.

Finally, in Sections 10.7–10.10, we will take a more detailed look at some 'energy scenarios' that have been constructed by governmental and non-governmental organisations in order to explore the various possible patterns of energy supply and demand in the future – and in particular the roles that renewables might play in such scenarios. We will also examine various measures that might be adopted by governments, companies, institutions and individuals, in order to promote an increasing contribution from renewable energy sources in the future.

10.2 EXISTING ENERGY SYSTEMS

Figure 10.1, sometimes called a 'Sankey diagram' after its originator, shows an overall picture of energy flows in the UK. Energy flows from so-called 'primary' energy sources, such as oil and gas wells, coal and uranium mines and hydro power stations, through installations such as oil refineries and fossil or nuclear power stations, in which the primary fuels are converted into deliverable energy forms.

In the current UK system these 'delivered' energy forms are of five main kinds:

• *liquid fuels*: almost entirely oil and its derivatives – petroleum (gasoline), diesel, kerosene, etc.;

• *gaseous fuels*: mostly methane ('natural gas'), plus some 'bottled' gas (propane and butane);

• *solid fuels*: almost entirely coal and its derivatives, but with small contributions from fuel wood, refuse incineration and straw burning;

• *electricity*: almost all from fossil-fuelled or nuclear power stations, with a small (2%) hydroelectric component;

• *heat*: in some countries (but only to a limited extent in the UK) substantial quantities of energy are supplied to buildings directly in the form of hot water or steam. This energy is provided either by centralised boilers in 'district heating' (DH) schemes, or in the form of 'waste' heat from power stations, in 'combined heat and power' (CHP) schemes.

These energy forms then flow into the various networks that have been developed for the distribution of electricity, gaseous, solid and liquid fuels, and heat, and are thus delivered to 'final consumers' in the main energy-using sectors of the economy.

Broadly, these sectors can be categorised as:
• domestic;
• services;
• industry;
• transport.

Within each of these sectors, 'delivered' energy in its various forms is used to satisfy our needs. But of course no-one actually 'needs' electricity, gas, oil or coal, as such. They need the energy service or services that such

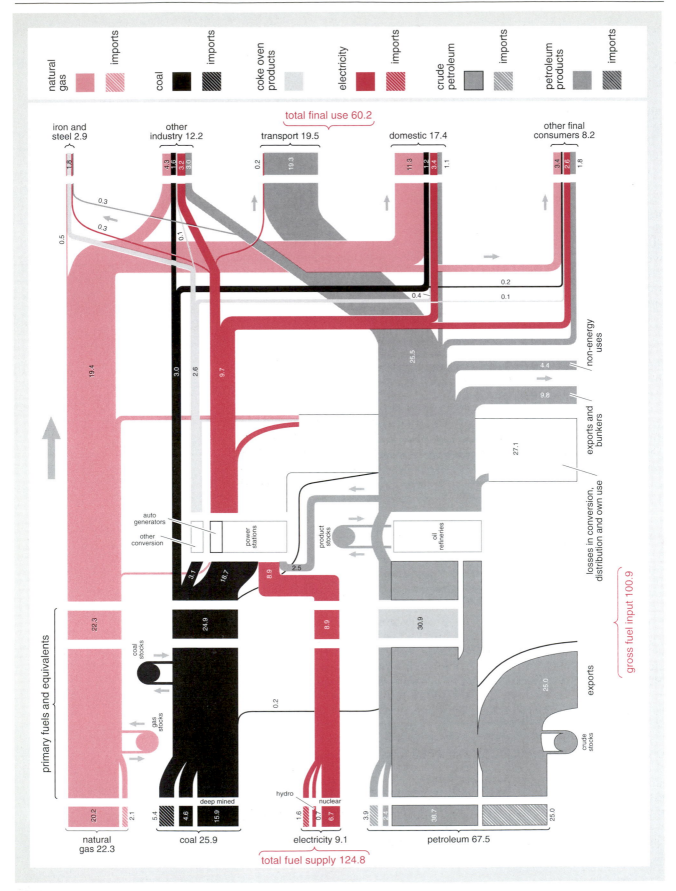

natural gas | imports | coal | imports | coke oven products | electricity | imports | crude petroleum | imports | petroleum products | imports

total final use 60.2

iron and steel 2.9

other industry 12.2

transport 19.5

domestic 17.4

other final consumers 8.2

1.8

4.3 1.6 3.0

0.2 19.3

11.3 1.2 3.4 1.1

3.4 2.6 1.8

0.3

0.3

0.5

0.1

19.4

3.0

2.6

9.7

25.5

0.4

0.2

0.1

non-energy uses

4.4

exports and bunkers

9.8

auto generators

other conversion

power stations

product stocks

oil refineries

27.1

losses in conversion, distribution and own use

gross fuel input 100.9

3.1 18.7

8.9

2.5

primary fuels and equivalents

22.3

coal stocks

24.9

8.9

8.9

30.9

0.2

exports

25.0

gas stocks

crude stocks

hydro

nuclear

1.6 0.7 6.7

deep mined

20.2 2.1

5.4 4.6 15.9

3.9 2.4 38.7 25.0

natural gas 22.3

coal 25.9

electricity 9.1

petroleum 67.5

total fuel supply 124.8

◄ *Figure 10.1 'Sankey diagram' showing the main flows of energy in the UK, 1992. Units: thousand million Therms (10^9 Therms = 105.5 PJ). Note that hydro and nuclear electricity contributions are expressed in terms of the primary energy content of the coal that would need to be burned to generate the equivalent amounts of electricity. (Source: DTI, 1993)*

fuels provide. Almost all our current energy service requirements can be categorised under the broad headings of:

- heat;
- motive power;
- electricity-based services.

Heat is required in many forms – from tepid water to superheated steam – for washing, cooking, space heating and industrial processing. It can be provided either by burning fuels close to where the heat is needed, by piping heat in from a more distant CHP or DH plant, or by using electricity, either in resistance heaters or in more sophisticated devices like microwave ovens.

Motive power is needed, obviously, for transport (cars, trucks, buses, trains, ships and aircraft, etc.) and to drive machinery. In most cases the form of delivered energy currently used to supply it is oil. However, a small but significant proportion of energy for motive power is in the form of electricity – some of it for electric railways, but a great deal in the almost unnoticed but ubiquitous form of power for electric motors. These are now used in enormous numbers for everything from watches to miniature cassette recorders, from washing machines to air conditioning systems, from industrial machinery to elevators.

Services based on the use of *electricity*, that most versatile of energy forms, include heat, lighting and motive power, which can also be provided by other forms of delivered energy. Electricity is also *essential* for use in those systems that simply cannot function with any other energy form – most notably, the vast array of electronic systems used by our society, including computers and communications systems but also more specialised applications such as electro-chemical processes.

10.3 HOW MUCH RENEWABLE ENERGY IS AVAILABLE?

Having looked very briefly at the UK's energy needs and how they are currently met by a variety of energy sources, let us now consider what contribution could be made by renewables.

Table 10.2 shows the UK Department of Energy's 1988 view of the total potential for renewable energy resources in the UK. The estimated total technical potential is very substantial. For electricity producers the total, equivalent to 57.2 GW of installed capacity, represents almost twice the 1990 UK electricity demand – and even this only includes those renewable energy options that appeared promising to the government at the time. It excludes, for example, electricity from biomass, active solar heating and photovoltaics.

A more recent report to the UK government by the Renewable Energy Advisory Group (REAG, 1992) came to similar conclusions. Figure 1.16 in Chapter 1 shows the Group's estimates of the 'accessible potential' of various electricity-producing renewable energy technologies, at a price of less than 10p per kWh in the UK. The Group's definition of 'accessible potential' is 'the amount of renewable energy which it would be technically possible to derive taking into account only basic constraints'. (See also Appendix 1.) As can be seen, the total accessible potential, at 1060 TWh a

Table 11.2   Technical potential and estimated contribution by 2025 of renewable energy resources in the UK

	Technical potential (TWh per year)	Estimated contribution (TWh per year)
Electricity producers		
Wind power		
– onshore	45	0–30
– offshore	1640	?
Tidal	54	0–28
Geothermal (hot dry rocks)	210	0–10
Wave	50	0–0.2
Small-scale hydro	2	0.3–0.7
Total electricity	**501**	**0.3–68.9**

	Technical potential (PJ per year)	Estimated contribution (PJ per year)
Heat producers		
Passive solar	216–378	27–54
Biofuels		
– wet and dry wastes (inc. landfill gas)	594	81–270
– forestry	At least 540	27–135
Total heat	**1350–1512**	**135–439**

Note: biofuels can be used to produce either heat or electricity, or both (CHP).
(Source: Department of Energy, 1988)

Figure 10.2 Diagrammatic representation of the current UK electricity system. Electricity is generated in power plants, most of them like the one shown on the left; transmitted over long distances at high voltage by the National Grid Company; and distributed at various lower voltages by the Regional Electricity Companies (in England and Wales) to industrial, commercial, institutional and domestic users

year, is more than three times the current UK electricity demand. A similar figure of 1100 TWh per year was arrived at in 1994 by the Energy Technology Support Unit (ETSU, 1994) in its assessment of the 'accessible resource' for electricity - producing renewable energy technologies in the UK. Equally large potentials are available in most other countries, though the mixture varies according to their individual circumstances.

Although the potential contribution of a renewable energy source may be very large, there is usually an enormous gulf between this and the actual contribution that is likely to be achieved by a given time in the future. Calculating such 'estimated contributions' is more of an art than a science and involves a great deal of judgement about likely future developments in

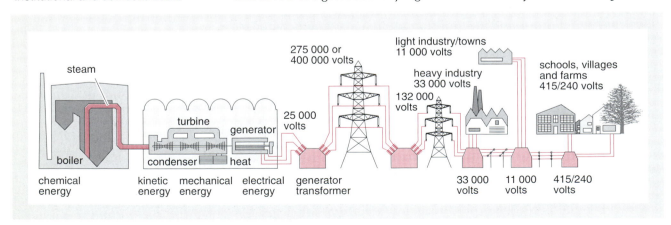

technology, market conditions, government regulations, public acceptability and similar factors. Figure 1.17 in Chapter 1 shows REAG's calculations of the estimated contribution of renewables to electricity generation in the UK by 2025. As can be seen, the estimated contribution depends primarily on the price of energy from each renewable source: if the price is low, the contribution could be large; if the price is high, the contribution is likely to be small. But then, as we shall see, the prices of the various energy sources do not always reflect their true costs to society.

The REAG report concentrated mainly on electricity and did not give estimates of the future contribution of renewables to UK needs for heat or transport fuels.

Figure 10.3 The Europe-wide network of natural gas distribution pipelines

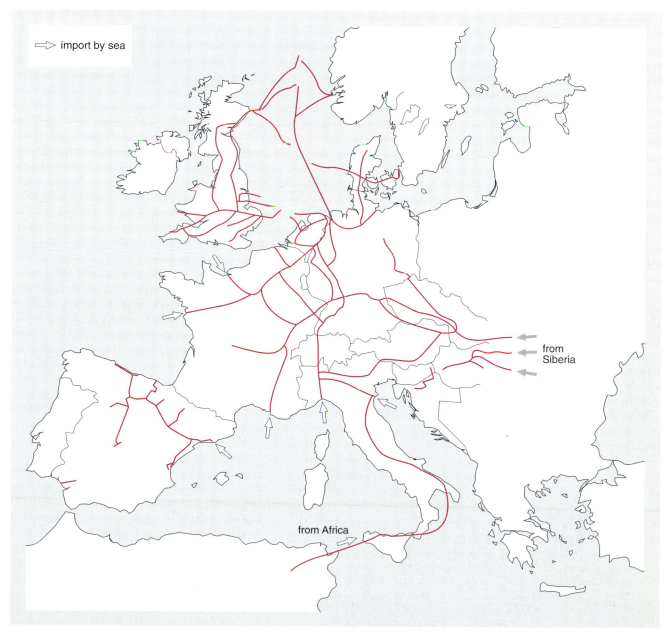

10.4 ARE RENEWABLE ENERGY SUPPLIES AVAILABLE WHERE WE WANT THEM?

So the potential contribution of renewables to UK energy needs could be very large in quantitative terms. Qualitatively, too, renewables can provide heat, motive power and electricity, in the same differing forms as can conventional sources. But can renewables supply our energy *where* we want it?

Most of our energy demand actually occurs within the relatively small areas of our major cities. Many of these are built in sheltered inland valleys, deliberately to *avoid* the worst excesses of wind and wave energy.

Many large industrial towns actually grew up around their fuel supplies, coal or wood. Some faded to obscurity when their fuel ran out. Others, like London for example, survived the destruction of their surrounding forests by importing fossil fuels. Even in the nineteenth century London was dependent on surrounding fields for its transport biofuel (hay for horses).

Figure 10.4 Geographical distribution of offshore wind, wave and tidal energy resources in the UK

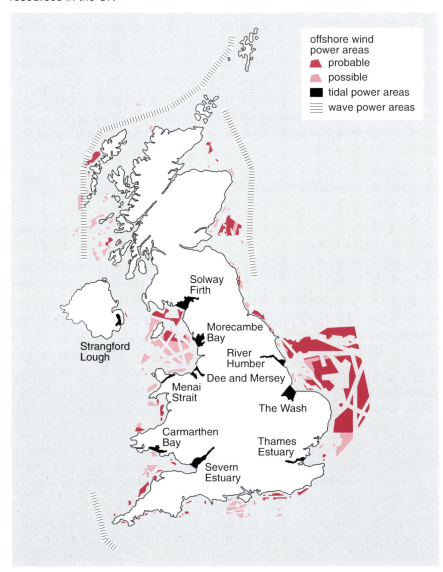

But with the advent of twentieth-century petroleum, some of these fields could be covered with houses.

In the first half of this century, most European cities ran mainly on coal, brought by rail or by sea. It was burned immediately where it was needed, or was converted into electricity or 'town gas' in local plants, often creating considerable pollution problems.

Nowadays, the picture is different. Electricity, oil, coal, solid fuel and natural gas are distributed country-wide. Electricity is generated in very large plants, usually of 500 MW or more output, and in the UK it is rare to find one really close to a major city. Coal-fired plants are often located near coal mines and where large amounts of cooling water are available. Similarly, most nuclear power stations are located on the coast where sea water can be used for cooling.

Electricity is distributed to users via the National Grid, a network of high-voltage cables that covers the UK and has a link across the Channel to France; and more locally via the lower-voltage grids operated (in England and Wales) by the Regional Electricity Companies (see Figure 10.2). This large-scale transmission of electricity has a price: about 8% of the electricity generated is dissipated in resistive losses in the cables used for its distribution.

In a similar manner, natural gas flows from the North Sea through a nationwide pipeline grid. Indeed, there is an impressive Europe-wide system of pipelines for natural gas distribution (Figure 10.3), stretching from Algeria in the south to Norway in the north and from Siberia in the east to the west of France and on to Spain.

Oil is transported to the UK by ship and pipeline, and is distributed within the UK mainly by road and rail, although some is sent through pipelines, and some is transported around the coast by ship.

Solid fuel is transported within the UK by road and rail, and to the UK by ship.

WHERE DO RENEWABLES FIT IN?

Overall, renewable energy sources are not evenly spread over the UK or the rest of Europe. Potential wind and wave resources are largely concentrated in the north and west and solar energy in the south. Tidal power potential is concentrated on a few large estuaries (see Figure 10.4). Biofuels are likely to be available in rural areas, but perhaps not those where food production is seen as more important than energy crops.

From an energy consumer's point of view, the importance of the spatial availability of renewable resources depends on the particular circumstances. On a Scottish island, wind or wave power are immediately to hand and could be attractive precisely because fossil fuel supplies may be physically difficult to obtain. On the mainland, where there is usually an electricity supply grid, we may not worry too much where renewable electricity supplies actually come from: they could be feeding into the grid hundreds of miles away.

Renewable heat supplies, on the other hand, are more likely to be located close to the point of demand, because of the large losses involved in heat transmission over long distances. Solar thermal panels can be fitted to the roofs of buildings. Passive solar measures are actually a part of the buildings themselves. In areas where geothermal energy is accessible and economic, boreholes can be drilled on the outskirts of the towns they serve. And refuse incinerators, given modern pollution control methods, can also be sited near town centres so that their waste heat can be put to good use.

The use of biofuels such as wood involves other spatial considerations. They need to be gathered and then transported from where they are grown, possibly in remote country areas, to where they will be used, probably in towns. This poses physical transport problems – though modern Scandinavian techniques can reduce wood to anything from small chips to a fine powder, both of which can be transported by truck or blown down a pipeline. In these forms, transporting wood is not very different from transporting coal or oil – although the energy density is considerably lower for wood.

Other biofuels, such as vegetable oils and sugars with the potential to be used as petroleum substitutes, need to be harvested, transported to processing plants and then inserted into the distribution chain to the customer. In many cases, however, liquid biofuels can be mixed with existing conventional fuels, and so fit into the existing distribution infrastructure.

This question of energy distribution may significantly affect any assessment of which renewables are best for a particular location. For example, experiments in local electricity generation using photovoltaic panels are being carried out in rural parts of Germany precisely because the existing electricity transmission lines are highly prone to failure in winter. In other countries, such as India, the cost of setting up a nationwide grid to provide electricity to every village is seen by many as prohibitive: it is considered better to devote resources to providing locally or regionally autonomous renewable energy supplies.

But for the bulk of the UK and other European countries, extensive electricity grids have already been set up. And although photovoltaic panels on the roofs of buildings could provide highly localised electricity supplies, other renewable energy sources are likely to be a lot further away. We are more likely to choose our mix of renewable resources on a regional basis than a local one.

Transmitting renewably-generated electricity raises a whole set of environmental questions about power lines, some of which are likely to be new. Much renewable power seems likely to be generated in areas previously untouched by industrial development. Many could be prime tourist areas.

At the moment, however, the electricity produced by most renewable energy installations, such as wind farms, is not fed directly into the National Grid but into local grids at around 11 kV, using relatively unobtrusive power lines. But for large-scale offshore wave and wind power the impact could be more significant: although the generators themselves might not be very prominent, they could in some circumstances require new grid connections running through hundreds of miles of countryside.

So searching out the areas with the highest wind speeds and the biggest waves might not be the best environmental solution. Scotland and Wales have vast renewable energy resources, but are remote from the main areas of energy demand: yet who wants more large pylons in the landscape? It might be better to generate electricity in more sheltered areas that are closer to the demand. Could offshore wind power in the Thames Estuary prove a better solution to supplying electricity to London than transmitting it from Wales or Cornwall? Ultimately, from an environmental point of view, it might even be worth moving the most energy-intensive industries to suitable towns in those areas with the biggest renewable energy potential.

REGIONAL ENERGY STUDIES

Given the diversity of renewable energy supplies, it is important to look in detail at their potential at a regional level. In the UK, such studies have been carried out in the North West Electricity (NORWEB) area, the South West Electricity area, Scotland and Northern Ireland. These have been complemented by a number of studies of the potential at the county and local level. (See the Further Reading in Appendix 1.) These projects are essential to identify exactly which renewable energy schemes are best suited to which area. They also raise awareness among residents, local authorities and the business community, and lay the organisational groundwork for setting up practical working projects.

10.5 ARE RENEWABLE ENERGY SUPPLIES AVAILABLE WHEN WE WANT THEM?

Our demand for energy is not constant. It varies widely over the day, the week and the year. We need more energy for heating buildings in winter than in summer. As a result the UK consumes three times as much natural gas in a typical December as it does in a summer month.

Generally, in the 'developed' countries, there are few constraints on our demand for energy. Our electricity supply systems are organised in such a way that power is virtually certain to be available whenever we turn on a switch. Gas is always there waiting for us to turn on the cooker. Every major highway has petrol stations every few kilometres ready to serve us when we drive in.

Complex infrastructures have been put into place to enable supply to meet demand. A greater need for, say, gas will set off a whole series of pumps distributing supplies from gas-holder to gas-holder through a nationwide set of mains. Any failure of the infrastructure to deliver energy without delay – be it gas, electricity, heating oil or petrol – causes a consumer outcry.

However, as we have seen, many renewable sources are intermittent. Wind, wave and solar energy are dependent on weather conditions that are partly predictable and partly random. They are not 'firm' supplies – that is, we cannot absolutely guarantee that they will be available when we need them. Hydro power is also dependent on weather conditions (though rainfall is predictable to some extent) but its availability is improved by the built-in storage provided by the reservoirs that form part of most hydro installations. Tidal power is more reliable: it is intermittent, but entirely predictable. The exceptions are biofuels, most of which can easily be stored and used on demand almost as easily as fossil fuels.

We'll look first at renewable sources of heat, then electricity, then transport fuels.

RENEWABLES AS HEAT SUPPLIERS

Heat is a relatively easy topic to consider. We can distribute it in many ways. In the UK at present this is mostly done by transporting fuel (gas, coal or oil) around the country and burning it *in situ*. Alternatively, we could distribute heat through city-wide district heating networks as is widely done in Denmark.

As we saw in Chapter 2, there are demonstration schemes in which heat is stored 'interseasonally', from summer to winter. But most heat stores, such as that shown in Figure 10.5, hold only sufficient supplies for a day or so. Using such a heat store frees renewable energy system designers from having to concern themselves with how the heat demand of a building varies over the day: but they do need to think about how it varies over the year.

We can split our heat demand into two parts:

- an all-year-round 'base load', largely water heating and industrial process heating;

- a need for space heating which peaks in mid-winter.

In countries where there is extensive district heating, part of the base load heat demand is often met by burning something that is produced

Figure 10.5 The 'Pimlico accumulator'. This large storage cylinder in central London can hold a day's heat for 4000 nearby homes

uniformly all year round – domestic rubbish. Even more of this demand can be met using waste heat from fossil-fuelled (or in the future biomass-fuelled) power stations (see Figure 10.6).

Meeting the winter space heating demand from renewable sources is a little more difficult. As we have seen in Chapter 2, there is plenty of sun to meet the summer demand, but it vanishes rapidly when winter comes. We have to choose between finding renewable heat sources to supply leaky uninsulated buildings, or insulating them so that they don't need so much energy to start with.

Experience in Scandinavia and Germany has shown that it is economically viable to insulate existing buildings to levels where their space heating demands are dramatically reduced. With new buildings, the economics are even more attractive, and the demands can be even lower. They can then be heated easily with relatively low-temperature district heating systems or quite small quantities of renewably generated electricity.

ELECTRICITY: HOW THE CURRENT UK SYSTEM WORKS

Electricity is a much more flexible and valuable commodity than heat, but it suffers from one problem: it is rather difficult to store. Generally it has to be made immediately to suit the demand. In the UK, electricity demand varies enormously over the year, and hour by hour throughout the day. Figure 10.7 shows typical national daily demand patterns for summer and winter. At night demand is relatively low, but it picks up early in the morning, flattens out during the day and reaches a peak in the early evening. This demand pattern is met by a mixture of generating plant. The first 7–8 GW is met by nuclear base-load stations. These have high capital costs but low running costs. Once built, it pays to run them continuously, whenever they are available to generate.

Next comes a mixture of coal-, oil- and gas-fired power stations. Some will run for most of the year, others will just fill in the seasonal and daily peaks. Under the present electricity generating system in England and Wales, the contribution which each power station makes depends on the price at which its owner can sell power through the National Grid Company, on the quantity of electricity it can supply and on the timing of the contribution. Generally, for a particular type of plant (coal, oil, gas, etc.), the most efficient plants run for the longest portion of the year and the less efficient ones are used at periods of high demand, e.g. mid-winter.

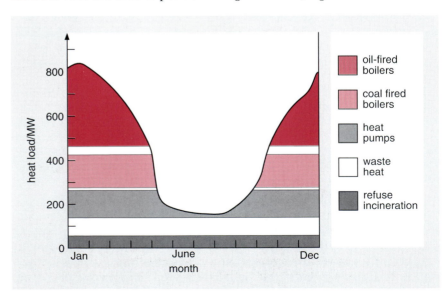

Figure 10.6 Variation of heat load over the year in a Swedish district heating scheme. Waste heat from refuse incineration and combined heat and power generation provide an all-year-round base load heat supply (Source: Swedish Trade Council)

Finally come the plants that fill in the fine detail of demand. The flexibility of hydro power makes it very good at doing this, but where hydro is not sufficient the controllers of the grid can turn to gas-turbine generators. These can be started very quickly in response to demand, but are fairly expensive to run. However, as they only operate for relatively few hours a year this does not matter too much. (These gas turbines, used as 'peaking' plant, should not be confused with the more sophisticated 'combined cycle gas turbine' (CCGT) power stations that are currently being operated by various UK electricity companies. These produce relatively cheap electricity and can be used as base load plant.) Alternatively, pumped storage plants, as described below and in Chapter 5, can be used.

The story is similar in other countries, though the proportions of fuels and generating plant may vary considerably.

The electricity distribution network that the National Grid provides gives enormous flexibility of operation. The electricity demands of Oxford do not have to be generated there, but can be met from a power station in Yorkshire or a storage plant in Wales. The electricity systems of Europe are linked across national borders (including an under-sea 'interconnector' between the UK and France), allowing power plants to share loads or export surpluses of electricity.

PUMPED STORAGE OF ELECTRICITY

Although we use electricity in an intermittent manner, turning on a light here and a heater there, on average it usually adds up to a smoothly varying demand that the grid system can cope with relatively easily. However, if for some reason all our demands become synchronised this can cause problems. Simultaneously showing the same TV programmes over the whole country can send a large proportion of the population rushing to put the kettle on at the same time. This can result in a demand surge of over 1 GW in a matter of minutes (see Figure 10.8).

Another major problem can occur if there is a sudden breakdown of a large power station. Generating capacity of 600 MW or more could suddenly disappear and it might be an hour or more before another station could get up enough steam to take over.

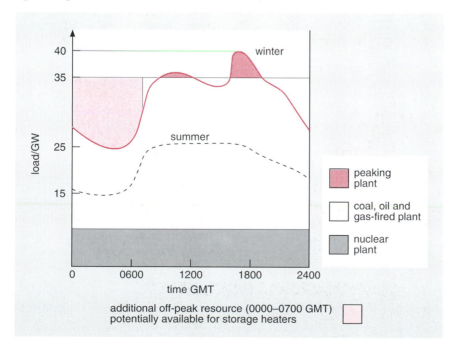

additional off-peak resource (0000–0700 GMT) potentially available for storage heaters

Figure 10.7 Variation in demand for electricity in England and Wales over a day in winter (solid line) and summer (dotted line), 1983, and notional allocation of generating plant to meet demand (Source: ETSU)

Before pumped storage plants were built, these surges were met by keeping 'spinning reserve' – extra fossil-fuelled power stations with steam up and turbines running, just waiting in case electricity was needed. But this wasted fuel.

The UK currently has three pumped storage plants, two in Wales and one in Scotland, at Cruachan (see Chapter 5). Of the Welsh plants, one, at Ffestiniog, was built in 1961 and the other, at nearby Dinorwic, in 1983. They use electricity at times of low load to pump water from a low-level lake to a high-level one. At times of sudden peak demand they use the stored potential energy of the water to generate electricity with as little as 10 seconds' notice. Their combined peak output power is over 2 GW, about 5% of the UK's typical winter electricity demand. Other countries have similar schemes. Switzerland has 8 GW of pumped storage plant and offers its services to the electricity systems of all its neighbouring countries.

DEMAND MANAGEMENT

While pumped storage can cope with sudden short-term fluctuations in supply, there are a number of other techniques of matching demand to fit the supply. These are known as 'demand management'. It would be convenient for fossil-fuelled, nuclear and most renewable electricity supplies if the electricity demand varied as little as possible over the day and night.

One way of encouraging this is through the use of 'off-peak' electricity tariffs. Electricity for heating (or other) purposes is supplied at cheaper rates at night and the heat can then be stored through to the next day. This allows existing power stations to continue running into the night, rather than having to build extra ones to cope with higher peak demands. Electricity supplied to industrial and commercial users may have quite complex price structures that discourage use at times of high demand (weekday winter evenings in the UK) and encourage it at times of low demand (mainly nights and weekends).

In the UK, only a relatively small amount of electricity is used for heating purposes. In France, with its high reliance on nuclear power, the proportion

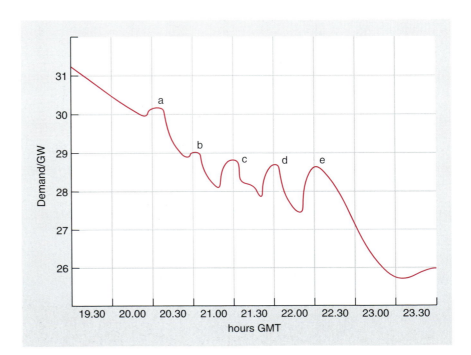

Figure 10.8 Changes in electricity demand during the showing of a James Bond film on UK television in 1975. Demand peaks at (a) and (e) mark the beginning and end of the film, and (b), (c) and (d) the commercial breaks (Source: Central Electricity Generating Board)

is much higher. The effect of the promotion of off-peak electricity in flattening out the winter demand profile is quite considerable (see Figure 10.9).

Electronic metering and communication systems now under development open up a whole range of new possibilities for demand management over a very short time-scale. These take advantage of the fact that some electrical loads can be switched off for short periods without causing significant problems. For example, although several million people apparently need to have a cup of tea or coffee simultaneously before James Bond returns to their screens, it would not matter much if their refrigerators were all turned off for five minutes in partial compensation. Experiments using remote radio switching of non-essential loads have been carried out in the UK and a number of other countries, and it is likely that the use of such techniques will increase.

INTEGRATING RENEWABLE ELECTRICITY

Where do the renewables fit into all this? The answer depends on the particular renewable source and the extent to which the timing and quantity of its output matches demand.

Hydro power is perhaps the most desirable of renewable electricity sources from the point of view of flexibility of supply. Water can be stored in dams for months or even years, yet the generators can be wound up to full power and turned off again in minutes.

And if we make electricity from biomass, we have most of the flexibility of conventional fossil fuel. We can store up wood for the winter, although household rubbish may be a little more difficult. Liquid and gaseous biofuels can also be stored and made available on demand. From an energy efficiency point of view, bio-fuelled electricity generating plant should,

Figure 10.9 Typical daily electricity demand profiles for France for the years 1965, 1975 and 1989. Over the years, the practice of offering cheap electricity at night has flattened the daily demand profile (Source: P Careme, Electricité de France)

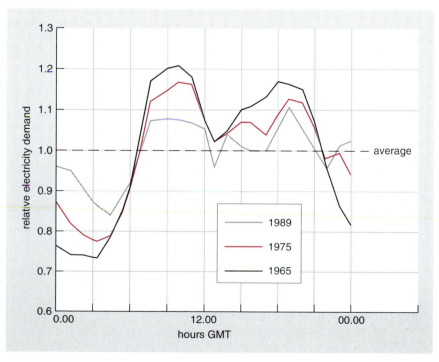

wherever practicable, be of the combined heat and power (CHP) type, where the 'waste' heat is put to use rather than thrown away. The reliability and flexibility of hydro and biomass power plants mean that they will probably play an important role in any future electricity generating system using a high proportion of renewables. Geothermal energy is also reliable and might also play a significant role in suitable locations (though in the UK its economic prospects are currently seen as unattractive).

Wind, wave and photovoltaic devices, on the other hand, only produce power when the weather activates them. Wind and wave power are more likely to be produced in winter, when the energy is really needed. But solar energy is likely to produce most in summer when the demand in the UK is already low. However, solar and wind/wave energy sources could in principle be used in a complementary supply mix to provide an overall output that roughly matches demand over the year.

The output of wind, wave and solar sources is unpredictable (although weather forecasts can help) but it pays to use the output when it is there, since there are no fuel costs. As these sources do not usually incorporate significant amounts of energy storage, using them means turning off some fossil-fuelled (hydro or bio-fuelled) plant at fairly short notice when they become available and turning it back on again when their output drops.

Various studies have suggested that the intermittent nature of many renewable electricity supplies would not be a problem up to about a 20% contribution to the grid. But when we start to talk of contributions of 50% or more, a more flexible electricity supply system would need to be developed. This would require the increasing use of power plant with rapid response times, such as gas turbines, together with various forms of demand management and energy storage. (See Halliday *et al.*, 1984 and Grubb, 1991.)

The National Grid can also be used to smooth out some of the variability of renewable supplies, by using different sources at different locations. When the wind stops blowing in Scotland, it may still be blowing in Wales. If a cloud passes over a photovoltaic panel on one side of London, the sun may well be shining on the other.

In the case of tidal power the situation is different. The supply is intermittent, but highly predictable. For a scheme such as the proposed Severn Barrage, generating only on the ebb tide, it would take the form of a six hour pulse of power every 12.4 hours (see Figure 10.10). The size of the pulse depends on the lunar cycle.

It would be easy to schedule a number of conventional power stations to shut down when the tidal one is about to start generating. A better arrangement might be to have two barrages, such as the Severn and the Solway Firth schemes, whose outputs would be conveniently six hours out of phase. When one had finished its cycle, the other would be about to begin. Alternatively, tidal schemes could be designed to operate on both the ebb and flow. Although the economics might not be so favourable, the relative evenness of the output would be easier to integrate into the overall electricity system.

One serious problem is that the peak power output of the largest tidal scheme, the Severn Barrage, at around 8 GW, would be a significant proportion of the UK's total electricity demand. If energy conservation as well as renewables were to be given a very high priority in the future, it might be difficult to absorb all this output, together with the output of other renewables, at times of low demand such as a summer night.

(A further problem is that very large power plants, such as large tidal barrages, would require new high-voltage transmission lines to connect the power to the grid: the cost and environmental impact of these would be significant.)

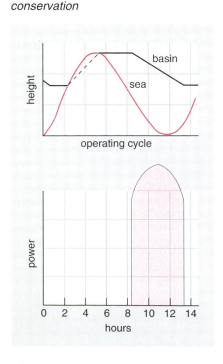

Figure 10.10   A tidal power station such as the Severn Barrage would produce enormous bursts of power of up to 8 GW in magnitude and six hours long. These could be difficult to integrate into the UK electricity system, especially if national electricity demand were cut by conservation

There are various approaches to the problem of electrical energy storage. In addition to pumped storage, as described above, these include conventional batteries (and more advanced batteries under development), the use of flywheels as short-term energy stores, and sophisticated techniques such as storage in superconducting electromagnets.

Another potentially attractive approach involves the production of hydrogen from renewable energy sources. This could provide a way of storing energy from renewables for later use in electricity (or heat) production, and could also provide a solution to the problem of supplying a renewable fuel for use in vehicles (see below).

RENEWABLE TRANSPORT FUELS: THE SOLAR HYDROGEN ECONOMY?

As we have seen, it is technically feasible (but not necessarily straightforward) to design and build renewable energy systems that can supply electricity where and when we need it. In the case of renewables as a source of energy for transport, the problems are more complex.

Of course, as we saw in Chapter 4, biomass can be used to provide liquid (or gaseous) fuels for vehicles. And renewable sources of electricity, such as hydro, could be (and in many countries are) used to supply a substantial proportion of the power for railway and tram systems, with other energy sources providing back-up. But for cars, buses, trucks and other manoeuvrable road vehicles that cannot easily be connected constantly to an electricity supply, the only significant alternative to liquid or gaseous fuels is the use of batteries. At present, these are heavy and expensive, and can store only enough energy for a limited range of travel between recharges – although developments in battery technology, coupled with increases in vehicle energy efficiency, may improve the performance and economics of battery vehicles in the future.

However, it may be simpler to turn renewably-produced electricity into an intermediate fuel that can be stored and then used in a more conventional way.

One fuel that is particularly interesting is hydrogen. Hydrogen has the advantage that when burned in air it does not produce carbon dioxide, carbon monoxide, sulphur dioxide or volatile organic compounds, unlike the combustion of fossil fuels. The only by-products of hydrogen combustion are water, and a very small amount of nitrogen oxides; and emissions can be reduced to zero if fuel cells (see Box 10.1 below) are used instead of combustion.

Hydrogen is already produced in large quantities and shipped around the world as a feedstock for the chemical industry. In 1986 total global production of the gas was equivalent to about 2% of the world's delivered energy consumption (winter 1991).

Currently, most hydrogen is produced by conversion from natural gas using steam. (Gas produced from biofuels can also be used.) But this process, in which methane is 're-formed' into hydrogen, necessarily produces an undesirable by-product, namely carbon dioxide:

$$2H_2O + CH_4 \rightarrow CO_2 + 4H_2$$
steam + methane $\rightarrow$ carbon dioxide + hydrogen

However, renewable 'solar' hydrogen can be produced without any CO_2 by-products, in two principal ways:

• By the **electrolysis** of water. If direct current electricity is passed between two electrodes immersed in water, hydrogen and oxygen can be collected at the electrodes. The electricity can be generated from conventional or renewable sources (Figure 10.11). In the case of renewables it could come from prime sites virtually anywhere: hydro power in Canada, solar plants in the deserts of Africa, wind power on the Scottish islands, or geothermal energy in Iceland.

• By the **thermal dissociation** of water into hydrogen and oxygen using concentrating solar collectors, probably in desert areas. To do this directly would require very high temperatures, over 2000 °C, but with more complex processes using extra chemical compounds the same result may be achievable at temperatures of under 700 °C. These processes have not yet been developed on a commercial scale.

Using hydrogen as a fuel is well understood. The old 'town gas', however, produced in the UK from steam and coal before the arrival of natural gas, consisted mainly of a mixture of hydrogen and carbon monoxide. Space rocket motors run on a mixture of liquid hydrogen and liquid oxygen. Hydrogen can also be stored either in gaseous form, or as a liquid, or by absorbing it into various metals, where it reacts to form a metal 'hydride': the hydrogen can later be released by heating.

Like natural gas, hydrogen can be shipped in bulk in a liquid form in insulated low-temperature tankers, or can be pumped like natural gas in pipelines. The possible uses of hydrogen from renewables as a fuel are wide-ranging and could include:

- replacing existing hydrogen production from fossil fuels (methane);
- adding a proportion of hydrogen to existing natural gas supplies to reduce their CO_2 production;
- as a transport fuel, using metal hydride storage;
- for electricity generation using fuel cells (see Box 10.1).

Currently, the price of hydrogen from renewables cannot compete with other fuels. However, its proponents claim that, if untaxed or taxed at a much lower rate, 'solar' hydrogen could be as cheap as energy from fossil fuels, including their taxes. It would be fair, they argue, for hydrogen to remain untaxed, as it does not cause the pollution and other problems of fossil fuels. They also argue that there are reasonable prospects that the price of 'solar' hydrogen will decrease in the future.

A number of major projects to evaluate the potential of hydrogen from renewables are currently under way. One is the ambitious German–Saudi Arabian 'Hysolar' project, in which a large photovoltaic array in the Saudi desert is being used to produce hydrogen which will then be shipped by tanker to Germany for use in buses, cars and other vehicles modified to burn hydrogen. Initially, these vehicles will use internal combustion engines, but it is envisaged that fuel cells, which are much more efficient, will be employed at a later stage.

Figure 10.11 Main elements of system for producing 'solar' hydrogen using photovoltaic electricity for the electrolysis of water into hydrogen and oxygen

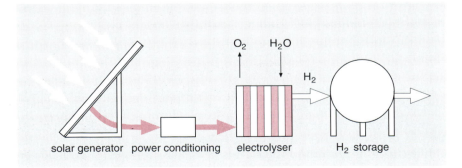

solar generator   power conditioning   electrolyser H_2 storage

In a similar collaborative project between Germany and Canada, it has been proposed (Gretz, 1989) that hydrogen produced from hydro power in Quebec be transported in liquid form by tanker to Hamburg, where it would be used in public transport systems and, later, to fuel an experimental hydrogen-powered aircraft proposed by Airbus Industrie (Figure 10.12).

10.6 CHANGING PATTERNS OF ENERGY USE

One of the main difficulties faced by any proposal to increase the proportion of renewables in our energy supply 'mix' is that the existing fossil fuel supplies are convenient, cheap and relatively abundant – at least in the medium term. Coal and oil have high energy densities and can be shipped easily in bulk half-way round the world at minimal cost. We have created infrastructures to process and distribute highly refined petroleum and natural gas. These fuels can all be stored and are ready to be used when we need them.

It might seem that changing the fuel supply mix would require unnecessary upheaval, but in fact fuel supplies are continuously changing as new supplies appear and old ones become more inconvenient. Even over a space of 20 years there can be major shifts.

Figure 10.12   *The proposed Euro-Quebec hydrogen pilot project. Hydrogen produced by electrolysis from hydro power in Quebec is to be shipped to Germany for use in households, power stations and road and air transport*

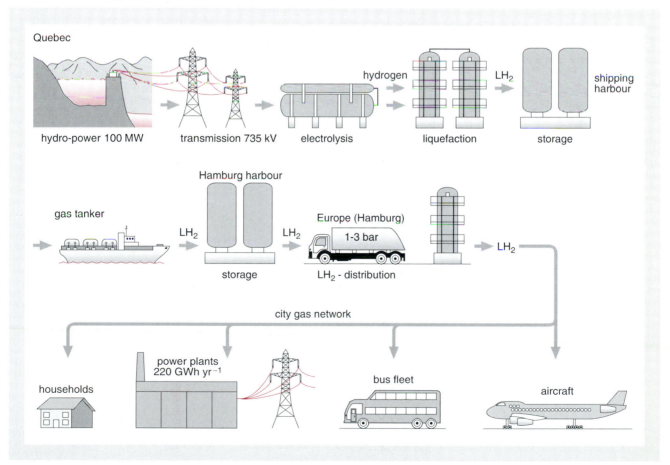

BOX 10.1: FUEL CELLS

In Chapters 1 and 2, we saw how all heat engines are inherently limited in the efficiency with which they can convert heat into motive power, and hence into electricity if the engine is driving a generator. Normally, most of the energy in the input fuel emerges as 'waste' heat (although of course this can often be harnessed and put to good use).

However, the fuel cell (Figure 10.13) is a device that enables fuel to be converted to electricity with much higher efficiency than an engine. A fuel cell is similar in some respects to a conventional rechargeable electric battery (such as that used in cars), except that in a fuel cell the energy required to enable it to continue providing electricity comes not from recharging but from a constant external supply of fuel. The principle of operation of the fuel cell is similar to electrolysis but in reverse: gases such as hydrogen and oxygen (or air) are pumped in and DC electricity is the output. The only by-products are water and there are virtually no pollutants. There is some 'waste' heat, but much less than in most combustion-based generation systems, and there are no moving parts.

Although the fuel cell was invented by Sir William Grove in the middle of the nineteenth century, development work did not really start until the late 1950s. Small systems were developed for the US Gemini and Apollo space programmes in the 1960s. More recently, Japan has started investing substantially in fuel cell development, and its Ministry of International Trade and Industry (MITI) has a goal of installing 2000 MW of fuel cell capacity by 2000 and 8000 MW by 2010. An 11 MW fuel cell co-generation plant was installed in Tokyo in 1991. The European Union also funds a substantial fuel cells R&D programme. In the UK, the Department of Trade and Industry collaborates with the Engineering and Physical Sciences Research Council and commercial firms to support a number of innovative fuel cell R&D projects.

So-called 'alkaline fuel cells' (AFCs) which run on pure hydrogen can achieve electricity production efficiencies of 60%. Most current large systems are 'phosphoric acid fuel cells' (PAFCs) of around 40% efficiency, but are designed to make their own hydrogen from natural gas using the steam 're-forming' process described earlier.

Currently, most fuel cell designs require the use of small quantities of 'noble metals' such as platinum, as catalysts. Although most of the metal in spent fuel cells can be recycled, if their use became very widespread, there might be catalyst supply problems.

However, some types of fuel cell under development do not require noble metal catalysts. These include the 'solid oxide fuel cell' (SOFC) and the 'molten carbonate fuel cell' (MCFC), which operate at high temperatures, and the 'proton exchange membrane fuel cell' (PEMFC); although the latter requires platinum, the quantities can apparently be reduced to low levels.

Fuel cells need further improvements in efficiency and reliability, and reductions in cost, before they can compete with conventional internal combustion engines, but many believe these goals are achievable over the next decade or so. They may also be very compatible with intermittent wind and electricity supplies, since their power output can be changed very rapidly, in some cases within fractions of a second.

Figure 10.13   Principle of operation of the phosphoric acid fuel cell (PAFC)

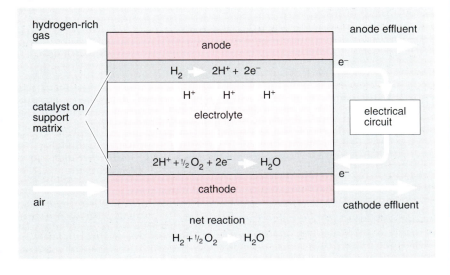

Let us look at three countries with different outlooks on fuel use: the UK, Denmark and France. Figures 10.14, 10.15 and 10.16 show the changing patterns of their respective primary energy consumptions over the period 1960–92. (Note that the population of Denmark is only about one-tenth of that of the UK or France, so its total primary energy consumption is correspondingly lower.)

THE UNITED KINGDOM

Historically, the UK has had plentiful supplies of fossil fuel. At the beginning of this century, like many European countries, it relied on coal for heating and 'town gas' for heating, lighting and cooking. Advances in large-scale coal-fired electricity generation in the first quarter of the century brought widespread electric lighting.

By the 1950s, increases in generation efficiency had made electricity cheap enough to be sold for heating purposes. Coal burned at the power station began to replace coal burned in the fireplace. Also cheap oil was available both for heating and for fuelling the rapidly increasing number of road vehicles.

With competition from cheap electricity, sales of town gas remained static and then began to fall, despite a new process to make it from oil. When in the early 1960s nuclear power arrived, it looked as if the UK gas industry might eventually collapse completely.

Then in the late 1960s, North Sea gas arrived. It sold at half the price of town gas and, because of its higher calorific value, doubled the energy-carrying capacity of gas mains. In the space of a decade, the gas industry had made up all its lost ground. By 1975 it had become the dominant fuel in the UK for heating, replacing coal, and now in the 1990s is eating severely into coal's dominance in electricity generation.

DENMARK

Whilst Britain's fuel changes have come about from an abundance of indigenous supplies, other countries have had to make radical fuel changes from a position of scarcity.

Denmark has little indigenous fossil fuel and since the war has been dependent on imported coal and oil. As shown in Figure 10.15, in the 1960s there was a massive increase in oil imports and a switch away from home-produced lignite and imported hard coal. As a result, in 1973 the country was gravely embarrassed financially by the fourfold increase in oil price.

The response was a considerable programme of energy conservation which has held the country's total energy demand constant despite continuing economic growth. Cuts in energy use for space heating through the use of improved building insulation standards and of combined heat and power generation have been quite spectacular. Between 1972 and 1985 the total area of heated building floor area increased by 30%, but the total amount of energy used to heat it decreased by 30%.

There has also been a switch back from oil to coal and, more recently, home-produced natural gas. Reliance on oil dropped from 93% in 1972 to only 55% in 1985. More recently, since 1988, Denmark has made considerable efforts to start building up its renewable resources – solar power, biofuels and particularly wind power.

FRANCE

Like Denmark, France is not rich in indigenous fossil fuels, though it has a certain amount of coal and natural gas and considerable hydro power capacity. Again, during the 1960s the country imported increasing amounts of oil and natural gas. However, the response to the oil price rises of the 1970s was to increase its nuclear power programme massively.

The total primary energy consumption of France has continued to rise throughout the 1970s and '80s. This is unlike the UK where it has remained static, largely through the decline of heavy industry, and Denmark where it has been kept in check with active energy conservation.

Figure 10.14   Primary energy consumption in the UK, 1960–92 (Source: Eurostat)

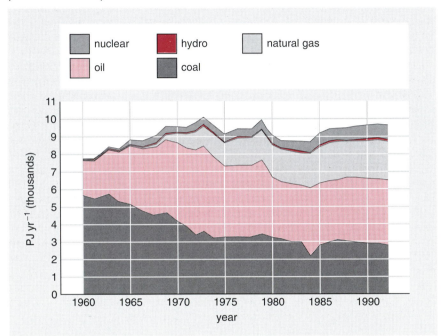

Figure 10.15   Primary energy consumption in Denmark, 1960–92 (Source: Eurostat)

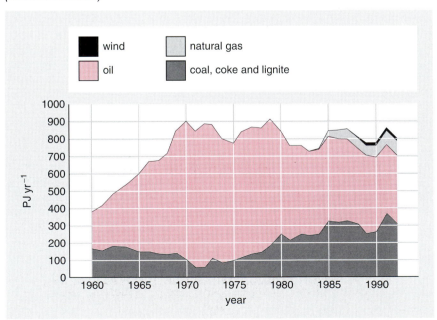

10.7 ENERGY SCENARIOS: EUROPE

Just as past patterns of energy use have changed from year to year according to different national circumstances, so will future patterns. Energy researchers have attempted to explore the possibilities using **energy scenarios**. These are pictures of what might happen, given various assumptions about available technologies, economic growth, fuel prices and changes in patterns of life-style.

For example, an 'alternative energy scenario' for Denmark was produced in 1983 by a group of energy researchers from Danish universities. It outlined a programme aimed at cutting oil and coal imports to zero by 2030, to be achieved by an increase in the proportion of renewables (wind, solar and biofuels) but most importantly, by a sharp reduction in total energy demand. The projection, shown in Figure 10.17(right), contrasts with the official Danish government projection (also shown), which suggested continued growth in energy demand (see Norgaard and Meyer, 1989).

The fact that actual Danish energy consumption up to 1992, as shown in Figure 10.17(left), has not followed either of these 1983 projections makes the point that energy scenarios are only pictures of 'what might be', not 'what will be'.

Returning to the UK, we can contrast a 'business as usual' scenario produced by the former Department of Energy (now part of the Department of Trade and Industry) in 1992 (Figure 10.18) with an earlier 'low energy' scenario produced by Earth Resources Research (ERR) in 1982 (Figure 10.19(b)). Also shown once again, for comparison, is the actual pattern of UK demand 1960–1992 (Figure 10.19(a)). Perhaps the most striking component of the Department of Energy 'business as usual' scenario is a continuing rise in petroleum consumption. This is virtually all due to projected increases in transport energy use, principally by private cars. More recent projections by the Department of Trade and Industry (1995) paint a broadly similar picture of future UK energy supply.

Figure 10.16   Primary energy consumption in France, 1960–92 (Source: Eurostat)

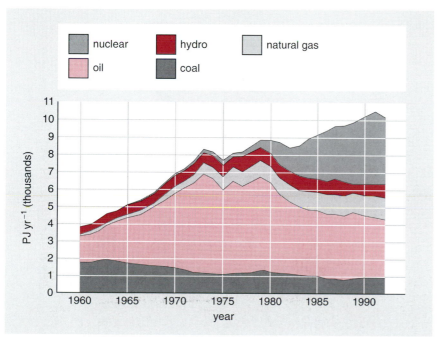

By contrast, the ERR scenario, like its Danish counterpart, assumed a massive reduction in energy demand, so that about half of total energy consumption could be met by a rising renewable energy contribution by 2025.

On a European scale, the ALTENER Programme, which projects a doubling in the proportion of renewable energy supply in the European Union, from around 4% in 1991 to about 8% by 2005, has already been mentioned (Section 1.4). An EC-funded study of the prospects for achieving the ALTENER targets (Wishart, 1993 and European Commission, 1994) concluded that the proportion of renewables in the EU could be as high as 13% by 2010 if the proposed Carbon Energy Tax, full social costing of energy sources, and other supporting measures were adopted. However, the renewable energy share might be as little as 6.5% by 2010 if no supporting action were taken.

We shall be examining some more energy scenarios at the end of this section.

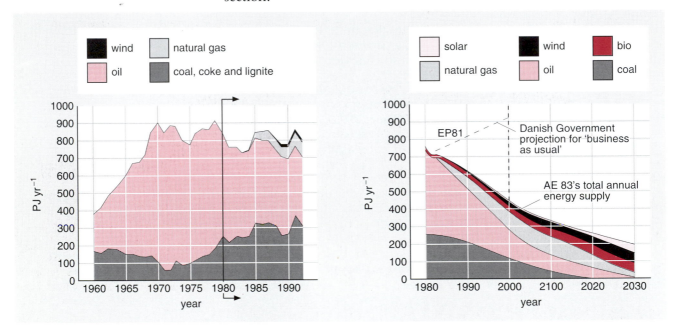

Figure 10.17   (Left) Primary energy consumption in Denmark, 1960–92, compared with (Right) Alternative energy scenario for Denmark, produced in 1983 (AE83), contrasted with Danish Government's 'business as usual' projection (EP81), produced in 1981 (Sources: Eurostat; and Norgaard and Meyer, 1989)

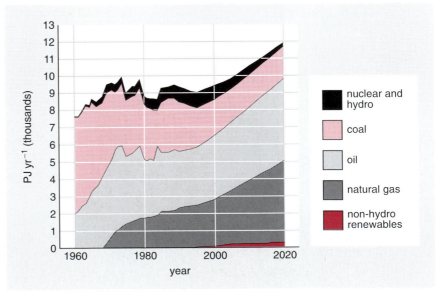

Figure 10.18   A 'business as usual' energy scenario for the UK produced by the Department of Trade and Industry (Sources: Eurostat and Energy Paper 59)

10.8 BALANCING ECONOMIC OPTIONS

In drawing up a particular scenario, energy analysts have to make reasonable choices about what technologies are likely to be viable at a particular time. At the beginning of this section we showed a table of technical potentials for renewables in the UK and their estimated contribution by 2025 (Table 10.2). A critical factor in assessing these potentials is their cost. We do not just have a 'potential for renewables' in isolation: rather, it is a 'potential at a particular price'. The more we are prepared to pay, the greater the potential resource and the wider the choice of options. This is well

Figure 10.19   (a) UK primary energy consumption, 1960–92, compared with (b) Alternative Energy Scenario for the UK produced by Earth Resources Research in 1982 (Sources: Department of Trade and Industry; Earth Resources Research)

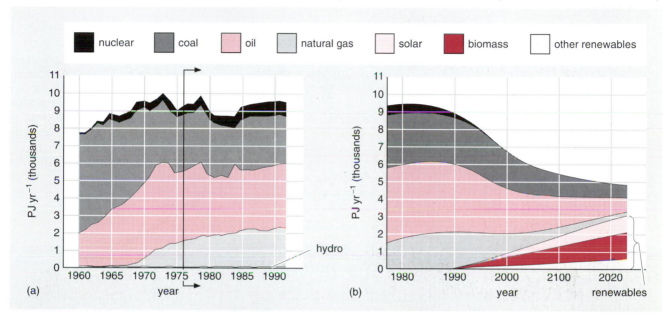

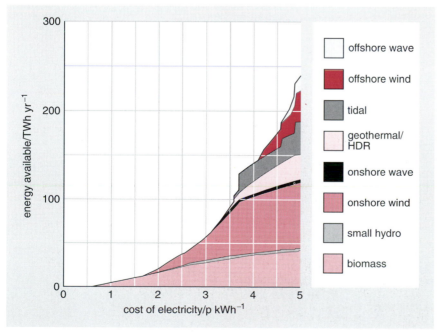

Figure 10.20   Renewable electricity generation: resource-cost curve for the UK, from Watt Committee Report (Laughton, 1990) (1987 costs; 5% discount rate)

illustrated by the resource-cost graphs shown in Figure 10.20 (from the Watt Committee), Figure 1.17 in Chapter 1 (from the REAG Report) and Figure 10.21, from the Energy Technology Support Unit. Estimates of cost vary, of course, according to the assumptions on which they are based. (These issues are explored in more detail in the Appendix).

RENEWABLES AND CONSERVATION

In practice, we have even wider choices to make, not just between different renewable supplies, or between renewables and conventional supplies, but between these and extra investment in energy conservation or improved energy efficiency. This is most important because:

- conservation and efficiency measures are usually more cost-effective than many renewable supply options;
- conservation and efficiency improvements narrow the gap between demand and the supply of renewable energy.

We can extend the idea of a resource–cost curve to mixtures of conservation/efficiency and renewable supply, as in the Swedish example shown in Figure 10.22.

What is striking about such curves is the diversity of options available. Many conservation options cost little or nothing. At a given energy price there may be choices between investments in biomass or onshore wind, or more efficient refrigeration or lighting.

This diversity is important to consider when we add in the difficulties of deciding between fossil fuel, nuclear and renewable energy supplies on environmental grounds.

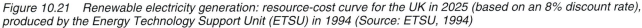

Figure 10.21   Renewable electricity generation: resource-cost curve for the UK in 2025 (based on an 8% discount rate), produced by the Energy Technology Support Unit (ETSU) in 1994 (Source: ETSU, 1994)

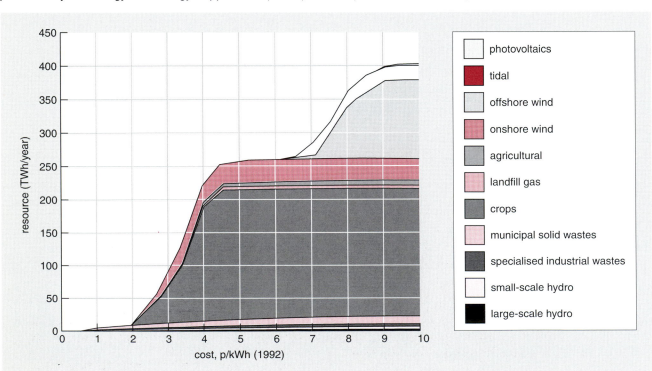

BALANCING ECONOMIC AND ENVIRONMENTAL CONSIDERATIONS

This is perhaps the most difficult area. There are several benefits of using renewable energy supplies in preference to conventional sources:

- they cut carbon dioxide emissions;
- they cut emissions of acid rain pollutants, sulphur dioxide and nitrogen oxides;
- they decrease a country's reliance on imported fuel and add to diversity of energy supply.

But what about the pollution produced in manufacturing a wind turbine or that made by burning biofuels?

Table 10.3 summarises one estimate of the waste products involved in the main forms of energy generation: fossil, nuclear and renewables.

Whilst renewable energy technologies are generally 'clean' in operation, the manufacture, transport and installation of the plant involved will normally necessitate the use of some fossil fuels and hence the emission of some greenhouse gases and pollutants. However, the total pollutants per unit of energy produced by renewables are typically two orders of magnitude smaller than those produced by fossil fuels. Nuclear power also produces a low tonnage of waste, but this, being radioactive, requires extreme care if satisfactory disposal is to be ensured.

A key consideration when evaluating the potential of renewables (or any other energy source) is the net energy balance. In other words, when the energy consumed in constructing, fuelling and operating the system is deducted from the energy produced over its lifetime, what proportion remains?

There are a number of approaches to such questions, each of which gives a rather different answer. In one study (Mortimer, 1991) the 'net energy requirement' – that is, the primary energy input required to produce one unit of energy output – of a range of renewables and conventional sources

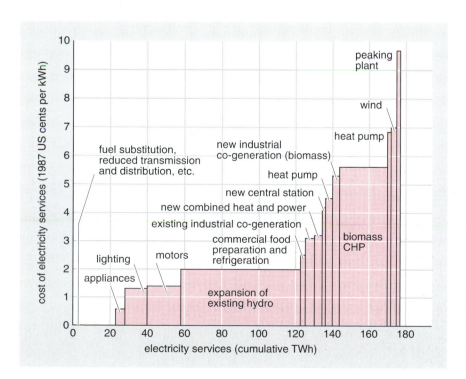

Figure 10.22   Resource-cost curve for investments in electricity conservation measures and/or new electricity supply technologies in Sweden (Source: Bodlund et al., 1989)

was calculated. The study suggested that renewable energy space- and water-heating systems, including most of those using biofuels, require a relatively small primary energy input for every unit of energy output. However, at the other extreme, a large orbiting solar satellite PV system could consume as much energy to construct and deploy as it ever generated. Similar doubts were expressed about small wind turbines with extensive battery back-up and some biofuel technologies. However, the data on which many of these assessments were based are now quite old, and for many renewables there have been significant technological developments that should result in a more favourable net energy balance.

The more general environmental impacts of each specific renewable energy source have been discussed in the preceding sections. To these impacts must be added the fact that, for all large-scale electricity generation technologies, including fossil fuel and nuclear plants, there are aesthetic objections to transmission cables, especially if transmission is at high voltage requiring large pylons (unless cables can be placed underground). This is a another good reason for pursuing a policy of energy conservation.

How, then, can the multitude of conflicting economic and environmental considerations affecting the choice between conventional fuels, energy conservation and renewables be resolved?

Table 10.3   A comparison of environmental impact of electric power generation technologies

Emissions of pollutants from electric power generation: the total fuel cycle[a] (tons per gigawatt hour)

Energy source	CO_2	NO_2	SO_2	TSP	CO	HC	Nuclear waste	Total
Conventional coal	1058.2	2.986	2.971	1.626	0.267	0.102	NA	1066.1
Natural gas IGCC	824.0	0.251	0.336	1.176	TR	TR	NA	825.8
Nuclear	8.6	0.034	0.029	0.003	0.018	0.001	3.641	12.3
Photovoltaic	5.9	0.008	0.023	0.017	0.003	0.002	NA	5.9
Biomass[b]	0*	0.614	0.154	0.512	11.361	0.768	NA	13.4
Geothermal	56.8	TR	TR	TR	TR	TR	NA	56.8
Wind	7.4	TR	TR	TR	TR	TR	NA	7.4
Solar thermal	3.6	TR	TR	TR	TR	TR	NA	3.6
Hydropower	6.6	TR	TR	TR	TR	TR	NA	6.6

* With biomass fuel regrowth program.

TSP: Total suspended particulates.

NA: not applicable.

TR: trace elements.

HC: Hydrocarbons

IGCC: Integrated Gas turbine Combined Cycle

Note: the total fuel cycle includes resource fuel extraction, facility construction and plant operation.

(a) Meridian Corporation, *Energy System Emissions and Material Requirements*. Prepared for the Deputy Assistant Secretary for Renewable Energy, US Department of Energy, Washington DC, February 1989, pp. 25–29.

(b) Carbon dioxide data adapted by the Council for Renewable Energy Education from Dr Robert L. San Martin, Deputy Assistant Secretary for Renewable Energy, *Environmental Emissions from Energy Technology Systems: The Total Fuel Cycle*, US Department of Energy, Washington DC, spring 1989, p. 5. Other emissions data from Assistant Secretary for Environment, Safety, and Health, *Energy Technologies and the Environment, Environmental Information Handbook*, Office of Environmental Analysis, US Department of Energy, October 1988, pp. 333–334.

(Source: table prepared by the Council for Renewable Energy Education)

There is no simple answer to this. Clearly, government policies, and the various influences upon them, play a key role in the resolution of such issues at a national level. At the local level, local authorities have established mechanisms, in particular the town and country planning system, for resolving energy-related issues as they affect specific localities. The Department of Environment (DoE) from time to time publishes 'Planning Policy Guidance' (PPG) notes to local authorities to help them in their assessment of specific topics. In the case of projects which are likely to have a significant effect on the environment, developers will usually have to produce an 'Environmental Statement'.

The situation as it affects renewables has been summarised by Muirhead (1993) as follows:

'To assist Local Authorities, a PPG on renewable energy (PPG 22) was published by the DoE in February 1993. It strongly supports the concept of renewable energy development and urges Authorities to look sympathetically at proposals for the generation of power by alternative means to fossil fuels. It includes:

- advice on how local Planning Authorities should include renewable energy in their development plans
- a recommendation that Local Authorities take account of the government's policy on renewable energy, together with other policies (e.g. on conservation and Green Belts)
- the observation that renewable energy can usually only be exploited close to the source
- an estimate of the contribution renewable energy sources can make towards reducing greenhouse gas emissions....

'In addition, European law has been implemented through the Town and Country Planning Act (Assessment of Environmental Effects) 1988, which requires the impact on the environment of certain kinds of development to be thoroughly assessed before planning assent can be granted. Projects *"which are likely to have a significant effect on the environment by virtue ... of their nature, size or location"* will require the submission of an Environmental Statement setting out the developer's assessment of a project's likely environmental effects and the measures for modifying or mitigating those effects.

'The Environmental Statement should consider the effects on humans, fauna, soil, water, air, climate and the landscape, the interaction between any of the foregoing, and cultural heritage and material assets. Consideration also needs to be given to use of natural resources, emission of pollutants, creation of nuisances and the elimination of waste or mitigation of its disposal. These are particularly important when considering applications for the development of renewable energy projects, as it will also be necessary to consider the scheme's environmental benefits in terms of off-setting the need to burn fossil fuels and thus reducing greenhouse gas emissions.'

In the case of very large projects, such as nuclear power stations, major Public Inquiries, chaired by a government-appointed Inspector, have sometimes been set up. It is possible that in the case of a very large renewable energy project, such as the Severn Barrage, the government would choose to set up a Public Enquiry and consider the verdict of the Inquiry Inspector before reaching a decision on whether or not to allow the project to proceed.

10.9 PROMOTING RENEWABLES

If governments wish to encourage the development and deployment of renewables, how can they do so?

The most straightforward form of encouragement is simply to publicise renewable energy, using marketing and promotional techniques to ensure that potential users (private individuals, companies and public bodies) are fully informed of the latest technologies available, their costs and their benefits.

Governments can go further, and subsidise demonstration schemes in which working examples of renewable energy are created to convince potential users that it is worth investing in the technology.

Another important role for government is in removing institutional or legal constraints that may unfairly inhibit the development of renewables – for example, restrictions on selling electricity to utilities, or anomalies in the rating (local taxation) system that may penalise 'private' generators.

A more proactive role for government would be in introducing laws or regulations that favour the development of renewables. These might specify, for instance, that all new houses must have solar collectors for water heating (as is the case in Israel); or that all new office buildings should, where possible, use passive cooling measures rather than air conditioning; or that all cars in cities by a specific date must be 'zero emission' vehicles (as has been stipulated by the State of California), which would tend to favour cars powered by renewables.

More controversial would be actions by governments either to subsidise renewables or to add to taxes on conventional fuels. Subsidies could include capital grants, premium prices for electricity produced, or tax relief on profits. Taxation measures could include the imposition of taxes on conventional fuels based on their energy or carbon content, to discourage fossil fuel use and to raise revenue that could be spent on subsidies for renewables (or energy conservation).

However, the idea of an energy subsidy offends those who believe in free energy markets. Free trade in energy has long been a policy goal of the European Union, for example.

The dilemma was well illustrated when the Danish government was taken to court in 1990 by the European Commission for imposing an energy tax, since it was argued that this constituted a barrier to free trade in energy. The Danes successfully replied that their tax was imposed to safeguard the environment and that this was a far more important aim of the Community.

Another problem is that subsidies require tax revenue to pay for them. Additional taxation tends to be resisted by those who have to pay.

Let us now look at some examples of both taxation and subsidy.

THE EC CARBON/ENERGY TAX

In 1992 the European Commission proposed a 'carbon/energy' tax an idea that provoked much heated debate. This would have been levied partly on energy and partly on the carbon content of the fuels used. The original intention was to introduce the tax in 1993 at the rate of $3 per barrel of oil, or equivalent, building up to $10 a barrel in 2000. The tax would have affected fossil fuels, nuclear energy and also large-scale hydroelectric schemes. Other renewables would have been exempt.

The overall intention was that energy prices to final consumers would rise by 25–30% in real terms, with the largest increases falling on users of coal and oil. Although energy-intensive industries with substantial overseas trade commitments would have been exempt, the proposals produced protests from the business community that the tax would impair their international competitiveness.

Although most advocates of free markets accept that all users of energy should pay for both its 'internal' and 'external' costs, in practice it seems that energy taxes for industry will be acceptable only if all competing industries in the world pay equally.

The tax was also opposed by those who believe that all extra taxation will push up prices and increase inflation. However, the intention of the EC energy tax was that it should be 'fiscally neutral', that is, it would allow other taxes to be reduced. Although this would encourage renewables by making them more competitive with fossil fuels, it would not raise the extra funds necessary for subsidies or training programmes for workers.

The European Commission estimated that the carbon/energy tax would reduce national economic growth rates by 0.05–0.1% per annum.

The UK government extended VAT to domestic fuel supplies from 1994 onwards, against stiff political opposition, and it has been argued that because this will encourage energy conservation the EC carbon/energy tax is unnecessary.

Among the advantages of levying VAT on domestic fuel are that it is easy to collect and should encourage many households to invest in energy conservation, improved efficiency and perhaps renewables.

The disadvantages are that it penalises poorer households who pay higher proportions of their income on energy and cannot afford energy conservation/efficiency investments; and that it applies equally to all fuels irrespective of carbon content and therefore does not particularly favour renewables.

The advantages of the carbon/energy tax are that it encourages the use of fuels with lower or zero carbon content, so favouring renewables; it applies to all sectors of the economy and it is levied on producers, who may not pass it on fully to consumers.

Among the disadvantages are that it imposes additional burdens on energy-intensive industries, which leaves them at a competitive disadvantage if there is not world-wide agreement. It also raises prices to consumers, which may disadvantage poorer households disproportionately.

THE UK NON-FOSSIL FUEL OBLIGATION

Currently, the UK operates a form of energy taxation, through the Non-Fossil Fuel Obligation (NFFO) and its associated Fossil Fuel Levy. The scheme set up under the 1989 Act that privatised the UK electricity industry, largely to provide a subsidy for nuclear power. Under the scheme, companies that supply electricity to the public are required to obtain a specified quantity of their electricity from generating stations that do not use fossil fuels.

A levy on electricity consumers (set at 11% in 1992) compensates the electricity industry in England and Wales for the extra costs involved in purchasing energy from non-fossil sources. The levy in 1990/91 raised a total of £1.175 billion. Although approximately 99% of this went to supporting the nuclear industry, the rest went to renewables. However, the amount paid to renewables has increased in subsequent years.

NFFO subsidises renewable energy projects by enabling premium prices to be paid for every kilowatt hour of electricity produced. For projects approved before 1993/94, premium prices are paid only up to the end of 1998, after which the 'free market' determines the price. The 1998 deadline was imposed because the European Commission would only allow the UK to subsidise its nuclear industry for a limited period – although the EU subsequently raised no objection to support for renewables over a longer period.

In practice, renewable energy projects in England and Wales under the pre-1994 NFFO scheme are paid anything from 6p to 11p per kWh for their electricity. This contrasts with the 2.5–3p per kWh that a large fossil fuel generator would normally be paid. The high prices paid to renewables were largely the result of the 1998 deadline, which meant that the capital cost of projects had to be recouped within a very short period. This resulted in much higher prices per kWh than would have been the case if the projects had been costed over a longer period.

However, from 1994 onwards, premium prices under the NFFO scheme are paid for up to 15 years. This has resulted in substantially lower prices, ranging from around 3.5p/kWh for electricity from landfill gas, through 4-6p/kWh for power from wind farms, to around 8.5p/kWh for electricity produced through the gasification of forestry wastes. The original NFFO arrangements apply only to England and Wales, but comparable schemes were set up in 1993 for Scotland and Northern Ireland.

The NFFO-type schemes are the main mechanisms by which the UK government intends to progress towards its target of installing a total of 1500 MW 'Declared Net Capacity' (see Box 10.2) of new renewable energy generating capacity by the year 2000. By then, the annual contribution of renewables to UK electricity supply should have increased from about 2% to around 5%.

Contracts for 620 MW of capacity from renewables were signed by the Non-Fossil Purchasing Agency on behalf of the Regional Electricity Companies under the terms of the first and second NFFO rounds of 'Renewables Orders' in England and Wales. In 1994, contracts for a further 630 MW of renewable electricity generating capacity were announced, under the terms of the third NFFO round of 'Renewables Orders'. Further NFFO rounds are planned for 1995 and 1997.

As the NFFO process continues, the government envisages a 'convergence' between the premium prices paid to renewables under the schemes and the normal market prices, with the expectation that eventually renewables will become commercially viable without further premium price support.

Payments under NFFO are based on the amount of electricity actually produced, which gives a strong incentive to renewable energy generators

---

BOX 10.2: DECLARED NET CAPACITY

The term 'Declared Net Capacity' (DNC) is sometimes used to describe the output of non-fossil fuelled power stations or other electrical generating plant, particularly in UK government publications.

The 'rated' output of a power station or generating plant (sometimes referred to as its 'nameplate' rating – a reference to the metal plates attached to electrical generators which specify their maximum capacity) is the maximum output of the plant that can be sustained on a continuous basis without damage.

Generating plant is not always operated at its rated capacity, however. In particular, the output

of some forms of renewable energy generating systems is variable and not always as high as the 'nameplate' rating of the generator might suggest. For example, a wind turbine equipped with a generator capable of producing up to 500 kW will only produce this level of power when the wind is blowing quite strongly, typically at around 13–15 metres per second. To facilitate comparisons between different types of generating plant, the concept of 'Declared Net Capacity' has been devised. Here, the output of a generating plant (such as a wind turbine) is expressed in terms of the nameplate power rating of an equivalent generator which, if operated continuously,

would produce the same annual output. Under the DNC system, a wind turbine is considered to have a DNC of 43% of its nameplate rating. A solar power plant is considered to have a DNC of 17% of its nameplate rating; wave or tidal plant is considered to have a DNC of 33% of its nameplate rating; and hydro, biofuelled and geothermal plants are considered to have DNCs of 100% of their nameplate ratings. These percentages are intended to reflect the approximate relative annual energy outputs of different types of renewable energy plant with the same nameplate ratings.

to maintain output. Lessons have been learned from earlier subsidy schemes, for example in California, where tax credits based on capital costs sometimes led to wind farms of dubious mechanical reliability being set up. On the other hand, this output-related payment has been criticised for leading to wind farms in the UK being built in the highest wind speed areas, which are also the most environmentally sensitive.

In 1995 the government decided to privatize the majority of the UK nuclear electricity industry, and to phase out its NFFO subsidies. Whether there will be further changes to NFFO support for electricity from renewables remains to be seen.

BIOFUELS AND AGRICULTURAL SUBSIDIES

The growing of biofuels is profoundly bound up with general agricultural policy. Any large-scale growing of energy crops will have to take into account the need to grow crops for food.

Since the end of the Second World War, most western European countries have given their farmers subsidies to increase agricultural production. As a result, the food shortages of the 1950s have given way to embarrassing production surpluses which have to be kept in storage.

Recent attempts to reduce these subsidies have included a policy under which farmers are paid to 'set aside' part of their land on which food will not be grown. This has encouraged some farmers to look at alternative sources of income, such as wind farming or growing biofuels.

Farmers in the UK can also receive forestry subsidies for planting biofuels such as arable coppice (see Chapter 4). In addition, in the recent calls by the UK government for renewable energy proposals under NFFO-type schemes (see above) encouragement has been given to farmers to generate electricity from biofuels, for which premium prices would be paid over a period of up to 15 years.

In Sweden and Austria, the production of fuel wood is subsidised from the proceeds of taxes on conventional fuels. In principle, similar arrangements might be applied in the rest of the EU, funded by revenues accruing from a future carbon/energy tax.

10.10 LONG-TERM GLOBAL ENERGY SCENARIOS

If renewables were to be given the kinds of support outlined above, what contribution could they make to global energy needs, in the medium to long term?

THE WORLD ENERGY COUNCIL SCENARIOS

One of the most comprehensive studies of the possible patterns of world energy demand over the next few decades was published in 1993 by the World Energy Council (WEC, 1993a), a non-governmental organisation with members from the major energy industries in some 100 countries. The WEC study used four scenarios to illustrate what it considered to be the various possibilities for world energy supply and demand to the year 2020. In all four scenarios, the world population increases, in line with United Nations estimates, from the 1992 level of 5.3 billion to 8.1 billion in 2020.

In WEC's 'Reference' scenario, the world economy grows at a 'moderate' average rate of 3.3% per annum, resulting in a total world gross domestic product (GDP) of some $56 trillion (million million) by 2020, and a total world primary energy demand of 13.4 thousand million tonnes of oil equivalent (Gtoe).

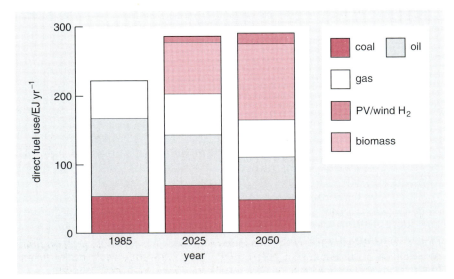

Figure 10.23   Total primary energy demand (Gtoe) and projected supply mix in World Energy Council energy scenarios for 2020 (see text) (Source: World Energy Council, 1993a)

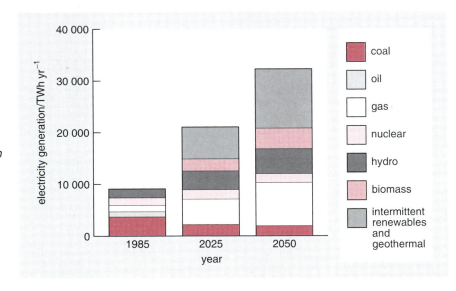

Figure 10.25   Electricity generation in the renewables-intensive global energy scenario. The contribution of renewables (hydro, biomass, 'intermittent renewables' and geothermal) could grow to over 60% by 2050, despite the forecast trebling of electricity consumption over the period (Source: Johannson et al., 1993)

Figure 10.26   Direct use of fuels in the renewables-intensive global energy scenario. The direct use of fuels for purposes other than electricity generation is projected to grow by about one-fifth – much less than the growth in electricity generation. The contribution of renewables could reach 40% by 2050 (Source: Johannson et al., 1993)

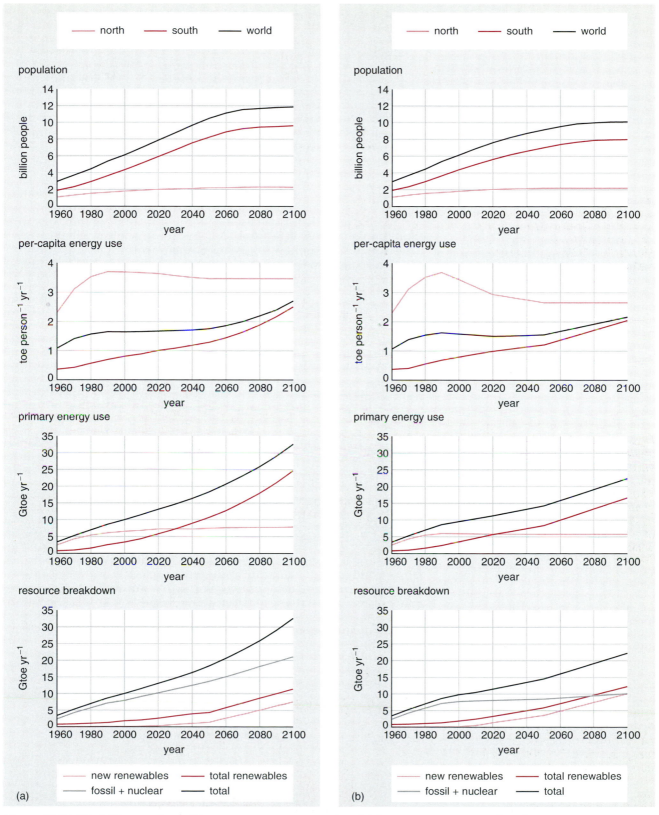

Figure 10.24 World Energy Council long-range energy scenarios: (a) 'Long-range current policies' scenario, assuming continuation of current energy policy trends; (b) 'Long-range ecologically driven' scenario, assuming a higher priority given to environmental considerations (Source: World Energy Council, 1993b)

In its 'High' scenario, economic growth rises to around 3.8% per annum, resulting in a GDP of some $65 trillion by 2020, and a total primary energy demand of over 17 Gtoe, about twice the current level.

In its 'Ecologically-driven' scenario, where it is assumed that a greater premium is placed on energy conservation and renewable energy, economic growth is still assumed to be 3.3% per annum, but primary energy demand rises only to 11.3 Gtoe by 2020.

The WEC study distinguishes between 'traditional' renewables such as wood fuel, which it estimates contributes some 10% to world primary energy needs, large-scale hydro power, which currently contributes an estimated 6%, and the 'new' renewables such as wind power, solar thermal and photovoltaics, which currently make a much smaller contribution, estimated by the WEC at around 2%. (The WEC total for all renewables, which adds up to 18%, is somewhat smaller than the figure of 20% that was given in Chapter 1. This is due to the slightly different assumptions and definitions used in the WEC study.)

The overall contributions of the main energy sources – fossil, nuclear, 'traditional' and 'new' renewables – in the recent past and for each of the four WEC scenarios, is given in Table 10.4 and Figure 10.23.

In the 'Reference' scenario (B), the total contribution of all renewables (i.e. large hydro, 'traditional' and 'new' renewables) is projected to rise to about 21% of the 13.4 Gtoe demand by 2020.

In the 'Ecologically-driven' scenario (C), the all-renewables share rises to just over 27% of the estimated 11.3 Gtoe total by 2020.

But in the 'High' scenario (A), although the contribution of renewables in absolute terms almost doubles from its current level, rising from 1.6 Gtoe to 3.1 Gtoe in 2020, the share of renewables stays the same, around 18%, because the overall total demand, at 17.2 Gtoe, is much larger.

The main WEC study does not give projections for the period beyond 2020. But in another report commissioned by the World Energy Council (WEC, 1993b), which deals specifically with renewables rather than energy in general, some additional scenarios for energy supply and demand in the longer term are given.

The WEC renewables study includes a 'Long-range current policies' scenario (Figure 10.24(a)) in which total world primary demand increases from 8.8 Gtoe in 1990 to some 32 Gtoe by the year 2100, of which 'new' and 'traditional' renewables would then be contributing around 33%.

In a second 'Long-range ecologically-driven' scenario (Figure 10.24(b)), total primary energy demand rises to about 22 Gtoe by the end of the next century, with a renewables contribution of some 12 Gtoe, just over 50%.

Table 10.4 Past and future annual fuel use in WEC scenarios (Gtoe)

	1960	1990	A	B_1	B	C
				in 2020		
Coal	1.4	2.3	4.9	3.8	3.0	2.1
Oil	1.0	2.8	4.6	4.5	3.8	2.9
Natural gas	0.4	1.7	3.6	3.6	3.0	2.5
Nuclear	–	0.4	1.0	1.0	0.8	0.7
Large hydro	0.15	0.5	1.0	1.0	0.9	0.7
'Traditional' renewables	0.5	0.9	1.3	1.3	1.3	1.1
'New' renewables	–	0.2	0.8	0.8	0.6	1.3
TOTAL	3.3	8.8	17.2	16.0	13.4	11.3

THE RENEWABLES-INTENSIVE GLOBAL ENERGY STRATEGY

As we saw in Section 1.4, a scenario in which renewables might achieve a 50% contribution to global energy needs even sooner than the end of the next century was submitted in an expert report to the United Nations Conference on Environment and Development (UNCED) in 1992.

The report (Johansson *et al.*, 1993) describes a 'renewables-intensive global energy strategy' (RIGES) in which the underlying assumptions are similar in many respects to those on which the World Energy Council's scenarios are based. These include a growth in world population to 8.19 billion in 2025 and 9.53 billion in 2050, and a growth in world GDP averaging 3.5% per annum to 2025 and 3.0% per annum between 2025 and 2050.

The RIGES assumes a more vigorous pursuit of energy efficiency and conservation than the WEC 'Ecologically-driven' scenario, though its authors maintain that the investments in energy efficiency which they advocate can all be justified on economic grounds. Similarly, it assumes a vigorous development of renewables, particularly biofuels for use in transportation. Towards the middle of the next century, an increasing proportion of transport fuels would be either ethanol or methanol, produced by various more efficient technologies now under development, or hydrogen either derived from biomass or by electrolysis from wind or photovoltaics. Electric motors powered by fuel cells would increasingly be used instead of internal combustion engines in vehicles.

In the electricity sector, biomass (grown sustainably) would also play a key role, supplemented by the 'intermittent renewables', wind and photovoltaics. The use of oil for electricity generation would be eliminated, and the share of coal would decrease to less than half, whilst the role of natural gas would expand enormously. Efficient, fast-acting gas-turbine generators, powered initially by natural gas but later by gas from biomass, would be used to provide back-up for the intermittent renewables.

As can be seen in Figure 10.25, the RIGES suggests that renewable energy sources (hydro, biomass, intermittent renewables and geothermal) could increase their share of electricity generation from the present level of around 20% (mainly large-scale hydro) to over 60% by 2050. This could occur despite a forecast trebling of electricity consumption over the period.

In the direct use of fuels for purposes other than electricity generation, which is forecast to rise by only one-third over the period, the RIGES suggests that renewables (mainly biomass and hydrogen from wind or photovoltaics) could attain a share of around 40% of world demand (Figure 10.26).

THE SHELL SCENARIOS

In 1995, planners at the Shell International Petroleum Company published the results of a detailed study of the long-term future prospects for the world's energy system (Shell, 1995 and Booth and Elliott, 1995). Their study included an analysis of the way in which the world's energy supplies have gradually become more diversified over the last 100 years or so. When first introduced, oil, natural gas and nuclear power were considerably more expensive than coal, but thanks to technological developments and volume production each eventually gained a substantial share of the overall energy market. The Shell planners see new renewable energy technologies following a similar path. The cost of wind power, for example, has dropped dramatically over little more than a decade to a point where it is beginning to gain a significant foothold in the market. They envisage modern biomass technology and photovoltaics following a similar pattern over the next couple of decades.

The Shell analysts have created two exploratory scenarios in which they sketch out two possible evolutionary paths that the world's energy system might follow during the next century. The first scenario, "Sustained Growth" envisages world energy demand, in the absence of any special efforts being made to introduce energy efficiency improvements, increasing from the current level of around 400 EJ to approximately 1500 EJ by 2060. World population increases to 11 billion by the end of the century, world GDP growth averages 3% per annum, and world energy demand growth averages 2% per annum. By the middle of the next century, sources of energy are likely to be more diversified than at present, with new renewables supplying around half the global commercial energy demand and fossil fuels beginning to decline, not so much because of absolute limitations on supply but because renewables have become more competitive.

In the second Shell scenario, called "Dematerialisation", the world economy becomes much more frugal in its use of materials and energy. Technological developments in currently-unrelated areas converge to create breakthoughs in the efficiency of products and processes. Energy demand rises at around 1% per annum to around 1000 EJ by 2060, with the renewables' contribution slightly lower than in "Sustained Growth" because of the lower overall demand.

THE GREENPEACE FOSSIL-FREE ENERGY SCENARIO

Even more optimistic about the prospects for renewables in the next century is the 'fossil-free energy scenario' (FFES), developed for Greenpeace International by the Stockholm Environment Institute's Boston centre and published in 1993 (Lazarus *et al.*, 1993).

Like the WEC and UNCED scenarios, the Greenpeace scenario is largely based on conventional assumptions about population increases and economic growth. In line with UN projections, the world's population is assumed to increase to over 11 billion by 2100, and world GDP to increase 14-fold between 1988 and 2100. The authors state that they have reservations about these assumptions on environmental and social grounds, but have retained them in order to allow their scenario to be compared with others.

In the fossil-free energy scenario, world primary demand increases by a factor of approximately 2.5, to around 1000 EJ (approximately 24 000 Mtoe) by the end of the next century (Figure 10.27). All fossil and nuclear fuels are assumed to be entirely phased out by the end of the period, and replaced

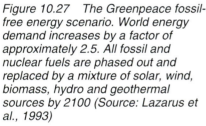

Figure 10.27 The Greenpeace fossil-free energy scenario. World energy demand increases by a factor of approximately 2.5. All fossil and nuclear fuels are phased out and replaced by a mixture of solar, wind, biomass, hydro and geothermal sources by 2100 (Source: Lazarus et al., 1993)

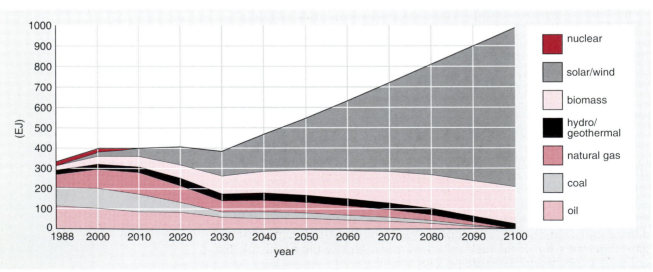

by a mixture of solar, wind, biomass, hydro and geothermal energy. A primary objective of the Greenpeace scenario is to show that greenhouse gas emissions from fossil fuels can be eliminated (although greenhouse gas emissions from other sources would have to be tackled using other measures). If this could be achieved, the study suggests that rises in mean global surface temperature by 2100 could be stabilised at around 1.5 °C, compared with rises of over 4 °C predicted in more conventional scenarios.

In considering the renewable energy options needed to meet estimated demand by 2100, the FFES authors downgraded the contribution of large hydro schemes, because of concerns about their environmental and social effects. No municipal waste incineration was included, and it was assumed that all biomass fuels would be produced sustainably.

Improvements in energy efficiency, to be achieved using 'market or near-market' technologies, would result in overall primary energy demand levelling out and then actually falling slightly around 2030, before rising again towards the end of the century. However, the authors suggest that this later increase could be avoided through further improvements in energy efficiency technologies.

The main renewable energy technologies contributing to the supply mix by the end of the next century, in the FFES scenario, include co-generation of electricity and heat (CHP) from biomass wastes, using such technologies as the biomass integrated gasifier steam injection gas turbine system (BIG/STIG: see Chapter 5); the use of more efficient 'second generation' fuel cells for electricity (and heat) production; and increasing use of wind turbines, photovoltaics and solar thermal electric power generation. Hydrogen, produced either by electrolysis from solar/wind sources or from biomass, provides an increasing proportion of transport fuel and a means of storing power from intermittent sources.

10.11 CONCLUSION

The Greenpeace scenario of a totally fossil-free energy future may seem Utopian to many. Clearly, the technical, social and political challenges involved in achieving anything like the replacement of fossil and nuclear fuels with renewables in just over 100 years would be immense.

But there seems little doubt that the world population, and the world economy, will continue to grow substantially over the next century or so. An accompanying rise in global primary energy use would seem extremely difficult (even if not technically impossible) to avoid.

If a substantial share of this additional energy is not to be supplied by renewables, then it will have to come from fossil and nuclear fission sources, with all the familiar environmental and/or resource depletion concerns that the use of these sources entails. (Energy from nuclear fusion, as distinct from nuclear fission, is still very much at the laboratory research stage. Even if practical fusion energy systems could be developed, they would be very unlikely to make a significant contribution to energy supplies before the middle of the next century.)

Although it may be possible to allay public concern about expansion in nuclear energy, there is a growing environmental pressure to cut fossil fuel use. In 1991 an enquiry commission of the German Bundestag (Parliament) called for world-wide cuts of 80% by 2050 in carbon dioxide emissions by all industrial nations. At the Rio summit in 1992, the UK government, like many others around the world, made a commitment to reducing CO_2 emissions to 1990 levels by the year 2000. And in 1993 the Clinton administration in the USA announced ambitious plans to curb greenhouse gas emissions from fossil fuel use, involving a greatly increased role for energy efficiency and renewable energy sources.

Clearly, the extent to which renewables can increase their share of world-wide energy supplies will depend on many factors. These include the scope for reductions in the relative price of energy from renewables compared with conventional energy sources; the extent to which investment in research and development on, and production of, renewable energy technologies can bring about improvements in efficiency and reductions in costs; the outcome of debates about the environmental and social costs of conventional sources, and the extent to which these costs are reflected in prices; the future pattern of world economic and population growth, and their effect on the level of demand for various forms of energy; the impact of these considerations on the priorities of governments; and the environmental and social acceptability of renewables to the public.

However, it is difficult to avoid the conclusion that renewables are likely to pay a greatly-increased role in future energy supplies. Even if the most "pessimistic" of the World Energy Commission's energy scenarios proves correct, the renewables' contribution to world energy needs by 2020 will still rise to double its present level. And if history should prove the more "optimistic" Greenpeace analysis to be more accurate, renewables could be supplying all the world's energy needs in just over 100 years' time.

We hope that this book will not only help to promote understanding of the potential of the renewables, but also play a part in facilitating their deployment on a world-wide basis, as countries progress towards a sustainable world economy.

REFERENCES

Blomen, L. M. J. (1989) 'Fuel cells: a review of fuel cell technology and its applications', in Johansson *et al.* (1989).

Bodlund, B. *et al.* (1989) 'The challenge of choices: technology options for the Swedish electricity sector', in Johansson *et al.* (1989).

Department of Energy (1988) *Renewable Energy, The Way Forward*, Energy Paper No. 55, HMSO.

Department of Trade and Industry (1995) *Energy Projections for the UK*, Energy Paper 65, HMSO.

European Commission (1994) *The European Renewable Energy Study*. Report published by Directorate General for Energy (DG 17).

Eurostat (1993) *Energy Statistical Yearbook 1992*, The Statistical Office of the European Communities.

Grubb, M. J. (1991) 'The integration of renewable electricity sources', *Energy Policy*, September.

Getz, J. (1989) 'The 100 MW Euro-Quebec Hydro-Hydrogen Pilot Project" in *Wasserstoff-Energietechnik II*, VDI-Berichte 602 und 725, VDI-Verlag, Dusseldorf.

Halliday, J. E. *et al.* (1984) 'A review of renewable energy integration strategies', *Proceedings of European Wind Energy Conference,* Hamburg, October, pp. 573–6.

Johansson, T. B., Bodlund, B. and Williams, R. H. (eds) (1989) *Electricity – Efficient End Use*, Lund University Press.

Johansson, T. B., Kelly, H., Reddy, A. K. N. and Williams, R. H. (eds) (1993) *Renewable Energy: Sources for Fuels and Electricity*, Island Press, Washington DC.

Laughton, M. A. *et al.* (1990) *Renewable Energy Sources,* Watt Committee on Energy, Report No. 22, Elsevier, London.

Lazarus, M. *et al.* (1993) *Towards a Fossil-Free Energy Future: The Next Energy Transition*, Stockholm Environment Institute – Boston Center.

Mortimer, N. (1991) 'Energy analysis of renewable energy sources', *Energy Policy*, May, pp. 374–85.

Norgaard, J. S. and Meyer, N. I. (1989) 'Planning implications of electricity conservation: the case of Denmark', in Johansson *et al.* (1989).

Olivier, D. *et al.* (1982) *Energy-Efficient Futures: Opening the Solar Option*, Earth Resources Research.

Renewable Energy Advisory Group (REAG) (1992) *Renewable Energy Sources: Report to the President of the Board of Trade*, Energy Paper No. 60, HMSO.

Wishart, G. (1993) 'Renewable energy in Europe: is there a future?', *Appropriate Technology*, Vol. 20, No. 3, December, pp. 21–4.

World Energy Council (WEC) (1993a) *Energy for Tomorrow's World,* St Martin's Press, London.

World Energy Council (WEC) (1993b) *Renewable Energy Resources: Opportunities and Constraints 1990–2020*, World Energy Council, London.

ETSU (1994) *An Assessment of Renewable Energy for the UK*, HMSO, 308 pp.

FURTHER READING

SOLAR HYDROGEN

Anahara, R. *et al.* (1993) 'Present status and future prospects for fuel cell power systems', *Proceedings of the IEEE*, Vol. 81, No. 3, March, pp. 399–408.

Winter, C.-J. (1991) 'Solar hydrogen energy trade', *Energy Policy*, June.

ENERGY SCENARIOS

Department of Energy (1992) *Energy-Related Carbon Emissions in Possible Future Scenarios for the UK*, Energy Paper No. 59, HMSO.

German Bundestag (ed.) (1991) *Protecting the Earth*, Vol. 2 (Third report of the Enquete Commission of the 11th German Bundestag).

Norgard, J. and Viegaud, J. (1994) *Low Electricity Europe - Sustainable Options*, European Environment Bureau Report, Brussels, 122pp.

RENEWABLE ENERGY POLICY IN THE UK

House of Commons Energy Select Committee (1992) *Renewable Energy,* Vol. 1 of Energy Select Committee Report, HMSO.

ETSU (1994) *Energy Technologies for the UK: An Appraisal of UK Energy Research, Development, and Demonstration*, ETSU Report R83 (2 volumes) HMSO.

National Audit Office (1994) *Report on the Renewable Energy Research, Development and Demonstration Programme,* January, HMSO.

Department of Trade and Industry (1994) *New and Renewable Energy: Future Prospects in the UK* (Energy Paper 62), HMSO, 114 pp.

Energy Select Committee (1992) *Fourth Report on Renewable Energy,* Volume 1, March, HMSO.

ENVIRONMENTAL IMPACTS

Clarke, A. (1989) *Comparative Environmental Impact of Renewables*, working paper, Open University Technology Policy Group, Milton Keynes.

Eyre, N. J. (1989) *Gaseous Emissions due to Electricity Fuel Cycles in the UK*, ETSU Report.

GENERAL

Department of Environment (1994) *Climate Change 1994: the UK Programme*, HMSO.

Eurostat (1993) *Compilation of Energy Statistics for the European Union*, monthly, The Statistical Office of the European Communities.

Kelly, H. and Weinberg, C. (1993) 'Utility strategies for using renewables', in Johansson *et al.* (1993).

COST AND RESOURCE ESTIMATING

A.1 INTRODUCTION

Once it has been established that a given renewable energy technology works, it is important to determine how much energy it could produce, and how much that energy would cost. These questions form the subject-matter of this section.

The cost of an energy technology can be one of its most critical aspects, so it is important to understand exactly how a costing is done, what it means and how it relates to other costings. The matter is not as simple as it might at first seem: there are many ways of producing and quoting costs (most of them arguably valid) and the different assumptions and methods that are used are usually not given alongside the figures that are quoted. Costs are also frequently taken out of context.

Costing is important because it gives a quantitative value which is relatively easy to calculate and which can be used as a yardstick for comparing energy technologies against one another. No reasonable person is going to undertake a project without having some idea of how much it will cost.

What must always be remembered, however, is that cost, in the financial sense, is not the only parameter on which judgements should be based. For example, there may be differing environmental and social implications associated with each technology, whose importance might reverse a decision based purely on financial cost. Environmental and social factors are in some cases reflected in financial costs, to some extent at least, through the cost of complying with environmental regulations, or through taxes and subsidies. Attempts have also been made to assign specific financial 'costs' to environmental and social implications, so that they can be included in the conventional cost analyses; but, as will be discussed later, these attempts have yet to prove satisfactory. Nevertheless, costing is a very useful tool if well understood and used correctly, and is therefore worthy of considerable study – as well as being essential for raising project finance. Costing is the subject-matter of Section A.2 below.

Estimating the amount of energy that is available – the resource size – can be an equally controversial matter for some technologies, especially the less developed ones, such as wave energy. Even for the more established technologies, resource estimates are often given without stating the assumptions behind their calculation, allowing invalid and misleading comparisons to be made. The terminology used to describe resource estimates is the subject-matter of Section A.3.

Many of the renewable energy technologies have an additional complication which must be understood when quoting costs. Unlike electricity from coal, for instance, which has a relatively fixed price (assuming a given source of coal), the cost and amount of electricity that can be generated by a wind turbine, for example, depends on *where* the turbine is located and the wind speeds at that site. This leads to the concept of a resource–cost curve, which is the subject-matter of Section A.4.

Finally, there are factors to be taken into account when we look at resource and cost estimating in the real world. Many of the input values for the cost calculations are in fact unknown and must therefore be estimated, using one of a variety of techniques. This can lead to large uncertainties in the final calculated cost. There are also differences in the ways in which different organisations assess their costs, reflecting their differing concerns and financial criteria. All this leads to additional difficulties when attempting comparative resource or cost estimating. This is the subject-matter of Section A.5.

However one looks at it, estimating the cost of, and the resource available from, a renewable energy technology is not easy. However, the importance and usefulness of the results we obtain make this challenging task more than worth while.

A.2 COSTING

INTRODUCTION

Perhaps the most useful way to express the cost of renewable energy is in terms of the number of pence it costs to produce each kilowatt-hour of electrical or thermal energy output.

This is by no means the only way in which to express cost, however. Often a figure in pounds per kilowatt of installed capacity is quoted, and many other, often more complicated, economic indicators are used in the world of financial appraisal (see the sub-section on 'Other economic indicators' in Section A.5, and Table A.8, for an explanation of other terms used). Of these, the **payback period**, that is, the time taken to recover the initial capital costs, is perhaps the most familiar. For many projects, it is a useful and sufficient figure on which to base economic decisions. However, if the payback period turns out to be quite long, or if the project being costed has an uneven and complex cash flow profile, and a more accurate appraisal of the economics is required, then a simple calculation of payback period may be unacceptable. In this case, of all the economic indicators available, a figure in pence per kilowatt-hour is probably the most intuitively obvious measure of cost, and one that most people can easily understand.

Before we look at costs in more detail, it is worth considering how a *cost* differs from a *price*.

A **cost**, as calculated in this section, assumes that we (a private individual, a company, or perhaps a government department) can make some profit out of our investment: the value of this return on our investment is included in the calculation of the cost. The cost is therefore a measure of the minimum amount for which we must sell our energy in order for its generation to be a profitable enterprise. As we shall see later, what is deemed an acceptable level of profitability depends on *who* is investing money in the project, and in some instances the profit could be quite minimal.

Price, in contrast, is largely a measure of market forces. The more that people want to buy a product, and the less of it there is for them to buy, the higher the price they are willing to pay for it. If the price at which we can sell our energy is greater than the calculated cost, our profits will be greater than the minimum we consider acceptable. Conversely, if the price that we can obtain for our energy is less than its cost, we will either have to accept lower profits or decide not to invest our money in the project. If we know what the market price is, we can therefore use our calculated cost to decide whether to invest in a project or not. If we are investigating several alternative projects, all of which are profitable at current prices, then we can use the cost to decide which will bring us the greatest return on our investment.

THE THEORY OF DISCOUNTING

How do we calculate a cost in pence per kilowatt-hour (p kWh^{-1})? Let us take as an example a wind turbine that generates electricity. As a first attempt, we could divide the capital cost of the turbine by the lifetime of the machine to work out the annual capital costs, and add the annual operating and maintenance costs to give the total annual cost. We could then divide this by the estimated annual energy output of the turbine to give the cost in pence per kilowatt-hour.

Example A.1 illustrates this calculation

There is a problem with this calculation, however, because although the output of electricity (in the example) is the same every year, the costs are not. The capital cost – the cost of buying or manufacturing the wind turbine, and of erecting it and connecting it to the transmission system – occurs at Year 0, or even over a period of years leading up to the start of operation. In contrast, the operating and maintenance costs occur every year thereafter, until the plant stops operating in Year 25. Whereas at first sight it might seem reasonable simply to add all these costs together, further consideration leads us to adopt a more sophisticated approach.

INTEREST RATES AND DISCOUNT RATES

In practice, a pound tomorrow is not worth the same as a pound today. We must look at the important concept of **the time value of money**. There are several separate processes involved and it is important to understand them. They are:

1. Our normal **time preference for money**. Given a choice we would generally rather have a pound today than a pound in the future. Put another way, we would need to be offered a pound plus some additional sum, say x%, next year to forgo the use of one pound today.

2. Our ability to lend out money and charge **interest** on it.

3. The effect of **inflation** which progressively erodes the ability of money to purchase real goods.

Different individuals' time preferences for money will vary and depend on their financial circumstances, but on average it is these that determine interest rates as quoted by banks. Someone opening a savings account at a bank is giving up the use of a pound today, but expects to be able to withdraw somewhat more than a pound at some time in the future. They will only open the account if the rate of interest offered is sufficiently attractive to overcome the attractions of spending the money now.

Let us say that they invest £100 at a 10% rate of interest per annum. They would expect to be able to withdraw £110 in one years time. Let's also say that this £110 has to be paid to settle some bill that we know will arise at that time. By investing only £100 now we can pay off a larger bill in the future. If this bill is due quite a long time in the future then the effects can be very marked. After ten years' investment at 10% interest, £100 would have a '**future value**' of £260. Put another way, the '**present value**' of £260 in ten years time at an interest rate of 10% is only £100.

We are **discounting** future payments, effectively saying that sums of money in the future can be expressed in terms of smaller sums today. This concept leads to a technique of economic appraisal known as **discounted cash flow (DCF) analysis**. This allows us to express a series of bills at various times in the future as a single lump sum in the present. For example, we may have three bills, £100 today, £110 in one year's time and £260 in ten year's

---

Example A.1
The capital cost of a proposed wind turbine generator is £20 000, and the estimated operating and maintenance costs are £400 a year. The plant is expected to produce an output of 28 000 kWh a year for 25 years.

Calculate the cost of the electricity in pence per kilowatt-hour on the assumption that this is simply the total cost per year divided by the output per year.

Solution
The total cost per year
= £20 000/25 + £400 = £1200

The cost per kWh
= 120 000p/28 000 kWh
= 4.3p kWh^{-1}

BOX A.1: DISCOUNTING AND FUTURE GENERATIONS

Discounting is complex and controversial in a wider social sense. Although individuals and enterprises usually have a preference for money now rather than in the future (and this would be so even if inflation did not exist), it can be argued that *society* should take a longer-term view. Some economists and philosophers believe that societies should regard the welfare of future generations as being just as important as that of the present generation. This would imply that (after allowing for inflation) the real discount rate that societies should apply when evaluating the costs and benefits of public investments should be *zero*.

There is, however, a counter-argument that, although such considerations imply that societal discount rates should be very low, they should *not* be zero because economic growth will make future generations wealthier in real terms. This would imply that a societal discount rate of around 2% (the actual rate of real growth in incomes in the UK over the past 40 years) would be more appropriate. These complex theoretical arguments are discussed in more detail in Broome (1992) and Pearce *et al.* (1992).

time. As we have seen above, the separate 'present values' of each of these is £100. We can add them together to have a **net present value (NPV)** of £300. This is the total amount of money that we have to have available today to settle all these bills, given that we can invest some of the money at an interest rate of 10%.

If the interest rate were different, say only 5%, then the net present value would be different. As we shall see later on, using a net present value calculation is a convenient tool for dealing with payments over long periods of time.

In practice the terms 'discount rate' and 'interest rate' tend to be used interchangeably. They are not necessarily quite the same thing, though. The discount rate is literally the rate at which we 'dis-count' the value of future income or expenditure. It may be similar to a bank's quoted interest rate but it may have an extra allowance to cover project risks or, for example, the fact that the wind may not blow equally strongly every year (see section A.5).

We can now go back and look at our wind turbine in example A.1 through the eyes of a potential investor. Would they do better to invest £20,000 in this turbine or to put the money in a bank or building society? Their investment in the turbine project must be able to compete with the **opportunity cost** , which can be defined as the value of the next best opportunity forgone in financing a given investment. If money can be safely invested to produce an 8% return in say, chemicals or electronics, then why bother with wind unless it can produce better returns?

The opportunity cost approach sees discount rates as something determined in a competitive marketplace, but it is also worth examining our basic time preference for money in more detail.

Even if we were not allowed to invest our money in any way, as considered above, we would still normally prefer to have it today rather than tomorrow. This is for a number of reasons: pure impatience; the uncertainty as to whether we will be alive next year; the uncertainty as to whether the money will still be available to us next year; the fact that if, like many people, we expect to be better off next year, the money will have relatively less value to us then. However, there are some exceptions to this general tendency to prefer money now to money in the future. These include saving to provide an income in old age (which some people would continue to do even if their savings earned zero interest), or to provide for children's education. In these cases, individuals are prepared to forego some present income in return for future benefits. The 'time preference' view of discounting is not easy to quantify, nor is its relationship to the 'opportunity cost' approach to discounting clear (see also Box A.1).

In practice, because the 'opportunity cost' approach is more easily quantified than the 'time preference' approach, the former is usually adopted as the basis for choosing a discount rate, with the average bank interest rate setting a lower limit on its value. However, it must be remembered that the exact choice of discount rate is not an easy matter; the difficulties involved are discussed in more detail in the sub-section on 'Real-world' complications' in Section A.5.

INFLATION

We must also be aware of the difference between the concept of discounting and that of **inflation**. Inflation describes the rate at which the general level of prices of goods and services increases over a given time period. It is important to note that it is only *prices* in monetary units that are changing, and not the actual *value* of the goods. A loaf of bread will feed the same number of people after its price has increased as before. Unfortunately, the value of goods is usually expressed in the same units as the price, that is, in pounds, dollars, yen, etc. To be strictly accurate in quoting prices, we should also quote the *monetary year* that is being used. Thus, if a loaf of bread costs £1 in 1990 and £1.10 in 1992 (because of inflation, and ignoring discounting for the moment), then we can say that it is worth £1 in 1990 monetary units, and £1.10 in 1992 monetary units. However, it is not the value of bread that has changed, but the value of the pound sterling that has decreased, which is why we need to pay more in terms of pounds (a higher *price*) to buy the loaf.

How does this relate to the idea of discounting described earlier? It is very important to realise that discounting and inflation are completely separate things.

Inflation describes how *prices rise with time*, which is caused by the changing value of pounds, dollars, etc., which in turn can be caused by changing exchange rates, changes in monetary supply and other economic factors. Discounting, on the other hand, describes the *time value of money* – the fact that, because of uncertainty about the future, we normally prefer to have money today rather than money tomorrow, and that if we have money now we can invest it to make even more money later. The inflation rate could be zero, but we could still invest our money in a bank and earn interest on it.

As an example, suppose that we invest money in a business that buys old cars for renovation. If we invest £1000 in an old car in 1995, renovate it and sell it in 1996 for £1500, the return on the investment is 50%, assuming that the inflation rate is zero. If the annual inflation rate is 10%, however, then the price at which we can sell the renovated car in 1996 becomes £1650 (£1500 + (£1500 × 10%)). The return on the investment in purely monetary terms is now greater, but because inflation has increased the price of everything we might want to purchase with this money, by the same 10%, we are in fact no better off in real terms than if inflation were zero. Thus, although inflation has increased the return on our investment in *monetary* terms, it has not affected the *real* value of the investment. If we are using this investment opportunity as a basis for choosing a discount rate, then the value of 50% is independent of any inflation rate.

Because monetary inflation is only about prices and not real values, we can (and usually should) separate it out from our calculations by ignoring it and basing our calculations on the monetary units of a given year. If we choose to work in 1990 monetary units, for example, then we can describe all past, present and future costs in 1990 monetary units, converting costs where necessary into 1990 monetary units by referring to an accepted index of prices, such as the **Retail Price Index (RPI)** (see Figure A.1). If we do this

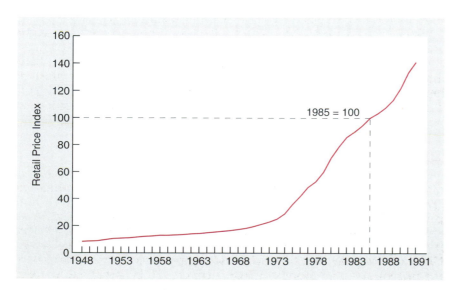

Figure A.1   Changes in the UK Retail Price Index, 1948–91 (Source: based on data given in Central Statistical Office, 1993)

439

when calculating the cost of electricity, for example, this will then also be in 1990 monetary units. We can see inflation as being the rate of change of the RPI with time. We have performed our calculation in 'real' terms, using 'real' costs and the 'real' discount rate rather than 'monetary' costs. Note that if we had chosen to use the bank interest rate as a basis for our discount rate, then we would have had to be careful to use the 'real' interest rate (which is equal to the 'monetary' interest rate minus the inflation rate) rather than the simple 'monetary' interest rate. It is worth noting that since both 'monetary' interest rates and inflation rates vary with time, so can the 'real' interest rate, which is the difference between the two. As Figure A.2 shows, historically there have been wide fluctuations in the real interest rate in the UK. Since about 1982, the rate has been positive and stable at around 5%.

Figure A.2 Real interest rates net of inflation, 1953–1994

THE BASIC DISCOUNTING FORMULAE

Although the philosophy of discounting and the choice of interest rates is a source of controversy, its application is relatively straightforward, and the formulae below are standard functions in computer spreadsheet packages. As we have seen the **present value** of a future sum of money is an important quantity. Its general formula is fairly easy to explain.

Given a discount rate of 10%, then a sum of £100 today is equivalent in value to

£100 x (1+0.1) in one years time

£100 x (1+0.1) x (1+0.1) in two years time

£100 x (1+0.1) x (1+0.1) in three years time

or £100 x $(1+0.1)^n$ in n years time

or in general for an interest rate r

$$V_n = V_p \times (1+r)^n$$

or $$V_p = \frac{1}{(1+r)^n} V_n \qquad (1)$$

This is just the present value of one sum of money at some time n years in the future. If we have a whole sequence of sums of money spread over a long time, then the total present value of all of these is the 'Net Present Value' (NPV).

BOX A.2: ANNUITISATION: A SIMPLIFIED APPROACH TO COSTING

The concept of capital expenditure having an annuitised value that depends on the discount rate and the project's financial lifetime is an extremely useful one. It leads to a simplified approach to calculating the average cost of energy that can be useful in many situations. Table A.1 shows the annuitised values for every £1000 of capital for various different real discount rates and project lifetimes. Using the table, it is easy to calculate the annuitised cost of a given capital sum over a given period. The annual running cost (fuel, maintenance, etc.) must, of course, be added to the annual cost of the capital. When this is done, the average cost of energy is given by the simple formula:

$$\text{Cost of energy} = \frac{(\text{Annuitised capital cost} + \text{Average annual running costs})}{\text{Annual average energy produced}}$$

This simplified approach, whilst sufficiently accurate for many purposes, is not adequate where annual costs are variable. In this case, costs for each year must be converted to their present values at Year 0 (see Figure A.5).

Table A.1 Annuitised value of capital costs (annual cost in £ per £1000 of capital) for various discount rates and capital repayment periods

Capital repayment period* (years)	Real discount rate (%)						
	0	2	5	8	10	12	15
5	200	212	231	250	264	277	298
10	100	111	130	149	163	177	199
15	67	78	96	117	131	147	171
20	50	61	80	102	117	134	160
25	40	51	71	94	110	127	155
30	33	45	65	89	106	124	152
35	29	40	61	86	104	122	151
40	25	37	58	84	102	121	151
45	22	34	56	83	101	121	150
50	20	32	55	82	101	120	150
55	18	30	54	81	101	120	150
60	17	29	53	81	100	120	150

* This is not necessarily equal to the total lifetime of the project.

If all of the payments are equal, then we have an **Annuity**, continuing for a fixed number of years to repay an initial capital sum. Its most familiar form is as regular mortgage repayments and the total present value V_p of n annual payments each of value A is given by:

$$V_p = \frac{1 - (1 + r)^{-n}}{r} A \qquad (2)$$

or, if we invert the equation, we can say that A is the **annuitised value** of a present capital payment V_p.

$$A = \frac{r}{1-(1+r)^{-n}} V_{\mathrm{p}} \qquad (3)$$

We can tabulate values of A as a function of r and n as shown in Table A.1. Nowadays, project costings are worked out on computer spreadsheets. However, in the past, banks and finance houses used simple books of precalculated values such as Table A.1 to work out the annuity on a single capital sum over a particular number of years. These are still useful to give quick answers.

For example, it can be seen that the cost of 4.3p kWh^{-1} calculated in Example A.1 is an underestimate when compared with the result calculated in Example A.2, using a DCF analysis.

DETAILS OF THE COST CALCULATION

Let us now look in more detail at the components that make up the overall costs and electricity output, and at our DCF calculation.

In Examples A.1 and A.2 we used two cost categories: the capital cost, and the operating and maintenance costs. In practice, a scheme is more accurately described by a list of costs (a 'cost breakdown'), an example of which is shown in Table A.2. Note, however, that the two cost categories still apply – capital costs (those occurring once at the start of a project) and running costs (those recurring throughout the project lifetime) – with the addition of a third category, disposal costs (those occurring at the end of the project). Each of these costs occurs at different times throughout the project, and a cash flow diagram can be constructed as shown in Figure A.3. Note that for a project where we knew the annual income from selling the energy, we could for each year subtract this income from the costs, thereby reducing the height of the cash flow profile and probably making it negative in some years. In the examples in this section, however, we are concerned only with calculating the *cost* of energy from a project, and so the cash flow profile essentially becomes a cost profile.

The running costs can be further subdivided into two: variable costs and fixed costs.

Variable costs are normally proportional to the energy output of the plant and are thus usually quoted in pence per kilowatt-hour of output; examples include fuel costs and some maintenance costs. In the renewable energy field, fuel costs are most significant for the biofuels, where buying or producing the biofuel and transporting it to the combustion plant can be quite expensive. It is worth noting, however, that fuel costs for

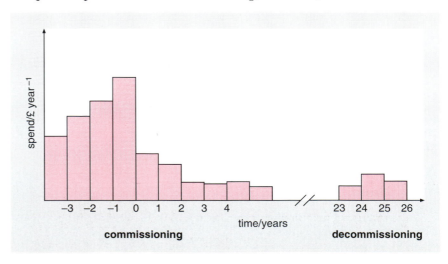

Figure A.3 Cash flow profile

municipal and other wastes can often be zero or negative as the producers of the waste are willing to pay for it to be taken away.

Fixed costs, in contrast, are independent of energy output and can thus be quoted as a straightforward annual cost (pounds per year) or sometimes as a cost per kilowatt of capacity (pounds per kilowatt per year). Examples include insurance and staff costs.

Table A.2 Generalised cost breakdown

Capital costs

Preparation	Development and planning
	Engineering and design
Building	Site preparation
	Production facility
	Manufacture/construction
	Delivery to site
Integration	Installation
	Commissioning
	Connection to transmission/ distribution network
Support investment Insurance	Capital spares
Project management	Supervision
	Quality control
	Other
Contingency	

Running costs

Operation	Fuel costs
	Staff costs
	Rent, rates, etc.
	Utilities
	Insurance
Maintenance	Inspection
	Service
	Overhaul
	Repair
	Spares usage
Overheads	

Disposal costs

Decommissioning
Sale

(Source: Based on Department of Energy, 1989)

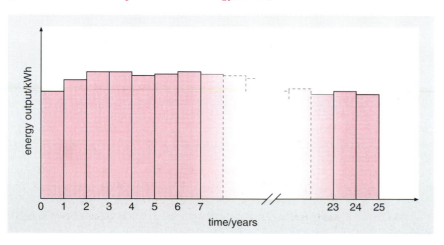

Figure A.4 Energy flow profile

BOX A.3: A TIDAL BARRAGE - AN EXAMPLE OF DISCOUNTED CASH FLOW ANALYSIS

In order to calculate the overall energy production cost from a really complex project, it is necessary to use detailed discounted cash flow and energy analysis. This can be carried out quite rapidly on a computer spreadsheet. Figure A.5 shows a printout of such a calculation for a Tidal Barrage scheme. The process involves five steps:

1. Itemising year by year all the capital and maintenance expenditure from the very first work on the drawing board right through the whole life of the project. In this case it involves eight years construction before any energy is produced at all and costings over 50 years operation including replacement of the turbines after 25 years.

Figure A.5 Example printout from a spreadsheet to calculate the cost of electricity from a tidal barrage

[All costs are in millions of 1988 pounds]   Commissioning Date

Year:	1	2	3	4	5	6	7	8	9	10	11	12	13	14	15	16	17	18	19
Capital Costs																			
Civil works	328	952	1060	928	657	658	313												
Turbine & generator works	119	352	410	266	275	275	278	278	164										
On-barrage transmission		27	61	74	78	78	49	17		Annual costs and output continue as below throughout the sixty-five year life of the tidal barrage, with replacement of generating plant after 25 years and again after 50 years.									
Feasibility studies, management & engineering	193	62	46	43	26	26	25	8	5										
Parliamentary & environment	42																		
Drainage, sea defences, port works, compensation					30	30	30	10	10										
Off-barrage transmission	42	43	127	128	170	170	85	43	42										
Running Costs																			
Operation & maintenance					5	15	20	29	34	40	40	40	40	40	40	40	40	40	40
Off-barrage					1	4	7	18	24	30	30	30	30	30	30	30	30	30	30
Plant replacement costs					Replacement costs of 90 million pounds in years 35 & 60														
Totals																			
Total annual costs	724	1409	1670	1426	1238	1256	836	435	296	70	70	70	70	70	70	70	70	70	70
Present value of costs	658	1164	1255	974	769	709	429	203	126	27	25	22	20	18	17	15	14	13	11
Annual output (TWh)								12	17	17	17	17	17	17	17	17	17	17	17
Present value of O/P (TWh)								6	7	7	6	5	5	4	4	4	3	3	3

Cost calculations	
Discount rate	10.0%
Costs	
Total to commissioning	9290 million pounds
Total to Year 75	14.1 billion pounds
Net present value to Yr 75 [1]	6.6 billion pounds
Output	
Total to Year 75	1151 TWh
Net present value to Yr 75 [2]	85 TWh
Cost of electricity [1]/[2]	7.8 pence per kWh

The output of the plant may also vary with time. (An energy output diagram can be constructed as shown in Figure A.4.) Load growth may be experienced in the first year or so, as teething problems are overcome or a phased start-up is used, for example with a large tidal barrage which is commissioned in sections. Over the lifetime of the plant there may be a slow fall in output as the equipment ages and efficiency drops. There may be variable availability of the plant over the years as unexpected 'outages' occur, resulting from equipment failure. Finally, the load factor itself may vary from year to year as climatic conditions, for instance, vary.

The shape of the cash flow profile is important, because of the effect that discounting has in devaluing future costs and income. A project for which

2. Itemising the year by year energy generation over the life of the scheme.

3. Calculating the Net Present Value of every year's capital and maintenance expenditure. In this case it has been calculated at year 0, the time when work first started.

4. Calculating the Net Present Value (in kilowatt-hours) of every year's electricity generation, again discounted back to year 0.

5. Working out the cost of electricity in pence/kWh as

$$\frac{\text{Net Present Value of Costs (pence)}}{\text{Net Present Value of Electricity (kWh)}}$$

It may seem odd to discount electricity generation in kilowatt-hours, but it has value, just like money. It is just that we cannot assign its magnitude until the calculation is done.

To understand why it is reasonable to discount the value of energy, it may be useful to compare two different hypothetical energy projects. Let us suppose that these two projects have identical capital and running cost profiles, that each project has the same lifetime, that identical discount rates apply, and that the total amounts of energy produced over the lifetime of each project are also identical.

However, in one project most of the energy is produced in the first few years, whereas in the other project most of the energy is produced near the end of the project's life.

Clearly, given that there is always some uncertainty about the future, the project that delivers its energy early is preferable to the one that delivers its energy late. It is therefore legitimate to 'discount' the value of the energy that is delivered later in time.

In this example, the capital costs are very large (£9 billion) and the construction time is long, so it is necessary to use a calculation procedure that can take care of the interest that has to be paid out during the construction period. After construction, the running costs are very low. The high capital costs make this kind of project very sensitive to the choice of discount rate, as is discussed in the Tidal Energy chapter.

In Example A.2, where the wind turbine construction time is very short and the energy output and running costs are likely to be the same year after year, we calculated the energy costs in a simpler manner. The capital cost was 'annuitised' over the project lifetime, running costs were added and the total annual payment was divided by the total annual electricity output to give the average energy cost in pence/kWh. We could alternatively have adopted the approach above, working out the Net Present Value of all the capital and running costs and dividing by the Net Present Value of the electricity produced (in kWh). The two methods are equivalent.

the initial capital costs are very large, and annual costs low, will usually be less attractive financially than one with a more even cash flow profile. Although the sum of the costs, with no discounting, might be the same for each project, discounting will benefit the project in which costs are spread out into the future. This adversely affects those renewable energy projects that are capital-intensive, such as wind farms and tidal barrages, making the cost in pence per kilowatt-hour very sensitive to, and greatly increased by, discounting. However, many biofuel projects, like fossil fuel projects, have more even cash flow profiles and are less affected by discounting. The use of high discount rates can thus make capital-intensive projects, including many renewable energy schemes, seem less attractive economically than fossil fuel projects, which tend to be less capital-intensive.

CONCLUSION

Discounted cash flow analysis is a simple technique for taking account of the time value of money in cost calculations. The technique is appropriate for individuals and enterprises. However, the conditions under which it is appropriate for assessing the long-term costs and benefits to society of public investments are a matter of some debate.

The calculations performed in this section are relatively clear cut and we might therefore wonder why costings arrived at by such methods are often controversial. The controversy usually arises because of disagreement about the specific *values* to be used in the calculations: that is, about the figures to be used for the *components* of the costs (and indeed, which components should be included in or excluded from the calculation: for example, transmission, disposal and contingency costs are often omitted); and about the specific *parameters* that should be applied, for example load factor, discount rate and lifetime. These issues are discussed further in Section A.5. Whenever a cost is quoted, an indication should ideally be given of the scope of the cost breakdown and the parameter values used.

A.3 RESOURCE TERMINOLOGY

DESCRIBING RESOURCE SIZE

Just as important as the cost of renewable energy is the amount of it we can obtain – the resource size. Unfortunately, there are many ways in which resource size can be calculated and there are many terms used to describe this resource. These terms are often only loosely defined or even not defined at all, and one term is often used by different people to mean different things.

There is, unfortunately, no widely accepted standard terminology for defining renewable energy resources. We must therefore be aware of the potential for confusion, giving full definitions of terms when quoting resource sizes ourselves, and seeking definitions when resources are quoted by others.

Despite this state of confusion, there are certain concepts which recur and which it is worth being aware of. The first concept is that of the total amount of a particular form of energy which exists in nature and which we are trying to extract. For example, we can consider all the energy in the sun's rays falling on the earth each year, or all the energy in the wind up to a given height passing over the UK each day. A subset of this is the resource that we can extract *in practice* after various factors are taken into account: for example, the efficiency of a wind turbine, limitations on how densely turbines can be placed, whether they can be positioned in National Parks, etc. The particular constraints that are imposed will limit the size of the resource thus defined, and different definitions include different sets of constraints.

One particular constraint that often merits the creation of a term on its own is that of economics – the amount of energy that can be produced at, or for less than, a given cost. In reality, economic constraints are applied almost by default in all resource size definitions, as it is usually assumed that a given project would not justify spending more than a certain amount of money. It is necessary to be careful, however, as the cost that is assumed to limit the resource is often either not stated, or else varies considerably. In general, terms like 'economic resource' can be misleading, and it would be better instead to quote 'the resource available up to 6p kWh^{-1}', for example. The relationship between economics and resource size is examined in more detail in Section A.4.

It is also worth being aware that a resource size can change with time for some technologies, particularly the biofuels. If we are talking about the resource available for generating electricity by burning municipal solid waste, for example, then a population increase by the next decade is likely to increase the resource available – unless, that is, we adopt stringent recycling policies in the future, in which case the availability of the resource could be sharply reduced. Thus, it may be necessary to give a date and even a predicted scenario to accompany the resource size quoted.

Finally, it is important to make a distinction between a 'resource', which refers to an amount of energy *that is available*, and a 'contribution', which refers to an amount of energy *that society might actually use* at present or at some time in the future. The latter takes into account factors such as market penetration, availability of funding, outcome of public inquiries, etc., and should always be accompanied by a reference to the scenario under which the prediction is made.

Whichever term is used, it is important to be clear about the units that are employed. For example, is a quoted landfill gas resource being described in terms of electrical output, heat output or combined heat and power output? Or is it in terms of the thermal energy content of the gas before it is burned? In addition, although resource sizes are usually quoted in terms of the energy available *each year*, other timescales can be used: for example, the energy available per hour or per day. Units of power are also sometimes used (for example, megawatts or gigawatts).

Table A.3 shows a possible set of resource terms that might be used. This illustrates some of the problems with resource terminology. The set consists

Table A.3 A possible set of terms for resources and contributions

TOTAL RESOURCE – the total energy content of the renewable energy source in a given time period

   TECHNICAL RESOURCE – the total resource, limited by our technical ability to extract energy from it

      PRACTICAL RESOURCE – the technical resource, additionally limited by basic practical incompatibilities (for example, roads, buildings, lakes, etc., which reduce the available land)

         ACCESSIBLE RESOURCE – the practical resource, additionally limited by institutional restrictions (for example, National Parks, Sites of Special Scientific Interest (SSSIs), Areas of Outstanding Natural Beauty (AONBs), etc.)

            PUBLIC SECTOR VIABLE RESOURCE – the accessible resource, additionally limited by what the public sector considers financially viable

            COMMERCIALLY VIABLE RESOURCE – the accessible resource, additionally limited by what the commercial sector considers financially viable

            ACCEPTABLE RESOURCE – the viable resource, additionally limited what is acceptable to society (for example, visual intrusion, planning permission, public inquiries, etc.)

ACHIEVABLE CONTRIBUTION (by a given date) – the accessible resource, as predicted for a given date, limited by the mechanics of implementation (for example, how fast tidal barrages can be built, wind turbines manufactured, planning permission obtained, etc.)

ESTIMATED CONTRIBUTION (by a given date) – the accessible resource, as predicted for a given date, limited by the mechanics of implementation, plus economics, market conditions and government policy (for example, government strategy, subsidies, resistance of people to change, commercial and political will, etc.)

Figure A.6 Diagrammatic representation of hydroelectricity resource terms for Kenya

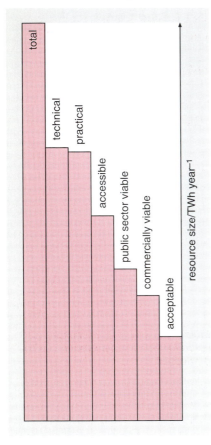

Table A.4 An example of possible resource definitions and constraints for hydroelectricity in Kenya

TOTAL RESOURCE – the potential energy available each year in all the rivers, lakes and reservoirs in Kenya given standard rainfall conditions (this is unlikely to change much with time, unless 'global warming', for example, brings about significant climate change in Kenya)

TECHNICAL RESOURCE – the total resource, constrained by turbine efficiency, spacing and design (as hydroelectric generation is a mature technology, this is unlikely to change with time)

PRACTICAL RESOURCE – as there are no real practical limitations, this will be the same as the technical resource

ACCESSIBLE RESOURCE – the technical resource, constrained by any legislation to limit development in National Parks, etc. (this might change with time if there are any changes in legislation)

PUBLIC SECTOR VIABLE RESOURCE – that part of the accessible resource that is viable according to public sector criteria (this would change if the Kenyan Government changed its criteria of viability)

COMMERCIALLY VIABLE RESOURCE – that part of the accessible resource that is commercially viable (this might change as the Kenyan economy varies)

ACCEPTABLE RESOURCE – the viable resource, constrained by any public opposition (this is unlikely to occur except for large schemes, but might change with time as public perceptions and opinions change)

of seven main terms arranged hierarchically so that terms lower down the list include the constraints of terms higher up. Also shown are two definitions for contributions by a given date.

Note how the lower terms become progressively more subjective: it would be reasonable to quote a range of values for some of these resource sizes (that is, an upper and lower limit to the resource size). Note also how some terms might not be well defined for certain technologies. For example, the commercially viable resource might be definable for waste combustion where a commercial sector exists, but not for wave energy where it currently does not.

We might wish to use two additional qualifiers with these resource terms. First, we might add an economic qualifier (for example, an upper cost in pence per kilowatt-hour, using a stated discount rate, project lifetime, etc.). Second, we might add a date qualifier (a date for which the resource is predicted): this may be significant in the case of biofuels, for example.

Thus, we might refer to the accessible resource for municipal solid waste combustion, predicted for the year 2005, at below 4p kWh^{-1} (in 1992 monetary units and assuming a 10% discount rate and a 15-year project lifetime).

Table A.4 shows how these terms and constraints could be defined for one particular type of renewable resource: hydroelectricity in Kenya. Figure A.6 presents a diagram of these terms. Note that the precise details of these definitions could vary, depending on which renewable energy technology we are talking about. Table A.5 lists how the term 'total resource' could be defined for different technologies in Kenya.

Figure A.7 A typical resource–cost curve

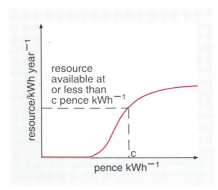

Table A.5 An example of possible definitions of 'total resource'* for different technologies in Kenya

Technology	Definition
Wind (onshore)	All the energy in the wind passing over Kenya up to a specified height
Offshore wave	All the energy in the waves across a given offshore deep water contour off the coast of Kenya
Shoreline and nearshore wave	All the energy in the waves that strike the Kenyan shoreline
Tidal	All the energy in all tidal estuaries in Kenya
Hydro	The potential energy in all the rivers, lakes and reservoirs in Kenya
Geothermal	All the thermal energy (at temperatures above ambient) in the earth's crust below Kenya, to a given depth
Active solar and photovoltaics	All the energy in the solar radiation falling on Kenya
Agricultural and human wastes	The energy content of waste arising in Kenya, assuming 100% utilisation of new waste by each option
Energy forestry and crops	Energy content of possible yields from all existing forests and crops in Kenya, assuming sustainable harvesting

* Total resource is the total energy content of the renewable energy resource available each year.

A.4 RESOURCE–COST CURVES

VARIATION OF RESOURCE SIZE WITH COST

In the previous section, we saw that economics can be used to put a constraint on the size of a resource. This leads us to the concept of a resource–cost curve. For a given definition of resource (for example, technical resource) we can vary the economic constraint (i.e. the acceptable cost in pence per kWh) and obtain a corresponding variation in resource size, from which we can plot a curve showing the variation in resource with cost (see Figure A.7).

For example, consider the wind energy resource in the UK. Because of the variation of annual mean wind speeds across the country, the cost of electricity produced will vary with the location. Wind turbines on the very best sites might generate electricity at a cost of 3p kWh^{-1}, for example, whilst those on the worst sites might generate at a cost of 20p kWh^{-1} or more. So it is impossible to give a simple answer to the question 'What is the cost of wind-generated electricity?'. We can either give the cost for electricity generated by a given scheme at a particular location, or we can quote a cost for which a certain resource size can be generated in the UK. However, neither of these gives the whole answer. Not only does our resource size vary with the economic constraints we choose to put on it, but also the cost of producing energy from a given technology varies with location.

This cost variation is a characteristic of many renewable energy technologies. The shapes of the resource–cost curves vary, depending on the renewable energy technology and, of course, on the area over which the resource is studied (for example, France will have a different curve from that of the UK). Many of the renewable energy technologies, such as hydro, can have long, sloping curves, indicating a large spread of costs highly dependent on location (see Figure A.8, for example). However, some of the biofuels can have step-like curves (see Figure A.9), indicating that location is not very important and that the cost of the fuel does not vary much. The latter curves can be quite similar to those for electricity generation from fossil fuel and nuclear plants.

Figure A.8 Possible resource–cost curve for small-scale hydroelectricity production

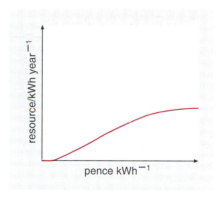

Figure A.9 Possible resource – cost curve for a biofuel

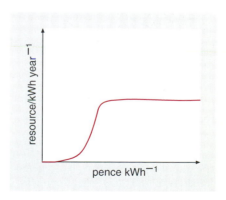

CONSTRUCTING RESOURCE–COST CURVES

Let us examine in more detail the building up of a resource–cost curve.

We can take as a first example the wind energy resource in California. If we divide California up into one kilometre squares, then for each square we can calculate the resource size and the average cost for generation within it, based on the mean annual wind speed. For each cost band or 'tranche' (for example, 8.5–9.5 cents kWh^{-1}), we can sum the resource available within all the kilometre squares in which energy can be generated at a cost between these limits. We can then plot a cumulative curve as shown in Figure A.10.

As another example, we can consider tidal energy in the UK. In this case, we can take a different approach, as the number of potential tidal barrage projects is limited and each forms a discrete component of the total resource. For each barrage site in the UK, we can calculate the cost of generating electricity and its potential output. We can then order the barrages by cost before plotting output against cost (see Figure A.11). Because of the limited number of tidal sites in the UK, together with the substantial variations in cost between sites, this inevitably leads to a more irregular profile than for, say, wind.

Figure A.10 Constructing a resource–cost curve for wind energy in California

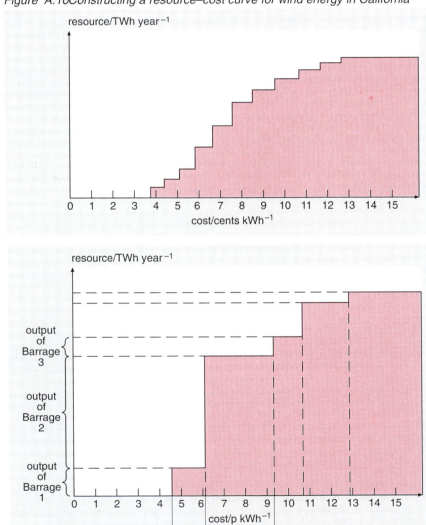

Figure A.11 Constructing a resource–cost curve for tidal energy in the UK

A.5 DIFFICULTIES WITH COMPARATIVE RESOURCE–COST ESTIMATION

INTRODUCTION

As we have seen in the previous section, it is not a straightforward matter to quote a cost for renewable energy. This makes it difficult when trying to compare the costs of the different renewable energy technologies. How can we compare resource–cost curves quantitatively? It is similarly difficult to compare the cost of renewable with non-renewable energy, and we should be wary of the many attempts to so do.

However, there are other factors to consider with comparative resource costing. These relate primarily to uncertainties in the data on which the costings are based, and are also due to what can be called 'real-world' complications. These factors are discussed below. It is worth noting that although many of the issues discussed are relevant in single source costing, they take on a further significance in comparative costing, because of the need for consistency in order to make cost comparisons valid.

COST ESTIMATING

Uncertainties arise because many of the renewable energy technologies are relatively novel, and it can be difficult to predict with accuracy what the capital costs and other parameters (for example, the plant lifetime, availability, load factor) are going to be. However, a variety of cost estimating techniques have been developed to help.

If detailed design plans are available, a detailed 'bottom up' costing can be performed. If bolts cost xp each and we have 1000 of them, we can calculate the cost of all the bolts, and similarly of all the other components, and the total costs can then be summed. In the same way, the cost of the labour used to assemble all the components can be estimated and added to the total.

A much cheaper and quicker, but less accurate method involves more aggregated relationships. For example, if wind turbines usually cost £x for each tonne they weigh, and we have one weighing y tonnes, we can again estimate its cost from the weight. This method is often called 'top down' or 'parametric' costing, because an aggregated component is related to a parameter such as weight or height which is a partial descriptor of the item. At its broadest level, relationships such as 'anything concrete costs £y per cubic metre' or 'all mechanical and engineering plant costs £z per tonne' can be used. Parameters can be anything appropriate to the component being costed: weight, volume, length, electrical rating, etc. In addition, factors can be multiplied to take account of the cost of assembling the components, and of their differing complexity (if steel costs £x per tonne, but the component to be costed has been moulded into an intricate shape, we can multiply the cost by a complexity factor to reflect the extra work that has gone into it). These 'top down' methods can be useful for cost estimates of very novel technologies and for so-called 'cost modelling' purposes. However, the results are generally subject to greater uncertainties than those of more detailed 'bottom up' costings.

It is not only capital costs that can be difficult to estimate. Running costs can also be uncertain, and estimates are often based on past experience with other, not necessarily related, projects. In some cases, as an initial approximation, annual running costs are estimated on the basis that they will be equal to a given percentage of the capital cost.

Whatever method is used to estimate costs, there is always an uncertainty in the result, as well as in the predicted values for the other parameters mentioned above.

'REAL-WORLD' COMPLICATIONS

'Real-world' complications can be even more difficult to deal with. The simplest complication is related to the form of the energy output. Whereas a given cost for hydroelectricity is easily compared with the cost of electricity generated from landfill gas, costs are not so easy to compare if the gas is used directly for heat. Is it really valid to compare costs for producing two different products? We could assume that we only ever use the gas to produce electricity, for the sake of simplicity, but in the real world this may not be the case. We may, for example, use the gas to generate combined heat and power (CHP). Not only are the products different, but the cost in pence per kilowatt-hour will vary, depending on whether heat, electricity or CHP is our product.

Further differences arise when we consider *who* is generating the energy. In Section A.2, it was described how even a small difference in the choice of discount rate can have a large effect on the calculated cost, particularly for many renewable energy technologies. The discount rate that is used is thus an important value, but how do we decide what it should be?

We have seen that bank or building society real interest rates can set a lower limit on the effective discount rate (in the 'opportunity cost' sense: see Section A.2), and these are perhaps of most relevance to private individuals for whom they are the main forms of alternative investment.

Businesses, however, will need to consider the rates of return available to them from their most profitable alternative projects, and these will vary between businesses. Sometimes an average rate of return on projects over past years is used as a basis for choosing a discount rate.

The private sector will also take the *risk* involved in a project into account. If half of a business's projects fail, then those that succeed will be expected to produce twice the average rate of return. This all means that the private sector may use very high discount rates: typically 15–20%, up to 30% or even higher for very risky projects. It will probably also calculate cost over a reduced 'project lifetime' of, for example, 10 years, rather than the real lifetime of the scheme, which for a tidal barrage may be over 100 years.

The UK public sector, in contrast, currently uses 8% as its standard discount rate in assessing public investments. This is based on the government's judgement of what is the 'social opportunity cost of capital' and is the source of some debate. There are arguments for increasing the rate to private sector levels, and other arguments for setting it much lower, even equal to zero (as we saw in Box A.1).

Public bodies in the UK are currently required to make an 8% rate of return, in real terms, on their total assets, and since this level of return may not be possible on all assets, discount rates higher than 8% may need to be used when appraising new investments. In general, the UK government encourages public sector bodies selling their output in the market to use discount rates similar to those of the private sector.

In some other countries, however, the public sector is encouraged to use relatively low discount rates when appraising the relative merits of public investments.

It is thus evident that the public and private sectors, within countries and between countries, can differ in their choice of discount rate (and other economic parameters), and that even within each sector there can be valid differences and significant uncertainties in the choice.

As an example of how assumptions and quoted costs can vary, consider evidence presented to the House of Commons Select Committee on Energy during its 1992 investigation into renewable energy (House of Commons Select Committee on Energy, 1992). It was told that, for wind energy, over a project lifetime of 20 years, electricity could be produced for 5–7p kWh^{-1}, but that reducing the project lifetime to six years would raise the cost to 9–12p kWh^{-1}. Other sources giving evidence to the Committee said that a 15-year contract would put the cost at around 5p kWh^{-1} (using a discount rate of 20%). The British Wind Energy Association quoted costs from 2.4 to 7.6p kWh^{-1} (for various wind speeds, and discount rates from 5 to 15%), assuming a 20-year project lifetime. Similar variations were given for tidal energy, ranging from 5p kWh^{-1} (20-year lifetime) to 6p kWh^{-1} (16.5-year lifetime) for the Severn Barrage; 6.75p kWh^{-1} for the Mersey Barrage (25-year lifetime); and 8.6p kWh^{-1} for the Conwy Barrage (15- to 20-year lifetime).

Not only do the values chosen for certain parameters vary, but there are also components that may actually be omitted, depending on who is doing the cost calculation. Subsidies (for example, from governments, the European Community, the World Bank, etc.) are an example, as are transmission and grid reinforcement costs, and factors such as taxation and depreciation. There is also a variety of historical or 'sunk' costs, such as money that has been spent on research and development, and money spent developing the National Grid. These might be considered a component of the true cost of the energy produced, but might not seem relevant to a private contractor calculating the cost of energy from a new wind farm, for instance.

It is also worth remembering that costs can quite validly change with time. In the Select Committee investigation quoted above, the Committee reported that for wind turbines 'further savings would occur with volume production. These savings were expected to be 20–25% of present costs even without major changes to the technology.'

For electricity from photovoltaic cells, the Committee reported that:

… production costs have been falling rapidly, from $14 per peak watt in 1977 to $4 per peak watt of capacity today. BP Solar expects costs to fall further, to $1–$2 per watt. The cost of electricity generated has fallen even more dramatically, from $3.39/kWh in 1980 to $0.30/kWh in 1988. Further reductions in cost are expected. These will arise from increases in efficiency, economies of scale resulting from higher volumes of production, and technical improvements in the raw materials.

It is worth noting that not only do unit costs decrease with volume of production, but they are also reduced for bulk purchases.

Costs may also vary between countries. The UK is renowned for the high wind speeds experienced in certain regions, and we would therefore expect wind energy to be cheaper in the UK than other less windy countries – other factors being equal. On the other hand, solar energy in the UK is likely to be more expensive than that produced in Israel, for instance, where the intensity and duration of sunshine is greater. Waste combustion plants might be more economic in Japan, where land for waste disposal is at a premium, than perhaps in Texas where disposal to landfill is easier.

Finally, there are a whole host of 'external' costs (or 'externalities') that may be included in the cost equation. For example, we could include costs resulting from air pollution (measured in terms of damage to human health, crops and buildings, etc.), noise pollution (measured perhaps in terms of the reduction of property prices in noisy areas), or costs resulting from the risk of major accidents in mines or power stations. External costs may be negative: for example, the security of supply resulting from an energy source being indigenous can be treated as a benefit, with an associated negative cost. Conversely, it has been suggested that the costs of the 1991 Gulf War constituted an external cost to oil of $23.50 per barrel imported into the USA (House of Commons Select Committee on Energy, 1992).

Some external costs are already to some extent internalised (i.e. incorporated into market prices) by means of taxes or the cost of complying with government regulations. In the future, other external costs, such as those of 'global warming', may be reflected in new taxes, like the proposed European carbon tax, or new regulatory measures.

Table A.6 shows the results of one study of the external costs of the production of electricity from various different technologies in the UK. The figures are illustrative rather than definitive, but give an idea of the possible magnitudes of additional costs, and the type of external effects, that need to be considered. The large variation in costs derived by different studies is illustrated in Table A.7 and this suggests that there is a lot of work yet to be done. Indeed, how to quantify these very often subjective 'costs' is a problem that may never be satisfactorily resolved.

For all these 'real-world' complications, who is to say who is right and wrong, and what should or should not be included in the 'real' cost? Even if everyone could agree on a costing for wind energy, for example, it may be argued that it is not valid to apply the same criteria to tidal energy, and even for a given technology the cost can vary depending on *how* it is operated within a *system* (for example, the electricity supply systems of England and Wales, Scotland and Northern Ireland). Whenever quoting comparative costs, therefore, all the above factors should be borne in mind, and wherever possible the assumptions behind the costings should be stated in full.

Table A.6 Illustrative estimates of the environmental external costs (in pence per kilowatt-hour) for electricity production from selected energy sources

Cost category	Old coal	New coal	Oil	Gas	Nuclear	Solar	Wind	Hydro
Health								
– Mortality	0.32	0.32	0.29	0.02	0.01	0.07	0.04	0.03
– Morbidity	0.12	0.12	0.12	0.04	0.01	0	0	0
– Disaster	NE	NE	NE	NE	0.45	0	0	0
Crop damage	0.10	0.05	0.05	0.02	0	0	0	0
Damage to forests	0.84	0.07	0.98	0.03	0	0	0	0
Reduction of biological diversity	NE	NE	NE	NE	NE	NE	NE	NE
Damage to buildings	3.22	0.28	3.77	0.11	0	0	0	0
Noise	NE	NE	NE	NE	NE	NE	NE	NE
Global warming damage	0.40	0.34	0.35	0.16	0.01	0	0	0.01
Visibility impact	NE	NE	NE	NE	NE	NE	NE	NE
Water pollution	0.40	0.04	0.049	0.01	0	0	0	0
Land contamination	NE	NE	NE	NE	NE	NE	NE	NE
TOTAL	**5.40**	**1.22**	**6.05**	**0.39**	**0.48**	**0.07**	**0.04**	**0.04**

NE: not estimated but probably positive.

(Source: Adapted from Pearce *et al.*, 1992)

454

Table A.7 Assessment of external costs by different studies

Author	Fossil fuels	Nuclear
Hohmeyer	0.8–3p kWh^{-1}[a]	1.3–6.7p kWh^{-1}
Friedrich and Voss	0.17p kWh^{-1}[b]	0.02–0.03p kWh^{-1}
Ottinger	Coal 1.5–3.4p kWh^{-1}[c]	
	Oil 1.5–3.9p kWh^{-1}	
	Gas 0.5–0.6p kWh^{-1}	
Stocker *et al.*	Coal 2p kWh^{-1}[d]	
	Gas 1p kWh^{-1}	
	Combined cycle gas 0.75p kWh^{-1}	
Hagen and Kaneff	Combined cycle coal 0.6p kWh^{-1}[e]	2.9p kWh^{-1}
Ferguson	(Acid pollution) £0.02–£2 kWh^{-1}	0.2–5p kWh^{-1}[f]
	(Global warming) £0.1–£10 kWh^{-1}[g]	
Koomey	0.9–2.4p kWh^{-1}[h]	

Hohmeyer, O. (1988) *The Social Costs of Energy Consumption*, Springer.

Hohmeyer, O. (1990) 'Latest results of the international discussion on the social costs of energy – how does wind compare today?', *Proceedings of the EC Wind Energy Conference*, Madrid, Spain, September, pp. 718–24.

Friedrich, R. and Voss, A. (1989) 'Die Sozialen Kosten der Elektrizitatserzeugung', *Energie Wirtschaftliche Tagestragen*, Vol. 39, No. 10, pp. 640–649.

Ottinger, R. L. (1990) *Environmental Costs of Electricity*, Oceana Publications.

Stocker, L., Harman, F. and Topham, F. (1991) *Comprehensive Costs of Electricity in Western Australia*, Ecologically Sustainable Development Working Group on Energy Production, Canberra, Australia.

Hagen, D. and Kaneff, S. (1991) *Application of Solar Thermal Technology in Reducing Greenhouse Gas Emissions – Opportunities and Benefits for Australian Industry*, ANUTECH Pty.

Ferguson, R. (1990) Newcastle University, UK.

Koomey, as cited in Hill, R. and Baumann, A. (1991) *External Cost Benefits of Energy Technologies*, Newcastle Polytechnic, UK.

(a) Includes estimates of costs of clean-up of acid rain and the greenhouse effect.
(b) Does not include estimates of climate damage.
(c) Costs of clean-up of acid rain and the greenhouse effect.
(d) Pollution costs only.
(e) Pollution costs only.
(f) Acidic deposition and global warming damage costs.
(g) Health/catastrophes.
(h) Pollution costs.
(Source: House of Commons Select Committee on Energy, 1992)

OTHER ECONOMIC INDICATORS

It is worth being aware of some of the other methods of appraising and expressing the economics of a project. Table A.8 lists some examples of other economic indicators. The preferred indicator depends on the exact nature of the projects being appraised, the cash flow profiles and the requirements of the appraisal.

In contrast to the method used up to now in this section (where a required level of profitability is assumed and a cost is calculated at which the developers of a project can afford to sell the energy), all of the methods listed in Table A.8 assume that the price at which the energy is sold (in pence per kilowatt-hour) is known. The income from selling it is included in the cash flow calculations (thus the annual return equals the annual income minus the annual costs) and a measure of profitability is calculated. Note that, as mentioned in Section A.2, the *price* at which energy is sold

Table A.8 Other economic indicators

Indicator	Definition	Comments
Simple payback period (years)	$= \dfrac{\text{Capital cost}}{\text{Average annual return}}$	Number of years taken to recover capital, ignoring discounting. Simple but crude.
Simple return on investment, ROI (or rate of return, ROR)(%)	$= \dfrac{\text{Average annual return}}{\text{Capital cost}}$	Pseudo measure of profitability, ignoring discounting. Simple but crude.
Net present value, NPV (£)	= Sum of all annual returns discounted to year zero minus discounted capital cost	The larger the NPV, the better. Projects with NPV > 0 are considered worth while.
Internal rate of return, IRR (%)	= Value that discount rate must take to make NPV equal to zero	IRR is a measure of profitability. Accept project with highest IRR or any project with an IRR exceeding minimum acceptable rate of return.
Benefit–cost ratio, B/C	$= \dfrac{\text{Present value of all benefits (income)}}{\text{Present value of all costs}}$	Projects with B/C > 1 are worth while. The higher the B/C, the better.

may not be the same as the *cost* of generating it, because prices are subject to market forces. If consumers are willing to pay a high price, that is what they will be charged, but if there is a glut of energy being produced, it may be necessary to reduce the price.

In Table A.8 the first two indicators (simple payback and simple return on investment) are crude measures, which ignore any discounting. The last three indicators, however, do include discounting and are in fact three different ways of expressing the same thing. In particular, note that when the net present value (NPV) is zero, the cost is equal to the price, and that the internal rate of return (IRR) gives a measure of the real rate of return on the investment available in the market-place.

It is also possible to measure the value of the renewable energy being produced in terms of the value of an alternative source of energy for which the renewable energy is a substitute. This method is often used when assessing solar water heating schemes, and is also applicable to costing energy conservation technologies. The capital and annual costs are calculated as before, but the annual income is expressed in terms of the value of conventional fuel saved (rather than any money that might be made by selling the solar-heated water to someone else). For example, if a solar hot water heating system reduces a gas or electricity bill by £100 per year, this is taken as the annual income generated by the scheme, and incorporated into any cash flow calculations as such. It is worth noting that when the energy is costed in this manner, any relative rate of change in the fuel prices (above or below general inflation) must be taken into account in the calculation.

SENSITIVITY ANALYSES

Although many uncertainties exist, it is possible to investigate the magnitude of their effect on the cost calculations by undertaking a series of sensitivity analyses. We vary each parameter around some central value (for example, a 'best estimate' for a capital cost) and see to what extent it alters the calculated cost in p kWh^{-1}. If it has little effect, we need not worry too much about it, but if there is a large effect, we need to be careful to obtain a reasonably-accurate estimate of the value of that parameter. For example, the discount rate is more important for a project with a high capital-to-running cost ratio than for one with a low ratio. Since it is often impossible to obtain accurate estimates for particular parameters, the cost in pence per kilowatt-hour is often expressed in terms of a range rather than a single value, to make clear such genuine uncertainty.

The results of a series of sensitivity analyses can be conveniently displayed in a 'spider diagram' (Figure A.12). We must remember that it may not be reasonable to vary all parameters by the same amount; for example, the load factor might be known quite accurately, whereas the capital costs may not. In this case, although the load factor has the steeper curve, the curve for capital cost may be of more importance.

Figure A.12'Spider diagram' illustrating sensitivity of cost of electricity generation for a municipal waste project

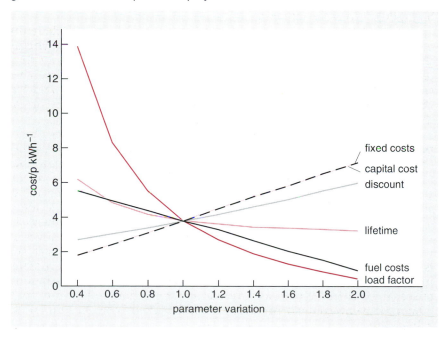

REFERENCES

Broome, J. (1992) *Counting the Cost of Global Warming*, Report to the Economic and Social Research Council, White Horse Press.

Central Statistical Office (1993) *Economic Trends: 1993 Supplement*, HMSO.

Department of Energy (1989) *Electricity Producing Renewable Energy Technologies: Common Costing Methodology*, Vol. 2, ETSU GEN 2006-P2, Yard.

House of Commons Select Committee on Energy (1992) Fourth Report, *Renewable Energy*, HMSO.

Pearce, D., Bann, C. and Georgiou, S. (1992) *The Social Costs of Fuel Cycles*, Report to Department of Trade and Industry.

FURTHER READING

The following regional studies of renewable energy potential contain good examples of cost and resource estimation:

ETSU (1993) *Prospects for Renewable Energy in Northern Ireland*. A report by ETSU in collaboration with the Department of Economic Development and Northern Ireland Electricity plc.

South West Electricity plc (1993) *Renewable Sources of Electricity in the SWEB Area*. A report by South West Electricity plc and the Energy Technology Support Unit (ETSU).

ACKNOWLEDGEMENTS

Grateful acknowledgement is made to the following sources for permission to reproduce material in this book:

CHAPTER 1

FIGURES

Figure 1.2: BP Statistical Review of World Energy, 1993, British Petroleum Company Limited; *Figures 1.7 and 1.9:* Blunden, J. and Reddish, A. (1991), 'UK Energy: End use by function' (1980) figure 1.14, p. 191, and 'Energy efficiency of different transport modes' figure 5.3, p. 40, *Energy Resources and Environment*, Hodder & Stoughton, by permission of the authors; *Figures 1.16 and 1.17:* Renewable Energy Advisory Group, Department of Trade and Industry (1992), *Energy Paper* **60**, figures 1 and 3c, pp. 14 and 19, HMSO.

TABLES

Table 1.2: Holdren, J. P., 'Energy in transition' p. 114, illustration by Goodman, M., *Scientific American*, September 1990, International edition. Copyright © 1990 by Scientific American Inc. All rights reserved; *Table 1.3:* Sørensen, B., 'Renewable energy: a technical overview' first published in *Energy Policy*, **19**(4), May 1991, p. 387, by permission of Butterworth-Heinemann, Oxford UK and the author; *Table 1.4:* Harrison, L., 'Europe gets clean away', *Windpower Monthly*, September 1992.

PHOTOGRAPH

Figure 1.10: Group Lotus Limited.

CHAPTER 2

FIGURES

Figures 2.1, 2.21, 2.42: ETSU, Department of Trade and Industry, *Active Solar Heating in the UK, Department of Energy R&D Programme 1977–1984; Figure 2.2:* courtesy of Eastern Electricity; *Figure 2.4, 2.16:* Szokolay, S. V. (1975), 'Solar radiation spectrum related to the full electro-magnetic spectrum', figure 1.4, p. 7 and 'Thermosyphon water heating', figure 3.1, p. 29, *Solar Energy and Building*, Architectural Press (Butterworth-Heinemann); *Figures 2.5, 2.6, 2.25, 2.36, 2.37:* adapted from Mazria, E. (1979), *The Passive Solar Energy Book*, Rodale Press Inc., ©

Edward Mazria; *Figures 2.7, 2.8:* CEC Directorate for General Science, 'Solar radiation', *European Solar Radiation Atlas Volume 1: Report EUR 9344*, Office for Official Publications of the European Communities; *Figure 2.11:* Department of Energy (1981), *Passive Solar Housing in the UK*, figure 34, p. 20, ETSU/Department of Trade and Industry; *Figure 2.15:* adapted from *Energy Projects in Milton Keynes: Energy Consultative Unit Progress Report 1976–1981*, Milton Keynes Development Corporation (1982), Commission for the New Towns; *Figures 2.28, 2.29:* Siviour, J. B. (1977), *Houses as Passive Solar Collectors ECRC/M1070*, The Electricity Council Research Centre, Capenhurst, Chester CH1 6ES; *Figures 2.33, 2.34, 2.35:* Department of Energy (1987), *The UK Department of Energy's Passive Solar Design Programme*, pp. 7, 9, 13, ETSU/Department of Trade and Industry; *Figure 2.52:* Cavanagh, Clarke and Price (1993), 'Schematic illustration of an OTEC floating platform', in Johannson, T. B. *et al.* (1993) *Renewable Energy Sources for Fuels and Electricity*, p. 540, Island Press Inc.

PHOTOGRAPHS

Figure 2.24: Dr M. G. Davies; *Figure 2.26:* Bob Everett; *Figure 2.31:* Commission for New Towns and J. Bogart; *Figure 2.43:* Mary Evans Picture Library; *Figure 2.44:* Phototheque EDF, photo: Marc Morceau; *Figures 2.45, 2.46:* copyright © James L. Ruhle and Associates; *Figure 2.47:* Hank Morgan/ Science Photo Library; *Figure 2.48:* Luz International; *Figure 2.49:* The Environmental Picture Library, © Steve Barham.

CHAPTER 3

FIGURES

Figure 3.3: Fraunhofer – Institut für Solare Energiesysteme; *Figure 3.9:* reprinted from McVeigh, J. C., *Sun Power*, Copyright © 1983, page no. 15, with kind permission from Elsevier Science Ltd, UK; *Figures 3.10, 3.14 and 3.29 (right):* Green, M. A. (1986) *Solar Cells*, Prentice-Hall; *Figures 3.16, 3.23, 3.27:* Burnham, L. (1993) *Renewable Energy Sources for Fuels and Electricity*, Island Press; *Figure 3.22:* from Wilson, H. G., MacCready, P. B. and Kyle, C. R., 'Lessons of Sunraycer', Copyright © 1989, Scientific American Inc. All rights reserved.; *Figure 3.31 (right):*

Graetzel, M. (1989) 'Photovoltaic Cell', *The Artificial Leaf*, Elsevier, by permission of the author; *Figure 3.33:* Treble, F. C. (1993) *Solar Electricity*, International Solar Energy Society; *Figure 3.34: BP275 Photovoltaic Module Part No. 360 314*, BP Solar Ltd.

PHOTOGRAPHS

Figure 3.1: Fraunhofer – Institut für Solare Energiesysteme; *Figure 3.4:* The Science Museum; *Figures 3.6 and 3.7:* AT&T, Bell Laboratories; *Figure 3.8:* Rutherford Appleton Laboratory; *Figure 3.19:* Mobil Corporation; *Figure 3.20:* Faculty of Technology, The Open University; *Figure 3.21:* Crystalox Ltd; *Figure 3.24: Sun World*, Vol. 15, No. 1, March/April 1991; *Figure 3.25:* Siemens Solar Industries; *Figure 3.26:* BP Solar Ltd; *Figure 3.28:* 3M; *Figure 3.29 (left):* Kundo-Staiger GmbH; *Figure 3.30:* Texas Instruments; *Figure 3.31 (left):* Godfrey Boyle; *Figure 3.35 (top):* BP Solar Ltd; *Figure 3.35 (middle):* BT Pictures, a BT photograph; *Figure 3.35 (bottom):* British Petroleum; *Figure 3.36:* BP Solar Ltd; *Figure 3.37 (middle left):* Deutsche Aerospace; *Figure 3.37 (middle right):* BP Solar Ltd; *Figure 3.37 (bottom left):* Mark Edwards/Still Pictures; *Figure 3.37 (bottom right):* BP Solar Ltd; *Figure 3.38:* CADDET Centre for Renewable Energy, courtesy of Misawa Homes; *Figure 3.39:* Godfrey Boyle; *Figures 3.40 and 3.42:* Systèmes Solaires, 45 rue de Richelieu, F.75001 Paris; *Figure 3.41:* RWE Energie; *Figure 3.43:* ENEA, Centro Richerche Energia Casaccia; *Figure 3.44:* Sacramento Municipal Utility District; *Figure 3.45:* National Photovoltaics Program, US Department of Energy; *Figure 3.47 (right):* © Werkbild TNC Consulting AG and Systèmes Solaires, 45 rue de Richelieu, F.75001 Paris; *Figure 3.47 (left):* Godfrey Boyle.

CHAPTER 4

FIGURES

Figure 4.4: Hall, D. O., 'The contribution of biomass to global energy use', *Energy Policy*, **19**(8), October 1991, by permission of the author; *Figure 4.10: Making Fuels from Wastes and Crops*, Energy Technology Support Unit, Crown copyright, reproduced by permission of the Controller, HMSO; *Figure 4.11: ETSU Technology Summary 198: Biofuels/*

Landfill Gas (1980), Energy Technology Support Unit, Crown copyright, reproduced by permission of the Controller, HMSO; *Figure 4.13: Wood: Fuel for Thought*, Energy Technology Support Unit, October 1991, Crown copyright, reproduced by permission of the Controller, HMSO; *Figures 4.20 and 4.21: ETSU Project Summary Unit 192: Biofuels/MSW Digestion* (1990), Crown copyright, reproduced by permission of the Controller, HMSO; *Figure 4.23: Wood as Fuel*, Energy Technology Support Unit, Crown copyright, reproduced by permission of the Controller, HMSO; *Figure 4.24* (map): Coombs, J. *Leben News*, April 1992, Commission for the European Communities.

PHOTOGRAPHS

Figures 4.2, 4.3 (planting willow cuttings), 4.7, 4.16, 4.22, 4.24, 4.26: ETSU/Department of Trade and Industry; *Figure 4.3 (short rotation coppice):* Holt Studios International, photograph by Nigel Cattlin; *Figure 4.25:* The Environmental Picture Library, © John Tomkins; *Figure 4.27:* Needham Chalks Limited.

CHAPTER 5

FIGURES

Figures 5.1: Hill, G. (1984) Map in *Tunnel and Dam*, Scottish Power; *Figures 5.7, 5.8 and 5.9:* Strand, S. (1979), *The History of the Machine*, Nordbok International; *Figure 5.31:* Flood, M. (1983), 'Turbo turbine', *Solar Prospects*, p. 123, Elron Press Ltd; *Figures 5.34 and 5.39:* Salford Civil Engineering Limited (1989), *Small Scale Hydroelectric Generation Potential in the UK*, ETSU, reproduced by permission of the Controller of HMSO; *Figure 5.38 (a) and (b): Cruachan: Power from the hollow mountain*, Scottish Power.

PHOTOGRAPHS

Figures 5.2, 5.4 and 5.5: Scottish Power; *Figure 5.15 (a):* Associated Press Photo; *Figure 5.15 (b):* Popperfoto; *Figure 5.17:* Sue Cunningham Photographic; *Figure 5.19:* Gilbert Gilkes and Gordon Limited; *Figure 5.25:* The Weir Group plc; *Figure 5.27 (a):* Scottish Hydro-Electric plc and Associated Illiffe Press; *Figure 5.36:* Popperfoto; *Figure 5.38 (c):* Scottish Power.

CHAPTER 6

FIGURES

Figures 6.1 and 6.4: Baker, A. C. (1991) *Tidal Power*, Peter Peregrinus; *Figures 6.7, 6.13, 6.17, 6.19, 6.22–6.25:* reproduced with the permission of the Controller of HMSO; *Figures 6.8:* Twidell, J. W. and Weir, A. J. (1986) *Renewable Energy Resources*, E & F Spon; *Figures 6.9–6.11, 6.16, 6.21, 6.26 and 6.30:* Taylor, R. H. (1983) *Alternative Energy Sources for the Centralised Generation of Electricity*, Adam Higler; *Figure 6.12:* Lewis (1963) 'The tidal power resources of the Kimberleys', *The Journal* December 1963; *Figures 6.14 and 6.15:* Carson, J. L. and Samuelson, R. S. (1978) *Power*, March 1978; *Figure 6.31:* 'Barrages to harness the power of the open sea', *New Scientist*, 3 December 1988; *Figure 6.32:* IT Power News.

TABLES

Tables 6.2, 6.3 and 6.7: reproduced with the permission of the Controller of HMSO; *Tables 6.4 and 6.5:* Baker, A. C. (1986) 'The development of functions relating cost and performance of tidal power schemes and their application to small scale sites', *ICE Symposium on Tidal Power*, Thomas Telford; *Table 6.6:* Baker, A. C. (1991) 'Tidal power', *Energy Policy*, **19**(8).

PHOTOGRAPHS

Figure 6.2: Phototheque EDF, photo Michael Brigaud; *Figure 6.20:* ETSU/Department of Trade and Industry.

CHAPTER 7

FIGURES

Figure 7.4: Vestas Danish Wind Technology A/S; *Figure 7.6:* Swift, D. (1988), *Physics for GCSE*, Simon & Schuster; *Figure 7.7:* Farndon, J. (1992), *How the Earth Works*, Dorling Kindersley Ltd; *Figure 7.8:* Kovarik, T., Pipher, C. and Hurst, J. (1979), *Wind Energy*, Quality Books Inc.; *Figure 7.10:* Park, J. (1981), *The Wind Power Book*, Cheshire Books, USA; *Figure 7.13:* Needham, J. with the collaboration of Ling, W. (1965) *Science and Civilisation in China Vol. 4, Part II*, Cambridge University Press; *Figure 7.28:* Rice, M. S. (1971), 'Clark Y', *Book of Airfoil Sections for Light Air Craft*, Aviation Publications; *Figures 7.29, 7.33 (a), (b),*

and (c): Freris, L. L. (1990), *Wind Energy Conservation Systems*, Prentice-Hall International UK; *Figure 7.30:* Creagh-Osborne, R. (1985), *This is Sailing – a complete course*, United Nautical Publishers, by permission of A&C Black (Publishers) Limited; *Figure 7.31:* Lysen, E. H. (1982), *Introduction to Wind Energy*, Ministerie van Buitenlandse Zaken; *Figures 7.41, 7.44, 7.47 and 7.48: Time for Action: Wind Energy in Europe* (1991) European Wind Energy Association; *Figure 7.43:* Rand, M. (1990), *Developing Wind Energy for the UK*, Friends of the Earth and the author; *Figures 7.50 and 7.51: Report to the President of the Board of Trade* (1992), Renewable Energy Advisory Group, © Crown Copyright. Reproduced with the permission of the Controller of Her Majesty's Stationery Office.

TABLE

Table 7.1: Vestas Danish Wind Technology A/S.

PHOTOGRAPHS

Figure 7.1: Marlec Engineering Ltd; *Figures 7.2, 7.5, 7.14 and 7.20:* Altechnica; *Figures 7.17 and 7.45:* WEG Ltd; *Figure 7.18:* Howden Wind Turbines; *Figure 7.19:* Stewart Boyle; *Figure 7.21:* VAWT Ltd; *Figure 7.22:* Derek Taylor; *Figure 7.49:* Bonus ES/Elkraft.

CHAPTER 8

FIGURES

Figures 8.1 (top), 8.22 (a), 8.26, 8.28, 8.30, 8.31 and 8.33–8.35: Thorpe, T. W. (1992), *A Review of Wave Energy*, ETSU R72 December; *Figures 8.39:* Long, A. E. and Whittaker, T. J. T. (1988), 'Wave power – a challenge to the engineers', *Proceedings of the Institute of Civil Engineers*, **84**, pp. 355–374, Thomas Telford Publications; *Figures 8.5, 8.7, 8.8, 8.16, 8.17, 8.18, 8.19, 8.20, 8.21, 8..22 (b), 8.23 (a), 8.25 and 8.32:* reprinted by permission of the Council of the Institution of Mechanical Engineers from *Wave Energy*, ETSU R26, Department of Energy Research and Development Programme 1974–1983, 1985, reproduced by permission of the Controller, HMSO; *Figure 8.13:* Falnes, J. and Lovseth, J. (1991), 'Ocean wave energy', first published in *Energy*

Policy, **19**(8), October 1991, pp. 768–775 and reproduced here with the permission of the authors and Butterworth-Heinemann, Oxford, UK.

TABLES
Tables 8.1 and 8.2: Thorpe, T. W. (1992), *A Review of Wave Energy*, ETSU R72 December.

PHOTOGRAPHS
Figure 8.1 (bottom): Les Duckers; *Figures 8.2 and 8.3:* ETSU/Department of Trade and Industry; *Figure 8.29:* Applied Research and Technology Ltd.

CHAPTER 9
FIGURES
Figure 9.6: from Cargo, D. N. and Mallory, B. F. (1974) *Man and his Geologic Environment*, Addison-Wesley and the authors; *Figure 9.7:* Henley, R. W. and Ellis, A. J., 'Geothermal systems ancient and modern: a geological review', in *Earth Science Reviews*, Vol. 19, No. 1, 1983, Elsevier Science B. V. and the authors; *Figure 9.9:* Stephen Hallinan, 'Gravity studies of the Guayabo Caldera and the Miravalles geothermal field, Costa Rica', PhD thesis, Milton Keynes, 1991, by permission of the author; *Figure 9.17:* Mortimer, N. D. and Monett, S. T. (1991) *The Cost Modelling of Hot-Dry Rock Systems*, vol. 2, ETSU, by permission of the Controller, HMSO; *Figures 9.23, 9.24 and 9.25:* Downing, R. A. and Grey, D. A. (1986) *Geothermal Energy: the potential in the UK*, British Geological Survey, by permission of the Controller, HMSO and British Geological Survey; *Figure 9.26:* acknowledgement is made to CSM Associates Ltd for permission to reproduce copyright owned material. Further reproduction requires authority from and acknowledgement to CSM Associates Ltd.

PHOTOGRAPHS
Figure 9.3 (top): Fratelli Alinari; *Figures 9.3 (bottom), 9.8. 9.14, 9.18, 9.19:* Geoff Brown.

CHAPTER 10
FIGURES
Figure 10.1: reproduced by permission of the Controller of HMSO; *Figure 10.7:* ETSU, reproduced by permission of the Controller of HMSO; *Figure 10.8:* Central Electricity Generating Board; *Figure 10.14–10.16:* Eurostat; *Figures 10.18 and 10.19:* Renewable Energy Advisory Group, reproduced by permission of the Controller of HMSO; *Figure 10.22:* Bodlund, B. *et al.,* 'The challenge of choices: technology options for the Swedish electricity sector', in Johansson, T. B., Bodlund, B. and Williams, R. H. (eds.) (1989), *Electricity – Efficient end use and new technologies, and their planning implications*, Lund University Press; *Figures 10.25 and 10.26:* Johansson, T. B., Kelly, H., Reddy, A. K. N. and Williams, R. H. (eds.) (1992), *Renewables for fuels and electricity*, Island Press; *Figure 10.27:* Lazarus, M. *et al.*(1993), *Towards a Fossil-free Energy Future: The next energy transition*, Stockholm Environment Institute.

TABLES
Table 10.1: Laughton, M. A. *et al.*(1990), *Renewable Energy Sources,* © 1990 Watt Committee on Energy, Elsevier Applied Science; *Table 10.3:* Council for Renewable Energy Education.

PHOTOGRAPHS
Figure 10.5: Bob Everett.

APPENDIX (COST AND RESOURCE ESTIMATING)
FIGURE
Figure A.2: Goulding, J. R., Lewis, J. O. and Steemers, T. C. (1992) *Energy in Architecture – The European passive solar handbook*, Batsford.

TABLES
Table A.2: Electricity producing renewable energy technologies final report Vol. 2, ETSU © Crown Copyright. Reproduced with the permission of the Controller of Her Majesty's Stationery Office; *table A.6:* Pearce, D., Bann, C. and Georgiou, S. (1992) *The Social Costs of Fuel Cycles*, University College, London.

INDEX

In this index page numbers in italic refer to items in diagrams, page numbers in bold refer to Tables and references to items in boxes are shown with a B following the page number.